EDUCATION AND SOCIAL INQUIRY

EDUCATION
AND
SOCIAL INQUIRY

Allan C. Ornstein
Loyola University of Chicago

F. E. PEACOCK PUBLISHERS, INC.
ITASCA, ILLINOIS 60143

Copyright © 1978
F. E. Peacock Publishers, Inc.
All rights reserved
Library of Congress
Catalog Card Number 77-83362
ISBN 0-87581-225-2

For Joel

Always Aim High

CONTENTS

PREFACE

This book is geared for courses in three areas of social inquiry in education—social foundations of education, sociology of education, and social policy. However, we are not trying to integrate three distinct areas of educational and social inquiry into a single volume; rather we will discuss the similarities and dissimilarities in scope and method of these three fields of study. The similarities (especially in the literature and in orientation) and the way the chapters are organized mean the book can be used in any one of these three fields, as well as being appropriate for urban education studies. It is true that the descriptions and explanations tend to coincide more with sociology of education than with social foundations or social policy. But the content and our interpretation of it are concerned with educational phenomena and educationally related social phenomena that are of concern in all three.

The book encompasses traditional education-related areas of social inquiry: the sociocultural context of education, education as a social institution, education as a changing process, classroom and teaching practices, and conflict and reform strategies in schools and society. Our purposes are to identify and describe the social forces underpinning education and to analyze the issues, differences, and trends they generate.

There are four parts in the book. Part I, a single chapter, defines the *field* of social inquiry in education, pointing up the differences among social foundations, sociology of education, and social policy. In Part II there are four chapters which deal with *students,* focusing on (1) socialization, (2) social class, (3) race and ethnicity, and (4) social stratification and inequality. Part III, divided into three chapters, is about *teachers:* (1) their decisions about teaching, (2) their effectiveness as teachers, and (3) their profession. Part IV is comprised of three chapters which deal with the nature of *schools* in terms of (1) school systems, (2) reform options, and (3) governmental roles and influences.

Some important features distinguish this book from others. First, one chapter is devoted to describing the similarities and differences among the various fields of social inquiry; most other texts on the subject do not explicitly deal with these subtleties. Second, the book is divided into three broad social and educational topics — students, teachers, and schools, and pertinent social issues and ideas are woven around these topics. Third, the perspective is sociological, so the concepts and analyses consider the educational institution as a social system. The result is a comprehensive picture which promotes understanding of education and the social process. A crucial point is recognition of the political and ideological differences in education. Not only is the nature of education political, reflecting choices and priorities, but the analysis of the data (as in all social science texts) reflects a value judgment which is both political and ideological. In short, observers and interpreters of social behavior can never be fully objective — no matter how hard they try. Finally, since social inquiry is an empirical science, the book places heavy emphasis on data-based studies. The important contemporary research is summarized and interpreted in easy-to-read form.

A special note of thanks goes to the typists for this book, Marie Dowd and Mary Travers. Appreciation also is extended to Tom LaMarre, the editor of F. E. Peacock Publishers, Inc., who had faith in the project from the start. My gratitude is also extended to Gloria Reardon, the copy editor, who worked many hours to shape the book in final form.

Chicago, Illinois

Allan C. Ornstein
Professor of Social and
Urban Foundations of Education

PART I

INTRODUCTION

A book on social inquiry and education must examine the various social approaches to education. Chapter I serves as an introduction by presenting three such approaches: social foundations of education, sociology of education, and social policy. Relationships among the three fields of study are noted, as are the differences between the researcher and the advocate in these three social areas of education.

In examining these three fields of study, it is interesting to note that increased public interest and concern with education at all levels of society has stimulated a substantial amount of writing and research in social foundations of education and, more recently, in sociology of education. Even more recent is the use of social science to measure the effects of educational policy outcomes as a basis for legislative and legal decisions. This has brought the need to provide more and better information on various social problems, such as poverty, welfare, crime, drugs, and racial conflict. Together, these developments have led to the emergence of the new field of social policy.

CHAPTER 1

DEFINING THE FIELD

Education is basically a social process which is concerned with how the student develops as an individual and in group relations. Its objective is to prepare the individual for participation in society, and it serves as a vehicle by which the culture of the group can be transmitted and perpetuated.

The idea of education as a social process involves various approaches to analyzing educational ideas and issues. There are basically three social approaches in education: (1) social foundations, (2) sociology of education, and (3) social policy. There is considerable overlap among the three approaches, and this leads to confusion over subject boundary areas, content, and methodology. These differences also create problems of semantics and dissonance among professors in terms of who should teach what.

The similarities and differences that exist among these three social approaches in education will be clarified in this chapter by examining the origins and methodology of each one.

SOCIAL FOUNDATIONS OF EDUCATION

The dependency of education upon the basic sciences was recognized during the late 19th century by those concerned with building a system of public schools in the United States and establishing programs to prepare teachers for them. The developing social and psychological sciences brought recognition of the complexity of the teaching-learning process and the need for a more adequate theory to guide educational practice. A number of foundation areas in education developed: philosophy of education, history of education, psychology of education, and sociology of education, followed in the mid-20th century by such specialties as anthropological and cultural foundations and, more recently, urban foundations.

Social Foundations as a Field of Study

The first formal program in the foundations of education was established at Teachers College, Columbia University, in the 1920s, under the chairmanship of William Kilpatrick.[1] It was largely based on progressive educational ideas and was spearheaded by a wing of the progressive movement—the members of the John Dewey Society for the Study of Education. The idea of the foundations program was to give prospective teachers an understanding of social issues and their impact on the schools; its key concept was to "see society as a whole and see education as a total enterprise in relation to the society and culture."[2] In administrative terms, this brought together two departments in the Columbia program: Psychological Foundations and Social and Philosophical Foundations.

The push toward social foundations was stimulated by a number of educators who interpreted philosophical and social issues of the day as demand for the democratization of schools and who felt that students and schools should be studied in relationship to the changing society. This was clearly reflected in the writings of that era, which started with John Dewey's *Democracy and Education* in 1916, included the works of Archibald Anderson, William Bagley, Boyd Bode, John Childs, George Counts, William Kilpatrick, Harold Rugg, and perhaps ended with William O'Stanley's *Education and School Integration* in 1953. This period roughly coincides with the height and eventual decline of the progressive movement in education.

Social foundations has been recognized as a legitimate area of specialization since the 1930s, but it failed to attain the status of an original, productive field of inquiry. The boundary areas of the field were never well defined. Some colleges and universities adopted the Columbia

[1] Earl E. Edgar, *Social Foundations of Education* (New York: Center for Applied Research in Education, 1965).
[2] R. Freeman Butts, in a letter to W. H. Cowley, cited in C. J. Brauner, *American Educational Theory* (Englewood Cliffs, N.J.: Prentice-Hall, Inc., 1964), pp. 202-4.

University plan, which combined philosophical and social foundations of education; others took an interdisciplinary approach involving several foundation areas or developed separate courses and fields of inquiry limited to social issues. Furthermore, the relevancy of the subject matter to the preparation of teachers has been criticized, so some educators question the wisdom of maintaining departments, or even offering courses, in the social foundations area.[3]

Currently, social foundations of education denotes two related areas: (1) social aspects of schooling and (2) issues regarding educational purposes and practices. The tendency is for the first area to involve concepts and practices which are sociological, while the second area involves philosophical questions. Together these two areas represent the need for a branch of study in education which specializes in identifying, integrating, and interpreting knowledge in the social sciences which pertains to the social dimension of education.[4] This can be translated into a course or a department in education which is concerned with relating educational philosophies and goals to social facts and situations that impinge upon the individual's and group's contacts with the institutions of society.

In efforts to determine the aims and purposes of such an approach, spirited arguments are offered which suggest what to teach, propose social goals, and offer conclusions reached by accepting certain premises: Education is preparation for life; Education is experience; We learn by doing; There must be no indoctrination; The curriculum must be relevant to the child's needs: Democracy and education. Recent issues related to the field are concerned with affective education, classroom processes, the role of the teacher, the influence of the home and community, the role of the local, state, and federal governments, career education, sex stereotyping, race and ethnicity, and equal educational opportunity. Such questions as education for what, education for whom, and the proper definition of education stem from the past and are still relevant today.

Concepts and Methods of Social Foundations

Social foundations is oriented toward value and policy statements for purposes of diagnosis and planning. Usually, a consistent and cogent body of knowledge evolves which is adequate to realize desired school goals and

---

[3] James B. Conant, *The Education of American Teachers* (New York: McGraw-Hill Book Co., 1963); James D. Koerner, *The Miseducation of American Teachers* (Boston: Houghton Mifflin Co., 1963).

[4] Cole S. Brembeck, *Social Foundations of Education*, 2nd ed. (New York: John Wiley & Sons, 1971); Harold L. Hodgkinson, *Education, Interaction, and Social Change* (Englewood Cliffs, N.J.: Prentice-Hall, Inc., 1966).

is consistent with systematic reasoning. Often, however, this knowledge is not based on empirical findings, nor is it easily verified by applying the methods of social science research.

The thrust of social foundations is practitioner oriented, whereas sociology of education is research oriented. The concepts and methods of social foundations have practical utility for teachers, school administrators, and school board members, who usually lack training in social science research and are generally unable to assess empirical studies and methodologies. Their major concern is to build a justifiable school program whereby ends and means make sense, and questions of purpose and technique are consistent with social conditions and a valid ethic of education.

Questions dealing with racial conflict, achievement and IQ, compensatory education, and so on, have meaning to educators, and pro and con arguments related to these issues are based on a deductive model with value-laden conclusions, while considering what is compatible for the real world of schooling. These arguments may use analytical, descriptive, or evaluative reasoning, but rarely do practitioners employ empirical data, even simple casual explanatory statements, in their formulation of purpose and technique. Many professors of social foundations courses tend to employ the same nonempirical procedures.[5]

However sensitive or aware educators in social foundations are about dealing with problems and issues in their field, they have not been encouraged to substantiate their claims with empirical methods of their own. This may be because the educator who is armed with quantitative findings often runs a high risk of failure. Careful research and impressive designs and analysis, however well received by the researcher's peers, rarely have any impact on school personnel, and though high-quality research standards may indeed be the proper measure of scientific progress, they are not necessarily the ideal way of advancing educational progress. The traditional highly structured research system of mutual criticism, referenced publication, peer group evaluation, and recognition through awards and appointments constitutes an intellectual marketplace and an academic process in institutions of higher learning, but this rarely leads to change in the real world of teaching.

Most contemporary criticism of the research community in education is directed not at its effectiveness in advancing knowledge, which is now taken for granted, but at its lack of capacity to couple knowledge to action, to project knowledge into the practitioner's arena, and to produce insights

---

[5] Donald A. Hansen, "The Uncomfortable Relation of Sociology and Education," in D. A. Hansen and J. E. Gerstl (eds.), *On Education—Sociological Perspectives* (New York: John Wiley & Sons, 1967), pp. 3–35.

relevant to the solution of the real problems that exist in classrooms and schools. This is exactly where specialists in social foundations can be of help. Although many of them do not have the expertise to conduct their own empirical research, they are familiar with the concepts, and they recognize results which describe and explain conditions in society that the school should take into account.

The contribution of specialists in social foundations lies in their ability to recognize a school need and to translate research into meaningful and manageable units which practitioners can adapt to real social conditions in education. These specialists, according to Richard Deer, can "conceptualize the school situation in such a way that those phenomena which are studied by the social sciences can be fitted together with the practitioners' task of selecting the best policies for their school."[6] By the same token, they can analyze and synthesize conclusions from researchers in jargon which the practitioner can understand and utilize. Thus social foundations can serve as a bridge between the researcher and the practitioner, both of whom are looking at social conditions which impact on schooling and society and are vital factors in educational decisions. This presents professors and students in social foundations courses with an opportunity to strengthen their area of study and to benefit both the research in and the practice of education.

SOCIOLOGY OF EDUCATION

As sociology and education have emerged as separate disciplines in American colleges and universities, some discomfort has developed between professors of sociology and professors of education in attempts to define the area where both fields merge and its substance, purpose, and methods. Sociology is a scientific approach to the study of how man interacts with and is shaped by the groups and institutions of society, that is, how the individual adjusts to the cultural setting. Education connotes a particular subdivision of society to be studied; it is a social process which utilizes sociology, like the other social sciences (philosophy, history, psychology, and political science), for its purposes.

For the sociologist, education is merely a component or branch of the field of sociology, "an institutional abstraction taken from society in the same manner that the family, politics, religion, etc., are studied by the sociologist for specific study."[7] For the educator, sociology is one of the

---

[6] Richard L. Deer, "Social Foundations as a Field of Study in Education," in J. Chilcott, N. C. Greenberg, and H. B. Wilson (eds.), *Reading in the Socio-Cultural Foundations of Education* (Belmont, Ca.: Wadsworth Publishing Co., 1969), p. 23.

[7] Robert R. Bell and Holger R. Stub, *The Sociology of Education: A Sourcebook* (Homewood, Ill.: Dorsey Press, 1968), p. 1.

many social sciences to be considered in trying to understand the educational process and the way the individual reacts to the cultural milieu.

Attempts to differentiate between sociology of education and educational sociology add to the discomfort existing between sociologists and educators. Traditionally, the term "sociology of education" has denoted a sociologist specializing in research on education, an area or source of data which could be analyzed through sociological methods under the science of sociology and be taught in departments of sociology. Educational sociology has suggested the application of sociology to the educational process, an area or source of data which relies on educational theory and comprises a course (or group of courses) offered in schools of education.[8]

Today, the subtle differences between sociology of education and educational sociology have been blurred by time and by common development. Although there is still debate involving who should teach these courses, professors of sociology or professors of education, both basically deal with similar subject matter: race, ethnicity, social class, and various other social indicators influencing school achievement; an understanding of the behavior and roles of students, teachers, administrators, and school board members; the functions of local, state, and federal governments as they relate to education; and an analysis of classrooms, schools, and school systems as social systems and institutions of society. There does tend to be greater stress on research, theory, and methods if the course is taught by a sociology professor rather than in the school of education. For the most part in this text, we will use the term "sociology of education" because this is the term currently used by most professors, regardless of whether they are based in sociology or education departments.

Sociology of Education as a Field of Study

Sociology of education arose from a merger of sociology and education, but it was developed separately by sociologists and educators. As a product of a mixed marriage, the field has always had trouble in establishing its identity. Although it owes a debt to many more sociologists (Auguste Comte, Emile Durkheim, Herbert Spencer, Edward Ross, Charles Cooley, Albion Small, Lester Ward) than educators (Horace Mann, John Dewey, Franklin Bobbitt), the subject for many years remained outside the

---

[8] Robert C. Angell, "Science, Sociology and Education," *Journal of Educational Sociology*, March 1928, pp. 406-13; Edward B. Reuter, "The Problem of Educational Sociology," *Journal of Educational Sociology*, September 1935, pp. 15-22.

mainstream of sociology. It was conceived in the main as a part of the study of education and referred to as educational sociology.

By 1914, as many as 16 institutions of higher learning were offering courses in educational sociology.[9] In 1916 the first department of educational sociology was established at Columbia University, and in the next decade course offerings in this field of study increased. Thus, in 1926, when Harvey Lee surveyed 505 institutions, 38 percent offered a course in educational sociology, and 10 percent required it.[10] Twenty years later, George Herrington found that 28 percent of 239 institutions offered the course, and only 6 percent required it.[11] By 1953, 18 percent of 100 institutions sampled offered a course in educational sociology; only one university offered as many as three courses.[12,13]

Why the apparent decline in educational sociology from the 1920s to the 1950s? It seems safe to say that the original interest in sociology of education and educational sociology was not sustained; apparently, schools of education made few attempts to develop such programs on a large scale. The study by Herrington in 1947 indicated that there were only five schools of education (Michigan State University, New York University, Ohio State University, Stanford University, and University of Chicago) offering a sufficient number of courses to consider the discipline as a major or minor, and more than 50 percent of the professors teaching such courses lacked formal training in the field.[14] Then, too, the study by Lee and another by Clyde Moore suggest that the courses had little similarity in content, and the result was a hodgepodge of subjects put together by professors in sociology and education.[15]

During this period of decline, several of the early sociologists thought of educational sociology as a branch of sociology which would provide understanding of the educational process, but the field evolved as a course designed to prepare teachers for their future tasks.[16] As a consequence,

[9] D. H. Kulp, *Educational Sociology* (New York: Longmans Green, 1932).

[10] Harvey Lee, *The Status of Educational Sociology* (New York: New York University Press, 1928).

[11] George S. Herrington, "The Status of Educational Sociology," *Journal of Educational Sociology*, November 1947, pp. 129-39.

[12] Bernard N. Meltzer and Jerome G. Manis, "The Teaching of Sociology," in *The Teaching of the Social Sciences in the United States* (Paris: UNESCO, 1954).

[13] A question arises as to the comparability of these percentages. Although the latter two studies implied that the data were comparable, we believe no adequate statistical data were presented to support these assumptions.

[14] Herrington, "Status of Educational Sociology."

[15] Lee, *Status of Educational Sociology*, Clyde B. Moore, "The Aims, Contents, and Methods of a General Course in Educational Sociology," *Education*, November 1924, pp. 159-70.

[16] Lloyd A. Cook and Elaine F. Cook, *A Social Approach to Education* (New York: Crowell, 1950); Joseph S. Roucek et al., *Social Foundation of Education: A Textbook in Educational Sociology* (New York: Crowell, 1942).

many sociologists lost interest in this area of study, and educators increasingly connected it with philosophical and social foundations of education. Few professors of education had a background in sociology, and it was natural (and still is today) for many of them to teach sociology of education as a social foundations course or one that is oriented to practice rather than research.

Furthermore, few sociologists wanted to be associated with teaching courses in schools of education; this was the period when many professors of the arts and sciences even refused to lunch at the same table with professors of education.[17] The teaching of sociology of education in departments of sociology was also criticized. With either arrangement, sociologists seemed to be prostituting themselves and watering down courses to the demands of education students. Although sociologists complained that the courses did not place sufficient emphasis upon research and theory, education students frequently criticized them because they were not practical or related to teaching.[18] The general feeling among professors was that teachers could get better training in sociology from other courses than those specifically designated as sociology of education or educational sociology.[19]

The many recent issues having a joint sociological and educational impact have given new interest and importance to the sociology of education (far exceeding that in the first half of the 20th century) and have helped create new communication links between sociologists and educators. These issues center around the growth of bureaucracy and technology; the government role in education; youth alienation and student unrest; crime, drugs and delinquency; urban decay and metropolitan growth; social class, race, ethnicity, and cultural pluralism; student achievement, IQ, and social inequality; and the ever-increasing debates over compensatory education, desegregation, and community control of the schools.

The importance of these issues has done much to stimulate interest and research in sociology of education, an interest that has become full blown during the past 10 or 15 years. The national prominence of leading social scientists (such as James Coleman, Christopher Jencks, Daniel Bell, Nathan Glazer, Daniel Moynihan, Arthur Jensen, and Thomas Pettigrew) who combine social and educational issues is unique in the short history of

---

[17] Conant, *Education of American Teachers.*

[18] Ronald G. Corwin, *Sociology of Education* (New York: Appleton-Century-Crofts, 1965); Judson T. Landis, "The Sociological Curriculum and Teacher Training," *American Sociological Review,* February 1947, pp. 113–16.

[19] Wilbur B. Brookover and David Gottlieb, *A Sociology of Education* (New York: American Book Co., 1959); Lloyd A. Cook, *Community Backgrounds of Education* (New York: McGraw-Hill Book Co., 1938).

sociology of education. The visibility of these social scientists and the controversies over their research results have done much to stimulate interest in the field. Awareness of the relationship between sociology and education has been enhanced, interest among sociologists in sociology of education as a body of organized knowledge has been renewed, educators have been forced to deal with theoretical and research aspects of the literature, and communication between professors of sociology and professors of education has been facilitated.

Furthermore, the negative attitude that sociologists once had toward applied endeavors such as education has diminished considerably. Since it is increasingly difficult for sociologists to find employment in "pure" sociological fields, they have come to accept the value of applied-sociology endeavors and to understand that their roles may go beyond the research and theory responsibilities of traditional sociologists.[20] At the same time, educators and practitioners in other fields have come to appreciate the knowledge sociologists can contribute and usually welcome them as part of an interdisciplinary team.

At present there is a boom in sociology of education in teacher training, and there is little indication that the subject will be taken over, as in the past, by educators, or that it will become divorced from the main body of sociology. The educational questions discussed today by commentators and by the public in general are best explained with a knowledge of both sociology and education. While there is no adequate sociological or educational theory which can answer all of these questions, those in academic circles who search for knowledge recognize the importance of sociology of education. It appears that the future of the field is now assured.

Concepts and Methods of Sociology of Education

In a theoretical sense, sociology of education is based upon the procedures of sociologists and social scientists. By nature, it is an abstracting and generalizing discipline, whereas social foundations is oriented toward predictive statements to be applied in practical situations. Although both fields employ summary statements for purposes of assembling data, specialists in sociology of education sometime seek generalizations which may have little function or use for teachers, whereas specialists in social foundations press for concrete and practical applications.

---

[20] Donald E. Gelfand, "The Challenge of Applied Sociology," *American Sociologist,* February 1975, pp. 13-18.

The problems with which both of these social approaches deal overlap considerably, but the methods for solving them often differ. The specialist in sociology of education attempts to solve problems and arrive at explanations with the aid of empirical findings and verifiable knowledge, that is, knowledge that can be validated and communicated to other people. Theories are presented which consist of generalizations concerning the interpretation of facts and their relationships to each other; a given theory remains valid only as long as it is verifiable. Validity of knowledge may be deductive (moving from the general to specific, involving the formulation of abstract concepts) or inductive (moving from the specific to general, involving experiments and controlled variables).

Although specialists in social foundations also seek verification, they do not always achieve it with the same degree of precision and exactitude. They also systematize knowledge, but they often organize the data on the basis of philosophical premises and practice-oriented assumptions rather than strict scientific methods. They do not always rely on empirical and verifiable data to seek causes but stress deductively formulated procedures and ideas supported by expert opinion. Also, many of the explanations in the social foundations approach are based on assumptions which cannot be proven easily with hard data. In short, most social foundations specialists base their prescriptions on philosophical constructs and applied reasoning, whereas the majority of sociologists of education use factual-based data and empirical verification procedures. The former group of specialists is more susceptible to value-laden judgments and subjective considerations, and the latter is more concerned with objectivity and the pursuit of facts.

Specialists in social foundations, because of their philosophical orientation, are system builders, that is, they deal in large generalizations arrived at by individual thinkers and individual researchers whose findings are summarized, quoted, and discussed (sometimes out of context) by others in the field. Sociology of education, especially in the present day, is marked by individual and group research on specialized topics, usually with small empirical studies, in the belief that knowledge can be advanced with short, manageable pieces of research. One merit of system builders is that they make clear their assumptions, judgments, and values, whereas other types of researchers may conceal their premises and prejudices and hide or slant data that do not coincide with their politics. Thus specialists in social foundations can be more open about their biases, whereas those in sociology of education, since they are required to be objective in their research, sometimes disguise them.

The specialist in sociology of education seeks to isolate factors and study their relationships; the procedures are complex, and multiple relationships frequently make it difficult to isolate one factor from another. The factors studied exist not only in the external world of schools and society but also in the subjective world of consciousness and unconsciousness, where they cannot be reduced to factors that can be studied like those in the external world. Thus the researcher may be faced with human motives, attitudes, and feelings he or she is unable to control or to separate for the objective pursuit of knowledge. The researcher may resort to various torturous methods to establish objectivity and to fit (sometimes force) an established methodology into a frame of reference or to apply it to a problem under consideration. This may lead to disputes over methodology and criticism of a researcher's procedures.

Despite the disputes over method in sociology of education, there is general agreement that only through verified knowledge and sound research techniques can theoretical claims be supported and a scientific outlook be arrived at. There is no universal agreement on method, but there is unanimity on the need for unbiased explanation, using many permissible methods.

SOCIAL POLICY

Only in a broad sense is social policy related to education; that is, education is only one of several areas with which social policy is concerned. However, in the context of a new equalitarian trend which links education, occupation, income, and equal opportunity, the area of education is becoming an increasingly important aspect of social policy.

It is difficult to pinpoint the boundaries of social policy, since the subject involves several social science areas (especially sociology, education, economics, and political science) and social services (schools, housing, welfare, employment, and medical care) and the relationship of these factors to the policial process and to various governmental policies and programs. Such an involved relationship suggests that the boundaries do not have clear parameters and the subject is diffuse; thus the specialist in social policy must have a broad education and be versed in the political process.

Students and professors of social policy in American colleges and universities exist in a variety of academic disciplines and professional schools, such as sociology, education, social work, and urban planning. Pressures to develop social policy as a separate field have recently increased, but presently this approach uses the subject matter and methods of other social sciences. Social policy therefore should be considered an interdisciplinary field. David Donnison asserts that social policy "cannot be studied in isolation from major social sciences. Its methods are dictated by the problem in hand," and they are drawn from several disciplines; thus much of the best research in social policy "goes on under other titles."[21]

Actually, the academic boundaries of social policy represent much more than simple cross-disciplinary team efforts. Rather, social policy recognizes that the social world cannot be easily carved into neat academic disciplines; the study of drug users and abuses, crime, unemployment, or reasons for school failure, for example, can be examined from many viewpoints and from the vantage of many social sciences. Social policy starts with the real world and attempts to search out practical solutions, regardless of the zealous guardianship of academic boundaries; it attempts to study and solve social problems on the basis of knowledge from many social sciences.

It follows that there is little logic to justify social policy as a separate field of study other than to try to bring unity to the field. Although the evidence that interdisciplinary research is fruitful remains inconclusive, despite the claims made in its behalf,[22] those who are committed to social policy usually have more in common with one another than they have with others from their own academic disciplines. The student who is drawn into social policy usually comes from another field but establishes new loyalties and adopts methods to pursue his own inquiries. Whereas traditionally students of social policy are drawn from the areas of social work, urban planning, and social administration, an increasing number of these students seem to come from the disciplines of sociology and education. Social policy centers and departments are now being established in some institutions of higher learning. Those who major in social policy before acquiring credentials from a traditional social science area have no other field to which they owe allegiance, and to the extent they are solely educated in social policy, they may lack another base from which they can function within most colleges and universities.

Social Policy as a Field of Study

Interest in social policy as a field of study is recent and coincides with the nation's shift in the 1960s from foreign priorities to domestic priorities, from the issues of the Cold War and Sputnik to the issues of the War on Poverty and the civil rights movement. Currently, this interest is being sustained by issues involving schooling and welfare reform, tax reform,

---

[21] David W. Donnison, "The Evolution of Social Administration," *New Society,* October 20, 1966, p. 610.

[22] Joseph Ben-David, "How to Organize Research in the Social Sciences," *Daedalus,* Spring 1973, pp. 39–51; Martin Rein, *Social Policy: Issues of Choice and Change* (New York: Random House, 1970).

and equal rights for all. The influx of federal monies to programs designed to solve domestic problems has been enhanced by growth in the role of government in educational and social reform, and increased use of social science research as a basis for legislative and judicial decisions. As the nation becomes increasingly aware of its social and educational problems, there is a concurrent need to expand social services and to develop realistic social policies—and interest in the study of social policy grows.

In part, social policy is a system of knowledge, beliefs, and action—ideas about the causes of social problems, assumptions about how society works, and suggestions for how problems can be resolved.[23]

A social policy might be described as a grand strategy: a large and loose set of ideas about how society works, why it goes wrong, and how it can be rectified. Such a strategy includes value judgments and beliefs about the target group or institution for which the policy is being developed.

In the early 1960s, for example, a national policy concerning educational opportunity began to take shape, based in part on recognition of the educational problems of poor and minority group children and assumptions that poverty, unemployment, and delinquency were related to the absence of particular cognitive skills and attitudes, and acquiring them would lead to economic success and greater social equality. The emerging policy, which came to be called *compensatory education,* assumed that providing schools with more resources would enable them to solve, or at least counteract, students' educational deficiencies.[24]

When the evaluative reports of the various programs indicated unsatisfactory results, one group of social scientists tended to place blame on the students (or target group), and a second group tended to blame the teachers and schools. To complicate matters, a third group of social scientists later entered the policy arena to claim that schools make very little difference in determining educational outcomes, and other variables related to social background are more important. To be sure, social policy can generate heated debate; the "evidence" that is set forth, even when it is empirical, is often based on and reflects a larger set of preconceived ideas and judgments the researcher holds about the social world.

To understand social policy, it is necessary to distinguish between *policy* and *program.* Policy establishes guidelines directed toward the future which are pursued or are intended to be pursued and which provide a framework for decisions; the major guidelines include such elements as goals, strategies, directed efforts, alternative decisions, and future plans and

[23] Martin Rein, "Social Policy Analysis as the Interpretation of Beliefs," *Journal of American Institute of Planners,* September 1971, pp. 297-310.

[24] David K. Cohen and Michael S. Garet, "Reforming Educational Policy with Applied Social Research," *Harvard Educational Review,* February 1975, pp. 17-43.

Figure 1.1 / Social Policy and Program Formation

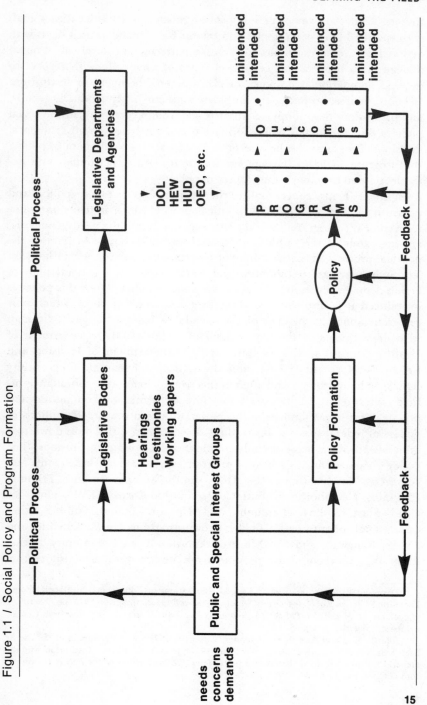

intents.[25] Another way of defining social policy is to consider it as a goal, with specified lines of strategies and intents for arriving at it; it deals with action plans, choices among alternative patterns, and levels of resource allocation to bring about certain changes of social life with respect to defined populations (the poor, blacks, women, the aged) or institutions (schools, houses, hospitals, the employment sector).[26] Individuals, groups, and institutions may adopt (voluntarily or through coercion) certain social policies, but the actual policy formation is often based on governmental decisions. Programs can be interpreted as an action component of policy; the program includes the aggregation of resources, personnel, and activities needed to achieve some aspect of policy.

Figure 1 helps conceptualize the relationship between policy and program, as well as the larger political process which impacts on policy formation and programs. Social policy is derived from the needs, concerns, and demands of the public and special-interest groups. As part of the political process, legislative bodies of government react to these influences. Through hearings, testimonies, and working papers a general plan of action is made which may be considered social policy. Once this policy is introduced it is implemented through grants and contracts (which now represent about 20 percent of the spendable federal budget[27]) through such departments as the Department of Labor (DOL), Department of Health, Education, and Welfare (HEW), Department of Housing and Urban Development (HUD), and the Office of Economic Opportunity (OEO). These groups, and their respective agencies and compliance offices, interpret legislative decisions, impose regulations on public and private institutions, and have the power to award or cut off millions of dollars of federal funds to institutions. In some cases, this boils down to a life-or-death decision, especially for financially pressed institutions. The policy is carried out via a host of programs supported by these grants and contracts. For example, the DOL funds Manpower and Training Programs, Neighborhood Youth Corps, and Job Corps; HEW is noted for Head Start, Follow Through, and Upward Bound, among other educational programs; HUD's best known programs are Model Cities and Urban Renewal; and OEO is well known for its Community Action Programs. In theory, the programs are designed to establish certain

---

[25] Desmond L. Cook and Robert Lange, "Limitations of Educational and Social Policy Evaluation," *Journal of Research and Development in Education,* Spring 1975, pp. 92–100.

[26] *What Is Meant by Policy?* (Syracuse, N.Y.: Educational Policy Research Center, Syracuse University, n.d.).

[27] John F. Due and Ann F. Friedlaender, *Government Finance: Economics of the Public Sector,* 6th ed. (Homewood, Ill.: Dorsey Press, 1977); John A. Steinhart, "Institutions and the General Purpose," in P. C. Ritterbush (ed.), *Scientific Institutions of the Future* (Washington, D.C.: Acropolis Books, 1972), pp. 7–27.

outcomes. Information about the programs is usually fed back as part of the political process and used as a basis for policy and program revision.

In general, it is easier to evaluate programs than policy, since programs deal with outcomes that can be quantified, while policy deals with alternatives and value choices related to the distribution of money, issues of equity, and the competing demands of special-interest groups. Furthermore, most policy-making bodies do not define a precise set of outcomes; rather they justify a general set of conditions and needs. Thus social policy can be evaluated not by conventional measurement and empirical techniques but through philosophical and political debates, which may involve heated arguments and much rhetoric and emotionality. Program evaluation, while supposedly quantitative, may not always be accurate or even honest, since knowledge assumes political importance related to the allocation of funds and jobs and determination of which individuals and groups will benefit.

It is also easier to revise programs than policy. Programs can be shifted, eliminated, or enlarged simply by modifying the amount of money earmarked for them. Once a policy is set in motion, however, bureaucratic layers grow, and bureaucrats become more entrenched and committed; those who benefit resist any major alteration in the policy, regardless of whether the general public derives benefit from it.

While most social scientists advocate basing social policy deliberations on data-based information, policy seldom results from a review of documented facts. Rather it emerges from a general awareness of dissatisfaction with current conditions or recognition that a social problem exists. If dissatisfaction is not expressed, or if a social problem is not defined, then there is no reason to be concerned or to establish a policy to rectify that problem. A social problem does not exist unless it is recognized by society to exist. Robert Merton is somewhat more inclusive: "The first and basic ingredient of a social problem consists of a substantial discrepancy between widely shared standards and actual conditions of social life."[28]

When individuals concerned with rectifying a problem recognize that they can accomplish little by themselves, they may form into special-interest groups (civil rights groups, welfare groups, gay-rights groups), which have a better chance of influencing policy makers. The interest group publicizes the problem to the public, focusing on recognized and unrecognized discrepancies and perhaps exaggerating them. If it is sophisticated in the art of policy making, the group will probably define

---

[28] Robert K. Merton, "Social Problems and Sociological Theory," in R. K. Merton and R. Nisbet (eds.), *Contemporary Social Problems* (New York: Harcourt, Brace & World, 1971), p. 799.

the problem in terms of widely cherished norms and values. It also may make excessive demands on policy makers, or the system in general, with the intent of negotiating a political compromise with other interest groups, in order to realize a social policy most in accordance with its own self-interests.

Once the attention of policy makers is obtained, a feeling of urgency develops. According to Alice Rivlin, much time and energy is devoted to gathering data describing the conditions of the group of people or the problem.[29] Little reliable information usually exists to verify these conditions, and much of it is often conflicting. Furthermore, policy makers (local, state, or federal) do not always read the scientific literature concerning the policy on which they are deciding, and those that do usually do not understand the technical aspects of the data. When testimony is given the story does not always get across.[30]

Legislative bodies therefore depend on "experts" to summarize and interpret the data, to offer their judgments, and to give advice on subjects related to policy issues. These experts, because they are human and limited by their own biases, often present a view that coincides with their own version of the "truth." They write their documents and present their testimonials in the way they perceive the world, sometimes promoting their own ideological views. They are ostensibly social scientists concerned with objectivity, but many of them play the role of advocate and are quite selective in presenting their data. There is no absolute way for policy makers to discern what information is objective or subjective, what is accurate or misleading, and what data are purposely stressed or omitted in reports and discussions. Men and women who claim to represent the research community but who may fall short of being objective students of social science can influence legislative bodies solely by their aura of expertise.

Activists or representatives of interest groups are by nature subjective and will readily slant their views in favor of the policy they are promoting. The nature of their politics takes precedence over loyalty to truth, and it is within their role to show fidelity to a prescribed ideology, to provide selective data, and to promote dogma. Most students of social policy, however, should be able to distinguish when the pursuit of scientific inquiry is being subverted for political and ideological reasons.

Since policy affects people, there is a tendency for people to exert all the influence they can to affect policy and thus ensure that what emerges is in

---

[29] Alice Rivlin, *Systematic Thinking for Social Action* (Washington, D.C.: Brookings Institute, 1971).

[30] Allan C. Ornstein, Daniel U. Levine, and Doxey A. Wilkerson, *Reforming Metropolitan Schools* (Pacific Palisades, Ca.: Goodyear Publishing Co., Inc., 1975).

their best interests. Needless to say, special-interest groups do not necessarily seek what is best for the larger society; their goals may not make for better social policy in educational or social programs, for example, although much of the rhetoric of interest groups would have the public believe otherwise.[31] Deliberations upon educational and social issues should recognize their political nature and the potential for policy formation. To say that compensatory education, welfare spending, or affirmative action policies are not political or that they mainly involve moral concerns is at best naive, since this ignores the reality of how policy is derived.

Methods and Concepts of Social Policy

Specialists in social policy are expected to utilize the tools of social science to document social aspects of the culture. However, their theories and research must be lodged in the reality under analysis, and they must recognize the facts of human interaction; they cannot remain divorced from the real world, since many of the social problems they analyze are debated in political circles and have implications for policy formation. While they are obligated to conduct research in terms of specific rules (frequently as a participant-observer or action researcher), they may be forced to modify their approaches, sometimes at the risk of validity, to conform to the sentiments of the people or the community being studied.

Specialists in social foundations and sociology of education can employ relatively impersonal research methods such as simulations in safe environments, surveys, and experiments with randomly selected respondents. Social policy researchers, however, must often enter the world they wish to describe and explain. They must locate relevant social settings in which subjects form groups and play out their attitudes and behaviors. As Martin Deutsch notes, the social scientist who deals in policy "can play a unique role in lowering barriers of social change by his activities when he arrives at relevant problems. He can not only study them, but also, by the kind of questioning of tacit assumptions proposed, he can assault the obstacles to their solution."[32]

As society becomes more aware of its social problems, conflicts between interest groups surface, and social scientists are the first to be caught in

---

[31] Allan C. Ornstein, "Evaluating Teachers and School Administrators: The Politics of Accountability," *Journal of Research and Development in Education,* Spring 1975, pp. 73–81; Allan C. Ornstein, *Race and Politics in School/Community Organizations* (Pacific Palisades, Ca.: Goodyear Publishing Co., Inc., 1974).

[32] Martin Deutsch, "Organizational and Conceptual Barriers to Social Change," *Journal of Social Issues,* Autumn 1969, p. 9.

flare-ups between groups. With increasing concern about the policy implications of research, minority groups have come to view researchers as a threat to their own welfare. Thus the rights of entry and the issue of censorship have surfaced.[33] Precisely because social research deals with delicate matters and often has policy implications, the independent social scientist is often considered a potential threat to groups (including majority groups) who have something to hide, who seek to define the "truth" as they wish to or to disseminate only "positive" research findings. The more an interest group has something to hide or wishes to propagandize, the more protective it is likely to be. The price of entry to the group for the researcher may be to provide those studied with the purpose of the data and the right to screen and edit the data before it is disseminated. Some interest groups may even ensure the findings before the research is conducted by hiring "inside" researchers or those whose ideology coincides with members of the group.[34]

The problem is aggravated by a number of people who now argue that an outsider is unable to understand or adequately present the problems of minority groups. Moral assumptions, political ideology, and racial and ethnic background may be valued more than research objectivity and technical qualifications. The cherished values of social science research are considered merely as sacred cows by those who believe that scientific authority and methodology are not relevant to one who is committed to social change and "real" reform.[35]

It is doubtful whether most social scientists are willing to accept these ideological perspectives, however. As scientists, they are committed to standards of scholarship and inquiry. They recognize that research does not always give the policy maker the type of data needed to implement policy and know they must not confuse profundity with incomprehensibility. Nevertheless, they acknowledge the need to be objective and maintain that very little is contributed to scientific knowledge by those who would dethrone scientific methodology. In a politically

[33] Roscoe C. Brown, "How to Make Educational Research Relevant to the Urban Community—The Researcher's View," paper presented at the annual meeting of the American Educational Research Association, New York, February 1971; Wilson Record and Jane C. Record, "The White Social Scientist in the Black Community," *Journal of Research and Development in Education*, Spring 1975, pp. 63-72.

[34] Francis G. Caro, "Issues in Evaluation of Social Programs," *Review of Educational Research*, April 1971, pp. 87-114; Francis G. Caro, "Evaluative Researchers and Practitioners: Conflicts and Accommodation," *Journal of Research and Development in Education*, Spring 1975, pp. 55-62.

[35] James A. Banks and Jean D. Grambs (eds.), *Black Self-Concept* (New York: McGraw-Hill Book Co., 1972); Joyce Ladner (ed.), *The Death of White Sociology* (New York: Random House, 1973); Gary T. Marx, *Muckraking Sociology* (New York: Frederick A. Praeger, Inc., 1972).

charged research and policy milieu there may be undue pressure to forgo the rigors of method and technique, to limit the researcher's entry, and to censor data. When these things are done, however, the research that is forthcoming is suspect.

These new pressures make it essential for social scientists to understand that their role "is not in the formation of social policy, but in the measurement of its results."[36] Casual insights and opinions by people or ideological stances by special-interest groups are interesting and absorbing, but they are hardly a sufficient basis on which to implement policy for a large political, social, or educational system. What is needed is empirical data, or at least objective data, on what works under what conditions. To provide these data, attempts have been made to establish social indicators such as race, ethnicity, income, occupation, educational level, one-family and two-family households, or number of children. Like the economic indicators on which planners and policy makers rely, these indicators can be used as a basis for decisions regarding social policies and programs.[37]

Apart from their objective help in establishing policy and assessing program outcomes, these indicators have the potential to develop a sophisticated central information system and facilities for long-range planning. Social indicators can be used for four basic purposes:

1. *Social Information.* Indicators can be used to define and collect social information for policy makers. The range of information could include both quantitative and qualitative data.

2. *Social Goals.* Indicators can be used to establish social goals that enable policy makers to establish targets. In this usage, social indicators are seen as part of an analytical and measurement phase of policy, in terms of both short-term and long-term planning.

3. *Social Reporting.* Indicators can be used to compile executive reports (such as the Coleman report or the Moynihan report) designed to affect policy or used in annual reports (such as the dean's report to the president of a university or a company president's report to its stockholders) to provide data on existing policies. These reports can be used to provide needed information concerning social as well as institutional problems.

4. *Social Accounting.* Indicators can be used for purposes of social accounting — that is, a comprehensive report which includes not only a

---

[36] Daniel P. Moynihan, *Maximum Feasible Misunderstanding* (New York: Free Press, 1969), p. 193.

[37] Raymond A. Bauer (ed.), *Social Indicators* (Cambridge, Mass.: MIT Press, 1967); Bertram M. Gross and Jeffrey D. Straussman, "The Social Indicator Movement," *Social Policy,* September 1974, pp. 43-54.

description of a specific social policy but also how that policy is related to the larger society and possibly the changing world (such as the Club of Rome 1972 report entitled "The Limits of Growth").[38] The report is based on a highly structured set of interrelated indicators which provides an ordered array of individual and group information concerning people, institutions, subsystems and total systems, and inputs and outputs.

The social indicators movement came of age in the mid-1960s, along with Lyndon Johnson's administration's concern with the War on Poverty, civil rights, urban disruptions, educational opportunity, and the War in Vietnam. It is especially supported by researchers with statistical, technical, and interdisciplinary competence who carry out studies at a few large universities or for research and policy organizations such as Rand Corporation or the Brookings Institute. Some social scientists have sought to erode the growing influence of the social indicator movement on social policy; humanists, revisionists, radicals, polemicists, and others have rejected them as nothing more than social statistics and have sought to stress instead a value-generating orientation for policy formation.

Policy research of any type has the potential for supporting or rejecting educational strategies, so long as it is *understandable* by the consumer (i.e., the policy maker or the courts). Good research is usually characterized by large data sets, statistical methodologies, and data analysis, all of which tend to be obscured in a strictly technical analysis. The greater the methodological sophistication, the greater the chance the research will be beyond the experience and competence of the potential consumer and therefore will not be considered.

Policy research also must be *credible* to the consumer. For example, research on the mass sterilization of human beings would not be considered, since it is viewed as amoral and unethical by the vast majority of people. A more practical example is studies which support the non-cognitive benefits of compensatory education; the cognitive benefits are very much more the concern of policy makers, and therefore more credible to them.

Finally, the research evidence must involve a remedy that is *politically feasible*. For example, it would not be worthwhile to present data on the merits of separating disadvantaged children from their families in order to improve their environment and chances for education. Educators, legislators, and judges frown on interfering with child-rearing practices, yet such a proposal has been seriously advanced in some research studies.

---

[38] This report warns that the world hasn't enough resources to continue much longer at the present pace of economic and population growth. Greater shortages of energy and raw materials are predicted between 1985 and 2000.

Given these three necessities, it is understandable why a good deal of social policy research is never seriously considered by policy makers.[39]

RESEARCH, SOCIAL VALUES, AND ADVOCACY

We have noted that one essential difference between social foundations and sociology of education is that the former is oriented toward predictive statements required in diagnosis and planning, while the latter is based on abstracting and generalizing.[40] Both employ summary statements to describe an assembly of data, but the educator typically uses these to press for concrete, specific, how-to-do approaches, while the sociologist is concerned with abstract generalizations, theory, and questions of method, which may have little immediate utility. Social policy presents a compromise whereby policy makers tend to seek concrete, specific data for purposes of decision making, while social scientists who report the data tend to rely on empirical and abstract approaches.

Those who can make a major contribution to research in education or some social aspect of it come to the job with a first-rate set of tools and procedures, a disciplined way of thinking. One reason for the abundance of second-rate and third-rate research in education is that many of these professionals work with dull tools, or no tools at all; they simply lack technical competence.[41] Education has no monopoly in generating poor research, but the large number of doctorates in education (about one third of all the doctorates conferred each year are in education) tends to dilute educational research.

There is very little study of research methodology in education courses, since most professional education is pedagogically oriented, and the research that does creep into these courses is mainly by people associated with other disciplines. Statistics, which is the core of research, is not a required course for potential teachers, and those who take a graduate course in statistics to fulfill degree requirements usually see it as an obstacle to be overcome and then forgotten. They are often taught statistics in rote or cookbook fashion, without genuine understanding of inference procedures or intellectual justification.[42]

---

[39] Henry M. Levin, "Education, Life Chances, and the Courts: The Role of Social Science Evidence," paper presented at the Conference on the Courts, Social Science, and School Desegregation, Hilton Head Island, South Carolina, August 18, 1974.

[40] Hansen, "Relation of Sociology and Education."

[41] Harold Howe, "The Trouble with Research in Education," *Change*, August 1976, pp. 46–47.

[42] Patrick Suppes, "The Place of Theory in Educational Research," *Educational Researcher*, June 1974, pp. 3–10.

Research involving social aspects of education tends to draw people who have expertise in social foundations, sociology of education, and/or social policy. Many of these researchers, especially those from sociology of education and social policy, tend to rely on special vocabularies, statistical procedures, and mathematical analysis, and they are doing so with growing sophistication and complexity to produce new insights into social problems and issues in education. But these tools and techniques are not understandable to a high proportion of those who are responsible for the everyday operation of the schools, much less the policy makers who will make the decisions about education and other social problems. Furthermore, practitioners and policy makers are intimately acquainted with education and have their own opinions about schools and colleges. They think they are authorities, and their opinions are more or less firm. Research studies that do not agree with their views or are not clear to them strike them as particularly annoying or, even worse, without merit. There is, then, a conflict between the generators of research and the consumers of research which operates not only in these three fields of social inquiry in education but in nearly all fields of education.

Those who engage in research in education or some social aspect of it, or in any of the social sciences, could be more objective about the potential of research for solving its problems of students, teachers, and schools. If we can go to the moon, it is often argued, why can't we figure out the most advantageous classroom size, the results of increasing expenditures on schools, the effects of desegregation, or how to teach children to read? The answer is, of course, that the social and educational issues that concern us are vastly more complex than the relatively simple matter of reaching the moon.[43] We are not dealing with nuts and bolts, or electrical or nuclear units, but with individual beings whose behavior is influenced by a host of factors which vary unpredictably with changing life experiences, and over which we have little control. Educators work with minds, attitudes, knowledge, beliefs, attitudes, and skills. Because these have few objective and empirical referents which researchers can observe or measure, efforts to present social and educational research have produced ambiguous results— certainly nothing as concrete as research in medicine or science.

From Researcher to Advocate

While researchers in education and social science could be a little more modest in their claims, and less positive in the way they present their find-

---

[43] Howe, "Trouble with Research in Education"; F. Raymond McKenna, "Why Is There No Science of Education?," *Phi Delta Kappan,* February 1976, pp. 405-9.

ings, it is most essential that they maintain objectivity and report their data without propagandizing. Increasingly, however, there are people in various fields who are rejecting the notion of value-free research because they feel the need to present a point of view or to promote a position in some social or political debate. In presenting, analyzing, and interpreting data, there is a tendency to propagandize, to carefully select "proofs" and arguments which support their political beliefs. In other words, they have given up their role as *researcher,* at least in the traditional sense, to play the role of *advocate.*

There is nothing wrong in taking a practical stand or position on an educational or social issue. But too often there is a tendency to deal in extremes, to pick out the "good" guys and the "bad" guys, to select policies which benefit one group at the expense of other groups. Policy issues are too complex to simplify into good versus bad. In this world of advocacy, there is also a tendency to engage in rhetorical overkill and occasionally to substitute name-calling for logic. And there is a tendency toward confusion, even dishonesty, if the social scientist switches to the role of advocate and still gives the illusion of being objective, implying that the study or explanation of social events is divorced from personal prejudices and biases or hinting that the facts have been carefully weighed and the conclusions have scientific validity. Sadly, many social scientists act unprofessionally when testifying as supposedly impartial witnesses before courts of law or governmental bodies, and deliver advocacy testimony under the guise of scientific objectivity. As Robert Havighurst contends, "It seems clear that a number of contemporary social scientists are not distinguishing between their own political preferences and their role as [researchers and] students of society."[44]

A lawyer is an advocate who defends the interests of his client, selecting from the evidence those facts likely to fortify his case and ignoring those likely to damage it. The researcher, whatever his political views and aversions, should not knowingly suppress even the most unpalatable evidence. The main weakness of advocacy is that it prefers the lawyer's approach to that of the traditional social scientist. With the advocate, the larger crisis of valuation is admitted into the internal choices.

The social scientist, like the nuclear physicist, seeks knowledge related to situations that exist. He is concerned with the nature of the result he is producing and the social process to which he is contributing. He is concerned with the question of how the data will be used and what kinds of decisions will result. But it is one thing to assume responsibility for one's

---

[44] Robert J. Havighurst, "Sociology in the Contemporary Educational Crisis," *Journal of Research and Development in Education,* Fall 1975, p. 15.

research and quite another to slant an experiment, to bury data, or to interpret it in the interest of ascertaining the "truth" according to a predetermined viewpoint. This is when the advocate, under the guise of "social responsibility," becomes irresponsible. Moreover, he may resort to rhetoric so as to put others who disagree with his political sentiments on the defensive. In his quest for truth-telling (that is, his effort to generate data to substantiate his personal beliefs), he may distort the data.

The fields of education and sociology have lately seen a good deal of advocacy by people who have taken a position on an issue and then have selected certain available facts to support their views. A closer look at these educational and social debates suggests that the data that have produced the advocacy have social policy implications. Information may be used by many groups in different ways. Perhaps it will help or hinder college open admissions for nonachieving students, or lead to increased or decreased welfare payments for disadvantaged groups, or be used to modify school spending. Thus in education and sociology, knowledge has both short-run and long-run policy implications.

Specialists in social policy recognize the political potential of information and see the need to emphasize one position or the other; therefore, most of them play the role of advocate. Indeed, it is difficult to find anyone involved with social policy who is in the middle, who is a neutral observer, or who is able to deal with controversial issues objectively. The stakes are high in social policy, as too many groups vie for a limited share of the pie. Even policy analysts who are considered primarily researchers often play the role of advocate and either refuse to admit it or try to mask it. This does not mean that those who are involved with social policy cannot deal with the objective world. Rather, because specialists in social foundations and sociology of education are usually less committed to an extreme political position, they are comparatively more capable of limiting their biases in the areas of their investigation or discussion.

CONCLUSIONS

There are basically two major questions regarding the fields of social foundations, sociology of education, and social policy. These questions present themselves at many levels of inquiry: from college and university departments, to the professional literature found in scholarly journals and textbooks, to research and development centers at local, state, and national levels.

The first question is how to *organize* the search for knowledge so as to obtain the greatest rate of social progress for a given investment of human and material resources in each field. By social progress we mean not the mere accumulation of information but the advancement of socially oriented human behavior and the improvement of social conditions. Such progress assumes that knowledge can be produced in many forms, ranging from analysis, synthesis, and interpretation of ideas and trends; to the development of models, paradigms, and theories; to the advancement of basic and applied research.

The second question is how to *use* this knowledge for the good of society. The practical benefits of knowledge cannot be realized unless it contributes to the education or welfare of the public and people use it to make decisions. Thus knowledge has implications for individuals, groups of people, and society in general.

Specialists in social foundations and sociology of education tend to focus on the first question, whereas those in social policy tend to be more interested in the second. Of course, dichotomies in social science are never perfect, and there is an overlap in the way people in these three fields perceive the two questions.

ACTIVITIES

1. Select three professors you know—one with an interest in social foundations, one in sociology of education, and one in social policy. Casually interview each professor with respect to a common topic, such as the effectiveness of compensatory education, desegregation, or teacher training. Look for ways in which they analyze the topic and reflect their particular field of study. Write these up as case studies.
2. Try to bring to your class three students, one each in social foundations, sociology of education, and social policy. Let them present their reasons for majoring in their respective fields and answer related questions. Try to discern similarities and dissimilarities in the discussion.
3. Try to reach a consensus among class members as to the differences between policies and programs.
4. Sponsor a discussion among fellow students as to the emerging conflict between the social scientist as a researcher and as an advocate.
5. Invite a guest speaker to discuss the functions and dysfunctions of sociological and social science knowledge.

DISCUSSION QUESTIONS

1. What are the basic distinctions between social foundations, sociology of education, and social policy?
2. What are the basic concepts and methods used in each of these three fields?
3. In what way do you feel the social sciences have failed the black community? Helped the black community?

4. How would you describe the roles of the social scientist and the advocate? At what point, if it can be determined, do you feel the social scientist surrenders his or her role as an objective observer and becomes an advocate?
5. Why is the advocate more likely to be found in social policy activities than in social foundations or sociology of education?

SUGGESTED FOR FURTHER READING

Black, James A., and Champion, Dean J. *Methods and Issues in Social Research.* New York: John Wiley & Sons, 1976.

Corwin, Ronald G. *Education in Crisis.* New York: John Wiley & Sons, 1974.

Gordon, C. Wayne (ed.). *Uses of the Sociology of Education,* 73rd Yearbook of the National Society for the Study of Education, Part II. Chicago: University of Chicago Press, 1974.

Kahn, Alfred J. *Social Policy and Social Services.* New York: Random House, 1973.

Kerr, Donna H. *Educational Policy: Analysis, Structure, and Justification.* New York: David McKay & Co., 1976.

Miller, Harry L. *Social and Urban Foundations.* 3rd ed. New York: Holt, Rinehart & Winston, 1978.

Myrdal, Gunnar. *Objectivity in Social Research.* New York: Pantheon Books, 1969.

Ornstein, Allan C. and Miller, Steven I. (eds.) *Policy Issues in Education.* Lexington, Mass.: D. C. Heath & Co., 1976.

Prichard, Keith W.; and Buxton, Thomas H. *Concepts and Theories in Sociology of Education.* Lincoln, Neb.: Professional Educators Publications, 1973.

Stinchcombe, Arthur L. *Constructing Social Theories.* New York: Harcourt, Brace & World, 1968.

PART II

STUDENTS

From the perspective of educators and social scientists involved in education, the most important individual to be considered is the student and his or her relationship to school and society. From the standpoint of schools, students are what schools are all about. All of the resources, facilities, programs, and people are organized for purposes of educating students. From the standpoint of society, the socialization process fits the individual child, who becomes the student, into an organized way of life and an established cultural tradition. Socialization begins very early in life and is a lifelong process; the school serves as only one of the many agents of socialization.

The four chapters of Part II examine numerous social factors affecting first the child and later the student. The examination begins in Chapter 2, with a discussion of culture and socialization: how the individual participates in new social forms and institutions, how the human animal becomes a human being and acquires a self, how the individual gains an identity, interacts with others, takes on ideals and values, and under various social conditions advances through the stages of life.

Chapter 3 considers the relationship of social class to education. While intelligence and ability measured as accurately as possible can affect school achievement, social class factors are also important in determining who goes how far in formal education. Along with a theoretical discussion of social class and deprivation, this chapter examines classic and current studies on the relationship of social class and achievement in school. The discussion starts with the Elmtown's youth and River City studies and continues beyond the Coleman and Jencks controversy.

Chapter 4 examines the meaning of minority status and related concepts, pointing up the differences between discrimination and prejudice and their effects on minority groups. Next there is a discussion about the changing population profiles of cities and suburbs, as well as school systems. Racial and ethnic studies on family structure, mental ability, and school achievement are detailed, and the effects of nonracial and nonethnic variables in education are described.

Chapter 5 is concerned with stratification and inequality. Difficulties of definition and measurement are delineated, and the perceptions of inequality and equality are evaluated and analyzed. Related concepts such as prestige, wealth, income, and education are noted, along with the notions of discrimination and reverse discrimination.

A final note about Part II, especially Chapters 3, 4, and 5: Because the issues in social class, race, ethnicity, and inequality generate lively controversy and even emotion, it is assumed that there may be little consensus of opinion among readers; moreover, it is expected that the aspects of these topics to which the author addresses himself will yield substantial clues to the controversial battlefield.

CHAPTER 2

CULTURE AND
SOCIALIZATION

Culture is an abstraction of society; it refers to the specific ways of life of a group of people. A culture is learned by individuals as the result of belonging to a given group; it is constituted of whatever is learned and shared by others. Every culture has a structure, a pattern of life. What appears to be queer behavior or different behaviors to someone from outside a culture may be normal to a person within it. According to Clyde Kluckhohn, even those who pride themselves on their individualistic behavior follow the customs of their culture most of the time.[1] The facts that we brush our teeth, put on pants or a dress (not a loincloth or grass skirt), eat three meals a day (not four or five), and sleep in a bed (not on the floor or in a sheep pelt) reflect our culture.

Culture not only provides the lens through which people perceive the world, it also guides them in responding to what they perceive. In a world defined by culture, language is perhaps the clearest illustration of the communication of shared meanings, but nonverbal behavior and physical objects also encapsulate cultural meanings. Some people communicate with smoke signals and others by telephone, for example; which method they use is largely determined by culture.

Culture provides the individual with ready-made explanations of the origin and role of man, the nature of the universe, and its natural laws.

---

[1] Clyde Kluckhohn, *Mirror for Man* (New York: McGraw-Hill Book Co., 1949).

These explanations may be mystical and superstitious, or logical and scientific. Culture determines whether a child who asks why days turn into evenings will be told that the gods are sleeping or that the earth is rotating around the sun. In short, culture provides people with the meaning of things and events and a way of thinking and behaving. It gives meaning to life; it is a group's knowledge and customs embodied in memories, books, and objects for present and future use; it is, according to Ruth Benedict, "that which binds men together."[2]

All people learn to conform to the culture patterns that prevail in their societies. It is true that the individual's genetic inheritance plays a role in his or her unique development, but culture also explains racial, national, ethnic, and social class differences, and it is the major impetus for moving man from the Stone Age to the nuclear age.

Today, the majority of social scientists reject both hereditarian and environmental determinism as the method whereby the individual is socialized into the culture. Neither heredity nor environment alone can explain the behavior patterns that distinguish one person from another. The key to human growth and development is embodied in the interaction effects of heredity and environment, what some social scientists call socialization.

THE SOCIALIZATION OF THE INDIVIDUAL

The infant enters the world as a biological organism preoccupied with its own physical comforts. It develops as a human being, with a set of attitudes and values, likes and dislikes, goals and purposes, and a self-concept of the sort of person he or she is. The person gets these characteristics through a process called socialization — that is, the learning process which turns the organism from an animal into a person with a human personality. Put more formally, socialization is the process whereby one internalizes the norms of one's group so that a distinct self — a unique individual — emerges.

Harlow and Davis: The Need for Group Experiences

Socialization begins with the people who care for an infant and attend to its needs. Dependency is a biological given. Newborn children are totally incapable of providing for themselves; they must be fed and sheltered, handled and loved, and their basic needs must be attended to.

Harry Harlow demonstrated the need for body contact in his famous

---

[2] Ruth Benedict, *Patterns of Culture* (Boston: Houghton Mifflin Co., 1934), p. 14.

experiments with monkeys. He raised monkeys in isolation, with only a heated terry-cloth-covered wire framework as a substitute "mother" from which they received their bottles and to which they clung when frightened. None of these animals raised in isolation developed normally. As adult monkeys, they were almost entirely asocial; many were apathetic and withdrawn, and others were hostile and aggressive. Apparently the substitute mother met the infant's need for food and security but was unable to carry it through any further stages of psychosocial development.[3] Other animal experiments have shown similar failures of isolated animals to develop the behavior normal for their species.[4]

For obvious reasons, no similar experiments have been performed with human infants. However, we do know of at least one child who was raised in near isolation. As reported by Kingsley Davis, Anna was the illegitimate child of a farmer's daughter. After trying to place the child in a foster home, Anna's mother brought her home as a last resort. The family refused to acknowledge her existence, and the mother put Anna in an attic room, where she remained for nearly six years. Except for feeding the child just enough to keep her alive, the mother ignored her. When social workers discovered Anna, she could not sit up or walk, much less talk. In fact, she was so apathetic, so uncommunicative, that they first assumed she was deaf, mentally retarded, or possibly both. Anna was placed in a special school and made progress in body coordination, communication, and learning, but she died four years later.[5] What Anna proved between the time she was discovered and her premature death was that practically none of the behavior usually associated with human beings arises spontaneously. In short, both animals and human beings need group experiences if they are to develop normally.[6]

Culture and Personality

Although infants are much the same the world over — all babies have the same biological needs and all require social learning — techniques of child rearing vary widely among different societies. There are as many ways of

---

[3] Harry F. Harlow and R. Z. Zimmerman, "Affectional Responses in the Infant Monkey," *Science*, August 21, 1959, pp. 421–32; Harry F. Harlow and Margaret K. Harlow, "A Study of Animal Affection," *Natural History*, December 1961, pp. 48–55.

[4] Maurice A. Krout, *Introduction to Social Psychology* (New York: Harper & Row, 1942), pp. 102–5.

[5] Kingsley Davis, *Human Society* (New York: Macmillan Co., 1948).

[6] Studies of institutionalized children support this conclusion. Even with the best physical care — good food, regular changes and baths, clean sheets, bright and airy rooms, etc. — infants who are not handled and played with develop slowly; mortality rates in orphanages are alarmingly high. See John Bowlby, *Separation: Anxiety and Anger* (New York: Basic Books, 1973).

holding, feeding, clothing, and training children as there are cultures. Human beings come into this world with a unique genetic makeup, but culture largely influences socialization, which in turn influences their growth and development. For example, John Whiting and Irwin Child's cross-cultural, early fifties study of child-rearing practices in some 50 nontechnological societies showed that the Marquesans believe that nursing spoils a child and therefore wean their infants at a very early age. The Chenchu of India, in contrast, continue nursing until a child is five or six years old. In the 1950s, American middle-class parents were relatively severe in their feeding methods: babies were usually put on a rigid schedule as soon as possible and were weaned at about six months. With regard to sex training, Whiting and Child pointed out that the Manus of New Guinea consider masturbation shameful, while the Alorese of Indonesia frequently masturbate their children to pacify them; the Hopi tell their children that premature sex will lead to deformity, but the Baiga of Southern Asia encourage sex games among very young children.[7] As for Americans, they are strict about sex activity and masturbation; they encourage modesty and inhibit sexual play.

In general, the way in which a child is raised will have an effect on his or her personality and behavior, and, consciously or unconsciously, parents encourage those personality traits a child will need to function in society. For example, based on surveys of over 100 societies, Herbert Barry et al. found that methods of child rearing in agricultural societies stress cooperation—a valuable personality trait when people must perform routine tasks to ensure a continuous food supply. Hunting and gathering societies, on the other hand, encourage individual initiative and daring, traits that may be beneficial when one must take chances or risk one's life in the hunter-gatherer society.[8]

Erich Fromm has argued that the basic American personality trait is "other-directedness"—the tendency to be sensitive to what other people think and feel. While Fromm, a psychologist, disapproves of Americans' need for social approval, he concedes that other-directedness may be related to technological societies and flexibility.[9]

All of these studies imply that different societies tend to produce different personality types. Agricultural societies seem to produce cooperative

---

[7] John W. M. Whiting and Irwin L. Child, *Child Training and Personality* (New Haven, Conn.: Yale University Press, 1953).

[8] Herbert Barry, Margaret K. Bacon, and Irwin L. Child, "A Cross-Cultural Survey of Some Sex Differences in Socialization," *Journal of Abnormal and Social Psychology*, November 1957, pp. 327–32.

[9] Erich Fromm, "Psychoanalytic Characterology and Its Application to the Understanding of Culture," in S. S. Sargent and M. W. Smith (eds.), *Culture and Personality* (Glen Gardner, N.J.: Libertarian Press, 1949), pp. 1–12.

people; hunting societies, self-reliant people; technological societies, other-directed people. These correlations are merely generalizations, however.

Benedict and Mead: Modal Personality

When sociologists speak of the modal personality type, they do not mean that all members of a particular society are exactly alike. As Ruth Benedict wrote, "No culture yet observed has been able to eradicate the differences in temperament of the persons who composed it."[10] However, members of a society do have much in common; they are nursed or fed on schedule, toilet trained a certain way, educated in similar fashion, marry one or several spouses, live by labor and perform common economic tasks, believe in one God or in many deities. These shared experiences temper individual differences so that individuals behave in similar ways. According to Benedict, the norms of society govern interpersonal relations and produce a modal personality; that is, the attitudes, feelings, and behavior patterns most members of a society share.

In a study of the American modal personality, anthropologist Margaret Mead stressed the idea that this is the land of unlimited opportunity. Whether this be fiction or fact, the belief that any boy can become President places a heavy burden on most Americans.[11] By implication, the boy who does not become President (or a doctor, lawyer, engineer, or corporate executive) has shirked his "moral responsibility to succeed." Most other people in the world blame poverty, fate, or the government for failure to succeed; Americans (except some minority groups) tend to blame themselves.

Whereas European parents usually raise their children to carry on a family tradition, first- and second-generation American parents want their children to leave home for a better life. Americans tend to evaluate their own self-worth according to how high they have climbed above their father's status and how they compare with their friends and neighbors. We are a materialistic, ever-striving group of people. At no point do Americans feel they have truly "arrived"; the climb is endless, and it is very much a part of the middle- and upper-middle-class value system.

THE SELF AND SOCIALIZATION

The existence of any society depends on the presence of people who share in the culture, take active roles in the society, and manifest the

---

[10] Benedict, *Patterns of Culture*, p. 253.
[11] Margaret Mead, *And Keep Your Powder Dry* (New York: William Morrow & Co., 1941).

actions that make it an ongoing process. But such people are not ready-made. At birth the human organism knows almost nothing and can do almost nothing; totally helpless and dependent on others, it has to learn and develop with the aid of others.

In the course of growing older, people develop a kind of amnesia about their early years. Perhaps a few incidents stand out, but how many can remember being put on a toilet seat or being spoon-fed while in a high-chair? Adults find it almost impossible to recall a time when they were without speech, uncoordinated, or not self-conscious. The sense of identity that adults take as a given emerges gradually, step by step, from early infancy. The analysis of socialization in this section focuses on the interaction between children and the people around them, and how this interaction shapes the sense of self.

Cooley: The Emergence of Self

It was Charles Cooley who, at the turn of the 20th century, first suggested that the "self" is largely a social product.[12] We take the words "I" and "me" for granted; we experience ourselves as distinct individuals, separate from all others. But there cannot be an "I" without a corresponding "they." The "self" is a social product that emerges as the child grows and interacts with others, first with his parents, then with other children and adults. In particular, the self-concept heavily depends on the feedback received by the individual as a child.

Cooley used the image of a looking glass to explain how others influence the way we see ourselves: "Each to each a looking glass / Reflects the other that doth pass." By this, he meant that we gain a feeling about ourselves by imagining what others think about us, or the way they perceive us. According to Cooley, the self has three main components: our imagination of the way we appear to others; our perception of the way others see that appearance; and the way we feel about those judgments.

Criteria for these judgments vary, but all societies evaluate physical appearance, and the way people react to a person's looks will affect that person's feelings about himself. In some cases, hair and skin color influence both social standing and self-image. For years, black children growing up in the United States learned that their dark skin and kinky hair were not considered attractive by whites. Consequently, many black people straightened their hair and used skin bleach. Even among themselves, light-skinned blacks had more status than dark-skinned blacks. Similarly, many Americans — white and black — believe that "blondes have more

---

[12] Charles H. Cooley, *Human Nature and the Social Order* (New York: Scribners, 1902).

fun." Some brunettes, as a result, grow up thinking they are at a disadvantage compared to their blonde friends.

It is important to note that Cooley's looking-glass theory is in part based on the "imagination [of the way] we perceive in another's mind some thought of our appearance, manners, aims, deeds, character," and so on.[13] One's self-image, then, does not necessarily reflect reality. Some minorities, for example, tend to hold others responsible for failure, regardless of whether this is true or not; intelligent, well-read women often go through life thinking themselves dull; some successful businessmen attribute their triumphs to luck and others to skill; punitive parents often see themselves as kind and loving. In other words, the way we see ourselves may not coincide with the way others see us. In checking the social looking glass, people tend to see what they want and expect to see; this is often conditioned by the self in the context of the socialization process.

Mead: Internalization of the Role of Others

Like Cooley, George Mead noted that children imitate adults in their actions, and this is significant in their learning. For Mead this meant that by taking the roles of others, the child leans how they respond to objects around them, and he is able to *internalize* these responses as his own. By taking their roles he learns to feel and think as they do.[14] For example, young children spend much of their time in the world of make-believe. For hours they play at being mothers and fathers (watch a child scold a doll, using the voice tone and words of its mother), mailmen, or doctors, often embarrassing adults with the accuracy of their portrayals.

In short, the child becomes one of the people who are important in his or her social and psychological world, those whom Mead called *significant others*. By exploring various roles firsthand, children learn how different activities look from the perspectives of parents, siblings, and others. In doing so, they learn to look at themselves through the eyes of other people.

In time, the characters children pretend to be become part of their internal self; they learn how people will respond to them without actually having to act out the situation. Thus, a five-year-old child may stop with his hand halfway in the refrigerator and say to himself: "No, you'll spoil your appetite." In ordinary terms, the child develops a *conscience*, what Mead called the *me*, whereas Freud called it the *superego*. Actually, it is the internalization of the norms of society. It enables the individual to respond morally to his own actions and thoughts and to judge himself as

---

[13] Ibid., p. 152.

[14] George H. Mead, *Mind, Self and Society* (Chicago: University of Chicago Press, 1934).

he perceives he might be judged by others. Such a capacity for self-judgment connotes that the individual has a self which has developed through the individual's social interaction with others.

Freud: A Psychoanalytical View of the Individual and Society

No discussion of socialization would be complete without some mention of Sigmund Freud. Although the number of orthodox Freudians in psychology today is small, Freud's work represents a major turning point in our view of human behavior. In his earlier papers Freud shocked — perhaps outraged — his contemporaries, who held Victorian views about infant sexuality. These papers were based on his impression that many of the women patients he was treating had been seduced by their fathers in early childhood. In his writings, Freud criticized the common belief that infants and children are asexual. Instead, he described the family unit as a hotbed of passions and the scene of guilt-ridden father-daughter, mother-son romances. No sooner were these ideas published than Freud realized that he was wrong; his patients had *imagined* — not experienced — seduction. Nevertheless, the effect on their inner lives was much the same. This led to Freud's unprecedented theory of the unconscious mind — one of the most important discoveries of this century.

As an offshoot of his view of the unconscious, Freud assumed that all human behavior could be explained in terms of cause and effect. This applied to seemingly accidental slips of the tongue (we speak of Freudian slips), the way people describe things (we speak of Freudian symbols), and dreams. In Freud's description of the self and the socialization process he begins with egocentric, aggressive, pleasure-seeking infants.[15] In the first years of life, all of the child's energies are directed toward oral gratification (sucking and eating), the pleasure release of tension in defecation, and the joys of masturbation. (This is the basis of what Freud called the *pleasure principle*.) Freud described not only sexual and aggressive urges, which he believed were biological givens, but all bodily functions as the concern of the *id*. Modern society, by way of parents, interferes with children's pleasure-seeking activities; their demands for food are met only at certain times, they are forced to control their bowels, and their masturbation is restricted. As children struggle to accommodate to these social demands, there begins to develop what Freud called the *ego*. The ego is the rational part of the self that interprets information obtained through the senses and finds socially acceptable ways of satisfying biological needs.

---

[15] Sigmund Freud, *The Standard Edition of the Complete Works of Sigmund Freud* (London: Hogarth Press, 1953).

As children grow up, their desires are still powerful, but so are their fears. Realizing that their parents have enormous power over them, they conform to what their parents want them to do. Children begin to internalize their parents' concepts of right and wrong, including their moral ideals. They learn to repress socially unacceptable ideas and, ideally, to redirect their energies into socially approved channels. The *superego,* or conscience, develops at this period; moreover, it forces the id underground. The desires and fears of childhood, which are stimulated by the reemergence of sexuality in adolescence, remain active in the unconscious, influencing the way the individual behaves throughout life.

Later in life, the superego is internalized by the norms and beliefs of society. The id continues to press for gratification. The ego serves to control these lustful (sexual and aggressive) drives, while at the same time modifying the unrealistic demands of the perfection-seeking superego. Driven one way by biological needs, the other by the norms of society, we are, according to Freud, forever discontented.[16]

Sex Roles and Sex Differences

Not only does society demand conformity to its basic values and mores, it also assigns specific roles to each of its members, expecting them to conform to certain established behavioral patterns. A good example of this type of socialization is found in sex roles; that is, the ways boys and girls and men and women are "supposed" to act. Sex roles vary from culture to culture, but within a given culture they are rather well defined, and, what is more, they are enforced through an elaborate schedule of selective reinforcement. For example, the preschool boy is ridiculed for playing with dolls, and girls are supposed to be "feminine."

An important contribution to the notion of sex roles has been made by David Lynn, who differentiated between parental identification, by which the child internalizes the personality characteristics of his parents, and sex-role identification of a given sex in a specific culture.[17] The initial parental identification of both male and female children is with the mother, but the boy must shift his original mother identification to establish the masculine role identity. At this period differences begin: a girl has the same-sex parental model for identification all hours of the day, but a boy sees the father only briefly. Besides, the father participates in

---

[16] Sigmund Freud, *Civilization and Its Discontents.* Originally published in German in 1930 (New York: W. W. Norton & Co., 1961).

[17] David B. Lynn, "Sex Role and Parental Identification," *Child Development,* March 1962, pp. 555-64; David B. Lynn, "Divergent Feedback and Sex-Role Identification in Boys and Men," *Merrill Palmer Quarterly,* January 1964, pp. 17-23.

some feminine roles, that is, roles which until very recently have been defined in American society as feminine (washing dishes, cleaning), so that he must distinguish the masculine role from the stereotype spelled out for him by society through a system of reinforcements and rewards. As a result, as the boy's identification with the mother role diminishes, it is gradually replaced by a learned identification with a culturally defined masculine role. This is accomplished mainly through negative admonishments such as "Don't be a sissy," which does not tell him what he should do instead, however.

The girl simply learns the female identification as it is presented to her, partly through imitation and partly through the mother's reinforcement and reward of selective behavior. The boy has the problem of making the proper sex-role identification in the partial absence of a male model, and this is even more difficult in a female-headed household where the father is completely absent. The girl acquires a learning method that basically involves a personal relationship and identification with the mother. By contrast, the boy must define his goals, restructure some of his experiences, and abstract underlying principles. The result is greater learning problems for boys and greater dependency on the part of girls.

When children come of school age, they find that the schools are largely staffed by females, especially on the elementary level, which is a critical age in child development. The schools are dominated by female norms of politeness, cleanliness, and obedience. The curriculum, tests, and classroom activities are female oriented—safe, nice, antiseptic. The school frowns on vulgar language and fighting; it suppresses the boys' maleness and often fails to permit action-oriented, tough sports. Thus the disadvantage that the boy finds at home in developing his masculine identity is compounded by the schooling process.[18]

In this connection, Patricia Sexton presents controversial data showing that schools are feminizing institutions which discriminate against the male and subvert his identity.[19] Her data show that approximately three out of four students regarded as problems are boys, and since teachers tend to fail problem students, approximately two out of three students who fail are boys. The male student who is a high achiever tends to be fat and flabby, especially at the elementary and junior high school level; those who gravitate to masculine activities, such as conflict sports and mechanics, tend to do poorly in academic areas—and they are often at odds with their teachers, who are predominantly female (and with male teachers, too, who by virtue of their role tend to enforce the feminized school norms).

---

[18] Allan C. Ornstein, "Who Are the Disadvantaged?" *Young Children,* May 1971, pp. 264–72.

[19] Patricia C. Sexton, *The Feminized Male* (New York: Random House, 1969).

Sexton maintains that the schools' values and the resulting discrimination against boys, compounded by the mother's inability to relate to sons in helping them establish a healthy male identification, are negative and cumulative. In part they explain why boys largely outnumber girls in school dropout rates, deviant and delinquent acts, mental illnesses, and suicides.

Although Sexton's conclusions may be somewhat overgeneralized and extend beyond her data, there is no question that girls receive higher grades throughout elementary school, with the gap being gradually reduced in high school. More boys are nonreaders; more boys fail; more boys are disciplinary cases; and more boys drop out of school. And more men than women are prisoners or have mental breakdowns, and men die at a younger age. No doubt sex roles and sex differences in school are at least in part related to role expectations which are incorporated into the self-concept very early in life. However, there is research which suggests that such roles may also be biochemically related and may stem from inherited predispositions of males and females, as well as maturation differences.[20,21]

SOCIALIZATION AND DEVELOPMENTAL THEORIES

A number of theories have been originated which focus on global aspects of human growth and development. They emphasize the study of behavior as a totality, starting with infancy, and in a sense they represent an aspect of Gestalt psychology, which considers the totality of the development of the human organism. Developmental theories are addressed to the cumulative effects of change that occur as a consequence of learning or failing to learn appropriate tasks during the critical stages of life. Failure to learn an appropriate task at a given stage of development tends to have detrimental effects on the developmental sequence to follow.

Development proceeds through a rather fixed sequence of relatively continuous stages, and it is assumed that maturation as well as appropriate cultural experiences are necessary to move the individual from stage to stage. Shifts from one stage to the next are based on maturation but are subject to variations as a result of differences in the amount and the quality of stimulation the individual experiences cumulatively over long spans of

---

[20] Josef E. Garai and Amram Scheinfeld, "Sex Differences in Mental and Behavioral Traits," *Genetic Psychological Monograph*, May 1968, pp. 169-229; George J. Mouly, *Psychology for Effective Teaching*, 3rd ed. (New York: Holt, Rinehart & Winston, 1973).

[21] Maturation can be defined as a broad continuum of growth and development based on previous growth and development and influenced by age as well as genetic and environmental factors.

development. Stages tend to set certain upper limits at given points in the developmental process because each stage is built on earlier stages of development.

Erikson: The Eight Stages of Man

Erik Erikson, one of Freud's students, began in the early 1950s to outline his comprehensive theory of human development. Erikson's developmental model brings Cooley, Mead, and Freud together and integrates the physiological, psychological, and cultural elements of the socialization process.[22] His major concern is with the feelings people develop toward themselves and the world around them; he describes socialization as a lifelong process which begins at birth and continues into old age.

Erikson describes eight stages of human development, each constituting a crisis in identity (Erikson gave us the term *identity crisis*) which is brought on by physiological changes to which the individual must adapt. He describes both positive and negative responses to these crises and asserts that elements of both exist in most people. When things go well, the maturing individual works out solutions to these crises that result in a stable identity. The eight stages are:

1. *Trust v. Mistrust (Infancy).* During this stage children are totally dependent on adults, primarily their mothers. Children whose mothers respond warmly and consistently to their needs begin to develop feelings of *basic trust.* Infants whose mothers are undependable and rejecting find the world a fearful place and develop *basic mistrust* toward themselves and other people.

2. *Autonomy v. Shame and Doubt (Early Childhood).* This is the period of muscular maturation, of grasping, reaching, crawling, controlling bowels — of "holding on" and "letting go." If parents allow the young ones to explore and develop at their own pace, they gain confidence in their ability to govern themselves — that is, their *autonomy.* But if children are constantly neglected they develop feelings of *self-doubt.* and if they are overdisciplined they develop feelings of *shame.*

3. *Initiative v. Guilt (The Play Stage).* At four or five, the child is eager to make things cooperatively and to combine with other children to construct objects. In their play and fantasies, they begin to act out adult roles, transforming (and mastering) the world in their imaginations. Children's feelings of *initiative* and self-worth grow if their parents and others important to them respect their efforts. Ridicule and disinterest

---

[22] Erik H. Erikson, *Childhood and Society* (New York: W. W. Norton & Co., 1950).

make children wonder about their actions and goals, and they develop feelings of *guilt*.

4. *Industry v. Inferiority (School Age)*. As the social setting shifts from the home to the school and larger community, children enter the impersonal world of unrelated children and adults. They learn to win recognition by producing things and by adjusting themselves to the tool world, and ideally they take pride in *industry*. However, if they fail to do well in school, or if they are rejected because of their social class or race, they tend to develop a sense of *inferiority*.

5. *Identity v. Role Confusion (Adolescence)*. At this stage childhood has ended, and a sense of *identity* develops if the youth has confidence in himself or herself, if past experiences have been derived from a sense of sameness and continuity, and if there is a future purpose. If a person cannot integrate his various roles into a clear identity the self remains diffuse, and there is *role confusion*.

6. *Intimacy v. Isolation (Early Adulthood)*. The young adult is willing to fuse his identity with others, to make a commitment, to enter into close friendships or marriage. This involves some risk—the risk of being hurt, of losing that person. Young people who are sure of themselves will be able to develop *intimate* relationships; those without a clear identity will keep to themselves or move from one short-lived relationship to another. They may feel safe, but they develop a sense of loneliness or *isolation*.

7. *Generativity v. Stagnation (Middle Age)*. This period involves the adult's concern in establishing and guiding the next generation, preferably one's own offspring. *Generativity* is the feeling that one is making a significant contribution, if not as a parent then by working to better society or leaving some mark which immortalizes one's existence. For some people, however, middle age is painful, and they feel a sense of *stagnation*.

Table 2.1 / Erikson's Eight Stages of Life

Age	Stage	Predominant Social Setting
Infancy	Trust v. Mistrust	Family
Early childhood	Autonomy v. Shame and Doubt	Family
Ages four to five	Initiative v. Guilt	Family
Ages six to twelve	Industry v. Inferiority	School
Adolescence	Identity v. Role Confusion	School; peer group
Early adulthood	Intimacy v. Isolation	Couple
Adulthood and middle age	Generativity v. Stagnation	New family; work
Old age	Integrity v. Despair	Couple or family; retirement

Source: Adapted from Erik H. Erikson, *Childhood and Society* (New York: W. W. Norton & Co., 1950), pp. 47-74.

8. *Integrity v. Despair (Old Age)*. This is a period of reflection, of evaluating the fruit of the other seven stages. One must come to terms with death, and this means coming to terms with life—with what one has done with one's time on earth. Acceptance of one's life results in *ego integrity,* whereas *despair* comes from looking back and seeing one's life as a series of missed opportunities and realizing that it is too late to start over. This feeling is difficult for a young person to understand.

Erikson's eight stages of life are summed up in Table 2.1. The underlying assumptions for charting the life cycle are that human growth develops according to predetermined stages, and society encourages the proper rate and sequence of the life cycle. Each of the critical stages is systematically related to the others, and all depend on the proper development of the previous stage. While the tempo and intensity of each stage will vary, depending on one's experiences, failure to integrate one of the eight stages will have a modifying influence on all later stages and may impair psychosocial development. Each culture develops the particular style of integrating these stages, and the way people work out solutions to their developmental problems reflects in part the norms and values of that culture.

Piaget and Kohlberg: Moral Development

While conscience and moral standards may be seen in the preschool years, not until the child is about age four do moral standards begin to develop at a rapid rate. As the younger child gradually abandons his relative hedonism—behavior pretty much governed by whatever he wants to do at a particular moment—his early conscience and moral development tends to be erratic, largely confined to prohibitions against specific behaviors, and based on external rather than internal sanctions. Gradually, however, from about four to six years, conscience in most children is confined less to specific behaviors and begins to incorporate more generalized abstract standards; it becomes determined less by external rewards or punishments and more by internal sanctions.[23]

Jean Piaget's theories of moral development were based on techniques of investigation which included conversing with Swiss children and asking them questions about moral dilemmas and events in stories. For example, he might ask a child, "Why shouldn't you cheat in a game?" Piaget's observations suggested that from age 5 to 12 the child's concept of justice

---

[23] Paul H. Mussen, John J. Conger, and Jerome Kagan, *Child Development and Personality* (New York: Harper & Row, 1969).

passes from a rigid and inflexible notion of right and wrong, learned from his parents, to a sense of equity in moral judgments. Eventually it takes into account the specific situation in which a moral violation has occurred.[24] For example, the five-year-old child is likely to view lying as bad, regardless of the situation or circumstances in which it occurs. As the child grows older, he becomes more flexible and realizes that there are exceptions to the rule, that is, there are some circumstances under which lying may be justifiable.

With increasing age, a child becomes a member of a larger, more varied peer group. Rules and moral judgments are less absolute and rigid and more dependent on the needs and desires of the people involved. Wrote Piaget, "For very young children, a rule is a sacred reality because it is traditional; for the older ones it depends upon a mutual agreement."[25] For example, 150 children between the ages of 6 and 12 were told stories involving a moral issue involving obedience to parents and a sense of justice. The percentage of children whose solutions involved "obedience to adults" decreased steadily with advancing age.

In another part of the study, children were asked to cite illustrations of what they considered as unfair. "Behaviors forbidden by parents" were mentioned by 64 percent of children between 6 and 8 years old, but by only 7 percent of children in the 9- to 12-year-old bracket. Inequality in punishment and treatment were mentioned by 73 percent of the children between 9 and 12 but only 27 percent of the children between 6 and 8.

On the basis of numerous studies of these types, Piaget concluded:

. . . there are three great periods in the development of the sense of justice in the child. One period, lasting up to age of 7-8, during which justice is subordinated to adult authority; a period contained approximately between 8-11, and which is that of progressive equalitarianism; and finally a period which sets in toward 11-12, and during which purely equalitarian justice is tempered by consideration of equity.[26]

Using both American and Swiss children as subjects, Eugene Lerner confirmed Piaget's findings regarding age changes in moral judgments. He found a progressive decline in suggestions for solving dilemmas by subordination to adult demands or acceptance of authority between ages 6 and 13.[27] Gardner Murphy also confirmed Piaget's work; he concluded:

---

[24] Jean Piaget, *The Moral Judgment of the Child* (London: Routledge & Kegan Paul, 1932).

[25] Ibid., p. 192.

[26] Ibid., p. 314.

[27] Eugene Lerner, *Constraint Areas and Moral Judgment of Children* (Menasha, Wis.: Banta, 1937).

Figure 2.1 / Kohlberg's Six Stages of Moral Development at Four Ages

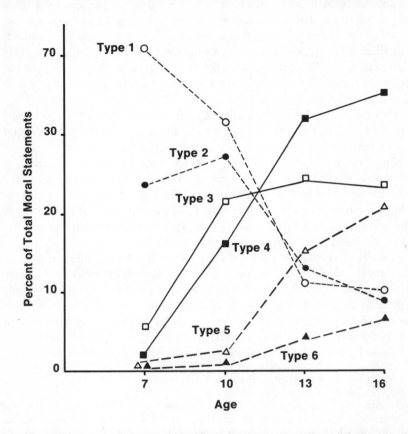

Source: Lawrence Kohlberg, "The Development of Children's Orientations toward a Moral Order," *Vita Humana*, vol. 6 (1963), p. 16. Reproduced by permission of S. Karger AG, Basel.

"Moral realism yields gradually during childhood to . . . a sense of balance or justice. Rightness is a matter of the mutual consideration of needs."[28]

More recently, Lawrence Kohlberg studied the development of children's moral standards by asking them to evaluate deviant acts which they were told were followed by reward, and conforming acts which they were told were followed by punishment. He presented similar questions to

[28] Gardner Murphy, *Personality: A Biosocial Approach to Origins and Structure* (New York: Harper & Row, 1947), p. 386.

children of various age groups and cultures and concluded that the way we think about moral issues is not simply a reflection of our culture but also based on stages of growth or age.

Six developmental types of moral judgments grouped into three moral levels (stages) were outlined by Kohlberg, corresponding to the four different age groups illustrated in Figure 2.1. The six types and three levels are discussed below.

1. *Preconventional Level.* Children at this level have not yet developed a sense of right or wrong. The level is comprised of two types: (1) children do as they are told because they fear punishment, and (2) children realize that certain actions bring rewards.

2. *Conventional Level.* At this level, children are concerned about what other people think of them. As a result, their behavior becomes largely other-directed. There are also two types in this level: (3) children seek their parents' approval by being "nice," and (4) children begin thinking in terms of rules.

3. *Postconventional Level.* Children's morality is based on what other people feel or on their precepts of authority. This level also includes two types: (5) children are able to view morality in terms of contractual obligations and democratically accepted laws, and they view morality in terms of individual principles of conscience.

Kohlberg views his theory as supporting the general developmental view of morality set forth by Piaget, although he differs on specifics.[29] Whereas Piaget stresses that there are very real differences in the way children think about morality at different ages, Kohlberg found considerable overlap at various ages in the use of his six moral types, as shown in Figure 2.1. However, in line with Piaget, the frequency of the more primitive types declined with age, and those of mature types increased. Kohlberg says:

As opposed to Piaget's view, the data suggest that the "natural" aspects of moral development are continuous and a reaction to the whole social world rather than a product of a certain stage, a certain concept . . . or a certain type of social relations.[30]

Unless a reasonable degree of moral development takes place during childhood and adolescence — that is, unless standards of right and wrong

---

[29] Lawrence Kohlberg, "The Development of Children's Orientations toward a Moral Order, I: Sequence in the Development of Moral Thought," *Vita Humana*, vol. 6 (1963), pp. 11–33; Lawrence Kohlberg, "Development of Moral Character and Moral Ideology," in M. L. Hoffman and L. W. Hoffman (eds.), *Review of Child Development*, vol. 1 (New York: Russell Sage Foundation, 1964), pp. 383–431.

[30] Lawrence Kohlberg, "Moral Development and Identification," in N. B. Henry and H. G. Richey (eds.), *Child Psychology*, Sixty-second Yearbook of the National Society for the Study of Education, Part I (Chicago: University of Chicago Press, 1963), pp. 322-23.

are established—the child, and later the adult, is likely to engage in asocial behavior, encouraged by her or his own urges for uncontrolled sexual and aggressive behavior. On the other hand, if the learning or socialization of internal standards and prohibitions (superego development) is unduly strong, crippling guilt may develop, in association with a wide variety of actions and thoughts. Without trying to get too involved in Freudian psychology, we can say that defenses erected against painful guilt feelings may lead to the development of psychological and psychosomatic symptoms. Ideally, it is up to young men and women to work out an adequate sense of morality and at the same time avoid self-condemnation, in the context of the culture in which they live.

Piaget: Cognitive Development

The most comprehensive view of cognitive growth and development also has been formulated by Jean Piaget.[31] During the past 50 years, the Swiss psychologist has put together a detailed theory of mental operations. However, it is only within the past 20 years that his work in cognition has come to the attention of American educators and has become popular among American social scientists.

Piaget describes cognitive development in terms of four stages, the characteristics of which can be summarized as follows:

1. The different stages form a sequence or succession—a progressive organization of mental operations.
2. The stages are hierarchical, forming an order of increasingly sophisticated and integrated mental operations; these stages imply a distinct qualitative difference in children's modes of thinking and solving the same problems.
3. Although the succession of stages is constant, stages of attainment vary within certain limits which are a function of culture and environment.
4. While cultural factors may speed up or slow down cognitive development, they do not change the sequence.

With this in mind, the four basic stages of intellectual development are defined as:

1. *The sensimotor stage (approximately the first two years)*. The child progresses from reflex operations, in which surrounding schema are undifferentiated, to complex sensorimotor actions, in which there is a progressive organization of the schema. The child comes to realize that

---

[31] Jean Piaget, *Judgment and Reasoning in Child Development* (New York: Harcourt, Brace & World, 1948); Jean Piaget, *The Psychology of Intelligence* (London: Broadway, 1950).

objects have permanence; they can be found again. The child begins to establish simple relations among similar objects.

2. *The preoperational stage (approximate ages two to seven)*. In this stage, objects and events begin to take on symbolic meaning for the child; the chair is for sitting; birthday parties are a time for celebration; school is a place to learn. At the latter part of this period, the child becomes aware of the concept of number and amount. The child shows an increased ability to learn more complex concepts from his experiences but must be provided with concrete or familiar examples from which to extract criteria that define the concept.

3. *The concrete operations stage (approximate ages 7–11)*. The child begins to organize data into logical relations and gains facility in manipulating data in problem-solving situations; these operations occur, however, only if concrete objects are available or if actual past experiences can be drawn upon. The child is able to make judgments in terms of reversibility and reciprocal relations; for example, left and right are spatial relations, "being a foreigner" is a reciprocal process. Understanding develops of the conservation of a liquid—a long narrow glass may hold the same amount of water as a short wide one.

4. *The formal operations stage (ages 11 onward)*. This stage is characterized by the development of formal and abstract thought operations. The adolescent is able to analyze ideas and make spatial and temporal relations. He can think logically about abstract data; he can evaluate data according to acceptable criteria. Instead of being bound to the concrete here and now, he can formulate hypotheses and deduce possible consequences from them.

Piaget's cognitive stages presuppose a *maturation* process in the sense that development is a continuation based on previous growth. Although the stages are defined as separate phases, they do overlap and are by no means precise or binding at a given age. A child's *hereditary* capabilities and *environmental* experiences (or culture) determine the quality of growth for that child at each cognitive stage, and the environmental experiences are affected by the family as well as teachers and schools. There is some controversy over whether the stages can be accelerated through appropriate experiences. Evidence supports the notion that planned training cannot substitute for the massive experience which occurs with age; this is a matter of maturation, at least until mastery of the concept of conservation, somewhere in Stage 3.[32]

[32] Hans Furth and Harry Wachs, *Thinking Goes to School: Piaget's Theory in Practice* (New York: Oxford University Press, 1974); Lawrence Kohlberg, "Early Education: A Cognitive-Developmental View," *Child Development*, December 1968, pp. 1013–62.

Piaget's theories are of special relevance to elementary school teachers, who must understand how children develop intellectually and at which stages of intellectual functioning certain cognitive activities should be presented. They also have significant implications for compensatory programs such as Head Start and Follow Through, and they point up the general need to provide children with appropriate sensorimotor activities and concrete objects with which to develop their mental structures.

Havighurst: Educational and Developmental Tasks

Robert Havighurst has identified six periods in human development: (1) infancy and early childhood, (2) middle childhood, (3) adolescence, (4) early adulthood, (5) middle age, and (6) late maturity. Developmental tasks are defined as "the tasks the individual must learn" for purposes of "healthy and satisfactory growth in our society. They are the things a person must learn if he is to be judged and to judge himself to be a reasonably happy and successful person." A developmental task is a task that occurs at a certain stage or period in the life of that individual. "Successful achievement . . . leads to his happiness and to success with later tasks, while failure leads to unhappiness, disapproval by the society, and difficulty with later tasks."[33]

The schooling of the individual is concerned with the developmental tasks of the second part of the first period and the next two periods of life. These are listed below.[34]

1. Early childhood
   a. Forming concepts and learning language to describe the social and physical reality.
   b. Getting ready to read.
   c. Learning to distinguish right from wrong and beginning to develop a conscience.
2. Middle childhood
   a. Learning physical skills necessary for ordinary games.
   b. Building wholesome attitudes toward oneself.
   c. Learning to get along with age-mates.
   d. Learning appropriate male and female roles.
   e. Developing fundamental skills in reading, writing, and mathematics.
   f. Developing concepts for everyday living.

---

[33] Robert J. Havighurst, *Human Development and Education* (New York: Longmans, Green & Co., 1953), p. 2.

[34] Robert J. Havighurst, *Developmental Tasks and Education*, 3rd ed. (New York: David McKay Co., 1971).

    g. Developing morality and a set of values.

    h. Achieving personal independence.

    i. Developing (democratic) attitudes toward social groups and institutions.

3. Adolescence

    a. Achieving new and more mature relations with age-mates of both sexes.

    b. Achieving a masculine or feminine social role.

    c. Accepting one's physique and using the body effectively.

    d. Achieving emotional independence of parents and other adults.

    e. Preparing for marriage and family life.

    f. Preparing for an economic career.

    g. Acquiring a set of values and an ethical system to guide behavior.

    h. Achieving socially responsible behavior.

Research findings confirm that achievement of a developmental task at one age level is followed by good performance on the same task at subsequent age levels, and is generally associated with achievement of other tasks at the same age level. In a few cases, successful achievement of one developmental task has been used by individuals to compensate for poor achievement on other tasks.[35] In order for the child or adolescent to *accomplish successfully* the developmental tasks required in this society, he or she must master self-acceptance, as well as the subject matter of the school. These two givens are related. For example, an emotionally disturbed child or one who has a poor self-concept usually does not acquire knowledge and related cognitive skills as efficiently as one who is not disturbed or has a healthy concept of self. Boys and girls who acquire learning outcomes efficiently in school tend to have positive self-concepts and are socially mature.

If the developmental tasks of childhood and adolescence are not adequately achieved, the individual is likely to experience difficulties in adulthood. Most of these early tasks are school-related and directly or indirectly learned in school. As a result, the school serves as the crucial institution for influencing the individual's present and future quality of life.

AGENTS OF SOCIALIZATION

The transformation of the young child into a member of society—the process called socialization—clearly depends upon contact with other

---

[35] Ibid.; Herbert J. Klausmier and William Goodwin, *Learning and Human Abilities,* 2nd ed. (New York: Harper & Row, 1966).

human beings. Thus socialization is dependent on interaction. For children, the process begins with the family and continues in peer groups and the school; for adults, it continues on the job and with marriage.

The Family as a Socializing Agent

Though family structure varies from one society to another, the family is the major socializing agent in each one; as such, it is the first medium for transmitting the culture to the child. Because the family is the whole world to very young children, its members teach children what matters in life, often without realizing the impact they are making. The desire to achieve, the need for popularity, the belief that a girl must be docile, and so on are passed from parent to child, The behaviors adults encourage and discourage and the ways in which they discipline the child also affect his or her basic orientation toward the world. However, values and child-rearing styles are not uniform from family to family, even within a single culture.

Interclass Differences. The typical middle-class family is comprised of both a husband and a wife and two or three children. The husband/father is traditionally seen as the major provider and head of the family, and the wife/mother is seen as responsible for maintaining an integrated relationship in the family and overseeing the development of values and emotions in the children. Although husband and wife roles are changing, due to the increasing number of middle-class, educated, working women, as well as the perceptions of male and female roles associated with the women's liberation movement, there is still stress on the children's achievement in school and, in general, on accomplishment and work.

In lower class or poor families, parent roles and behavior are quite different from those in the middle class. Bernard Berelson and Gary Steiner, without reporting on the magnitude of the differences, summarize variations in child behavior expectations in lower-class as compared to middle-class families as follows:

> . . . lower-class infants and children are subject to less parental supervision but more parental authority, to more physical punishment and less use of reasoning as a disciplinary measure, to less control of sexual and other impulses, to more freedom to express aggression (except against the parent) and to engage in violence, to earlier sex typing of behavior, . . . to less development of conscience, to less stress toward achievement, to less equalitarian treatment vis-à-vis the parents, and to less permissive upbringing than their middle-class contemporaries.[36]

Berelson and Steiner represent the current majority view of family and social-class differences and child-rearing techniques. However, this view is

---

[36] Bernard Berelson and Gary A. Steiner, *Human Behavior* (New York: Harcourt, Brace & World, 1964), pp. 479–80.

criticized by some social scientists as being culturally biased and anti-lower class. To be sure, arguments concerning family and social class differences are heated today (as will be discussed in Chapters 4 and 5). Even greater controversy and value-laden judgments are involved when racial differences are introduced into the discussion.

The Roles of Mother and Father. In current child development literature, incidental learning through role identification is most often cited as being influential in the areas of achievement, motivation, and behavior. Adult role modeling is especially important in achieving sex-role identification. The traditional school of thought emphasizes the importance in child development of a warm and satisfying relationship between mother and child in the early years of socialization. The mother is clearly the most important figure in the child's interpersonal matrix, especially during infancy and early childhood. However, the role of the father is gaining attention, as the research emphasis shifts to social-class differences and the allocation of parental responsibilities in child rearing. The purpose of research on these topics is to examine the effects of socioeconomic class attitudes toward the division between mother and father of the responsibilities for training and disciplining their children.

For example, Melvin Kohn and Eleanor Carroll interviewed 200 middle-class and 200 working-class families and found that middle-class mothers emphasize equality of the mother-father roles in training the child, while the father's role as disciplinarian is given only secondary importance. Working-class mothers expect their husbands to be firm disciplinarians but expect little from them in terms of supportive training. Working-class fathers feel that child rearing, in all its aspects, is properly the mother's responsibility.[37]

Earlier research reference to the father's role was made largely in terms of his influence as a sex-role model for boys. Robert Sears et al. have demonstrated the importance of the father not only as a sex-role model but as the source of power in the family, an agent of moral training, and one who sets high achievement standards.[38] Children in families where the father is absent are handicapped in these areas of development.

The ways children reared in father-absent families are affected are well known, and the topic is particularly relevant to the black family in this country today. David Lynn and William Sawrey examined the effects on boys and girls in 40 father-absent and 40 father-present Norwegian families of equal socioeconomic levels. The absent fathers were all

---

[37] Melvin L. Kohn and Eleanor E. Carroll, "Social Class and the Allocation of Parental Responsibilities," *Sociometry*, December 1960, pp. 372–92.

[38] Robert R. Sears et al., *Child Rearing and Identification* (Stanford, Ca.: Stanford University Press, 1965).

sailors — away for an average of nine months each year. It was found that more father-absent boys than father-present boys showed signs of immaturity, strove harder for masculine identification, and had poorer peer adjustments. Father-absent girls were better able to make peer adjustments than father-absent boys, though their problems in this area were more pronounced than those for father-present children, regardless of sex.[39] In other words, boys seem to be more severely disadvantaged by their father's absence.

In his report to the President, Daniel Moynihan reviewed the situation for black families in American society.[40] His emphasis was on the disorganized family structure, noting a large and growing number of illegitimate births and the absence of the father from the family. The report, to be discussed in Chapter 4 in detail, points out that for a vast number of poorly educated, unskilled blacks, the fabric of conventional family relationships is all but absent. In his reanalysis of the well-known Coleman report on educational opportunity,[41] Moynihan continued this theme; he showed that while average reading scores for whites are above averages for blacks at all grade levels, in both groups there is a tendency for achievement to decline in homes where the father is absent and to increase in homes where he is present.[42] Confirming data presented by Martin Deutsch and Bert Brown show a direct relationship between the father's absence and children's IQ. For both boys and girls, and blacks and whites, the IQ of children with fathers in the home is higher than those of children who have no father at home.[43]

The Peer Group as a Socializing Agent

While the family is the first and therefore most basic of the primary groups with which the individual is associated, interactions soon become frequent in the peer group — the play group for the small child, and the teen-age clique for the adolescent. Within these interactions the highly personal authority of the parent is gradually replaced by the impersonal authority of the groups. The peer group provides significant learning experiences in how to interact with others, how to be accepted by others, and how to achieve status in a circle of friends.

---

[39] David B. Lynn and William L. Sawrey, "The Effects of Father-Absence on Norwegian Boys and Girls," *Journal of Abnormal and Social Psychology*, September 1959, pp. 258–62.

[40] Daniel P. Moynihan, *The Negro Family: The Case for National Action* (Washington, D.C.: U.S. Government Printing Office, 1965).

[41] James S. Coleman et al., *Equality of Educational Opportunity* (Washington, D.C.: U.S. Government Printing Office, 1966).

[42] Daniel P. Moynihan, "Sources of Resistance to the Coleman Report," *Harvard Educational Review*, Winter 1968, pp. 23–36.

[43] Martin Deutsch and Bert Brown, "Social Influences in Negro-White Intelligence Differences," *Journal of Social Issues*, April 1964, pp. 24–35.

Peers are relatively equal, as opposed to the power structure in the family and the school. Parents and teachers can force children to obey rules they neither understand nor like, but peers have about equal authority, and thus the true meaning of exchange, cooperation, and equity can be learned more easily in this setting. The importance of peer groups increases over the years, reaching maximum influence in adolescence, when they in part dictate behavior in school.

Student Achievement and Peer Conformity. In a landmark study on adolescent culture, James Coleman examined ten midwestern high schools and found a powerful peer influence among adolescents.[44] As many as 54 percent of the boys and 52 percent of the girls found it hardest to accept parental disapproval; 43 percent of both sexes were most concerned with their friends' reactions, and teacher disapproval was of concern to only a small percentage. Coleman interpreted these data to mean that the balance between parents and peers reflects the transitional experience of adolescence—leaving the family, but not completely, for the peer group, and consequently being influenced by both parents and friends.

Students surveyed by Coleman favored such activities as dating, talking on the telephone, being in the same class, eating together with friends in school, "hanging around together," or just being with the group outside of school—activities which still seem relevant today. Esteem was gained by a combination of friendliness and popularity, an attractive appearance and personality, and possession of skills and objects (cars, clothes, records) valued by the culture. The images of the athletic star for boys and the cheerleader for girls were most esteemed, and the brilliant student, especially the brilliant female, was unimportant and fared poorly as a dating choice. Coleman concluded that the peer group had a low commitment to the basic goals of the school and to some degree was a subversive element in adult society; in fact, students with the most status were less adult oriented (less concerned about parental or teacher approval) than the rest of the students.

While most data on peer status infers that students from middle-class, relatively well-educated families tend to have the most status in schools, Coleman found that the correlation between a student's family status and her or his school status was modified by the socioeconomic composition of the schools. He wrote, "The leading crowd of a school, and thus the norms which the crowd sets . . . tends to accentuate [the] background characteristics already dominant, whether they are upper-or-lower-class."[45] Other research tends to confirm the same conclusion; that is, the effects of

---

[44] James S. Coleman, *The Adolescent Society* (New York: Free Press, 1961).
[45] Ibid., p. 109.

academic achievement and social acceptance within each school are closely related when achievement is valued by the dominant group.[46] On the other hand, there seems to be a tipping point where the value of academic achievement can be threatened — if another group with sufficient numbers is unruly, unable to achieve, or possesses different values and behaviors which conflict with achievement in school.[47]

Fifteen years later, Coleman, as chairman of a ten-member Presidential panel on youth, pointed out that extended schooling in our society accentuates the self-consciousness of youth and makes the transition to adulthood more difficult.[48] Schools have the paradoxical effect of bringing into being a substantial group of young people who have a preference for the continuation of irresponsible and even deviant behavior.

Prolonged schooling isolates young people from adults and thus tends to shift socialization from the family to the peer group. Excluded from the major institutions of our society, young people are "outsiders," and consequently they adopt the political and social views of outsiders. An outsider, according to Coleman, has no stake in the existing system. Whereas once youth wanted to hurry their childhood to arrive at adulthood, the opposite has begun to be true. Once they learn to live by their own subculture, many youth are reluctant to leave it and to become assimilated into the adult culture from which they were never really apart. In effect, many students become alienated from the adult world because of the way the schools are organized. The Coleman panel concludes that schools must transform unsocialized adolescents into responsible adults and attempt to teach them the principles of self-management and adjustment to existing institutions in the larger society.

The Counterculture of the 1960s. During the 1950s most American youths were lethargic about social and political issues and represented no threat to adult society. Most adults, therefore, were taken by surprise by the youth activists of the 1960s. The goals of these young people were basically centered around implementation of a relevant school curriculum, promotion of student rights, concern for poor people and blacks, the promotion of ecological interests, and ending the war in Vietnam. They

---

[46] Sarane S. Boocock, *An Introduction to the Sociology of Learning* (Boston: Houghton Mifflin Co., 1972); Francis J. Ryan and Joseph S. Davie, "Social Acceptance, Academic Achievement and Academic Aptitude among High School Students," *Journal of Educational Research*, November 1958, pp. 101-6; O. E. Thompson, "Student Values in Transition," *California Journal of Educational Research*, March 1968, pp. 77-86.

[47] See Edward C. Banfield, *The Unheavenly City*, 2nd ed. (Boston: Little, Brown & Co., 1974); Nathan Glazer, "For White and Black, Community Control Is the Issue," *New York Times Magazine*, April 27, 1969, pp. 36-37 ff.; Nathan Glazer, *Affirmative Discrimination: Ethnic Inequality and Public Policy* (New York: Basic Books, 1975).

[48] James S. Coleman et al., *Youth: Transition to Adulthood*, report of the Panel on Youth of the President's Science Advisory Committee (Chicago: University of Chicago Press, 1974).

valued humane attitudes and freedom in personal lifestyles and expressed disdain for adult authority and traditional political groups.

According to Charles Reich, the counterculture of the 1960s was born out of dissatisfaction with the kinds of lifestyles and options then being offered by society. One of the major threads of the movement was the dissatisfaction of its members with the present state of the country. Its ranks were largely populated by college-age youth of middle-class and suburban backgrounds as well as civil rights activists, and by older teenagers as the ideas filtered down to the high schools. The ideology of the counterculture was based on a new humanism, what Reich called *Consciousness III*. His *Consciousness I,* with its emphasis on hard work, sexual morality, and achievement, was rejected, as was *Consciousness II,* which emphasized impersonal efficiency, technocracy, bureaucracy, materialism, and racism.[49]

In general, the counterculture movement drew on the romantic naturalism of Jean Jacques Rousseau in Western civilization and the popularized version of Zen Buddhism in the East. The movement viewed man as positive. As an extension of the "flower children" and the expression of the "make love, not war" slogan of the 1960s, it incorporated alternative lifestyles such as free schools, communes, and encounter groups.[50] Drugs, the Jesus movement, and various religious, demonic, and witchcraft cults also characterized segments of the movement—augmented by academic communities such as Greenwich Village, New York; Hyde Park, Chicago; and Berkeley, California.

Few would quarrel with the counterculture movement for envisioning a society in which the norms would be people rather than machines, peace rather than war, love rather than hatred, cooperation rather than conflict, truth rather than hypocrisy, good rather than bad. The Judeo-Christian belief in man and the search for truth and serenity are not altogether different from the expressed hopes of Consciousness III. What was new was the cynicism of youth and the irrational belief that machines, war, and all other evils would go away. The reality of the situation was that a sufficient number of middle-class youth were willing to "cop out" of leadership roles in our society and choose not to "play the game" in our institutions and sectors of our economy. But the era of student unrest seems at the present to represent a bygone era.

The Tranquility of the 1970s. The decade of the 1970s started with a crescendo as young people actively protested against various aspects of schools and society. But it quickly waned in high schools and colleges, and

[49] Charles A. Reich, *The Greening of America* (New York: Random House, 1970).
[50] Theodore Roszak, *The Making of a Counterculture* (New York: Viking Press, 1969).

there was an apparent upsurge in conservatism among young people, particularly middle-class youth.

Much about the 1970s remains a puzzle to social scientists. Little is heard now about the social and humane goals of the counterculture of the 1960s, which had been pushed with a good deal of zeal and publicity. From most perspectives, it seems that the counterculture on which many youths and liberal adults had pinned such' hope was either dead or had gone underground by the mid-1970s.

On the basis of extensive survey data of college and noncollege youth between 1967 and 1973, Daniel Yankelovich has interpreted what occurred in the late 1960s and early 1970s.[51] First there was a revolution in moral and social values which continued through the 1960s; largely achieved among college students, it was adopted by some noncollege youth in the 1970s. Second, there was a "political revolution," induced by the civil rights movement and the war in Vietnam, which was very evident on many high school and college campuses. According to Yankelovich the latter has more or less ceased in terms of overt action, but the revolution in moral and social thinking still affects today's youth, representing new values, or what he terms a "new naturalism."

Yankelovich found that youth today generally questions the institutions of marriage, the nuclear family, sexual morality, hard work, excessive materialism, and religion. But the most dissatisfied young people now are not college students but high school graduates who have ended their formal education and have gone directly into the work force and may have married. As the contagion of the middle-class, campus values of the 1960s has spread to the lower middle class and blue-collar workers, dissatisfaction among this younger working force, who make up about 75 percent of the present youth population, has greatly increased.

Related studies of high school graduates and college youth tend to confirm the Yankelovich findings; moreover, the new research indicates that youth today is concerned with school grades and career opportunities — perhaps reflecting the tightening job market and the decreasing number of good jobs available for graduates. Furthermore, they seem to be becoming increasingly materialistic and surprisingly conservative politically.[52] This represents a shift in the pendulum, in some respects back toward the 1950s.

---

[51] Daniel Yankelovich, *The Changing Values on Campus* (New York: Washington Square Press, 1972); Daniel Yankelovich, *The New Morality* (New York: McGraw-Hill Book Co., 1974).

[52] See Brigitte Berger, "The Coming Age of People Work," *Change*, May 1976, pp. 24–30; Martin Mayer, *Today and Tomorrow in America* (New York: Harper & Row, 1976); James O'Toole, "The Reserve Army of the Unemployed," *Change*, May 1975, pp. 26–33 ff.

The School as a Socializing Agent

The avowed purpose of education is to teach children the information and skills they need if they are to become productive members of their society. In traditional society, the family was the major socializing and educational agent for children and young people. In modern societies, including the United States, the school serves as the major institution devised by the adult generation to maintain and perpetuate the culture; it imparts the knowledge and tools necessary for survival and ensures the transmission of values to future generations. In short, the school provides a sense of continuity and past experience of the culture; it is a highly formal system for educating the young, an institution children are required to attend in order to be socialized and enculturated into the larger society.

The purposes of schools are basically twofold: to enhance the potential of the individual, and to perpetuate society. The specific purposes of schools have changed over time, but generally they include the teaching of basic skills in reading, writing, and arithmetic and the development of good citizens and productive workers. The most famous statement on the purposes and nature of schooling is the *Cardinal Principles of Secondary Education,* prepared by the Commission on the Reorganization of Secondary Education and published in 1918. Although the work of the Commission was directed at secondary schooling, the statement is applicable to all levels of formal education and is still relevant today.

The Commission stated that "education in a democracy, both within and without the school, should develop in each individual the knowledge, interests, ideals, habits, and powers whereby he will find his place and use that place to shape both himself and society toward ever nobler ends."[53] The Commission then listed seven areas of daily living with which the broad purposes of the school program were to be concerned: (1) health, (2) fundamental skills, (3) home membership, (4) vocation, (5) civic education, (6) leisure, and (7) ethical character. These seven "cardinal principles of education" constitute a point of view worthy of consideration by all planning groups today. Although the wording of new reports may differ, the broad purposes of education remain basically the same.

The Culture of the School. The school has a subculture of its own — a set of values and behaviors that it reinforces and rewards. Education in school, compared with that in the family or peer group, is carried on in relatively formal ways. Groupings are formed not by voluntary choice but in terms of age, aptitudes, and sometimes sex. Students are tested and

---

[53] Commission on the Reorganization of Secondary Education, *Cardinal Principles of Secondary Education* (Washington, D.C.: U.S. Government Printing Office, 1918), p. 9.

59

evaluated; they are told when to sit, when to stand, how to walk through hallways, and so on. There are many rules, rituals, and ceremonies which enhance group behavior and conformity, ranging from punishment to reward. These include student codes, disciplinary procedures, and awards for attendance, achievement, conduct, or service to the school. In addition, school assemblies, athletic events, and graduation ceremonies, and the school insignia, songs, and cheers all enhance the culture of the school and socialize the students.[54]

It is generally accepted that the orientation of the school is basically middle class. The strong emphasis on punctuality, responsibility, hard work, honesty, and achievement are middle-class values. Similarly, the language spoken by teachers is middle class, and the curriculum and tests tend to coincide with middle-class culture. Students from lower-class backgrounds are at a disadvantage; they usually lack inner control and are not always "good"; they often speak a different language than the formal one spoken by their teachers and lack the academic skills necessary for school success. In general, they possess a set of values that does not coincide with the values of the school. As a result they experience cultural shock when they first begin school, and they are put at a disadvantage throughout most, if not all, of their school careers.[55]

Other Socializing Agents

Other formal agencies share in socializing the child, but their influence is much less than that of family, peer group, and school. Among these are the church, scouting groups, and similar character-building organizations. The mass media, especially television, is extremely influential in shaping the attitudes and behaviors of children as well as adults.

Recent evidence makes it clear that television has become "a second school system," as children sit entranced for hours in front of the television set. Children under five years old watch TV for an average of 24 hours a week, or about one fifth of their waking hours. By the time a child graduates from high school, he or she will have spent "an average of 15,000

[54] See Edgar Z. Friedenberg, *Coming of Age in America* (New York: Random House, 1965); Robert J. Havighurst and Bernice L. Neugarten, *Society and Education*, 4th ed. (Boston: Allyn & Bacon, 1975); Jules Henry, *Culture against Man* (New York: Random House, 1963).

[55] See Allison Davis, *Social-Class Influences upon Learning* (Cambridge, Mass.: Harvard University Press, 1948); Keith W. Prichard and Thomas Buxton, *Concepts and Theories in Sociology of Education* (Lincoln, Neb.: Professional Educators Publications, 1973); Sandra A. Warden, *The Leftouts: Disadvantaged Children in Heterogeneous Schools* (New York: Holt, 1968).

hours watching television and only 11,000 in school." Before the child reaches 18, he will "have seen 350,000 commercials urging them to want, want, want."[56] The power of television over young minds is great, probably more than most people realize. Recently there has been a growing body of research on the effects of TV advertising, as well as violence and sexuality, on children.

Socialization in Later Life

Socialization, of course, does not end at age 18 or upon graduation from high school. Entering college or the work force, moving into one's own apartment, getting married, becoming a parent, changing jobs or neighborhoods (or even spouses), and growing old all require learning new roles and "playing the game" by certain rules. For example, when one makes the transition from school to work, it sometimes is extremely important to hide one's anger or keep one's mouth shut if one wants to remain in the new organization. Or, when two people live together they are still the same people they were before, when they lived separately, yet there are changes. One may have to reassure the other that wanting some time alone does not mean rejection. Premarital sex certainly makes wedding nights less awkward and embarrassing, but once the lover role is changed to that of the spouse lovemaking may diminish; moreover, there are many more responsibilities to be considered. Who is going to do the laundry or go to the store is no longer predetermined.

As people grow older they are expected to move aside, retire from work, and to exchange their responsibilities as parents for the supposed pleasures of grandparenting. These expectations are quite different from those in many traditional societies, where older people are revered. In this country, even offering advice to children and grandchildren may be seen as interference. And old people must learn to cope with diminished physical power as well as diminished responsibilities. According to Margaret Mead, older people become victims of the socialization process. For years they have been expected to do certain things at certain times—and with old age, the only thing to do is to stay out of the way of the young and "to look cheerful when they come to visit."[57] This country has not found a way to utilize old people in a meaningful role. Those who reach old age will almost certainly be faced with some feelings of loneliness, uselessness, or despair.

---

[56] Evelyn Kaye, *The Family Guide to Children's Television: What to Watch, What to Miss, What to Change, and How to Do It* (New York: Pantheon Books, 1974), pp. 7, 54.

[57] Margaret Mead, "A New Style of Aging," *Christianity and Crisis*, November 15, 1971, p. 242.

CONCLUSIONS

Socialization is the process of interaction whereby the individual internalizes the culture. The process begins in the family when the infant interacts with an adult (usually a parent) who loves it and cares about it. The family and, later, peer groups and schools are the primary agents of socialization in children. Adults undergo 'continuing socialization when they encounter new roles in new situations.

Many students of social behavior have contributed to our understanding of the socialization process. Cooley used the image of the looking glass to explain how others influence the way we see ourselves; the self is a social product which emerges as the child interacts with other people, and it reflects the feedback he or she receives from others. Mead expanded on Cooley's theory to explain that by taking the role of others in play, children learn to imitate people close to them and develop a generalized impression of what people expect of them.

Whereas Cooley and Mead viewed socialization as a gradual process, Freud argued that it is thrust upon the child against his or her will. For Freud, socialization is the taming of the id, the respository of innate sexual and aggressive urges. The superego, or conscience, begins to develop as the child internalizes his or her parents' (and later society's) ideas of right and wrong. Gradually, the child develops an ego — the conscious part of the self that seeks socially acceptable ways of satisfying biological cravings.

A number of sociologists and psychologists have explained the dimensions of the socialization process with the aid of various developmental theories. Erikson described human development in terms of eight stages, ranging from infancy to old age. In many ways he brings the ideas of Cooley, Mead, and Freud together, integrating them in a social-psychological and physiological explanation of socialization. Piaget has added much to our knowledge of cognitive and moral development; he showed that there are real differences in the way children think at different ages. Piaget concludes there are four stages of cognitive development and three stages of moral development which are related to age. Kohlberg also added to our knowledge of moral development by specifying six types and three levels of the way people think about moral issues. Both Piaget and Kohlberg view moral development as a socialization of standards, somewhat coinciding with Freud's superego development. Havighurst views human development in terms of six stages from infancy and early childhood to old age, whereby the individual learns appropriate tasks within each stage. The second half of the first stage and the next two stages coincide with the schooling of the individual.

Socialization is a lifelong process which takes place as the individual inculcates the values of the surrounding culture—those he or she learns in childhood, adolescence, and adulthood. The self emerges in socialization when the individual learns to be conscious of himself as a social object and to respond to himself with approval and disapproval.

ACTIVITIES

1. Construct a set of statements on the topic "Who am I?" What relationships to others are implied?
2. Using a tape recorder, transcribe a short TV dialog between parent and child. What interactions are evident which help illustrate the child's id, ego, and/or superego?
3. Examine the literature on changing sex roles. Individual reports may be written, or a dialog or debate can be conducted by students supporting and opposing various points of view.
4. Explain how your present classroom illustrates the socialization process. Explain the subtle ways in which students are taught which further illustrate this process.
5. As a research project, compare and contrast the social unrest of the 1960s with the tranquility of the 1970s in high schools and colleges.

DISCUSSION QUESTIONS

1. How does an individual acquire a concept of self? Once acquired, explain how the concept of self can change.
2. How can an individual be socialized to deviant behavior?
3. How may a parent employ moral persuasion in the deliberate socialization of the child?
4. How do the schools transmit the culture?
5. What are the major socializing agents which transmit the culture? How does each affect the individual in different stages of life: childhood, adolescence, adulthood, maturity, old age?

SUGGESTED FOR FURTHER READING

Erikson, Erik H. *Childhood and Society.* New York: W. W. Norton & Co., 1950.
Friedenberg, Edgar Z. *Coming of Age in America.* New York: Random House, 1967.
Kluckhohn, Clyde. *Mirror for Man.* New York: McGraw-Hill Book Co., 1949.
Linton, Ralph. *The Study of Man.* New York: Appleton-Century-Crofts, 1936.
Mead, Margaret. *Culture and Commitment.* Garden City, N.Y.: Doubleday & Co., 1970.
Mills, C. Wright. *Power Elite.* New York: Oxford University Press, 1956.
Montagu, Ashley. *On Being Human.* New York: Schuman Publishers, 1950.
Rogers, Carl. *On Becoming a Person.* Boston: Houghton Mifflin Co., 1961.
Toffler, Alvin. *Future Shock.* New York: Random House, 1970.
Yankelovich, Daniel. *The New Morality.* New York: McGraw-Hill Book Co., 1974.

CHAPTER 3

SOCIAL CLASS AND EDUCATION

As fields of inquiry, social foundations and sociology of education have placed great emphasis upon social class and social stratification. A review of textbook materials reveals that almost one third of the space devoted to examining sociology of education considers concepts involving social class or social stratification.[1] While many present-day sociologists and educators stress these concepts, they were emphasized to an even greater degree in the past.

Social stratification, to be discussed in Chapter 5, may refer to almost any size population, ranging from small groups to society in general. Individuals or groups are ranked by status in some form which creates inequality with respect to privileges, power, and prestige.[2] The status may be ranked according to education, jobs, skills, income, social class, political positions, racial and ethnic origins, or other factors. Social class is only one form of social stratification, but it is perhaps the most important and the most frequently studied.

Social class is a division of people in society who have relatively similar *social* and *economic* backgrounds. The term "socioeconomic status" (SES) is

[1] Keith W. Prichard and Thomas H. Buxton, *Concepts and Theories in Sociology of Education* (Lincoln, Neb.: Professional Educators Publications, 1973).

[2] Albert J. Reiss, "Some Sociological Issues about American Communities," in T. Parsons (ed.), *American Sociology* (New York: Basic Books, 1968), pp. 66–74.

sometimes used interchangeably with the term "social class." Persons and groups comprising a specific social class have many things in common with regard to shared values, attitudes, behaviors, and lifestyles. As a group, they tend to form a predictable pattern which distinguishes them from members of other social classes. However, it is important to note that social class differences cannot be used to predict the behavior of individuals; the concept makes sense only for large groups.

Social class differences should not be attributed to any one single factor. Rather, the concept is based on a composite of factors, such as home or/ and background, cultural tradition, education, income, occupational status, or racial or ethnic identity. Any single-variable theory, such as the Marxist view which regards social class differences as being primarily based on economic factors, or the view that assumes that all black-white differences in the United States are associated with the one factor of discrimination, is overly simple and frequently results in an ism or ideology.

DEFINITION OF SOCIAL CLASS

The divisions that separate or cause the different social classes in any society are at best difficult to determine. W. Lloyd Warner and his associates at the University of Chicago identified six major dimensions which, in combination, produced an index for measuring social class: occupation, amount of income, source of income, house type, dwelling area, and level of education. These dimensions were used in a series by Warner and his colleagues to study the American social class structure in small towns and cities of various sizes in the 1940s.[3] Another noteworthy analysis of the major dimensions of social class for purposes of empirical studies was developed by Joseph Kahl in the 1950s. This included seven dimensions: prestige, occupation, possession of wealth, social interaction of people, class consciousness of oneself, value orientation, and power (or the ability to control the actions of others).[4] Other researchers have tested combinations of these and other indicators and have found them to be correlated with measures of attitudes, behaviors, and beliefs. In general, occupation, education, and income have been found to be the most widely used components for defining social class.

The usual procedure for studying social class utilizes one of three approaches:

---

[3] W. Lloyd Warner and Paul S. Lunt, *The Status System of a Modern Community* (New Haven, Conn.: Yale University Press, 1942); W. Lloyd Warner, Marcia Meeker, and Kenneth Eells, *Social Class in America* (Chicago: Science Research Associates, 1949).

[4] Joseph A. Kahl, *The American Class Structure* (New York: Holt, Rinehart & Winston, 1957).

1. *The Objective Approach.* The social scientist establishes a number of dimensions or variables which can be statistically analyzed. The categories are formed not by the people or members of the classes being studied but by the investigator. The categories that are used can be empirically defined and rely on questionnaires, surveys, or census data. Variables such as occupation, education, and income can be used, but such variables as class consciousness or power would be considered too difficult to operationalize or control statistically.[5]

2. *The Subjective Approach.* This approach to social class views it as a social rather than statistical category. It includes two possible procedures. One is based on a theory and elaborated with logic and the literature. The second is based on consciousness on the part of an individual, that he or she is a member of a given social class; the method used is simply to ask the individual to evaluate his own class position. With the first procedure, the social scientist develops the social class categories. With the second procedure the individual who is being studied provides valuable information and helps to formulate the classes. Here it is important to note that the class with which the individual identifies may be the one he aspires to rather than the one to which he actually belongs.[6]

3. *The Reputational Approach.* This approach was developed by Warner, who was also important in originating the categories used in the objective approach. It requires the investigator to obtain judgments of the position of another group of people along the social class continuum. The procedure is for the investigator to move into the community and live there for a time, visit and talk with the people, observe them, and ask them to rank other members of the community in socially superior and inferior positions. It was during this interviewing procedure that the Warner group discovered that certain terms and labels were used by individuals to describe other people who were above them, on the same level, and below them in the social structure.[7]

Social Class Descriptions

Numerous designations have been developed to categorize different levels of a social class continuum. The three most popular designations are:

---

[5] Harry L. Miller and Roger R. Woock, *Social Foundations of Urban Education* (Hinsdale, Ill.: Dryden Press, 1970); James W. Vander Zander, *Sociology* (New York: Ronald Press, 1965).

[6] Ibid.

[7] W. Lloyd Warner and Paul S. Lunt, *The Social Life of a Modern Community* (New Haven, Conn.: Yale University Press, 1942); Warner and Lunt, *Status System of a Modern Community.*

1. Three subgroups: upper class, middle class, and lower class.
2. Five subgroups: upper class, upper-middle class, lower-middle class, upper-working class, and lower-working class.
3. Six subgroups: upper-upper class, lower-upper class, upper-middle class, lower-middle class, upper-lower class, and lower-lower class.

These subgroups should be considered only as broad designations; they cannot account for a variety of patterns to be found within each class level or do justice to an individual who is categorized as being at a specific class level. They suffice only to point out salient group differences in lifestyles as they relate to such factors as home background, race, education, income, and occupational status.

While it can be demonstrated that there are wide differences between the attitudes and behaviors of subgroups at different ends of the social class continuum, less is known about differences between adjacent classes. Lower-class and middle-class students may exhibit different orientations toward school, but it is less clear how members of the lower-middle class and upper-middle class differ in their values regarding schooling. Many apparent social class differences described in the literature may be more efficiently explained by occupational role, income, ethnic background, or family structure than by a broad category such as social class.

Inquiry into differences among social classes usually results in concern with lower-class descriptions and problems, because this is the situation which needs to be understood and improved. Indeed, there is a great deal of reform literature dealing with lower-class groups. However, it often fails to recognize the variety of subcultures which exists within this class, as well as every other social class. A universal solution to problems of the lower class is impossible. Many lower-class families comprise two-headed households, but many others lack a male head. Some lower-class groups, although not necessarily the majority, are in the class mainly because of discrimination. They have accepted the value of social mobility but have been unsuccessful in escaping from the lower class. Many other lower-class groups are reconciled to a culture of poverty perpetuated from one generation to the next; society is not the main cause of their plight.

The social class continuum has perpetuated a stereotype which sees all lower-class people as disadvantaged. Reform programs based on such a stereotype can be detrimental to the vast numbers in the lower class to whom it does not apply. Not only do most descriptions of lower-class groups tend to be negative, they also adopt the theme of deviance from the acceptable standards of the larger society. These descriptions have been formulated by middle-class social scientists who are, for the most part, white. Moreover, their intellectual biases are often reflected in reform literature which tends to be critical of working-class and middle-class groups.

Descriptions of different social classes tend to ignore the similarities among all the groups. For example, all classes share a revulsion toward incest and theft among themselves. Family relations generally prevail over friendships. There are some pragmatic expectations associated with education. Young girls and boys learn to fill the roles expected of females and males.

It must be recognized that terms such as upper, middle, and lower class and their subgroups are not mutually exclusive categories. Within and among studies, there is an overlap among class levels. Terms used to define a particular class level do not necessarily have the same definition or incorporate the same variables from study to study. The term "middle class" in one study, for example, may not mean the same thing in another, yet discussions and textbooks will accept this term as universally understood and will build on it to elaborate a theory or point of view. In reverse, dissimilar terms may be used in the same or different studies and yet suggest the same thing. For example, in most textbooks written since the 1960s, the term "lower class" is used interchangeably with "poor," "disadvantaged," and "deprived." This suggests that the terms are global and not well defined.

With all these shortcomings you might wonder why social scientists refer to social class at all. The reason is that any concept of group membership is useful in education (or any social or economic facet of society) if it correlates with or predicts, with a fairly high degree of accuracy, important factors for its members. Among the various social group concepts, social class has great influence. There is much less sensitivity to using it to illustrate attitudes, behaviors, or extremes than there would be to use such group concepts as ethnicity, race, or religion; that is, it is more palatable to discuss differences by social class than differences among these other group concepts. Since a substantial proportion of blacks exist within the confines of the lower class, however, a discussion of the lower class sometimes leads into a discussion of blacks; if and when this occurs, the assumption that blacks can be equated with the lower class is grossly inaccurate and biased.

Regardless of whether social class distinctions are based on exhaustive procedures or casual indicators, social class is used in education to predict IQ test scores, grades, achievement, dropouts, course failure, truancy, suspensions from schools, and so on. These predictions are not perfect and apply only to group differences, not to differences on an individual basis.

They do make sense, and they provide useful data which have policy implications for education.

Value Differences by Social Class

The values which distinguish social classes in American society are of importance to teachers, and they affect school outcomes. A number of investigators have focused on the influence social class differences can have on learning in school; of particular importance are the writings and research of W. W. Charters, Allison Davis, Robert Havighurst and Harry Miller.[8] They represent the majority opinion; their works extend over a period of 30 years and include study of both black and white groups. Their descriptions of the middle and lower classes are relevant in at least five areas of particular interest for educators.

1. *Time Orientation.* The middle-class child is taught from an early age to defer gratification. He is taught that activities such as going to school and studying, although restricting in themselves, will provide future benefits. The lower-class child is not provided with this model. He does not see direct evidence of success from long-range planning. Although there is an occasional example of a relative who "makes it" through education, given the lack of evidence of present successes, most lower-class children are unwilling to delay gratification of needs and desires in the hope that eventually greater rewards will result; their time orientation is toward the present.

2. *Personal Orientation.* The lower-class child is usually unable to interact successfully with the middle-class world, which is object-oriented, impersonal, and bureaucratic. Inability to communicate in formal English and to read the necessary forms results in rejection of this world, with its career-oriented goals and an impersonalized setting. Instead, personalized friendships with peer groups and loyalty to one's family are substituted. The result is often strong cliques or gang membership and extended family loyalties.

---

[8] W. W. Charters, "Social Class Analysis and Control of Public Education," *Harvard Educational Review,* Fall 1953, pp. 268–83; W. W. Charters, "Social Background of Teaching," in N. L. Gage (ed.), *The Handbook of Research on Teaching* (Chicago: Rand McNally, 1963), pp. 715–813; Allison Davis, *Social Class Influences upon Learning* (Cambridge, Mass.: Harvard University Press, 1948); Robert J. Havighurst, "Who Are the Socially Disadvantaged?" *Journal of Negro Education,* Summer 1964, pp. 210–17; Robert J. Havighurst, "Social Class Perspectives on the Life Cycle," *Human Development,* Vol. 14, No. 2 (1971), pp. 110–24; Robert J. Havighurst et al., *Growing Up in River City* (New York: John Wiley & Sons, 1963); Miller and Woock, *Social Foundations of Urban Education.*

3. *Self-Image.* Compared to the middle class, lower-class members receive little recognition within the larger community, unless they are notorious. They are poor and powerless, and often are viewed only as welfare recipients. Unemployment rates are high among out-of-school teen-agers and adults, and what employment is offered is usually quite menial and low-salaried. Their low position in the social system tends to be internalized and reflected at an early age in their own judgments about themselves. Lower-class youngsters tend to have poor images of themselves and tend to doubt their ability to succeed in school and adult life, which in turn detrimentally affects their performance in school and society.

4. *Motivation.* Motivation to succeed is more prevalent in middle-class than lower-class families; these differences lead to variations in achievement need held by parents, which in turn are embraced by their children. Middle-class parents place greater emphasis on success, due partially to their more positive self-images and mobility; in turn, their children adopt similar attitudes and behaviors. Lower-class parents place less emphasis on achievement and provide unsuccessful role models. The achievement orientation has its beginnings in middle-class parent-child interaction and is internalized by the child at an early age. Those lower-class children who manage to internalize such values frequently overcome their social and economic handicaps and perceive the need for school success.

5. *Physical Aggressiveness.* The system of rewards and punishments in lower-class families and peer group relations is based on physical aggression. In contrast, in middle-class society aggression is in the form of covert behavior: gossiping, backbiting, and verbal manipulation. Physical power and aggression, in fact, are functional in lower-class life. A youngster living in the slums must learn to defend himself, run fast, sometimes even steal to survive. When these behavior patterns are carried over to the schools, they are interpreted by teachers and counselors as unwarranted and unacceptable. Further, lower-class children expect physical punishment as a means of control for severe infractions, but the disciplinary and socialization measures they encounter in the schools are based on words and threats, which are meaningless to them.

An important dimension of social class values is that, to the extent that differences do exist, the majority opinion in the professional literature presumes that nearly all are related to the lifestyle of the lower class and are therefore bad. This view is illustrated in Robert Havighurst's summary description:

. . . there is substantial doubt that the socially disadvantaged children in our big cities have any positive qualities of potential value in urban society in which they are systematically better than the children of families who participate fully in the mass culture. The writer does not know of any comparative study which shows American lower-lower class children to be superior in any positive respect to American upper working-class or middle-class children.[9]

The positive strengths of the lower class are easily ignored. Frank Riessman's list of strengths provides a needed perspective:

. . . cooperativeness and mutual aid that mark the extended family; avoidance of the strain accompanying competitiveness and individualism; equalitarianism, informality, and warm humor; freedom from self-blame and parental over-protection; the children's enjoyment of each other's company and lessened sibling rivalry; the security found in the extended family and in a traditional outlook.[10]

Riessman points out that schools lack techniques for assimilating the lower class into the existing academic mainstream. He notes that teachers and counselors often exhibit a "discrimination without prejudice," a lack of respect for these children based on their inability to accept value differences. He argues that the lower class possesses not only a culture, but one that is functional for them and worthy of emulation.

Certainly many subcultural groups among those who can be defined as underprivileged do have a culture of their own, different from the core culture. Riessman and others do more than recognize this culture; they defend lack of conformity with the rules of the schools. But a child has to learn not to offend the teacher, regardless of whether he has freedom from self-blame, or not to use physical violence when he feels wronged, regardless of whether he respects power and physical strength. No child should be encouraged to break school windows for kicks or put a knife to the teacher because he was insulted in class—the kinds of things some observers defend by tacit approval and by blaming school people and defending younsters who resort to vandalism or violence.[11]

On the other hand, it is crucial for teachers to remember that lower-class values are based on realistic evaluations of the lower-class environment. Ronald Corwin summarizes it well:

Middle class persons, however, have difficulty understanding that values so clear and useful to them are not useful or appropriate to the slum boy who encounters other social dangers. And conversely that lower class value systems are functional in the slum environment. . . . What appears to the middle class teacher to be a

---

[9] Havighurst, "Who Are the Socially Disadvantaged?" pp. 216–17.

[10] Frank Riessman, *The Culturally Deprived Child* (New York: Harper & Row, 1962), p. 10. Also Frank Riessman, "Low Income Culture: The Strengths of the Poor," *Journal of Marriage and the Family*, November 1964, p. 419.

[11] Edgar Z. Friedenberg, *The Vanishing Adolescent* (Boston: Beacon Press, 1959); Jules Henry, *Culture against Man* (New York: Random House, 1963); William Glasser, *Schools without Failure* (New York: Harper & Row, 1960).

negative attitude on the part of lower class children . . . is in fact a positive orientation towards the peer group and a realistic assessment of the situation.[12]

THE DEPRIVATION THEORY

Interest in the special learning problems of lower-class students, particularly those of the inner city, has been sustained since the early 1960s, when the term "lower class" became synonymous in the literature with "poor," "disadvantaged" and "deprived." Although the terms are often used synonymously, the deprivation theory is an environmentalist view (as opposed to a hereditarian view) of the relation between cognitive growth and the child's learning experiences; indeed, middle-class and upper-class children sometime fail to master one or more cognitive skills, too. But the majority of lower-class children fall into the disadvantaged and deprived category, due to their social and economic background. And, thus, while the flood of ideas and programs have been rapid, and numerous approaches have evolved for counteracting the effects of deprivation on the achievement of children, they have focused on lower-class children.

Current research indicates that the educational deficits lower-class children bring with them to the classroom inhibit the schools' efforts to work with them effectively. At home, these children are not provided with necessary experiences to explore, manipulate, and discuss — processes which are important for cognitive growth and development — nor do their parents have sufficient time or knowledge to take an active role in teaching them tasks that may subsequently facilitate academic achievement and orient them to the rules and routines of school life. Lower-class students consistently perform poorly on tests of scholastic aptitude and achievement which require a formal language or a conceptual style of thinking. The child's social and family milieu is the most important determinant of cognitive development, much more than the impact of schools; this is consistently shown by research to be discussed later in this chapter.

The concept of cultural deprivation traces academic inadequacy in school to environmental deficiencies at home, especially in the early years in the cognitive growth and development of the child. The relationships between environment and cognitive growth are complex and interrelated suggesting the quantitative and qualitative effects of environment on (1) visual discrimination, (2) auditory discrimination, (3) language formation, and (4) concept formation. In each of these four areas of cognitive development there are various stages of development, but each one affects

---

[12] Ronald G. Corwin, *A Sociology of Education* (New York: Appleton-Century-Crofts, 1965), p. 162.

the others; therefore, development in one area will affect development in the other areas. The four cognitive areas are built on the developmental characteristics of earlier stages of growth and development. An individual who is unable to develop a characteristic fully (say, the ability to discriminate sizes and shapes) at a particular stage in life will fall behind in the development of that characteristic in latter stages, and other characteristics that are dependent on it will be inhibited as well. This idea is well established in biology and animal and infant behavior studies.

Although there is danger in extrapolating from animals to humans or from infants to adults, David Ausubel has extended this reasoning to hypothesize that there is a tendency for deficits in cognitive development to occur if the child is deprived of necessary stimulation during "critical periods" when he is most susceptible in terms of potential capabilities.[13] The corollary of this hypothesis is that individuals who fail to acquire these skills at appropriate times are forever handicapped in attaining them. The deficits become irreversible and cumulative, since current and future rates of intellectual growth are always based on or limited by the attained level of development. (New growth, in others words, proceeds from existing growth.) The child with an existing deficit in growth which was incurred from past deprivation also is less able to profit from new and more advanced levels of environmental stimuli. Thus the deficit tends to increase cumulatively and leads to permanent retardation—forming what is called the "cumulative intellectual" deficit. This helps explain the increasing academic retardation of slow readers or nonreaders as they proceed through school, for example.

Early Years of Development

The deprivation theory holds that the early years of development are more important than later years. Although all human characteristics do not reveal the same patterns of development, the period of most rapid development of human characteristics, including cognitive skills, is during the preschool years. Benjamin Bloom presents longitudinal data (extended over a period of several years) which strongly suggest that from birth to age 4 the individual develops 50 percent of his potential intelligence; from ages 4 to 8 another 30 percent is developed, and between ages 8 and 17, the remaining 20 percent appears.[14] Supplementary evidence suggests that 33

---

[13] David P. Ausubel, "How Reversible Are the Cognitive and Motivational Effects of Cultural Deprivation?" *Urban Education,* Summer 1954, pp. 16–38; David P. Ausubel, *Educational Psychology: A Cognitive View* (New York: Holt, Rinehart & Winston, 1968).

[14] Benjamin S. Bloom, *Stability and Change in Human Characteristics* (New York: John Wiley & Sons, 1964).

percent of learning potential takes place by the time the child is age six, or before he usually enters school, and another 17 percent takes place between six and nine.

Based on the above estimates for intelligence and learning, Bloom considers the home environment crucial, not only because of "the large amount of cognitive development which has already taken place before the child enters the first grade but also because of the influence of the home during the elementary school period." These estimates also suggest the very rapid rate of cognitive growth in the early years and the great influence of the early environment (largely the home) on this development; thus it is suggested that all subsequent learning "is affected and in a large part determined by what the child has [previously] learned by the age of 9 or by the end of grade 3."[15] Even the prenatal stages of development (the mother's health and diet and chemical changes related to smoking, alcohol, personality stress, etc.) affect the child's intellectual development.

This does not mean that once a learning deficit occurs remediation is impossible, but it does clearly imply that it is more difficult to effect changes for older children, and a more powerful environment is needed to do so. Two-year deficits in reading or math for the ninth-grade student are more difficult to overcome than two-year deficits for a third-grader, for example. Bloom shows that learning differences can be reduced over time with appropriate environmental and training conditions, however.[16] Through his own research in mastery learning, as well as by utilizing others' research, Bloom concludes that most students can become similar with regard to learning ability, rate of learning, and motivation for further learning. It should be noted, however, that information on the extent to which intellectual deficits of one maturation period or age can be made up in another is limited, and differences in the difficulty of reversing deficits of different magnitudes or at different stages of cognitive development cannot be compared precisely.

The Nature and Extent of Deprivation

The theory of deprivation is supported by research which indicates that a child in lower-class surroundings will often suffer from a deprived environment or limited stimuli, which negatively affects his opportunities for adequate development in the four areas of cognitive development discussed above. Conversely, a child of middle or upper socioeconomic

---

[15] Ibid., p. 110.

[16] Benjamin S. Bloom, *Human Characteristics and School Learning* (New York: McGraw-Hill Book Co., 1976).

status usually has an enriched environment or ample high-quality stimuli which positively affects his opportunities for adequate development in these four areas. Thus the child's social class is related to his environmental experiences, which influence his learning capabilities and academic achievement.

These relationships are group patterns, and individual differences are possible among children in both deprived and enriched environments. For example, it is possible for a lower-class child to have an enriched home environment and for a middle-class counterpart to have a deprived home environment. Similarly, it does not necessarily hold that all children from deprived environments are going to have limited school abilities, while all children from enriched environments are going to experience academic success. Rather, social class and home environment will handicap or assist children in developing their mental capabilities.

Although the deprivation theory builds on the importance of the environment, this should not be interpreted as acceptance of a one-factor theory for explaining cognitive growth and development. No matter how complex a single factor can be, usually other intervening variables must be considered. Most of those who subscribe to the deprivation theory, and who are in effect staunch environmentalists, agree that heredity sets limits on individual potential for intellectual growth. Within unprescribed limits, however, environment influences the measurement and development of intelligence.

J. McVicker Hunt, the well-known environmental psychologist, has summarized thousands of research studies dealing with intelligence. He alludes to this controversy: The rate of cognitive development "is in substantial part, but certainly not wholly, a function of environmental circumstances." He is unable to determine the interaction between heredity and environment but believes that the greater the variety of environmental situations to which the child must accommodate his behavioral structures, the more differentiated and mobile he becomes: "Thus, the more new things a child has seen and the more he has heard, the more things he is interested in seeing and hearing."[17] The emphasis on environment implies the detrimental effects of an impoverished environment; this, in turn, leads to the concept of environmental deprivation or stimulus deprivation.

In this connection Martin Whiteman and Martin Deutsch have developed a Deprivation Index which correlates higher than social class

---

[17] J. McVicker Hunt, *Intelligence and Experience* (New York: Ronald Press, 1961), pp. 258–59. Also see J. McVicker Hunt, *The Challenge of Incompetence and Poverty* (Urbana, Ill.: University of Illinois Press, 1969).

does with achievement (reading) and ability (IQ) scores.[18] The multiple correlation expresses the relation between the effect of seven environmental conditions (social background, economic aspects, motivational aspects, family setting, parental interaction, children's activities with adults, and school experiences) with fifth-grade reading scores, .49, and IQ scores, .70. Separately the environmental conditions tend to show only a fair degree of correlation with achievement and ability; .32 and .30 are the highest correlations between any specific environmental condition and reading and IQ, respectively. This implies that these environmental conditions exert maximum effect on achievement and ability by means of their cumulative interaction, rather than as separate variables of some deprivation condition. Moreover, these combined environmental conditions correlate higher than social class or economic background does with IQ or reading. This suggests that the Deprivation Index may be a more accurate predictor of school success, and social class studies concerning ability and achievement could be supplemented by another set of variables such as those in the Deprivation Index.

The importance of the impact of environmental conditions on learning can be shown by examining the various factors which affect growth and development in the four cognitive areas: visual discrimination, auditory discrimination, language formation, and concept formation. These provide the framework for understanding the role of environment and how deprivation or inadequate development in one cognitive area affects the other areas.

Visual Discrimination

In lower-class homes the visual stimuli presented tend to be of minimum quantity and quality. There is little color variety and few pictures and books or household objects. The stimuli that are available tend to be repetitious and lacking in color, shape, and size variations.[19] Although the home may be overcrowded and cluttered with objects, they are presented in unorganized fashion, and the effect is often chaotic. This environment

[18] Martin Whiteman and Martin Deutsch, "Social Disadvantage as Related to Intellective and Language Development," paper presented at the Conference on Cultural Deprivation and Enrichment Programs at Yeshiva University, New York, April 1965. Later published in Martin Deutsch et al., *The Disadvantaged Child* (New York: Basic Books, 1967).

[19] Martin Deutsch, "Perspectives on the Education of the Urban Child," in A. H. Passow (ed.), *Urban Education in the 1970s* (New York: Teachers College Press, Columbia University, 1971), pp. 103-19; Herbert L. Pick and Anne D. Pick, "Sensory and Perceptual Development," in P. H. Mussen (ed.), *Carmichael's Manual of Child Psychology* (New York: John Wiley & Sons, 1970), pp. 773-847.

often overloads the child; the conflicting and disorganized stimuli are confusing. The child has difficulty in distinguishing relevant stimuli, and her or his range of visual stimuli is obstructed.

According to Deutsch, the lack of diversity of visual stimulation gives the child "few opportunities to manipulate and organize and discriminate the nuances of the environment."[20] The child's lack of perceptual development limits his capacity to utilize cues, to extract information, and to make subsequent classifications and judgments. The child makes fewer cognitive decisions and has less opportunity to sustain, accumulate and use knowledge; he experiences few language-symbolic operations and obtains less practice in concepts of visual comparison and relativity.[21]

Thus, by virtue of having seen fewer things, the lower-class child makes fewer specific responses and associations. Furthermore, since he encounters fewer tasks, he is less able to handle new and potential learning experiences, in the sense that appropriate responses have not been learned. For example, in a full-size picture of a boy riding a bicycle in the park, with trees and grass in the background, the boy and the bicycle should be the relevant stimuli, but to the deprived child they could be submerged by the background of trees and grass or other irrelevant objects. The teacher, however, takes it for granted that the child understands the picture.

Learning to write is also linked to the child's perceptual-motor skills. Writing is the substitution of verbal symbols for visual imagery and drawing. In learning to write, the child associates perceptual symbols with internalized representations. Limited motor-perceptual development will cause the child to have difficulty discriminating among graphic symbols (o–c or M–W, for example) and writing them.[22]

The effect of poor visual discrimination is also linked with reading retardation, for reading is based in part on a form of perceptual discrimination and spatial organization. Readers discriminate among words by recognizing letters, and poor readers find it difficult to discriminate on the basis of the shape and form of selected letters and

---

[20] Martin Deutsch, "The Disadvantaged Child and the Learning Process" in A. H. Passow (ed.), *Education in Depressed Areas* (New York: Teachers College Press, Columbia University, 1963), p. 170.

[21] Jerome S. Bruner, "The Cognitive Consequences of Early Sensory Deprivation," in P. D. Solomon (ed.), *Sensory Deprivation* (Cambridge, Mass.: Harvard University Press, 1961), pp. 195–207; John P. Zubeck (ed.), *Sensory Deprivation: Fifteen Years of Research* (New York: Appleton-Century-Crofts, 1969).

[22] Linda O. Lavine, "Differentiation of Letterlike Forms in Prereading Children," *Developmental Psychology*, March 1977, pp. 89–94; Joachim F. Wohlwill, "From Perception to Inference: A Dimension of Cognitive Development," in *Cognitive Development in Children: Five Monographs of the Society for Research in Child Development* (Chicago: Society for Research in Child Development, 1970), pp. 73–93.

words.[23] The child may have difficulty in discriminating graphic symbols in reading, as well as writing.

Auditory Discrimination

The child who lives in a tenement is surrounded by many noises and sounds that lack meaning, at least in terms of learning to discriminate auditory stimuli. People are piled up together; the population is dense on the streets and in the dwellings. Constant noise from outside and in the hallways adds to the din of many people living together. Too much noise in the environment, it has been shown, causes the child to "tune out."[24] In addition, the slum child usually has limited verbal interaction with parents or other adults, and assistance in listening to verbal responses is rarely given. In crowded, stressful living conditions, conversation which is directed toward the child is generally noninstructional, and few of the words used are multisyllabic.

Limited auditory practice and adult feedback lead to failure to develop attention and memory powers; attentiveness is related to the child's ability to listen and remember what he or she has experienced. Lack of sustained auditory contact with a verbally mature parent or significant adult impedes the development of memory; it is by recalling shared experiences with an adult that the child practices and develops her or his memory and learning experiences.[25] The middle-class child usually has the benefit of numerous dialogues with verbally mature adults to assist him in the development of verbal responses and memory, whereas the lower-class child seldom has.

The child raised in a noisy environment, with limited adult conversation directed toward him, will also become deficient in auditory discrimination, and subsequently in related speech, language, and reading skills. To learn new words for purposes of speaking or reading, the individual must listen to and modify speech sounds. He compares his sounds with those of a parent, friend, or teacher, detects differences, and modifies

---

[23] David McNeill, "The Development of Language," in P. H. Mussen (ed.), *Carmichael's Manual of Child Psychology,* Vol. 1, 3rd ed. (New York: John Wiley & Sons, 1970), pp 1061-1161; Murray Sidman and Barbara Kirk, "Letter Reversals in Naming, Writing, and Matching to Sample," *Child Development,* September 1974, pp. 616-25.

[24] Cynthia Deutsch, "Environment and Perception," in M. Deutsch, I. Katz, and A. R. Jensen (eds.), *Social Class, Race, and Psychological Development* (New York: Holt, Rinehart & Winston, 1968), pp. 58-85; Reinier Plomp, "Auditory Psychophysics," in M. R. Rosenzweig and L. W. Porter (eds.), *Annual Review of Psychology* (Palo Alto, Ca.: Annual Reviews, 1975), pp. 207-32.

[25] Jane B. Ralph, "Language Development in Socially Disadvantaged Children," *Review of Educational Research,* December 1965, pp. 389-400; Milton Schwebel and Jane B. Ralph, *Piaget in the Classroom* (New York: Basic Books, 1973).

his speech or reading. For the lower-class child, the verbal sounds at home and school are often different. The more practice and feedback the child has had with hearing and discriminating words and phrases, the more referents he has to build new words and the easier it is to learn the language.

In the early grades there is a positive relationship between lack of auditory discrimination and poor pronunciation and reading, since phonics plays an important role in these learning areas and related achievement levels.[26] To the child with limited auditory facilities, *for, four,* and *foe* sound alike (and therefore are considered the same), as do *can, cane,* and *came.* Eric Lenneberg points out that a sentence of ten words consists of extraordinary detail: "some 60 phonemes . . . characterized by 9 to 12 distinctive features," and each word broken down into several "intonation stress characteristics." Blind repetition of all these sounds is nearly impossible, since a list of several nonsense syllables cannot be remembered. But when the language and its auditory cues are understood, "sequences of phonemes within words and sequences of words within sentences fall within familiar patterns that help organize the stimuli."[27] A child who has not gained facility in auditory discrimination will fail to organize and repeat long sentences. The child may understand the general meaning of the sentence, but when asked to repeat it he is often unable to do so accurately, and he mixes or provides his own words.

Language Formation

The child's language basically evolves through the labeling of his environment, that is, his description and reaction to audiovisual stimulation. Learning to speak and use language requires the child to learn to discriminate among the corresponding visual and auditory symbols of words and to make proper classifications. What the child sees and hears serves as a source for understanding what he is verbalizing, as well as for categorizing, stating, and using conceptual referents. By learning the language, the child is also able to discriminate and classify various concepts of size, form, and sounds.[28]

---

[26] Alan S. Cohen, *Teach Them to Read* (New York: Random House, 1969); Ellis Richardson et al., "The Relationship of Sound Blending and Reading Achievement," *Review of Educational Research*, Spring 1977, pp. 319–34.

[27] Eric H. Lenneberg, "Speech as a Motor Skill with Special Reference to Nonaphasic Disorders," in *Cognitive Development in Children: Five Monographs of the Society for Research in Child Development* (Chicago: Society for Research in Child Development, 1970), p. 401.

[28] Daniel E. Berlyne, *Structure and Direction in Thinking* (New York: John Wiley & Sons, 1965); Lev S. Vygotsky, *Thought and Learning,* trans. E. Kaufman and C. Valtar (New York: John Wiley & Sons, 1962).

Table 3.1 / Mother and child at home: Illustrating the development of language

Case I		Case II	
Mother:	Put away your blocks.	Mother:	Put away your blocks.
Child:	Why?	Child:	Why?
Mother:	Put them away.	Mother:	You have finished playing with them.
Child:	Why?	Child:	Why?
Mother:	They mess up the house.	Mother:	Because we should learn to put away our toys when we are finished using them. If the toys are left on the floor, the house will look untidy.
Child:	Why?	Child:	Why?
Mother:	I told you to put them away, didn't I?	Mother:	Now put the blocks away, darling, and don't make such a fuss.

Source: Adapted from Basil Bernstein, "Social Structure, Language, and Learning," in A. H. Passow, M. Goldberg, and A. T. Tannenbaum (eds.), *Education of the Disadvantaged* (New York: Holt, Rinehart & Winston, 1967), p. 236.

To help the child handle the multiple attributes of words and associate them with the proper referents, a good deal of exposure to and practice with language is presupposed. This involves verbal interaction with and feedback from an adult who is significant to the child (e.g., a parent). The lower-class child's verbal experiences with an adult, however, are often meager in terms of formal verbal expression; the conversation is often short and functional or authoritarian; the vocabulary is limited in terms of correct English, and the meanings are conveyed less in words and more in gestures. There is often little opportunity to engage in games such as "Peek-a-Boo" and "Pat-a-Cake," hear fairy tales, or get explanations of why the sky is blue or clouds make rain. Verbally and emotionally, parent-child encounters restrict the child's verbal skills and subsequent concept formation.

The differences in such encounters are shown in Table 3.1, which contrasts two approaches used by mothers to explain reasons for putting away blocks. This example is based on a classic dialogue reported by the English psychologist Basil Bernstein.[29] In terms of language development, the child in case I is disadvantaged relative to the child in case II. The child in the first case is not given a full explanation of why he should remove his toys from the floor; he receives no corrective or reinforcing

[29] Basil Bernstein, "Social Structure, Language, and Learning," in A. H. Passow, M. Goldberg, and A. T. Tannenbaum (eds.), *Education of the Disadvantaged* (New York: Holt, Rinehart & Winston, 1967), pp. 225–44. Also see Basil Bernstein, *Class, Codes, and Control* (London: Routledge & Kegan Paul, 1971).

feedback. If this repeatedly occurs, the child may stop asking "Why?" The child in the second case has a better opportunity to learn; he receives full explanations and corrective feedback, as well as engaging in reasoning and considering concepts of causality, and he learns that blocks are toys.

In case I, the mother's vocabulary is limited and categorical. The child receives few opportunities to learn new words and concepts and little practice in hearing complex sentences. The emotional relationship between the child and mother is more authoritarian, her behavioral demands are abrupt and basically unexplained, and the child is directed to do the work alone. The child's change in behavior is brought about by verbal conditioning. This child may well fail to develop facility with the structure of the language and will be apt to experience cultural and language shock upon entering school. In case II the mother exposes the child to more words and more elaborate sentences. She attempts to satisfy the child's curiosity, in effect stimulating the child to learn. Her warm relationship, and her "we" rather than "you" do it attitude, helps the child develop his cognitive and emotional processes. The child's change in behavior is related to verbal learning; he is learning responsibility and self-discipline, too. In school, he will find that teachers speak with language patterns similar to his mother's.

The cumulative deficiency in language formation for the child in case I, or the disadvantaged child (usually the lower-class child), tends to lead to the development of a restricted language code, or what Bernstein calls "public" language. This is characterized by:

1. Short, grammatically simple, and often incomplete sentences.
2. Simple and repetitive use of conjunctions.
3. Few subordinate clauses.
4. Dislocated subjects and verbs as well as context.
5. Infrequent use of adjectives and adverbs.
6. Infrequent use of pronouns as subjects for conditional clauses.
7. Frequent use of statements to produce illogical conclusions.
8. Frequent use of sequence reinforcers (e.g., "Get it?" "Understand?").
9. Use of ill-defined idiomatic phrases.
10. A sentence organization of implicit rather than explicit meaning.

The middle-class child tends to speak a "formal" language in which the characteristic patterns are opposite to this disadvantaged language style: accurate grammatical order, a wide range of vocabulary, appropriate structure and relationships within and between sentences, and a conceptual hierarchy for the organizing of experiences. The original studies of interaction statements made between parents and children and of social class language differences were conducted by Bernstein in England, which is a crucial argument for those who disagree with his findings. Nevertheless, his findings have been replicated in this country a number of times, with both black mothers and children[30] and white mothers and children.[31]

The argument for a nonformal or lower-class language also concerns a distinctive black language. It has more subtle and linguistic sounds, rooted in the assumption expounded by Noam Chomsky that the acquisition of a language depends on being placed in the environment of the language.[32] This idea has been elaborated and popularized by Joey Dillard, who argues that black children possess a language that is different from the "school register" but has direct application to their immediate environment.[33] The argument also has political and social implications, suggesting that the school is insensitive to the child's language mode, rather than that the student is at fault for not learning formal English.

Regardless of the student's ethnicity or racial background, the characteristic patterns of language interaction between lower-class children and adults inhibit the development of standardized language patterns, as well as the vocabulary to register and classify data. The interaction that characterizes most middle-class families tells the child when an explanation he has offered is correct or incorrect, answers his questions about why things are so, and supplies many words and concepts. This is the language used by schools and the larger society, and the standard by which people judge others in social and job-related contexts.

Concept Formation

Language and thought are closely linked, and educators agree that conceptual development is in part dependent on language. The development of language permits the child to classify more stimuli and to make a response to a subject or event, despite spatial or temporal distance from it. Language permits the child to increase his knowledge, deal with a variety of stimuli, and label and store up concepts.

---

[30] Robert D. Hess and Virginia D. Shipman, "Early Experiences and the Socialization of Cognitive Modes in Children," *Child Development*, December 1965, pp. 369-86; Eleanor Pavenstadt, "A Comparison of the Child-Rearing Environment of Upper-Lower and Very Low-Lower Class Families," *American Journal of Orthopsychiatry*, January 1965, pp. 92-96.

[31] Kate L. Logan and Herbert C. Wimberger, "Interaction Patterns in Disadvantaged Families," *Journal of Clinical Psychology*, October 1969, pp. 347-53; David J. Bearison and Thomas Z. Cassel, "Cognitive Decentration and Social Codes: Communicative Effectiveness in Young Children from Differing Family Contexts," *Developmental Psychology*, January 1975, pp. 29-36.

[32] Noam Chomsky, *The Sound Patterns of English* (New York: Harper & Row, 1968).

[33] Joey L. Dillard, *Black English: Its History and Usage in the United States* (New York: Random House, 1972).

When, as in lower-class families, the visual and auditory stimuli at home and parent-child verbal interactions are limited, the child has less opportunity to learn to label and categorize stimuli, to note their differences, and to ask questions and receive feedback. For example, Robert Hess and Virginia Shipman found that lower-class mothers seem at a loss in giving clear instructions and explanations, or motivating their children to learn about the things they see and hear.[34] Moreover, it has been pointed out that the child's lack of experiences reduces opportunities to link experiences with interpretations or to convert objects and events into abstractions in formulating the relationships and generalizations needed to identify signals and relate them to previously learned categories.[35] The child who has a disorganized home life often is unable to comprehend clearly the experiences of separateness and difference, or to organize and think in a logical order. Disorganization at home, plus lack of routine or a recognizable sequence of activities recurring over time, gives the child fewer opportunities to systematize and conceptualize events and to think of time as other than the immediate or the present — not the past or future.

There are studies which show that "sense of control" correlates with social class.[36] The middle-class child learns early which of his acts and words will bring about desired results. He internalizes a set of probabilities, reinforced by an organized home life, which helps him decide the relative merit of several behaviors. Those that most effectively and most consistently meet with success he practices, thus gaining mastery over his own skills and environment. As a result, he comes to school with many developed cognitive strategies for problem solving, most of which correspond with the demands of the school.

Among the most important coping strategies the child brings to school are a formal language and verbal concept code. Fred Strodtbeck contends that power through language is the "hidden curriculum" of the middle-class home.[37] The child has learned that power can be attained and maintained

[34] Hess and Shipman, "Early Experiences and Socialization."

[35] David Elkind, "Conservation and Concept Formation," in D. Elkind and J. H. Flavell (eds.), *Studies in Cognitive Development* (New York: Oxford University Press, 1969), pp. 171–90; Herbert J. Klausmeier and Frank H. Hooper, "Conceptual Development and Instruction," in F. N. Kerlinger and J. B. Carroll (eds.), *Review of Research in Education 2* (Itasca, Ill.: F. E. Peacock, Publishers, 1974), pp. 3–54; Scott A. Miller, "Cognitive Certainty in Children: Effects of Concept, Developmental Level, and Method of Assessment," *Developmental Psychology*, May 1977, pp. 236–45.

[36] James S. Coleman et al., *Equality of Educational Opportunity* (Washington, D.C.: U.S. Government Printing Office, 1966); Bernard C. Rosen, "The Achievement Syndrome: A Psychocultural Dimension of Social Stratification," *American Sociological Review*, June 1956, pp. 203–11.

[37] Fred L. Strodtbeck, "The Hidden Curriculum of the Middle-Class Home," in C. W. Hunnicutt (ed.), *Urban Education and Cultural Deprivation* (Syracuse, N.Y.: Syracuse University Press, 1964), pp. 15–31.

through words and by conversation, so he extends and elaborates his use of words and verbal concepts into a power instrument which is as effective at school as it is at home. Where power through words is not achieved, as in the case of the disadvantaged, there is less motivation to use words and ver- bal reasoning to exercise power. The strategies the disadvantaged child develops are physical in nature — a kind of random striking out both as a response to frustration and as a means of control. Such behavior impedes the use of problem solving and conceptual strategies in school.

Great social class differences have also been found in the rate of acquiring the basic differential concepts (big-little, light-dark, near-far). Carl Bereiter and Siegfried Englemann's controversial approach to teaching preschool and primary grade disadvantaged children is based on research which indicates that the disadvantaged require experiences with language in a highly structured form. They must be drenched with language in order to conceptualize their experiences. Their approach, with its emphasis on drill and more drill, does not teach children to raise questions. They contend the child is not ready to be taught in this manner; he must acquire the rudiments of language before he can conceptualize.[38]

Many present theories of thinking (Jerome Bruner, Robert Gagné, Jean Piaget, Hilda Taba) are based on sequences and stages of hierarchies of mental development. If, as in the lower-class home, there is no recognizable sequence of activities recurring in time, if there is less systematic ordering of stimuli, if there is less opportunity to think in a logical order of elaboration, then at best the methods and cognitive stages or hierarchies the child in such an environment uses to solve problems will differ from the norm. This connotes a learning process based on cultural influence. In many cases, such a child will not gain facility in conceptual thinking; rather he or she will adapt a low-level, concrete, or possibly rote learning style.

To end on a positive note, we can note Frank Riessman's contention that in other areas of thinking the disadvantaged child is quick and flexible, for example, in dealing with or judging people, in physical activities, and in figuring out ways of "beating the system." Although slowness is part of his or her mental style, this should not be misconstrued as dullness. The assumption is that the slow thinker is not dull, rather, he has a different cognitive strategy. Riessman characterizes the disadvantaged child's mental style as (1) physically and visually oriented rather than aurally oriented, (2) content oriented rather than form oriented, (3) externally centered rather than introspective, (4) problem oriented rather than

---

[38] Carl Bereiter and Siegfried Englemann, *Teaching Disadvantaged Children in the Preschool* (Englewood Cliffs, N.J.: Prentice-Hall, Inc., 1966).

abstract oriented, (5) inductive rather than deductive, (6) spatially oriented rather than temporally oriented, (7) slow and careful rather than quick and facile, (8) dependent on more concrete examples to grasp ideas, (9) rigid rather than open to reason, and (10) pragmatic and anti-intellectual.[39] It should be recognized that Riessman's theories are based mainly on intuition, not research.

Policy Implications

To summarize the cognitive deficiencies of the culturally deprived child, David Ausubel's statement is appropriate:

It is reasonable to assume that whatever the individual's potentialities are, cognitive development occurs largely in response to a variable range of stimulation. . . . Characteristic of the culturally deprived environment, however, is its restricted range and a less adequate and systematic ordering of stimulation sequences. The effect of this restricted environment includes poor perceptual [and auditory] discrimination skills; inability to use adults as sources of information, correction and reality testing, and as instruments of satisfying curiosity; and an impoverished language system and a paucity of information concepts and relative propositions.

His abstract vocabulary is deficient and his language-related knowledge, such as number concepts, self-identity information, and understanding of the physical and geometrical and geographical environment limited.[40]

In examining the deprivation theory, social scientists have contributed various useful dimensions to the understanding of the problem. Some of the data are complementary but differ in their emphasis and suggest different reasons for the major problems of deprivation. Each of the research studies and theories on the topic presents a logical and consistent piece of the truth, in the absence of more definitive and more fully tested explanations. Singly and in combination, the various studies have given rise to curricular and organizational programs to counteract the deprivation of children which together are termed compensatory education. These programs have not yet produced adequate results, and in many cases there has been failure. Nevertheless, the movement toward compensatory education—especially Head Start—is a direct result of the hypotheses and research derived from the theory of deprivation.

The deprivation theory is criticized by some educators for being culturally biased and for ignoring the cultural systems of students from backgrounds outside the mainstream. The alternatives advocated, how-

---

[39] Riessman, *Culturally Deprived Child;* Frank Riessman, *Helping the Disadvantaged Pupil to Learn More Easily* (Englewood Cliffs, N.J.: Prentice-Hall, Inc., 1966).
[40] David P. Ausubel, "The Influence of Experience on Intelligence," paper read at the NEA Conference on Productive Thinking, Washington, D.C., May 1963, pp. 2-3.

ever, rest on a radical alteration of mainstream institutions, a separation theory, or an antiformal educational strategy. Such rhetoric often ignores the fact that every citizen must learn to read, write, and count in our society. In every case in the United States where groups have overcome poverty and discrimination, they have developed these abilities through formal education and by working within mainstream institutions.

To be sure, it is necessary to consider the components of cultural and educational deprivation in order to devise a realistic program which can meet the needs of lower-class or disadvantaged children and youth. We must be concerned with broad capabilities, not for the sake of debate but to translate into interventionist programs the conditions and sequences of learning that are most fruitful at the various developmental stages.

Finally, to blame teachers for their inability to cope with the learning problems of the lower class may be an expression of legitimate frustration on the part of educational reformers, but it may also be an attempt to disguise the fact that schools alone cannot counteract the impact of family life. Society may direct the schools to educate the child, but it cannot perform these functions effectively when the child comes to school with limited cognitive abilities. This does not mean that we should allow public officials and schools off the hook; rather, we must also hold parents partially responsible for the quality of their children's input and subsequent schooling. If we place total blame on teachers for poor student performance while ignoring family factors, the influence of the home is masked, and numerous political motives which lead to unrealistic policies can emerge.

SOCIAL CLASS AND SCHOOL SUCCESS

Certain relationships between social class and school success have been documented in countless studies and seem to hold no matter what measure of social class or socioeconomic status (SES) is used: the higher the social class of students' families, the higher are the students' academic achievement and related achievement variables, such as school grades, test scores, retention at various grade levels, honors and awards, amount of schooling, and college plans, and the lower are such variables as course failures, truancy, behavior problems, suspensions, and dropouts. Similarly the higher the social class, the higher are the students' aspirations and the more positive are parental influences.

While literally thousands of studies over the past 50 years have dealt with the theme of social class and school success, we will divide them into two periods: early and current. In the early period the term "social class" was predominantly used, and social class characteristics such as occupation of the breadwinner, family income, and parents' education were correlated with a variety of school achievement variables. In the current period, the term "socioeconomic status" is generally employed, the statistical procedures are more advanced, and the data tend to be larger in scope compared to the earlier period, which relied on smaller samples. There is also a shift in emphasis from the impact of social class to the impact of school characteristics (with SES combined and in some cases parceled out) on achievement.

In both periods three basic problems persist. First, investigators do not agree on the definitions of social class or socioeconomic status, and therefore different criteria are used to distinguish levels of class or status. Second, school quality varies not only by social class but also by geographic setting and region; and geographical differences are rarely controlled. Third, there are many interactive relationships of social class. While sex, intelligence, ethnicity, and race are usually considered, many other interaction factors such as family size, birth order, mother's age, and time spent with children are not, though they are also related to school success.

EARLY RESEARCH PERIOD: THE EFFECTS OF SOCIAL CLASS

The research in the early period is generally concerned with social class and its relationship to school achievement. Achievement data usually contrast students of lower and higher social classes, pointing up the higher rate of school dropouts among lower-class children, their concentration in nonacademic curricula, lower grades, higher failure rates, and lack of participation in extracurricular activities. Data related to social class also examine differences in reading and IQ test scores and how social class and IQ combined impact on school achievement.

The earlier period generally relied on simple correlation data to show the effects of social class on achievement. Many studies sampled schools in small towns or a particular large-city school system. We will focus on two studies in small towns, two in large cities, and one on a national level; they are all considered classic studies.

Social Class and Achievement: Studies in Small Towns

August Hollingshead moved into Elmtown (a pseudonymous midwestern town) and studied the relationship of social class differences and education for 752 high school students.[41] He divided the group into five social classes:

---

[41] August B. Hollingshead, *Elmtown's Youth* (New York: John Wiley & Sons, 1949).

Table 3.2 / Social Class Differences and Education in Elmtown

PART A. PERCENT WITH TYPE OF CURRICULUM

Social Class	College Preparatory	General	Commercial
I–II (Upper)....................	64	36	0
III (Middle)	27	51	21
IV (Upper-Lower)...............	9	58	33
V (Lower-Lower)	4	58	38

PART B. PERCENT WITH GRADE POINT AVERAGES

Social Class	85–100	70–84	50–69
I–II	51	49	0
III	36	63	1
IV	18	69	13
V	8	67	25

PART C. NUMBER AND PERCENT OF FAILURES AND SUBSEQUENT DROPOUTS

Social Class	Number of Students	Number of Failures	Percent of Failures	Number of Subsequent Dropouts
I–II.............	35	1	2.9	0
III.............	155	8	5.5	1
IV.............	233	63	27	42
V	72	64	89	62

Source: August B. Hollingshead, *Elmtown's Youth* (New York: John Wiley & Sons, 1949), pp. 172–74, 462. Reprinted by permission of John Wiley & Sons, Inc.

Table 3.3 / Intelligence and Social Class in Relation to School Progress in River City

	Boys			Girls		
	High School Dropout	High School Graduation Only	College	High School Dropout	High School Graduation Only	College
IQ Quartile						
IV (high)	4	13	27	3	23	36
III...............	18	17	22	12	24	18
II	25	25	7	27	26	3
I (low)	37	15	3	26	17	4
Social Class						
Upper and upper-middle ...	1	4	15	1	2	18
Lower-middle.....	9	22	27	10	28	22
Upper-working....	38	25	15	23	46	20
Lower-working....	36	19	2	34	14	1
Total number .	84	70	59	68	90	61

Source: Adapted from Robert J. Havighurst et al., *Growing Up in River City* (New York: John Wiley & Sons, 1962), p. 51. Also see Robert J. Havighurst and Bernice L. Neugarten, *Society and Education*, 3rd ed. (Boston: Allyn & Bacon, 1967), Table 3.2, p. 74. Reprinted by permission of John Wiley & Sons, Inc.

I and II, upper; III, middle; IV, upper-lower; and V, lower-lower. Among the factors studied were type of curriculum, grade-point averages, and failures and subsequent dropouts.

As shown in Part A of Table 3.2 Hollingshead found that as many as two thirds of the students classified as in the two highest social classes were in the college preparatory curriculum, and only a little over one tenth of the lower two groups were in that track. Similarly, no student from the top two social classes took commercial courses, but one third of the lowest two social classes were enrolled in the commercial track, considered the least prestigious and easiest.

More than half of the students in the highest two social classes had mean grade scores of 85-100, and the remaining had mean grade scores of 70-84. Less than 15 percent of the two lower social classes had mean scores of 85-100, whereas about two thirds had 70-84 averages, and one fifth had 50-69 averages. This is shown in Part B of Table 3.2.

The relationships of failing in one or more subjects and subsequent dropouts with social class were analyzed for 495 10th graders. In the two highest classes there was only one failure, or 2.9 percent. There were 8 failures in class III, or 5.5 percent, and 63 failures in class IV, or 27 percent; moreover, in class IV, 42, or two thirds of the failures, subsequently dropped out of school. In class V, 64 out of 72 students received at least one failing grade, or 89 percent, and 62 out of these 64 left school the subsequent semester. This is shown in the third Part C of Table 3.2.

Robert Havighurst et al., in a study of a midwest community they called River City, studied the relationship between social class and intelligence and the child's progress through school.[42] As shown in Table 3.3, both factors were found to be strong predictors of school progress. The intelligence data came from tests given in the sixth grade, with the IQs divided into quartiles. It was reported that in the highest quartile more than 50 percent of the students (63 out of 120) went to college, while only 5 percent (7 out of 132) dropped out of school before graduation. In contrast, in the lowest quartile 5 percent (7 out of 120) continued their education beyond high school and almost 50 percent (63 out of 132) dropped out before high school graduation.

The relationship was not as great, however, between four social classes and school progress. In the highest social class, less than 25 percent (33 out of 120) of students went to college, while only 1 percent (2 out of 152) dropped out of high school. In the lowest social class, less than 3 percent (3 out of 120) went to college, and almost 25 percent (40 out of 152) dropped out of high school.

---

[42] Robert J. Havighurst et al., *Growing Up in River City* (New York: John Wiley & Sons, 1962).

Table 3.4 / Income Differences and Elementary Education in Detroit (1961)

Schools by Average Family Income Groups	Number of Schools in Each Group	Iowa Achievement Test Mean Scores			Percent of Students Reading Below Grade Level	IQ Mean Scores with Ranges from 2.0 to 6.0
		Fourth Grade	Sixth Grade	Eighth Grade		
I. ($3,000+)	135	3.48	5.32	6.77	96%	2.79
II. ($5,000+)	107	3.73	5.61	7.38	82	3.31
III. ($7,000+)	85	4.42	6.47	8.22	5	4.55
IV. ($9,000+)	20	4.84	7.05	8.67	0	5.09

Income Groups	Number of Gifted Students Per 10,000	Detention Students Per 10,000	Special Behavior Classes Per 10,000	Percent of Nonpromotions	Percent of Dropouts
I. ($3,000+)	0	85.7	37.7	7.4%	15.5%
II. ($5,000+)	3.6	40.2	14.8	4.9	3.0
III. ($7,000+)	27.0	6.9	4.2	2.9	1.5
IV. ($9,000+)	78.0	2.7	0	1.2	.7

Source: Adapted from Patricia C. Sexton, *Education and Income: Inequalities in Our Public Schools* (New York: Viking Press, 1961), pp. 24, 28, 39, 54, 60, 71-72, 97.

Furthermore, it was found that patterns of school progress — in terms of grades, IQ scores, social adjustment, behavior, attendance, and so on, and eventually who drops out, graduates, or goes to college — are clearly established at the elementary school level. By examining the records of sixth-grade students, "it is possible to discover the probable dropouts with considerable accuracy, and also to discover those who will go farthest in school . . . and go on to college."

Social Class and Achievement: Studies of Big Cities

Two studies of big-city public schools in this period were conducted by Patricia Sexton in Detroit and Robert Havighurst in Chicago. Both were concerned with entire school systems, from grades K-12, but Sexton emphasized the elementary schools and Havighurst stressed the secondary schools.

Using the 1957 census tract, Sexton categorized the schools by average family income of $3,500 to $11,055, and then combined these levels into four major groups ranked from lowest to highest as follows: (I) $3,000-4,999, (II) $5,000-6,999, (III) $7,000-8,999, and (IV) $9,000 + .[43] Table 3.4 indicates that achievement scores tend to go up as income levels rise. Students in all 242 schools in the two lowest income levels were achieving below grade level; furthermore, the differences between groups I and IV tended to widen with each passing grade level. Low reading levels

[43] Patricia C. Sexton, *Education and Income: Inequalities in Our Public Schools* (New York: Viking Press, 1961).

also were associated with income. In the lowest group of schools, 96 percent of the students were reading below grade level, whereas in none of the schools in the highest group did students have a mean score below the national grade level. IQ mean scores for children in the first and fourth grades were grouped into five equal categories, from 2.0 to 6.0, and it was found that these scores directly related to income groups, too.

Sexton also compiled data on other school variables. She found that gifted students came exclusively from schools in the upper income groups; the number of gifted students per 10,000 was 78 for group IV and zero for group I. Detention students came mainly from low-income schools, 86 per 10,000 students compared to 2.7 per 10,000 for upper-class students. Special programs designed for students who were considered behavior

Table 3.5 / Relation of Socioeconomic Ranking of High Schools with Student Achievement Levels and College Plans in Chicago (1964)

Social Class Ranking of High Schools[a]	Percent of High Achievers[b]	Percent Low in Reading[c]	Percent Who Say They Will Go to College[d]	Percent Black Enrollment
1	52%	0%	94%	0%
2	49	0	88	0
3	54	0	91	0
4	54	0	81	2
5	40	12	71	26
6	47	0	67	0
.	.	.	.	.
.	.	.	.	.
.	.	.	.	.
18	32	8	46	3
19	11	16	46	28
20	43	0	70	3
21	21	15	76	88
22	26	0	39	11
23	25	12	42	19
.	.	.	.	.
.	.	.	.	.
34	10	46	65	80
35	14	29	39	44
36	8	36	61	99
37	4	37	51	91
38	4	42	53	100
39	6	41	53	100

[a] Social class ranking indicated in descending order from high to low. Six of the first 12 schools are listed to represent the highest one third, ranks 18–23 represent the middle third, and ranks 34–39 represent the lowest category.

[b] Percent of 9th- and 11th-grade students in top three stanines on standard tests of reading. For the city as a whole, 23 percent are in the top three stanines.

[c] Percent of ninth-grade students reading at sixth-grade level or lower.

[d] Students who were graduating in June were asked in the Spring whether they expected to go to college.

Source: Robert J. Havighurst, The Public Schools of Chicago (Chicago: Board of Education of the City of Chicago, 1964), pp. 208–9.

problems were attended by 38 per 10,000 students in schools in the lowest income group and none in the highest one. The nonpromotion rate was six times higher in group I than group IV, and the dropout rate was 22 times higher in group I than group IV. Thus from the standpoint of school *success*—say achievement, reading, and IQ scores—and giftedness, the trend which favors upper-class children is established at an early age. And, from the standpoint of school *failure*—say detention, behavior problems, nonpromotions, and dropping out—the trend among low-income children is established early in their school careers, too. Indeed, the gap between both groups tends to widen at the secondary school level.

In the Havighurst study of the Chicago public schools, 39 high schools were ranked according to a socioeconomic index from high to low.[44] Table 3.5 shows that average achievement level and reading ability were closely related to the socioeconomic level of the school. The percentage of students claiming they would go to college was related to the social class ranking of the schools, but to a lesser extent; a surprisingly large percentage of students in low-ranked schools claimed they would further their education. The last column of the table indicates that lower achievement and reading scores are related to the percent of black students in the schools, even when social class is controlled. Yet a larger percentage of nonachieving blacks than whites say they will enter college. Because the basic skills of these students do not seem to warrant success in college, it can be concluded that blacks are either more motivated to succeed or exhibit more unrealistic job and educational aspirations than their counterparts.

Making it to college and receiving a degree represent the most coveted reward offered by the schools. College completion usually means getting a better job than average, with good pay, better working conditions, greater security, and more status. Regardless of what the literature may say, most low-income youth understand this, though they may not appraise the value of a college education the same way middle- and upper-middle-class income students do and may not prepare for it in the elementary grades the same way.

Social Class and Achievement: Nationwide

Perhaps the most comprehensive social class study of this period was conducted by Robert Herriott and Nancy St. John.[45] The study

[44] Robert J. Havighurst, *The Public Schools of Chicago* (Chicago: Board of Education of the City of Chicago, 1964).

[45] Robert E. Herriott and Nancy H. St. John, *Social Class and the Urban School* (New York: John Wiley & Sons, 1966).

included data from 41 cities with populations of 50,000 or more during the 1960–61 school year. A sampling procedure was designed to obtain a 5 percent sample of the entire school population. For the elementary school, data were reported for four social class categories (high, moderately high, moderately low, and lowest), while only the first and last categories were used for the senior high schools.

Among the parental and student correlates of the schools' social class composition reported for elementary and senior high school levels were family stability, parental involvement, student behavior, student ability, student achievement, and educational level. For both elementary and senior high schools, the school principals surveyed reported their appraisal of students and parents in specific incidences (teachers reported on student behavior). Their answers led to the following findings:

1. The lower the school's social class composition, the greater the proportion of students who experienced family instability.
2. The lower the school's social class composition, the smaller the proportion of parental involvement in the schools.
3. The lower the school's social class composition, the greater the proportion of students whose behavior was substandard.
4. The lower the school's social class composition, the smaller the porportion of students with IQs greater than 120, and the larger the proportion of students with IQs less than 90.
5. The lower the school's social class composition, the greater the proportion of students who were performing below grade level.
6. The lower the school's social class composition, the smaller the proportion of students who were expected to go to college, and the greater the proportion who were expected to drop out of school. (Replies for item 6, educational level, were likely to be subjective and derived from impressions rather than facts, especially for the elementary school students.)

Interpretation of the Early Studies

The data and conclusions of these early studies clearly indicate wide differences in school achievement among social classes, but there is considerable controversy regarding the explanation of these differences. In the social sciences there is no substantial agreement concerning the explanation of human nature and social behavior. Facts about people do not speak for themselves; they must be interpreted in a frame of reference. Since this frame of reference is both conceptual and value-ridden, there is often disagreement about the interpretation of facts.

There are two basic explanations for the poor performance of lower-class students in schools, and the explanation one adopts largely depends on one's political and social view of the world. The first explanation represents a moderate to conservative view of the world. In this view, lower-class children come to school with a number of handicaps stemming from their family situation — limited cognitive skills, lack of motivation, poor ego development, and atypical or unsocial behavior. This puts them at a disadvantage compared to their middle- and upper-middle-class counterparts. As growth and development proceed the cognitive differences become cumulative, so that as the child is passed from grade to grade the achievement gaps increase. This explanation coincides with the deprivation theory discussed above.

The second explanation, which represents a more liberal to radical view, is based on the assumption that teachers are of the middle class and schools are middle-class institutions, and they discriminate against students of a different class or culture. The curriculum is also middle-class oriented, as are standardized tests and the general routines: the child must be taught how to read, attendance must be taken, discipline must be maintained, and there is an emphasis on neatness, cleanliness, punctuality, and hard work. Failure to achieve in school or to go to college reflects the impersonal discrimination of the system. The child and his parents are not accountable for learning; rather teachers and schools must be held accountable for any differences that may exist in the output (the achievement rates of the students).

There is little reason to debate these two explanations. It would be difficult if not impossible to modify each reader's view of how the social world works, since this reflects a particular philosophy and ideology, embellished by many years of selective knowledge and experience as well as personal bias.

Perhaps somewhere in the middle of these two explanations lies the golden mean. School is a sorting and selecting process based on ability and achievement. Although not intentionally, it also sorts and selects in relation to social class. Schools may be middle-class institutions, but they reflect the biases of society. It is less likely that members of the larger society will adjust their performance to accommodate existing subcultures than that those who live outside the mainstream will have to adjust their attitudes and behaviors to the society so they can function healthily and gain mobility within the system.

CURRENT RESEARCH PERIOD: THE EFFECTS OF SCHOOLS

The new period of social and educational research which evolved in the 1950s and blossomed in the 1960s and 1970s aroused considerable interest among social scientists and legislators. New modes of statistical analysis made it possible to analyze the "effects" of schools — by studying first the school context or climate, then the more direct influence of peer groups, and finally the impact of several school characteristics or the educational program on student achievement and aspirations.

At first the overall data found social class composition of the schools, and the more direct measure of peer influence, to be related to student performance. Data developed by James Coleman, Christopher Jencks, and their successors, however, indicated that school characteristics have no discernible relationship to the level of student achievement.

The School Context

The technique in the school context or climate studies consists of combining the attributes or attitudes of all members of a social group or system to form a single measure by which individual members can be identified. Alan Wilson's studies of the Berkeley and San Francisco–Oakland Bay area schools, conducted in the 1950s and 1960s, are the most prominent example of this type of research. In the first study, Wilson ranked 14 elementary schools according to occupational and educational level of families from which the students were recruited.[46] He formulated three school groups: "Hills," containing a high proportion of students whose parents ranked high in occupational and educational status; "Foothills," schools which had families in mixed occupational and educational levels; and "Flats," schools containing a high proportion of students whose parents were of the working class (semiskilled and unskilled) and had dropped out of high school.

Table 3.6 / Mean Reading-Achievement Test Scores of Sixth-Grade Students by Father's Occupation and School Composition

Occupational Category	Hills Schools (upper white collar)	Foothills Schools (lower white collar)	Flats Schools (working class)
Professional and executive	107	103	—[a]
White collar and self-employed.	103	96	81
Manual workers	102	92	78
Total N	302	206	196

[a] Mean is not reported because of insufficient number of cases.

Source: Adapted from Alan B. Wilson, "Social Stratification and Academic Achievement," in A. H. Passow (ed.), *Education in Depressed Areas* (New York: Teachers College Press, Columbia University, 1963), Table 4, p. 223.

[46] Alan B. Wilson, "Social Stratification and Academic Achievement," in A. H. Passow (ed.), *Education in Depressed Areas* (New York: Teachers College Press, Columbia University, 1963), pp. 217–35.

The key question Wilson wanted to answer was whether differences in school social context influenced the achievement and aspiration of the students from varying social classes. The findings indicated that the answer is yes; while the socioeconomic status of the students' parents did have an effect upon educational achievement, this effect was modified for all social groups by the dominant class character of the schools' student body. Thus, as Table 3.6 shows, the mean reading–achievement test scores of the children of white-collar workers in the Hills, for example, was 103; in the Foothills, 96; and in the Flats, 81, and so on for the other groups of workers.

These findings coincided with an earlier study of Wilson's which ranked eight high schools in their similar groups: A, predominantly upper middle class; B, predominantly lower middle class, and C, predominantly working class.[47] Two thirds of the sons from the professional group in the group A schools attained A or B median grades, while 50 percent did so in group B and 18 percent did so in group C. As many as 40 percent of the sons of the manual workers in group A schools attained A or B median grades, 27 percent in group B, and 13 percent in group C. Similarly, 93 percent of the sons of professionals in group A schools wanted to go to college, compared to 77 percent in group B and 64 percent in group C. And, 59 percent of the sons of manual workers in group A planned to go to college, compared to 44 percent in group B and 38 percent in group C.

These relationships led Wilson to conclude that the cumulative effects of the primary variable (students' social class origin) and contextual variable (schools' dominant class character) affected student achievement and aspirations. Wilson found similar relationships when he used the father's education and the mother's education as independent variables, and also when he used IQ scores of the students. In all of these cases when parents' educational attributes or student abilities were held constant, the attributes of the school had a clear and consistent effect upon students' educational performance and aspirations.

A third Wilson study, conducted under the auspices of the U.S. Commission on Civil Rights, was concerned with both the socioeconomic and racial context of schools.[48] This sample from the San Francisco–Oakland Bay area included elementary and high school students. School composition was measured by the proportion of students who were black and the proportion who were of the lower class (those whose family heads

[47] Alan B. Wilson, "Residential Segregation of Social Classes and Aspirations of High School Boys," *American Sociological Review*, December 1959, pp. 836–45.

[48] Alan B. Wilson, "Educational Consequences of Segregation in a California Community," in U.S. Commission on Civil Rights, *Racial Isolation in the Public Schools* (Washington, D.C.: U.S. Government Printing Office, 1967), pp. 165–226.

were unskilled laborers, domestics, unemployed, or on welfare). Neighborhood composition was measured as with the school measure, except several demographic characteristics of a student's immediate neighborhood were analyzed from the census tracts.

Examination of the mean reading achievement scores for the sixthgraders in the sample, controlling one independent variable at a time, indicated that the greatest differences were produced by the school context; the mean reading level of the students who had attended primary schools with populations of less than 10 percent lower SES children was 7.4, compared with a mean of 4.9 for children in schools where a majority of their classmates were of lower SES. School context produced a greater difference than neighborhood context or individual family status and race did.

A clear relationship was also established between IQ scores for students in the 8th and 11th grades and the percentage of lower-class schoolmates in elementary schools attended. The mean IQ level of students who attended elementary schools with populations of less than 10 percent lower SES children was 110 at the 8th grade and 107 at the 11th. Where the majority of classmates were of lower SES, the mean IQs in these grades was 92 and 90 respectively. Again, the consequences of social class segregation were affirmed.

Although the racial composition of the school and the racial composition of the neighborhood had a clear negative effect on student achievement (reading scores) and ability (IQ scores), the main effect was produced by the social class composition of the school. This led Wilson to conclude that

[T]he effect of neighborhood segregation upon achievement is entirely through the resulting segregation of neighborhood schools on social class lines. Restructuring the composition of the schools, even in the absence of residential rearrangements, can be expected to have an effect upon the academic achievement of students.[49]

Wilson's findings imply that school desegregation strategies should be conducted along class as well as racial lines. Because black students are disproportionately concentrated in lower SES schools and neighborhoods, however, they are more likely than whites to be subject to adverse school effects.

Wilson's findings agree with those of Daniel Levine and his associates in their study of 155 schools in the Kansas City, Missouri, metropolitan area.[50] They found that the proportion of students expecting to go to

---

[49] Ibid., pp. 180–81.

[50] Daniel U. Levine et al., *Opportunities for Higher Education in a Metropolitan Area: A Study of the High School Seniors in Kansas City* (Bloomington, Ind.: Phi Delta Kappan, 1970).

college was related to the SES of the student and the school. The number of middle-class seniors planning to attend college varied from 87 percent of those attending middle-class schools, to 80 percent of those in comprehensive (both middle-class and working-class students) schools and 47 percent of those in working-class schools. Among working-class seniors, the corresponding figures were 80 percent, 61 percent, and 58 percent.

In another study, Levine et al. showed a significant relationship between reading scores and SES characteristics of elementary students in approximately 600 schools between 1969 and 1975 in five large cities: Chicago, Cincinnati, Cleveland, Kansas City, Missouri, and St. Louis.[51] These characteristics centered around concentrations of poverty (percent of families below poverty level, monthly rents, population per acre, housing deterioration, etc.) and family disorganization (female-headed households, adult-youth dependency ratios, people per room, etc.). Such variables were found to affect the school climate and were relatively stable predicators of reading achievement over the years in each of the cities. Furthermore, they overlapped with one another, thus suggesting they were reflecting different aspects of the same problems of poverty and family disorganization.

The findings of these studies on contextual effects raised some questions concerning the effects of intelligence on educational achievement and aspirations. When William Sewell and his associates studied 10,000 high school seniors in Wisconsin, they found a weaker positive relationship between school social class composition and students' achievement and college plans when SES and intelligence of students were controlled for simultaneously. Specifically, Sewell computed a multiple correlation between the students' sex, social class, family attitudes, and intelligence and the dependent variable of students' college plans. The resulting multiple correlation coefficient was .48, and the addition of social class composition of the school increased it only slightly, to .50.[52]

Peer Group Influences

Another group of studies found that peer group formation has a greater effect on student achievement and aspiration than family background or

---

[51] Daniel U. Levine et al., *Concentrations of Poverty and Reading Achievement in Five Big Cities* (Kansas City, Mo.: Center for the Study of Metropolitan Problems in Education, University of Missouri–Kansas City, 1977). The exact number of schools varied over the years, between 575 and 624.

[52] William H. Sewell and J. Michael Armer, "On Neighborhood Context and College Plans," *American Sociological Review*, April 1966, pp. 159–68; William Sewell and Vinal P. Shah, "Social Class, Parental Encouragement, and Educational Aspirations," *American Journal of Sociology*, March 1968, pp. 559–72; William Sewell, Archibald O. Haller, and George W. Ohlendorf, "Educational and Early Occupational Status Achievement Process: Replication and Revision," *American Sociological Review*, December 1970, pp. 1014–27.

Table 3.7 / Correlations of School Status and Friends' Status with College Plans of High School Seniors

	Zero-Order Correlations			Partial Correlations		
Parents' Educational Level	(1) School Status with College Plans	(2) Friends' Status with College Plans	(3) School Status with Friends' Status	(4) School Status with College Plans[a]	(5) Friends' Status with College Plans[b]	(6) N
Both parents—college..	.10	.15	.49	.03	.12	172
One parent—college ...	.16	.29	.36	.06	.26	183
Both parents—high school	.15	.28	.50	.01	.24	147
One parent—high school	.07	.19	.34	.01	.18	178
Neither parent—high school	.14	.31	.40	.02	.28	295

[a] Holding friends' status constant.
[b] Holding school status constant.
Source: Ernest Q. Campbell and C. Norman Alexander, "Structural Effects and Interpersonal Relations," *American Journal of Sociology*, November 1965, p. 286.

school composition. Using a sample of male seniors in 30 North Carolina high schools, C. Norman Alexander and Ernest Campbell asked each student to name the two fellow students he "went around with most often."[53] The data obtained showed a clear relationship between the educational plans of individual respondents and the plans of the students they named as their best friends, even controlling for SES, and regardless of whether their friends reciprocated the sociometric choice. A student at any given social class level was more likely to have college aspirations, and to actually attend college, when his best friends also had college plans. The relationship was even stronger when the friendship choices were reciprocated.

In a follow-up study, Alexander and Campbell integrated these findings with school SES context and formulated a three-stage model whereby each respondent was scored on (1) his own social class, (2) his friends' social class, and (3) his school's social class (the average SES of all students in his school).[54] The correlations between school and friends' social class and a student's college plans are shown in Table 3.7. Column 1 shows that there is a slight positive relation of college plans to school status, column 2 that the relation is stronger with friends' status, and column 3 that the relation is stronger still when the effects of these two variables are combined.

[53] C. Norman Alexander and Ernest Q. Campbell, "Peer Influences on Adolescent Educational Aspirations and Attainments," *American Sociological Review*, August 1964, pp. 568–75.

[54] Ernest Q. Campbell and C. Norman Alexander, "Structural Effects and Interpersonal Relations," *American Journal of Sociology*, November 1965, pp. 248–89.

These researchers also predicted that school status and the tendency of individuals to choose friends of the same status were related in themselves, and friends could be an influencing variable that mediates the relationship between school status and college expectations. This is exactly what happened. When friendship status was held constant, as in column 4, there was only a negligible variation to be explained by school status. By contrast, when school status was held constant, as in column 5, the relationship between friends' status and college plans remained strong. The investigators concluded that "these two sets of partial correlation coefficients support the influence that the structural effects of school status are best conceived of as due to the interpersonal influences of an individual's significant others."[55]

The two studies by Alexander and Campbell do not imply that differences among schools' formal educational programs have no effect on college plans of students. Rather, they suggest that when school social composition is separated it approaches a zero relationship to achievement and aspiration, and peer group influences are more important. We can go one step further and infer from the data that school integration will have little effect on students' aspirations unless there is also strong interpersonal contact among social class groups. Of course, attitudes toward learning are determined partially by the composition of the student body as a whole, which constitutes the pool from which one's friends are chosen.

The significance of direct contact with peers was also the theme of a study by James McPartland which viewed peers as classmates rather than friends.[56] McPartland's analysis of 5,000 ninth-grade New England and Middle Atlantic students indicated that for black students the academic advantage of being in an integrated school depended upon being in the same classes with middle-class white students. School integration based on race has almost no effect on verbal achievement of black students; it "increases with the proportion of their classmates who are white. The only [black] students who appear to derive benefit from attendance at mostly white schools are those in predominantly white classes within the school."[57]

Parallel to Alexander and Campbell's findings, McPartland's indicate that while the social (in this case racial) context of the school affects the likelihood of contact between students of different backgrounds, an individual student's academic gains are directly affected by only those

---

[55] Ibid., p. 288.

[56] James McPartland, *The Relative Influence of School Desegregation and of Classroom Desegregation on the Academic Achievement of Ninth Grade Negro Students* (Baltimore: Johns Hopkins University Press, 1967).

[57] Ibid., p. 5.

students with whom he or she has direct and interpersonal relations. Furthermore, these findings are similar to what was obtained in the Coleman study on equal educational opportunity, to be discussed below. Controlling social class and racial characteristics of individual students and schools, McPartland found that for both white and black students in the 6th, 9th, and 12th grades, tests on verbal ability were related more strongly to the backgrounds of fellow students than to differences in the school or the school program.

These peer group studies reaffirm the importance of social class (family characteristics) for student achievement and aspiration. They also show that school social composition affects student performance, and that, more specifically, its positive and negative effects derive from peer influence.[58] The positive impact is that if lower-class (and minority group) students attend a middle-class (and majority group school) school and form friendships with middle-class students, then the achievement and aspirations of these lower-class students *increases* to a greater extent than if they were attending a lower-class school. The negative impact is that middle-class (majority group) students will exhibit a *decrease* in academic achievement and aspirations in proportion to the number of lower-class (minority group) students in these school and peer groups. Based on an extensive review of the research, Robert Bain and James Anderson put it this way:

It seems evident that the greater the proportion of students from a certain social class who attend a school, the greater the numerical opportunity and probability that a given student who attends that school will form friendships from among students of that given social class. Once a student forms a friendship with another, he will tend to be influenced by the attitudes and values including social class-linked attitudes and values of that friend.[59]

The effects are not equal, however. Lower-class students are more likely than middle-class students to be influenced by school and peer group effects, and the research suggests that lower-class youth would rather be friends with middle-class youth than vice versa.[60] The studies discussed above, as well as others, tend to confirm that students in the lower-class group who attend middle-class schools gain more in achievement and aspirations through classroom associations and friendships than middle-

---

[58] Also see the discussion on student achievement and peer conformity in Chapter 2.

[59] Robert K. Bain and James G. Anderson, "School Context and Peer Influences on Educational Plans of Adolescents," *Review of Educational Research*, Fall 1974, p. 440. Copyright 1974, American Educational Research Association, Washington, D.C.

[60] Norman E. Gronlund, *Sociometry in the Classroom* (New York: Harper & Row, 1959); Edward O. Laumann, "Subjective Social Distance and Urban Occupational Stratification," *American Journal of Sociology*, July 1965, pp. 26–36.

class students lose in attending lower-class schools.[61] The resulting implications are twofold: (1) schools matter more for some students than
others, and disadvantaged groups are especially susceptible to the school
climate set by peer group attitudes and values, and (2) a redistribution of
students among schools and classrooms can have a positive effect upon
achievement and aspiration levels of lower-class students (and minority
groups, since they are concentrated in lower classes), although it tends to
have a negative effect on middle-class (majority group) students. This
latter point is rarely mentioned by researchers for political and social
reasons.

School Characteristics

A number of large-scale studies prior to the Coleman report showed that
schools have an effect on student achievement. The first, by William
Mollenkopf and S. Donald Melville, involved 100 high schools nationwide
which differed with respect to size, region, staff training, percentage of
graduates going to college, and financial support. Achievement and
aptitude tests were given to some 9,600 students in grade 9 and 8,400
students in grade 12.[62]

Regression analysis was used to correlate school averages on these tests
with 34 different school characteristics. Four of these characteristics
showed relatively high relationships with tests scores: (1) geographical
location (whether or not the school was in the South), (2) urbanism
(whether the school was in an urban, suburban, or rural area), (3) cost of
instructional support per student, and (4) the number of specialists on the
school staff (psychologists, guidance counselors, etc.).

A problem that beclouds this and later studies of the effects of school
factors on student achievement is the role of the SES variables. The
correlation of socioeconomic status with student achievement is high—so
high indeed that it is difficult to separate with certainty how much impact
the school alone had on the students. Mollenkopf and Melville caution the
reader at length about drawing conclusions from correlational data or
disentangling home and family variables from school variables. They
nevertheless suggest—somewhat grudgingly—"that the results support the

---

[61] Besides the studies by Wilson, Levine et al., Campbell and Alexander, McPartland and
Coleman et al., see Denise Kandel and Gerald S. Lesser, "School, Family and Peer Influences
on Educational Plans of Adolescents in the United States and Denmark," *Sociology of
Education*, Summer 1970, pp. 270–87; John A. Michael, "On Neighborhood Context and
College Plans," *American Sociological Review*, October 1966, pp. 702–6.

[62] William G. Mollenkopf and S. Donald Melville, *A Study of Secondary School
Characteristics as Related to Test Scores* (Princeton, N.J.: Educational Testing Service,
1956).

Table 3.8 / Correlations of Selected School Characteristics with Seventh-Grade Student Achievement and SES

Variable	Raw Correlation	SES Partialled Out
Teacher experience...................	.56	.37
Per-student expenditure...............	.51	.31
Special staff per 1,000 students	.24	.12
Classroom atmosphere................	.24	.23
Social class of parents...............	.61	—

Source: Adapted from Samuel M. Goodman, *The Assessment of School Quality* (Albany, N.Y.: New York State Education Department, 1959), Table 9, p. 32, Table 10, p. 35.

conclusion that certain characteristics descriptive of the school situation do have a distinct influence on the achievement of students."

A later study by Samuel Goodman involved 70,000 students in grades 4, 7, and 10 in 103 school systems in New York State.[63] Correlational results focused mainly on seventh-grade performance; the variables found to be most strongly related to student achievement are listed in Table 3.8. Together, this and the Mollenkopf-Melville study begin to provide some notion of how much we can generalize about school characteristics. Both studies found that student expenditures and special staffing were associated significantly with achievement, but they differed sharply on the importance of teacher experience. Goodman found this to be the most important variable, next to social class. Mollenkopf and Melville found it to be negligible.

Goodman's study gives a fairly good indication of the effect of SES on the relationship of the four most important school characteristics with achievement. The table shows the correlation of social class per se and achievement (.61) and then separates SES from the other variables, thus suggesting there is still room for teacher experience, per-student expenditures, and classroom atmosphere to have something to do with how much students learn. In other words, the second column shows that variables independent of the students' social class also affect achievement.

The Goodman and Mollenkopf-Melville studies, as well as the Coleman study (soon to be discussed), were forced to rely on cross-sectional rather than longitudinal data. Most educators would prefer to observe students and to see how schools influence measures of change over extended periods of time. Indeed, it is likely that school characteristics associated with student gains in achievement at a given point in time could be quite different over an extended period.

Marion Shaycoft provides some information on this point. She analyzed 6,583 students who were tested in Project Talent in 1960, when they were

[63] Samuel M. Goodman, *The Assessment of School Quality* (Albany, N.Y.: New York State Education Department, 1959).

Table 3.9 / Correlates of Student Achievement, Grades 6 and 9

School Characteristics	Mexican-Americans	Puerto Ricans	Indian-Americans	Asian-Americans	Blacks North	Blacks South	Whites North	Whites South	Total
Student Body Characteristics									
Proportion of pupils with encyclopedia in the home	X	X	X	X		X			5
....		X							1
Proportion of school's graduates in college	X	X	X	X		X		X	6
Proportion in college prep curriculum	X		X						2
Average attendance as percentage of enrollment	X	X	X						3
Proportion of pupils who are white	X	X	X						3
Average number of white pupils in preceding year	X	X	X	X	X	X	X	X	8
Mean nonverbal test score	X	X	X	X	X	X	X	X	8
Mean verbal test score	X	X							2
Proportion of pupils who think teacher expects their best work	X	X							2
Proportion of pupils whose mothers went to college			X	X				X	3
Characteristics of Instructional Personnel									
Teacher's estimate of quality of own college	X	X	X	X		X			5
Teacher's verbal score	X	X	X	X					4
Teacher's race	X	X							2
Teacher's preference for teaching middle class	X	X				X			3
Teacher's attitude toward integration	X	X	X						3
Teacher's salary				X					1
Finances and Program									
Per-pupil expenditure				X					1
Comprehensiveness of curriculum				X	X				2
Mathematics offering	X		X						2
Totals	14	14	12	10	3	6	2	4	

Note: An X is any column indicates that the characteristic correlates .2 or higher with one or more achievement test variables at either grade 6 or 9 or both.

Source: Adapted from *Supplemental Appendix to the Survey on Equality of Education Opportunity* (Washington, D.C.: U.S. Government Printing Office, 1966), pp. 143, ff.

Table 3.10 / Noncorrelates of Student Achievement, Grades 6 and 9

Student Body Characteristics

Number of twelfth-grade pupils
Pupil mobility (transfers in and out)
Average hours pupils spend on homework
Proportion of pupils who read over 16 books the preceding summer
Teacher's perception of quality of student body
Proportion of students whose mothers expect their best work

Characteristics of Instructional Personnel

Teacher's socioeconomic status
Teacher's experience
Teacher's localism
Teacher's highest degree received
Teacher's absences
Amount of teacher turnover
Availability of guidance counselors
Pupil-teacher ratio

Program, Facilities, Other

Extracurricular offerings
Tracking
Movement between tracks
Accelerated curriculum
Policy on promotion of slow learners
Foreign language offering
Number of days in session
Length of school day
Number of science labs
Volumes per pupil in school library
School location (urban-rural)
Teacher's perception of quality of school

Source: *Supplemental Appendix to the Survey on Equality of Education Opportunity*, pp. 143, ff.

in grade 9, and retested in grade 12. She concluded that the impact of schooling upon cognitive development over this three-year period was considerable; there were gains on all 42 tests analyzed, and the larger gains were associated with subjects taught in school rather than areas of general information or skills that could be acquired elsewhere. Furthermore, on 40 of the 42 gain scores there were statistically significant variations among schools.[64]

From Shaycoft's data it is possible to conclude that the quality of schooling makes a difference in student achievement, but the data do not tell us how pronounced it is or what school characteristics are most important. And, while her study indicates that qualitative differences in the schools are associated with achievement, there is no guarantee that dif-

[64] Marion F. Shaycoft, *The High School: Growth in Cognitive Skills* (Pittsburgh, Pa.: American Institute for Research and University of Pittsburgh, 1976).

ferences in student achievement among schools reflect differences in the students' social class—or other factors outside the school. For example, it is conceivable that upper- and middle-class students attend specific schools, and these schools account for the greatest differences among schools in gain scores.

Coleman and Jencks: The Importance of Nonschool Variables

In startling contrast to the studies on social class and school success discussed above, the studies by James Coleman and Christopher Jencks concluded that the schools have little influence upon children's intellectual achievements. The results of these studies are difficult to present concisely, since the analysis includes a host of variables and a large number of subgroups.

The Coleman survey deals with 625,000 children and 4,000 schools, and the report is about 1,300 pages long, including 548 pages of statistics.[65] It is the largest educational research enterprise conducted in the United States, and almost everyone of whatever persuasion can find something in it to quote.

The general approach sorts 45 school characteristics or variables into correlates and noncorrelates of student achievement (see Tables 3.9 and 3.10). For this purpose, a correlate was loosely defined as any school characteristic that correlates .2 or better with any *one* of three achievement measures—reading, mathematics, and general information. Of the 45 variables, 19 showed some relationship with at least one out of three achievement tests, and 26 failed to do so.

The 19 correlates which tend to be associated with student achievement cluster around *student* and *teacher* characteristics, and especially around students; these are *hard-to-change* characteristics. Those that are unassociated with student achievement are by and large *school* characteristics and *easy-to-change* variables. In effect, the report says that schools in general have little impact on learning, and the variables associated with learning, such as the students' or the teachers' mean verbal test scores, are difficult to change. Changes effected by spending extra money—such as teachers' experience, teacher turnover, student-teacher ratio, tracking, and length of school day—are easier to bring about but have little relation to achievement. Thus the correlation between expenditures per student and learning was essentially zero at each grade level examined, as Table 3.9 shows.

---

[65] James S. Coleman et al., *Equality of Educational Opportunity* (Washington, D.C.: U.S. Government Printing Office, 1966).

The Coleman findings raise difficult policy questions for the nation's educators. If increases in student expenditures, higher teacher salaries, reduced classroom sizes, and other conventional remedies for low achievement have virtually no effect, what grounds are there to seek increased funds for education? Compensatory education advocates were being told, in effect, that extra spending makes no difference in outcomes because it does not correlate with student achievement.

The data led to the conclusion that schools can do very little to effect changes in student achievement; rather, home characteristics and peer group influences are, in that order, the two major variables associated with achievement. In a subsequent interview, Coleman put it this way:

All factors considered, the most important variable—in or out of school—in a child's performance remains his family background. The second most important factor is the social-class background of the families of the children in the school. Those two elements are much more important than any physical attributes of the school.[66]

An important qualification of this conclusion is that schools seem to have greater impact on some minority group children, as indicated in Table 3.9 (we will return to this theme in the next chapter, on race and ethnicity). Nevertheless, Coleman's finding of a small relationship between school facilities and student achievement, a conclusion which contradicts the Mollenkopf-Melville, Goodman, and Shaycoft reports on effects of school characteristics, has inspired searching analysis of the topic and arguments for and against the report since its publication.

The major criticism leveled against it is that the criterion of academic achievement is almost exclusively a measure of verbal abilities, which are more likely to be the product of the child's home than his school experience.[67] However, most other studies rely on the same test measurements, and when the results appear more positive this factor is not mentioned. If Coleman can be criticized for this bias, it follows that almost all other studies on school achievement are also misleading.

Another criticism pertains to Coleman's method of analysis, in particular his heavy dependence upon regression analysis, which unavoidably leads to an underestimate of the effects of school investment.[68] When independent variables in a multiple repression analysis are related, controlling for the first will reduce the correlation of the second. For

---

[66] James S. Coleman, "Class Integration—A Fundamental Break with the Past," *Saturday Review*, May 27, 1972, p. 59.

[67] Henry S. Dyer, "School Factors and Equal Educational Opportunity," *Harvard Educational Review*, Winter 1968, pp. 38–56.

[68] Samuel Bowles, "Towards Equality of Educational Opportunity," *Harvard Educational Review*, Winter 1968, pp. 89–99.

example, controlling for social class of the student indirectly controls also for part of the variation of school resources. The additional predictive power associated with the addition of school resources to the analysis thus represents a downward estimate of the real relationship between school resources and achievement.

These statistical problems were recognized by Coleman; it was for this reason that he permitted a low correlation of .2 to represent the level of acceptance, whereas most studies would require a higher correlation. Moreover, Coleman accepted relationships on any one of three tests for any one of two grade levels as significant; each of the 45 variables had six opportunities to show a correlation with achievement. Had he required a higher correlation, or had he used only one test with only one grade level, there would have been almost zero correlates.

Most important, the reanalysis of the Coleman data by other investigators,[69] and other recent large-scale statistical studies of the determinants of student achievement,[70] show similar results. A large fraction of the variation in student achievement is accounted for by out-of-school variables, such as the students' home characteristics. Another large fraction is attributable to the so-called peer group effect, that is, the characteristics of the students' classmates. Of the variation that is explained by school factors (no more than 30 percent), only part can be attributed to teachers.

While Coleman showed that there was not much schools could do to improve the achievement levels of students, Christopher Jencks went one step further and indicated that differences in school achievement as well as economic attainment are more related to socioeconomic origin than to schooling.[71] In his four-year study of the reanalysis of the U.S. Census, the Coleman report, and several smaller studies, Jencks concluded that:

1. The schools do almost nothing to close the gap between the rich and poor, the disadvantaged or advantaged learner.
2. The quality of education has little effect on what happens to students (as regards future income) after they graduate.
3. School achievement depends largely on a single input, that is, the

---

[69] George W. Mayeske et al., *A Study of Our Nation's Schools* (Washington, D.C.: U.S. Government Printing Office, 1966); Frederick Mosteller and Daniel P. Moynihan (eds.), *On Equality of Educational Opportunity* (New York: Random House, 1972).

[70] Harvey Averch et al., *How Effective Is Schooling? A Critical Review and Synthesis of Research Findings* (Santa Monica, Ca.: Rand Corp., 1972; Raymond Boudon, *Education, Opportunity and Social Inequality* (New York: John Wiley & Sons, 1973); Herbert J. Kiesling, *The Relationship of School Inputs to Public School Performance in New York State* (Washington, D.C.: Rand Corp., 1966).

[71] Christopher Jencks et al., *Inequality: A Reassessment of the Effect of Family and Schooling in America* (New York: Basic Books, 1972).

family characteristics of the students — and all other variables are either secondary or irrelevant.

4. About 45 percent of IQ is determined by heredity, 35 percent by environment, and 20 percent by a covariance or interaction factor.

5. There is no evidence that school reform (such as compensatory spending or integration) can substantially reduce the cognitive inequality that exists among students.

Committed to egalitarianism, Jencks concluded that it would require actual redistribution of income to achieve complete economic equality, regardless of ability.

The main policy implications of these findings are that schools cannot contribute significantly to equality. Jencks maintains that educators at all levels of instruction are not improving the lives of students, but this is not really their fault; rather the problem lies with the children's social class and other home characteristics. Economic equality in our society will have to be achieved by changing not the schools but our economic institutions. The reforms of the 1960s and 1970s failed because they tried to effect changes that were not feasible. To reduce social and economic inequality, it is necessary to shift the emphasis from equal opportunity to equal results.

Jencks's positions on heredity and environment, his support of standardized tests for predicting school success and measuring academic skills, his belief that schooling is without value, and his espousal of the merits of income redistribution, regardless of differences between those who are smart and ambitious or dumb and lazy, aroused criticism from the political left and right alike. The *Harvard Educational Review* devoted a feature issue to the study. In trying to answer his critics, Jencks strongly responded that those who are politically oriented or are advocating a specific position will "deplore anything that undercuts [their] arguments." He said sufficient criticism had been leveled at the book so that educators, laymen, and policy makers "feel free to accept or reject its conclusions according to their prejudices." The critics' arguments are unconvincing; "most of the issues they raise [were originally] covered in the text . . . or appendices." This does not necessarily mean that the study's conclusions were correct, but "the assumptions are plausible" and those who reject the data "are under obligation to offer an alternative view of how the world works, along with some empirical evidence that their view is more accurate then ours."[72]

In a related study, Jencks, with Marsha Brown, found few relationships between high school characteristics and measures of school effectiveness.

---

[72] Christopher Jencks, "Inequality in Retrospect," *Harvard Educational Review*, February 1973, pp. 104-5, 113.

Using portions of the Project Talent study (an extensive survey conducted during the early 1960s for purposes of estimating the range and levels of ability among American high school students), they concluded that, at least for white students, changes in high school characteristics are unlikely to change academic outcomes. They also argued that the equalization of high school characteristics would do little to reduce differences in student achievement, student entrance into college, and subsequent occupational levels.[73]

The Jencks and Brown study pretested and posttested some 4,900 students on six different reading and math tests in the 9th and 12th grades in 98 high schools across the country. They made estimates of the contribution of various high school characteristics to the variation of these test scores and estimated how high school quality affected high school graduation, college plans, and career plans five years after high school. The findings indicated that high schools which are effective in boosting student performance on one standardized test are only marginally effective in boosting scores on other tests. Those that are unusually effective in raising test scores across the board are no more effective than the average in getting their students to finish their education and enter high-status occupations.

Of all the measures of school characteristics, class size was the only one whose correlation was consistent for all measures of cognitive impact, and these correlations were too small to be significant. The correlation was also precisely the opposite of what most educators would assume. According to Jencks and Brown, large classrooms have a positive effect on student achievement. Other characteristics such as student expenditures, teacher salaries, teacher experience, and socioeconomic composition have little impact on cognitive growth between the 9th and 12th grades and on college plans and occupational success.

The fact that socioeconomic composition does not seem to affect student achievement scores is at odds with Coleman's conclusions, but the rest of the findings tend to coincide with Coleman and the earlier Jencks study. The implications of this study by Jencks and Brown are that more money, smaller classrooms, more graduate work for teachers, higher salaries for teachers, socioeconomic desegregation, and possibly other traditional remedies do not have much effect on educational attainment.

The International Association for the Evaluation of Educational Achievement (IEA)

The IEA study evolved from an international conference in the 1950s at which researchers from a dozen countries agreed to assess children's

---

[73] Christopher Jencks and Marsha D. Brown, "Effects of High Schools on their Students," *Harvard Educational Review,* August 1975, pp. 273-324.

achievement on a cross-national basis; it is the largest cross-cultural study on academic achievement. The first major survey, in the area of mathematics, involved 133,000 elementary and secondary students, 13,500 teachers, and 5,450 schools in 12 technological countries including the United States. After this study the researchers embarked on a six-subject survey of science, literature, reading comprehension, English and French as foreign languages, and civic education. Together with mathematics, these subjects cover practically all the principal subjects in the secondary curriculum. This survey involved 258,000 secondary students and 50,000 teachers from 9,700 schools in 19 countries (4 of them less developed).

The data analysis in the math survey was complicated but tended to show that teacher and school characteristics are relatively unimportant in determining math achievement. Student characteristics highly correlated with achievement, and the child's social class accounted for the greatest share of variation in learning. The study also showed that, at every age level and in most countries, boys out-performed girls in math.[74]

The six-subject survey was reported in nine volumes beginning in 1973. The reading survey is of most interest, at least to Americans. The conventional view of the relation of socioeconomic level to reading scores apparently holds true internationally. The general belief in the universal superiority of girls' reading does not hold up, however; age seems to be a factor with reading scores, and at the secondary school level reading scores of teen-age boys and girls are similar. The relatively low scores of American as compared to European students supports the general view that many students in this country are disadvantaged and have basic reading problems.[75]

The data from all six areas tend to confirm the importance of the student's culture, and particularly the home, to achievement. The total effect of home background is considerably greater than the direct effect of school variables. At age four the overall average is .42 for home factors, but only .26 for school; at age ten, it is .35 for home factors and .22 for school.[76] The data are also sufficiently detailed to conclude, as the science report does, "that learning is a continuous and cumulative process over generations."[77] Not only is the child's home environment important, but so is his family and culture, which is rooted in generations of environmental

---

[74] Torsten Husén, *International Study of Achievement in Mathematics: A Comparison of Twelve Countries,* vols. 1 and 2 (New York: John Wiley & Sons, 1967).

[75] Robert L. Thorndike, *Reading Comprehension Education in Fifteen Countries* (New York: John Wiley & Sons, 1973).

[76] James S. Coleman, "Methods and Results in the IEA Studies of Effects of School on Learning," *Review of Educational Research,* Summer 1975, pp. 335–86.

[77] L. C. Comber and J. P. Keeves, *Science Education in Nineteen Countries* (New York: John Wiley & Sons, 1973), p. 298.

(and genetic) change. While the home is the most important environmental factor, the impact of the school on a culture is shown to be generally more important in science and foreign language than other areas.[78] This is significant, since the Coleman and Jencks data are based on reading and mathematics scores in the United States. The suggestion that certain subjects might be more amenable to school influences is taken as an encouraging sign for those who feel that schools make a difference and educators should be held accountable.

Of course, there are many limitations to such a large-scale study. There is the question of common content across countries to warrant testing and then there are age differences by school levels across countries. (All 13-year-olds have not had or are supposed to have had the same amount of schooling cross-nationally.) Translation of content may be accurate, but it is difficult to assure that the vocabulary and resulting speed passages are similar. There is the sheer magnitude of the data; and because of the size of the population, there are numerous variables possibly not accounted for which may have affected the scores. With all of these problems, still, the studies constitute probably the best models in existence for cross-national research on social institutions and social behavior. This fact should not be lost, in the critique of these studies by secondary analysis.

CONCLUSIONS

Differences in values among social classes and the theory of deprivation point to family or home characteristics as the chief factor affecting student performance in school. Early studies on the effects of social class confirm this conclusion, demonstrating the relationship of students' family background and income to school achievement and other performance levels.

More recent studies show that school characteristics have an effect on student achievement, but the effects of schools per se ultimately can be explained away by characteristics of the individual students who comprise the student body. This has policy implications, including the issue of school integration, but it also confirms the important influence of family characteristics and peer groups on student achievement. Some studies found that the impact of school resources, including financial expenditures, is minimal, and so is the capacity of schools to effect changes in student achievement.

The revolutionary conclusions of some of these recent studies threaten cherished beliefs about schools. Starting in the mid 1960s, the research

---

[78] William E. Coffman and Lai-min P. Lee, "Cross-National Assessment of Educational Achievement: A Review," *Educational Researcher*, June 1974, pp. 13–16.

data tend to show that school reform has little effect on reducing cognitive inequality. Many of these studies have been challenged by other social scientists; nevertheless, they have performed a valuable service in helping to dispel some of the myths about what schooling can and cannot achieve. The education community has often claimed more than it was prepared to deliver, and a more realistic appraisal of what we can expect will be healthy.

If, as these studies contend, cognitive outcomes are not substantially affected by what the teacher or school does, if schools cannot deliver on their promises because of client problems, then the implications are clear. The results suggest that many of the resources for which school systems and local, state, and federal governments have been willing to pay a premium, such as reduced class size and special programs, may not be of much value. With financial pressures being felt by education budget makers everywhere, less costly "solutions" are eagerly sought; since the most costly item in all school budgets is teachers' salaries, hiring fewer teachers or letting class size increase is the easiest way to improve the cost benefit ratio of the school program. Eliminating compensatory programs that have not worked or produced desired results would also reduce spending; in fact, a radical change of input variables to reduce educational costs could be advocated. And, if variations in what children learn in school depend on variations in what they bring to school, not on variations in what schools offer them, a cultural autocracy could easily characterize the school's response to children who do not learn or conform in the way desired.

On the other hand, we should be wary of accepting too easily or uncritically the findings of the more recent studies discussed in this chapter. Social science research does not deal in exact measurements or certainties. There are too many variables which cannot be controlled and which interact in multiple ways.

It should be remembered, too, that the schools have served many people well in the past, although it could be argued that the clients were different. Like it or not, we have no other option at the present but to seek to improve the schools for all children and youth, even though the schools may be limited in serving all students equally.

ACTIVITIES

1. Rate your own social class, first by the subjective method and then by the objective method. Are the results similar? What criteria did you use for self-rating? How do your criteria differ from your classmates'?
2. Visit a city council meeting or similar local situation where the public is invited to voice its opinions. Cite examples of any display of vested interests which might be class related.

3. Look through catalogs or circulars of summer camps, private and preparatory schools, and colleges. What evidence of an attempt to cater to social class interests do you find?
4. List the factors determining how far a student goes in school, and how successful he or she is. Identify the relationship between intelligence, social class, and education.
5. Invite a professor to discuss the controversy generated from the Coleman and Jencks studies.

DISCUSSION QUESTIONS

1. Defend or argue against the idea that social class is a useless concept.
2. Discuss the consequences social class has for education.
3. Explain the concept of deprivation. How does early child environment affect mental growth and development?
4. How does the school serve as a sorting and selecting agency?
5. Make a case for or against the notion that schools make a difference in educational outcomes.

SUGGESTED FOR FURTHER READING

Bloom, Benjamin S. *Human Characteristics and School Learning.* New York: McGraw-Hill, 1976.

Boocock, Sarane S. *An Introduction to the Sociology of Learning.* Boston: Houghton Mifflin Co., 1972.

Coleman, James S., et al. *Equality of Educational Opportunity.* Washington, D.C.: U.S. Government Printing Office, 1966.

Davis, Allison. *Social Class Influences upon Learning.* Cambridge, Mass.: Harvard University Press, 1948.

Havighurst, Robert J. and Neugarten, Bernice L. *Society and Education.* 4th ed. Boston: Allyn & Bacon, 1975.

Hollingshead, August B. *Elmtown's Youth.* New York: John Wiley & Sons, 1949.

Jencks, Christopher, et al. *Inequality: A Reassessment of the Effect of Family in Schooling in America.* New York: Basic Books, 1972.

Passow, A. Harry; Goldberg, Miriam; and Tannenbaum, Abraham J. (eds.). *Education of the Disadvantaged.* New York: Holt, Rinehart & Winston, 1967.

Riessman, Frank. *The Culturally Deprived Child.* New York: Harper & Row, 1962.

Warner, W. Lloyd; Meeker, Marcia; and Eells, Kenneth. *Social Class in America.* Chicago: Science Research Associates, 1949.

CHAPTER 4

RACE, ETHNICITY, AND MINORITY GROUP EDUCATION

Among the issues that have occupied Americans in recent years, one of the most prominent has been the status of racial, ethnic, and other minority groups. The central political question in this country since the 1960s has been how to provide equality for all persons considered to be of minority status. Discrimination and prejudice, once considered only in terms of a black-white dilemma, have been analyzed to include Asian Americans, American Indians, Spanish Americans, and women, and the handicapped and older people are also seeking minority rights. Concern for protection against racism and sexism is now common, and individuals, private and public institutions, and the federal government are all involved. This chapter will investigate race and ethnicity; some other minority group problems are discussed in Chapter 5, on social stratification.

THE MEANING OF MINORITY STATUS

The term "minority status" is used to designate the standing of those members of society who are prevented from participating fully and equally in all phases of social life, who are subordinate to the majority, who can be distinguished on the basis of physical or cultural characteristics, and who have fewer life chances and rights than the majority. Charles Wagley and Marvin Harris have suggested five characteristics of a minority:

1. Minorities are subordinate segments of a complex society.
2. Minorities have special physical or cultural traits which [distinguish them from the majority group, and often] are seen as undesirable [as well].
3. Minorities have a group self-awareness brought about by the special traits they share and the special disabilities these traits cause them.
4. Membership in a minority is transmitted by a rule of descent — one is born in a minority — and this rule of descent is capable of imposing the minority status on future generations, even if by then the special physical or cultural trait of the minority has disappeared.
5. Members of a minority, whether by choice or by necessity, tend to practice endogamy — that is, to marry within the group.[1]

These characteristics seem to fit white ethnic minorities best, especially those who are in the process of assimilation or who have not yet begun it. As assimilation proceeds, some of the minority characteristics will become weaker — group awareness may decrease, marriage out of the group may increase, and distinctive cultural traits may be abandoned. Thus, there exists for white ethnics what may be called a "continuum of minoritiness," rather than a sharp break between minority and majority groups.[2] In the course of the 20th century, various immigrant groups from Europe to this country have moved along this continuum from a greater to a smaller degree of "minoritiness." Wagley and Harris's definition is somewhat less accurate for nonethnic minority groups, especially for women, blacks, and other nonwhites, as well as the aged and the handicapped, who constitute minorities by virtue of being politically and economically subordinate to the majority.

The sociological meaning of the term "minority" is sometimes misunderstood because it also has a quantitative meaning. Women could be thought of as a majority because they constitute more than half of the American population, but the sociological meaning of minority status is a matter of social standing and social power, not of numbers. The blacks in South Africa, for example, have a minority status even though they are more numerous than the whites, because the whites are in power and control the institutions of society. Conversely, the rich and ruling elite of a society always constitute a numerical minority, but they never occupy a minority status. In American society and Western culture in general, the aged constitute a minority both in absolute numbers and in regard to economic status and the treatment they receive, yet they have only recently begun to be recognized as a minority group.

To be sure, today in the United States minority status provides certain advantages not provided to others, including preferential treatment in

---

[1] Charles Wagley and Marvin Harris, *Minorities in the New World* (New York: Columbia University Press, 1958), p. 10.
[2] Joseph Julian, *Social Problems* (Englewood Cliffs, N.J.: Prentice-Hall, Inc., 1973).

social policy and in the economic sector. Just who is defined as a minority is becoming a political issue. Traditionally, those who were considered discriminated against and in need of constitutional protection could be distinguished on the basis of their "race, color, religion, and national origin." The Civil Rights Act of 1964 was designed to protect these groups against discrimination in the spheres of voting, jobs, and education (in 1968, housing was added). Due in part to the subsequent civil rights movement, in 1970 the civil rights enforcement agencies of the Departments of Labor and Health, Education, and Welfare, made their own interpretation of the Civil Rights Act. They omitted religious and white ethnic groups from their immediate concern and shifted from *protection of individuals* against discrimination to *preferential treatment of certain groups:* blacks, Asian Americans, American Indians, and Spanish Americans. In 1972, in the wake of the feminist movement, women were added to the list of preferential groups.[3]

Minorities as Social Categories

If the members of a society are to exclude some people from full participation in the culture and define them as a minority, both majority and minority groups must be identifiable to one another. The blacks of the Ituri Forest can treat the pygmies as a minority because they can easily identify pygmies by their stature.[4] Mexicans can distinguish among those of Spanish descent, Indian descent, and the offspring of mixed marriages by coloring, hair texture, and bone structure. English-speaking Canadians can treat French-speaking Canadians as a minority because language and family names make their differences apparent. Protestant Irish and Catholic Irish can be distinguished not only by church affiliation but also by regional language and accent. Minority identification can result from speaking a different language, having a different skin color, hair, or eye characteristics, or attending a different church from those identified with the people in the majority group. Thus minorities can be either physically or culturally identified as different. The Nazis forced Jews to wear armbands so that they could be more easily identified, since the latter were not readily identifiable.[5]

---

[3] See Nathan Glazer, *Affirmative Discrimination: Ethnic Inequality and Public Policy* (New York: Basic Books, 1975); Allan C. Ornstein, *Race and Politics in School/Community Organizations* (Pacific Palisades, Ca.: Goodyear Publishing Co., 1974); Allan C. Ornstein, "The Return of Racial Quotas," *Educational Forum,* November 1975, pp. 97–114.

[4] Carleton S. Coon and Patrick Putnam, "The Pygmies of the Ituri Forest," in C. S. Coon (ed.), *A Reader in General Anthropology* (New York: Holt, Rinehart & Winston, 1948), pp. 322–42.

[5] Raymond W. Mack and John Pease, *Sociology and Social Life,* 5th ed. (New York: D. Van Nostrand Co., 1973).

If only cultural behavior makes people identifiable as members of a minority, they can become socialized into the majority culture and thus be assimilated; this is the case for most white immigrants to the United States, and especially for second-generation ethnics. If physical differences such as skin color, hair type, or sex make people identifiable as minority members, the only ways to protect minority groups are by implementing and adhering to specific laws or, better yet, changing the beliefs and attitudes of the majority group, if possible.

In the United States there is controversy about the nature of the ideal society. Should our objective be the proverbial *melting pot,* in which each

Table 4.1 / Physical Characteristics of Three Main Races of the Human Species

Trait	Caucasoid	Mongoloid	Negroid
Skin color	Pale reddish white to olive brown; some dark brown.	Pale yellow to yellow-brown; some reddish brown.	Brown to brown-black; some yellow-brown.
Stature	Medium to tall.	Medium tall to medium short.	Tall to very short.
Head form	Long to broad and short; medium high to very high.	Predominantly broad; height medium.	Predominantly long; height low to medium.
Face	Narrow to medium broad; no projecting jaw.	Medium broad to very broad; cheekbones high and flat.	Medium broad to narrow; frequent projecting jaws.
Hair	Head hair: color light blond to dark brown; texture fine to medium, form straight to wavy. Body hair: moderate to profuse.	Head hair: color brown to brown-black; texture coarse; form straight. Body hair: sparse.	Head hair: color brown-black; texture, coarse; form light curl to woolly or frizzly. Body hair: slight.
Eyes	Color: light blue to dark brown; occasional side eye-fold.	Color: brown to dark brown; fold of flesh in inner corner very common.	Color: brown to brown-black; vertical eye-fold common.
Nose	Bridge usually high; form narrow to medium broad.	Bridge usually low to medium; form medium broad.	Bridge usually low; form medium broad to very broad.
Body build	Slim to broad; slender to rugged.	Tends to be broad; occasional slimness.	Tends to be broad and muscular, but occasional slimness.

Source: Adapted from Wilton M. Krogman, "The Concept of Race," in R. Linton (ed.), *The Science of Man in the World of Crisis* (New York: Columbia University Press, 1945), p. 50.

ethnic or racial group is an ingredient to be blended in a common culture? Or, should the objective be a *pluralist society,* in which each group retains its distinctive characteristics while respecting the culture of other groups and dealing with them on the basis of mutual respect and equality? And the ultimate question is: Can either one of these societies truly exist in American society?

Race as a Biological Concept

Most frequently, the basis used for labeling and identifying a minority is *race.* Race is a confusing term, because it is hard to differentiate from cultural and religious heritage. As the concept is used by geneticists and most social scientists, a race is a group of people who share a set of innate *physical* characteristics. It is often assumed that members of a race share an unchangeable set of physical characteristics that permanently set them apart from other races. This is not so; races are subject to the same process of genetic change as all other living organisms.

All persons belong to a single species, the human race. Within this species, groups of races were formed through a combination of mutations (some of which survived more easily in one environment than in another), long periods of relative isolation which resulted in inbreeding, and a selection of cultural standards of what were and were not considered desirable physical traits. As armies, traders, travelers, tribal migration, and individual emigration reduced isolation, intermarriages with other physical types resulted, and distinctive hereditary patterns were muted.

Consequently, there are no pure races within the human species, and it is impossible to devise a system of exact classification on the basis of inherited physical traits. We can only approximate such a classification; the difficulty of doing so is indicated by the vagueness of the categories in Table 4.1, which shows the three *major races* of the human species recognized by almost all social scientists. Subgroups or *geographical races* based on broad geographic areas[6] are shown in Figure 4.1.

Subordinate to a geographical race are different breeding populations, the groups geneticians and anthropologists often study. This is called the *local race.* Local races may be separated by physical or social barriers; they mate chiefly within their own group, and they are most like their neighbors in gene characteristics. They number in the hundreds, as contrasted to the three major classifications of race and the more than 30 geographical races.

---

[6] Theodore Dobzhansky, *Mankind Evolving* (New Haven, Conn.: Yale University Press, 1962); I. I. Gottesman, "Biogenetics of Race and Class," in M. Deutsch, I. Katz, and A. R. Jensen (eds.), *Social Class, Race, and Psychological Development* (New York: Holt, Rinehart & Winston, 1968), pp. 11–51.

Figure 4.1 / Geographical Areas of 34 Local Races

1. Northwest European
2. Northeast European
3. Alpine
4. Mediterranean
5. Hindu
6. Turkic
7. Tibetan
8. North Chinese
9. Classic Mongoloid
10. Eskimo
11. Southeast Asiatic
12. Ainu
13. Lapp
14. North American Indian
15. Central American Indian
16. South American Indian
17. Fuegian
18. East African
19. Sudanese
20. Forest Negro
21. Bantu
22. Bushman and Hottentot
23. African Pygmy
24. Dravidian
25. Negrito
26. Melanesian-Papuan
27. Murrayian
28. Carpentarian
29. Micronesian
30. Polynesian
31. Neo-Hawaiian
32. Ladino
33. North American Colored
34. South African Colored

Source: Adapted from Theodore Dobzhansky, *Mankind Evolving* (New Haven, Conn.: Yale University Press, 1962), p. 264.

While race classifications or names may be somewhat arbitrary, race differences are facts of nature which can be studied in terms of gene pools and specific traits, localized in time and space. Racial classifications, moreover, do not correlate with either cultural or social patterns. High cheekbones show some relationship to reddish-brown skin, and black hair is associated with brown-black skin, but none of these characteristics is associated with intelligence, musical ability, or any other innate abilities.

DISCRIMINATION AND PREJUDICE

Interest in the study of prejudice has increased since World War II, provoked by the death of 6 million Jewish people in Europe, the independence of former colonies and the rise of Third World powers, and the civil rights movement in this country, accompanied by urban violence, black separatism and white backlash, and feminist rights. Today, government-imposed affirmative action programs have reversed discrimination to favor minorities and help them "catch up" to majority status.

Different levels of actions flow from prejudice, from a mild ethnic slur to the most overt act, extermination. Five levels are noted by Gordon Allport. The first is a verbal expression of prejudice, such as: "I don't like blacks" or "All Jews are aggressive," or "Women belong in the kitchen." At the next level, the prejudiced person avoids members of the group he or she dislikes; this does no direct harm to the disliked person. The flight of whites from the city to the suburbs because of black in-migration in a neighborhood or an increase of black students in the local school population illustrates this kind of avoidance. The third level of action resulting from prejudice is discrimination; this does direct harm to members of the disliked group by excluding them from certain types of jobs, housing, and education. Segregation enforces discrimination by law or custom, resulting in an institutionalization of prejudiced behavior—separate toilet facilities, separate schools, separate neighborhoods for whites and blacks. At the fourth level there is physical abuse; members of the disliked group are beaten in the streets, as in the anti-Jewish pogroms in Eastern Europe or attacks on Japanese Americans in Los Angeles during World War II. The fifth and most violent level is extermination, such as the massacres of Indians in the United States or the lynching of blacks after the Civil War and Chinese workers in the far west before the turn of the 20th century.[7]

Institutionalized Discrimination

As a result of prejudice which imparts minority status, some people have the capacity to impose discrimination on others. Many people think of prejudice and discrimination as one and the same process; they are not. In many instances people who are prejudiced are unable or unwilling to act upon their beliefs and attitudes. For most of us, values, laws, and customs intervene between our individual attitudes and our capacity to act accordingly. We usually do not act on our own personal prejudices but are

---

[7] Gordon Allport, *The Nature of Prejudice* (New York: Doubleday, 1958).

constrained in our behavior by the social situation and social policy; in short, we tend to follow organizational or societal decisions.

Discrimination is a socially learned behavior of majority group members which is designed to support and justify their prejudices and rationalizations of continued dominance. Unwittingly, this discrimination is built into the very structure and form of society and affects the people in it. If members of a society have been socialized to believe that certain minorities are just "dumb" or "lazy," it is natural for them to formulate social policy and build institutions which discriminate against those minorities. And once discrimination is institutionalized by a society, it is difficult to change individual behavior. Equal protection of the laws is important, but the people and the policy makers must truly believe in equal opportunities.

The discrepancy between the ideal and the reality of the situations for black and white people in this country was the subject of what Gunnar Myrdal called the "American dilemma" in his classic study.[8] One's judgment of to what extent the discrepancy remains today in the wake of the civil rights movement and affirmative action policies, and to what extent it applies among other minority groups, is based as much as anything on one's own political beliefs and personal bias.

POPULATION TRENDS OF MINORITY GROUPS

In 1975, there were some 210 million Americans, including 184 million whites. Included in this figure were the following minorities: approximately 40 million first-, second-, and third-generation European ethnics (including 6 million Jewish Americans) and 11.2 million Spanish Americans (including 6.7 Mexican Americans and 1.7 Puerto Ricans). In addition, there were approximately 23.8 million black Americans, 1.5 million Asian Americans, and nearly 1 million American Indians. Women as a minority included another 60 million women who were not members of other minority groups.[9] Clearly more than 75 percent of the American population could be classified as occupying minority status and experiencing some amount of discrimination.

Of course, all persons of minority status do not have exactly the same life chances. Jewish Americans, Chinese Americans, and Japanese Americans, for example, have higher educational and income levels than other minority groups do. While blacks generally are burdened with low in-

---

[8] Gunnar Myrdal et al., *An American Dilemma* (New York: Harper & Row, 1944).
[9] *Population Profile of the United States; 1975,* Current Population Reports, Series P-20, no. 292 (March 1976), Table 25, pp. 39–40.

comes, some blacks are quite wealthy, and occupational segregation is greater for women than it is for blacks even though women have higher educational levels.

Patterns of Black Emergence

As recently as 1910, blacks and foreign-born European ethnics accounted for more than 25 percent of the nation's population. In this century (up to 1970), the black population has remained fairly constant, between 10 to 11.5 percent of the total population, while first-generation white ethnics, or foreign-born Europeans, have decreased from 15 percent in 1910 to 4.7 percent in 1970.[10] The birthrate among blacks has been traditionally higher than for whites (in 1940 it was 33 percent higher, in 1970 90 percent higher),[11] but in the past rapid white immigration from Europe and the high death rate of blacks offset this advantage. Since 1940, however, the immigration rate from outside the United States has dropped dramatically, from 29.1 million between 1901 and 1940 to 5.1 million between 1941 and 1975.[12] In addition, improved medical care for blacks has caused the ratio of black to white deaths per 1,000 to drop from 1.47 in 1900 to parity in 1970.[13] As a result of these factors, the black population is now growing considerably faster than the white population. From 1940 to 1960, the black population rose 46.6 percent, compared to the white population, which increased 34 percent.[14] From 1960 to 1970, the black population rose another 19 percent, while the white population rose only 14 percent.[15] Although there has been a recent decline in birthrates for both white and black women, by 1975 whites were at less than zero population growth, 1.8 children per white women, while the rate was 2.4 children for black women. These rates did not consider women under 18 years old, and, since young black women generally have considerably more births in their teen-age years than white women, the differential birthrates

[10] *Census of the Population, 1970, General Social and Economic Statistics* (Washington, D.C.: U.S. Government Printing Office, 1972), Table 69, p. 203; Table 86, p. 382; *Historical Statistics of the United States, 1789–1945* (Washington, D.C.: U.S. Government Printing Office, 1949), p. 25; *Statistical Abstract of the United States, 1972* (Washington, D.C.: U.S. Government Printing Office, 1973), Table 31, p. 29.

[11] *Report of the National Advisory Commission on Civil Disorders* (New York: Bantam Books, 1968), p. 238; *Social and Economic Status of the Black Population in the United States, 1974,* Current Population Reports, Series P-23, no. 54 (July 1975), Table 2, p. 12.

[12] *Advisory Commission on Civil Disorders,* p. 238: *Statistical Abstract of the United States, 1976* (Washington, D.C.: U.S. Government Printing Office, 1977), Table 166, p. 105.

[13] *Status of the Black Population, 1974,* Table 83, p. 125.

[14] *Advisory Commission on Civil Disorders,* p. 238.

[15] *Statistical Abstract of the United States, 1975* (Washington, D.C.: U.S. Government Printing Office, 1976), Table 32, p. 29.

were even larger than reported.[16] Given no changes in birthrates, it is estimated that by 1980 blacks will comprise 12 to 13 percent of the population and 15 percent of it some time between 1985 and 1990.

City and Suburban Trends

Between 1940 and 1970 the migration of blacks from the rural South was apparent as unskilled blacks were first drawn to the industrial centers created by World War II. Whereas 77 percent of the black population lived in the South in 1940, only 52 percent did in 1970. Since 1970, however, the number of blacks moving from the South has equaled the number moving to the South.[17]

Almost all black population growth is occurring within the cities. From 1950 to 1970, when the U.S. black population rose by 7.5 million, over 85 percent of that increase took place in cities and less than 15 percent in suburbs and rural areas. By far the greatest white population growth was in the suburbs. From 1950 to 1970, 80 percent of the white population

Table 4.2 / Changing Black Profiles of the Ten Largest U.S. Cities, 1950–1980 (blacks as percent of population)

City	1950	1960	1970	Percent of Change, 1950 to 1970	1980[a]
New York	9.8%	14.0%	21.1%	115.3%	32.0%
Chicago.	14.1	22.9	32.7	131.9	43.5
Los Angeles	9.0	13.5	17.9	98.9	22.3
Philadelphia	18.3	26.4	33.6	83.6	40.0
Detroit.	16.4	28.9	43.7	166.5	61.1
Houston	21.1	22.9	25.7	22.0	30.1
Baltimore	23.8	34.9	46.4	95.0	56.9
Dallas	13.0	19.0	24.9	91.5	30.7
Washington, D.C..	35.0	53.9	71.1	103.1	86.7
Cleveland	16.3	28.6	38.3	135.0	45.9

Note: Cities ranked in descending order according to 1970 population.
[a] Projections based on extrapolation from last 20 years (1950–70) by author.
Source: Adapted from David N. Alloway and Francesco Cordasco, *Minorities and the American City* (New York: David McKay & Co., 1970), Table 9, p. 19; *National Advisory Commission on Civil Disorders* (New York: Bantam Books, 1968), p. 248; *Statistical Abstract of the United States, 1972* (Washington, D.C.: U.S. Government Printing Office, 1973), Table 22, pp. 21–23.

---

[16] *Fertility of American Women: June 1975,* Current Population Reports, Series P-20, no. 301 (November 1976), Tables 19, 20, 22, pp. 36-37, 39; *A Statistical Portrait of Women in the United States,* Current Population Reports, Series P-23, no. 58 (April 1976), Table 5.1, p. 19; *Population Profile of the United States: 1975,* Table 16, p. 24.

[17] *Population Profile of the United States, 1975,* Current Population Reports, Table 16, p. 24; *Statistical Abstract of the United States, 1975,* Table 31, p. 28.

increase of 42.6 million took place in the suburbs; only 2 percent of the white increase was in the cities, and the remaining was in rural areas. [18]

Thus, the cities are becoming more heavily black, both absolutely and relatively (see Table 4.2). The total black population more than doubled from 1910 to 1970 (from 9.5 million to 22.6 million), but the number living in the cities rose fivefold (from 2.7 million to 12.7 million). [19] The urbanization process has been dramatic within the past 20 years; in 1970, 57 percent of the black population lived in the cities, compared to 28 percent of the white population. [20] Between 1950 and 1970 the cities added 10 million people, mostly black and other nonwhites, while the suburbs added 35 million people, the overwhelming majority being white. The greatest exchange of city-suburban population shifts occurred in New York City and its surrounding suburban areas; nearly 2 million blacks and Puerto Ricans moved into the city to replace nearly 2.5 million white residents fleeing to the suburbs. In Chicago, the shift was almost parallel; while about 700,000 blacks, Puerto Ricans, and Mexican Americans moved into the city, nearly 1 million whites out-migrated to the suburbs; the suburban ring increased from 1.5 million to 3.5 million whites. [21]

Nationwide, the black population in the suburbs increased by approximately 1 million between 1950 and 1970, bringing the total to about 3.5 million. Because the white exodus to the suburbs was so large, blacks who moved to the suburbs went somewhat unnoticed. The percentage of blacks living in the suburbs has remained constant during this 20-year period, at under 5 percent. [22] Thus we are fast becoming two separate nations: one black and living in the cities, the other white and living in the suburbs.

The preference of whites for the suburbs may well be a response to the massive migration of the new minority groups into the cities, but it is probably a mistake to interpret it only as white flight. People move to the suburbs for many reasons: better job opportunities, better schools for their children, less congestion, cleaner air, lower taxes, safer streets, and so on. Some of these reasons may be considered "code" words for escaping from

---

[18]*Advisory Commission on Civil Rights*, p. 243; *Statistical Abstract of the United States, 1975*, Table 16, p. 17; Table 31, p. 28; Table 32, p. 29.

[19] *Historical Statistics*, p. 25; *Advisory Commission on Civil Rights*, p. 239; *Status of the Black Population, 1974*, Table 1, p. 11.

[20] *Statistical Abstract of the United States, 1975*, Table 19, p. 18.

[21] Robert J. Havighurst and Daniel U. Levine, *Education in Metropolitan Areas*, 2nd ed. (Boston: Allyn & Bacon, 1971), p. 59; Ornstein, *School/Community Organizations*, p. 187.

[22] Ornstein, *School/Community Organizations*, p. 187; *Status of the Black Population*, Table 6, p. 15; *Statistical Abstract of the United States, 1975*, Table 16, p. 17.

blacks and other nonwhite minorities, but Americans in fact have been moving to the suburbs since the 19th century, when there were few blacks in the cities.

Some whites have moved from Northern cities to the Southern and Southwestern sunbelt areas for job opportunities and retirement purposes. Between 1970 and 1975, the South and West each experienced a net migration gain of 4.1 million. Other areas of recent growth are the rural areas and small cities of under 50,000 people. In the early 1970s the growth rate in metropolitan areas reversed itself for the first time in American history, and nonmetropolitan growth outstripped growth in urban areas.[23] Each year between 1970 and 1975, for every 100 people who moved to a metropolitan area, 131 moved out. Net migration gains occurred in nearly two-thirds of all metropolitan (suburban-rural) counties, compared with only one-quarter in the 1960s. In 1975, ten of the nation's largest standard metropolitan statistical areas were declining in population — New York, Philadelphia, Pittsburgh, Cleveland, Cincinnati, Detroit, Chicago, St. Louis, Los Angeles, and Seattle-Everett.[24]

By 1985 it is estimated the total black population will rise to about 31 million from its 1970 level of 22.5 million, gaining an average of 7.7 percent per year. The increase will be faster in the major cities, and it is estimated that 12 cities will have black majorities — including Baltimore, Birmingham, Camden, Cleveland, Detroit, New Orleans, Oakland, Philadelphia, Richmond, St. Louis, Savannah, and Trenton.[25] Unless there are major changes in population shifts, the suburbs ringing the cities will remain largely white.

These population shifts mean U.S. cities are being drained of their middle-class tax base, since whites are disproportionately middle class, and are being burdened with less affluent and poorer residents who demand more services. While revenues are declining, expenditures for every kind of essential public service (education, health, police and fire protection, welfare), are increasing. This drain on the resources of the cities has put them in a financial plight which is seen as a national problem. The loss of private industry and jobs in urban areas and the expansion of federal assistance to the cities are trends with far-reaching consequences for the states and the nation.

---

[23] *Population Estimates and Projections: Estimates of the Population of States with Components of Change, 1970–1975*, Current Population Reports, Series P-25, no. 640 (November 1976), Tables A–B, p. 1; Tables D–E, pp. 3–4.

[24] Peter Morrison, "Migratory Patterns Reversing," paper presented to the American Association for the Advancement of Science, Denver, February 1977.

[25] *Population Estimates and Projections*, Table 25, pp. 21–23.

Table 4.3 / School Enrollments in the Ten Largest Cities, 1968–1969, 1972–1973, and 1976–1977 (percentage of black, white, and other students)

	Enrollment (1976–77)	1968–69[a]			1972–73[b]				1976–77[c]			
		White	Black	Other	White	Black	Spanish	Other	White	Black	Spanish	Other
New York	1,100,000	44%	32%	24%	35.2%	36.1%	26.9%	1.8%	32.1%	37.4%	28.2%	2.3%
Los Angeles	601,500	54	23	23	46.0	25.2	23.9	4.9	37.0	24.1	32.1	6.8
Chicago	524,221	38	53	9	31.0	56.9	11.1	1.0	24.9	59.4	14.1	1.6
Philadelphia	263,654[d]	39	59	2	35.2	61.4	3.4	NR	32.0	62.0	6.0	NR
Detroit	235,895	39	59	2	30.8	67.6	1.6	NR	19.0	79.0	2.0	NR
Houston	210,025	53	33	14	43.9	39.6	16.5	NR	34.2	43.1	21.8	0.9
Baltimore	159,358	35	65	0	30.2	69.3	0.5	NR	25.0	74.5	0.5	NR
Dallas	139,080	61	31	8	50.5	38.7	10.3	0.5	38.1	47.0	14.0	0.9
Washington, D.C.	125,908	6	93	1	3.8	95.5	0.7	NR	3.5	95.1	0.8	0.6
Cleveland	122,706	42	56	2	40.0	57.6	2.0	0.4	37.8	58.5	3.0	0.7

Note: School systems are ranked according to 1976–77 enrollments in descending order.

NR = Not reported.

[a] 1968 represents the first year that black-white school enrollment figures were collected on a nationwide basis.

[b] 1970 represents the first year that Spanish-speaking enrollment figures were collected on a nationwide basis.

[c] 1976 figures were obtained by writing to the public information officer of each school system.

[d] Based on 1975–76 school population enrollments.

Source: Fall, 1972 Racial and Ethnic Enrollment in Public Elementary and Secondary Schools (Washington, D.C.: Office for Civil Rights, 1974), Table 3A, pp. 12–15; Table 3B, pp. 15–17; U.S. Senate Select Committee on Equal Educational Opportunity (Washington, D.C.: U.S. Government Printing Office, 1972), pp. 116–17.

School Enrollment Trends

As white families withdraw their children from city schools, they are replaced by a greater number of black students. This is because the black population has a higher birthrate, has more children of school age, and makes less use of the private schools. In most cities the proportion of black students in public schools has become greater than the black proportion of the city population. Between 1950 and 1965, for example, the black population in Oakland, California, grew from 12 percent to 30 percent (+ 18 percent), but the black school population grew from 14 percent to 45 percent (+ 31 percent), and in Washington, D.C., the black population increased by 20 percent (to 55 percent), while the black school population increased by 39 percent (to 89 percent). From 1960 to 1970, the black population in Atlanta increased to 52 percent (+ 14 percent), but black students in the school system increased to 69 percent (+ 29 percent).[26] In the same decade the black population in Detroit went to 44 percent (+ 15 percent), while the black student population went to 64 percent (+ 19 percent).[27]

Enrollment gains of black students vis-à vis black census trends are similar in all major cities.

Over an eight-year period, from 1968 to 1976, increases in the proportion of blacks in school enrollments were evidenced in all of the ten largest cities, as shown in Table 4.3. By 1976 blacks comprised a majority or near majority of public school students in 8 out of the 10 largest cities, as well as many other major cities; moreover, if the total nonwhite student population is included, all of the ten largest cities have fewer white students than nonwhite students. Evidence of the loss of white students is the fact that in the 100 largest school districts (which have half the nation's black students), total enrollments dropped by 280,000 students between 1970 and 1972,[28] even though there was a gain of 146,000 black students during this period.

The trend to proportionately greater black enrollments can be expected to continue because the black population is relatively younger. In 1975, 40 percent of the black population was under 18 years old, compared to about 32 percent of the overall population; the median age for blacks was 23.1

---

[26] *National Advisory Commission on Civil Rights,* p. 431; Robert G. Wegman, "White Flight and School Resegregation: Some Hypotheses," *Phi Delta Kappan,* January 1977, pp. 389–93.

[27] Allan C. Ornstein, *Metropolitan Schools: Administrative Decentralization v. Community Control* (Metuchen, N.J.: Scarecrow Press, 1974), p. 212; *Statistical Abstract of the United States, 1975,* Table 25, pp. 23–25.

[28] Wegman, "White Flight and School Resegregation," p. 390.

and for whites, 28.8.[29] Projections therefore are for a continuing increase in the proportion of the black population which is of school age.

THE STRUCTURE OF THE BLACK FAMILY: THE MOYNIHAN REPORT

The role of the family in predicting school achievement and dropout rates and other social trends, such as mental health, juvenile delinquency, and unemployment rates, is well documented in social science research. But the role of the black family in terms of differences between lower-class and middle-class blacks and blacks and whites in general has developed into a controversial issue since the release of the Moynihan report in the mid-1960s.[30]

Approximately 25 years prior to this report, Franklin Frazier, a black sociologist, wrote about family disorganization among blacks and its results in what was to become a classic text, *The Negro Family in the United States.*[31] Frazier said black family disorganization was rooted in the history of slavery, which meant a more important role for the female, greater significance being attached to variations in skin color, and a higher incidence of desertion, illegitimacy, and other forms of disorganization. Commenting on his thesis ten years later Frazier indicated that:

As a result of family disorganization, a large proportion of Negro children and youth have not undergone the socialization which only the family can provide. The disorganized families have failed to provide for their emotional needs and have not provided the discipline and habits which are necessary for personality development. Because the disorganized family has failed in its function as a socializing agency, it has handicapped the children in their relations to the institutions in the community. . . . Since the widespread family disorganization among Negroes has resulted from the failure of the father to play the role in family life required by American society, the mitigation of this problem must await those changes in the Negro and American society which will enable the Negro father to play the role required of him.[32]

In the presixties black viewpoint of Frazier, the child who comes from a disorganized home and enters school experiences cultural shock and finds classroom experiences dull, uninteresting, frustrating, and anxiety-producing. Thus the black child is at odds with the school and later with

---

[29] *Population Profile of the United States, 1975,* Table 39, p. 39; *Status of the Black Population, 1974,* Table 18, p. 17.

[30] Daniel P. Moynihan, *The Negro Family: The Case for National Action* (Washington, D.C.: U.S. Government Printing Office, 1965).

[31] E. Franklin Frazier, *The Negro Family in the United States* (Chicago: University of Chicago Press, 1939).

[32] E. Franklin Frazier, "Problems and Needs of Negro Children and Youth Resulting from Family Disorganization," *Journal of Negro Education,* Summer 1950, p. 277.

society. Because of a general lack of discipline, training, and family structure, the child lacks the inner control and self-discipline necessary for learning and exhibiting "appropriate" behavior in school. The black child either displays aggressive behavior, psychologically withdraws or is physically absent from school. His poor performance in school subsequently affects his life opportunities as an adult.

When Daniel Moynihan addressed himself to the same point of black family disorganization in the 1960s, he was criticized by liberals and blacks. The times had changed. Whereas prior to the civil rights movement blacks were on the defensive, any criticism of blacks by an outsider since the early sixties can invite vigorous criticism, name-calling, and even personal attack. Not only was Moynihan white, and therefore considered alien to the black experience, but blacks had become organized and astute in utilizing their sense of injustice and charges of racism to put social scientists, who are mostly white, on the defensive.

Moynihan postulated that family structure is a major product of social behavior and attitudes and serves primarily as a socializing agent in the creation of culture, social character, and social class. He considered the black family structure to be the major reason for the poor achievement and unemployment which was keeping blacks in the lower class. Distinguishing between stable and successful middle-class families and unstable and unsuccessful lower-class (black) families, he cited numerous statistics on illegitimacy, broken homes, lack of education, crime, narcotics addiction, and so on to support his conclusion that "the family structure of low-class Negroes is highly unstable, and . . . is approaching complete breakdown."[33]

Among the statistics Moynihan cites were the following:

1. The illegitimacy ratio was 8 times higher for nonwhites than for whites: "The white rate was 2 percent in 1940; it was 3.07 percent in 1963. In that period the Negro rate went up from 16.8 percent to 23.6 percent."[34]

2. Almost 25 percent of the black families were headed by females. Black families were more likely than whites of the same income level to break up: "Only a minority of Negro children reach the age of 18 having lived all their lives with both their parents."[35]

3. Fertility rates for nonwhites compared to whites were 1.4 higher in 1960, "but what might be called the generation rate [was] 1.7 higher" —

---

[33] Moynihan, *Negro Family*, p. 5.

[34] Ibid., p. 5. More than 90 percent of the nonwhite population is black. Nonwhite was used in portions of the report because this is the method that the Census Bureau used to collect some of the data.

[35] Ibid., p. 9.

meaning the ratio of nonwhite to white children born per thousand to women between 15 to 19 years. Family size changed little for whites between 1950 and 1960, from 3.45 to 3.58, but it increased from 4.07 to 4.30 for nonwhites during the same period.[36]

4. The breakdown of the black family "has led to a startling increase in welfare dependency": as many as 56 percent of nonwhite children compared to 8 percent of white children were classified as dependent. "The majority of Negro children receive public assistance under the AFDC program [Aid to Families with Dependent Children] at one point or another in their childhood."[37] Particularly alarming was the fact that AFDC cases had increased steadily since 1958, while unemployment among blacks had declined.

5. The breakdown of the black family structure had led not only to increased welfare dependency but also to many other pathologies for which figures were cited: poor school performance, high dropout rates, and high rates of juvenile delinquency, violent crimes, and narcotics—higher than for whites, both absolutely and relatively, despite the 9:1 difference in population ratio.

Moynihan viewed the influence on boys of the absence of fathers in the Negro home as an explanation for a variety of these pathologies and for the rise of a matriarchal society among blacks. He did not explicitly propose any solution, except in stating the need for "a national effort towards the question of family structure . . . [with] the object to strengthen the Negro family so as to enable it to raise and support its members as do other families."[38]

Although Moynihan's thesis largely coincided with Frazier's, its social and political implications at the time touched off a fury in academic circles, journals, and the mass media. Moynihan's interpretation of the data in the Coleman report[39] and supplementary census data added fuel to the controversy. His later conclusions were:

1. The fact that blacks and whites have wide differences in verbal achievement scores cannot be explained solely by peer group or school factors but must also take into account family structure. Both black and white students show a strong tendency for achievement to decline in homes where the father is absent; furthermore, the family-head variable is a

---

[36] Ibid., p. 25.

[37] Ibid., p. 12.

[38] Lee Rainwater and William L. Yancey, *The Moynihan Report and the Politics of Controversy* (Cambridge, Mass.: MIT Press, 1967), pp. 47–48.

[39] James S. Coleman et al., *Equality of Educational Opportunity* (Washington, D.C.: U.S. Government Printing Office, 1966); see Chapter 3.

stronger predictor of school achievement than the family-income variable.[40]

2. The general rate of illegitimacy among black women declined compared to whites; it was 7 times higher than for whites in 1970, compared to 10 times higher in 1960. The absolute difference was still large, however: 5 percent of all white births were illegitimate compared to 31 percent of black births; 10 percent of all white first births but 48 percent of all black first births were illegitimate.[41]

3. The number of female-headed black families increased to 30.6 percent in 1971, compared to 9.4 percent for whites (but it was 33.9 percent for Puerto Ricans).[42] By 1975 black families with female heads had increased to 36 percent, compared to 10.5 percent for whites. In 1968, the majority of black children were in female-headed families; by 1975 the number reached 85 percent.[43]

4. Family economic status was even more closely linked to the sex of the family head. The number of blacks below the poverty line declined 49.4 percent between 1959 and 1968 for families with male heads but increased 23.6 percent for those with female heads. By 1974, two thirds of all black families below the poverty line were headed by females.[44]

Moynihan refers to "a deepening schism" among black families, a term originally used by the black social scientist Andrew Brimmer in a speech at Tuskegee University. While a growing stable, successful black middle class is closing the gap on their white counterparts in terms of education and income, there is also a growing unstable, unsuccessful black group.[45] According to a study of racial indicators by Michael Flax, blacks are catching up to whites on a number of social indicators and will reach parity by the late 1970s in a host of educational and job categories. But there are no catching-up projections for percent of illegitimate births, percent of female-headed families, and percent of children living with two

---

[40] Daniel P. Moynihan, "Sources of Resistance to the Coleman Report," *Harvard Educational Review*, Winter 1968, pp. 23–36; Frederick Mosteller and Daniel P. Moynihan (eds.), *On Equality of Educational Opportunity* (New York: Random House, 1972).

[41] Daniel P. Moynihan, *Coping: On the Practice of Government* (New York: Random House, 1975); *The New York Times*, April 20, 1971, p. 1.

[42] *Selected Characteristics of Persons and Families of Mexican, Puerto Rican, and Other Spanish Origin, March 1971,* Current Population Reports, Series P–20, no. 224 (October 1971), Table 5, p. 7; Table 11, p. 13; Daniel P. Moynihan, "The Deepening Schism," *Public Interest*, Spring 1972, pp. 3–24.

[43] *Household and Family Characteristics, March 1975,* Current Population Reports, Series P–20, no. 291 (February 1976), Table 1, p. 9.

[44] Moynihan, "The Deepening Schism"; *Status of Black Population, 1974,* Table 26, p. 45.

[45] Andrew Brimmer, "The Deepening Schism," paper presented at Tuskegee University. Nashville, Tenn., April 1970.

parents, all of which indicate a disintegrating family structure for lower class blacks.[46]

Moynihan is not alone in his thesis; other well-known social scientists have presented similar data indicating disorganized and pathological family structures, especially among lower-class blacks; most blacks are said to live in a self-perpetuating "culture of poverty."[47] But it is Moynihan who is most readily associated with the thesis and thus most threatening to liberal and black interests. He probably was singled out for opposition because his original report was earmarked for Congress to promote federal action on social and educational programs. Moynihan is well known in both academic and policy-making circles, and other scholars who support his views have less influence on social policy.

Criticisms of the Moynihan Thesis

Among the major criticisms of the Moynihan thesis that a disintegrating family structure keeps blacks from social, economic, and political parity with whites is that reference to "the weakness of the black family" in effect "blames the victim." The idea is seen as a race-relations game which has been imposed on blacks for centuries, with different arguments but similar intentions. The notion that the black family is unstable and does not prepare black people for productive lives is regarded as most detrimental to black progress because it is potentially acceptable to those who determine social policy and control the communications media.

According to these critics, the Moynihan report and similar literature place the source of the plight of blacks with the family unit rather than with society. The problems facing black families are not internal, however, as Moynihan suggests; rather they are external and associated with the materialism and racism which emanate from society.[48] The report does not suggest national action to crack down on prejudice and discrimination, as it should; rather it implies that federal action must be initiated to correct

---

[46] Michael Flax, *Blacks and Whites: An Experiment in Racial Indicators* (Washington, D.C.: Urban Institute, 1971).

[47] Edward C. Banfield, *The Unheavenly City*, 2nd ed. (Boston: Little, Brown & Co., 1974); H. Etzowitz and C. M. Schaflander, *Ghetto Crisis: Riots or Reconciliation* (Boston: Little, Brown & Co., 1969); Nathan Glazer and Daniel P. Moynihan, *Beyond the Melting Pot*, 2nd ed. (Cambridge, Mass.: MIT Press, 1970); Harry L. Miller, *Social Foundations of Urban Education*, 3rd ed. (New York: Holt, Rinehart & Winston, 1978); Oscar Lewis, "The Culture of Poverty," *Scientific American*, October 1966, pp. 19–25; Hyman Rodman, "Family and Social Pathology in the Ghetto," *Science*, August 1968, p. 756–61.

[48] Andrew Billingsley, "Black Families and White Social Science," *Journal of Social Issues*, Summer 1970, pp. 127–49; Rainwater and Yancey, *Moynihan Report and Politics of Controversy*.

the matriarchal structure of the black family. Not only does it serve as a possible rationalization of past and continued discrimination, it also makes a strong case for segregation.[49]

The critics also say that the report is of no use to scholars and students trying to understand family functioning in the black community because it ignores the positive characteristics of the black family while concentrating on its negative features. Noting that the report ignores black assets and never makes positive comparisons of black differences from whites, several black social scientists have described the assets of the black family, relying mainly on their experience and intuitive knowledge.[50] They cite such positive characteristics as:

1. Strong kinship bonds and family cooperation, including the absorption by the family of young and elderly relatives and children born out of wedlock.
2. An attitude of self-help and an ability to cope with and beat the system, but willingness to accept help when appropriate.
3. Flexible family roles, including equalitarian family patterns in two-headed households and confident females who can function as the heads of families.
4. Strong education and work orientations.
5. A strong religious orientation, especially in its role as a community organization and a part of the civil rights movement.
6. Low suicide rates — a possible indicator of stability.
7. The fact that most black families have both mothers and fathers.

According to critics of the Moynihan thesis, the plain fact is that most black families are headed by males, and those that are headed by females may not be at a disadvantage in any social or psychological measure. The argument is that father absence is only one of several interacting factors which influence a growing child. Even if a significant relationship can be demonstrated between father absence and one of the adverse effects attributed to it, the impact is dwarfed by other factors, such as the ability of

---

[49] Robert Blauner, *Racial Oppression in America* (New York: Harper & Row, 1972); Albert Murray, "White Norms, Black Deviation," in J. A. Ladner (ed.), *The Death of White Sociology* (New York: Random House, 1973), pp. 96-113.

[50] Andrew Billingsley, *Black Families in White America* (Englewood Cliffs, N.J.: Prentice-Hall, Inc., 1968); James E. Blackwell, *The Black Community: Diversity and Unity* (New York: Dodd, Mead & Co., 1975); Robert B. Hill, *The Strengths of Black Families* (New York: Emerson Hall, 1971); Robert Staples, *The Black Family: Essays and Studies* (Belmont, Ca.: Wadsworth Publishing Co., 1971).

the mother to give adequate supervision, the economic situation of the family, and community influence.[51]

In general, the critics see the Moynihan thesis as another example of analysis of black culture and life by a white social scientist in a white perspective. Andrew Billingsley says, "The reason black families have fared so much worse than white families in social science is that they are black and [the social scientist] is white. . . . These social scientists have been victimized by their own Anglo-European history and culture."[52] Since few white scholars have overcome their biases and even a number of black social scientists have adopted them, differences between blacks and whites are considered as deviations from the acceptable (white) norm. Until recently, all nonwhite cultures have been regarded as subject to assimilation.[53]

The counterargument by Moynihan, in brief, is that denial of black problems has become a successful strategy for liberals and blacks since the civil rights movement. But denying that problems exist will not make them go away. "A literature of denial [has] steadily accumulated on the general theme that there is nothing wrong with these family arrangements, that what was wrong was a sick society," and whatever pathologies are admitted are seen "as a 'natural' and healthy adaptation."[54]

RACE AND INTELLIGENCE

On the heels of the Coleman report's finding, that family rather than school characteristics affect learning, and the Moynihan report's support for the role of the family, a series of research studies by the new hereditarians further challenged the views of the environmentalists in regard to intelligence. The basic role of genetic inheritance as a determinant of intelligence represented the majority opinion among social scientists from the mid-19th to the mid-20th century, when the environmentalists began to raise serious doubts about the cultural biases of IQ tests and to stress the importance of environmental factors in determining intelligence. Acceptance of the environmentalists' views by the

---

[51] Elizabeth Herzog, "Social Stereotypes and Social Research," *Journal of Social Issues,* Summer 1970, pp. 109–25; Elizabeth Herzog and Hylan Lewis, "Children in Poor Families: Myths and Realities," *American Journal of Orthopsychiatry,* April 1970, pp. 375–87.

[52] Billingsley, "Black Families and White Social Science," pp. 133–34.

[53] Nathan Hare, "The Challenge of the Black Scholar," in J. A. Ladner (ed.), *The Death of White Sociology* (New York: Random House, 1973), pp. 67–78; Murray, "White Norms, Black Deviation."

[54] Moynihan, *Coping,* p. 358.

majority of social scientists has coincided with the civil rights movement in the United States and the new prominence of the non-Western world in foreign affairs.

The New Hereditarians: The Jensen Study

The new hereditarians maintain that intelligence is determined far more by heredity than by environment. Arthur Jensen, the best known, based his conclusions on a review and reanalysis of previous research on IQ, as well as his own research using representative samples of whites, blacks, Mexican Americans, American Indians, and Asian Americans.[55] His findings, published in a lengthy paper in the *Harvard Educational Review* in 1969, included the following points:

1. IQ tests are not culturally biased, because certain aspects are similar for white and black groups: correlation of raw scores with age, internal consistency reliability, item difficulty (i.e. percent passing), item correlation with total score, and loading of items or questions on total score.

2. An extensive review of studies of IQ involving parents and offspring, and identical twins reared together and apart, found that 80 percent of the variations in IQ are explained by heredity, 20 percent by environmental factors.

3. After controlling for social class, blacks average 15 points below the white average on IQ tests; this is due to genetic differences between the two races, but the test scores apply only for groups as a whole and should not be considered on an individual basis.

4. Blacks and other "disadvantaged" children have difficulty in abstract reasoning, which forms the basis for IQ measurements and for higher mental skills. Unfortunately, the schools have assumed that all children can master higher cognitive skills. Conversely, blacks and other "disadvantaged" children tend to do well in tasks involving rote learning—memorizing mainly through repetition. These aptitudes can be used to help raise their scholastic achievement, up to a point.

5. Compensatory education, which is costing taxpayers billions of dollars a year, has failed, and will continue to do so because it is trying to compensate disadvantaged children using learning processes and concepts that are geared for students who have facility in abstract reasoning. The K-

---

[55] Arthur Jensen, "How Much Can We Boost IQ and Scholastic Achievement?" *Harvard Educational Review*, Winter 1969, pp. 1–123.

12 curriculum should be revamped to fit the characteristics and learning needs of the disadvantaged more closely.[56]

Jensen pointed out that the nature of the differences of intellectual skills among races and the role of genetics in intelligence had not been fully explored. He strongly attacked the environmentalists who dominated the field and argued that almost all children have the same potential for developing mental abilities, and differences in IQ scores are the result of social, psychological, and economic deprivation. Pointing out the overwhelming failures in compensatory education, he called for a fresh look at classroom and school failure. It should start, he declared, with a reexamination of the nature of intelligence.

Criticism of Jensen's findings has been widespread, but the most comprehensive analysis is by six environmentalists (Carl Bereiter, William Brazziel, Lee Cronbach, David Elkind, J. McVicker Hunt, and Jerome Kagan) who were invited by the *Review* to respond to Jensen's article.[57] Their main points were:

1. IQ tests are biased, and the scores do not necessarily measure intelligence.

2. IQ outcomes are affected by a host of environmental factors, such as prenatal care and malnutrition, which are difficult to measure.

3. There is considerable disagreement on the importance of environment; some see the environment-heredity interaction as impossible to separate and measure, while others maintain the environment accounts for 80 percent of variations in IQ.

4. Jensen's research is based on relatively small samples, and he fails to consider studies contrary to his findings.

5. Race prejudice could account for any differences in IQ that might exist between blacks and whites.

6. Although billions of dollars have been spent on compensatory education without impressive results, it may be that the threshold has not been reached where the amount of money spent per child makes an impact. In addition, if compensatory programs are to have maximum effect they must be begun almost as soon as the child is born.

7. The curriculum advocated by Jensen would track disadvantaged students, especially minority group children, into second-rate, nonacademic programs.

[56] Also see Arthur R. Jensen, "IQ Tests are Not Culturally Biased for Blacks and Whites," *Phi Delta Kappan*, June 1976, p. 676; Arthur R. Jensen, "Test Bias and Construct Validity," *Phi Delta Kappan*, December 1976, pp. 340–46.

[57] "How Much Can We Boost IQ and Scholastic Achievement?: A Discussion," *Harvard Educational Review* (Spring 1969), pp. 273–356.

The arguments snowballed and became quite heated in the professional literature. Jensen's classes were continuously disrupted; some of his colleagues at the University of California at Berkeley unsuccessfully tried to censure him and have him dismissed, and they devised a review panel to screen further research. Jensen and his family were frequently threatened and he was harassed and heckled at appearances before professional audiences. Like many theorists, he was often misquoted, and those of his critics who read the original study often could not follow the statistics.[58]

Jensen continues the controversy today, maintaining that the environmentalists have failed to refute his findings.[59] He expresses concern over the environmentalists' argument that the differences in IQ and school achievement are caused mainly by racial discrimination, and none are due to heredity, because he believes the resulting frustration and hostility of blacks (and the recent reverse discrimination against whites) may become acceptable forms of behavior.

Other New Hereditarians

Other contemporary hereditarians who are relatively well known are Hans Eysenck, Richard Herrnstein, Edward Wilson, and William Shockley. Eysenck summarizes the Jensen controversy, emphasizing the role of heredity in determining inequality in education and income and concluding that quotas for college admissions and jobs are a political attempt to redress the imbalance resulting from hereditary differences between groups.[60]

Herrnstein supports Jensen's view that IQ is largely hereditary but purposely avoids the racial issue. Rather, he argues that IQ is a crucial factor in determining social class within a stratified system. The closer a society comes to the ideal of equal opportunity, the more those with high IQs will rise to the top and those with low IQs will remain at the bottom.

---

[58] Martin Deutsch, "Organizational and Conceptual Barriers to Social Change," *Journal of Social Issues,* Autumn 1969, pp. 5-18; Ornstein, *School/Community Organizations;* Allan C. Ornstein, "Should Any Topic Be Off Limits to the Social Scientist?" *Chronicle of Higher Education,* May 13, 1974, p. 24; Wilson Record, "Who Is Impartial?" *Time,* August 7, 1972, pp. 46-47; Wilson Record, "More Than a Matter of Color," paper presented at the Annual Conference of the American Sociological Association; New York, August 1973; Michael Scriven, "The Values of the Academy," *Review of Educational Research,* October 1970, pp. 541-49.

[59] Arthur R. Jensen, *Genetics and Education* (New York: Harper & Row, 1972); Arthur R. Jensen, "The Differences Are Real," *Psychology Today,* December 1973, pp. 83-87; Arthur R. Jensen, "Relationship of Level I and Level II Cognitive Processes to a Test of Associative Responding," *Journal of Educational Research,* January 1977, pp. 127-30.

[60] Hans J. Eysenck, *The IQ Argument: Race, Intelligence, and Education* (New York: Library Press, 1971).

Like Eysenck, he fears the decline of merit and competency as the push for egalitarianism calls for equal results.[61]

Wilson is a controversial hereditarian whose views fall within a field called sociobiology, the systematic study of the biological bases of social behavior in every kind of organism, including man. He presents a massive amount of research on the determining influences of behavioral characteristics, such as weight and height, the propensity for illness and mental disorders, and intelligence, and shows them to be influenced more by genetics than environment.[62]

Shockley, a Stanford University physicist who was a co-winner of the Nobel prize for the invention of the transistor, entered the controversial arena concerning intelligence. He accepts Jensen's research on the role of heredity and black-white differences in IQ and supports the data with mathematical equations. But he goes further to suggest a theory of "dysgenics," which he defines as "retrogressive evolution through the disproportionate reproduction of the genetically disadvantaged," and proposes such countermeasures as cash incentives to limit the number of offspring for people of low IQ. While his mathematical work is rarely criticized, his assertions on dysgenics are considered unworthy of serious consideration by most social scientists.[63]

The Limits of Social Research

Liberals and blacks have attempted to discount the theories of the new hereditarians as the products of racists or ideas devised to support racist practices. They charge that the new hereditarians have applied the rules of statistical inference too strictly, but liberals have not admitted "the best trained environmentalists writing about the subject have gone as far and often further in the opposite direction."[64] Much of the criticism has been emotional and without scientific support, based on abbreviated versions and secondary summaries of the studies, so that it contains demonstrable errors of interpretation. The name-calling and harassment with which critics have met the arguments of these new hereditarians involve issues

---

[61] Richard J. Herrnstein, "IQ," *Atlantic,* September 1971, pp. 43-64; Richard J. Herrnstein, *IQ in the Meritocracy* (Boston: Little, Brown & Co., 1973).

[62] Edward O. Wilson, *Sociobiology* (Cambridge, Mass.: Harvard University Press, 1975).

[63] William Shockley, "Models, Mathematics, and the Moral Obligation to Diagnose the Origin of Negro IQ Deficits," *Review of Educational Research,* October 1970, pp. 369-77; William Shockley, "Negro IQ Deficit: Failure of a 'Malicious Coincidence' Model Warrants New Research Proposals," *Review of Educational Research,* June 1971, pp. 227-48; William Shockley, "Dysgenics, Geneticity, Raceology: A Challenge to the Intellectual Responsibility of Educators," *Phi Delta Kappan,* January 1972, pp. 297-307.

[64] Scriven, "Values of the Academy," p. 548.

regarding free inquiry and academic freedom, as well as the social scientist's responsibility to publish sensitive data which have the potential to polarize groups.

There is the danger that social scientists concerned with research in race relations, minority education, or related subjects such as tests and measurements will find that conclusions which run counter to liberal-black opinion are not worth the personal and professional costs involved. Increasingly, only one point of view is being heard, while almost any idea not flattering to minorities, regardless of its objectivity, is being labeled as racist. Not only is there an underlying, self-imposed censorship in many college classrooms, so that topics such as the basis of intelligence are best ignored or slanted to suit minority interests and ideologies, but many researchers feel compelled to bury or modify their findings. Such an atmosphere is not conducive to the principles of free research and discussion.[65]

However, to many liberal and black spokesmen, academic freedom and scientific inquiry are not the major issues in research outcomes. Rather it is the policy statements and political decisions that can come from the research. They recognize that research can harm a racial or ethnic group by detrimentally affecting the policies directed to its needs and interests.

The federal government recently detailed an extensive control system over "improper" social research, and several major universities have introduced screening boards to consider the impact research will have on persons belonging to identifiable groups and to curtail studies with potentially sensitive results. Some members of the black and Spanish-speaking communities have sought to prevent white social scientists from conducting research in their schools and neighborhoods, and the right to screen and approve or disapprove findings before they are submitted to any agency or journal has been demanded. In short, there is a move to control the flow of information from ghetto areas.[66]

The feelings of blacks and other minorities who consider themselves victims of past studies, which considered neither the social responsibilities

---

[65] See Herrnstein, *IQ in the Meritocracy;* Ornstein, "Should Any Topic Be Off Limits to the Social Scientist?"; Norman Podhoretz, "The New Inquisitors," *Commentary,* April 1973, pp. 7-8; Record, "Who Is Impartial?"; Wilson, "Liberalism versus Liberal Education."

[66] *The New York Times,* December 9, 1973, Section 4, p. 5; "Protection of Human Subjects," *Educational Researcher,* November 1973, pp. 10-17; Roscoe C. Brown, "How to Make Educational Research Relevant to the Urban Community—the Researcher's View," paper presented to the Annual Conference of the American Educational Research Association, New York, February 1971; Deutsch, "Barriers to Social Change"; Allan C. Ornstein, "Research on Decentralization," *Phi Delta Kappan,* May 1973, pp. 610-14; Wilson Record and Jane C. Record, "The White Social Scientist in the Black Community," *Journal of Research and Development in Education,* Spring 1975, pp. 63-72.

of the researchers nor the consequences of their findings must be recognized. The assumption is that the white social scientist is unaware of her or his role as a perpetuator of institutional racism. Many black social scientists now claim that only blacks are qualified to conduct research in the black community. They call for new criteria of judgment and emphasis on concepts that show the positive aspects of black life and ask for allowances to be made for research that is not tightly controlled.[67] While the implications of these claims are censorship of research, ensuring "positive" findings, advancing political ideology, and creating research jobs based only on race, they reflect a combination of long years of frustration and moral criticism, as well as the economic aspirations of black social scientists.

Whatever the justification for the increasing regulation of social research and the demands of some minority spokesmen, their actions underscore some difficult questions about the nature and purpose of scholarly inquiry pertaining to race relations. What are the limits of this research? Are there areas of inquiry that should be placed off limits? Do some groups have the right to censor data? When does freedom of inquiry conflict with the responsibilities of the researcher? When are claims of racism, or even of responsibility, used as strategies to curtail research? Should the researcher pursue knowledge wherever it leads? To be sure, it is difficult to find a neutral commentator who is capable of answering, much less willing to answer, these questions.

RACE, ETHNICITY, AND SCHOOL ACHIEVEMENT

Along with social class, the student characteristic that has been the subject of most educational controversy and analysis is race. Recent research has focused upon the differences in school success among black and other minority group children and their white counterparts, and the extent to which race or ethnicity is a function of differential school achievement and opportunities for schooling. In Chapter 3 we examined the educational evidence related to social class, in particular family characteristics, peer groups, and school climate. Here we will examine the effects on school achievement of being black or of an ethnic heritage.

---

[67] See Hill, *Strengths of Black Families;* Ladner, *Death of White Sociology;* Judith K. Shanahan, "The White Researcher in the Black Community: A Dilemma," paper presented at the Annual Conference of the American Educational Research Association, New Orleans, February 1973; Madelon D. Stent, "Researchers, Consultants, and Urban Schools," paper presented at the Annual American Educational Research Association, New Orleans, February 1973; Chuck Stone, "The Psychology of Whiteness v. the Politics of Blackness," *Educational Researcher,* January 1972, pp. 4-6, 16.

The Coleman Report

The Coleman report included a sample of 625,000 students in grades 1, 3, 6, 9, and 12 and children from six racial and ethnic groups: blacks, Asian Americans, American Indians, Mexican Americans, Puerto Ricans, and whites other than Spanish speaking (referred to as the "majority," or simply white). Achievement of the average black, Mexican American, Puerto Rican, and American Indian was much lower than the average white child at all levels; Asian Americans came closer to the norm. Moreover, the differences widened at higher grades, as shown in Table 4.4, which considers only grades 6, 9, and 12. Blacks and Puerto Ricans had the lowest test scores; they start approximately one-half year behind whites in reading and mathematics at the first grade, and end up three years behind in reading and more than four years behind in mathematics by the 12th grade. The following excerpt best summarizes the data:

With some exceptions—notably Oriental Americans—the average minority pupil scores distinctly lower on these tests at every level than the average white pupil. The minority pupils' scores are as much as one standard deviation below the majority pupils' scores in the first grade. At the 12th grade, results of tests in the same verbal and nonverbal skills show that, in every case, the minority scores are *farther* below the majority than are the 1st graders'. . . . Thus, by this measure,

Table 4.4 / Achievement Test Scores of Minority Group Compared to White Students

| Minority Group | School Grade | Grade Levels Behind White Students | | |
		Verbal Ability	Reading Achievement	Math Achievement
Blacks	6	1.6	2.0	2.0
Mexican Americans	6	1.7	2.2	1.9
Puerto Ricans	6	2.4	2.9	2.5
American Indians	6	1.4	1.8	1.7
Asian Americans	6	0.6	0.8	0.7
Blacks	9	2.5	3.0	2.6
Mexican Americans	9	1.9	2.2	2.2
Puerto Ricans	9	2.5	2.9	3.0
American Indians	9	1.7	1.9	2.0
Asian Americans	9	0.6	0.5	0.0
Blacks	12	3.5	2.9	4.7
Mexican Americans	12	2.9	2.8	3.4
Puerto Ricans	12	3.0	3.2	4.1
American Indians	12	2.9	2.7	3.2
Asian Americans	12	1.0	1.1	0.2

Source: Adapted from James Coleman et al., *Equality of Educational Opportunity* (Washington, D.C.: U.S. Government Printing Office, 1966), Tables 3.121.1–3.121.3, pp. 274–75.

Table 4.5 / Attitudes toward School and Academic Work of Twelfth-Grade Students, by Race and Ethnicity

Percent of Students Who:	White	Black	Mexican American	Puerto Rican	American Indian	Asian American
Part I						
Would "do almost anything" to stay in school	45	46	37	35	36	44
Want to be among the best students	33	58	33	36	38	46
Spend three or more hours on homework daily	31	23	22	21	17	42
Have never missed any school because of truancy.	66	76	59	53	60	76
Have read at least one book during previous summer	75	80	69	72	73	74
Part II						
Plan to go to college next year	40	34	26	26	27	53
Have consulted college officials	37	25	22	25	26	33
Have read a college catalog.	61	54	46	45	50	70
Plan to have a professional occupation.	37	27	18	21	21	43
Part III						
Feel they "just can't learn"	39	27	38	37	44	38
Feel "good luck is more important than hard work for success"	4	11	11	19	11	8
Feel "every time I try to get ahead something or somebody stops me."	14	22	23	30	27	18
Feel "people like me don't have much of a chance to be successful in life."	6	12	12	19	14	9

Source: Adapted from Coleman et al., *Equality of Educational Opportunity*, Tables 2.43.1–2.43.3, pp. 193–99; Tables 3.13.1–3.13.16, pp. 278–90.

the deficiency in achievement is progressively greater for the minority pupils at progressively higher grade levels.

For most minority groups, then, and most particularly the Negro, schools provide no opportunity at all for them to overcome this initial deficiency; in fact, they fall farther behind the white majority in the development of several skills which are critical to making a living and participating fully in modern society. Whatever may be the combination of nonschool factors — poverty, community attitudes, low educational level of parents — which put minority children at a disadvantage in verbal and nonverbal skills when they enter the first grade, the fact is the schools have not overcome it.[68]

Coleman and his colleagues next turned to the task of examining the school orientation of the various racial and ethnic groups in their sample, particularly their academic motivation, educational and occupational aspirations, and feelings about themselves. As shown in Table 4.5, Part I, white and black students have similar attitudes toward school and academic work; blacks express an even higher valuation of academic achievement. But black and white students differ in the steps they will take to implement their educational aspirations (Part II). Black respondents have fewer concrete plans to attend college or to enter a professional occupation. There are also wide differences between black and white students in their sense of control, as shown in Part III. This variable is among the most powerful predictors of test scores for minority students, and for black students it was found to be the most important variable.

Mexican American, Puerto Rican, and American Indian students have lower positive responses than blacks on almost every attitude toward academic achievement and plans beyond high school, and they express greater inability to control their environment. Asian Americans, however, show aspirations and activities that are generally higher than whites; although they have somewhat lower scores on the control dimension than whites, they are higher than other minority groups; in any case, sense of control is not an important variable related to achievement for Asians.

For whites and Asian Americans at grade 12, self-concept is more highly related to verbal test scores than is control of environment; for all other minority groups, the relative importance is reversed, and the students' sense of control of environment is strongly related to achievement. These two variables, self-concept and control, are the most powerful predictors of test scores — more than family background, peer group influence, or school characteristics. Coleman states that there is:

. . . a different set of predispositional factors operating to create low or high achievement for children from disadvantaged groups. For children from advantaged groups, achievement or lack of it appears closely related to what they believe about themselves. For children from disadvantaged groups, achievement or

---

[68] Coleman et al., *Equality of Educational Opportunity,* p. 21.

144

lack of achievement appears closely related to what they believe about their environment: whether they believe the environment will respond to reasonable efforts, or whether they believe it is, instead, merely random or immovable. In different words, it appears that children from advantaged groups assume that the environment will respond if they are able to affect it; children from disadvantaged groups do not make this assumption, but in many cases assume that nothing they will do can affect the environment—it will give benefits or withhold them but not as a consequence of their own action.[69]

Summing up the Coleman data:

1. White and Asian Americans tend to have similar achievement scores and tend to be higher achievers than other minority group children.
2. Achievement discrepancies of black, Mexican American, Puerto Rican, and American Indians compared with white (and Asian) students tend to increase by grade level.
3. White and black students at the twelfth grade exhibit a similar valuation of school achievement, whereas Mexican Americans, Puerto Ricans, and American Indians put less value on education.
4. Asian Americans outperform all other minority groups, as well as whites, on intellectual value and aspiration.
5. Minority group students, except Asians, are less likely to have a sense of control over their environment; students with a low sense of control are low achievers in school.

Nonracial and Nonethnic Variables

Although race and ethnicity have a definite impact upon school success, and at least part of the effect is due to discrimination practiced against minorities, the exact relationship is difficult to estimate because race and ethnicity interact with many other variables which are important to school outcomes. Certainly, social class is one such important variable, as demonstrated in the preceding chapter. Additional variables which impact on achievement for minority groups and should be taken into account are:

1. Family characteristics, including family head, number of children, quality of language spoken at home, parents' education and attitude toward education.[70]

---

[69] Ibid., pp. 320-21.

[70] David J. Bearison and Thomas Z. Casel, "Cognitive Decentration and Social Codes: Communication Effectiveness in Young Children from Differing Family Contexts," *Developmental Psychology*, January 1975, pp. 29-36; Martin Deutsch et al., *The Disadvantaged Child* (New York: Basic Books, 1967); Robert H. Hess and Virginia D. Shipman, "Early Experiences and the Socialization of Cognitive Modes in Children," *Child Development*, December 1965, pp. 369-86; Eleanor Pavenstadt, "A Comparison of the Child-Rearing Environment of Upper-Lower and Very Low-Lower Class Families," *American Journal of Orthopsychiatry*, January 1965, pp. 92-96.

2. For immigrant groups, old immigrants (white ethnics) and new immigrants (Spanish speaking and Asian Americans) alike, foreign born v. native born, as well as generation—first, second, or third.[71]
3. For American Indians, tribal identification is one of the strongest predictors of intelligence and achievement scores.[72]
4. For children of minority groups, old and new, who are non-English-speaking, bilingual, or whose spoken language at home is not English, facility in standard English strongly correlates with intelligence and achievement scores.[73]

In a multiple ethnic study of school achievement, George Mayeske separated the effect of ethnicity on group achievement scores and then adjusted them for six social conditions: social class, family structure, student attitude toward self, educational motivation, geographical residence, and school mix (or integration).[74] Reanalyzing the Coleman Report, he measured the maximum relationship of ethnicity and these various conditions with achievement scores for white, black, Mexican American, Puerto Rican, American Indian, and Asian American children. Ethnicity alone accounted for a maximum of 24 percent at the sixth grade on the achievement scores for all the groups combined, and 20 percent at the twelfth grade. After social class was considered, the relationship dropped to approximately 10 percent, and by the time all of

---

[71] James G. Anderson and William H. Johnson, "Stability and Change among Three Generations of Mexicans: Factors Affecting Achievement," *American Educational Research Journal*, March 1971, pp. 285-309; David K. Cohen, "Immigrants and the Schools," *Review of Educational Research*, February 1970, pp. 13-27; Frank M. Cordasco and Eugene Bucchioni; *The Puerto Rican Community and Its Children on the Mainland* (Metuchen, N.J.: Scarecrow Press, 1972); Harry H. L. Kitano, *Japanese Americans: The Evolution of a Subculture* (Englewood Cliffs, N.J.: Prentice-Hall, Inc., 1969).

[72] Robert J. Havighurst, "Mental Development and School Achievement of American Indian Children and Youth," in *Final Report: National Study of American Indian Education*, Series IV, no. 3 (Bethesda, Md.: ERIC No. 040798, 1970); Robert J. Havighurst et al., "Environment and the Draw-A-Man Test: The Performance of Indian Children," *Journal of Abnormal and Social Psychology*, January 1946, pp. 50-63; Robert A. Roessel, "Intelligence and Achievement of the Indian Student," in J. C. Stone and D. P. DeNevi (eds.), *Teaching Multi-Cultural Populations* (New York: D. Van Nostrand Co., 1971), pp. 348-57.

[73] Charles B. Brussell, *Disadvantaged Mexican-American Children and Early Educational Experience* (Austin, Texas: Southwest Educational Laboratory, 1968); Cohen, "Immigrants and the Schools"; Estelle Fuchs, "Curriculum for American Indian Youth," in R.C. Doll and M. Hawkins (eds.), *Educating the Disadvantaged* (New York: AMS Press, 1971), pp. 206-15; Richard J. Margolis, *The Losers: A Report on Puerto Ricans and the Public Schools* (New York: Aspira, 1968).

[74] George W. Mayeske, *A Study of our Nation's Schools* (Washington, D.C.: U.S. Government Printing Office, 1970); George W. Mayeske, "On the Explanation of Racial-Ethnic Group Differences in Achievement Test Scores," in M. D. Gall and B. A. Ward (eds.), *Critical Issues in Educational Psychology* (Boston: Little, Brown & Co., 1974), pp. 117-24.

the six social conditions were considered, the percentage dropped to 1.2 percent at the sixth grade and 1.1 percent at the twelfth grade. In other words, differences among the ethnic groups in achievement approached zero as more variables related to differences in their social conditions were taken into account. Wrote Mayeske, "The findings suggest that no inferences can be made about the 'independent effect' of membership in a racial-ethnic group on academic achievement, for that membership, as it

Figure 4.2 / Test Performance of Mental Abilities by Ethnicity

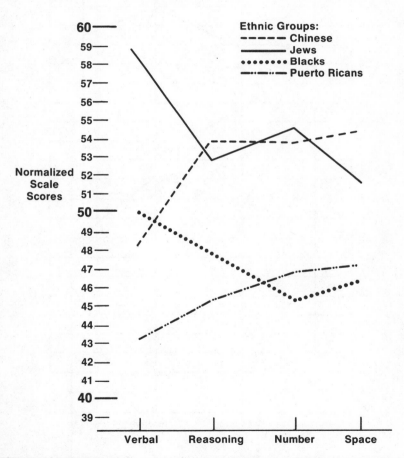

Source: Gerald S. Lesser, Gordon Fifer, and Donald H. Clark, *Mental Abilities of Children in Different Social and Cultural Groups,* Comparative Research Project No. 1635 (Washington, D.C.: U.S. Government Printing Office, 1964), Figure 2, p. 64.

147

Figure 4.3 / Test Performance of Mental Abilities by Ethnicity and Social Class

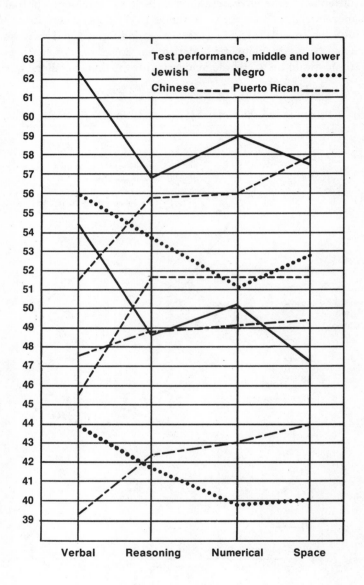

Source: Adapted from Lesser et al., "Mental Abilities of Children," Figures 3–6, pp. 65–68.

148

relates to academic achievement, is almost completely confounded with a variety of conditions."[75]

Racial and Ethnic Variables

The above data show that race or ethnicity and social class, as well as other social conditions, interact on achievement; they suggest that race or ethnicity should not be considered a major variable related to achievement in school. But a carefully designed, now classic study, which not only controlled for ethnicity and social class but also separated the test variable into several components, found the racial-ethnic variable to be the main predictor of mental ability. Gerald Lesser and his associates tested a group of 320 first-graders divided into four ethnic groups—Chinese, Jewish, black, and Puerto Rican evenly distributed by sex and social class.[76] Four different ability areas were tested: verbal, reasoning, number, and spatial relations. To ensure that the test differences reflected real differences in ability rather than differences in familiarity with test materials, special tests were constructed which presupposed a content familiar to all four ethnic groups and various social classes. To avoid tester-testee biases, the children were tested by trained psychologists of their own ethnic background. The abilities tested were verbal, reasoning, numerical, and spatial.

The results of the study by *ethnicity alone* are shown in Figure 4.2. Children in the four groups differed both in the absolute level of each mental ability and in the pattern among the four abilities. For example, Jewish students ranked way above the others on verbal ability and were relatively high in all ability areas, but they were surpassed in reasoning and spatial relations by the Chinese children (who were weak in verbal ability). Black children performed higher than Chinese and Puerto Rican children in verbal ability but were at the bottom or next to the bottom in three out of the four abilities.

The results of the study by *ethnicity and social class* are shown in Figure 4.3. To a surprising degree each of the ethnic groups showed a relatively consistent pattern, even when class was controlled. Social class did make some difference in the performance level at which the ability was manifested, but not in the pattern. Ethnicity was the major variable, not class; it influenced not only the pattern but also the level of the abilities. Lesser described his findings in a later article:

. . . once the pattern specific to the ethnic group emerges, social class variations within the ethnic group do not alter the basic organization.

---

[75] Mayeske, "Racial-Ethnic Differences in Test Scores," p. 123.

[76] Gerald S. Lesser, Gordon Fifer, and Donald H. Clark, *Mental Abilities of Children in Different Social and Cultural Groups,* Comparative Research Project no. 1635 (Washington, D.C.: U.S. Government Printing Office, 1964).

The failure of social-class conditions to transcend patterns of mental ability associated with ethnic influences was unexpected. Social-class influences have been described as superseding ethnic-group effects for such diverse phenomena as child-rearing practices, educational and occupational aspirations, achievement motivation, and anomie. The greater salience of social class over ethnic membership is reversed in the present findings on patterns of mental ability. Ethnicity has the primary effect upon the organization of mental abilities, and the organization is not modified by social-class influences.[77]

A replication of the study by the same authors (a rare phenomenon in social science research) with a similar sample of children in a different city duplicated almost the exact data by ethnicity and class. But the group did something very unusual for social scientists; they voted, with Lesser dissenting, to withhold their findings from publication, feeling that the earlier work had been misused to bolster what they saw as a racist theory; in short, they buried the data which they construed as too sensitive.

Achievement by Asian and Jewish Students

It is important to note that the Coleman and Lesser studies as well as other research[78] show that one nonwhite minority group does not fit the

Table 4.6 / Median Years of School Completed by Chinese, Japanese, and Jewish Populations Compared to Other Populations

1970[a]		1974[a]	
Total U.S.	12.2	Total U.S.	12.3
White	12.2	White	12.4
Nonwhite	10.1	Nonwhite	11.1
Japanese	12.7	Jews	14.0
Chinese	12.3	Episcopalians	13.5
Filipino	11.7	Presbyterians	12.7
Black	9.9	Methodists	11.5
Spanish[b]	9.4	Lutherans	11.2
Central and South America	12.1	Baptists	10.7
Cuban	12.1		
Mexican	8.3		
Puerto Rican	8.4		
Other Spanish	12.1		

[a] Years of school based on persons 25 years and over.
[b] Mexican and Puerto Rican groups comprise 70 percent of the Spanish-speaking population in the United States.
Source: *Ethnic Origin and Educational Attainment,* Current Population Reports, Series P-20, No. 220 (April 1971), Table E, p. 7; *Digest of Educatiōnal Statistics, 1975,* Table 11, p. 14; Greeley, *Denomination and Inequality,* Table 6, *Japanese, Chinese and Filipinos in the United States* (Washington, D.C.: U.S. Government Printing Office, 1973), pp. 52, 110, 169; *Statistical Abstract of the United States,* 1975, Table 190, p. 118.

[77] Susan S. Stodolsky and Gerald S. Lesser, "Learning Patterns in the Disadvantaged," *Harvard Educational Review* (Fall 1967), p. 570.
[78] Robert J. Havighurst and Bernice L. Neugarten, *Society and Education,* 4th ed. (Boston: Allyn & Bacon, 1975).

pattern of low scholastic achievement: On virtually every variable of intellectual value, aspiration, and achievement, the Asian American child is equal to, or outperforms, his white counterpart. Despite their verbal handicap (due probably to their immigrant status, segregated living, and language spoken at home), Asians receive higher school grades and educational levels (see Table 4.6) than whites, and proportionately more go on to college; major in difficult subjects such as mathematics, science, and engineering; are enrolled in graduate schools and the medical sciences; and receive doctorates.[79] In areas of relatively high concentrations of Asian population such as New York City, Chicago, Los Angeles, and San Francisco, Chinese and Japanese students are seen by their teachers as "good" students, hard-working and bright, and schools that have a high proportion of Oriental students are generally seen as "good" schools.

Some clues to the success of Asian students, especially the Chinese and Japanese, are offered by longitudinal studies which compare first-, second-, and third-generation Asian Americans with samples of middle- and lower-class non-Asians on a variety of educational and occupational indices. Asian-heritage children are able to achieve more than other groups who appear far less handicapped by ethnic or cultural differences. They tend to value politeness, respect for authority and parental wishes, hard work, personal achievement, and long-range goals. There is a very tight and close family structure, controlled by parental authority and strong social sanctions. Family honor and high expectations of performance reinforce achievement-oriented behavior.[80]

Similar achievement patterns are noted among Jewish Americans. The high performance scores among Jewish students noted in the Lesser study were consistent with the studies of immigrants of the early 1900s, in which first- and second-generation Jewish students typically scored higher than

---

[79] *Enrollment of Minority Graduate Students at Ph.D. Granting Institutions* (Washington, D.C.: American Council on Education, 1974), pp. 5-6; Table 1, p. 11; Table 3, p. 13; Derald W. Sue and Austin C. Frank, "A Typological Approach to the Psychological Study of Chinese and Japanese American College Males," *Journal of Social Issues*, April 1973, pp. 129-48; Stanley Sue and Harry H. L. Kitano, "Stereotypes as a Measure of Success," *Journal of Social Issues*, April 1973, pp. 83-98.

[80] Sarane S. Boocock, *An Introduction to the Sociology of Learning* (Boston: Houghton Mifflin Co., 1972); William Candhill and George DeVos, "Achievement, Culture, and Personality: The Case of the Japanese Americans," in S. W. Webster (ed.), *The Disadvantaged American* (San Francisco, Ca.: Chandler Publishing Co., 1966), pp. 208-28; Milton Gordon, *Assimilation in American Life* (New York: Oxford University Press, 1964); Kitano, *Japanese Americans*; Gene N. Levine and Darrel M. Montero, "Socioeconomic Mobility among Three Generations of Japanese Americans," *Journal of Social Issues*, April 1973, pp. 33-48; Sue and Frank, "Chinese and Japanese American College Males"; Sue and Kitano, "Stereotypes as a Measure of Success."

other European immigrant groups on IQ tests, achievement tests, school retention rates, and educational levels—and at about the same level as native whites.[81] Although it is possible (but unlikely) that Jewish families had a social and economic edge over other European immigrant groups, it is unlikely they had a similar advantage over native whites. The differences in achievement and staying power were much more likely to result from variations in culture and motivation. Thus, even when controlling for social class, IQ, and achievement differences, immigrant Jews were still overrepresented in U.S. high schools and colleges. In fact, quotas were established to limit the numbers of Jewish students in some colleges, universities, and professional schools up to the 1950s.[82]

These performance scores are also consistent with the longitudinal studies of gifted children by Lewis Terman and Melita Oden.[83] Jewish subjects, while not differing significantly in IQ scores from the group as a whole, received higher grades, achieved more years of education and higher incomes, and concentrated more heavily in the professional occupations.

Jews can also be classified as a religious group; in fact, they prefer this to an ethnic category, since they have immigrated from several different countries. Studies of the main religious groups—Protestant, Catholic, and Jewish—found Jewish children to have the highest mean scores on achievement tests, motivation and aspiration tests, and plans to go to college, even when social class is controlled.[84] Similarly, Andrew Greeley's National Opinion Research Center studies on religion and ethnicity show that among members of five different Protestant denominations, Catholics, and Jews, the latter had the highest mean levels of education (see note in Table 4.6) and entry into professional occupations. After con-

---

[81] Leonard Ayres, *Laggards in Our Schools* (New York: Russell Sage, 1909); Gustave A. Feingold, "Intelligence of the First Generation of Immigrant Groups," *Journal of Educational Psychology*, February 1924, pp. 65–82; Riverda H. Jordon, *Nationality and School Progress* (Bloomington, Ind.: Public Schools Publishers, 1921); U.S. Immigration Commission, *The Children of Immigrants*, 5 vols. (Washington, D.C.: U.S. Government Printing Office, 1911).

[82] Ayres, *Laggards in Our Schools;* Feingold, "Intelligence of the First Generation of Immigrant Groups"; Nathan Glazer and Daniel P. Moynihan, *Beyond the Melting Pot* (Cambridge, Mass.: MIT Press, 1963).

[83] Lewis M. Terman and Melita H. Oden, *The Gifted Child Grows Up* (Stanford, Ca.: Stanford University Press, 1947).

[84] David C. McClelland et al., "Religious and Other Sources of Parental Attitudes Towards Independence Training," in D. C. McClelland (ed.), *Studies in Maturation* (New York: Appleton-Century-Crofts, 1961), pp. 389–97; A. Lewis Rhodes and Charles B. Nam, "The Religious Context of Educational Expectations," *American Sociological Review*, April 1970, pp. 253–67; Fred L. Strodbeck, "Family Interaction, Values and Achievement," in D. C. McClelland et al. (eds.), *Talent and Society* (New York: D. Van Nostrand & Co., 1958), pp. 135–94.

trolling for social class, moreover, Jews made the most of their family background; they are the most rapidly upward mobile group.[85]

Simply put (although very little in social science is simple), there may be something in the Jewish culture, as well as among the Chinese and Japanese, that places emphasis on school and work accomplishment. These minority groups outperform other minority groups as well as majority groups in terms of ability and achievement scores, staying power in school, college enrollments, and professional careers. The standard argument which explains deficient achievement for minority groups in terms of poverty, prejudice, and discrimination breaks down in this case. If anything, these achieving groups came to this country with few resources and have also experienced prejudice and discrimination.

Anthropologists and sociologists such as Ruth Benedict, Margaret Mead, David Riesman, and Nathan Glazer suggest that differences in educational achievement may be explained by cultural factors in different ethnic groups: the language styles in the home, child-rearing practices, interaction between mother and child, extent of parental authority, stress on education, customs and traditions. All these can exert a differential reinforcement for performance in school. The fact is that when we explore ethnic differences in education and achievement, we usually wind up in debates like the prevailing arguments over black-white differences. Discussing differences between groups raises incredibly difficult problems, because spin-off questions about heredity and intelligence and political concerns inevitably arise. There may be something about differences in the degree to which groups achieve educationally which extends beyond the debate about heredity or environment.

If differences between groups have little to do with society or the way schools operate, what are we to do? Nathan Glazer asks: "How elaborate are we to make the efforts to wipe out these differences, and how successful can we hope to be no matter how elaborate our efforts? Are our measures to equalize to include the restriction of opportunities for those groups who find school achievement easy?"[86] These are hard questions, and the answers to them are not easy to come by. But they are beginning to polarize society, and we will discuss them in the next chapter.

CONCLUSIONS

Minority status in a society is accorded those who have physical characteristics or behavioral patterns which differ from those of members

---

[85] Andrew M. Greeley, *Ethnicity, Denomination, and Inequality* (Beverly Hills, Ca.: Sage Publications, 1976).

[86] Nathan Glazer, "Ethnic Group and Education: Towards the Tolerance of Difference," *Journal of Negro Education*, Summer 1969, p. 195.

of the dominant group; as a result of this status, they are often discriminated against. Society's treatment of minorities, if allowed to operate without political strictures, may range from some form of accommodation to attempts to exterminate the group. If the minority is distinguished from others by its behavior rather than by physical characteristics, its members may become assimilated in the larger society. Minorities whose appearance and culture are similar to the majority's will be more acceptable to the dominant group and will have an easier time being assimilated.

When minority status is defined in terms of race, assimilation is more difficult, since members of such minorities are readily identified by physical characteristics. Though there is no pure race, racial type, or racial behavior, and no pure correlation between any physical trait and innate ability, minorities continue to be discriminated against on the basis of racial stereotypes and imagined characteristics. Such a situation has long placed blacks at a disadvantage with whites and, to a lesser extent, between women to a disadvantage with men.

The weight of the evidence examined in this chapter supports the idea of the interaction effects of minority status (race or ethnicity) and social class on educational achievement. The disadvantage to which minority groups are placed in society explains in part why their members typically score below the national norm in academic achievement and other school performance scales. The exception is Chinese, Japanese, and Jewish children; a mixture of cultural and family factors seems to give them a good base for academic achievement.

ACTIVITIES

1. Referring to census data, identify and comment upon demographic developments during the 1960s and 1970s within a metropolitan area of your choice. Make projections for the 1980s. Defend your reasoning. Also devote attention to how these developments affect the schools.
2. Invite to class representatives of a variety of minority groups. (Do not overlook white ethnic groups, if substantial clusters of Americans from such backgrounds exist nearby.) Organize a debate concerning minority rights.
3. Discover and take advantage of opportunities to visit two or more different ethnic neighborhoods other than your own. Report your observations to the class.
4. Look for opportunities to develop relationships with people of different ethnic and religious affiliations, whether they represent minorities or majorities. Find, if you can, opportunities for activities through community action programs, settlement house work, youth agencies, and churches.
5. Tutor at least one child of minority group background or from a disadvantaged home.

DISCUSSION QUESTIONS

1. America is the land of opportunity for minority groups and majority groups alike. Defend or argue against this statement.
2. In what way are women defined as a minority group?
3. Have the immigrant white ethnic groups been forgotten by government officials and social reformers?
4. What are the major educational problems of black children, Spanish-speaking children, and American Indian children?
5. Identify the relationships between race, ethnicity, social class, and school achievement, giving particular attention to the theory of (1) innate group differences and (2) environment.

SUGGESTED FOR FURTHER READING

Dahl, Robert A. *Democracy in the United States.* 3rd ed. Chicago: Rand McNally & Co., 1975.

Frazier, Franklin E. *The Negro in the United States.* Rev. ed. New York: Macmillan Co., 1957.

Glazer, Nathan, and Moynihan, Daniel P. *Beyond the Melting Pot.* 2nd ed. Cambridge, Mass.: MIT Press, 1970.

Gordon, Milton. *Assimilation in American Life.* New York: Oxford University Press, 1964.

Greeley, Andrew M. *Ethnicity, Denomination, and Inequality.* Beverly Hills, Ca.: Sage Publications, 1976.

Grier, William, and Cobbs, Price M. *Black Rage.* New York: Basic Books, 1968.

Herrnstein, Richard J. *IQ in the Meritocracy.* Boston: Little, Brown, 1973.

Hill, Robert B. *The Strengths of Black Families.* New York: Emerson Hall, 1972.

Lewis, Oscar. *La Vida.* New York: Random House, 1966.

Novak, Michael. *The Rise of the Unmeltable Ethnics.* New York: Macmillan Co., 1972.

CHAPTER 5

SOCIAL
STRATIFICATION AND
INEQUALITY

In a complex society like ours, a considerable degree of upward mobility from one social class to another implies there is equality, at least equality of opportunity. A substantial amount of stratification, however, gives evidence of inequality. The extent to which our society, or for that matter any society, offers equality or inequality of opportunity will affect the kind of education the student can expect to receive, and in turn, the kind of education available to students from various social and economic backgrounds will affect mobility and stratification patterns operating within the society.

Equality and inequality can be discussed from social, philosophical, economic, and educational points of view. The issues in the idea of equality go back to the ancient Greeks and Hebrews, involving both intense debate and a unifying idea among intellectuals through the ages. In modern times the pursuit of equality was first evidenced by the Puritans in the 17th century, and it has been the mark of every political revolution in the West. While religious controversies were more intense in the past, there are now signs that "equality is taking on a sacred aspect," even "approaching dogmatic status" among a good number of social scientists.[1]

---

[1] Robert Nisbet, "The Pursuit of Equality," *Public Interest*, Spring 1974, p. 103.

Concern for political and social equality is being replaced by issues involving equality of education and income in the United States today.

In preindustrial society, inequalities were justified by ascription or inferred quality derived from inherent characteristics such as birth and caste. Industrial society justified inequalities by achievement based on economic success. The birth of the American nation saw equalitarianism combined with excellence; that is, equality óf opportunity was professed as an ideal, but it was recognized that inequalities would emerge due to people's differing abilities. With growing doubts about this theory, a new egalitarian trend is emerging which deemphasizes merit and competency and calls for protection of specific groups defined as minorities. The goal of equality of opportunity is being replaced by equality of results.

HISTORICAL AND PHILOSOPHICAL ISSUES
OF EQUALITY AND INEQUALITY

All societies (with the exception of a few small esoteric or utopian groups) require some hierarchy of organizational structure with levels of superiority, subordination, authority, and power. In order to function and survive, they eventually adopt some form of unfreedom, inequality, and restriction of individual behavior. Originally these restrictions were not experienced as repressive but were presumed to be linked to the divine or natural order. When reason is applied to society, the hierarchy must be rationally legitimatized and justified; it should conform, at least appear to conform, to the principles of justice.

In preindustrial society such justification was based on ascription; differences of power, status, and wealth were believed to be derived from ancestry, birth, or caste. People were privileged or unprivileged by accident of birth and not for what they accomplished, and mobility from one class to another was severely limited. With the rise of industry and commerce, the role of ascription was replaced in modern Western society by achievement, and ascriptive stratification was replaced by meritocratic stratification, wherein merit was awarded for achieving whatever society valued. The difference between an ascriptive and achievement-oriented society lies in the yardstick for merit; in the case of ascription, it is belonging to a group; in the case of achievement, it is doing and performing.[2]

In modern Western industrial society, achievement as the legitimizing principle goes hand in hand with concepts of equality and mobility. For

---

[2] Walter A. Weisskopf, "The Dialectics of Equality," *Annals of the American Academy of Political and Social Science*, September 1973, pp. 163–73.

157

most Americans, legitimate equality is epitomized by equality of opportunity, and it is recognized that all jobs in society are not equally pleasant or important, and, because different talents and abilities are required for different occupations, the reward system varies. With unequal rewards required to serve all of society's needs, social stratification results.

But the political left sees this stratification as producing a meritocracy which in its own way is as evil as any of the historic forms of aristocratic privilege. In his text on inequality, Christopher Jencks states that "the crucial problem today is that relatively few people view income inequality as a serious problem. We will not only have to politicize the question of income inequality but alter people's basic assumptions about the extent to which they are responsible for their neighbors and their neighbors for them."[3] Similarly, John Rawls equates justice with absolute equality and argues that if some citizens have more goods than others it has been accomplished by the loss of freedom for those who have fewer goods.[4]

A Change in Meritocracy

The phrase "postindustrial society," coined by Daniel Bell, describes the scientific-technological societies evolving in developed countries in the second half of the 20th century. The singular feature of this new society is the importance of theoretical knowledge as the source of production, innovation, and policy formulation. Emerging from the older economic systems in both advanced capitalistic and socialistic countries is a knowledge society based on the preeminence of professionals and technicans. In the United States in the 1950s and 1960s, Bell notes, "this group outpaced . . . all others in the rate of growth, which was twice that for clerical workers (the category that held the lead in the 1940s) and seven times more than the overall rate for workers."[5] The stratification structure of this new society produces a highly trained research elite, supported by a large scientific and technical staff.

Thus the basis of achievement in the postindustrial meritocracy is education, whereas in the bourgeois meritocracy of the 19th century it was economics. Merit and differentials in status, power, and income are awarded to highly educated and trained experts with credentials; they are

---

[3] Christopher Jencks et al., *Inequality: A Reassessment of the Effect of Family and Schooling in America* (New York: Basic Books, 1972), p. 263.

[4] John Rawls, *A Theory of Justice* (Cambridge, Mass.: Harvard University Press, 1971).

[5] Daniel Bell, *The Coming of Post-Industrial Society* (New York: Basic Books, 1973), p. 108.

seen as the decision makers who will inherit the power structure in business, government, and even politics.[6]

This trend toward a meritocracy of the intellectual elite has aggravated inequalities. Because of their socioeconomic deprivation and limited education, minorities as groups are unable to compete successfully in a society based on educational credentials of achievement. Without the appropriate certificates they are not needed by the economy; they are not exploited, but they are underpaid for their services; not discriminated against but not in demand. An achievement-oriented society based on academic credentials and standardized tests (which compare individuals in relation to a group score, say on IQ, achievement, or aptitude) condemns most of them to the low end of the stratification structure.

It is not surprising that those who find it difficult to compete within this system condemn the selection procedures. Hence the black community and the political left, which generally supports their efforts, attack IQ tests and standardized tests of achievement and professional entrance examinations as culturally biased and as highly unreliable and invalid predictors of achievement and job performance. The rejection of measurements which register the consequences of deprivation has political and social implications which we shall discuss later in this chapter.

SOCIAL MOBILITY AND SOCIAL STRUCTURE

Social scientists study social mobility in order to ascertain the relative openness or fluidity of a social structure. They are interested in the difficulties different persons or groups experience in acquiring the goods and services that are valued in the culture and may be acquired through unequal contributions.

In ascription societies, the stratification system is closed to individual mobility because prestige (or status) is determined at birth. The amount of education one will receive, the occupational status one will enter, one's income, and one's whole lifestyle cannot be changed. In an open-class society, although people start with different advantages, opportunities are available for them to change their initial positions. The life chances of a welfare recipient's son born in the slums differ considerably from those of a banker's son born in the suburbs, but in an achievement-oriented society the former can achieve as much as or more than the latter.

The emphasis on vertical social mobility in the American social

---

[6] C. Wright Mills, *The Power Elite* (New York: Oxford University Press, 1956); Max Weber, *Economy and Society* (New York: Bedminister Press, 1968).

structure is one of the most striking features of our class system. Kurt Mayer writes:

> . . . the United States has placed greater emphasis on social mobility than any other large nation in modern times. Americans have firmly proclaimed the idea of equality and freedom of achievement and have acclaimed the large numbers of individuals who have risen from humble origins to positions of prominence and affluence. Indeed, the belief in opportunity is so strongly entrenched in the culture that most Americans feel not only that each individual has the "right to succeed" but that it is his duty to do so. Thus we are apt to look with disapproval upon those who fail or make no attempt to "better themselves."[7]

There is evidence of considerable social mobility in the United States. Studies of *intra*generational mobility — the occupational career patterns of individuals in terms of their mobility between jobs and occupations during their lifetime — reveal that a very large proportion of American men have worked in different communities, different occupations, and different jobs. Nonetheless, there are certain limits to the variety of such experiences — most notably, occupational mobility is confined primarily to either side of a dividing line between manual and nonmanual occupations; little permanent mobility takes place across this basic line.[8]

*Inter*generational mobility studies involve a comparison of social status of fathers and sons at some point in their careers (for instance, as assessed by their occupations at approximately the same age). About two thirds of the American male population moves up or down a little in the class hierarchy in every generation, as shown in a classic study on mobility (Table 5.1). Another study which compared fathers' and sons' occupations

Table 5.1 / Social Mobility of American Males, 1962

Son's Occupation	Percent Who Have Changed from Father's Occupation		
	Moved Up	Moved Down	Not Changed
Professionals	88%	0%	12%
Managers.	85	6	9
Clerks.	78	18	4
Factory laborers	40	54	6
Farmers	3	15	82
Farmer laborers	0	86	14

Source: Peter M. Blau and Otis D. Duncan, *The American Occupational Structure* (New York: John Wiley & Sons, 1967), p. 39.

[7] Kurt B. Mayer, *Class and Society* (New York: Random House, 1955), p. 69. Copyright Random House, Inc., 1955.

[8] Otis D. Duncan, "The Trend of Occupational Mobility in the United States," *American Social Review,* August 1965, pp. 491-99; Seymour M. Lipset, "Social Mobility and Equal Opportunity," *Public Interest,* Fall 1972, pp. 90-108.

found that if the son is not in the same occupational category as his father, the next most likely place is in the occupational category either immediately above or below.[9] These studies show that more sons are upward mobile than downward mobile, but the extent of mobility from one generation to the next is limited.

International comparisons show that the United States is the most upwardly mobile of all industrialized societies,[10] but the political left has argued that in advanced stages of industrialized society, such as that achieved in the United States, social classes are likely to become more rigid. However, recent studies show that mobility has not slackened off; if anything, American society is more mobile than in the past.[11] This is supported by a 1970 survey of the backgrounds of executives which revealed only 10.5 percent of the current generation to be sons of wealthy families, compared to 1950, when the figure stood at 36 percent, and the turn of the century, when it was 45.5 percent.[12] Moreover, in the post–World War II period the proportion of those in the top echelons of American business from economically "poor" backgrounds nearly doubled, from 12.1 percent in 1950 to 23.4 percent in 1964; simultaneously there was an appreciable decline in the percentage from wealthy families, from 36.1 percent in 1950 to 10.5 percent in 1964.[13] Factors contributing to these developments include the replacement of family-owned enterprises by public corporations, recruitment of management personnel from the ranks of college graduates, competitive promotion policies, and the demand for people with ability and mobility to cope with the complexities of the postindustrial society.

Mobility of Women

The study of father-to-son mobility is reasonably straightforward, but it is more difficult to compare the intergenerational mobility of women. The mothers of many working women were never considered to be in the labor force or worked outside the home only briefly; in the past, only a small percent of women pursued occupational careers. Another complicating factor is that women often interrupt their work careers after marriage.

---

[9] Seymour M. Lipset and Richard Bendix, *Social Mobility in Industrial Society* (Berkeley: University of California Press, 1959).

[10] Leonard Broom and Philip Selznick, *Sociology*, 5th ed. (New York: Harper & Row, 1973); Gerhard E. Lenski, *Power and Privilege* (New York: McGraw-Hill Book Co., 1966).

[11] Duncan, "Occupational Mobility in the United States"; Lipset, "Social Mobility and Equal Opportunity"; Bradley R. Schiller, "Equality, Opportunity and the 'Good Job'," *Public Interest*, Spring 1976, pp. 111–20.

[12] Robert S. Diamond, "A Self-Portrait of the Chief Executive," *Fortune*, May 1970, pp. 180–81, 320–23.

[13] Lipset, "Social Mobility and Equal Opportunity."

Although women's work in the home is of social and economic value, the intergenerational mobility of women has usually been described by comparing the occupational status of their fathers and their husbands (if any). Thus the daughter of a skilled worker who marries a professional man is considered upwardly mobile. This is certainly vertical social mobility, but it tells nothing about women who do not marry. What it indicates is that there is intermarriage between social classes, and female mobility is achieved not so much by performance as by whom they marry. It is true that men and women of similar education and intelligence tend to marry,[14] and in this sense women's education and intelligence are indirectly related to their mobility. The fact that the best indicator of a woman's mobility is her husband's occupation and income is a testimony to the socioeconomic inferiority of women and the biases within social science.

Prestige of Occupations

Nationwide polls on the relative prestige of various occupations offer useful information about the existence of a status structure and the consequences the criteria of status have for members of society. People with varying occupations, incomes, and amounts of education share different norms and behave differently. Thus class structure based on occupation leads to the development of class subcultures; in turn, the patterns fostered in the subcultures become criteria of placement in the class structure.

In the two best known studies of occupational prestige, made by the National Opinion Research Center in 1947 and 1963, approximately 90 occupations were rated by national samples. The high and low ratings of these two samples are shown in Table 5.2, ordered by rank in the later

Table 5.2 / Prestige Ratings of Occupations, 1947 and 1963

	March 1947		June 1963	
Occupation	NORC score	Rank	NORC score	Rank
U.S. Supreme Court justice.	96	1	94	1
Physician.	93	2.5	93	2
Nuclear physicist.	86	18	92	3.5
Scientist	89	8	92	3.5
Government scientist	88	10.5	91	5.5
State governor	93	2.5	91	5.5
Cabinet member in the federal government . . .	92	4.5	90	8
College professor.	89	8	90	8

[14] Robert J. Havighurst et al., *Growing Up in River City* (New York: John Wiley & Sons, 1962); Richard J. Herrnstein, *IQ in the Meritocracy* (Boston: Little, Brown & Co., 1973).

Table 5.2 / Prestige Ratings of Occupations, 1947 and 1963 (Cont.)

Occupation	March 1947 NORC score	Rank	June 1963 NORC score	Rank
U.S. representative in Congress.............	89	8	90	8
Chemist.................................	86	18	89	11
Lawyer..................................	86	18	89	11
Diplomat in the U.S. foreign service	92	4.5	89	11
Dentist.................................	86	18	88	14
Architect...............................	86	18	88	14
County judge	87	13	88	14
Psychologist...........................	85	22	87	17.5
Minister................................	87	13	87	17.5
Member of the board of directors of a large corporation	86	18	87	17.5
Mayor of a large city	90	6	87	17.5
Priest..................................	86	18	86	21.5
Head of a department in a state government..	87	13	86	21.5
Civil engineer	84	23	86	21.5
Airline pilot............................	83	24.5	86	21.5
Banker.................................	88	10.5	85	24.5
Biologist	81	29	85	24.5
Sociologist	82	26.5	83	26
Instructor in public schools	79	34	82	27.5
Captain in the regular army	80	31.5	82	27.5
Accountant for a large business	81	29	81	29.5
Public school teacher	78	36	81	29.5
.	.	.	.	.
.	.	.	.	.
.	.	.	.	.
Streetcar motorman......................	58	68	56	70
Lumberjack.............................	53	73	55	72.5
Restaurant cook.........................	54	71	55	72.5
Singer in a nightclub	52	74.5	54	74
Filling station attendant	52	74.5	51	75
Dockworker.............................	47	81.5	50	77.5
Railroad section hand	48	79.5	50	77.5
Night watchman.........................	47	81.5	50	77.5
Coal miner..............................	49	77.5	50	77.5
Restaurant waiter........................	48	79.5	49	80.5
Taxi driver	49	77.5	49	80.5
Farm hand..............................	50	76	48	83
Janitor.................................	44	85.5	48	83
Bartender	44	85.5	48	83
Clothes presser in a laundry...............	46	83	45	85
Soda fountain clerk	45	84	44	86
Sharecropper—one who owns no livestock or equipment and does not manage farm	40	87	42	87
Garbage collector........................	35	88	39	88
Street sweeper..........................	34	89	36	89
Shoe shiner.............................	33	90	34	90
Average.............................	70	...	71	...

Source: Adapted from Robert W. Hodge, Paul M. Siegel, and Peter H. Rossi, "Occupational Prestige in the United States, 1925–63," *American Journal of Sociology,* November 1964, Table 1, pp. 290–92.

study. Viewed as a whole the prestige scores correlate highly with the income and education attainments of workers in the occupation. There are some deviations from this rule, however; ministers and teachers rank higher in prestige than in income, but nightclub singers and dockworkers have less prestige than would have been expected from their incomes.

Obviously the prestige of occupations is not a simple function of economic rewards and educational requirements. Responsibility, independence, aesthetic aspects, and work site also influence ratings. Some manual occupations rank higher than nonmanual occupations. The increased importance of and higher wages for some kinds of blue-collar work, and perhaps a change in attitude toward manual labor, may influence further shifts in the prestige of blue-collar and white-collar jobs.

Educational Prestige

In the United States, education is an important determinant of an individual's place in the stratification system. Not only does level of education help determine the prestige of an individual's occupational attainment, but the college and university from which one is graduated correlates with employment opportunities and subsequent earnings. As long as institutions of higher learning are judged on meritocratic lines,

Table 5.3 / Leading Institutions of Higher Education in Selected Professions, 1973 and 1976

Margulies–Blau (1973) Rankings	Cartter-Solomon (1976) Rankings
EDUCATION	
1. Stanford University	1. Stanford University
2. Teachers College, Columbia University	2. Harvard University
3. Ohio State University[a]	3. University of Chicago
4. University of Chicago	4. University of California—Los Angeles[a]
5. Harvard University	5. University of California—Berkeley[a]
LAW	
1. Harvard University	1. Harvard University
2. Yale University	2. Yale University
3. University of Michigan[a]	3. Stanford University
4. Columbia University	4. University of Michigan
5. University of Chicago	5. University of Chicago
BUSINESS	
1. Harvard University	1. Stanford University
2. Stanford University	2. Harvard University
3. University of Chicago	3. Massachusetts Institute of Technology[a]
4. University of Pennsylvania[a]	4. University of Chicago
5. Carnegie-Mellon University	5. Carnegie-Mellon University

[a] Public institutions; all others are private.

Source: Adapted from Rebecca Z. Margulies and Peter M. Blau, "The Pecking Order of the Elite: American Leading Professional Schools," *Change,* November 1973, pp. 24–25; "The Cartter Report on the Leading Schools of Education, Law, and Business," *Change* (February 1977), p. 46.

those who attend the leading institutions will have relatively more opportunities available. For example, a graduate from Harvard Law School commands about $5,000 more in beginning salary than does the average law school graduate.

Whether those who attend leading institutions are made more productive by their education, or they were admitted and graduated because they were relatively more capable in the first place, is difficult to determine. The point is, going to college does lead to higher incomes, at least in the past it has, and going to prestigious colleges leads to even higher incomes.

Table 5.3 shows the pecking order of America's leading professional schools in education, law, and business. The rankings on the left are based on a 1973 survey of opinion of the deans of 3 professional schools, and those on the right are based on a 1976 survey of professors in these fields. The rank positions of the institutions tend to coincide in the two surveys, at least for the five leading institutions in the three fields of study. Private institutions outrank public institutions about 4:1. Stanford, Harvard, and the University of Chicago are the three leading institutions in the country, and professors rated the California schools more highly than did deans.

Regardless of the inherent value of national rankings of colleges and universities, or the way such rankings are commonly used and misused, the fact is such surveys do matter. These assessments play a part in determining who will be hired in the top colleges, law firms, and corporations; and who will be able to better command higher entry salaries and have an advantage for future promotions to still higher level jobs and income.

Prestige of Communities

Early studies using the reputational technique (described in Chapter 3) were conducted by a number of sociologists and educators in the 1930s and 1940s. These studies found that people in small, homogeneous communities tend to use similar criteria in evaluating one another. At the lower economic levels, money was a more important criterion, and manners, taste, family background, and tradition counted for more at the higher levels. Considering the community as a whole, occupation and income were the most important bases for prestige in Morris, Illinois ("Jonesville")[15] and an Ozark community in Missouri ("Plainsville").[16] Family background and length of residence were salient in small cities in

---

[15] W. Lloyd Warner et al., *Democracy in Jonesville* (New York: Harper & Row, 1949).

[16] James West (Carl Withers), *Plainsville, U.S.A.* (New York: Columbia University Press, 1945).

Massachusetts ("Yankee City"),[17] and the Deep South ("Old City"). [18] In these communities, an upper class of prominent old families outranked the lower upper class in prestige, although on the average, the latter had more money. In a study of Burlington, Vermont, ethnicity and religion combined with income, occupation, and length of residence to determine prestige and stratification. The families of the old stock were at the top of the stratification order; the broad categories were made up of "foreigners," people born outside the country and not acceptable to the Yankee tradition, who were generally laborers, and "newcomers," who generally owned small businesses but had not been assimilated into the local community.[19]

Five or six classes could be identified in each community. In "Plainsville," however, there were only two major classes, the "prairie people" and the "hillbillies." In each of these communities, it became apparent that people had definite views and used various terms to identify people perceived as their equals or as above or below them. The striking similarities of how people perceive others in terms of morality and respectability within the stratification structure of "Old City" is illustrated in Figure 5.1.

These classic investigations and many others show that for people who live in small communities prestige is based on the fact that people know each other. There is considerable flexibility in the standards used to judge people, including occupation, income, education, nativity, ethnicity, religion, and length of residence. In small, homogeneous, older communities, residents of long standing — provided they have some wealth and education — receive the highest ranking; only gradually is there an acceptance of the "new" rich and shorter term residents into the top stratum. Moral values and style of life are frequently applied as standards of judgment too, although these are often linked with economic, ethnic, and religious distinctions.

These early studies of small, static communities are not representative of most cities and suburbs of today. In larger and more heterogeneous communities, where prestige criteria are less uniform than in smaller and older towns, there is usually no local prestige hierarchy. Not only do many people not know each other (neighbors are often strangers in high-rise apartments), but prestige criteria differ among whites and blacks, various

---

[17] W. Lloyd Warner and Paul S. Lunt, *The Social Life of a Modern Community* (New Haven, Conn.: Yale University Press, 1941); W. Lloyd Warner and Paul S. Lunt, *The Status Systems of a Modern Community* (New Haven, Conn.: Yale University Press, 1942).

[18] Allison Davis, Burleigh B. Gardner, and Mary R. Gardner, *Deep South* (Chicago: University of Chicago Press, 1941).

[19] E. L. Anderson, *We Americans: A Study of Cleavage in an American City* (Cambridge, Mass.: Harvard University Press, 1973).

ethnic communities, the educated and less educated, professional and blue-collar workers, young and old, and other subcultures.

ECONOMIC STRATIFICATION IN THE UNITED STATES

The United States is an example of a relatively open-class system in which birth or lineage is only one factor in the determination of social

Figure 5.1 / Elements in the "Old City" Stratification Structure

UPPER-UPPER CLASS		LOWER-UPPER CLASS
"Old aristocracy"	UU	"Old aristocracy"
"Aristocracy," but not "old"	LU	"Aristocracy," but not "old"
"Nice, respectable people"	UM	"Nice, respectable people"
"Good people, but 'nobody' "	LM	"Good people, but 'nobody' "
	UL	
"Po' whites"	LL	"Po' whites"

UPPER-MIDDLE CLASS		LOWER-MIDDLE CLASS
"Society" { "Old Families"	UU	
"Society," but not "old families"	LU	"Old aristocracy" (older) "Broken-down aristocracy" (younger)
"People who should be upper class"	UM	"People who think they are somebody"
"People who don't have much money"	LM	"We poor folk"
	UL	"People poorer than us"
"No 'count lot"	LL	"No 'count lot"

UPPER-LOWER CLASS		LOWER-LOWER CLASS
	UU	
	LU	
"Society" or the "folks with money"	UM	"Society" or the "folks with money"
"People who are up because they have a little money"	LM	"Way-high-ups," but not "Society"
"Poor but honest folk"	UL	"Snobs trying to push up"
"Shiftless people"	LL	"People just as good as anybody"

Source: Adapted from Allison Davis et al.; *Deep South* (Chicago: University of Chicago Press, 1941), p. 65.

167

position. The emphasis on achieved status has meant that economic stratification persists. Then, too, human slavery at one time existed along with the open-class system, and this later gave way to a caste system based on race. The persistence of prejudice and discrimination continues today in more subtle ways, often with economic consequences, and opportunities for women and other ethnic and religious groups have been restricted in the past.

The Distribution of Wealth

Social stratification refers to the unequal distribution of the valued assets of a society. In modern industrial societies, this refers to the distribution of wealth (cash and assets which can be transferred to cash).

Table 5.4 / Estimated Wealthholdings of the Top 0.5 Percent and 1 Percent of the Adult Population, United States, 1922–1956, 1972

Year	0.5 Percent of Adult Population (percent of wealth held)	1 Percent of Adult Population (percent of wealth held)
1922	29.8%	31.6%
1929	32.4	36.3
1933	25.2	28.3
1939	28.0	30.6
1945	20.9	23.3
1949	19.3	20.8
1953	22.7	24.2
1954	22.5	—
1956	25.0	26.0
1972	18.9	24.1

Source: Robert J. Lampman, *The Share of Top Wealth-Holders in National Wealth, 1922-1956* (Princeton, N.J.: Princeton University Press, 1962), Table 6, p. 24. With permission of the National Bureau of Economic Research. 1972 data from *Statistical Abstract of the United States, 1976* (Washington, D.C.: U.S. Government Printing Office, 1977), Table 694, p.427.

Table 5.5 / Distribution of Income and Wealth by Fifths, United States, 1970

Group	Percent of Income	Percent of Wealth
Lowest fifth	3%	1%
Second fifth	11	2
Middle fifth	16	5
Fourth fifth	24	15
Highest fifth	46	77
	100%	100%

Source: Adapted from Herbert J. Gans, "The New Equalitarianism," *Saturday Review*, May 6, 1972, pp. 43–46; Herbert J. Gans, *More Equality* (New York: Random House, 1973), pp. 13–14; *Statistical Abstract of the United States, 1976*, Table 651, p. 406.

Valid and reliable data on wealth are not easy to come by, since wealthy people are astute in hiding their wealth, for tax purposes, and seldom wish to discuss the subject with researchers, while the poor and the lower middle class tend to exaggerate their economic worth.

One of the most careful studies of wealth in the United States considered the data between 1922 and 1956.[20] Robert Lampman pointed out that of all wealth in the United States in 1953, about 20 percent was government owned, and the remaining 80 percent was privately owned. That year, the richest 1.6 percent of the adult population owned 27.6 percent of all private wealth, and 50 percent of the population owned only 8.3 percent. While the estate of the richest 1.6 percent was over $186,000, that for the remaining 98.4 percent was $7,900. He also noted that wealth is continuously stratified. For example, in 1956, the top 1 percent of the adult population owned 26.1 percent of the nation's private wealthholdings, but the top 0.5 percent accounted for 25.0 percent; in other words, the top 0.5 percent of the population accounted for almost all of the wealthholdings of the top 1 percent.

Lampman further showed that the top wealthholders decreased between the Depression and World War II, but the decline for these two top groups leveled off in 1949 and thereafter inequality increased for the years up to 1956. These figures are shown in Table 5.4, along with comparative figures up to 1972. Practically no change in this share was found for the years 1958–75. In fact, since 1810 to the present, the wealthiest 0.5 percent have held a share of the wealth ranging from 18 to 32 percent, with an average of 22 percent; while the wealthiest 1 percent has had a share of wealth ranging from 21 to 36 percent, with an average of 25 percent.[21] In other words, there has been no real change in the distribution of wealth among the superrich within the last 170 years.

The distribution of wealth can also be described in terms of that held by fifths of the population or consumer units (families and persons not living in families).[22] In Table 5.5 the categories are ordered by income and wealth; the poorest fifth of all Americans obtained in 1970 only 3 percent of the nation's annual income and less than 1 percent of its wealth, while the top fifth received 46 percent of the income and owned 77 percent of the wealth. Inequality was even greater among the top 5 percent, who earned 19 percent of the nation's annual income and owned 53 percent of the

---

[20] Robert J. Lampman, *The Share of Top Wealth-Holders in National Wealth, 1922–1956* (Princeton, N.J.: Princeton University Press, 1962).

[21] Jonathan H. Turner and Charles E. Starnes, *Inequality: Privilege and Poverty in America* (Pacific Palisades, Ca.: Goodyear Publishing Co., 1976), Table 3, p. 9; p. 20; Figure 1, p. 24; *Statistical Abstract of the United States, 1976* (Washington, D.C.: U.S. Government Printing Office, 1977), Table 694, p. 427.

[22] See, for example, *Statistical Abstract of the United States, 1976.*

private wealth; and 1 percent of the people earned 7 percent of the income and controlled more than 25 percent of the wealth.

The same inequality of wealth exists in the business world. In 1970, there were approximately 2 million corporations: 0.10 percent controlled 55 percent of the total corporation assets, and 1.1 percent controlled 88 percent. At the other end of the continuum, 94 percent of the corporations owned only 9 percent of the total assets.[23]

Thus the upper classes, and especially the superrich, control a greater share of private wealth than they earn of the nation's income, and wealth and not income is the true barometer of inequality. Income can fluctuate on a yearly basis and is more susceptible to being taxed. Wealth consists of assets accumulated over several years, sometimes over different generations within a family. It is long term and mainly represents investment assets, which tend to generate more wealth, and most of it is tax exempt or has already been taxed. Wealth also represents political leverage and power.

Inequality in wealth has tremendous political implications. Ferdinand Lundberg's classic analysis, *The Rich and the Super-Rich*, shows how a small number of families control the major share of the wealth and power of the country.[24] Although his data is based on 1962 census and federal reserve data, the implications are relevant today. Some 200,000 families worth $500,000 or more represented less than 0.4 percent of all households but 22 percent of the private wealth. However, that 22 percent translates into much more potential power, since the nature of the wealth was mostly in corporate equities and investments, which are what confer economic control and in turn political influence. Lundberg notes that the economic power of the upper 200,000 is greater than indicated by their ownership of 22 percent of all assets: "Experts concede that a 5 percent ownership stake in a large corporation is sufficient in most cases to give corporate control. It is my contention that general corporate control lies in this group of 200,000, very probably."[25]

Lundberg's conclusion was based on the fact that those who owned 22 percent of the nation's assets concentrated their holdings for the most part in large corporations and utilities. With only 5 percent of ownership in any individual corporation required to control it, these families in effect controlled the large corporations. A man who owns 5 percent of a corporation capitalized at $4 billion is worth only $200 million, but this 5 percent of ownership gives him control of the corporation; his potential

[23] *Statistical Abstract of the United States, 1971* (Washington, D.C.: U.S. Government Printing Office, 1972), Table 727, p. 467.

[24] Ferdinand Lundberg, *The Rich and the Super-Rich* (New York: Lyle Stuart, 1968), p. 23.

[25] Ibid., p. 24.

operative power is $4 billion. Politically, this person has a large voice, not only because of the campaign contributions by which the corporation can influence administrators and legislators, but by virtue of the offices the corporation has in various states and foreign countries; the lobbyists it employs to protect its interests; the advertising it places, whereby it influences the mass media; the charitable institutions and causes it funds; and the taxes it pays (if any) to local, state, and federal governments. As Lundberg summed it up, "the actual power of such concentrated ownership, therefore, is much greater than its proportion in the total investment assets."[26]

The Distribution of Income

Because most Americans do not have substantial wealth, they must depend upon earned income. Income is more equally distributed than wealth, and it can be more easily redistributed through tax reform and social policy. Nevertheless, inequality in the distribution of income exists.

One conventional measure of inequality is the number of families who earn less than half the median family income. Between 1955 and 1975, when the median as reported by the U.S. census rose from $4,421 to $13,719 (see Table 5.6) the number earning half that amount remained constant at about 19.5 percent. (The increase in family income mainly reflects inflation and an increase in the number of family members, especially wives, who are earning income.) Moreover, the distribution of

Table 5.6 / Distribution of Families by Income Level, United States, 1955-1975

Family Income	1955	1965	1975
under $2,000	17.6%	8.9%	2.1%
$ 2,000-$ 2,999.	11.0	7.2	2.4
$ 3,000-$ 3,999.	14.6	7.7	3.4
$ 4,000-$ 4,999.	15.4	7.9	4.1
$ 5,000-$ 5,999.	12.7	9.3	4.1
$ 6,000-$ 6,999.	9.5	9.5	4.2
$ 7,000-$ 9,999.	12.9	24.2	12.8
$10,000-$14,999.	4.8	17.7	22.3
$15,000-$24,999.	0.9	6.2	30.3
$25,000 and over	0.5	1.4	14.1
Median income	$4,421	$6,957	$13,719
Half the median.	$2,210	$3,478	$ 6,859

Source: *Statistical Abstract of the United States, 1976,* Table 647, p. 404.

---

[26] Ibid., p. 24

Table 5.7 / Distribution of Income for Families and Individuals, by Fifths, United States, 1955–1975

	1955	1965	1975
Families			
Lowest fifth	4.8%	5.2%	5.4%
Second fifth	12.2	12.2	11.8
Middle fifth.	17.7	17.8	17.6
Fourth fifth.	23.4	23.9	24.1
Highest fifth.	41.8	40.9	41.1
Highest 5 percent	16.8	15.5	15.5
Individuals			
Lowest fifth	2.4%	2.9%	4.0%
Second fifth	7.3	7.6	9.0
Middle fifth.	13.4	13.6	14.7
Fourth fifth.	24.8	25.0	24.3
Highest fifth.	52.0	50.9	47.9
Highest 5 percent	21.9	20.0	18.7

Source: *Statistical Abstract of the United States, 1976,* Table 651, p. 406.

income has changed very little over the past 20 years. Table 5.7 indicates that in 1955 the highest fifth (20 percent) of the population of families that had the highest incomes received 42 percent of all income, while the poorest 20 percent received only 5 percent. For individuals the income gap was even wider—52 percent and 2 percent, respectively. As the table shows, the situation changed very little in 1975.

Taxes and Equality

Taxes should have the significant effect of equalizing income. But people who earned $2,000 or less in the early seventies paid half their incomes in direct and indirect taxes, as compared with only 45 percent paid in taxes by people who earned $50,000 or more. Middle Americans were not much better off; those earning $10,000 to $15,000 a year paid 4 percent less of their incomes in taxes than those earning $25,000 to $50,000.[27]

The history of the income tax in this country is based on the idea of *raising needed revenues,* not *redistributing income.* It was based first on the principle of a *proportionate tax,* not on a *flat tax* which penalizes the poor, and later on a *progressive tax,* whereby the rich would be taxed a greater proportion, as the demand for federal expenditures grew in the 20th century. It is also based on *equity,* that is, it is supposed to be a fair

---

[27] Herbert J. Gans, *More Equality* (New York: Random House, 1973); Herman P. Miller, *Rich Man, Poor Man* (New York: Crowell Collier & Macmillan, 1971).

rate whereby people pay taxes in proportion to their wealth, not on *equality*, which is rooted in 19th-century socialist and communist aims of expropriating the wealth of the rich.[28] The political left today, however, argues for a tax based on redistributing income; this is supposed to lead to equality and a "just" social policy.

Opposition to evening-out efforts is supported by the economic rationale that they would reduce the individual's incentive to maximize his or her income. Most Americans work hard to maximize their incomes, with the goal of increasing their standards of living. Not only would any planned program for redistributing income curtail this incentive, it would also reduce investments and taking the kinds of corporate risks that result in increased production, employment, and national income. Thus economic growth would be curtailed, and the American standard of living would drop. As long as economic growth continues, the argument goes, lower income families are bound to share in the rising total income; redistribution of money would make almost everyone worse off eventually because each family would simply receive a more equal portion of a "shrinking pie." As everyone becomes better off (indeed, today, people of all income groups are better off economically than yesterday), it takes even larger increments of income for any one family to improve its relative position.[29] Unless we are willing to soak the rich, which suggests a politically extreme measure inappropriate in a democratic society, it is argued that there is insufficient money to redistribute it to accommodate the egalitarian philosophy.

The harsh fact is, however, that the present income tax system in the United States is increasing inequality. Through tax loopholes (inheritance trusts, oil depletion allowances, depreciation allowances, crop supports, and tax-exempt bonds and insurance policies) this country has unwittingly devised a reverse welfare program which provides the rich with the bulk of subsidies, the "have littles" or working and middle classes with a few hundred dollars, and the poor with a few dollars per year. The public is coming to realize that the rich, who have enormous political power, do not pay their full share of taxes, but the average person, surprisingly, does not appear resentful of this inequality. The American dream lingers on in the minds of most people: through education and hard work it is still possible to rise to the top, and anyone who does so is entitled to the economic rewards.

---

[28] Edgar K. Browning, "How Much More Equality Can We Afford?" *Public Interest* (Spring 1976), pp. 99–110; Irving Kristol, "Taxes, Poverty, and Equality," *Public Interest* (Fall 1974), pp. 2–28.

[29] Kristol, "Taxes, Poverty, and Equality"; Stanley Surrey, "Taxes as a Moral Issue," *Saturday Review*, October 21, 1972, pp. 51–52.

Table 5.8 / Percentage Increase in Taxes for Selected Income Groups with Closing of Tax Loopholes

Income Group	Increase in Taxes
Under $3,000	18%
$ 3,000–$5,000	16
$ 5,000–$10,000	17
$ 10,000–$15,000	22
$ 15,000–$20,000	23
$ 20,000–$25,000	24
$ 25,000–$50,000	28
$ 50,000–$100,000	45
$100,000–$500,000	73
$500,000–$1,000,000	98
Over $1,000,000	96

Source: Stanley S. Survey, *Pathways to Tax Reform* (Cambridge, Mass.: Harvard University Press, 1973), p. 11. Copyright Harvard University Press, 1973.

One of the earlier accounts of the inequality produced by the tax system was Philip Stern's *The Great Treasury Raid*.[30] He estimated that through tax privileges, a family that earns $1 million receives $720,000 in subsidies (or tax write-offs), the family earning $10,000 to $15,000 annually receives $650 in subsidies, and the family at the $3,000 level receives $16 in subsidies. Ten years later, when Stern updated his analysis in *The Rape of the Taxpayer,* he maintained that the "wonderful world" of tax shelters had grown.[31] A greater percentage of government officials, business executives, doctors, actors, and ballplayers were avoiding their share of taxes by investing in such tax dodges as real estate, oil, cattle, farming, tax-exempt bonds, and living abroad, and they managed to eliminate the tax on their incomes altogether or to reduce it to paltry amounts. Thus the actual average tax rate for individuals with incomes between $200,000 and $1 million ranged between 29 and 33 percent, although it should have been between 58 and 63 percent. Moreover, many individuals with incomes of over $100,000 paid no tax; many others paid less than 10 percent.

One way to visualize the extent to which tax loopholes work for the rich is to pose the hypothetical question: Whose taxes would increase if tax loopholes were removed? Table 5.8 summarizes the percentage increase in taxes that would result from closing the most conspicuous loopholes for individuals, excluding old-age benefits.

The 1970 congressional statistics show that the percentage of people who escaped federal taxes rose steadily as income increased. Only 0.12 percent of those earning $15,000 to $20,000 paid no tax, but the percentage was almost four times as high (0.45 percent) in the $100,000 to $200,000 bracket and nine times as high (1.07 percent) among those reporting

[30] Philip M. Stern, *The Great Treasury Raid* (New York: Random House, 1964).

[31] Philip M. Stern, *The Rape of the Taxpayer* (New York: Random House, 1973).

incomes between $500,000 and $1 million. Similar patterns exist among corporations. The average tax for corporations was 35 percent; for the largest it was 25 percent, although it should have been 48 percent for all of them. Eight major corporations which each earned a net of $650 million or more (after expenses) paid no federal income tax in 1971 and 1972, though they paid out a total of $418 million in dividends. At the same time, the federal government provided these eight corporations with $77 million in tax refunds and tax credits.[32]

The federal government loses between $50 to $60 billion a year through tax loopholes.[33] But so long as wealth and political power are locked up by the same people, almost every decision to devise a more equitable income solution becomes a battle between the "have littles" and the "have nots," while those on the top maintain their advantages. In the past, the United States avoided political upheaval because economic growth increased more rapidly than population growth. Without changing income distribution, most Americans were able to obtain greater incomes and increase their standards of living. Now, however, inflationary rates may exceed increases in salaries, and continued growth and productivity will probably taper off due to a host of resource, energy, and employment factors. Furthermore, ecologists claim that increased expansion must lead to the exhaustion of resources and the eventual economic decline of the entire world. As the expectations of lower-class and middle-class people increase, there are bound to be increased conflicts over the concepts of equality and inequality.

Income distribution figures or years of schooling are often reported between blacks and whites (as we shall report later in this chapter), but the real discrepancies exist between rich and poor and cut across race. In a multiracial and ethnic society, differences between groups are more visible and emotion-arousing than the larger differences between the very wealthy (1 or 2 percent of the people, or those who have inherited concentrations of wealth) and the rest of the population.

Genuine tax reform would include the following principles:

1. Tax all income on the same basis.
2. Eliminate the billions of dollars in revenues lost through tax loopholes, which the lower- and middle-income groups must make up by being overtaxed.

---

[32] See Edmund S. Muskie, "Tax Reform and Ethnic Diversity," in M. Wenk, S. M. Tomasi, and G. Baroni (eds.), *Pieces of a Dream: The Ethnic Workers' Crisis with America* (New York: Center for Migration Studies, 1972), pp. 105–11.

[33] Herbert Stein, "Money Made by Money is Already Taxed More than Money Made by Men," *Saturday Review*, October 21, 1973, pp. 47–48; Gus Tyler, "Debate: Nixon, the Great Society and the Future of Social Policy," *Commentary*, May 1973, pp. 53–57.

3. Reduce tax rates for the majority of the populace; increase them for the 1 or 2 percent in the highest income brackets.
4. Eliminate the privileges of the corporations, without passing the effects on to the consumer.
5. Make it impossible for anyone to inherit or receive in his or her lifetime a gift amounting to more than $1 million (or any comparable figure), which would be taxed at the level required for earned income.
6. Have public hearings on tax reform so lawyers and accountants who are paid by corporations or the rich cannot establish new loopholes behind closed doors.
7. Let the people know they are being cheated so they will elect congressmen who are committed to tax reform.

The assumption is that these reform measures could reduce economic stratification, or inequality in wealth and income, over a gradual period of time without violent upheaval or conflict within the political and economic system. Without trying to soak the rich, they would ensure greater economic equality among groups and make more money available for the federal government to spend on social, educational, and health programs. The value of education also would be enhanced, since inheritance and tax loopholes would be reduced.

EDUCATION AND STRATIFICATION

Education is related to stratification in two ways:

1. In part, other people's evaluations of an individual's status derives directly from how much and what kind of education he or she has had.
2. Many other important criteria of social class, such as occupation and income, are partially determined by amount of education.

The Value of Education

There is a vast amount of evidence that, on average, those who receive comparatively more years of schooling earn more income. Table 5.9 shows that men who finish college earn twice as much as men who have only an elementary school education. Similarly, more than 60 percent of college graduates have professional occupations, while only 15 percent of those with a high school education and 1 percent with an elementary school education attain such occupations.[34]

Most educators share the public's faith in these relationships, as indicated in Robert Havighurst and Bernice Neugarten's summary of the

---

[34] See, for example, *Digest of Educational Statistics, 1975* (Washington, D.C.: U.S. Government Printing Office, 1976), Table 16, p. 20.

Table 5.9 / Lifetime Income and Type of Occupation for Men by Years of School Completed, 1972 and 1974

Years of School Completed	Average Income from Age 18 to Death, 1972	Percent of Professional and Technical Workers, Age 16 and Over, 1974	Percent of Laborers, Age 16 and Over, 1974
Elementary school			
Less than 8 years	$279,997	0.3%	12.9%
8 years	343,730	0.7	10.1
High school			
1–3 years	389,207	2.3	30.6
4 years	478,873	15.1	34.0
College			
1–3 years	543,435	16.9	10.8
4 years	710,569	64.8ª	1.6ª
5 or more years	823,759		

ª Distribution of occupations by college is divided into two categories, 1–3 years or 4 or more years.
Source: *Digest of Educational Statistics, 1975* (Washington, D.C.: U.S. Government Printing Office, 1976), Table 16, p. 20, Table 19, p. 22.

Table 5.10 / Selected Age Groups Enrolled in Secondary School and College, United States, 1900–1975

	Percent of 14–17-Year-Olds Enrolled in Secondary Schools	Percent of 17-Year-Old High School Graduates	Percent of 18–21-Year-Olds Enrolled in College
1900	11.4	6.4	3.9
1910	15.4	8.8	5.0
1920	32.3	16.8	7.9
1930	51.4	29.0	11.9
1940	73.3	50.8	14.5
1950	76.8	59.0	26.9
1960	86.1	65.1	31.3
1970	93.4	76.5	45.2
1975	93.2	74.6	50.3*

* 1975 data of students enrolled in college based on *Chronicle of Higher Education*, September 13, 1976, pp. 12–13.
Source: *Digest of Educational Statistics, 1974, 1975* (Washington, D.C.: U.S. Government Printing Office, 1975, 1976), Table 33, p. 33; Table 80; p. 80; Table 41, p. 43; Table 63, p. 65.

position: "Education has become the principal avenue of opportunity in twentieth century America. . . . Realizing that the avenue of opportunity is provided by the educational system, parents have encouraged their children to go further and further in school."[35] Henry Levin et al. surveyed the research on this topic and found that: "While the studies differ in their findings on the relative magnitude of the schooling-earnings effect, virtually all studies on the subject show evidence of a significant effect."[36]

---

[35] Robert J. Havighurst and Bernice L. Neugarten, *Society and Education*, 4th ed. (Boston: Allyn & Bacon, 1975), p. 62.
[36] Henry M. Levin et al., "School Achievement and Post-School Success: A Review," *Review of Educational Research*, February 1971, p. 8.

177

The emphasis on education in the United States is evident in the following facts: In 1975 more than 58 million students were enrolled in schools and colleges; 69 percent of all Americans between the ages of 5 and 24 were enrolled in some program of formal education. College enrollments in the United States more than doubled between 1960 and 1970, from 3.6 million to 7.9 million, and rose to 9.3 million in 1975-76. And of all American children between the ages of 7 and 17, more than 95 percent were enrolled in school in 1975.[37] In no other country in the world and at no other time in history has such a large proportion of a population been in school. Our growing faith in the value of formal education over the past 75 years is shown in Table 5.10; the percent of the population between ages 14 and 17 enrolled in school increased from 11 in 1900 to 93 percent in 1975. In 1900 6 percent of all 17-year-olds had completed high school, compared to 75 percent 75 years later, and 4 percent of the population between 18 and 21 was attending college, compared to 50 percent in 1975.

These increasing enrollments, of course, do not necessarily indicate a proportionate commitment to the intrinsic value of higher education. The demonstrable economic rewards can make it attractive to those who would otherwise quickly terminate their formal educations when legally possible. With parental and peer pressure as well as equalitarian opinion added to the economic rewards, almost everyone is encouraged and expected to go on to higher education. There are programs to encourage further education for self-improvement of retired adults; among drug addicts and prison populations, regardless of intellectual capabilities; and for elementary and high school dropouts who have never been able to get much out of schooling, much less college.

The number of people who must be persuaded, encouraged, and pushed into higher education is increasing as lower admission standards, open enrollment policies, and college credit for life experience (e.g., three credits in sociology for living in the inner city) increase.[38] While it is important for the citizenry to be educated to their fullest potential, there are some problems with mass higher education—among them, as we shall see,

---

[37] *Digest of Educational Statistics, 1975* (Washington, D.C.: U.S. Government Printing Office, 1976), Table 79, p. 79; *Statistical Abstract of the United States, 1976*, Table 191, p. 120.

[38] For a discussion of these issues, see Nathan Glazer, "Who Wants Higher Education, Even When It's Free?" *Public Interest,* Spring 1975, pp. 130-35; Martin Haberman, "New Entry Requirements and New Programs for College Students," in A. C. Ornstein and S. I. Miller (eds.), *Policy Issues in Education* (Lexington, Mass.: D. C. Heath & Co., 1976), pp. 95-112; Martin Mayer, "Higher Education for All?" *Commentary,* February 1973, pp. 37-47; Edward M. White, "Sometimes An A Is Really an F," *Chronicle of Higher Education,* February 3, 1975, p. 24.

an increasing oversupply of college-educated people vying for a shrinking number of jobs that require a degree. Second-rate college diplomas or degrees in large numbers also devaluate all diplomas, especially since it has become increasingly difficult to test for academic outcomes and professional competence and thus to evaluate college graduates.

Relationship of Education to Income

There are a number of ways in which education and income are related. Two will be discussed here: the traditional and the revisionist.

The Traditional View. Traditionalists hold that most inequalities are not created by some central authority but arise out of the individual's innate or acquired skills, capabilities, and other resources. In a society based on unrestricted equality, where the government does not interfere, the individual with greater skills and capabilities will be at an advantage. There will be room for those who excel to climb to the top, but there will also be the possibility that others will not do well in school or will lose their jobs and will drop a level or two in social stratification.

In this view, education is conceived as a process involving the acquisition of skills and the inculcation of better work habits in order to increase the individual's productivity. Since income is related to productivity, the more education an individual has, the higher will be his income. Education also serves as a screening device to sort out individuals into different jobs; the more highly educated individuals will obtain the better jobs.

There are varying degrees of traditionalism which offer a number of overlapping explanations for this viewpoint:

1. There are marked differences in individual abilities; those who are more capable will achieve higher levels of education and thus better jobs. Stratification, based on individual merit, and performance, will develop. Even in a society where there is inherited wealth, there will still be room at the top for those who are capable.

2. In hiring, it is often difficult for employers to identify potential good employees, but they have observed the qualities that make present workers more productive on the job. Although the correlation between schooling and productivity is not perfect, competitive firms can offer individuals who have done well in school and have completed more years of schooling the better jobs.

3. The more educated get the better jobs because they have been made more productive by the schools. In a modern, technological society, additional years of schooling constitute a signal of this greater productivity.

4. As long as there is an excess number of applicants for a job, the employer has to use some criterion to decide whom to hire or promote. In

some societies, it may be the applicant's race or ethnic group; in our society, it is largely the amount of education. This explanation is distinguished from the first three in that the more educated are not seen as necessarily the most productive; rather, education is a convenient criterion which most people would regard as fair and as making sense.[39]

The Revisionist View. Recently various scholars representing various ends of the political left have argued that the traditional view is incomplete and inadequate. Ivar Berg, one of the first and more moderate revisionists, maintains that while education often provides better jobs and higher incomes, it offers no guarantee of either, and under certain conditions too much education can create difficulty on the job.[40] On some jobs productivity has very little to do with education; other factors, such as personality, drive, common sense, and experience, are far more relevant than the diplomas or degrees people have acquired. Most important, with the passage of time there is a tendency for many people to be in jobs that utilize less education than they have (service industries, manual labor, the civil service); furthermore, on some jobs educational advancement can catapult people out of employment, since they can be replaced by others who are just as capable but have less education and therefore command lower wages.

A number of critics argue that the schools have not promoted education or social or economic mobility but have discriminated against and limited the life chances of the poor and racial and ethnic minorities.[41] They contend that members of these groups have always had a hard time in the schools; in the early 1900s it was the European immigrants who were most likely to receive failing marks, to repeat grades, and to drop out of school, and now blacks and Spanish students are more likely to do so than white, middle-class students. Not only have the schools failed to recognize the legitimacy of cultures and social classes different from the predominant middle class, but through reliance on intelligence tests, achievement tests, and vocational counseling they have limited the educational opportunity

---

[39] The traditional view is further detailed by Daniel Bell, Nathan Glazer, Irving Kristol, Daniel Moynihan, Robert Nisbet, and James Wilson, who frequently write for *Commentary* and *Public Interest.* Also see Robert Nozick, *Anarchy, State and Utopia* (New York: Basic Books, 1974), and Joseph E. Stiglitz, "Education and Inequality," *Annals of the American Academy of Political and Social Science,* September 1973, pp. 135–45.

[40] Ivar Berg, *Education and Jobs: The Great Training Robbery* (New York: Frederick A. Praeger, Inc., 1970).

[41] David F. Cohen, "Immigrants and the Schools," *Review of Educational Research,* February 1970, pp. 13-27; Colin Greer, *The Great School Legend: A Revisionist Interpretation of American Public Education* (New York: Basic Books, 1972); Clarence J. Karier, Paul Violas, and Joel Spring, *Roots of Crisis: American Education In the Twentieth Century* (Chicago: Rand McNally & Co., 1973).

of these groups. These critics ignore the evidence provided by the numerous ethnics who have risen to the top, and minimize the fact that other social indicators, such as family structure and deprivation, also impact on school achievement.

A stronger revisionist view which approaches Marxism is that the educational system reflects the social and economic system.[42] These advocates see American society as racist, sexist, and capitalistic, based on stratification and inequality, and maintain that the schools cannot be reformed until society is reformed. To them, the relationships among students, teachers, and administrators replicate the hierarchical divisions of labor and the discriminatory practices of society. Students are ranked and tracked, and sorted by social class, race, and sex, thus mirroring society. If people are trained to be subordinate and kept sufficiently fragmented in consciousness, this viewpoint maintains, they will remain disorganized and unable to shape their material existence. Any kind of meritocracy is rejected on the grounds that it would undermine egalitarianism, and a good society and equality are virtually synonymous. They envision an egalitarian educational and social system, to be achieved by replacing the capitalist system with enlightened socialism and by redistributing income. Not only does such a solution send the majority of Americans into their political trenches, but such an approach to education condemns anything suggesting high standards as a mask for "elitism" and "racism."

Intervening Variables

The traditional and revisionist points of view agree that there is a correlation between mobility (movement from one social class to another, based on occupation and income) and education. However, whereas the traditionalists argue that education is the main avenue of opportunity, the revisionists criticize it as a vehicle by which inequality is perpetuated. Both groups probably overstate their cases as to the influence of education.

The correlations among occupation, income, and education are based on averages. The spread around the mean is considerable, which reduces the real predictability for each occupational and income group. In a classic study on occupational mobility of over 20,000 male Americans, Peter Blau and Otis Duncan show that the direct correlation between schooling and occupational status is a modest .32, though significant, and that when all

---

[42] Samuel Bowles and Herbert Gintis, *Schooling in Capitalist America* (New York: Basic Books, 1976); Martin Carnoy and Henry M. Levin, *The Limits of Educational Reform* (New York: David McKay & Co., 1976); Rawls, *Theory of Justice.*

variables are considered education accounts for only 10 percent of the variation in occupational status.[43]

Figure 5.2 helps explain the relationship. The width of the bar is

Figure 5.2 / Relationship Between Educational Attainment and Occupational Status for Males, 20–64 Years Old

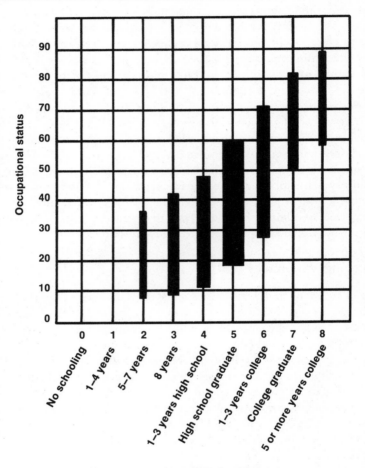

Educational attainment

Note: Does not include men with farm backgrounds; based on a 1962 census.
Source: Peter M. Blau and Otis D. Duncan, *The American Occupational Structure* (New York: John Wiley & Sons, 1967), p. 144.

---

[43] Peter M. Blau and Otis D. Duncan, *The American Occupational Structure* (New York: John Wiley & Sons, 1967).

182

proportional to the number of subjects in the population at each educational level, and its length represents the spread above and below the mean in each group. Thus, for example, a high school graduate on the average has a lower occupational status than a man who has attended college, but a considerable number of high school graduates have better jobs than those who have three years of college. Similarly, more than half of the men who leave college before graduating do as well as those who finish, and one third do as well as those who do graduate work. And, at the other end of the scale, half the men who did not complete elementary school are doing as well as those who completed high school.

In a related research project, Duncan found that education is only one of several variables influencing a person's occupational status and income

Figure 5.3 / Determinants of Level in the Stratification System

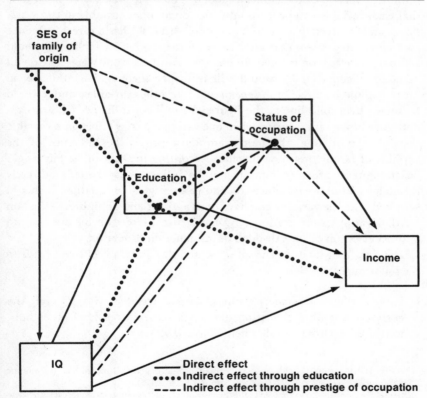

Source: Adapted from Otis D. Duncan, David Featherman and Beverly Duncan, *Socioeconomic Background and Achievement* (New York: Seminar Press, 1972).

183

later in life.[44] What accounts for the assumed relationship between education and occupation and income are a number of underlying variables related to education, such as the family's origin or socioeconomic class. For example, parents with high incomes are able to provide more education for their children, just as they spend more on food and housing, and therefore the children of the affluent obtain more education and go on to higher paying jobs. Parents with high educational levels themselves are more likely to expect and to motivate their children to continue further in schooling. There is also a relation between social class and intelligence of parents and, in turn, the inherited IQ and education of children; thus, those with higher measured IQ scores are more likely to attain higher levels of education.

A synthesis of the relationships between intelligence, socioeconomic position, education, occupation, and income is indicated in Figure 5.3, a simplified version of the Duncan model.[45] To understand it we must note that each variable can have an influence on another variable in two ways: direct and indirect. If we say, for example, that IQ has a direct influence on income, this means that after controlling for other variables, IQ would still have an effect on income. In other words, if everyone were alike on all variables except IQ, IQ would still influence income; its influence on income would be direct or *independent* of the other variables, and it would be shown by a solid line in the figure. An indirect influence (shown by a dotted or broken line) occurs when one variable has its effect on a variable through a third one; the best example of this is the influence of the variable of family origin on income. According to Duncan, family origin has no direct influence on income; its influence is exerted indirectly through its influence on education and on prestige of occupation. It should be noted that one variable can have both a direct and an indirect effect on another variable; for example, IQ has a direct effect on income and an indirect effect on income through its influence on education.

The data on which the model presented in Figure 5.3 is based leads to the following conclusions:

1. Family origin or socioeconomic class is correlated with IQ, but the correlation is low, indicating that IQ is either a result of other non-measured environmental or heredity variables.

---

[44] Otis D. Duncan, David S. Featherman, and Beverly Duncan, *Socioeconomic Background and Achievement* (New York: Seminar Press, 1972).

[45] Actually Duncan shows that several other variables, such as motivational level, the type of wife a man marries, and quality of schooling, are minor factors in increasing the ability to predict occupational status or income.

2. IQ has a direct influence on how much education a person gets. Independent of education, IQ also has some direct influence on the status of occupation and income.

3. The socioeconomic status of a family has its main influence on education; it has some direct influence on occupational status and virtually no direct influence on income.

4. Education is highly correlated with occupational status and therefore has an indirect influence on income.

5. The main determinant of how much money a person earns is the status of his occupation. IQ and education have less important direct effects on income.

A large body of sophisticated research on social mobility within the past 20 years generally supports the above conclusions, at least for white males.[46] Of this research, the most controversial and well known is by Christopher Jencks, who studied the effect on income for the following variables: (1) father's occupational status, (2) father's years of schooling, (3) father's IQ, (4) respondent's IQ at age 11, (5) respondent's Armed Forces aptitude test, (6) respondent's years of schooling, (7) respondent's occupational status, and (8) respondent's income.[47] He found that the number of years of school does not predict income very much. For white males with the same family background and initial ability, an additional year of elementary or secondary education increases future income about 4 percent; an additional year of college, about 7 percent; and an additional year of graduate school, 4 percent. Controlling for IQ, the top fifth of the population earns seven times as much as the bottom fifth, whereas it should only account for 1.4 times as much; this suggests other factors related to inequality of income. All the eight variables (including education and IQ) combined only explain 25 percent of the existing differences in income. This means that if everyone had the same family origin, if everyone had the same IQ and education, and if everyone had the same occupational status, most of the existing differences would remain. This Jencks calls "luck." If by "luck," we mean all those variables not included in the Duncan model or not accounted for by Jencks, then Jencks is correct.

---

[46] See Jerald G. Bachman, Sawyer Green, and Llona Wirtanen, *Youth in Transition*, vol. 3 (Ann Arbor, Mich., Survey Research Center, 1971); W. Lee Hansen, Burton A. Weisbrod, and William J. Scanlon, "Schooling and Earnings of Low Achievers," *American Economic Review*, June 1970, pp. 409-18; Donald Feldstein, "Who Needs High School?" *Social Policy*, May 1974, pp. 20-23; Frederick Mosteller and Daniel P. Moynihan (eds.), *On Equality of Educational Opportunity* (New York: Random House, 1972).

[47] Jencks et al., *Inequality: Reassessment of the Effect of Family and Schooling*.

To call all these variables "luck," however, is not a very good choice of words because it implies that people have little control over their economic fate. Jencks argues that two brothers who are brought up in the same family and who have approximately the same IQ and years of schooling may earn considerably different incomes. One becomes a surgeon who earns $500,000 a year, the other a college professor who earns $30,000 a year. There is considerable difference in their income, but this difference is not a result of luck; it is the result of decisions over which both brothers had full control. Rather than conclude that individual success is largely based on luck, it might make more sense to say that economic success is only partly related to family origin, ability, or education, and there are many other intangible factors influencing income differences among individuals.

Although we may disagree with Jencks's reference to the unexplained variance of income as luck, he may be right in concluding that equalizing opportunity or equalizing education will not reduce inequality. Jencks, who is a revisionist, argues for the redistribution of income — taxing the middle and upper classes and distributing revenues to the poor.

Jencks has been criticized from both the political left, especially black spokesmen, and the political right. From the left came attacks on his measurement of IQ heredity (which he estimated to be 45 percent of the total variance) and his link between IQ and income. Moreover, there was criticism of the implications of his data that schooling is not important (which made it more susceptible to cuts in funding). His major proposition that schools make little difference to academic and economic outcomes runs counter to the widespread belief that educational reform is the best way of reducing poverty and equalizing incomes. Jencks, or anyone else, should not be allowed to let school people off the hook. From the political right came an attack on his views that inequality could only be reduced through income redistribution; these critics pointed out that there are spin-off effects to rewarding unskilled workers, welfare recipients, and able-bodied people who do not want to work, and this would adversely affect the general work ethic and productivity rates.[48]

To put all this research in perspective, we can conclude that the United States is far from an open or fluid society in which ability, performance, and motivation are the only determinants of rank in the stratification system, but these factors are more important than social origins. It should be clear that the degree to which a society is open or fluid, and the degree

---

[48] For a discussion of these points, see the February 1973 issue of the *Harvard Educational Review.*

of mobility—upward or downward—have little to do with the amount of existing inequality. A society can be extremely fluid and still have a great deal of inequality, so long as ability and performance are the criteria used in assigning people to their various stratified positions.

Higher Education and Current Employment Trends

For decades the American educational system has provided both training and education, promising that higher earnings and occupational status will follow further education. We have elaborated on the investment returns of education, indicating that with increased education we should expect to have better jobs and to earn more money in our lifetime (see Table 5.9). While in the past education, and especially higher education, often fulfilled these promises, today it offers no guarantee of doing so. Furthermore, the cost of higher education has dramatically increased in recent years, so it now means some sacrifice for the majority of parents and students.

These developments have fostered a new outlook toward higher education which is expressed in part by Caroline Bird in *The Case against College*.[49] She argues that college is a waste of time and money for the majority of students. At best it is a social center or aging vat, and at worst a young folks' home or even a prison that keeps them out of the mainstream of economic life for a few more years. The baby boom is over, and colleges and universities, having expanded in the 1960s to cope with it, now find a dramatic decline of their traditional market; they also are squeezed by the pressures of inflation. To keep their mammoth plants financially solvent, many institutions have begun to use hard-sell recruiting techniques and are lowering their standards to attract more students.

Bird's most persuasive argument against going to college is that it is no longer the best economic investment for a young man or woman. On the basis of 1972 census data, a man who had completed four years of college could expect to earn $199,000 more between the ages of 22 and 64 than a man who had had only a high school education. If a 1972 high school graduate bound for an Ivy League college had put $34,181 (the amount his four years of college would cost him) into a savings bank at 7.5 percent (long-term) interest, compounded daily, he would have had at age 64 a total of $1,129,200, or $528,200 more than the earnings of a male college graduate, and more than five times as much as the $199,000 extra the more educated man could expect to earn between 22 and 64.

The big advantage of taking money set aside for college in cash, if it

---

[49] Caroline Bird, *The Case against College* (New York: David McKay & Co., 1975).

were possible to do so, would be that it could be invested in something with a higher rate of return than a diploma. The student who did not go to college in 1972 but banked his $34,181, earned an average salary for a high school graduate, and lived on his job earnings, would at 28 have earned $13,000 less on his job from age 22 to 28 than a college-educated person would. But he would have $73,113 in his savings passbook—enough to buy out his boss and to go into business for himself. If he had the brains to go to an Ivy League college in the first place, he would be likely to make more money in his lifetime, without ever stepping on a college campus.

Jencks puts this into perspective with his argument that there is no real evidence that the higher income of a college graduate is due to a college education. College may simply attract people who are slated to earn more money anyway; those with higher IQs, better family background, a more enterprising temperament. "Luck," or the unexplained variance related to income, may be more important than education.

Unfortunately, few high school graduates get the opportunity to bank all the money for their college education in advance, and those who do would probably attend college. And few colleges cost $34,181 for four years, or $8,500 per year; for example, in 1975 the College Entrance Examination Board estimated that the average cost for undergraduate residence at a public university was $2,790, and at a private university it was $4,568 including tuition, room, board and sundry expenses. Only a few leading private institutions run more than $7,000 per year.[50] Bird's estimate, based on Princeton, is atypical. Finally, there are grave difficulties in assigning a dollar value to college. Higher education is increasingly essential and worthwhile in a complex society, regardless of economic consequences; furthermore, college graduates still make considerably more than high school graduates, though proportionately not quite as much more as in the 1960s.

Nevertheless, the golden age of college ended at the outset of the 1970s, when the 25-year boom in the job market for college-educated people turned into a bust. Richard Freeman points out that when only a small proportion of young Americans attended college, the financial rewards for the college trained were sizable and stimulated many to extend their education.[51] In response, institutions of higher learning expanded (almost one new institution per week at the 1970–72 peak), and Americans flooded

---

[50] *Student Expenses at Postsecondary Institutions, 1977–78* (New York: College Entrance Examination Board, 1977).

[51] Richard B. Freeman, *The Over-Educated American* (New York: Academic Press, 1976); Richard B. Freeman and J. Herbert Holloman, "Declining Value of College Going," *Change*, September 1975, pp. 24–31, 62.

the halls of ivy. There was little incentive to examine the value of college education carefully when whatever was being taught was paying off in good jobs for graduates. Furthermore, going to college coincided with the democraticization of schooling, the equalitarian philosophy of the day, and the notion of upward mobility—the kind of reasoning few people would oppose. However, it also meant (which Freeman fails to point out) that a large number of unqualified students were swept into college on this wave of new egalitarianism, thus further deevaluating the college diploma, both intellectually and economically.

It has become evident that the number of job offerings is not growing as rapidly as the increasing number of students graduating from college. The proportion of Americans with four or more years of college increased sixfold from 1940 to 1975, from 216,000 to 1.3 million, and the growth has accelerated in recent years.[52] Coinciding with this growth of college graduates seeking work, the growth of most sectors of the economy which employ educated personnel has leveled off, even declined in some areas. Teaching is a good example of a minus-growth industry requiring college graduates. A few sectors of the economy (computer science, business and finance, and health services) are still growing, but not enough to maintain levels of employment for graduates. Thus there is an oversupply of highly trained and educationally qualified applicants for a shrinking (at least not expanding) employment market.

As a consequence, college graduates found it increasingly difficult to obtain the jobs for which they were trained, and the relative incomes of college-educated workers declined. In 1969, the last good year in the college job market, 0.9 percent of college graduates lacked employment, compared with a nationwide average of 3.5 percent. By late 1972, even before the economy had entered a serious recession, 9.3 percent of the class of '72 lacked work of any kind, and the rate was as high as 15.4 percent for those who had majored in the humanities and 16 percent for social science majors. The college-educated unemployment rate was far in excess of the national average (5.6 percent) and above that for high school graduates of about the same age (7.7 percent). Between 1970 and 1974, not only did length of unemployment among college graduates exceed that of other workers, but the 1974 starting-salary advantages of college graduates over wage and salary earnings dropped sharply (15 percent),[53] to return to 1954

---

[52] *Digest of Educational Statistics, 1974* (Washington, D.C.: U.S. Government Printing Office, 1975), Table 115, p. 101; Also see *Projections of Educational Statistics to 1983–84* (Washington, D.C.: U.S. Government Printing Office, 1975), Table 21, pp. 44–45.

[53] Freeman and Holloman, "Declining Value of College Going," pp. 25–26.

Figure 5.4 / Starting-Salary Advantages of College Graduates over Average Wage and Salary Earnings, 1954–1974

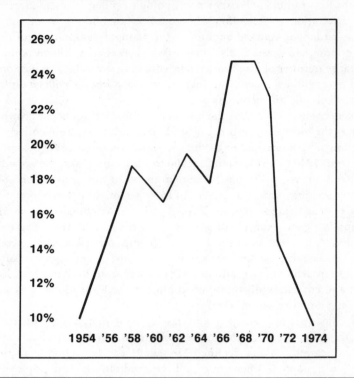

Source: Richard B. Freeman and J. Herbert Holloman, "The Declining Value of College Going," *Change,* September 1975, p. 25.

levels, as shown in Figure 5.4, even though inflation had spiraled close to 50 percent during this 20-year period.

Nonprofessional, nonmanagerial jobs were being held by over 30 percent of male and 25 percent of female college graduates in the mid-1970s. Between 1969 and 1974 the number of male college graduates working as salesmen and cab drivers and the proportion of female graduates employed in clerical and waitress positions increased by more than 30 percent. More than 50 percent of all college graduates accepted positions unrelated to their college majors throughout the midseventies, compared to 10 percent in the early sixties.[54] In 1975 job offers to college

[54] Ibid.

graduates fell 25 percent as compared with 1974; offers at the bachelor's level dropped 24 percent; at the master's level, 18 percent; at the Ph.D. level, 37 percent. The job market for college graduates improved slightly in 1976 and 1977, but it was still a tight market and worse than in any year between 1970 and 1974.[55]

Analysis of the turnaround in opportunities for college graduates suggests that they represent a major break with the past and may not be simply cyclical or temporary in nature. Under normal economic cycle patterns, the position of college graduates relative to the less educated improves in recessions and declines in booms. In past economic declines, blue-collar workers have lost jobs when unemployment rises, not college graduates or professionals. The fact that starting salaries of college graduates fell relative to average earnings from 1970 to 1975 suggests an overall change in supply-demand shifts in the economy.[56]

The collapse of the college market could be long-lasting. Trends in both the job market and numbers of college graduates show that supply of graduates may exceed demand by 3 percent in 1980 and by more than 10 percent by 1985. The job deficit for college graduates is expected to total 12,500 per year until 1980, increasing to 140,000 per year between 1980 and 1985, barring an unforeseen drop in bachelor's degree recipients.[57] If these supply-demand trends (they coincide with the teacher supply-demand projections in Chapter 6) are accurate, the early 1980s will be the harshest economic period to be faced by college graduates. Of course, some groups and fields will be affected less than others. Those graduating with a Ph.D. will find it more difficult than those at the bachelor's or master's levels. Females and blacks will have more opportunities than white males, due to affirmative action policies. Health services, engineering, and computer science will be selectively good markets, and graduates in the humanities and social sciences will have to travel a very rough road.

Not until the mid-1980s will the supply-demand trend improve for college graduates. Continued weakness in the job market for graduates, plus a decline in the traditional college age group, should eventually reduce college enrollments, and subsequently there should be an upswing in demand for college-educated people. These forecasts are, of course, relative to business cycle developments as well as the back-to-college

[55] Frank S. Endicott, *Trends in Employment of College and University Graduates in Business and Industry, 1975, 1976, 1977, 1978,* 29th, 30th, 31st and 32nd annual reports (Evanston, Ill.: Northwestern University, 1974, 1975, 1976, 1977).

[56] Freeman, *Over-Educated American.*

[57] *Occupational Manpower and Training Needs* (Washington, D.C.: U.S. Government Printing Office, 1975).

pattern of middle-aged men and women[58] and the number of students allowed into college, regardless of qualifications.

Concurrent with these job trends, James O'Toole warns of the prevalence of job dissatisfaction which is expressed in low productivity.[59] A Ph.D. from Stanford University manages to find work as a salesman, a young woman with a B.A. in teaching finds typing is her only marketable skill, another graduate finds a job behind a ticket counter for an air line. The effect trickles down; job displacement reaches its fullest force at the bottom of the ladder, where poorly educated workers are often bumped off the last rung. A high school dropout is told that a high school diploma is required to deliver groceries. Moreover, most high school graduates desire not only good jobs in terms of income and status but also interesting and meaningful jobs.

Thus the rules are changing; no longer does education seem to be the key to job satisfaction and economic rewards. In a sort of Catch 22, four years of college are not enough; to succeed you must go back to college and earn a master's or Ph.D. degree, and then, when you look for a job, you will be overqualified.

We have reached a disjunction in industrialized society where, according to O'Toole, "We are unable to produce an adequate number of jobs that provide the status and require the skills and educational levels" now demanded of the work force. By way of a Malthusian analogy, "levels of educational attainment have tended to grow in geometric progression, while the number of jobs that require higher levels of educational attainment have tended to grow at a much slower pace." There are not enough good jobs to go around to everyone who is educationally qualified for one or who thinks he or she deserves one. The economic sector is unable to make good the promises of and expectations raised by schooling.

There is already some evidence that the national policies designed to upgrade the educational levels of society may result in frustration and low morale among young people, and in turn this will lead to low productivity and increased social dissatisfaction. O'Toole says that placing "intelligent and/or highly qualified workers in dull and unchallenging jobs . . . is a prescription for pathology—for the worker, the employer, and the society."[60] In the past, the job discontent of blue-collar workers was ignored; in fact, they were often treated as dull-witted "hard hats." Now college

---

[58] Brigitte Berger, "The Coming Age of People Work," *Change,* May 1976, pp. 24-30; Allan M. Cartter, *Ph.D.'s and the Academic Labor Market* (New York: Carnegie Commission on Higher Education-McGraw-Hill, 1976); *Occupational Manpower and Training Needs.*

[59] James O'Toole, "The Reserve Army of the Underemployed," *Change,* May 1975, pp. 26-33, 63.

[60] O'Toole, "Reserve Army of the Underemployed," p. 28.

graduates are feeling the same dissatisfactions, and they have the educational backgrounds to create social unrest. This problem is compounded by a growing number of professional people (e.g., professors, teachers, social workers) whose salaries are being eroded by inflation.

In short, the nation may wind up with an overeducated, unemployed or underemployed, intellectual proletariat. Jobs that were once available without educational credentials are being redefined to require them, and college graduates may not perform well in jobs they feel do not utilize their education. The price will also be paid by those who do not go to college.

For most Americans, however, the value of education is sustained by the guiding principle of progress which has permeated our society. Progress and education have become synonymous in the sense that it is beyond doubt that only a highly educated populace can ensure a humane, rational world. Education is largely believed to underlie the universal solution to every problem, from juvenile delinquency to senility. As the panacea to all social ills, it is viewed as the major institution for combatting ignorance and inequality and ensuring a better tomorrow.

However, it is time to accept the diminished importance of education as a means to higher income and occupational status. Contradictions of schooling are beginning to surface, given the limitations of the economy. A shrinking number of high-paying, interesting jobs to meet the demands of a growing overeducated populace will cause job dislocations and dissatisfaction among educated people. The traditional relationship between schooling and stratification will have to be revised as more and more college-educated people compete for jobs. There are those who welcome this turn of events because it liberates education from a materialistic orientation. They believe it is time to stop selling education as an economic investment and return it to its classic goals and intellectual pursuits.

The one major exception to these trends is the success black college graduates have had in finding jobs. After having been historically paid less, they have reached parity with whites and in many cases exceeded it. For the time being we can expect many white job-seekers to be caught in a tightening employment vise, while opportunities for blacks and other minorities expand; these matters are discussed below.

DISCRIMINATION

Discrimination is said to exist when two or more groups differentiated on the basis of some characteristic which is irrelevant to an objective measure of selection or productivity are treated unequally in a particular activity. The differentiating characteristic may be race, sex, ethnic origin, religion, age, marital status, or any other physical or social characteristic. When a decision as to who to admit into graduate school or to hire for a job is made on the basis of the racial or sexual characteristics of the applicants rather than their qualifications as a student or employee, discrimination is occurring.

The bureaucratic decision by the federal government, particularly the Office of Civil Rights (under the jurisdiction of the Department of Health, Education, and Welfare), Office of Federal Contract Compliance (under the Department of Labor), Equal Employment Opportunity Commission, and Department of Justice, plus another 22 federal agencies with enforcement responsibilities, to give *preferential treatment* to selected minorities must not be confused with the original intent of the 1964 Civil Rights Act, which *prohibited discrimination* on the basis of race, sex, religion, and ethnic origin. According to federal guidelines, the goal of equ.: ' opportunity has become synonymous with equality of results for certain minority groups. On the basis of this change in the meaning of equality, the U.S. Commission on Civil Rights has stated that the number of minority persons found in the employment at every "level must be equal to their proportions in the population."[61] Concern has shifted from prohibiting discrimination to the actual employment of minorities in all sectors of the economy, and the same reasoning now applies for college admissions. The minorities to receive this protection include blacks, persons with Spanish surnames, American Indians, Asian Americans, and women — but not Italians, Poles, Greeks, and other white ethnics, poor whites, or Catholics and Jews. Needless to say, those eligible for preferential treatment are not the only ones who have been discriminated against in the past.

Ascertaining Discrimination

Using population proportions as a criterion for ascertaining whether discrimination exists is misleading, yet this is the way affirmative action plans and enforcement procedures are implemented. This section will consider examples of how these programs are applied in attempts to define and counter discriminatory practices in *education* and *occupations*. The specific topics are college admissions and college faculties.

Discrimination in Education? As an example of the difficulties involved in assessing whether or not discrimination is being practiced in college admissions, consider the enrollment patterns of a college which is 40 percent female and 60 percent male, and 3 percent black and 97 per-

---

[61] U.S. Commission on Civil Rights, *Federal Civil Rights Enforcement Effort* (Washington, D.C.: U.S. Government Printing Office, 1970), p. 47.

cent white, in contrast to nationwide population percentages, which are approximately 50 percent female and 12 percent black. We know that reading and achievement scores for men and women are similar, but it is possible that the underrepresentation of women in the hypothetical college might be a result of either self-selection on the part of female applicants or the fact that the college offers several programs (engineering, science, premedicine) which a considerably smaller percentage of women are interested in as careers. Fewer women apply for admission to the college, due mainly to social roles rather than discrimination on the part of the institution. But if it can be shown that the selection process was based on some nonrelevant criteria for admission, say the outdated notion that a seat to a woman would be wasted (i.e., she would get married and have children and would not pursue her career), it can be argued that sexual discrimination has occurred.

For blacks (and other minorities) the situation is different. We know from the Coleman report and other research (see Table 4.4) that the reading scores of black students in the 12th grade are more than three years below those of their white counterparts (and for Spanish-speaking groups the gap is almost as wide), and the Scholastic Achievement Scores for 12th-grade students in inner-city schools average more than 100 points below the norm.[62] The question arises: Is it possible for institutions of higher learning to have "adequate" representation of blacks or Spanish-speaking students without lowering standards? And the next question is: To what level should standards be lowered to admit disadvantaged students into college programs?

Across the country, as a result of egalitarian pressures, many students who are functional illiterates and who have reading and math scores as low as the fifth-grade level are being admitted into colleges and universities, provided only that they have been graduated from high school. Proposals to tighten admission standards (one proposal for the City University of New York is to cut off admissions at the eighth-grade reading level) have resulted in charges of "elitism" and "discrimination" and have been called schemes to drive blacks and Spanish groups off the college campuses.[63] There may be debates about social pressures, equality, and what is expected of institutions of higher learning, but it is embarrassing to

---

[62] *Chronicle of Higher Education*, September 13, 1976, p. 3; *College Board Seniors, 1975–1976* (New York: College Entrance Examination Board, 1976).

[63] See Bernard Bell, "College for All: Dream or Disaster?" *Phi Delta Kappan*, February 1975, pp. 390–95; *Chicago Sun Times*, January 15, 1975, p. 48; April 12, 1977, p. 1, 10; *Chicago Tribune*, April 17, 1977, p. 32; Nathan Glazer, "Who Wants Higher Education Even When It's Free?" *Public Interest*, Spring 1975, pp. 130–35; Jeffrey M. Katz, "What Price CUNY?" *Change*, June 1976, pp. 45–47.

academicians to give college credit for remedial reading and mathematics or to practice grade inflation despite declining student achievement scores and admission standards.

The kind of federal government pressure being felt by colleges and universities is illustrated by an HEW communication to a western university which was charged with discrimination against minorities because in one department "out of many applicants only one minority person was enrolled [for the term]." Another illustration is a compliance letter to an Ivy League university which demanded to know why there were no minority students in the Graduate Department of Religious Studies. The department head responded that a reading knowledge of Latin, Greek, or Hebrew was required. The HEW representative advised: "then end those old fashioned programs that require irrelevant languages. And start up programs or relevant things which minority group students can study without learning languages."

In this connection two leading black social scientists, Martin Kilson from Harvard University and Thomas Sowell of UCLA, point out that the Scholastic Aptitude Test and Graduate Record Examination scores for most entering blacks (even at the prestigious universities) are now in the 25th percentile on a national level, but such students are occupying seats at Harvard and Yale that would normally require scores above the 90th percentile.[64] On a nationwide basis a recent study by the Association of American Law Schools reports that all but 2 of 50 law schools surveyed indicated preferential treatment and the lowering of admission standards for minorities.[65] Similarly, Jack Shepard indicates that by 1971, 79 out of 100 medical schools reported that admission requirements were being lowered to admit additional minorities. More women also were being admitted into medical schools, but their scores were similar to those of white males.[66] The point is, a great many college and university seats are being reserved for minority students whose formal qualifications are questionable, while seats are being taken away from more qualified students.

For example, Stanford University Law School virtually guaranteed admission in 1972 to any minority student whose grade point average was not below that of the lowest scoring white in the 1971 class and whose Law School Admission Test (LSAT) was within 50 points of that of the weakest

---

[64] Martin Kilson, "The Black Experience at Harvard," *New York Times Magazine*, September 2, 1973, pp. 13, 31 ff; Thomas A. Sowell, *Black Education, Myths and Tragedies* (New York: David McKay & Co., 1974).

[65] Committee on Nondiscrimination and Integrity, "Statement for Immediate Release," June 9, 1972.

[66] Jack Shepard, "Black Lab Power," *Saturday Review*, August 5, 1972, pp. 33-35 ff.

student in the previous entering class. In 1973 Northwestern Law School was admitting blacks who scored below the 10th percentile on the LSAT, some of whom were from colleges whose accreditation was under question. The school was at the same time refusing admission to white students who scored in the 80th and 90th percentiles. The University of Illinois Medical School at Urbana reserved 60 out of 300 places in its incoming class for minorities in 1972. More recently, at California State University at Fresno the goals in the School of Social Work were to admit "one third black, one third Chicano, one tenth other minorities, and the remainder Caucasian students."[67] These examples are only the tip of the iceberg; they represent the early period of affirmative action in which the drift toward these quota policies became increasingly more pronounced. Such sentiments, according to the traditionalist viewpoint, can seriously erode the quality of higher education under the guise of egalitarian "reform." The egalitarians claim, however, that such procedures are necessary if minorities are to overcome historical discrimination.

The DeFunis case is one of the two best known examples of a student denied admission because of preferential treatment given to minorities. Marco DeFunis, Jr., a white male with a 3.62 average on a 4.0 scale, applied to the University of Washington Law School in 1971 and was rejected. He later discovered that 38 other applicants, all minorities, with lower grades and lower LSAT scores were accepted. DeFunis sued the university, charging he was the victim of reverse discrimination. He won his case in the state court and was admitted, but the decision was overturned in the federal district in 1973. The case reached the U.S. Supreme Court in 1974. In a seven-page unsigned opinion, with four justices dissenting, the Court ruled that the issue was moot; any decision reached by the Court would have been made after DeFunis had finished his studies. The dissenting judges argued that DeFunis was still in his last year of law school and still could be subject to a number of unexpected events that might prevent him from graduating. He thus might be faced with another admissions rejection. But most important to the dissenting judges was their belief that the case was not moot for a vast number of other students, and therefore the issue should be resolved for the interests of the public. (It can be assumed that a large number of students have had no idea that they were victimized by a quota system and so have not pursued their cases in the courts.) The nondecision in the DeFunis case evoked considerable criticism, and it certainly did not resolve the problem.

---

[67] See Allan C. Ornstein, "Affirmative Action and the Education Industry," in A. C. Ornstein and S. I. Miller (eds.), *Policy Issues in Education* (Lexington, Mass.: D. C. Heath & Co., 1976), pp. 139-59; Paul Seabury, "HEW and the Universities," *Commentary*, February 1972, pp. 33-44.

In 1974 a rejected white medical student by the name of Allan Bakke, at the University of California, Davis, filed a similar lawsuit. As many as 16 of 100 seats were reserved for minorities, and all of these applicants were rated substantially below Bakke. The California Supreme Court ruled (6–1) that he had been discriminated against because of his race, in violation of the 14th Amendment which guarantees equal protection of the law. In 1978, the U.S. Supreme Court will render a decision in what could be the most far-reaching civil rights decision since *Brown* v. *Board of Education* in 1954, on whether universities can judge white applicants and applicants from certain minorities by different standards. The issue is whether society has abandoned the principle that rights belong to individuals, not groups. At stake not only are coveted places in medical schools and universities in general, but ultimately millions of jobs affected by affirmative action policies.

Discrimination in Occupations? Now consider an employment situation for example, within a college department. If only 5 percent of the department's members are black and 20 percent are women, can it be inferred that discrimination is being practiced? It cannot, in view of the small size of most departments (less than ten members), which would distort the outcome of statistical analysis, and considering the pool of qualified people for a particular field of study.

One of the relevant criteria for hiring professors is the applicant's possession of a Ph.D. Between 1961 to 1973, the more than 2,500 institutions of higher learning awarded this degree to only two women in meteorology, six in agronomy, and less than ten in pharmacy, nuclear chemistry, theoretical chemistry, electromagnetism, optical physics, civil engineering, and sanitary engineering. Women earned 0.5 percent of the Ph.D.s in engineering, 2.3 percent in agriculture, 2.9 percent in physics, 3 percent in business administration, 3.5 percent in earth science, 4 percent in ecology, 7 percent in mathematics, and 7.6 percent in chemistry.[68] Although data are unavailable by fields of study for blacks, the figures can be expected to be substantially lower; the *total* supply of Ph.D.s awarded to blacks in all fields for *all* years through 1972 was between 1,500 to 2,280, depending on the research referred to, and nearly half were in the field of education.[69]

---

[68] Commission on Human Resources, National Research Council, *Summary Reports, 1967–1973: Doctorate Recipients from United States Universities* (Washington, D.C.: National Academy of Sciences, 1967–1974).

[69] William F. Brazziel, "Affirmative Action: Snail's Pace Gained," *Phi Delta Kappan*, March 1977, p. 492; Allan C. Ornstein, "What Does Affirmative Action Affirm? A Viewpoint," *Phi Delta Kappan*, December 1975, pp. 242–45, 255.

Although there has been an increase since 1972 in the Ph.D. output of women and blacks, even if the degree output each year for the next five years (the period usually provided by HEW to make up deficiencies in college departments) were multiplied by 1,000, this still would not provide a sufficient pool of women and blacks for most departments needing such personnel. Over half the departments in college and universities throughout the country had less than 50 women doctorates and two to three black Ph.D.s available on a nationwide basis from which to recruit during the 1958–67 period, when most hiring was done in higher education.[70] In addition, all women and blacks with doctorate degrees are not available for posts in college and universities. Therefore, it seems unreasonable to list hundreds of college and university departments as deficient.

In 1972 fewer than 1 percent of all Ph.D.s in this country were held by blacks and 15 percent by women. If candidates were selected at random from all those possessing this single qualification, this proportion should be present in most institutions of higher learning. Actually, blacks comprised 2.9 percent of college and university faculties, and women comprised 22 percent, in 1972.[71] It could be argued, then, that based on the Ph.D. criterion, blacks and women were already overrepresented, and collegiate institutions are being forced to "correct" black/white and female/male ratios that are already more than would normally prevail.

But possession of a Ph.D. is only a minimal qualification for a faculty job or for promotion. Other relevant criteria are demonstrated teaching ability and research. Although it is nearly impossible to define a "good" teacher (see Chapter 7), Richard Lester, in his report for the Carnegie Commission on Higher Education, summarized several studies which show men outnumber women professors in research and publication by about 4:1 in articles and 2:1 in books and monographs, and these differences increase with age and marriage.[72] Both male and female researchers conclude that married women must accommodate their careers to their

---

[70] Commission on Human Resources, National Research Council, *Doctorate Recipients from United States Universities, 1958–1966* (Washington, D.C.: National Academy of Sciences, 1967); Allan C. Ornstein, "Affirmative Action and the Education Industry," in A. C. Ornstein and S. I. Miller (eds.), *Policy Issues in Education* (Lexington, Mass.: D. C. Heath Co., 1976), pp. 139–59; Miro M. Todorovich, statement before the Special Subcommittee on Education and Labor, Congress of the United States, September 20, 1974.

[71] Alan F. Bayer, *Teaching Faculty in Academe: 1972–73*, ACE Research Report, vol. 8, no. 2 (Washington, D.C.: American Council on Education, 1973); Richard A. Lester, *Antibias Regulation of Universities*, Report for the Carnegie Commission on Higher Education (New York: McGraw-Hill Book Co., 1974), pp. 48, 51.

[72] Lester, *Antibias Regulation of Universities*, pp. 31–59.

family commitments, and differences between the sexes in societal and marriage roles realistically are crucial factors in terms of productivity and have second-order effects on promotions, salaries, and tenure.[73] There is a greater difference in publication between blacks and whites, in part due to past differences in quality of education and training.[74]

Depending on what survey you read, male-female salary discrepancies favor males by 2.5 percent to 17.5 percent. Data on racial differences are incomplete, although *current* trends suggest that blacks are favored by $3,000 to $4,000 at the assistant rank and as high as $8,000 at the associate or full rank.[75]

To be sure, these hiring trends are apparent in all sectors of the economy; they involve not only institutions of higher learning, which was used as the example here, but the public schools, health systems, civil service (policemen, firemen, post office workers, etc.), the armed forces, construction and trade industries, unions, businesses and corporations, any agency regulated by the government (railroad, communications, financing, social security, etc.), and all organizations employing 50 or more people or having contracts of $50,000 or more with the federal government. In total, about 95 percent of the employment market is affected.[76]

A Basis for Inferring Discrimination

Discrimination cannot be inferred from a simple distribution by admissions to college or occupation. In order to demonstrate that discrimination is being practiced, it would have to be shown that a group of equally qualified applicants for college or a specific job was hired in smaller proportions than another group with similar qualifications. But

---

[73] Helen S. Astin, *The Women Doctorate in America: Origins, Career, and Family* (New York: Russell Sage Foundation, 1969); Alan E. Bayer, *College and University Faculty: A Statistical Description*, ACE Research Report, vol. 5, no. 5 (Washington, D.C.: American Council on Education, 1970); Norton T. Dodge, *Women in the Soviet Economy* (Baltimore, Md.: Johns Hopkins University, 1966); Burton J. Malkiel and Judith A. Malkiel, "Male-Female Pay Differentials in Professional Employment," *American Economic Review*, September 1973, pp. 693–705.

[74] Bell, "College for All"; Orde Coombs, "The Necessity of Excellence: Howard University," *Change*, March 1974, pp. 36–41; Louis G. Heller, *The Death of the American University* (New York: Arlington House, 1974); Lester, *Antibias Regulation of Universities*; Sowell, *Black Education*.

[75] *Chronicle of Higher Education*, August 5, 1974, p. 9; June 9, 1975, pp. 1, 17; Lester, *Antibias Regulation of Universities*, p. 49.

[76] Nathan Glazer, "A Breakdown in Civil Rights Enforcement," *Public Interest*, Spring 1971, pp. 106–15; Nathan Glazer, *Affirmative Discrimination: Ethnic Inequality and Public Policy* (New York: Basic Books, 1975); *Newsweek*, November 7, 1977, pp. 34–36 ff.

the federal government now makes the assumption that if percentages present do not correspond with population proportions, the institution or organization is discriminating.

Compliance agencies flatly deny that they are promoting a quota system, preferring to speak of "goals." But the distinction between goals and quotas is mostly semantic, and in effect the pressure tactics used by the federal government—statistical bookkeeping and legal and monetary penalties—turn the goals into quotas. If minorities and women are found to hold positions or to be accepted as students in low percentages, the figures will be offered as prima facie evidence of discrimination. Using this kind of quantitative method alone, a case for discrimination against almost any group could be built. Compliance agencies defend their policies by saying that we must compensate for past injustices, failing to recognize or to admit that implementing this process creates new injustices. Of course, staff and investigators for these agencies, who are predominantly (85 percent) black and/or female, can be expected to have a healthy bias toward their own reference group.

If there were no differences between people in ability, motivation, or attitudes, and if there were no discrimination, then we would expect that the proportion of women and blacks (and other minorities) in each occupation would be the same as the proportion of women and blacks in the labor force. In fact, however, the proportion of women and blacks in various occupations varies greatly. For example, almost 100 percent of nurses are women, and almost 95 percent of engineers are men. More than 40 percent of professional basketball players are black, and more than 95 percent of engineers are white. From such statistics, it would be wrong to conclude that employers of nurses discriminate against men, or that employers of engineers discriminate against women and blacks, or that team owners discriminate against whites.

There are two basic processes which determine the distribution of college admissions or of occupations: self-selection and social selection. The choice of a particular educational level or occupation reflects in part the motivation of the individual. But everyone who might want to attend college or enter a particular occupation is not qualified. Social selection connotes the right of the college admission officer or employer to screen out candidates or to make choices on the basis of ability or education. Only if irrelevant criteria are used for selection—criteria based on sex, race, or religion, for example, rather than skill or achievement level—can it truly be said that discrimination is being practiced.

Tests of ability and achievement, however, are under attack as selection and screening devices. This includes all tests for college admission, professional licenses (ranging from teaching to practicing medicine), and jobs. The National Association for the Advancement of Colored People and other civil rights organizations have successfully argued in the courts in cities such as Boston, New York, Detroit, Chicago, and San Francisco that the written examinations used to select and promote teachers, firemen, and policemen are "biased" and discriminate against minorities, especially blacks. Of wider impact, the U.S. Supreme Court ruled in *Griggs* vs. *Duke Power* in 1971 that tests can no longer be considered a reasonable job requirement for minorities. All arbitrary barriers to employment that demand certain skills or test score results and have the effect of employing minorities in less than their proportion to the population are considered illegal. If test scores are involved, the employer must now demonstrate that the tests are a valid predictor of job success.

There is also strong pressure to eliminate bar and medical examinations; the contention is that a person who receives a degree from an accredited law or medical school is qualified and should be admitted to practice. This ignores the fact that admission requirements have been lowered for disadvantaged groups, and there is considerable pressure to pass them from level to level. Thus graduation from college or professional school does not guarantee equality of academic outcomes or professional competence.[77]

We do not argue that there has been no past discrimination in our society, but rather that current trends indicate a pattern of reverse discrimination. The federal government, assuming discrimination on the sole basis of population distribution, has established timetables and goals which give preferential treatment to selected groups, sometimes at the expense of others.

While some kind of policy is needed to bring minorities and women into the mainstream of society, the present affirmative action policy results in a denial of equal opportunity for nonprivileged groups, at the same time it puts a "less qualified" stamp on qualified minorities and women by association. Already people are asking, usually in private discussion, how a certain person got into medical school or was placed on the job. Besides filling a quota, did this person have any real qualifications? The questions are embarrassing and lead to further stereotyping among college students and employees and in the client-professional relationship. Indeed, many qualified minority members and women feel uneasy about affirmative action.

---

[77] For a discussion of these issues. see Orde Coombs, "The Necessity of Excellence: Howard University"; Glazer, *Affirmative Discrimination;* Robert M. O'Neil, *Discriminating against Discrimination* (Bloomington, Ind.: Indiana University Press. 1976); Wilson Record, "Who is Impartial?" *Time,* August 7, 1972, pp. 46–47; Paul Seabury, "The Idea of Merit," *Commentary,* December 1972, pp. 41–46.

Somehow we must find a way to recognize the entitlements of groups who claim special privileges without abridging the rights of other individuals. A social policy that encourages a double standard is not in the best interest of the public; it is bound to lead to new antagonisms between groups. What we need is a policy which provides the *individual* with the opportunity to fulfill his or her human potential: remedial help for people with limited skills, reward for people who work hard and are competent, and mobility between social classes. A just policy cannot be defined through mathematical formulas; society is not that simple. In a democratic society, the best policy is based on communication and compromises between groups who have different interests and competing demands. Policy must protect the rights of the individual while accommodating both minority and majority groups. Such a social policy is not derived from political or public whim, nor from zealous governmental bureaucrats; rather, it is derived from law and reason.

Race

Data on incomes of whites and blacks have left little doubt about the effects of past discrimination. It must not be forgotten that blacks came to this country in chains, and 100 years after the Civil War they were still subject to economic and social discrimination; this was most evident in the South, where two-thirds of blacks have resided until 1960.

With this historical background, and amidst all the rhetoric dealing with racism, there is emerging a new phenomenon—the black middle class. The most important variable in ranking of status in our society is money, and Table 5.11 shows the dramatic changes that have taken place in median family income of blacks and whites in recent years. The last

Table 5.11 / Median Income of White and Black Families, 1950–1975 (constant 1975 dollars)

Year	White	Black[a]	Ratio, Black to White
1950	$ 7,702	$4,178	.54
1955	9,271	5,113	.55
1960	10,604	5,871	.55
1965	12,370	6,812	.55
1970	14,188	9,032	.64
1975[b]	14,268	9,321	.65

[a] Actual figures are for blacks and other nonwhite races as defined by the Census Bureau. Since blacks comprise 90 percent of the nonwhite races category, this index is considered relatively good for all blacks in America.
[b] Not strictly comparable with earlier years due to revised procedure.
Source: *Statistical Abstract of the United States, 1976,* Table 650, p. 405.

Table 5.12 / Percentage of White and Black Families Earning $12,000 or More, 1950–1975 (constant 1975 dollars)

Year	White	Black
1950	25.0%	3.0%
1955	28.8	6.8
1960	38.2	15.0
1965	52.1	22.5
1970	60.6	35.4
1975	60.6	37.4

Source: *Statistical Abstract of the United States, 1976,* Table 648, p. 404.

column shows the ratio of median black family income to median white family income; the lower the ratio, the greater the income difference between blacks and whites. If black income equaled white income, the ratio would be 1.0. As the table shows, in 1950 black families earned about one half as much as white families; by 1975 their earnings were equal to 65 percent of white families'. Although a .65 ratio is still a long way from parity, there has been dramatic progress—a catching up—for black families since the 1960s, coinciding with the civil rights movement.

Progress is also evident in the percentage of black families earning about $12,000 compared to whites, as shown in Table 5.12. These trends are in constant 1975 dollars; that is, the erosion caused by inflation has been discounted. To qualify as earning $12,000 or more in 1950, a family had to earn about $7,500, the equivalent of $12,000 in 1975 (and $15,500 in 1978).

Viewing income distribution through the lens of $12,000, or what most would call a 1975 middle-class income for a family of four living in an urban area, the proportion of whites earning at least $12,000 increased from 25 percent to 60 percent from 1950 to 1975. For blacks the increase has been much more dramatic, from 3 percent to 37 percent. Whereas the increase for white families in this income bracket was 2.5 times, for blacks it was 12.5 times.

The march of blacks into the middle class can be seen even more clearly by looking at within-group variables. For example, about 50 percent of blacks now live in the South, compared to 68 percent in 1950. In 1975 black family income in the South was 58 percent of white family income, but outside of the South, black family income was 69 percent of white income.[78] A second variable within black-white income ratios is family status. Black families are much more likely to be female headed (see Chapter 4), but if black and white husband-wife families in 1974 are

[78] Derived from *Statistical Abstract of the United States, 1976,* Table 654, p. 407.

compared, the income for blacks nationwide was 75 percent of comparable white family income; outside the South it was 87 percent.[79]

The most encouraging income data probably is for young blacks. By 1970 the census figures showed that the median income of black husband-wife families living outside the South, where the head of the family was under 35 years old, was 96 percent that of comparable white families. Furthermore, a higher proportion of white wives was working than blacks—and still there was overall income equality between the two groups. In black and white families where both spouses worked, the income of black families was 104 percent that of white families, and for such families with the head of the family under 25 years old, the black income was 113 percent of the white income;[80] yes, more than whites. These figures must be revised even more in favor of blacks to reflect increasing affirmative action policies affecting all sectors of the economy. New and better jobs in most sectors of the economy are going to blacks and other minorities, especially to those who are college educated; as of 1973, black college graduates earned approximately $1,500 more than their white counterparts.[81]

The number of years of school completed by blacks between the ages of 25 and 29 has also jumped, from 8.6 years in 1950 to 9.9 years in 1960, 12.2 in 1970, and 12.5 in 1975, so that it now approaches that of the general population, which was 12.8 in 1975. In 1950, 22.2 percent of blacks graduated from high school, compared to more than double the figure for the general population, which was 52.8 percent. By 1975 the gap had been considerably reduced; 71.0 percent of blacks and 83.1 percent of whites completed high school.[82] And in 1950, 3 percent of the black population was enrolled in college; 25 years later the figure was 9 percent.[83] In short, racial differences in years of school completed for young black and white students are now very small.

---

[79] Ibid., Table 662, p. 411.

[80] *Difference between Income of White and Negro Families by Work Experience of Wife and Region: 1970, 1969 and 1959,* Current Population Reports, Series P-23, no. 39 (December 1971), Tables 1-2, pp. 6-8, 9-10. Also see Daniel P. Moynihan, *Coping: On the Practice of Government* (New York: Random House, 1975), pp. 352-53; Ben J. Wattenberg, *The Real America* (New York: Doubleday & Co., 1974), pp. 124-30.

[81] Edward C. Banfield, *The Unheavenly City,* 2nd ed. (Boston: Little, Brown & Co., 1974); Endicott, *Trends in Employment,* 30th Annual Report; Stanley H. Masters, *Black-White Income Differentials* (New York: Academic Press, 1974); William H. Sewell and Robert M. Hauser, *Education, Occupation and Earnings* (New York: Academic Press, 1975).

[82] *Statistical Abstract of the United States, 1976, op. cit.,* Table 198, p. 123; Table 199, p. 123.

[83] *Chronicle of Higher Education,* November 8, 1976, p. 7; Current Population Reports, *School Enrollment—Social and Economic Characteristics of Students, October 1974,* Series P-20, no. 286 (November 1975), Table 7, p. 25. Also see *Population Profile of the United States, 1975,* Current Population Reports, Series P-20, no. 292 (March 1976), Table 11, p. 17.

Thus, by the most important standards (income and education), blacks have made impressive gains in the period between 1950 and 1975, and these gains should continue. These advances are sometimes denied by civil rights advocates for the purpose of maintaining political and social pressure, but it can be concluded that young blacks can look to a brighter future, especially if they are educated; the older generation of unskilled blacks, trapped by past discrimination, will not get the same breaks. As the older generation dies off, black-white group differences in income and educational levels will increasingly disappear; and in some cases, blacks already surpass in income whites of similar age and family makeup.

Yet these figures do not tell the whole story. On the other side of the picture are the poor. The percentage of blacks living in poverty has declined from 55.1 percent in 1959 to 29.3 percent in 1974, even though the number of black families headed by women has increased during the same period (550,000 to 1,000,000). While 29 percent is an extremely high figure, compared to 8.9 percent for whites,[84] in the face of widening differences in family structure between blacks and whites, a widening discrepancy of income between these two groups might be expected; the opposite is true, however.

It is doubtful whether affirmative action programs can help unskilled, unmarried black women with several children or the black teen-ager who has dropped out of school, in view of their levels of education, the nature of the jobs for which they are qualified, and the alternative attraction of welfare. Furthermore, a substantial measure of income equality between skilled or educated blacks and whites was established prior to the implementation of affirmative action in 1972. Therefore it is doubtful that statistical representations and quotas imposed by the federal government are even needed to effect black progress. They were imposed at a point where, economically and educationally, the idea of advancement for blacks seemed solidly instituted in American society and was maintaining itself, despite the rhetoric and riots of the 1960s. Indeed, affirmative action has retarded black progress in some respects; it has divided the country, created a great deal of resentment among nonpreferred groups, and made it appear that blacks cannot otherwise compete with whites in schools and on the job.

Women

Women's earnings, whether measured as annual income or average hourly wages, have averaged about 60 percent of men's earnings during

---

[84] *Population Profile of the United States, 1975,* Table 23, p. 35; *Statistical Abstract of the United States, 1976,* Table 672, p. 415.

Table 5.13 / Median Income of Year-Round, Full-Time Workers, by Sex, 1960–1975

Year	Men	Women	Ratio, Women to Men
1960	$ 5,435	$3,296	.61
1970	9,184	5,440	.59
1975	13,114	7,719	.59

Source: *Statistical Abstract of the United States, 1976*, Table 670, p. 414. Also see *A Statistical Portrait of Women in the U.S.*, Current Population Reports, Series P-23, no. 58 (April 1976), Table 10.3, p. 48.

Table 5.14 / Percent Distribution of Income for Year-Round, Full-Time Workers, by Sex, 1971

Total Income	Attained by Women	Attained by Men
$ 1–$999	1.9%	1.3%
$ 1,000–$2,999	8.2	3.0
$ 3,000–$4,999	28.1	7.8
$ 5,000–$6,999	30.3	13.7
$ 7,000–$9,999	21.8	27.5
$10,000–$14,999	8.1	29.6
$15,000–$24,999	1.4	13.1
$25,000 and over	0.3	4.0

Source: *Money Income in 1971 of Families and Persons in the United States*, Current Population Reports, Series P-60, no. 85 (December 1972), Table 51, pp. 121–22.

the past 15 years, as shown in Table 5.13. In 1971, as Table 5.14 shows, 70 percent of full-time women workers had incomes of less than $7,000, compared with 25 percent for males, and more than 45 percent of men had incomes in excess of $10,000, but only 10 percent of women attained that level.

For years, a much larger percentage of women than men has been concentrated in the lower paid occupational groups. In 1973, for example, 51 percent of women and 14 percent of men were in two relatively low-paid occupations: clerical and service workers.[85] Women are also less likely to be promoted into higher level jobs. A man who starts at a lower level than his boss's secretary can work his way up the organizational hierarchy, while the secretary probably can only expect to become a better paid secretary.

Income discrepancies are partially explainable by differences in educational attainment levels. In 1975, for example, 17.6 percent of men age 25 and over had four years or more of college, compared with 10.6 percent of women.[86] Educational levels set job barriers that cannot be

[85] *Digest of Educational Statistics, 1975* (Washington, D.C.: U.S. Government Printing Office, 1976), Table 16, p. 20.
[86] *Statistical Abstract of the United States, 1976*, Table 200, p. 124.

easily surmounted. However, women have received less pay than men for work in the same occupational categories, even when their educational qualifications were equivalent.[87]

Society's sex roles also contribute to inequality. Some women leave the labor force to marry, and others become full-time homemakers when they bear children. Unable to accumulate experience and bargaining power, they must take uninteresting and poorly paid jobs when they return to work, either part-time or full-time. Their net income is further reduced if they must hire help to care for children. A high turnover rate, as women seek more interesting work or simply stay home for a time, reinforces the career disadvantages of sporadic employment and limited job experience, and their qualifications often become obsolete while they are not working.[88]

The woman who works full time and raises a family must devote considerable time and energy to family responsibilities. Married professional women spend on average 20 hours a week on care of children, plus another 18 hours on household chores.[89] Married men devote considerably less time to these duties, though the pattern is changing. If their job output is not to suffer, women must budget their time carefully. Furthermore, the husband's job mobility usually takes precedence; if he is transferred, the wife's employment opportunities and career progress may be adversely affected, and employers recognize that if her husband is transferred she will quit her present job.

Sex stereotyping also impairs a woman's chances for well-paid and prestigious jobs. The feeling among many employers is a single woman's job is temporary until she marries and has children, so there is little incentive to train her on the job for more responsibilities or to advance her. In the past a similar attitude prevailed in screening applicants for professional schools, particularly in law and medicine.

Efforts by the federal government to reverse a long-standing inequality of opportunity for women include the Equal Pay Act of 1963, which requires equal pay for equal work; the Secretary of Labor's Revised Order No. 4, effective 1972, calling for female (and minority) hiring quotas; and

---

[87] See *Digest of Educational Statistics, 1974 & 1975*, Table 20, p. 20; Tables 16–17, 20–21: *A Statistical Portrait of Women in the U.S.*, Current Population Reports, Series P-23, no. 58 (April 1976), Table 10.4, p. 49.

[88] Leonard Broom and Philip Selznick, *Essentials of Sociology* (New York: Harper & Row, 1975). Margaret M. Poloma and T. Neal Garland, "The Married Professional Women: A Study in the Tolerance of Domestication," *Journal of Marriage and the Family*, August 1971, pp. 531–40.

[89] Astin, *Women Doctorates in America;* Margorie Galenson, *Women and Work: An International Comparison* (Ithaca, N.Y.: Cornell University Press, 1973).

Title IX, effective 1975, which forbids sex discrimination in education, specifically in the instruction and treatment of students and in job opportunities among employees. These laws do not affect the majority of working women, who are in clerical and sales jobs, so much as they do college-educated women who are competing with men for high-paying jobs. Since the early 1970s, starting salaries for women college graduates have been increasingly approaching parity with those for men, and starting from 1975 to 1977 their starting salaries have been higher than for men in the majority of professional and business fields.[90] Critics of affirmative action argue that discrimination against females does not exist as much as the statistics would have us believe; the problem is rooted in the sex roles and especially marriage roles of society—and this is what needs to be modified.

CONCLUSIONS

Social stratification refers to the ranking of people in horizontal layers or strata. This finds expression in the unequal distribution among the members of any society of certain scarce, divisible, valuable things, which commonly include wealth, power, status, and, in modern technological society, education. Each constitutes an analytically distinct dimension for considering inequality and differences in social ranking.

The *extent* of inequality of the distribution of wealth, power, or status is basically a matter of fact and therefore is an objective matter. The *reasons* for the same distribution and its equity are basically a matter of judgment, and therefore are subjective. Two strikingly different theories have emerged to explain the existing social stratification or inequality in American society.

The first, the conservative or traditional viewpoint, which approaches this author's viewpoint, tends to support the economic system and argues that an unequal distribution of the social rewards (that is, inequality) is necessary to get essential tasks performed and to reward people on the basis of ability; it rejects proportional representation as discriminatory to the individual and endorses *equal opportunity for individuals*. The liberal or revisionist viewpoint is critical of the economic system and views inequality as an exploitative and discriminatory result of the struggle for a limited amount of goods and services in society. It rejects the notion of achievement based on ability as just another form of exploitation; it seeks propor-

---

[90] *The Condition of Education, 1977*, Vol. III, Part I (Washington, D.C.: U.S. Government Printing Office, 1977), Table 5.14, p. 219; Endicott, *Trends in Employment*, 30th, 31st and 32nd Annual Reports.

tional *equality of groups* and endorses preferential treatment of certain groups defined as minorities, if need be at the expense of individuals who belong to groups that are not favored nor permitted special privileges or support from civil rights agencies or federal compliance agencies.

Somewhere between these two viewpoints is the opinion of most people. The debates centering around social stratification and inequality are heated, sometimes quite simplistic and emotional, and involve more political than moral issues.

ACTIVITIES

1. Social mobility is so highly prized in our society that those who do not strive after it are considered to be "dropouts." Study a group of dropouts. What are their ideological disagreements with the rest of society? Analyze how and why they have come to this belief.
2. Have each student list the occupations of his parents and grandparents. Is the student upwardly mobile? Was his father or mother? What effect does a mother's social class have on the mobility of children? What effect does luck have on mobility? What effect does hard work have? Skill? Intellectual ability?
3. Design a society in which inequality would be abolished. Be sure to specify all the kinds of inequality that are to be abolished. What difficulties would be faced in carrying out the program, and what are the chances of success?
4. Organize a debate on the relationship between equity and equality.
5. Invite a guest speaker to explain how the federal government has attempted to promote social mobility and equality. Then, invite a second guest speaker to demonstrate how the government is influenced by wealth and big business.

QUESTIONS

1. What are some of the problems related to defining and measuring the concepts of inequality and equality?
2. Some people who could be upwardly mobile decide not to be. What are some of the reaons for such a decision?
3. Why is it necessary to differentiate intergenerational from intragenerational mobility?
4. Discuss the implications of the statement, "The closer society comes to the idea of equal opportunity, the more it will increase income gaps among people."
5. There appear to be two conflicting goals in American society—excellence and equality. How can any society achieve both goals? What limits must be placed on people in such a society?

SUGGESTED FOR FURTHER READING

Berg, Ivar *Education and Jobs: The Great Training Robbery.* Boston: Beacon Press, 1970.

Carnoy, Martin and Levin, Henry M. *The Limits of Educational Reform.* New York: David McKay & Co., 1976.

Freeman, Richard B. *The Over-Educated American.* New York: Academic Press, 1976.

Gans, Herbert. *More Equality.* New York: Random House, 1974.

Gardner, John. *Excellence: Can We Be Equal Too?* New York: Harper & Row, 1961.

Glazer, Nathan, *Affirmative Discrimination: Ethnic Inequality and Public Policy.* New York: Basic Books, 1975.

Katz, Michael. *Class, Bureaucracy, and the Schools.* New York: Frederick A. Praeger, 1972.

Mosteller, Frederick, and Moynihan, Daniel P. (eds.). *On Equality of Educational Opportunity.* New York: Random House, 1972.

Rawls, John. *A Theory of Justice.* Cambridge, Mass.: Harvard University Press, 1971.

Sewell, William H. and Hauser, Robert M. *Education, Occupation, and Earnings.* New York: Academic Press, 1975.

PART III

TEACHERS

You have had considerable experience with teachers, since you have been going to school for a long time and have had contact with many teachers of all different sorts. Some of your teachers you remember well, others you have forgotten, and still others you would like to forget. Your experience with teaching is based on a number of different teachers who taught you well, badly, or indifferently; teachers whom you liked, disliked, or were indifferent to. You have been on only one side of the desk, however — at least the majority of you have not taught yet, and your perspective on teachers is based on your views as a student. There is much to be learned by sitting on the other side of the desk — the teacher's side. Part III is intended to give you a look of this side and the aspects of education that concern teachers.

Chapter 6 considers two questions: Why teach, and who teaches? A number of related topics are discussed, including reasons for teaching; stereotypes of teachers, past and present; and kinds of people who teach (broken down into such variables as age, sex, race, ethnicity, and education). Two important issues are examined in detail: salary and supply-demand relationships.

What intellectual abilities and personal attributes are required for successful teaching? What behaviors characterize the effective teacher? Surely no one would quarrel with the need to define good teachers. But the problem, as we shall see in Chapter 7, is a complex one, and the more knowledge one has on the subject, the more one realizes the mysteries of unraveling the relationships. For our purposes, the discussion focuses on leadership theory, teacher style, and teacher behavior, and the numerous terms and methods used to measure teacher effectiveness.

For some time now, teachers have expressed their contention that teaching is a profession and have been critical of the failure of society in general, and political and governmental agencies in particular, to grant teachers the conditions and responsibilities appropriate to a profession. Chapter 8 examines teaching in terms of whether it meets the characteristics of a profession, which are outlined early in the discussion. Factors such as teacher status, teacher education, teacher roles (bureaucratic or professional), and teacher organizations are noted.

WHY TEACH,
WHO TEACHES?

This chapter deals with a number of concerns affecting teaching. It should help potential teachers decide whether they want to teach and veteran teachers to become acquainted with some of the trends impacting on their jobs. The first part deals with the basic question of the decision to teach. How do parents and previous experiences with teachers influence the decision? What social and psychological factors are influential? And what about those persistent answers to the question, Why teach? — "Because I don't know what else to do"; "I'll teach until I have a family"; "I love children."

The second part is concerned with teacher stereotypes in our society. Although there is usually some truth in a generalization, stereotypes tend to oversimplify group characteristics; they are distortions and caricatures which have limited validity. As for teachers, existing stereotypes for the most part have not been positive.

A discussion of certain characteristics of teachers follows, dealing with such considerations as age, sex, marital status, and educational levels. The social origins of teachers are also discussed, and it is pointed out that the social origin of teachers is not synonymous with the current social status of teachers.

The fourth and fifth parts of the chapter deal with two major concerns: salaries and supply-demand trends. Most people want to be well informed as to the economic probabilities of their work as they attempt to determine their lifestyles. Past, present, and future teacher compensation and teacher demand are examined in detail. How do today's salaries compare relatively with salaries of teachers during past years? Of course, the salaries themselves have gone up, as in other fields, but how about buying power? Can we be optimistic about the future? In the past it was common for college students to be told, "If you want to be certain of getting a job after graduation, go into teaching—there's always a job there." Again, can we be optimistic about the future? These concerns are pinpointed in the discussion.

THE DECISION TO TEACH

There are many reasons why people choose teaching as a career. One strong motivation for many teachers is their identification with adult models during their childhood—parents and, especially, teachers. Among the 1,066 college seniors surveyed in one noted study, women were found to be influenced by their parents only slightly more than by their teachers in their decisions to become teachers. However, men were influenced by their teachers more than twice as often as their parents.[1] The 230 juniors and seniors in another study rated teachers twice as high as parents in influencing their decisions to teach, and a teacher was mentioned most frequently by male respondents.[2] Both studies indicate that parents often encourage their daughters to become teachers but do not express similar feelings to their sons. Perhaps this is due to the wider range of professional choices for men in the past; also, there is the traditional view that teaching is a respected occupation for women but does not hold similar status for men.[3]

The view that the choice of teaching as a career is based on early psychological factors has also been given attention in the literature. For example, Benjamin Wright and Shirley Tuska contend that teaching is an expression of early yearnings and fantasies.[4] Dan Lortie contends that early teaching models are internalized during childhood and triggered in latter teaching.[5] John Stephens maintains that the act of choosing teaching

---

[1] "Yale-Fairfield Study of Elementary Teaching," in C. S. Brembeck, (ed.), *Social Foundations of Education* (New York: John Wiley & Sons, 1971).

[2] Clarence Fielstra, "Analysis of Factors Influencing the Decision to Become a Teacher," *Journal of Educational Research,* May 1955, pp. 659-67.

[3] Allan C. Ornstein, *Teaching in a New Era* (Champaign, Ill.: Stipes Publishing Co., 1976).

[4] Benjamin D. Wright and Shirley A. Tuska, "From a Dream to Life in the Psychology of Becoming a Teacher," *School Review,* September 1968, pp. 253-93.

[5] Dan C. Lortie, "Observations on Teaching as Work," in R. M. W. Travers (ed.), *Second Handbook of Research on Teaching* (Chicago: Rand McNally & Co., 1973), pp. 474-97.

as a career is rooted in childhood tendencies to talk, correct, prompt others, and moralize; hence, once in front of a classroom, teachers incessantly talk, correct their students or some author long dead, manipulate and socialize their students.[6] Although these three investigations have different theoretical commitments, the implications of their positions are similar; each argues that to a considerable extent the decision to teach is based on experiences which predate formal training and go back to childhood and psychological decisions.

The reason for deciding to teach is likely to be related to sex, age, and level of teaching (elementary or secondary). A breakdown of reasons according to these three variables was done in a National Education Association survey of 1,533 teachers.[7] The desire to work with young people and the value of education to society were the top two reasons given, evenly distributed for both sexes and various age groups. The third most important reason was related to interest in one's subject matter. Predictably, a much larger percentage of secondary than elementary teachers were drawn to teaching because of the subject; it was mentioned by 57 percent of the secondary teachers, compared to 14 percent of the elementary teachers. Almost 20 percent more men than women cited interest in a subject field. The reason of never considering anything else was cited by 10.5 percent of the men but 21 percent of the women. Among the women, 8 percent considered teaching as a second income in the family, compared to only 0.8 percent of the men. Younger teachers (under 40) were more likely to claim to be influenced by a desire to work with young people, interest in the subject, and long vacations. Older teachers (above 40) were influenced more by their families and the need for a second income. It should be noted that more of the older teachers were women, and their response reflects not only a different generation but a sex variable as well.

Most of the reasons cited above for choosing teaching as a career are positive (such as the top reasons reported by the NEA) or neutral (such as family or teacher influence and psychological factors). However, some reasons which may be considered negative or selfish (and which *are* shortsighted) have also been reported in the literature: job security; good pensions; long summer vacations; short work days. Women used to feel teaching was something to do until marriage or an insurance policy in case they wanted or had to work after marrying. The difficulty of preparation in other fields might precipitate a change to education; some college students are undecided what to do in the future, and teaching seems to be

---

[6] John M. Stephens, *The Process of Schooling* (New York: Holt, 1967).

[7] *Status of the American Public School Teacher, 1970–71*, Research Report 1972-R3 (Washington, D.C.: National Education Association, 1972).

a viable option; inability to succeed in other fields might cause a switch in careers; and the need for income while attending graduate school or preparing for another profession might be met by teaching.[8] These negative reasons are only speculative, however, and they are supported mainly by commentary, not by available research.

Teachers, of course, are usually intelligent people and will tend to give socially acceptable answers on surveys. It is likely that pure dedication and love of teaching or children are fables from the past, when the profession was imbued with the image of the schoolmarm and Mr. Chips. Whatever the reasons teachers decide to enter the profession, they are mixed (both positive and negative), and it should not be considered detrimental to admit to selfish reasons. This is established in our society; all physicians are not dedicated to healing the sick, for example, and the priority of some very competent doctors is to make money.

Rarely are the motives or values involved in taking teaching as a career examined in relationship to ethnicity, economic, or geographical trends. Why do certain ethnic groups look more favorably than others upon teaching as a means for upward mobility? How do fluctuations in teacher supply and demand, or beginning teacher salaries relative to other professions, affect the decision to enter teaching? How do population shifts, say from the cities to the suburbs or more recently from the North to the South, relate to teacher entry? The studies to provide this information are lacking; in fact, we know very little about the reasons why different groups of people choose teaching as a career. Different people have different reasons for considering teaching; selection procedures "may even operate," according to Frances Fuller and Oliver Brown, "to favor students motivated [mainly] by expediency."[9]

STEREOTYPES OF TEACHERS

There are approximately 2.5 million teachers in the public and private schools of the United States; they range from 21 to over 65 years of age and come from all social classes, religions, and ethnic groups. Of course, they have some common characteristics as a group (which we will discuss below in greater detail): they average about 35 years of age, two out of three are

---

[8] Elizabeth M. Eddy, *Becoming a Teacher* (New York: Teachers College Press, Columbia University, 1969); Allan C. Ornstein, *Introduction to the Foundations of Education* (Chicago: Rand McNally, 1977); B. O. Smith, *Teachers for the Real World* (Washington, D.C.: American Association of Colleges for Teacher Education, 1969).

[9] Frances F. Fuller and Oliver H. Brown, "Becoming a Teacher," in K. Ryan (ed.), *Teacher Education*. 74th Yearbook of the National Society for the Study of Education, Part II (Chicago: University of Chicago Press, 1975), p. 36.

women, they earn about $13,000 a year, and their family income is about $25,000. Almost all of them have college educations, and they are above average in intelligence. Teaching is the largest profession, and its members run the gamut of human types.

Historically, teachers have not been considered important figures worthy of emulation or heroic portrayal. To some extent this corresponds with our traditional antiintellectual, antischolarly bias.[10] The schoolmaster of colonial times ranked low in status, qualifications were minimal, and bond servants coming to America who were tailors or locksmiths brought higher prices than schoolmasters.[11] At the turn of the 20th century, illiterate ditch diggers or factory workers earned more money than teachers did.

While in Europe many of the liberal and nationalistic revolutions were spearheaded by intellectuals, and their political officials (yesterday and today) have included former teachers and professors, American political leaders have come chiefly from big business and law. Not until the Kennedy era were the "best and brightest" minds recruited on a large scale to serve an American president, and no more than a handful of our local, state, or national political leaders have ever been ex-teachers. The hero in America, according to Dixon Wecter, has never been a teacher or an ex-teacher.[12]

The traditional teacher stereotype we inherited was mainly based on novels and is reinforced by television and the movies. Teachers are often shown as silly, authoritative, rigid, and unmarried, as in Washington Irving's creation of Ichabod Crane, run out of town by the virile men of the community with a pumpkin smashed over his head. The image persists today with J. D. Salinger's character of Old Spencer, the history teacher, dressed in "ratty old clothes" and "picking his nose . . . getting his thumb right in there" while scolding Holden Crawford in *Catcher in the Rye.* The mass media depict professors as in the movie, "The Nutty Professor," starring Jerry Lewis; TV's "Professor Backward"; the cartoon Professor Whimple's "Crossword Zoo"; and Pat Paulsen's "Laugh-In" version.[13]

The authoritarian image of the teacher is illustrated by the school patron in Charles Dickens's *Hard Times;* in the passage below, Gradgin demonstrates his teaching method for a colleague:

---

[10] Richard Hofstadter, *Anti-Intellectualism in American Life* (New York: Alfred A. Knopf, Inc., 1963).

[11] Alma S. Wittlin, "The Teacher," *Daedalus,* Fall 1963, pp. 745–63.

[12] Dixon Wecter, *The Hero in America* (New York: Charles Scribner's Sons, 1941).

[13] George Gerbner, "Teacher Image in Mass Culture: Symbolic Function of the 'Hidden Curriculum,'" in D. R. Olson (ed.), *Media and Symbols: The Forms of Expression, Communication, and Education,* 73rd Yearbook of the National Society for the Study of Education, Part I (Chicago: University of Chicago Press, 1974), pp. 470-97.

219

Now what I want is facts. Teach these boys and girls nothing but facts. Facts alone are wanted in life. Plant nothing else, and root out everything else. You can only form the minds of reasoning animals upon Facts; nothing else will ever be of any service to them. This is the principle on which I bring up my own children, and this is the principle on which I bring up these children. *Stick to facts, sir.* [14]

Rigidity, as well as law and order in the classroom, are persistent themes, overlapping with the authoritarian stereotype. Miss Dove of Frances Gray Patton's *Good Morning, Miss Dove* used the same method for 35 years:

Miss Dove had no moods. Miss Dove was a certainty. She would be today what she had been yesterday and would be tomorrow. And so, within limits, would they. Single file they would enter her room. Each child would pause on the threshold as its mother and father had paused, more than likely, and would say—just as the policeman had said—in distinct formal accents: "Good morning, Miss Dove." And Miss Dove would look directly at each of them, fixing her eyes directly upon theirs, and reply "Good morning, Jessamine," or "Margaret," or "Samuel." (Never "Sam," never "Peggy," never "Jess.") She eschewed familiarity, as she wished others to eschew it. They would go to their appointed desks. Miss Dove would ascend to hers. The lesson would begin. [15]

Not only was Miss Dove cold, conventional, and critical toward her students, she was a poorly dressed, unhappy spinster.

There was nothing elusive about Miss Dove's appearance and it had, moreover, remained much the same for more than 35 years. . . . Her hair was more shadowy than it had once been but, twisted into a meagre little old-maid's knot, it had never had a chance to show much color. Her thin, unpainted mouth bore no sign of those universal emotions—humor, for instance, and love. . . . Her pale, bleached out complexion never flushed with emotion—a slight pinkness at the tip of her pointed nose was the only visible indication that ordinary human blood ran through her veins. . . . All in all, in bearing and clothing and bony structure, Miss Dove suggested that classic portrait of the eternal teacher . . . with nubbins of purloined chalk; a grown-up stranger, catching his first glimpse of her, might be inclined to laugh with a kind of relief, as if he'd seen some old, haunting ogress of his childhood turned into a harmless joke. . . . Even the elevated position of her desk—a position deplored by modern educators who seek to introduce equality into the teacher-student relation—was right and proper. [16]

Love eludes the attractive and eager "Our Miss Brooks," as well as the shy but amiable "Mr. Peepers." Sex degrades the neurotic Miss Brodie in her prime; it destroys Professor Rath of "The Blue Angel." In novels and films, teachers and professors are generally unable to find spouses; if they

---

[14] Charles Dickens, *Hard Times* (New York: E. P. Dutton—Everyman's Library 1967), p. 1.

[15] Frances G. Patton, *Good Morning, Miss Dove* (New York: Dodd, Mead & Co., 1954), p. 8.

[16] Ibid., pp. 19-21.

are married, the marriages are usually atypical or pathological. Theodore Dreiser's character, Donald Moranville Strunk, professor of history, is married to "one of the homeliest women." In "Who's Afraid of Virginia Wolf?" the marriage relationship of two professors is used to illustrate the decline of Western civilization. College students, who should be alert to stereotyping, have characterized the school teacher as a person "who cannot even command an attractive wife [or husband]"[17]

Contemporary television programs and films have presented more positive images of teachers; interestingly, they are almost all males, which may reflect something about Hollywood and the complaints raised by women activists today. James Franciscus played "Mr. Novak" in the mid 1960s, and, more recently, Sidney Poitier in "To Sir With Love," Lloyd Haynes in "Room 222," and Bill Cosby and Gabriel Kaplan as quick-witted teachers propelled teachers into positive role models.

Perhaps the best way to appreciate the changing image of teachers in American society is to note two profiles of the "average" teacher by Myron Brenton. The first one goes back a few decades, when the teacher was thought of as a meek public servant, controlled by autocratic administrators and school board officials, who was dedicated, poorly paid, and usually a female. The second and more recent image is that of a self-determined individual, usually a male (although females still represent the majority of the American teachers), militant, and bent on improving salaries and working conditions.[18]

The first profile was:

. . . decidedly a "she" (for as of a short time [35 years] ago, only 12 percent of the teaching force was composed of men). She was thirty-one years old . . . and had been teaching for a decade. She was not married. Her educational background consisted of from two to four years' worth of college. She earned $1,500 a year.

People generally ascribed a fierce sense of dedication to her, believing that this prompted her to go into the profession. A love for children and a pride in teaching may well have nourished her professional ambitions.[19]

The second profile:

. . . the most distinguishing feature of today's teacher is his militancy. Where's the spinster lady devoted to her boys and girls? Where's the Mr. Chips who used to teach when I was a boy? rhetorically demanded a father (whose son was affected by a teacher strike). The men talk aggressively; the women wear miniskirts. They parade around in front of the schools they've closed, with picket signs. . . .[20]

---

[17] Donald D. O'Down and David C. Beardslee, *College Student Images of a Selected Group of Professions and Occupations,* Cooperative Research Project no. 562 (Washington, D.C.: U.S. Government Printing Office, 1960), p. 14.

[18] Myron Brenton, *What's Happened to Teacher?* (New York: Coward-McCann, 1970).

[19] Ibid., p. 31.

[20] Ibid., p. 117.

Neither image is entirely correct, for teachers represent a multitude of profiles and personalities, but it is correct to say that the stereotype of teachers has undergone a recent change which reflects not only the new mass media portrayal of them but also their increased militancy. Commenting on the success of teacher militancy, Peter Janssen, an educational journalist, put it this way: "Nothing kills the Mr. Chips fantasy faster than a picture of striking teachers being loaded into police vans."[21]

The present image of the teacher presented in the media reflects a happier and healthier fate, a more stable personality, a purposeful and socially meaningful individual. Mass media are the cultural organs of modern society; the pictures they portray extend the institutional order and shape our beliefs and attitudes. The stereotypes they project have almost the same effect, after a while, as reality itself. Fantasy and reality serve as agents of social transformation; media images of schools and teachers and the world they symbolize affect people. And it is the people who pay the salaries of teachers, and their attitudes that in part determine the professional status of teachers.

The traditional images of teachers in American mass culture are those that humiliate and ridicule: failures in love, powerless in life, and rigid. When teachers are portrayed in a negative light, their clients are affected; there is little wonder that American students disrespect their teachers. European students, in contrast, have traditionally experienced positive images of teachers and exhibit great respect for their mentors. Giving teachers a messianic mission or superhuman or noble qualities is not the answer, either. It is only reasonable to expect realistic images of teachers as having both strong and weak qualities, as people who are worthy of being considered human beings — neither fools nor gods.

STATISTICAL GENERALIZATIONS ABOUT TEACHERS

To understand any occupation, we must know the kinds of people who are engaged in performing its functions. This is almost impossible unless accurate data on the social characteristics and backgrounds of members of the occupation are available. The collection of data about teachers' characteristics which are comparable over time is scanty; this is one reason why stereotypes exist about the people who teach. Getting representative data on a national level is difficult, not only because teacher membership is large but also because research-based institutions equipped to do the job have not been interested in obtaining such data in the past. The two

---

[21] Peter Janssen, "The Union Response to Academic Mass Production," *Saturday Review*, October 21, 1967, p. 65.

national groups which do most in the area of data collection about teachers are the National Education Association (NEA) and the U.S. Office of Education (USOE).

The NEA materials provide the most comprehensive data readily available for making statistical generalizations about teachers, but they induce some degree of ambiguity. Their sampling procedures are not of the highest quality; moreover, their personnel surveys have in the past purposely omitted selected items (i.e., race, ethnicity, religion) which were construed as sensitive to analyze and better omitted. Their presentations of the data are usually based on one set of variables and occasional use of another, without assessing multiple variables or interaction factors on a particular question or characteristic.

Although the USOE has produced statistical information on education since the turn of the 20th century, their data gathering information on teacher characteristics has been based, at least in the past, on NEA sources. Only very recently — with the passage of the 1965 Elementary and Secondary School Act and the 1967 Education Professions Development Act, and the affirmative action guidelines of the 1970s — have the researchers of the USOE set out to study and interpret their own questions related to the social characteristics and backgrounds of teachers.

Nevertheless, we can make some statistical generalizations about teachers — bearing in mind, of course, that we are dealing with means and medians, which must be approached with caution.

Number of Teachers

There were 2.7 million professional persons employed in public and private elementary and secondary day schools in the 1975-76 school year.

Table 6.1 / Estimated Number of Classroom Teachers in Elementary and Secondary Schools, 1965-1985 (in thousands)

Teaching Positions	1965	1975	1985
Total classroom teachers[a]	1,933	2,463	2,484
Elementary	1,112	1,354	1,498
Secondary	822	1,109	986
Public classroom teachers	1,710	2,203	2,188
Elementary	965	1,183	1,299
Secondary	746	1,019	889
Nonpublic classroom teachers	223	261	296
Elementary	147	171	199
Secondary	76	90	97

[a] The total number of teachers gradually increased to 2.475 million in 1976; thereafter, projections show slight decreases in the number each year until 1983; then there may be a slight turn about.

Source: *Projections of Education Statistics to 1985-86* (Washington, D.C.: U.S. Government Printing Office, 1975), Table 22, p. 48.

These included principals, supervisors, auxiliary personnel (i.e., librarians, guidance and psychological personnel) and classroom teachers. Of the total, 90 percent were classroom teachers.

As shown in Table 6.1, the total number of classroom teachers has increased from 1.9 million in 1965 to 2.5 million in 1975. The number of classroom teachers in public elementary schools increased from 965,000 in 1965 to 1.2 million in 1975, primarily as a result of decreased student-teacher ratios, from 27.6:1 in 1965 to 21.7:1 in 1975. Although enrollments in public elementary schools are expected to decrease by nearly 2 million students by 1980 (from 30.5 million to 27.8 million) corresponding decreases in student-teacher ratios are expected to offset enrollment decreases, and as a result the 1975 level of 1.2 million teachers will be maintained through 1980. By 1985, the student-teacher ratio is expected to have decreased to 19.4, which along with slightly increased enrollments, will account for an increase of 100,000 teachers (to a total of 1.3 million) in public elementary schools.[22]

The number of classroom teachers in public secondary schools increased from 746,000 in 1965 to 1 million in 1975 as a result of increasing student enrollments (15.5 million in 1965 compared to 19.2 million in 1975) as well as reductions in student-teacher ratios (from 20.8 in 1965 to 18.8 in 1975). Sharp enrollment drops are expected in the late 1970s and early 1980s, reflecting a trend which has affected elementary enrollments since the early 1970s and which started to affect the secondary schools in 1977; these enrollment trends will be too large to be offset by decreasing student-teacher ratios. As a result, the expected number of public secondary school teachers for 1985 is 889,000, or 110,000 fewer than in 1975.[23]

Catholic school student enrollments and teacher positions made up about 90 percent of the nonpublic school figures in 1965 and 75 percent in 1975; it is expected they will comprise 65 percent of the nonpublic figures by 1985. The number of classroom teachers in nonpublic elementary schools slightly increased, from 147,000 in 1965 to 171,000 in 1975, even though school enrollments in nonpublic schools decreased by 1 million, from 4.9 to 3.9 million students. The large decreases in enrollment were offset by a sharper reduction in student-teacher ratios, from 33.5:1 in 1965 to 22.8:1 in 1975. It is expected that both enrollments and student-teacher ratios will continue to decrease, resulting in a relative stability of the number of teachers in nonpublic elementary schools. The number of classroom teachers in nonpublic secondary school increased from 76,000 to

---

[22] *Projections of Educational Statistics to 1985–86* (Washington, D.C.: U.S. Government Printing Office, 1975), Table 4, p. 15; Table 22, p. 48; Table 23, p. 49.

[23] Ibid.

90,000 during 1965–75 and is expected to increase to 97,000 by 1985, as a result of stable enrollments and small reductions in student-teacher ratio.[24]

In interpreting the data in Table 6.1, it is important to remember that teacher trends, in both public and nonpublic institutions, are in part based on the assumption that student-teacher ratios will continue to decrease. While there is pressure among teacher organizations to sustain this decline, persistent financial and budgetary problems among school districts across the country may cause a leveling off or even a reversal in student-teacher ratios. It must also be kept in mind that schools are being squeezed by increasing costs of energy and supplies; between 1972 and 1975, heating oil rose 150 percent, paper products and supplies 100–250 percent, and milk by 100–125 percent. At the same time, there is public demand to freeze the amounts of local property taxes which can be levied to pay for these costs. Something must be trimmed in school budgets, and one of the easiest things is to increase classroom size, since 60 to 75 percent of the past budget has been related to salaries, and the research on the relationship of classroom size to student achievement is at best mixed. If inflationary trends continue, the original projections of classroom size and therefore of classroom teachers for 1985 will probably be modified; we can expect up to 10 percent fewer teaching positions.[25]

Age, Sex, Marital Status, and Academic Attainment of Teachers

The NEA has conducted several similar surveys over the past 25 years. When the data for the 1960–61 and 1975–76 school years are compared, the following trends emerge.[26] In 1976 the typical teacher was younger than in 1961 ((33 as compared with 41), and median years of teaching experience also declined (8 years in 1976 versus 11 years in 1961). Teachers in 1976 tended to be better educated than previously; only 1 percent did not hold bachelor's degrees, compared to 15 percent in 1961. As many as 37 percent held master's degrees or equivalent in 1976, up 14 percent from 1961. Men continued to have superior qualifications compared to women, but women have improved their credentials greatly over the past ten years, showing a large increase in bachelor's degrees and a small increase in master's degrees. For example, in 1961, 4 percent of the men and 19

---

[24] Ibid., *U.S. Catholic Schools, 1975–76* (Washington, D.C.: National Catholic Education Association, 1976).

[25] Ornstein, *Teaching in a New Era.*

[26] *Status of American Public School Teacher, 1970–71*, Table B, p. 9; Table 1, p. 12; Table 5, p. 15; Table 40, p. 63; *Highlights of Status of Public School Teachers, 1975–76* (Washington, D.C.: National Education Association, 1976), pp. 1–3.

Figure 6.1 / Selected Characteristics of Public Elementary and Secondary School Teachers, 1976

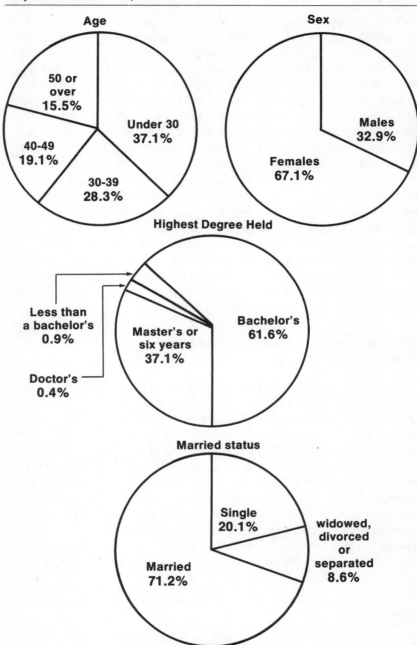

Age

50 or over 15.5%

Under 30 37.1%

40-49 19.1%

30-39 28.3%

Sex

Males 32.9%

Females 67.1%

Highest Degree Held

Less than a bachelor's 0.9%

Doctor's 0.4%

Master's or six years 37.1%

Bachelor's 61.6%

Married status

Single 20.1%

widowed, divorced or separated 8.6%

Married 71.2%

Source: *Highlights of Status of Public School Teachers, 1975–76* (Washington, D.C.: National Education Association, 1976), pp. 1–3; *Status of the American Public School Teacher, 1975–76* (Washington, D.C.: National Education Association, 1976), p. 49.

percent of the women held less than bachelor's degrees, while 40 percent of the men and 15.5 percent of the women held master's degrees. By 1976, only 0.5 percent of the men and 1.5 percent of the women lacked bachelor's degrees, and 45 percent of the men and 20 percent of the women held master's degrees.

Male teachers accounted for 33 percent of the total teachers in 1976 but only 31 percent in 1961. Women comprised 64 percent of the elementary teaching force in 1976 and only 33 percent of the secondary teaching force. In 1961, 67 percent of the teaching force were married, compared to 71 percent in 1976. That year, 8 percent of the men teachers and 24 percent of women teachers were single, divorced, or widowed.

It should be kept in mind that the 1960-61 and 1975-76 figures are based upon sample surveys and therefore are subject to the usual sampling variability. Some of the highlights of the 1976 selected characteristics (males and females combined) are shown in pictorial form in Figure 6.1.

Social Class Origins of Teachers

Prior to the 1920s, teachers were generally recruited from middle-class families, and relative to the rest of the American population, they were better educated. In those years, although teachers were poorly paid, teaching was considered one of the few occupations available to respectable and educated women. As the schoolmaster was replaced by the schoolma'am, an increasing number of middle-class and even upper-middle-class teachers entered the profession.

When more job opportunities became available to women in the 1930s and 1940s, due primarily to work-force shortages during World War II, the social composition of the teaching profession changed as more teachers were recruited from lower-class and working-class backgrounds. By 1939 the American teacher could be described as being predominantly lower-middle class in origin.[27] Two years later, Florence Greenhoe reported results of a national survey of more than 9,000 teachers which showed their fathers' occupations were 38 percent farmers, 26 percent small businessmen, 18 percent laborers, and only 4 percent professionals.[28] From his 1944 studies of "Home Town," "Yankee City," and "Old City" and his 1949 study of "Jonesville," Lloyd Warner and his associates concluded that the great majority of teachers across the country had come from lower-middle-class families, and only a small proportion were of upper-middle-class origin. However, Warner pointed out that teachers had come to be

---

[27] Willard S. Elsbree, *The American Teacher* (New York: American Book Co., 1939).

[28] Florence Greenhoe, *Community Contacts and Participation of Teachers* (Washington, D.C.: American Council on Public Affairs, 1941).

Table 6.2 / Father's Occupation of Chicago Public School Teachers, 1964

| | Percentage of Teachers | |
Occupation of Teacher's Father	Elementary	Secondary
Semiskilled and unskilled	17%	14%
Farm laborer	1	1
Skilled worker	31	27
Farm owner	3	4
Clerical or small business	22	23
Professional or managerial	26	31
	n = 5,150	n = 2,373

Source: Adapted from Robert J. Havighurst, *The Public Schools of Chicago* (Chicago: Board of Education of the City of Chicago, 1964), pp. 417–18.

Table 6.3 / Ethnic Composition of Teachers, 1974

Ethnic Group	Percent Distribution of Teachers
White	87.9%
Black......................	10.0
Spanish	1.4
Asian......................	0.4
Indian	0.2
Other.....................	0.1
Total	100%

Source: *The Condition of Education, 1977*, vol. 3, Part I (Washington, D.C.: U.S. Government Printing Office, 1977), Table 2.12, p. 168.

identified as middle class and were enforcing such values in the schools.[29] Ten years later Wilbur Brookover also concluded that teachers had come from working-class and lower-middle-class backgrounds but had become members of the middle class who emphasized school attendance, punctuality, honesty, responsibility, respect for property, and strict sex codes — in short, the values of middle-class America.[30] This teacher orientation was, to be sure, at the expense of lower-class children whose lifestyles and culture often conflicted with such ideals. In the 1950s and 1960s studies of prospective as well as experienced teachers continued to show that a majority came from lower-middle-class families,[31] but high-ranking school

[29] W. Lloyd Warner, Robert J. Havighurst, and Martin B. Loeb, *Who Shall Be Educated?* (New York: Harper & Row, 1944); W. Lloyd Warner et al., *Democracy in Jonesville* (New York: Harper & Row, 1949).

[30] Wilbur B. Brookover, *A Sociology of Education* (New York: American Book Co., 1955).

[31] W. W. Charters, "Social Class Analysis and the Control of Public Education," *Harvard Educational Review,* Fall 1953, pp. 268–83; Robert J. Havighurst, *The Public Schools of Chicago; A Survey for the Board of Education of the City of Chicago* (Chicago: Board of Education of the City of Chicago, 1964).

administrators and school board members were selected from upper-middle-class backgrounds.[32]

In recent years the heterogeneity of social backgrounds of teachers has continued to increase. On a national basis, the most pronounced change was between 1961 and 1971: the number of teachers from farm families decreased, from 27 to 19 percent, and the number of teachers from unskilled, semiskilled, and skilled workers (i.e., blue-collar families) increased, from 37 to 46 percent. These changes are accentuated by age differences; older teachers who will soon retire came predominantly from rural backgrounds and younger teachers predominantly from urban, blue-collar backgrounds.[33] Studies of teachers' fathers' occupations in large city school systems, such as Chicago, Pittsburgh, and Kansas City, Missouri, showed even greater proportions of teachers from working-class backgrounds.[34] For example, the listings of fathers' occupations of teachers in Chicago in 1964 in Table 6.2 indicate that 4 percent came from farms, while 48 percent came from working-class families.

Ethnic Factors among Teachers. Traditionally, teaching was a means of upward mobility for the sons and daughters of white ethnics during the first half of the 20th century. Irish, Germans, and Swedes became teachers in large numbers in the early 1900s, especially in cities. People with names suggesting Anglo-Saxon and Protestant backgrounds then comprised (and still make up today) the bulk of the teaching profession in smaller school systems. Jews, Poles, Italians, and Greeks came into the city school systems in large numbers between 1920 and 1950. Since World War II there has been a substantial increase of Asian American teachers, especially Japanese and Chinese, in western and far western cities. Teachers of Spanish-speaking ancestry are just beginning to enter the profession in sizable numbers in the urban centers of Florida, New York, Illinois, Texas, Arizona, and California. Nationwide, as shown in Table 6.3, they represent only 1.4 percent of the teacher population.

The position of black teachers is somewhat different from teachers of other ethnic groups. Before 1954 they taught in segregated school systems in the South, representing a large group of teachers in all-black schools. There were fewer black teachers in the North, and the majority of blacks

---

[32] Charters, "Social Class Analysis and Control of Public Education"; Robert L. Crain, *The Politics of School Desegregation* (Chicago: Aldine Publishing Co., 1968); Patricia C. Sexton, *Education and Income* (New York: Viking Press, 1961).

[33] *Status of American Public School Teacher, 1970–71*, Table 39, p. 61.

[34] Patricia J. Doyle, "The Pittsburgh Public Schools," in *Social Planning in Pittsburgh: A Preliminary Appraisal* (Kansas City, Mo.: Institute for Community Studies, 1969), pp. 93–110; Havighurst, *Public Schools of Chicago;* Robert J. Havighurst and Daniel U. Levine, *Education in Metropolitan Schools,* 2nd ed. (Boston: Allyn & Bacon, 1971).

who taught in these schools were (and still are) in inner-city or predominantly black schools.

While civil service occupations have always been a source of upward mobility for black persons, this has especially been true for teaching as a career. In 1974 blacks comprised 5.5 percent of the college-educated populace but 10 percent of the teacher population.[35] With the rise of the black power and community control movements, there has been a substantial increase in the number of black teachers in urban areas. By the mid-1970s, many large and medium-sized city school systems (i.e., Chicago, Cincinnati, Cleveland, Detroit, Gary, Kansas City (Mo.), Memphis, Philadelphia, Newark, St. Louis, Washington, D.C.) had close to 50 percent (or more) black teaching personnel.[36] The sharp increase in the number of black teachers in the cities also coincides with the elimination of verbally oriented written and standardized tests for teacher preparation, on which blacks traditionally have scored lower as a group than other ethnic groups with earlier middle-class origins and better communication skills. Today these tests have been labeled as culturally biased and an instrument designed to exclude blacks and other minorities from the system, but their advocates have defended them as providing a means for employment on the basis of merit and academic ability. They contend the elimination of such tests introduces a subjective and political element into hiring, which civil service examinations had attempted to eliminate.[37]

In a depressed job market, the conflict over teaching jobs is intensified and ethnic consciousness surfaces. Many of the Jewish teachers in New York City, the Irish teachers in Boston and Chicago, the Polish teachers in Baltimore, Buffalo, and Detroit, and the Italian teachers in Newark and Camden, New Jersey, feel threatened by the recent gains made by blacks and the more recent gains by Spanish-speaking groups in the teaching profession. Emotions increase as one group replaces another. The question arises: How are we to provide jobs for displaced groups and yet curtail group confrontations and ethnocentrism? The problem is apparent not only in the teaching profession but for all municipal workers and professions in the cities today. While depolarization on social and economic issues is urged, the current trends are for a resurgence of ethnic

[35] *Statistical Abstract of the United States, 1976* (Washington, D.C.: U.S. Government Printing Office, 1977), Table 198, p. 123; also see Table 6.3 in this chapter.

[36] Allan C. Ornstein. *Race and Politics in School/Community Organizations.* (Pacific Palisades, Ca.: Goodyear Publishing Co., 1974).

[37] Jerome E. Doppelt and George K. Bennett. "Testing Job Applicants from Disadvantaged Groups," *Testing Service Bulletin,* no. 57 (New York: Psychological Corporation, 1967); Paul Kurtz, "The Principle of Equality and Some Dogmas of Environmentalism," *Humanist,* March 1972, pp. 4-6.

tribalism and sometimes increasing hostility between black, brown, and white teachers, as it is for jobs in general.

SALARIES OF TEACHERS

A large part of current expenditures for public elementary and secondary schools is for salaries of instructional staff; it amounted to nearly 65 percent in 1976–77. The average annual salary for teachers increased from $6,830 in 1966–67 to $13,235 per year in 1976–77, as shown in Table 6.4. Using 1966 as a base year, this represented an annual in-

Table 6.4 / Average Annual Salaries of Public School Teachers, 1966–67 to 1976–77

School Year	Average Salary	Percentage Increase
1966–67	$ 6,830	
1967–68	7,432	8.7%
1968–69	7,952	7.1
1969–70	8,635	8.6
1970–71	9,269	7.3
1971–72	9,706	4.7
1972–73	10,164	4.7
1973–74	10,673	5.0
1974–75	11,595	8.6
1975–76	12,448	6.8
1976–77	13,235	6.3

Average annual salary increase $640
Average annual percent increase 6.8%

Source: *Digest of Educational Statistics, 1974* (Washington, D.C.: U.S. Government Printing Office, 1975), Table 56, p. 49; *Fall 1976 Statistics of Public Schools: Advance Report* (Washington, D.C.: U.S. Government Printing Office, 1976), Table 3, p. 7; *Statistics of Public Elementary and Secondary Schools, Fall 1975* (Washington, D.C.: U.S. Government Printing Office, 1976), Table 11, p. 36.

Table 6.5 / Projected Average Annual Salaries of Public School Teachers, 1977–78 to 1986–87

School Year	Expected Average Salary
1977–78	$14,124
1978–79	15,084
1979–80	16,109
1980–81	17,204
1981–82	18,373
1982–83	19,622
1983–84	20,956
1984–85	23,381
1985–86	23,902
1986–87	25,527

crease of $640, or an average percentage increase of 6.8. The consumer price index rose approximately 5.5 percent during this ten-year period, with the greatest increase being experienced in 1973–75. Thus teachers made real gains of only 1.3 percent in their salaries, but the average worker lost approximately 2 to 3 percent in real income during the same ten-year period.

Projected average annual salaries of public elementary and secondary teachers are shown in Table 6.5. The calculations are based on the average annual salary increase projected as a continuation of the 1966–67 to 1976–77 trend: $13,235 + 6.8\% \ t$, where $t =$ time in years. These

Table 6.6 / Average Salaries of Teachers by Regions and States, 1976–77

Region and State	Average Salary	Region and State	Average Salary
New England..............	$11,355	Plains...................	11,144
Connecticut	N.R.	Iowa..................	12,533
Maine..................	10,724	Kansas...............	11,769
Massachusetts..........	N.R.	Minnesota.............	N.R.
New Hampshire	10,250	Nebraska..............	11,172
Rhode Island...........	14,420	North Dakota...........	10,063
Vermont................	10,028	South Dakota	10,183
Middle Atlantic..........	14,920	Southwest................	11,949
Delaware	13,170	Arizona.................	13,743
District of Columbia......	16,460	New Mexico	12,032
Maryland	14,689	Oklahoma	10,480
New Jersey	14,500	Texas	11,542
New York...............	17,100	Rocky Mountain	11,782
Pennsylvania...........	13,600	Colorado	N.R.
Southeast	10,756	Idaho	10,987
Alabama...............	10,600	Montana...............	N.R.
Arkansas	9,733	Utah	12,170
Florida	10,811	Wyoming..............	12,190
Georgia	N.R.	Far West	14,694
Kentucky	10,950	California..............	16,500
Louisiana..............	11,092	Nevada................	13,415
Mississippi	9,397	Oregon................	13,500
North Carolina	12,034	Washington............	15,361
South Carolina	10,391	Alaska	21,020
Tennessee.............	11,120	Hawaii	17,192
West Virginia...........	11,436	United States	13,235
Great Lakes..............	13,848		
Illinois	14,656		
Indiana................	11,967		
Michigan	16,269		
Ohio	12,500		
Wisconsin	N.R.		

N.R. = no report.
Source: Adapted from *Fall 1976 Statistics of Public Schools*, Table 3, p. 9.

projected gains ignore the possibility of inflation and the effects inflation has on salary demands, and they assume that student teacher ratios will remain constant and that public sentiment toward educational spending and teachers in general will not drastically change (for it is the public's local property taxes that largely determine how much is spent on education and how much is devoted to teacher salaries). Therefore the projections are not exact, but they suggest that in 1986–87 the average teacher salary will be $25,527.

There are regional differences in compensation. In 1976–77, when the average teacher salary was $13,235, the best place to teach, as far as money is concerned, was in the MidAtlantic region, where the average salary was $14,920, or in the Far West (not including Alaska or Hawaii), where it was $14,694. The Great Lakes area ($13,848) comes closest to the average, and the Southeast ($10,756) and New England ($11,355) were the lowest paid areas. The difference between the lowest paid and highest paid regions was $4,164. These data are indicated in Table 6.6. Of course, comparative living costs must also be considered. The states in the MidAtlantic and Far West are the most expensive regions in which to live, while the South (with the exception of a few cities such as Atlanta and Daytona, Miami, and Orlando, Florida), is the least expensive.

Salary differences among states are also wide, ranging from $9,397 for Mississippi to $21,020 for Alaska (Alaska and Hawaii have the highest cost-of-living indices). In addition to Hawaii, four states (New York, California, District of Columbia, and Michigan) also reported average

Table 6.7 / Mean Starting Salaries for College Graduates with Bachelor's Degrees in Four Selected Fields Compared with Teaching, 1965–1977

Field	Class of			
	1965	1970	1975	1977
Engineering	$ 7,584	$10,476	$12,744	$14,904
	(54%)	(53%)	(45%)	(55%)
Accounting	6,732	10,080	11,888	12,804
	(37%)	(47%)	(35%)	(33%)
Sales and marketing	6,276	8,580	10,344	11,640
	(27%)	(25%)	(18%)	(21%)
Business administration	6,240	8,124	9,768	10,644
	(26%)	(19%)	(11%)	(11%)
Teaching.	4,925	6,850	8,768	9,618*

Note: Figures in parentheses represent percent difference or gap between what teachers and other beginners are paid.

* 1977 mean beginning teaching salary has been estimated, based on extrapolation from NEA data.

Source: Frank S. Endicott, *Trends in Employment of College and University Graduates in Business and Industry*, Annual Reports (Evanston, Ill.: Northwestern University, 1965, 1970, 1975, 1977); *Salary Schedules, 1975–76*, NEA Research Memo A-35, July 1976, Table 5, p. 6.

233

salaries in excess of $16,000. In four states (Arkansas, Vermont, and North and South Dakota) the average salary was only about $10,000.[38]

Salary differences are great within states, too, especially where the mean state pay scales are high. For example, in California maximum salaries in 1976–77 ranged from over $23,500 in Beverly Hills, Kern, and San Mateo to as low as $17,500 in Bakersfield, Barstow, and San Juan. In Southern states, where the mean salaries are low, the range is narrower but there are still considerable differences. In Tennessee, for example, if a teacher put roots down in Franklin County, the maximum salary was $13,060, while a teacher in Nashville could earn up to $18,300.[39]

A good yardstick of the economic position of an occupational group is to compare its salaries with those of other groups of workers having similar years of education. Table 6.7 shows that beginning teacher salaries at the bachelor's level have consistently been lower than the beginning salaries for four other occupational groups usually entered, like teaching, at the bachelor's level. The figures in percentages indicate the difference between what beginning teachers are paid and entry-level salaries in engineering, accounting, marketing, and business. The data show that while the gap between teacher salaries and each of the four other occupations declined between 1965 and 1975, it began to widen after 1975 — due probably to teacher supply and demand and school budget problems. In any case, beginning teachers are not paid as much as other workers in business and engineering, and the gap widens when such variables as graduate education and experience are taken into account.

Table 6.8 / Average Salaries of Teachers by Educational Preparation, 1965–66 and 1975–76

Educational Preparation	Salary 1965–66	Salary 1975–76
Bachelor's degree		
Minimum average	$4,925	$ 8,768
Maximum average	7,262	12,883
Master's level		
Minimum average	5,350	9,797
Maximum average	8,167	15,166
Doctor's level		
Minimum average	6,057	11,413
Maximum average	9,452	17,846

Source: Adapted from "Salary Schedules, 1975–76," Table 2, p. 3; Table 5, p. 6.

[38] *Fall 1976 Statistics of Public Schools, Advance Report* (Washington, D.C.: U.S. Government Printing Office, 1977), p. 9.

[39] *Survey of Teachers' Salaries, 1976–77, Advance Report* (Washington, D.C.: American Federation of Teachers, 1977).

The above average salaries do not reveal differences between the beginning teacher salary and that of the experienced teacher who usually holds a graduate degree. As shown in Table 6.8, the average salary for the beginning teacher with a bachelor's degree in 1975-76 was $8,768, up almost 80 percent from 1965-66. The teacher with a doctor's degree and sufficient experience to reach the maximum level in a school system earned an average salary of $17,846 in 1975-76, up slightly more than 80 percent from 1965-66. These figures are averages for the nation. The actual range in beginning salaries with the bachelor's degree in 1975-76 was a low of $7,000 and a high of $14,300. Salaries with the doctor's degree ranged from as low as $10,290 in poor school systems to as high as $28,000.[40]

Salary Issues

At present, teachers are usually paid on the basis of their experience and education. They move along a salary schedule according to prescribed levels, and eventually they reach a maximum salary. A question arises whether teachers should be paid on the basis of a uniform salary schedule, compensated solely on the basis of experience and education, or rewarded at least partially on the basis of merit.

Teachers will generally admit that they all do not possess the same abilities or strengths, but they tend to reject the idea of "merit" based on judgments of teacher effectiveness. As long as it is not possible to judge, on the basis of valid empirical evidence, what teacher excellence consists of, there is no solid foundation for merit pay. Moreover, it is argued that merit salaries could open a can of worms; the political, ethnic, and subjective factors that would emerge could lead to hostilities among teachers. Also, the idea of merit pay for superior performance could be used in reverse to penalize poor performance; this is already apparent in the trend to holding teachers accountable for outcomes, which is in part based on a negative assumption that teachers are not doing a good job and should be responsible for student learning.

Teaching fares well in the debate over sex equality and equal pay for equal work; female teachers generally now earn as much as male teachers in comparable positions. However, secondary school teachers earn approximately $1,200 more than elementary school teachers, and, as indicated above, a larger percentage of men than women teach at the secondary level. Thus a salary difference exists by level of teaching which indirectly leads to differing salary scales by sex. The argument for higher compensation for secondary school teachers is based on their need for more

---

[40] "Salary Schedules, 1975-76," *NEA Research Memo* A-35, July 1976, Table 4, p. 5.

preparatory study and higher qualifications, plus the traditional attitude that high school education is more important than elementary school education. Recent opinion, however, is that elementary school teaching is the more important, since it reaches children at an earlier age when they are more malleable, and future school success is built on their elementary education.

Another issue dealing with sex and salaries is that, of the 2.5 million persons employed as public school teachers, more than 1.5 million are women. Where the teacher is a married woman (76 percent of women teachers are married),[41] it can be assumed their spouses earn similar or higher salaries, and their combined salaries are likely to put these families in the top 5 percentile in the country, those having annual incomes of $30,000 or more. The salaries of married women teachers amounts to less than 50 percent of their family income, as opposed to married males (whose wives often are not working or are earning less on other jobs), whose salaries represent 75 percent of family income. These male-female differences are further evidenced by the fact that more than 60 percent of the male teachers supplement their salaries with part-time or summer work, as opposed to 20 percent of their female counterparts.[42] Thus in general male teachers feel greater pressures to support families and their family income is less than that of their female counterparts.

Teacher salaries rank at the top 5 percent of salaries paid working women,[43] in part because women have not had as many opportunities to advance in other fields. Thus the net gains in salaries have been more impressive for women than for men teachers. Similarly there is more status for women than for men in teaching. Parents express more satisfaction that their daughters are teachers than that their sons are, and women teachers are more satisfied than men are. If given the choice to make again, there is a 51 percent chance that *she* would certainly become a teacher, while there is a 33 percent chance that *he* would do so.[44]

Then there is the issue of future salaries for teachers. In an era of inflationary school costs, reduced student enrollments, and new research which purports to show that schools do not make much difference with

---

[41] *Condition of Education, 1977*, vol. 3, Part I (Washington, D.C.: U.S. Government Printing Office, 1977), Figure 2.08, p. 35; *Highlights of Status of Public School Teachers, 1975–76*, p. 3.

[42] *The New York Times* August 5, 1973, Sect. 3, p. 7; *Status of the American Public School Teacher, 1970–71*, Table 42, p. 65, p. 91; Appendix C. pp. 157, 198–204, 216.

[43] John K. Galbraith, *Economics and the Public Policy* (Boston: Houghton Mifflin Co., 1973). *Income in 1971 of Families and Persons in the United States*, Current Population Reports Series P-60, no. 85, reports that the 1971 male median salary was $9,399, compared to $5,593 for women. The male teacher median salary was $9,913; for female teachers it was $8,126.

[44] *Status of the American Public School Teacher, 1970–71*, Appendix C, p. 224.

regard to student learning, the budget squeeze has come to American schools, just about everywhere. Moreover, the general attitude at the local, state, and federal governmental levels is to avoid deficit spending and cut nonessential items in educational (and social) spending. In the school year 1976–77, for example, more than 50 percent of attempts to increase property taxes (which are mainly earmarked to pay for schooling) were rejected by local voters. Moreover, there is an oversupply of teachers, and the use of paraprofessionals in professional teaching roles is increasing.

All these trends put teachers on the defensive as we move toward the 1980s. As the public realizes that most educational spending is for salaries, jobs will be eliminated, classroom size will be increased, and raises will be at a minimum. The cuts that are made will be in response to apparent public pressure, which is increasing. To what extent people will place a higher value on education for their children than on their concern for rising school taxes is difficult to gauge.

Concern for these issues has been expressed by teachers and teacher organizations. Albert Shanker, president of the American Federation of Teachers, warns that what happened in New York City in the school year 1975–76 may happen across the country: Thousands of teachers were cut from the payrolls, classroom sizes were increased, and teachers gave up preparation time and free periods in order to pay for their salary raises.[45] The handwriting is on the wall. The gains made by teachers in the past will be at stake; striking teachers will be forced to hold the line, while trying to keep up with the cost of living. Kai Erickson, associate executive secretary of the Michigan Education Association (the state affiliate of the NEA), has mapped out a short- and long-range strategy to avoid the salary crunch.[46] It includes: (1) securing state unemployment benefits for teachers (only eight states currently provide such benefits for out-of-work teachers), (2) mounting a concerted effort to convince the public of the value of education as well as of smaller class size, (3) suing in the courts for increased educational funding and school budgets, (4) negotiating tax-free fringe benefits and cost-of-living adjustments for teachers, (5) increasing teacher retirement benefits and permitting early retirement without penalty or reduced costs, (6) reexamining the salaries of teachers and considering a $50,000-a-year master teacher contract, and (7) developing political coalitions with interest groups which will help teachers obtain such benefits.

While it is comforting to think that things will get better soon, the trends

---

[45] *The New York Times* September 21, 1975, Sect. 4, p. 6.

[46] Kai L. Erickson, "Some Suggestions to Soften a Somber Economic Picture for Teachers," *Phi Delta Kappan*, March 1975, p. 473.

indicate this is not going to happen. Few people see a bright light at the end of the tunnel in the 1980s. Whether the above proposals will be seriously considered is difficult to say; nevertheless, teachers may be faced with a serious economic and salary crisis which may continue through the

Figure 6.2 / Range of Excess Teacher Supply, Projections for 1980–81

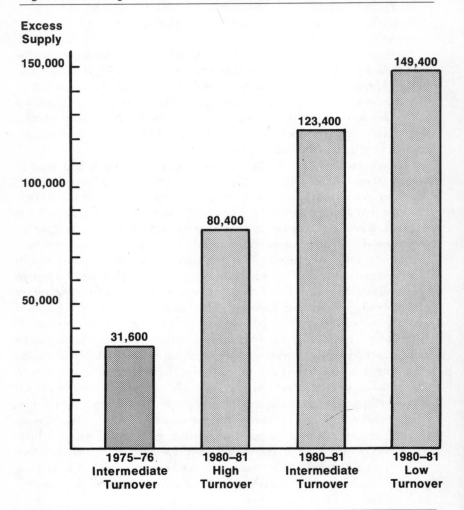

Note: Projections are based on 1975–76 data in which the HEW report contended there were some 31,600 excess teachers; this figure is considered low by most authorities, who report excesses between 60,000 and 100,000 for that school year. The fact that the base figure is low means that the projected figures between 80,400 and 149,400 are low, too.

Source: *Projections of Teacher Supply and Demand to 1980–81* (Washington, D.C.: U.S. Government Printing Office, 1976), Figure 1, p. 3.

1980s. Furthermore, the supply-demand curve is going to add to their difficulties.

SUPPLY AND DEMAND OF TEACHERS

From 1970 on, in school systems across the country, and especially in the large cities, several thousand young college graduates who took the National Teacher Examination (or a local school system test), with what they interpreted as a promise of jobs, found themselves on waiting lists without immediate job prospects. The situation has worsened each year, reflecting the increased supply of graduates desiring to enter the profession and the shrinking number of job openings.

In 1968 the demand for teachers exceeded the supply by approximately 2,000 positions. This was to be the last year teachers were to experience a favorable job market. The next year it was reported that there were 1,600 "excess" beginning teachers; thereafter, the annual "oversupply" of teachers has been steadily increasing. By 1975, the number of "surplus" beginning teachers was between 30,000 and 80,000, depending on which survey you were reading,[47] with several additional thousands of graduates no longer even applying for jobs. By the end of the decade there may have accumulated between 80,000 and 400,000 or more graduates who are qualified to teach and unable to find jobs.[48] These estimates usually take into consideration three basic sources of the *demand* for teachers: (1) changes in student enrollment, (2) changes in the ratio of teachers to students, and (3) teacher turnover, as well as two basic sources of teacher *supply:* (1) recent graduates eligible to teach for the first time, and (2) the reentry pool of teachers.

One of the lowest estimates of excess teachers is that of the Department of Health, Education, and Welfare. These estimates are projected up to school year 1980–81 and are shown in Figure 6.2 to range between 80,400 (based on a high rate of teacher turnover) to 149,000 (based on a low rate of teacher turnover), with an intermediate projection of 123,400 (based on an intermediate rate of teacher turnover). Remember, these are probably the lowest estimates of teacher oversupply; some go as high as 400,000, or even higher.

If the figure of 400,000 excess teachers appears gloomy, then consider

---

[47] *Condition of Education, 1977,* Table 2.09, p. 166; *Projections of Teacher Supply and Demand to 1980–81* (Washington, D.C.: U.S. Government Printing Office, 1976), p. 3.

[48] James Montgomery et al., "The Teacher Surplus: Facing the Facts," *Phi Delta Kappan,* May 1973, p. 627; *Projections of Teacher Supply and Demand to 1980–81,* pp. 2–3; Cyril G. Sargent, "Fewer Pupils, Surplus Space: The Problem of School Shrinkage," *Phi Delta Kappan,* January 1975, pp. 352–57.

Table 6.9 / Demand for New Teachers, 1970–1985

	Students Earning Bachelor's Degree in Education	Demand for New Teachers	Demand Filled by Reentering Teachers[a]
1970	176,000[b]		
1971	191,000	131,000	19,650
1972	194,000	164,000	24,600
1973	185,000	161,000	24,150
1974	167,000	155,000	23,250
1975	162,000	167,000	25,050
	(898,000)	(778,000)	(116,700)
Projected			
1976	160,000	138,000	20,700
1977	165,000	121,000	18,150
1978	167,000	109,000	16,350
1979	164,000	104,000	15,600
1980	162,000	102,000	15,300
	(820,000)	(574,000)	(86,100)
1981	160,000	116,000	17,400
1982	156,000	122,000	18,300
1983	150,000	140,000	21,000
1984	145,000	156,000	23,400
1985	137,000	168,000	25,200
	(748,000)	(702,000)	(105,300)

[a] Demand filled by reentering teachers is estimated to be 15 percent, based on "Teacher Supply and Demand in Public Schools, 1975," NEA Research Memo 2 (June 1976), p. 7.
[b] Earned bachelor's degrees in education for 1970 is not included in subtotals.
Source: Projections of Education Statistics to 1985–86 (Washington, D.C.: U.S. Government Printing Office, 1977), Table 18, p. 35; Table 24, p. 50.

the following. Between 1970 and 1985, as shown in Table 6.9, there should be a total of 2 million openings for new teachers, while teaching institutions will be preparing nearly 2.5 million beginning teachers — at first glance what appears to be a cumulative surplus of almost 500,000 beginning teachers. However, a new teacher is also considered one who is reentering active status and was not employed as a full-time teacher during the preceding school year. A beginning teacher is a person entering active employment as a full-time teacher for the first time. Therefore, the demand for *new* teachers is the sum of the demand for *beginning* and *reentering* teachers.

On the basis of estimates from studies of teacher turnover and reentering teachers, a minimum of 15 percent of the total number of new teaching positions should be filled each year by reentering teachers.[49] This means that the cumulative surplus for beginning teachers will not be 500,000 but closer to 800,000 (see Table 6.9). Another claim is that by 1985 "there will

---

[49] "Teacher Supply and Demand in Public Schools, 1975," NEA Research Memo (June 1976), p. 7.

be two teachers for every teaching job in the United States, with three million teachers employed and another three million [cumulative between 1975 and 1985] either unemployed or working in another field."[50]

The surplus of beginning teachers has effected changes in the mobility, reentry, and turnover patterns of experienced teachers. With the exception of those on leaves of absence or sabbaticals, many experienced teachers who want to return to the classroom after varied interruptions, or who move and seek positions in new locations, are finding it difficult to obtain employment. Both inter-school system and intra-school system mobility have declined. Many previously mobile teachers are being forced to enter the unemployment ranks because the number of positions open to them has been reduced.

These reentry problems are also influenced by decisions of school boards to select comparatively larger proportions of beginning teachers to fill vacancies. Financial pressures have encouraged a growing tendency to fill positions at beginning rather than experienced teacher salaries. Reports of teacher surpluses and dwindling educational dollars will probably result in a marked increase in the number of unemployed experienced teachers, a marked decrease in the rates of voluntary teacher turnover and mobility, and a move to replace tenure with "periodic review."[51] A spin-off trend may evolve whereby school systems will fine teachers each day they are on strike, as in New York City, or fire striking teachers en masse and replace them with teachers who are on waiting lists — and for less money. A few school systems in Illinois, Indiana, New Hampshire, and Wisconsin have already pursued this route. Such events may increase in the late 1970s and early 1980s since the U.S. Supreme Court in 1976 upheld the right of school boards to fire striking teachers.[52]

Why the Teacher Oversupply

What happened to cause these supply-demand shifts? Why are teachers confronted by unemployment in their chosen field on a scale unprecedented since the Great Depression? To be sure, population trends have changed. During the early 1950s and until the late 1960s, the schools were bursting with record enrollments that had their beginnings in the post-World War II baby boom. However, these high-birthrate groups had

---

[50] Albert Shanker, "Teacher 'Oversupply' or 'Underutilization,' " *The New York Times*, August 18, 1974, Sect. 4, p. 9.

[51] Charles W. Lavaroni and John J. Savant, "Replacing Tenure with 'Periodic Review.' " *Phi Delta Kappan*, February 1977, p. 499; Allan C. Ornstein, "Educational Poverty in the Midst of Educational Abundance: Status and Policy Implications of Teacher Supply/Demand," *Educational Researcher*, April 1976, pp. 13-16.

[52] *Hortonville Joint School District No. 1* v. *Hortonville Education Association*, 1976.

to rely on teachers born during the years of low birthrates; the "Depression babies" entered teaching during the 1950s to provide a trickle of teachers for a flood of students. But the birthrate leveled off around 1963, and by 1968–69 the number of entering first-grade public school students declined for the first time in decades—a trend which has picked up each successive year as it has progressively affected a higher grade level.

By the 1972–73 school year, the educational industry had been transformed from a growth to a declining industry. After 26 consecutive years in which K–12 enrollments established annual records, the total number of students declined, not dramatically but nevertheless from 51.4 million to 51 million students. This downward trend is expected to continue to affect the schools midway into the decade of the 1980s, bottoming out in 1983–84 with a total enrollment of 45.3 million, then gradually rising and reaching 46 million in 1985–86. These trends are shown in Table 6.10.

Table 6.10 / Enrollment in Grades K-12, Public and Private Schools, 1965 to 1985 (in thousands)

Year (Fall)	Total Public and Nonpublic K-12	Public			Nonpublic (estimated)		
		K-12	K-8	9-12	K-12	K-8	9-12
1965......	48,473	42,173	30,563	11,610	6,300	4,900	1,400
1966......	49,239	43,039	31,145	11,894	6,200	4,800	1,400
1967......	49,891	43,891	31,641	12,250	6,000	4,600	1,400
1968......	50,744	44,944	32,226	12,718	5,800	4,400	1,400
1969......	51,119	45,619	32,597	13,022	5,500	4,200	1,300
1970......	51,309	45,909	32,577	13,332	5,400	4,100	1,300
1971......	51,381	46,081	32,265	13,816	5,300	4,000	1,300
1972......	51,044	45,744	31,831	13,913	5,300	4,000	1,300
1973......	50,729	45,429	31,353	14,077	5,300	4,000	1,300
1974......	50,353	45,053	30,921	14,132	5,300	3,900	1,400
1975......	50,138	44,838	30,545	14,294	5,300	3,900	1,400
Projected							
1976......	49,696	44,393	30,072	14,321	5,300	3,900	1,400
1977......	49,021	43,721	29,463	14,258	5,300	3,900	1,400
1978......	48,154	42,854	28,753	14,101	5,300	3,900	1,400
1979......	47,224	41,924	28,199	13,725	5,300	3,900	1,400
1980......	46,409	41,109	27,876	13,233	5,300	3,900	1,400
1981......	45,818	40,518	27,819	12,699	5,300	3,900	1,400
1982......	45,413	40,113	27,923	12,190	5,300	3,900	1,400
1983......	45,370	40,070	28,158	11,912	5,300	3,900	1,400
1984......	45,624	40,324	28,446	11,878	5,300	3,900	1,400
1985......	46,058	40,758	28,830	11,928	5,300	3,900	1,400

Note: Does not include independent nursery schools and kindergartens, residential schools for exceptional children, subcollegiate departments of institutions of higher education, federal schools for Indians, federally operated schools on federal installations, and other schools not in the regular school system.
Source: *Projections of Education Statistics to 1985–86*, Table 3, p. 14.

To make matters worse, the mid-1970s was a period of economic recession, characterized by both rising unemployment and growing inflation. An abundant supply of college graduates preparing to enter the job market received far fewer job offers, resulting in underutilization not only of teachers but of other college-trained people.[53] More college-educated persons were scrambling for a dwindling number of professional jobs, including teaching.

Inflation exacerbated the tendency for the public to refuse to vote in the taxes which would be needed to employ additional teachers. Many school districts reduced commitments in special teaching areas, while others increased class size. As the purchasing power of the dollar decreased, whatever increases in the budget were voted could not be used to hire additional teachers.

THE IMMEDIATE JOB OUTLOOK

These teacher job trends, of course, are national in scope; they do not apply everywhere. The outer suburban ring of the metropolitan sprawl (and some rural areas) should experience population growth and increasing student enrollments. Whether young teachers, especially single persons who desire the excitement of the cities, wish to work in small towns is another question. There are also a few subject areas where the need for teachers is still evident: on the elementary level, teachers of art, music, physical and health education, and, especially, remedial reading and special education, and on the secondary level, teachers of mathematics, general science, and, especially, industrial and vocational education. Bilingual and bicultural teachers at both levels are in vogue in many urban centers, too.

But teacher supply and demand can no longer be considered simply in terms of the numbers who prepare to teach in different subject fields or even the locations where vacancies exist. Personal characteristics such as sex, race, and ethnicity also must be considered. As the school integration process moves forward, staff ratios are being considered along with student enrollments. Black teachers are at an advantage in predominantly white schools, and the opposite is true in predominantly black schools. A countertrend is also evident; under the thrust of community control, local determination of hiring standards, and ethnic pride and power, various minority groups are demanding teachers of their own groups. As tensions mount in the cities, meeting the demands of militant groups has become

---

[53] Richard B. Freeman, *The Over-Educated American* (New York: Academic Press, 1976); *Occupational Manpower and Training Needs, 1974* (Washington, D.C.: U.S. Government Printing Office, 1975).

the easiest and most frequently used method by which those in power survive and keep the peace. We may question the moral and legal implications of this trend, but there are reports to suggest that in some city school systems candidates who have recently obtained their teaching licenses have been placed on waiting lists, while unqualified people from local communities have been hired to staff the classrooms.[54]

As racial and ethnic patterns in the appointment of inner-city teachers take hold, greater competition among whites for teaching slots in the outer cities and suburbs can be expected. Anxiety and frustration over securing positions probably will be compounded by federal affirmative action guidelines whereby selected minority groups are accorded preferential treatment in the hiring process. Although affirmative action does not apply to women seeking teaching jobs in the public schools, since they already outnumber men 2 to 1, race and ethnicity factors can be expected to complicate the supply-demand curve.

Increased disillusionment and even bitter feelings among graduates seeking teaching positions are likely as many wind up taking temporary jobs, such as driving cabs or typing. Some will find substitute teaching jobs on an irregular basis; but a great many will of necessity seek employment in other fields. The gravity of the situation may further reduce undergraduate enrollments in schools of education. Regardless, as what has traditionally been the greatest source of employment for college graduates diminishes, the total job market will be affected, increasing the difficulty for many graduates seeking "suitable jobs."

Where Do We Go From Here?

While the discussion of teacher supply and demand has focused on negative and threatening aspects, an abundant supply of teachers does have some advantages. It provides unprecedented opportunities for improvements to be made in school programs and teacher education programs, the selective recruitment of students preparing to teach, and for the upgrading of teachers with substandard qualifications. The following ten points discuss these possibilities.

1. A major point that is raised by many educators and bears repeating is that there are actually not enough teachers on the job to meet the real needs of the schools and to achieve quality education. The problem is not an oversupply of teachers but an undersupply of the money needed to reduce class sizes, expand course offerings, hire special personnel, and

---

[54] Bernard Bard, "The Battle for School Jobs," *Phi Delta Kappan*, May 1972, pp. 553–58; Allan C. Ornstein, Daniel U. Levine, and Doxey A. Wilkerson, *Reforming Metropolitan Schools* (Pacific Palisades, Cal.: Goodyear Publishing Co., 1975).

enlarge the coverage of special programs to meet the needs of students who
warrant them.

Allan Ostar makes this comment:

How can we talk about a teacher surplus when perhaps half our communities are
without kindergartens; . . . when almost half of the adult population 25 years and
over is functionally illiterate; . . . when in our high schools we have less than one
counselor for every 500 students; when our rural and urban areas are woefully
inadequate in meeting the special educational needs of our underprivileged
children? There is no teacher surplus. There is an educational deficit which . . .
we now have an opportunity to correct.[55]

Harold Regier makes a similar point:

For a country that spends about 8 percent of the gross national product on
education, one can conclude that spending enough for education may be the real
problem . . . Given enough dollars, the conclusion may be that "too many
teachers" is fiction, but until the dollar problem is solved, it is a fact.[56]

2. A system of lifelong education is now possible for the first time. Albert
Shanker asks: "Why should any individual have only one chance of
success? Why should a person who made the mistake of dropping out of
school at an early age not be given a second chance — or a third — to return
to school?"[57] The AFT President advocates a lifelong educational system
for all Americans, starting at the prekindergarten ages, which are the most
important for cognitive growth and development, and providing new
programs to help mature adults retool their skills for employment opportunities and open up new interests and leisure-oriented activities.

We have gained immensely from the G.I. bill, which permitted veterans
to continue their education after military service. They profited in-
dividually in terms of education and employment, and the nation profited
collectively in terms of worker skills and production levels. Many other
people, possibly numbering in the millions, could profit by returning to
school and college. We need new educational options and alternatives, not
only for our youth but also for our adult populations. Wherever possible
the individual should pay, but for economically disadvantaged adults,
Shanker urges "Educare for the mind." The availability of thousands of
teachers for these programs would make it possible to get them off to a
start.

3. The supply-demand crisis in the teaching profession is related to the
problem of how education is financed and how much the public is willing
to invest in schools. As teaching ranks continue to decline and efforts to

---

[55] "Too Many Teachers?" *Changing Times*, October 1970, p. 44.
[56] Harold C. Regier, *Too Many Teachers: Fact or Fiction* (Bloomington, Ind.: Phi Delta
Kappa Educational Foundation, 1972), p. 37.
[57] Shanker, "Teacher 'Oversupply' or 'Underutilization,' " p. 9.

decrease school budgets are strengthened, teachers will rely on collective bargaining to demand lower student-teacher ratios and increased services for children. In the political arena, they will get involved in electing proeducation legislators and securing allies among parents and other citizens who are interested in seeing educational quality improved.

But the ideas to have more teachers for fewer students, or to create new jobs by providing needed services to children, will not gain easy acceptability, especially on a mass scale. In fact, such ideas may prove politically and economically impractical. In many cases school budgets have leveled off as a result of public demand or been lowered in real dollars as inflation spirals. The average taxpayer, worried about meeting his own family's immediate financial needs, usually fails to grasp the important concept that all real costs entail further social costs. Conventional cost benefit analysis is possible whenever a price tag is placed on some sort of input and output, whatever the goals of the program may be. However, this is an illusory price which fails to consider the dysfunctional effects of poor quality education and unequal educational opportunity, and the related social and economic costs of unemployment, poverty, crime and delinquency, poor mental health, and all the other social ills that lead to the problems, tensions, and polarization of contemporary society.

4. Past teacher shortages made it necessary to accept a wide range of teacher talent — and disproportionate numbers of students with lower academic ranks and standardized test scores than students of other professions.[58] Then the concern was with meeting the national need to educate a fast-growing student population; standards had to be lowered to the point where it became possible to recruit an adequate supply of teachers.

It would be common sense now for the teaching profession to evaluate its own certification process and to select, train, and appoint teachers on the basis of quality. With an abundant supply of teachers, higher levels of competence can be stressed. But while existing trends may encourage responsible teacher educators to take appropriate action to upgrade entry standards for teacher education programs, opposite forces also are at work. Professors of education may feel enrollments are declining to a level where their jobs are at stake, and so may further relax standards, or politics and affirmative action guidelines may replace objective examinations as a basis for selection.

---

[58] William S. Leonard and Benjamin D. Wood, *The Student and His Knowledge* (New York: Carnegie Foundation for the Advancement of Teaching, 1938); *Graduate Record Examinations: An Analysis of the Graduate Record Examination Scores by the Undergraduate Major Field of Study, 1963–64* (Princeton, N.J.: Educational Testing Service, 1965); *Standards for the Accreditation of Teacher Education* (Washington, D.C.: National Council for Accreditation of Teacher Education, 1977).

5. It must be recognized that, increasingly, thousands of students who enter college are seriously deficient in the ability to write clearly, read at the appropriate level, or perform simple mathematical problems. This trend is rapidly growing as open admission and access policies take effect in institutions of higher learning, and the decline of enrollments in private colleges results in pressure to lower admission requirements to stay in business. It is further compounded by the egalitarian push toward equal educational opportunity, which declares that everyone has a right to an education, including college. There are sufficient data to indicate that the career attitudes of a large portion of these new students correlate with a preference for teaching.[59]

Teacher educators and teachers alike are faced with the question: Should access to higher education without regard to past achievement affect admission into programs of teacher education? If teachers are serious about upgrading the profession in general, they must recognize the fundamental differences between general education and professional education. While students may have the right to a general education, they do not have the *right* to become teachers. The determination to lower college entry standards may reflect a public debate on the purposes of education, but the question of entry into teaching is essentially a matter for professional action.

6. Whereas in the past the concern was more with filling positions than maintaining quality levels of competence, upgrading teacher training is now possible on three different levels: for prospective teachers, for beginning teachers, and for experienced teachers. Candidates for teachers can be selected from the top percentiles of their high school graduating classes. The need for teachers who can do a good job of teaching their subject calls for higher academic and intellectual standards for certification. Despite the difficulties in correlating cognitive scores and teacher competence, it should be obvious that intellectual ability and training are required to teach secondary subjects. Also, the intellectual abilities of the teacher tend to bear a relationship to the educational standards established for students.

7. Beginning teachers need assistance in the classroom, especially those appointed to ghetto schools. Prospective teachers can read the literature in their courses and gain theoretical insights, but they need actual experience

---

[59] Martin Haberman, "Guidelines for the Selection of Students into Programs of Teacher Education," paper published by the Association of Teacher Educators and Eric Clearinghouse on Teacher Education, May 1972; Martin Haberman, "New Entry Requirements and New Programs for College Students," in A. C. Ornstein and S. I. Miller (eds.), *Policy Issues in Education* (Lexington, Mass.: D. C. Heath & Co., 1976), pp. 95–107; "Trends in Choosing Majors," *Activity*, January 1975, p. 1, ff., Leon Zelby, "Good Teaching — A Problem in Education," *Social Science*, Summer 1977, pp. 133–38.

and on-the-job assistance when they start teaching—yet this is when the college abandons them. For many beginning teachers, inservice education comes too late—at a time when many are overwhelmed by insurmountable problems and have already given up or are thinking of transferring to another school or quitting the profession.

Teachers develop competence and become aware of their role as teachers during the first two or three years of teaching, not while they are in undergraduate school. An internship period for beginning teachers would be helpful, one in which they are given lighter teacher loads and the rest of their time is devoted to preparation and assistance from experienced teachers, who should also be given abbreviated teaching loads in exchange for their services.

8. In the past, the demands of teaching were so great that adequate provision could not be made for professional growth. Teachers can now be provided with the additional time and support necessary to upgrade their skills, keep abreast of latest educational developments, and involve themselves in cooperation with universities. No program of teaching education can presume to give a beginning teacher all the knowledge and the skill she or he will ever need. Nor can any profession reasonably disclaim the need of its members for continuous in-service education and retooling programs.

It should be acknowledged that teachers can become less effective with the passage of time, rather than remaining on the level of effectiveness they had when they began teaching. Any science teacher who was graduated from college 10 or 15 years ago and who knows only the science learned at college is unfit to teach today. In every area of teaching, it is essential that teachers keep up with the latest developments in their subject matter and the profession. Some teachers need help in controlling and motivating their students; others need assistance in basic skills; they are attempting to teach their students skills they themselves never learned adequately. In short, the public must recognize that the cost of the continuing education of teachers is part of the price that must be paid for quality education.

9. An inservice course every few years two days a week for 15 weeks or so is not the way to improve teacher quality. A person burdened with a full teaching load and the related responsibilities of instructional planning and grading papers, who also has personal and family responsibilities, is hardly likely to benefit from piecemeal academic and professional studies. Such course work becomes merely a necessary prerequisite for a salary differential, rather than serious retooling or learning on a level of excellence required of professionals.

The armed services and private industry have for some time granted personnel paid leaves of absence for study at institutions of higher learning or special centers, ranging from a few weeks of intensive training to a few years. There is no good reason why teachers should not follow these examples, which have proven beneficial to the participating individuals and the general public.

10. Finally, a serious look at our teacher training institutions is in order. Some 1,350 institutions of higher learning are currently training teachers. Not only is this an astonishing number, when we consider that the demand for new college graduates preparing to teach will be about 165,000 to 170,000 per year between 1980 and 1985,[60] but as many as 40 percent of these institutions are not accredited by the National Council for Accreditation of Teacher Education.[61] Furthermore, all the accredited institutions do not offer quality programs. If regional or national standards were introduced, based on projected manpower pool needs as well as quality control, probably close to half of the teacher training institutions could be eliminated.

CONCLUSIONS

There are more than 2.5 million individuals teaching in American elementary and secondary schools. As a group, teachers defy stereotyping; they are almost as varied as the American people. There are many reasons why an individual chooses teaching as an occupation, and there is no one image that adequately portrays teachers. About the only thing teachers have in common is that, for several reasons, they have chosen to work with young learners whose lives they can influence. In this respect, they share the possibility of shaping future generations through being teachers.

Whether experienced or new, most teachers are concerned with salaries and supply-demand trends. Salaries have improved considerably in recent years, and for past generations there has been a demand for teachers. Whether substantial salary gains will continue is hard to predict, but the 1980s may not be as bright as the 1970s. Education is no longer a growth industry, and the demand for teachers is shrinking. Some potential candidates may be forced to make career changes, and experienced teachers may be forced to cope with salary crunches. Those who are considering teaching as a career should subject themselves to extensive self-analysis to verify the validity of such a choice. Those who are already

[60] *Projections of Educational Statistics to 1985–86;* see Table 6.9 above.

[61] Egon G. Guba and David Clark, "Selected Demographic Data about Teacher Education Institutions," paper presented at the First National Conference on Teacher Education, Indianapolis, November 1975; Vello A. Kuuskraa et al., *Condition of Teacher Education—1977* (Washington, D.C.: Lewin & Associates, 1977).

teaching should be prepared to face new tensions and trials as they seek to implement strategies for maintaining previous gains in salaries and working conditions while improving their opportunities for the future.

ACTIVITIES

1. Develop a simple questionnaire concerning motivations for teaching and try it out with the class.
2. View a current TV program involving a teacher. Briefly delineate how the teacher is portrayed. Is there any validity to this portrayal?
3. Interview three or four friends to find out what they envision when you say "school teacher."
4. Devise a salary schedule you believe would be fair, yet practical, for a school district today. Include different educational levels and experience of teachers; also consider family income level and wealth of the people in the area. Now compare your schedule with one or two nearby school districts.
5. Invite a local school administrator to class and ask her or him to discuss employment opportunities for teachers.

DISCUSSION QUESTIONS

1. How would you describe the "average" teacher today? 25 years ago?
2. Why are increasing numbers of men entering the teaching profession?
3. What advantages and disadvantages do you see in teaching in one's home town or neighborhood?
4. Discuss the pros and cons of merit pay for teachers.
5. What factors have caused the current teacher surplus? Why do some educators feel the teacher surplus is a myth?

SUGGESTED FOR FURTHER READING

Ashton-Warner, Sylvia. *Teacher.* New York: Simon & Schuster, 1963.

Brenton, Myron. *What's Happened to Teacher?* New York: Coward-McCann, 1970.

Broudy, Harry S. *The Real World of the Public Schools.* New York: Harcourt, Brace Jovanovich, 1972.

Holt, John. *How Children Fail.* New York: Pitman Publishing Corp., 1964.

Jersild, Arthur T. *When Teachers Face Themselves.* New York: Teachers College Press, Columbia University, 1955.

Kohl, Herbert. *On Teaching.* New York: Schocken Books, 1976.

Proefiedt, William A. *The Teacher You Choose To Be.* New York: Holt, Rinehart & Winston, 1975.

Silberman, Charles A. *Crisis in the Classroom.* New York: Random House, 1970.

Smith, B. O. *Teachers for the Real World.* Washington, D.C.: American Association of Colleges for Teacher Education, 1969.

Waller, Willard. *The Sociology of Teaching.* New York: John Wiley & Sons, 1965.

CHAPTER 7

Probably no aspect of education has been discussed with greater frequency, with as much concern, or by more educators and parents than has teacher effectiveness—how to define, how to identify, and how to measure it. Facets of this problem have been studied by state and local school systems, by individuals, and by teams of researchers. But findings about the competence of teachers are inconclusive; little is presently known for certain about teacher excellence.

There is general agreement that the goal should be a highly competent teacher in every classroom, but there is considerably less agreement on the meaning and evaluation of competence. In recent years, educators have focused on various methods to assess teacher effectiveness. Three of these methods are discussed in this chapter.

In the first part, the notion of teacher leadership is introduced. One may question the need for leadership among teachers and ask why schools properly designed for their purpose will not function adequately without leadership from teachers. The answer lies in the inescapable facts of classroom life: changing classroom conditions, internal dynamics of the classroom, and the nature of the membership in the classroom.

A quite different approach to the study of teacher competence is the concept of teacher style. The notion of teaching style is viewed as a general dimension: the teacher's stance, mode of behavior, flavor of performance, attitude toward tasks, the way materials are organized and students are instructed. Here we are talking about a general style which identifies the way the teacher goes about performing his or her work.

The final part of the chapter is concerned with more specific descriptions of teacher behavior. The discussion of theoretical and research approaches to the problem of identifying and measuring teacher behavior is complex and lengthy, illustrating that solutions to the problem of teacher behavior are not easy. Although the topic of teacher behavior is narrower than that of teaching style, in fact behavior may be viewed as one component of style. Its nonfacile and elusive nature provides little comfort for those who are confronted with the problem of assessing teacher behavior.

LEADERSHIP THEORY: IMPLICATIONS FOR TEACHERS

Leadership appears in the social science literature with three basic meanings: as an attribute of a position, as a characteristic of a person, and as a category of behavior. To be a teacher is to occupy a position of leadership, usually in the classroom, and to be a principal is to occupy a position of greater leadership. Yet it may be said that certain teachers exercise considerable leadership, and some principals exercise very little. Furthermore, leadership is a relational concept implying two terms: the influencing agent and the persons influenced. Without followers there can be no leader. Hence, leadership conceived of as an ability is a tricky concept, since it depends too much on the properties of the situation and the people to be "led." If a powerful, leading teacher were promoted to principal, would his or her leadership abilities still prevail? And if he could not lead as principal, what would become of (or how would we rate) his leadership abilities?

One common approach to the definition of leadership is to equate it with the differential exertion of influence. There would be no leader in a group of people who all were equally effective or ineffective in influencing others. Even where one individual has more effect upon his fellows than another, he would not ordinarily be considered a leader if the effect derives almost entirely from his position in the social structure rather than from his special utilization of that position. The teacher who passes along the order "Keep in line" when there is a fire drill, and the entire school is exiting, and the assistant principal is in full view of the class is not really exercising leadership. The same teacher, in charge of a class during a real fire may deploy members out of the building effectively, or have to switch routes because the prescribed exit is blocked. The teacher's behavior would then fall toward the positive end of the leadership continuum. This is not to equate leadership with the exercise of influence only under extreme pressure. Leadership does occur in formal structures and in routine situations such as the classroom; indeed, every act of influence on a matter of organizational relevance, whether it be in a school situation, military situation, hospital, and so on, is in some degree an act of leadership to the extent that such influential acts are prescribed for certain positions in the organization; even the routine functioning of the role system involves acts of leadership.

When we think of leadership in contrast to routine role performance in a given situation, we become particularly interested in the kinds of individual behavior which go beyond required performance or routine behavior. In other words, "We consider the essence of organizational leadership to be the influential increment over and above mechanical compliance with the routine directives of the organization."[1] In terms of the classroom situation, students react not only to the power and authority of the teacher but to his or her personality; it is this that often makes the difference between effective and ineffective teachers.

With respect to the legitimate power of teachers and their ability to reward and punish students, all teachers in a given school are created equal. They do not, however, remain equal. Some of them are much better than others in controlling students. John French and Bertram Raven have suggested five types of power: legitimate, reward, punishment, referent (refers to influence based upon liking or identifying with another person), and expert power.[2] Neither referent power nor expert power can be readily conferred by the organization (in this case, the school), and yet both are important in getting work done (in this case, in the classroom). The concept of influential increment has relevance here; referent and expert powers, to the extent they are displayed by the teacher, represent additions to power available from the school. Legitimate power, reward power, and punishment power are available sources derived from organizational policies, and people in leadership positions (in this case, teachers), utilize these powers in different ways and get different results. The utilization of these powers in the classroom has a marked effect upon the teacher's referent power, that is his influence based upon the appreciation and respect students accord him, and expert power, that is his opportunity to demonstrate knowledge and technical competence to the students.

In the same vein, Max Weber outlines three orientations which

---

[1] Daniel Katz and Robert Kahn, *The Social Psychology of Organizations* (New York: John Wiley & Sons, 1966), p. 302.

[2] John R. P. French and Bertram H. Raven, "The Basis of Social Power," in D. Cartwright and A. Zander (eds.), *Group Dynamics: Research and Theory,* 3rd ed. (New York: Harper & Row, 1968), pp. 255–69.

legitimate the exercise of power and control: charisma, tradition, and rational-legal processes.[3] While Weber conceptualizes these three orientations in relation to organizations, they are pertinent to the teacher's leadership and control of students in the classroom. Charisma is based largely on extraordinary gifts or abilities which are embodied in the person and influence others. Traditional authority rests on a legitimacy base and is rooted in established customs and institutions. Rational-legal authority is based on established laws, rules, and norms which have operated in the past and channel behavior.

In this typology, the nature of charisma parallels with referent and expert power; the teacher maintains her or his position and displays leadership by her capacities for understanding performance which are recognized by and beneficial to her students. This kind of authority depends on a strong respect for the demonstrated competencies and corresponds with the concept of influential increment. Tradition and rational-legal authority are similar to legitimate power, reward power, and punishment power. In effect, social relations operating in the classroom are treated as givens and are followed because they have endured over time.

Experienced teachers recognize that tradition and legal authority often do not suffice in classroom situations. Regardless of the teacher's role and the institutional support provided by the school, the teacher must earn the respect and trust of the students. The nature of leadership is crucial here; teachers cannot escape from this issue. If they lack leadership qualities, they will find it too difficult to teach and may eventually abandon teaching, seek positions where the task of controlling behavior is easier, or escape the classroom to undertake a nonteaching capacity.

Leadership in the Classroom

Analysis of leadership behavior involves not only what a leader does, but also what types of personal variables bear a positive relationship to leadership. The teacher may gain insight not only by regarding styles of leadership behavior but by considering the question: What traits are important in determining leadership? It is important to note, however, that personality traits related to leadership in one situation may not necessarily be predictive of leadership in other situations.

Our attempt to show some of the differences among patterns of leadership behavior will be limited to three examples. In general, they are

---

[3] Max Weber, *The Theory of Social and Economic Organization,* (New York: Free Press, 1947).

congruent with three basic leadership styles—nomothetic, idiographic, and transactional as delineated by Jacob Getzels and Egon Guba.[4]

1. *Nomothetic Style.* This style is characterized by behavior which stresses the requirements of the institution, its roles and expectations sometimes at the expense of the individual. Effectiveness is rated in terms of behavior directed toward accomplishing the organization or school's goals by following rules and regulations.

2. *Idiographic Style.* This style is characterized by behavior which stresses the individuality of people, their personality and needs disposition. Minimum emphasis is put on the institution's rules and regulations. The assumption is that the school can accomplish its objectives not by enforcing adherence to well-defined roles, but by making it possible for each person to seek what is most relevant and meaningful to him or her.

3. *Transactional Style.* This style is characterized by behavior which makes explicit the roles and expectations required for organizational goal accomplishment but also makes provision for individual differences and concerns. Both the institution and people are taken into account. Considered a midpoint or balance between nomothetic and idiographic behavior, this style judiciously utilizes each of the other two as the occasion demands.

These three leadership styles are conceived in terms of the classroom (or school) being a social system on which the teacher and students interact to

Figure 7.1 / The Nomothetic and Idiographic Dimensions of Leadership Behavior

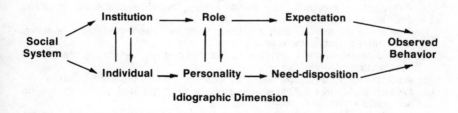

Nomothetic Dimension

Institution ⟶ Role ⟶ Expectation

Social System ⟶ Observed Behavior

Individual ⟶ Personality ⟶ Need-disposition

Idiographic Dimension

Source: Jacob W. Getzels and Egon C. Guba, "Social Behavior and the Administrative Process," *School Review*, December 1957, p. 429.

[4] Jacob W. Getzels and Egon C. Guba, "Social Behavior and the Administrative Process," *School Review*, December 1957, pp. 423–41.

Figure 7.2 / Interrelationships of the Cultural-Nomothetic and Biological-Idiographic Dimensions

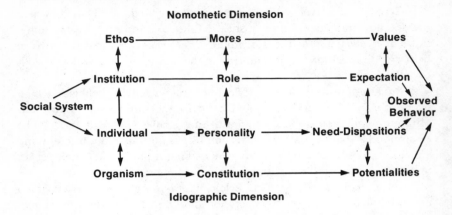

Source: Jacob W. Getzels and Herbert A. Thelen, "The Classroom Group as a Social System," in N. B. Henry (ed.), *The Dynamics of Instructional Groups*, 59th Yearbook of the National Society for the Study of Education, Part II (Chicago: University of Chicago Press, 1960), p. 73.

Table 7.1 / Leadership Dimensions, with Implications for Classroom Situations

1. *Representation.* The leader speaks and acts as the representative of the groups.
2. *Demand Reconciliation.* The leader reconciles conflicting demands and reduces disorder to the system.
3. *Tolerance of Uncertainty.* The leader is able to tolerate uncertainty and postponement without anxiety or upset.
4. *Persuasiveness.* The leader uses persuasion and argument effectively and exhibits strong convictions.
5. *Initiation of Structure.* The leader clearly defines his own role and lets followers know what is expected of them.
6. *Tolerance of Freedom.* The leader allows followers scope for initiative, decision, and action.
7. *Role Assumption.* The leader actively exercises the leadership role rather than surrendering leadership to others.
8. *Consideration.* The leader has regard for the comfort, well-being, status, and contributions of followers.
9. *Productive Emphasis.* The leader applies pressure for productive output.
10. *Predictive Accuracy.* The leader exhibits foresight and ability to predict outcomes accurately.
11. *Integration.* The leader maintains a closely knit organization and resolves intermember conflicts.
12. *Superior Orientation.* The leader maintains cordial relations with superiors, has influence with them, and strives for higher status.

Source: Ralph Stogdill, *Manual for the Leader Behavior Description Questionnaire—Form XII* (Columbus: College of Commerce and Administration, Ohio State University, 1963), p. 3.

produce what can be called observed behavior. By way of summarizing the characteristics of these leadership dimensions, the relationships between the nomothetic and idiographic dimensions are shown in Figure 7.1.

This leadership model was extended by adding a cultural dimension — factors such as ethos, mores, and values — to the nomothetic (top) axis and a biological dimension — factors such as the organism, constitution, and potentialities — to the idiographic (bottom) axis.[5] The ideal balance of emphasis for actual behavior is said to be achieved by interaction of these enlarged institutional and individual relationships. If all these dimensions are put into a simple representation, the relationship appears as in Figure 7.2. The fundamental leadership styles remain the same in this enlarged model.

According to this model, which was based on the classroom group, any group process or transaction in the classroom should be studied by considering the teacher and students in relationship to cultural (ethos, mores, and values) as well as biological (organism, constitution, and potentialities) factors. The leadership behavior of the teacher depends not merely on ability to perceive behavior to be responded to immediately but on looking behind the act and understanding the behavior as a transaction within the social system of the classroom. Educators have extended and popularized these three leadership dimensions in terms of administrative behavior.

Research studies at Ohio State University led to the identification of the 12 leadership behaviors listed in Table 7.1. Several studies involving leadership behaviors of school administrators, teachers, ministers, community leaders, industrial leaders, and U.S. Senators have utilized these subscales. Factor analysis of these studies reveals three clusters of effective leadership: (1) leaders who respond to social system needs, (2) leaders who respond to personal needs of those under their command, and (3) leaders who respond to the needs of both the system and persons. The three resulting behaviors are in many ways similar to the nomothetic, idiographic, and transactional leadership styles described by Jacob Getzels and his associates at the University of Chicago. They add to the debate over the relative merits of a system or person-oriented approach to leadership, and, indirectly, to the question whether classroom teachers should act according to the requirements of the school and its role and expectations, or those of the individual and his personality and needs disposition.

---

[5] Jacob W. Getzels and Herbert A. Thelen, "The Classroom Group as a Social System," in N. B. Henry (ed.), *The Dynamics of·Instructional Groups,* 59th Yearbook of the National Society for the Study of Education, Part II (Chicago: University of Chicago Press, 1960), pp. 53–82.

Focusing on the leadership qualities used by teachers to maintain control in the classroom, Willard Waller has outlined five techniques which also may be categorized along a system-personal continuum.[6] These five techniques are: (1) command, in which institutional dominance and subordination appear in their purest form; (2) sanction, whereby punishment is used to enforce the command; (3) manipulation, a means of controlling students through indirect devices; (4) temper, which is marked by weakly controlled or uncontrolled emotion; and (5) appeal, frequently used for dealing with minor infractions or for effecting a change in the general attitude of a student.

In the order of listing, Waller's five techniques to control students in the classroom range from utilization of the system (or institutional) approach to dependence upon personal influence. These are by no means all the techniques used by teachers in an attempt to teach students. Probably all teachers use these techniques, and more, but with different emphasis and in different degrees, while maintaining the emphasis on control and discipline. States Waller, "Education . . . is the art of imposing upon the young defined roles" accepted by those who maintain the schools. "The school is thus a gigantic agency of social control" in which teacher and student relationships are based on "a form of dominance and subordination."[7]

Leadership for Control and Discipline

Most teachers find it necessary to exercise control at sometime or another, and especially in inner-city schools. Aggressive or destructive behavior often has a contagious effect; as students see others violating rules, it becomes harder for them to resist joining in. Under these conditions, more aggressive students serve as models for the behavior of others, and a kind of antisocial learning can occur unless teachers intervene. In some schools, the level of hostility and disrespect for authority runs so high that more than half the teacher's time and behavior patterns are devoted to maintaining control.[8]

Here is what may be considered a typical summation of a teacher's first days of teaching in an inner-city school:

---

[6] Willard Waller, *The Sociology of Teaching* (New York: John Wiley & Sons, 1965).

[7] Ibid., pp. 296-97.

[8] See "Blackboard Battlefield: A Question of Survival," *Time*, February 19, 1973, p. 19; *The New York Times*, March 26, 1972, Sect. 4, p. 9; September 15, 1974, Sect. 4, p. 8; November 17, 1974, Sect. 4, p. 13; National Commission on the Reform of Secondary Education, *The Reform of Secondary Eduction* (New York: McGraw-Hill Book Co., 1973); Jack Slater, "Death of a High School, *Phi Delta Kappan*, December 1974, pp. 251-56.

I thought I knew what to expect in a school like this. I had been there for a year as a student teacher and I had seen lots of classes. But nothing seemed to help. My class was so unruly and so impossible to discipline that I didn't sit down for a minute for weeks. I was exhausted, and I didn't know how to help them or myself.[9]

Although the majority of new teachers look forward to the opening day or the start of their teaching careers and most of them are eager to devote extra hours in order to do a good job, they are not prepared for the realities of the inner-city classroom.

As Albert Shanker asserts, for many the first days, the first weeks, or the first year lead to disheartening experiences. The students enter the room with a bang! The teacher writes his or her name on the blackboard, but a few students are "shouting out ugly variations on the name." The teacher calls for order, and "the response is a combination of noise, pranks, and derisive laughter." Not knowing the students' names, the teacher has little control of the situation but attempts to seat them by plan. Some "refuse to respond by refusing to change their seats or to give their proper names." Disorder characterizes each day; the teacher feels helpless. How will he be able to reach these students? What happens if the principal walks in? "It is hard, at that moment, for the teacher not to view the student as enemies," as threats to his capacity to do the job and hold the job, especially if the scenario is continuously repeated, and, in fact, it often is.[10]

Little wonder, then, that when 244 first-year urban school teachers were rated by their supervisors, the following characteristics of ineffective teachers were identified: lack of control, 40; personality clash, 29; immaturity, 20; lack of organization, 17; and lack of confidence, 17.[11] All these characteristics could be lumped together as having something to do with leadership behavior regarding classroom control and discipline.

But the problems of leadership for purposes of control and discipline are not limited to beginning teachers; a rash of books has appeared describing the experiences of teachers of all sorts in the inner city and their problems of maintaining classroom order.[12] Furthermore, stress on control and discipline is necessary in all types of schools, although it may assume different forms. It may take the shape of what Edgar Friedenberg terms

---

[9] Carol R. Bloomgarden et al., *Learning to Teach in Urban Schools* (New York: Teachers College Press, Columbia University, 1965), p. 38.

[10] Albert Shanker, *Where Do We Stand?* (New York: United Federation of Teachers, 1973), pp. 6-7.

[11] Jack O. Vittetoe, "Why First Year Teachers Fail," *Phi Delta Kappan*, January 1977, pp. 429-30.

[12] See Elizabeth Eddy, *Walk the White Line* (New York: Doubleday & Co., 1967); Mary F. Greene and Orletta Ryan, *The School Children Growing Up in the Slums* (New York: Random House, 1965); Jim Haskins, *The Diary of a Harlem School Teacher* (New York: Grove Press, 1969); Alexander Moore, *Realities of the Urban Classroom* (New York: Doubleday & Co., 1967).

teacher "ressentiment," a kind of ill temper and suppressed anger toward students, or what Jules Henry called "education for docility," or encouragement of conformity, lest school people lose control over students.[13]

It should come as no surprise that Charles Silberman, in his influential description of American schools, noted:

A teacher will rarely, if ever, be called on the carpet or denied tenure because his students have not learned anything; he most certainly will be revoked if his students are talking or moving about the classroom — or even worse found outside the room, and he may earn the censure of his colleagues as well.[14]

If teachers and schools appear to be preoccupied with discipline, they are not alone. In a 1969 poll of 100 schools conducted by the Louis Harris organization for *Life Magazine,* nearly two-thirds of the parents surveyed believed that "maintaining discipline is more important than student self-inquiry," and the comparable figure for teachers was only 27 percent.[15] An annual poll of parents over nine years (1969–77) by George Gallup and associates for *Phi Delta Kappan* revealed that in all but one of the years, those who were surveyed named discipline as the no. 1 problem of the schools in their own communities.[16]

With all this concern for classroom discipline, a large body of professional literature on the subject is to be expected. Despite all the research, however, and the time and effort spent on it, the results are contradictory. About the only sure thing is that how much control or discipline should be exercised, and at what point that should be administered, are questions each teacher must answer for himself or herself. What works for one teacher may not work for another. One teacher may just point to an unruly student, and the student will immediately calm down. Another teacher may try the same technique on the same student and be ignored.

The choice of what measures to use and when to use them will naturally depend on the leadership qualities of the teacher, the social climate of the classroom, the problem at hand, and the amount of disorder the teacher and class can tolerate and still make progress in the tasks of teaching and learning. And, certainly, overemphasis of discipline or the sole equation of

---

[13] Edgar Z. Friedenberg, *The Dignity of Youth and Other Atavisms* (Boston: Beacon Press, 1965); Jules Henry, "Docility, or Giving Teacher What She Wants," *Journal of Social Issues,* April 1955, pp. 33–41; Jules Henry, *Culture against Man* (New York: Random House, 1963).

[14] Charles E. Silberman, *Crisis in the Classroom* (New York: Random House, 1970), p. 144.

[15] "What People Think About the High School," *Life,* May 16, 1969, pp. 22–23.

[16] *The Gallup Polls of Attitudes toward Education, 1969–73* (Bloomington, Ind.: Phi Delta Kappan, 1973); for the 1974 to 1976 polls, see *The Condition of Education, 1977,* vol. 3, Part I (Washington, D.C.: U.S. Government Printing Office, 1977), Table 1.5, p. 158. Also see Chapter 11, Table 11.5; for the 1977 poll, see the September 1977 issue of *Phi Delta Kappan.*

classroom control with teacher leadership should be avoided. Too much stress on discipline suggests a nonteaching, nonlearning situation — which in fact characterizes many inner-city schools. What is needed in all classroom situations is the proper mix of controlling and teaching techniques.

TEACHING STYLES

If you watch different teachers at work, you can sense that each one has a style for maintaining control and for teaching. While teacher leadership is associated with classroom power relationships and teacher-student roles and expectations, teaching style is associated with a generalized method of teaching and a particular psychological temperament. Some investigators have suggested descriptive models of teaching styles, and there are a variety of teaching styles, based on research, which show the relationships between them and the learning patterns of children. In this section we will present two interesting models of teaching styles, based on informal observations of teachers, and then discuss various research-based models.

Frank Riessman uses colorful terms to describe teaching styles. He listed them after visiting low-income schools in over 35 cities, and there is no research data to support the description.[17] Although originally written in the context of teaching disadvantaged students, it is relevant for all types of teachers and all types of students.

1. *Compulsive Type.*   This teacher is fussy, teaches things over and over, and is concerned with functional order and structure (which disadvantaged children like).
2. *Boomer.*   This teacher shouts out in a loud, strong voice; "You're going to learn"; there is no nonsense in the classroom. The ground rules are laid out early in the term, and students know that there is a point beyond which they cannot go without getting into trouble.
3. *Maverick.*   Everybody loves this teacher, except perhaps the principal. She raises difficult questions and presents ideas that disturb. Learning is linked to new ideas and new things in her classroom.
4. *Coach.*   He is informal, earthy, and may be an athlete, but in any case he is physically expressive in conducting his class. His classroom is characterized by activity and motion.
5. *Quiet One.*   Sincere, calm, but definite, this teacher commands both respect and attention.

---

[17] Frank Riessman, "Teachers of the Poor: A Five-Point Plan," *Journal of Teacher Education,* Fall 1967, pp. 326–36.

6. *Entertainer.* This teacher is not afraid to have fun with children. She has a flair for the comic and is free enough to joke and laugh with the students.
7. *Secular.* This person is relaxed and informal with children; she will have lunch with them, even use their own lavatories as opposed to the teachers'.
8. *Academic.* He is interested in knowledge and its transmission to the students. He is not so interested in right answers as in the substance of ideas.

Herbert Thelen's set of seven teaching styles that teachers in various schools seem to use is also expressed in colorful terms, descriptive in nature, and not research based.[18] Thelen's list is:

1. *Socratic Discussion.* This person is a wise, somewhat crusty philosopher who purposely argues with students for purposes of clarifying concepts and ideas.
2. *Town Meeting.* Student input is welcomed; they decide on courses of action required to solve problems.
3. *Apprenticeship.* The child is in class to learn; he listens carefully and learns through activities presented by the teacher.
4. *Boss-Employee Method.* The relationship between the teacher and student need not be harsh, but the teacher is obviously in command; students are in a subordinate role.
5. *Business Arrangement.* This is essentially the "contract plan" in which student and teacher agree on the work to be done; the students periodically consult with the teacher as the work proceeds.
6. *Good Old Team.* The image is of a group of players listening to the coach.
7. *Guided Tour.* This image represents a group of interested students closely following the instructions of the teacher. From time to time, the teacher calls their attention to certain objects, ideas, or questions.

There are many other teacher styles. Everyone must develop her or his own style of teaching—not copy someone else's. Both beginning and experienced teachers must feel comfortable in the classroom; if they are not genuinely themselves students will see through them and label them as phony. In short, teachers must develop their own repertoire, which will be relative to their own physical and mental characteristics. Hence there is no one ideal teacher type but a multiple set of teacher types.

---

[18] Herbert A. Thelen, *Dynamics of Groups at Work* (Chicago: University of Chicago Press, 1954).

Important Early Studies on Teaching Style

A number of hypothetical models have been derived from research and deduced from theoretical concepts. These teaching styles have been verified through systematic observation and the classification and comparison of teachers. Two classic studies of teacher styles by Harold Anderson and Ronald Lippitt and Ralph White laid the groundwork for classifying the *process* of what a teacher does in the classroom.

Results of the Anderson study introduced the concepts of the *dominative* vs. *integrative* style of teaching, based on observations of preschool and elementary children with different teachers over a period of time.[19] The dominative teacher used threats and shame and demanded conformity, whereas the integrative teacher exhibited approval for students' interests and was supportive and understanding. Dominative teachers produced dominative students, and integrative teachers stimulated further integration of students. Thus, the teachers' style influenced classroom patterns and student behavior.

Lippitt and White extended the general conclusions of Anderson, initially by developing an instrument for describing the "social atmosphere" of children's clubs and for quantifying the effects of group and individual behavior.[20] Since the publication of the original study in 1939, the results have been generalized in numerous research studies and textbooks; it has been the source of literally hundreds of research investigations on the subject of teaching style and teacher behaviors.

This classic study used classifications of *authoritarian, democratic* and *laissez-faire* styles of teaching as the basis for determining student performance. The authoritarian teacher directs all the activities of the program—a strong similarity to Anderson's dominative type of teacher. The democratic teacher encourages group participation and is willing to share the decision-making process with students. This style is related to the integrative teacher. In the laissez-faire group, few, if any, goals and directions are provided for group or individual behavior. This is representative of the ineffective teacher.

---

[19] Harold H. Anderson, "Domination and Integration in the Social Behavior of Young Children in an Experimental Play Situation," *Genetic Psychological Monograph,* August 1937, pp. 341–408; Harold H. Anderson, *Studies of Teachers' Classroom Personality, II and III: Applied Psychology Monographs* (Stanford, Ca.: Stanford University Press, 1946).

[20] Ronald Lippitt and Ralph K. White, "The Social Climate of Children's Groups," in R. G. Barker, J. S. Kounin, and H. F. Wright (eds.), *Child Behavior and Development* (New York: McGraw-Hill Book Co., 1943), pp. 485–508; Ronald Lippitt and Ralph K. White, "An Experimental Study of Leadership and Group Life," in E. E. Maccoby, T. M. Newcomb, and E. L. Hartley (eds.), *Readings in Social Psychology,* 3rd ed. (New York: Holt, Rinehart & Winston, 1958).

Table 7.2 / Flanders's Indirect and Direct Teacher Influences

I. Teacher Talk
  A. Indirect Influence
    1. *Accepts Feelings.* Accepts and clarifies the tone of feeling of the students in an unthreatening manner. Feelings may be positive or negative. Predicting or recalling feelings are included.
    2. *Praises or Encourages.* Praises or encourages student action or behavior. Jokes that release tension, but not at the expense of another individual, nodding head or saying "um hm?" or "go on" are included.
    3. *Accepts or Uses Ideas of Student.* Clarifying, building, or developing ideas suggested by a student. As teacher brings more of his own ideas into play, shift to category 5.
    4. *Asks Questions.* Asking a question about content or procedure with the intent that a student answer.
  B. Direct Influence
    5. *Lecturing.* Giving facts or opinions about content or procedure; expressing his own ideas, asking rhetorical questions.
    6. *Giving Directions.* Directions, commands, or orders which students are expected to comply with.
    7. *Criticizing or Justifying Authority.* Statements intended to change student behavior from unacceptable to acceptable pattern; bawling someone out; stating why the teacher is doing what he is doing; extreme self-reference.
II. Student Talk
    8. *Student Talk—Response.* Talk by students in response to teacher. Teacher initiates the contact or solicits student statement.
    9. *Student Talk—Initiation.* Talk initiated by students. If "calling on" student is only to indicate who may talk next, observer must decide whether student wanted to talk.
III. Silence
    10. *Silence or Confusion.* Pauses, short periods of silence and periods of confusion in which communication cannot be understood by the observer.

Source: Ned A. Flanders, *Teacher Influence, Pupil Attitudes, and Achievement* (Washington, D.C.: U.S. Government Printing Office, 1965), p. 20.

One result of the Lippitt and White investigation was that children taught by an authoritarian teacher failed to initiate activity and became dependent upon the teacher; some of the student groups exhibited aggressive and rebellious behavior toward this leader. The democratic teacher generated a friendly and cooperative group atmosphere; students' output was the highest in this group, and the students carried through work assignments without the aid of the teacher for periods of time. The laissez-faire style of leadership resulted in confusion and minimal student productivity.

One of the most ambitious research studies on teaching style was conducted by Ned Flanders between 1954 and 1962.[21] The main focus of

---

[21] Ned A. Flanders, *Teacher Influence, Pupil Attitudes, and Achievement* (Washington, D.C.: U.S. Government Printing Office, 1965).

Flanders's work concerned the development of an instrument for quantifying verbal communication in the classroom. Seven categories were assigned to teacher talk and two to student talk; the tenth category covered pauses, short periods of silence, and talk that was confusing or noisy. The first four teacher categories, as indicated in Table 7.2, represent various degrees of an *indirect* teaching style, and the next three represent a *direct* teaching style. The indirect teacher tended to overlap with Anderson's integrative teaching style and Lippitt and White's democratic teaching style. The direct teacher tended to exhibit characteristics similar to Anderson's dominative teacher and Lippitt and White's authoritarian teacher.

Flanders's sampling of students in Minnesota and New Zealand in grades five to eight found that students taught by indirect teachers learned more and exhibited more constructive and independent attitudes than students taught by direct teachers. All types of students in all types of subject classes learned more with indirect teachers.

Teachable Groups

Research of special interest on teaching style was done by Louis Heil and his associates at Brooklyn College who hypothesized that it is correlated with their students' achievement.[22] On the basis of observation of fifth- and sixth-grade classrooms, four student and three teacher styles were characterized. For students, these were:

1. *Conformers,* who exhibited control over impulses and quiet behaviors.
2. *Opposers,* who were characterized by conflict and oppositional relationships with authority figures, intolerance of ambiguity, and frustration.
3. *Waverers,* who were anxious, fearful, and indecisive.
4. *Strivers,* who showed a marked drive for recognition in academic and school activities.

Teachers were divided into three types:

1. *Turbulent,* characterized by little patience, poor routine, inconsistency, and more concern for ideas than people.
2. *Self-controlling,* who were organized, structured, and workmanlike, while at the same time exhibiting sensitivity to students' feelings.

---

[22] Louis M. Heil, I. Feifer, and Marion Powell, "Characteristics of Teacher Behavior Related to Achievement of Children in Several Elementary Grades," Mimeographed, 1960; Louis M. Heil and Carlton Washburne, "Brooklyn College Research on Teacher Effectiveness," *Journal of Educational Research,* May 1962, pp. 347–51.

3. *Fearful,* described as being anxious, dependent on the approval of supervisors and children, and unable to bring structure and order to the teaching process.

When achievement was controlled for IQ, neither the strivers nor the conformers were significantly affected by teacher style. But teacher style did make a difference for the opposers and waverers, which are considered typical behaviors of nonachievers and disadvantaged students. The turbulent and fearful teachers had difficulty teaching opposers and waverers; in fact, fearful teachers were ineffective for all kinds of students except strivers, who wanted to please all teachers.

From Heil's study, it would appear that certain teachers can teach difficult students, while other teachers are ineffective. This would obviously be supported by common sense. The findings, though apparently inconclusive, also are consistent with the idea of grouping students according to social, psychological, and cognitive behaviors and *matching* them with teacher styles. This would lead to the formation of "teachable" groups, a concept derived from Herbert Thelen's research. He contends that teachable students for one teacher may be quite different for another, that the "fit" between teacher and teachable students primarily results in successful grouping and more meaningful teaching-learning experiences. Further, any grouping which does not in some way attempt to fit students and teacher together can have only accidental success.[23]

Affective v. Cognitive Teaching Styles

To put the topic of teaching styles in perspective with a number of traditional and current ideas about learning which have divided educators into conflicting camps, two teaching styles emerge. Both are psychoeducational. The first teacher style stresses a *permissive-humane* approach, characterized by the Summerhill and open education programs (in both cases, children have freedom to do what they want, within reason and without fear of teacher censure). The second teacher style takes a *behavioral-engineering* approach, characterized by structure and a definite plan, such as the Bereiter-Engelmann drill method for teaching disadvantaged learners, the Skinnerian approach to programmed instruction, or the Hewett-Lindsley methods, which emphasize *what* the child is ready to learn and *how* to teach him.

The permissive-humane approach is rooted in progressive education and traditional field psychology (which includes Gestalt and phenomenological

---

[23] Herbert A. Thelen, *Classroom Grouping for Teachability* (New York, John Wiley & Sons, 1967).

processes, both of which are concerned with the whole organism). It is currently reflected in the movement toward affective learning (dealing with attitudes, feelings, and emotions) as well as child-centered and "relevant" educational practices. The behavioral-engineering approach is based on the philosophy of essentialism and traditional behavioral psychology (including stimulus-response, connectionism, and conditioning). It is currently reflected in the stress on cognitive learning and the basic three Rs, as well as teacher-centered practices. The teacher who employs the permissive-humane style serves as a therapist and teacher-counselor and is concerned with *process* (or treatment effects). The teacher who employs the behavioral-engineering style serves in the role of diagnostician and is concerned with behavioral modification and *products* (or outcomes).

These two teaching styles are represented in the literature in various ways, not as an either-or-dichotomy. The two styles can be abstracted from theoretical and research data, but they have not been explored as exclusive aspects of research on teaching. They merely represent "food for thought" in the light of historical and contemporary educational practices.

THEORETICAL APPROACHES TO STUDYING TEACHER BEHAVIOR

When we turn to the research on what actually constitutes a good teacher, we find that it is virtually impossible to identify these characteristics either precisely or neatly — the research has its limitations. There are literally thousands of studies on the subject, yet few facts have been established and few generalizations have been accepted. The problem is so complex that no one agrees upon what a "competent" or "effective" teacher is; therefore, we can define a "good" teacher anyway we like — so long as it makes sense. Furthermore, there will always be teachers who will break almost all the rules and yet be profoundly successful.

In spite of the countless research studies on what constitutes good teaching, the data have failed to produce useful results; many of the findings are either confirmations of "common sense" or highly questionable, and so-called acceptable findings are often later repudiated. Bruce Biddle maintains that the majority of researchers admit that "we do not know how to define, prepare for, or measure teacher competence," despite the urgent need for skilled teachers and for understanding teacher effectiveness.[24] Confusion over terms and the complexity of the teaching

---

[24] Bruce J. Biddle, "The Integration of Teacher Effectivness," in B. J. Biddle and W. J. Ellena (eds.), *Contemporary Research on Teacher Effectiveness* (New York: Holt, Rinehart and Winston, 1964), pp. 2–3.

act are major reasons for the negligible results for judging teacher behavior. The result is that the few viable discoveries up to now are pitifully small in proportion to the outlay in time, effort, and money.

In general, methods for organizing teacher behavior research generally fall into three categories: (1) model approach, (2) instructional (or interaction) processes, and (3) teacher characteristics (or lists).

The Model Approach

Man is constantly observing his environment, labeling objects, events, and ideas, and relating them to one another. Educators formulate models because it is challenging and fashionable to do so, and models tend to increase understanding of facts, correlates, and relations. While models provide initial comprehension it is often an illusion of comprehension (this is especially true of teacher behavior models). The models deal with flow arrows and circles, input and output variables, and sequences and subsequences—all of which result in a highly complex, theoretical formulation. Most model approaches tend to overwhelm or confuse because they try to encompass the whole and include all germane variables, to the point that the model often produces trivia or meaningless data.

Perhaps the best way to gain from the models approach in studying teacher behavior is to use it as a system of implications for understanding relations, rather than taking the information literally. Robert Snow asserts that the teacher behavior model should promote *theoretical* thinking about teaching. The reader (or listener or viewer) should create an analogy between some aspect of teaching and other known things, concepts, or roles listed in the model, in order to elaborate on ideas about teaching. Such analogies are not meant to be closely reasoned or binding in detail. They are merely suggestive and can generate hypotheses.[25]

William Morris adds three additional factors that deserve attention in learning to build or appreciate educational models: (1) a process of elaboration, which starts with simple points and evolves to richer points reflecting the complexity of actual situations, (2) a process of analogy (similar to Snow's), in which well-developed structures from other fields are incorporated for elaboration, and (3) a process of grouping and

---

[25] Robert E. Snow, "Heuristic Teaching as Protheses." In R. E. Snow (ed.); *A Symposium on Heuristic Teaching,* technical report no. 18 (Stanford, Ca.: Stanford Center for Research and Development in Teaching, Stanford University, 1970), pp. 104-10. Robert E. Snow, "Theory Construction for Research on Teaching," In R. M. W. Travers (ed.), *Second Handbook of Research on Teaching.* (Chicago: Rand McNally, 1973), pp. 77-112.

Figure 7.3 / A Seven-Variable Sequence Model for Teacher Effectiveness

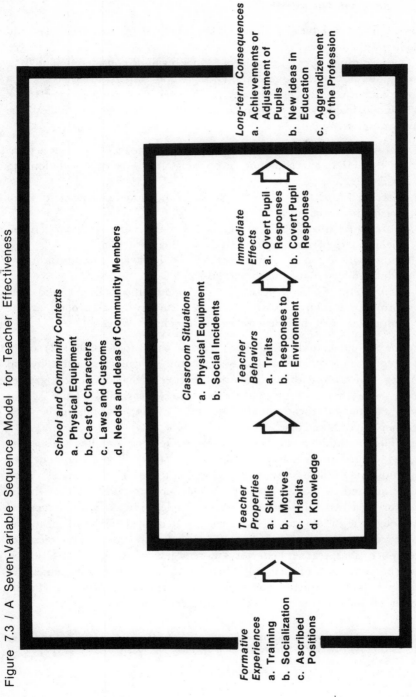

Source: From *Contemporary Research on Teacher Effectiveness*, Edited by Bruce J. Biddle and William J. Ellena. Copyright © 1964 by Holt, Rinehart and Winston. Reprinted by permission of Holt, Rinehart and Winston.

regrouping variables for purposes of making assumptions and deductions.[26]

Two examples of teacher behavior models will be considered. The first, by Biddle, postulates a cause-and-effect relationship or, more precisely, a cause-and-effect sequence between teacher behavior and teacher effects.[27] The model involves five main sequences and two contextual variables. The five sequences are:

1. *Formative Experiences.* These include the teacher's experiences prior to the classroom situation, everything from personal relations to teacher education.
2. *Teacher Properties.* These include the individual characteristics and personality traits of the teacher.
3. *Teacher Behaviors.* These include the product of interaction between the demands of the situation and the teacher's reactions.
4. *Immediate Effects.* These include the behavior and performance exhibited by the students in the classroom.
5. *Long-Term Consequences.* These include the behavior and performance exhibited by students after leaving the classroom, or the consequences of the teacher after the student leaves school.

The two contextual variables are (1) classroom situations and (2) school and community contexts. These are mainly sociological and physical settings which affect the students' and teacher's behavior. For the greater part, the teacher has little control over these two variables. Figure 7.3 is a representation of the postulated sequence of the relationship between teacher behavior and teacher effect.

While the Biddle model is relatively clear and easy to follow (this is why it was selected as an example), the function and utility of the model are questionable. Having established the existence of the model, what relevance and use does it have for the classroom teacher? Will the model improve teacher behavior research, much less the success of teachers? Although the Biddle model, like others, is highly rational and logical, one must ask whether teaching can be sliced into such concise categories. On many occasions, teacher behavior is more or less spontaneous and based on hunches and intuition. Teaching involves an uncontrived and sometimes uncontrollable character, and speed. The formulation of any model for teacher behavior is perhaps metaphysical, not to be taken literally.

---

[26] William T. Morris, "On the Art of Modeling." In R. M. Stogdill (ed.), *The Process of Modeling in the Behavioral Sciences* (Columbus, Ohio: Ohio State University Press, 1970), pp. 76–93.

[27] Biddle, "Integration of Teacher Effectiveness," pp. 1–40.

Louis Smith and William Geoffrey have developed a systems analysis model for analyzing classroom events.[28] In what is perhaps the most intensive study of a single classroom, Smith observed Geoffrey's seventh-grade class each day for an entire semester. Summary observations and interpretations were recorded by tape. The analysis of the early days focuses on the development of teacher-student roles, how the teacher establishes control and how students behave. The teacher not only sets rules and regulations but indirectly builds a belief system for students. Figure 7.4 shows one sequence of events involving a few moments in the

Figure 7.4 / Classroom Model of the Development of Monitor Roles and Belief Systems

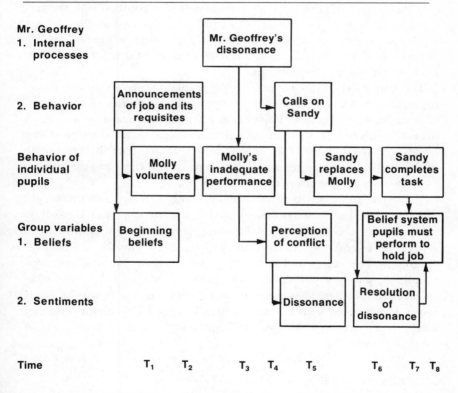

From *The Complexities of an Urban Classroom: An Analysis Toward a General Theory of Teaching* by Louis M. Smith and William Geoffrey. Copyright © 1968 by Holt, Rinehart and Winston. Reprinted by Holt, Rinehart and Winston.

[28] Louis M. Smith and William Geoffrey, *Complexities of an Urban Classroom* (New York: Holt, Rinehart & Winston, 1968).

classroom in which Geoffrey gives the role of "assignment monitor" to a girl named Molly and later substitutes another child in the role.

The boxes within the figure describe the sequences of behaviors and attitudes that evolve in these few moments; these classroom dynamics are further detailed in the left-hand column outside the figure. At the bottom of the figure are eight time sequences, $T_1 \ldots T_8$. At T_1 the teacher announces the requirements of an assignment monitor—such as good attendance and good handwriting. At T_2 Molly volunteers and a belief system emerges; that is, the student must be adequate to the task. During T_3 Molly misspells a word in writing the assignment on the board. Though spelling ability was not originally specified for the job, it seems that dissonance surfaces for both teacher and class—at T_4 and T_5. The belief that the student-monitor must do an adequate job conflicts with the fact that Molly is not performing adequately. This leads to the teacher replacing Molly with another student; the problem is resolved at T_6, followed at T_7 and T_8 with reinforcement of the belief that the assignment monitor must do an adequate job.

The authors elaborate on their model, explaining how Geoffrey moves to build a belief system among students which consists of two major themes: learning should be going on at all times, and learning is work. A detailed analysis of the teacher's behavior accompanies the discussion; how he develops the monitor's role, how he deals with questions, his reaction to student behaviors, the alternatives that were open to him, and the possible consequences of these alternatives.

While the analysis is both complex and enlightening, and the insight that the model provides is of immediate interest, the approach is based on the personality of Geoffrey and his students; therefore, it is difficult to generalize beyond the descriptions. The model is limited to Geoffrey's classroom. The events and time sequences are real, but they are over-simplified, purely hypothetical, and almost certainly different for other teachers and students. For example, in another classroom situation Molly could have reacted with hostility during T_4 and T_5, or another teacher would have accepted Molly's spelling mistake and retained her as monitor—and so on.

Instructional (or Interaction) Processes

Approaches to the study of the instructional process are based on assessing teacher-student interaction and may be divided into two groups. One tends to be descriptive and is based on nonsystematic observation. The observer usually enters the classroom, takes notes, develops insights, and is at liberty to analyze any facet of teacher, student, or teacher-student behavior. The observer is not limited by any instrument but uses an open-ended form and can concentrate on whatever she or he wants to write about or describe — ranging from the evenness of the window shades to the teacher's attire. Data are usually summarized in journalistic style, as exemplified by traditional supervisory observations of teachers and by the recent narratives of what goes on in the classroom written by John Holt, Herbert Kohl, Jonathan Kozol, and Alexander Moore.[29]

This procedure is perhaps the most unreliable and invalid of the instructional processes. The observer or narrator usually enters the classroom with a host of biases and preconceived attitudes about the teacher. Since there are no controls or guidelines and no reliability or validity checks, there is wide latitude for the observer to see what he or she expects to see. Because this approach ignores research methods it is not elaborated on in this text, merely noted so as to help distinguish the second type of instructional process.

The second approach to studying the instructional process tends to be analytical and is based on systematic observation of the classroom in which the observer tests preconceived hypotheses related to teacher-student interaction or, sometimes, teacher characteristics. The analysis deals with a specific behavior (i.e., "move" or "episode"), and a series of these behaviors constitute a larger behavior (i.e., "cycle" or "pattern"), described and recorded by an abstract unit of measurement which may vary in size and time (i.e., every three seconds a recording is made). The data is pre- and posttested, recorded or transcribed, and the results are statistically analyzed.

A few examples of this instructional process should suffice. Arno Bellack analyzed the linguistic behavior of teachers and students in the classroom.[30] Observation of what goes on reveals that classroom activities are carried out in large part by verbal interaction between students and teachers; few classroom activities can be carried out without the use of language. The research, therefore, focused on language as the main instrument of communication in teaching. Four basic verbal "pedagogical moves" were labeled.

1. *Structuring.* Structuring moves serve the function of focusing attention on subject matter or classroom procedures and beginning interaction between students and teachers. They set the context for subsequent

---

[29] See John Holt, *How Children Fail* (New York: Pitman Publishing Corp., 1964); Herbert Kohl, *36 Children* (New York: New American Library, 1967); Jonathan Kozol, *Death at an Early Age* (Boston: Houghton Mifflin Co., 1967); Moore, *Realities of the Urban Classroom.*

[30] Arno A. Bellack et al., *The Language of the Classroom* (New York: Teachers College Press, Columbia University, 1966).

behavior; for example, teachers frequently begin a class with a structuring move in which they focus on the topic to be discussed in class.

2. *Soliciting.* Moves in this category are designed to elicit a verbal or physical response. For example, the teacher asks a question about the topic with the hope of encouraging a response from the students.

3. *Responding.* These moves occur in relation to and after the soliciting moves. Their ideal function is to fulfill the expectations of the soliciting moves.

4. *Reacting.* These moves are sometimes occasioned by one or more of the above moves but are not directly elicited by them. Reacting moves serve to modify, clarify or judge the structuring, soliciting, or responding moves.

According to Bellack, these pedagogical moves occur in combinations or patterns called "teaching cycles." The cycle usually begins with the structuring or soliciting move by the teacher, both of which are initiative behaviors, continues with a responding move from a student, and ends with some kind of reaction by the teacher. In most cases, the cycle begins and ends with the teacher. The investigators' analysis of the classroom also produced several insights:

1. Teachers dominate verbal activities. The teacher-student ratio in terms of words spoken is 3:1. (This evidence corresponds with Flanders's research which found that teachers' talk represents 80 percent of classroom activity.)

2. Teacher and student moves are clearly defined — the teacher engages in structuring, soliciting, and reacting behaviors, while the student is usually limited to responding. (This evidence also corresponds with Flanders's finding that most teachers dominate classrooms in such a way as to make students dependent.)

3. Teachers initiate about 85 percent of the cycles. The basic unit of verbal interaction is the soliciting-responding pattern. Verbal interchanges occur at a rate of slightly less than two cycles per minute.

4. In approximately two-thirds of the moves and three-fourths of the verbal interplay, talk is content oriented.

5. About 60 percent of the total discourse is fact oriented.

In summary, the data suggest that the classroom is teacher dominated, subject centered, and fact oriented. The students' primary responsibility seems to be to respond to the teacher's soliciting moves.

In another study, B. Othaniel Smith and Milton Meux focussed on the linguistic behavior of the teacher.[31] These behaviors are divided into

---

[31] B. Othaniel Smith and Milton Meux, *A Study of the Logic of Teaching*, 2nd ed. (Urbana, Ill.: University of Illinois Press, 1970).

"episodes" and "monologs," and through these verbal aspirations the teacher exhibits a "pattern" which shapes the course of instruction. The episode is defined as one or more verbal exchanges between two or more speakers. Questions by the teacher and answers by the students constitute the most common episode. The monolog consists of a solo performance by a speaker addressing the group; the teacher who gives directions or a command is expressing a monolog. Effective teachers tend to pattern their behavior along episodes in which there is give and take between teacher and students. Various types of episodes are exhibited in the classroom, and the ideal one represents an alternation which occurs when several speakers respond to the original entry question. Thus the most effective linguistic behavior is not teacher-student, student-teacher, but the teacher interacting with several students.

A series of episodes or monologs comprises a cycle which includes one or more of several verbal entries. These are:

1. *Defining.* Entries comprising this group are concerned with how words are used to refer to objects. They are usually stated as "What does the word . . . mean?"
2. *Describing.* This connotes an explanation or description about something: "What did John find out?"
3. *Designating.* These entries identify something by name: "What animal did we see in the film?"
4. *Stating.* In this group are statements of issues, proofs, rules, theories, conclusions, beliefs, and so on. "What is the plot of the story?" is a question which asks for a statement of some sort.
5. *Reporting.* The entries in this group ask for a summary or a report on a book or document.
6. *Substituting.* In this group, the student is asked to perform a symbolic operation, usually of mathematic or scientific value.
7. *Evaluating.* These entries ask for judgment or estimate of worth of something.
8. *Opinioning.* The entries in this group ask for a conclusion, affirmation, or denial based upon evidence: "How do you feel President Carter will be judged by historians?"

A third example of instructional process is the study by James Gallagher of the kinds of questions that teachers ask.[32] His study led to four categories of questions:

[32] James J. Gallagher, "Expressive Thought by Gifted Children in the Classroom," in *Language and the Higher Thought Processes* (Champaign, Ill.: National Council of Teachers of English, 1965), pp. 56–65.

1. *Cognitive-Memory.* These questions require students to reproduce facts
   or remember content through processes such as rote memory or selective recall. An example is: "What is the capital of France?"
2. *Convergent.* These questions require students to produce new information which leads to the correct or conventional answer. Given or
   known information usually determines the correct response; novel
   information is usually considered incorrect. An example is: "Could you
   summarize the author's major points?"
3. *Divergent.* These questions require students to generate their own data
   or to take a new perspective on a given topic. Divergent questions have
   no "right" answer; they suggest novel or creative responses. An example
   might be: "What might the history of the United States have been if the
   South had won the Civil War?"
4. *Evaluative.* These questions require students to make value judgments
   about the quality, correctness, or adequacy of information, based on
   some criterion usually set by the student or by some objective standard.
   For example, "How would you judge the art of Picasso?"

Gallagher's study reveals that in most classrooms cognitive-memory
questions comprised more than 50 percent of the total questions asked.
(This is based on classrooms with gifted students; it is assumed that
teachers ask even more cognitive-memory questions with ordinary or slow
students.) Convergent questions were the second most frequently used
category, and few divergent or evaluative questions were asked. In fact,
Gallagher surmises that teacher-student discussions can operate normally
if only the first two categories of questions are available.

The instructional process ordinarily implies the use of verbal communication. In a parallel study, Charles Galloway developed guidelines for
observing nonverbal communication of teachers; that is, the silent
behavior of space, time, and body.[33]

Space. A teacher's use of space conveys meaning to students. For
example, teachers who spend most of their time by the blackboard or at
their desks may convey insecurity — a reluctance to venture into student
territory.

Time. How teachers utilize classroom time is an indication of how they
value certain activities. The elementary teacher who devotes a great deal of
time to reading but very little to mathematics is conveying a message to the
students.

Body Maneuvers. Nonverbal cues are used by teachers to control
students. The raised eyebrow, the pointed finger, the silent stare all

---

[33] Charles Galloway, "Nonverbal Communication," *Theory into Practice,* December 1968,
pp. 172–75.

communicate meaning. When the teacher's verbal and nonverbal cues are in contradiction, the students tend to read the nonverbal cues as a truer reflection of the teacher's real feelings, according to Galloway.

Perhaps the best way for teachers to become aware of their nonverbal behavior is to sensitize themselves to student feedback in terms of their own behavior. Videotapes of classroom experiences can be analyzed to pick out inconsistencies between verbal and nonverbal behavior.

In summary, it is important to recognize that the instructional processes are based on observing teacher and student behaviors. Although this method is popular for measuring teacher behavior, it has limitations. These include the small number of observations upon which a rating is usually based, and the possibility that the observer's reliability is limited. The teacher tends to put on an act while being observed, and the presence of the observer creates a "Hawthorne effect" whereby, because students and teacher are aware of a study being conducted, their behaviors are altered. Despite the inventory being tested for reliability and validity, the observer is influenced by his or her own values and interpretations of what constitutes a good teacher. Even the position of the observer is a factor to consider. If he sits in the back of the room, he sees a number of heads and shoulders, which partially blocks his vision of the students. If he positions himself on the side of the room, he accentuates his presence and increases the likelihood of behavioral changes among subjects.[34]

Teacher Characteristics (or Lists)

In the reams of research on teacher behavior, the greatest amount involves the study of teacher characteristics. This in itself causes a problem; inability to define or agree upon which teacher characteristics constitute "good" or "important" teacher behavior or "effective" teaching has confused and caused inconsistencies among the researchers. Confusion over a variety of terms, such as "teacher traits," "teacher personality," "teacher competency," "teacher performance," or "teacher outcomes," add to the general problem. Not only are there no clear or acceptable methods of categorizing teacher characteristics, but the lists of characteristics are sometimes vague and ill defined, and they vary from one researcher to another.[35]

---

[34] Allan C. Ornstein, "Can We Define a Good Teacher?" *Peabody Journal of Education,* April 1976, pp. 201-7.

[35] Bruce J. Biddle, "Methods and Concepts in Classroom Research," *Review of Educational Research,* June 1967, pp. 337-57; Gary D. Borich (ed.), *The Appraisal of Teaching: Concepts and Processes* (Reading, Mass.: Addison-Wesley Publishing Co., 1977); John McNeil and W. James Popham, "The Assessment of Teacher Competence," in R. M. W. Travers (ed.), *Second Handbook of Research on Teaching* (Chicago: Rand McNally, 1973), pp. 218-44.

Even when similar terms are used, the definitions and usage vary, so that similar terms have dissimilar meanings. Warm behavior for one investigator often means something different for another; further, it can be assumed that a warm teacher would have different effects on first-graders, sixth-graders, and twelfth-graders. Different effects would also be expected with low-income and middle-income students, members of different ethnic groups, boys and girls, or high achievers and nonachievers. These differences probably operate for every teacher behavior characteristic.[36]

Thus, the inability of researchers to agree on a particular list of characteristics for a particular school setting distorts the research findings,

Table 7.3 / Characteristics Important for Successful Teaching: A Review of the Research

1. *Resourcefulness.* Originality, creativeness, initiative, imagination, adventurousness, progressiveness.
2. *Intelligence.* Foresight, intellectual acuity, understanding, mental ability, intellectual capacity, common sense.
3. *Emotional Stability.* Poise, self-control, steadfastness, sobriety, dignity, nonneuroticism, emotional maturity, adjustment, constancy, loyalty, easygoing realism in facing life, not excitable, stable, integrated character.
4. *Considerateness.* Appreciativeness, kindliness, friendliness, courteousness, sympathy, tact, good-naturedness, helpfulness, patience, politeness, thoughtfulness, tolerance.
5. *Buoyancy.* Optimism, enthusiasm, cheerfulness, gregariousness, fluency, talkativeness, sense of humor, pleasantness, carefreeness, vivaciousness, alertness, animation, idealism, articulativeness, expressiveness, wit.
6. *Objectivity.* Fairness, impartiality, open-mindedness, freedom from prejudice, sense of evidence.
7. *Drive.* Physical vigor, energy perseverance, ambition, industry, endurance, motivation, purposefulness, speediness, zealousness, quickness.
8. *Dominance.* Self-confidence, forcefulness, decisiveness, courageousness, independence, insensitiveness to social approval, self-sufficiency, determination, thick-skinnedness, self-reliance, self-assertiveness.
9. *Attractiveness.* Dress, physique, freedom from physical defects, personal magnetism, neatness, cleanliness, posture, personal charm, appearance.
10. *Refinement.* Good taste, modesty, morality, conventionality, culture, polish, well-readness.
11. *Cooperativeness.* Friendliness, easy-goingness, geniality, generosity, adaptability, flexibility, responsiveness, trustfulness, warm-heartedness, unselfishness, charitableness.
12. *Reliability.* Accuracy, dependability, honesty, punctuality, responsibility, conscientiousness, painstakingness, trustworthiness, consistency, sincerity.

Source: A. S. Barr, "Characteristics of Successful Teachers," *Phi Delta Kappan,* March 1958, pp. 282–83.

[36] Allan C. Ornstein, "Systematizing Teacher Behavior Research," *Phi Delta Kappan,* May 1971, pp. 551–55.

as do linguistic usage, confusion over words, and interchangeable words. These types of discrepancies, the inability to agree upon operational terms and school settings, and the problem of similar and dissimilar categories, cause a lack of generalizability in the findings. Although a list of teacher characteristics may be reliable and valid for a particular study, the categories of one study usually cannot be compared with another. When the researchers are having so much trouble trying to make sense of what they are doing, it is little wonder that teachers are relatively unaffected by the research on teacher behavior. They do not take it seriously, and, for the greater part, they do not find it meaningful or applicable to the classroom situation.

Figure 7.5 / The Ryans Teacher Behavior Inventory

Pupil Behavior

1. Apathetic	N	Alert
2. Obstructive	N	Responsible
3. Uncertain	N	Confident
4. Dependent	N	Initiating

Teacher Behavior

5. Partial	N	Fair
6. Autocratic	N	Democratic
7. Aloof	N	Responsive
8. Restricted	N	Understanding
9. Harsh	N	Kindly
10. Dull	N	Stimulating
11. Stereotyped	N	Original
12. Apathetic	N	Alert
13. Unimpressive	N	Attractive
14. Evading	N	Responsible
15. Erratic	N	Steady
16. Excitable	N	Poised
17. Uncertain	N	Confident
18. Disorganized	N	Systematic
19. Inflexible	N	Adaptable
20. Pessimistic	N	Optimistic
21. Immature	N	Integrated
22. Narrow	N	Broad

Note N = not sure.

Source: David G. Ryans, *Characteristics of Teachers* (Washington, D.C.: American Council of Education, 1960), p. 86.

Although a particular list of teacher characteristics cannot be advocated or reduced to a simple formula, and although literally thousands of teacher characteristics have been studied over the years, A. S. Barr attempted to organize recommended behaviors into a brief, manageable list.[37] Reviewing some 50 years of research on the topic, he listed and defined 12 characteristics, as reported in Table 7.3.

David Ryans's monumental study of teacher characteristics, involving 6,000 teachers in 1,700 schools, yielded a bipolar list of four student characteristics and 18 teacher characteristics.[38] This list, which was used in conjunction with a seven-point rating scale to assess teacher behavior, is reproduced in Figure 7.5.

Respondents were asked to check the approximate position of the teacher on a scale ranging between the opposite behaviors, with N to be checked if they were not sure.

The 22 characteristics were defined in detail and devised by complex statistical procedures. The 18 teacher characteristics were further grouped and reduced into three "patterns" of teacher behavior, similar to the teaching style discussed above. The three patterns of teacher behavior were designated as:

1. Pattern X, reflecting understanding, friendliness, and responsiveness v. aloofness and egocentrism.
2. Pattern Y, reflecting responsible, businesslike, systematic v. evading, unplanned, slipshod teacher behavior.
3. Pattern Z, reflecting stimulating, imaginative, original v. dull, routine teacher behavior.

These three primary teacher patterns were the major qualities singled out for further attention. Elementary teachers scored higher than secondary teachers on the scales of understanding and friendly classroom behavior (pattern X). Differences between women and men teachers were insignificant in the elementary schools, but in the secondary schools women consistently scored higher in pattern X, as well as responsible and businesslike classroom behavior (pattern Y), and stimulating and imaginative classroom behavior (pattern Z). Younger teachers (under 55 years) scored higher than older teachers from the standpoint of patterns X and Z; older teachers exhibited an advantage when compared from the standpoint of pattern Y.

---

[37] A. S. Barr, "Characteristics of Successful Teachers," *Phi Delta Kappan*, March 1958, pp. 282-83.

[38] David G. Ryans, *Characteristics of Teachers* (Washington, D.C.: American Council of Education, 1960).

Figure 7.6 / The Tuckman Teacher Feedback Form (TTFF)

Teacher observed _____ Observer _____ Date _____

Place an X in that one space of the seven between each adjective pair that indicates your perception of the teacher's behavior. The closer you place your X toward one adjective or the other, the better you think that adjective describes the teacher.

1.	Original	___ ___ ___ ___ ___ ___ ___	Conventional
2.	Patient	___ ___ ___ ___ ___ ___ ___	Impatient
3.	Cold	___ ___ ___ ___ ___ ___ ___	Warm
4.	Hostile	___ ___ ___ ___ ___ ___ ___	Amiable
5.	Creative	___ ___ ___ ___ ___ ___ ___	Routinized
6.	Inhibited	___ ___ ___ ___ ___ ___ ___	Uninhibited
7.	Iconoclastic	___ ___ ___ ___ ___ ___ ___	Ritualistic
8.	Gentle	___ ___ ___ ___ ___ ___ ___	Harsh
9.	Unfair	___ ___ ___ ___ ___ ___ ___	Fair
10.	Capricious	___ ___ ___ ___ ___ ___ ___	Purposeful
11.	Cautious	___ ___ ___ ___ ___ ___ ___	Experimental
12.	Disorganized	___ ___ ___ ___ ___ ___ ___	Organized
13.	Unfriendly	___ ___ ___ ___ ___ ___ ___	Sociable
14.	Resourceful	___ ___ ___ ___ ___ ___ ___	Uncertain
15.	Reserved	___ ___ ___ ___ ___ ___ ___	Outspoken
16.	Imaginative	___ ___ ___ ___ ___ ___ ___	Exacting
17.	Erratic	___ ___ ___ ___ ___ ___ ___	Systematic
18.	Aggressive	___ ___ ___ ___ ___ ___ ___	Passive
19.	Accepting (people)	___ ___ ___ ___ ___ ___ ___	Critical
20.	Quiet	___ ___ ___ ___ ___ ___ ___	Bubbly
21.	Outgoing	___ ___ ___ ___ ___ ___ ___	Withdrawn
22.	In control	___ ___ ___ ___ ___ ___ ___	On the run
23.	Flighty	___ ___ ___ ___ ___ ___ ___	Conscientious
24.	Dominant	___ ___ ___ ___ ___ ___ ___	Submissive
25.	Observant	___ ___ ___ ___ ___ ___ ___	Preoccupied
26.	Introverted	___ ___ ___ ___ ___ ___ ___	Extroverted
27.	Assertive	___ ___ ___ ___ ___ ___ ___	Soft-spoken
28.	Timid	___ ___ ___ ___ ___ ___ ___	Adventurous

Source: Bruce W. Tuckman, "Feedback and the Change Process," *Phi Delta Kappan,* January 1976, p. 342. Copyright © Bruce W. Tuckman.

A similar but more recent list of teacher characteristics was compiled by Bruce Tuckman, who has developed a feedback system for stimulating change in teacher behavior.[39] His instrument (Figure 7.6) contains 28 bipolar items, also with seven spaces to rate teachers for each pair of adjectives.

---

[39] Bruce W. Tuckman, "Feedback and the Change Process," *Phi Delta Kappan,* January 1976, pp. 341–44.

The characteristics cluster into four teacher "dimensions," similar to the procedure followed by Ryans. Tuckman's dimensions are:

1. *Creativity.* The creative teacher is imaginative, experimenting, and original, as opposed to the noncreative teacher, who is routine, exacting, and cautious.
2. *Dynamic.* The dynamic teacher is outgoing, energetic, and extroverted as opposed to the nondynamic teacher, who is passive, withdrawn, and submissive.
3. *Organized.* The organized teacher is purposeful, resourceful, and in control as opposed to the disorganized teacher, who is capricious, erratic, and flighty.
4. *Warm.* The warm teacher is sociable, amiable, and patient as opposed to the cold teacher, who is unfriendly, hostile, and impatient.

The inventory developed by Tuckman is supposed to be used as a feedback system for stimulating change in teacher behavior. He offers 12 rules to be followed in using his teacher characteristic inventory to achieve this (Table 7.4).

Tuckman believes that teachers working in a team, visiting and rating each other in their own classrooms, can be taught how to use the inventory and will subsequently improve their instruction. After a round of mutual visitation, each teacher is given a summary of his or her ratings by other teachers in the group. This tells the teacher how his teaching behavior is perceived. At the same time, feedback is provided by the group in an informal and personal atmosphere, as opposed to a formal supervisory-teacher relationship or an impersonal rating sheet placed in the mailbox. Teachers learn how to create new strengths for themselves by discussing

Table 7.4 / Rules for Feedback and Change

1. Feedback should involve concrete behaviors or characteristics.
2. Feedback should provide clear data of exactly how one behaves.
3. The feedback source should be reputable and believable.
4. Feedback should be in terms that the teacher can understand and relate to.
5. The feedback recipient should have a clear ideal model of what his or her behavior should be.
6. The feedback recipient should know what others expect of him or her.
7. The feedback recipient should be committed to change.
8. The feedback recipient's commitment to change should be made public.
9. Feedback should create tension.
10. The feedback recipient should receive support.
11. Models for change which are relevant for teachers should be provided.
12. Feedback should be continuous.

Source: Bruce W. Tuckman, "Feedback and the Change Process," pp. 340–44; Bruce W. Tuckman, "The Effectiveness of Feedback for Changing Student Teachers' Humanistic Behavior," paper presented at the annual meeting of the American Educational Research Association, Chicago, April 1974. Copyright © Bruce W. Tuckman.

their weaknesses. As the last step in the feedback process, the teachers observe one another a second time to provide a basis for determining whether there has been a change in behavior in the recommended direction. Although teachers and schools may be reluctant to try out Tuckman's inventory, since change and growth are risk processes, the inventory is relevant for teachers, and it can be used in the classroom to improve instruction.

Before leaving the topic of teacher characteristics, we should note that these lists are the most common technique used for measuring teacher behavior. They are easy to use and to tally, and they reflect a tradition which goes back to beginning of the 20th century. On a typical form students, teachers, supervisors or administrators, parents, or researchers observe and rate the teacher's behavior. However, there is sufficient data to suggest that different groups markedly disagree in their judgments on identifying good teachers.[40] This is not surprising, since the judges are handicapped by their own personal biases and beliefs of what is or what should be a good teacher.

Because the rater is, of course, human, the ratings may be distorted by the (1) halo effect, whereby the rater evaluates or reacts to each characteristic in the direction of the general impression of the teacher, (2) the error of leniency, a tendency of the rater to rate low or high, no matter what the reason, (3) the error of central tendency, whereby the rater is reluctant to make extreme judgments about others and always marks toward the middle of the rating instrument,[41] and (4) constant error, whereby the rater tends to rate others in the opposite direction of his own attitudes and behaviors (for example, the rater who is businesslike tends to rate the teacher as less businesslike). Other factors that tend to affect raters are their: (1) sex, (2) race (ethnicity), (3) age, (4) intelligence, (5) understanding of directions, (6) understanding of purposes, (7) time required to complete the ratings, (8) possession of traits being measured, and (9) criteria employed to assess the various behaviors or traits.[42]

Raters also are observers, either at the time they are observing the teacher or, with regard to students, as they observe the teacher over a long period of time and under various conditions. The limitations of observing teachers, which were examined above in relation to the instructional

[40] Edward E. Hawkins and Emery Stoop, "Objective and Subjective Identification of Outstanding Elementary Teachers," *Journal of Educational Research*, April 1966, pp. 344–46; Maurice G. Kendall and Alan Stuart, *The Advanced Theory of Statistics*, vol. 3, 3rd ed. (New York: Hafner Publishing Co., 1975).

[41] This is the reason Ryans and Tuckman both use a seven-point rating scale instead of the traditional five-point scale.

[42] J. P. Guilford, *Psychometric Methods*, 2nd ed. (New York: McGraw-Hill Book Co., 1954); Ornstein, "Can We Define a Good Teacher?"

process, are also germane and limit the person who is attempting to rate the teacher on a list of characteristics or traits.

To sum up the research on teacher behavior, whether using the models approach, instructional process, or teacher characteristics, it is virtually impossible to delineate good teaching. The numerous studies have not scientifically isolated the components of successful teaching. Except for common sense — a friendly teacher is a better teacher than an unfriendly teacher — there is no adequate criterion against which teacher behavior can be validated.

According to B. Othaniel Smith, it is "inappropriate to ask whether . . . a system is a true classification of the relevant phenomena." The most we can hope is that the selection and classifications of teacher behaviors are wise and useful and that the method for classifying them is clear — bearing in mind that this "condition may never be completely satisfied by any system."[43] Donald Hamachek also defends the efforts to identify good teachers. "Even though there is no single best or worst kind of teacher there are clearly distinguishable characteristics associated with 'good' and 'bad' teachers. There is no one best kind of teacher because there is no one kind of student."[44]

CONCLUSIONS

Literally thousands of studies have been conducted on teacher effectiveness. Investigators have looked at teacher leadership, teaching styles, and teacher behaviors. Teacher effects have been judged by investigators themselves, supervisors and administrators, teachers, parents, and students. Teacher training, traits, personality, abilities, sex, weight, voice quality, and many other variables have been studied to determine what makes a good teacher. And yet, with all this research activity, the results have been modest and often contradictory. We know very little about teacher effectiveness, and many of our findings concerning teacher leadership, styles, and behaviors have been later repudiated.

Today many researchers have abandoned the field of teacher competence as too complex. Still others feel the field represents a simpleminded approach and have moved to more complex topics, such as the study of student outcomes, to hold teachers accountable, or the study of learning environments whereby the teacher's behavior is only one of many

[43] B. Othaniel Smith. "Recent Research on Teaching: An Interpretation," *High School Journal,* November 1967, p. 67.

[44] Don Hamachek, "Characteristics of Good Teachers and Implications for Teacher Education," *Phi Delta Kappan,* February 1969, p. 343.

variables considered, along with others such as students, peer groups, family, school, and community.

In the meantime, the dismal results of teacher effectiveness research provide little comfort for school people who are confronted with everyday, real problems in the field of teacher excellence. Practical decisions have to be made; applicants for teaching positions must be screened and recruited; teachers must be evaluated and provided with assistance. These judgments continue to be made chiefly by personal opinion and rarely on the basis of objective criteria.

ACTIVITIES

1. Describe the teacher's opportunities for leadership in the classroom.
2. Describe the importance of the teacher's personality in relation to teacher style.
3. Defend or criticize the textbook's characterization of the complexity involved in measuring teacher behavior.
4. After analyzing a number of plans for measuring teacher behavior, discuss the advantages and disadvantages of one plan from the student's view, teacher's view, school's view.
5. Develop your own instrument for measuring teacher behavior. Try it out in class, if possible.

DISCUSSION QUESTIONS

1. What are some of the problems involved in measuring teacher behavior?
2. What leadership qualities are needed to maintain classroom discipline with elementary school children, junior high school children, senior high school youth?
3. How would you describe your own teacher style?
4. How would you define a "good" teacher?
5. What are the advantages and disadvantages of using the model approach, instructional approach, or list of characteristics for assessing teacher behavior?

SUGGESTED FOR FURTHER READING

Allen, Dwight and Ryan, Kevin. *Microteaching*. Reading, Mass.: Addison-Wesley Publishing Co., 1969.

Borich, Gary D. *The Appraisal of Teaching*. Reading, Mass.: Addison-Wesley Publishing Co., 1977.

Flanders, Ned A. *Teacher Influence, Pupil Attitudes, and Achievement*. Washington, D.C.: U.S. Government Printing Office, 1965.

Gagné, Robert M. and Briggs, Leslie J. *Principles of Instructional Design*. New York: Holt, Rinehart & Winston, 1974.

Good, Thomas L., Biddle, Bruce J. and Brophy, Jere E. *Teachers Make a Difference*. New York: Holt, Rinehart & Winston, 1975.

Goodlad, John I. and Klein, M. Frances. *Behind the Classroom Door.* Worthington, Ohio: Charles A. Jones Publishing Co., 1970.

Jackson, Philip W. *Life in Classrooms.* New York: Holt, Rinehart & Winston, 1968.

Raths, Louis E., Harmin, Merrill and Simon, Sidney B. *Values and Teaching.* Columbus, Ohio: Charles E. Merrill Publishing Co., 1966.

Travers, Robert M. W. (ed.). *Second Handbook of Research on Teaching.* (Chicago: Rand McNally & Co., 1973.

Walberg, Herbert J. (ed.). *Evaluating Educational Performance* (Berkeley, Ca.: McCutchan Publishing Corp., 1974.

CHAPTER 8

THE NATURE OF
THE TEACHING
PROFESSION

The efforts of teachers to establish their professional status, despite the restraints of bureaucratic school systems and the power of school boards, is well documented. The problem of professional identity is linked to salaries and working conditions, as well as what the public thinks of the kind of service teachers render to society. The teacher's professional image, on the whole, is determined by occupational restraints within the system as well as comparative rankings with other occupations. Educators also have a general image of teachers; in school systems where the educational organization includes a great many hierarchical levels, the classroom teacher falls at the bottom. When teachers are recognized as the most important component in the educational structure, given major responsibility in school affairs, and rewarded in accord with their functions and productivity, the status of the teaching profession in comparison with other professions and within education should improve.

In this chapter we will focus on five aspects which can facilitate greater teacher professionalism. First we will explore the status of teachers, which in our society is somewhere between the highest and lowest ranking occupations. Professions such as medicine and law are ranked higher; occupations such as waiter or cab driver are ranked lower. Just where teachers fall compared to other occupations is difficult to assess and changes over time. Then we will examine the characteristics of professionalism in general and relate it to teachers. The status of the teaching profession suffers in several respects, particularly in that its standards are set and sanctioned by groups outside the teaching field. Next we will discuss teacher education as an aid to professionalism, and then role typologies for bureaucratic employees and professional employees will be compared to suggest role changes for teachers. Finally we will discuss the growth of professional militarism and the need for teaching organizations to exercise muscle and leadership to help enhance the status of teachers.

THE STATUS OF TEACHERS

The various stereotypes of teachers and the changing image of teachers — from a docile, underpaid person to a militant, better paid person — were examined in Chapter 6. These profiles affect the professional status of teachers, for what people think about teachers strongly influences such rankings. Other factors affecting this status are linked to the place of teachers in communities, their education and competencies, and their economic rewards.

The exact status of teachers is difficult to determine. It has changed with internal shifts within the profession and alterations in the status of other occupations. From a historical point of view, the status of teachers has gradually increased since colonial times. This status change is linked to our credential-oriented 20th-century society which believes in the importance of education, the higher entry standards of the profession, and the recent salary gains and improved working conditions of teachers.

Perhaps the most comprehensive studies of occupational prestige are those conducted by the National Opinion Research Center (NORC), affiliated with the University of Chicago. In 1947, when NORC rated 88 occupations as indicated by the opinions of people across the country, college professors ranked 7th and school teachers were 36th on the totem of status.[1] A related NORC study of 90 occupations with a similar sample conducted in 1963 showed teachers' ranking was 29.5, an increase of 7.5 points[2] (also see Table 5.2). The college professor still outranked the classroom teacher by more than 20 points, but the teacher had passed the factory owner, contractor, artist, musician, novelist, and economist; furthermore, the teacher had not been passed by anyone lower in the status order. Thus the classroom teacher had gained more respect in the eyes of

---

[1] C. C. North and Paul K. Hatt, "Jobs and Occupations: A Popular Evaluation," *Opinion News*, September 1, 1947, pp. 3-13.

[2] Robert W. Hodge, Paul M. Siegel, and Peter H. Rossi, "Occupational Prestige in the United States, 1925-63," *American Journal of Sociology*, November 1964, pp. 286-302.

America, but levels of stratification within the profession between college teachers and school teachers were still apparent.

In 1970 Paul Siegel, who worked at NORC, completed his doctoral dissertation by ranking 500 occupational titles.[3] No comparisons with the earlier NORC should be made, since different occupational titles and ranking systems were used. Teachers scored in the 90th percentile in the ratings of their occupation. Not only did college professors continue to place higher than classroom teachers, but secondary school teachers rated three points higher than elementary teachers. It seems, then, that stratification exists within the profession; not only by levels of teaching but also by sex. Positions predominantly filled by men — college teachers, school administrators, and high school teachers — have a higher position in terms of status and income rankings than do teachers in elementary schools — positions mainly filled by women.[4]

Changes in the status of teachers appear to be continuing; since the 1970s they have never been held in higher esteem by parents. A Gallup poll in 1972 reported that when parents were asked if they would like their children to take up teaching as a career, 67 percent said they would; only 22 percent said no, and 11 percent were undecided. While these percentages are impressive, it is worth noting that 75 percent said yes in 1969, and in the case of parents with children still in school it was even higher — 80 percent. (Comments by those interviewed shed light on the drop: teaching jobs are now scarce and "supply in many areas exceeds demand"; teaching has become "dangerous . . . with children permitted to run wild in many schools.") In 1972 and 1973, when asked to tell what was particularly good about the schools, "good teachers" and "up-to-date teaching methods" headed the list of reasons. In 1976 and 1977 "good teachers" and "good teaching methods" headed the reasons again.[5]

While teachers have relatively high status rankings when compared with other occupations, it is evident that they do not receive salaries in keeping with their ratings on occupational status scales. Many skilled blue-collar workers, such as plumbers, electricians, and construction workers, rank lower in status but receive higher salaries. One reason for the lower teachers' salaries may be linked to the fact that the profession has been

---

[3] Paul M. Siegel, *Prestige in the American Occupational Structure,* unpublished Ph.D. dissertation, University of Chicago, 1971.

[4] Martha M. McCarthy, "Woman School Administrators: A Status Report," National Association of Secondary School Principals, April 1977, pp. 49-57; Terry N. Saario, "Title IX: Now What?" in A. C. Ornstein and· S. I. Miller (eds.), *Policy Issues in Education* (Lexington, Mass.: D.C. Heath Co., 1976), pp. 127-59.

[5] *The Gallup Polls of Attitudes toward Education, 1967-1973* (Bloomington, Ind.: Phi Delta Kappa, 1973) also see the 1976 poll in Phi Delta Kappa Fastbask # 94, and September 1977 issue of *Phi Delta Kappan.*

dominated by women; traditionally, women have been paid less than men for similar jobs, and female-dominated jobs have been low paid in general. As late as 1961 females held 69 percent of the teaching jobs; men gradually entered the profession in the 1960s, and many of them were young and had militant sentiments. Salaries had almost doubled by the end of the decade 1960 to 1970, and should triple by 1980.[6]

The status of the profession also suffers because of its high rate of attrition—about 10 percent left the profession annually during the 1950s and 1960s. With jobs more difficult to come by, and with improved teacher salaries, the rate of attrition has slowed down to about 8 percent annually in the 1970s. Entrance requirements into the profession have

Table 8.1 / Characteristics of a Profession, with Implications for Teachers

Characteristic	Lieberman (1956)	Corwin (1965)	Ornstein (1976)
1. A sense of public service...............	X		
2. A defined body of knowledge beyond that grasped by laymen....................		X	X
3. Application of research and theory to practice (to human problems)...........	X	X	X
4. A lengthy period of specialized training...	X	X	
5. Control over licensing standards and/or entry requirements....................		X	X
6. Autonomy in making decisions about selected spheres of work...............	X	X	X
7. An acceptance of responsibility for judgments made and acts performed related to services rendered.....................	X		
8. Commitment to work and client; an emphasis upon service to be rendered......	X		X
9. Administrators facilitate work of professionals; administrators' functions are considered secondary and their work is considered undesirable................			X
10. A self-governing organization comprised of members of the profession...........	X		
11. Professional associations and/or elite groups provide recognition for individual achievement.........................			X
12. There is a code of ethics to help clarify ambiguous matters or doubtful points related to services rendered............	X	X	X
13. High prestige and economic standing....		X	X

Sources: Myron Lieberman, *Education as a Profession* (Englewood Cliffs, N.J.: Prentice-Hall, Inc., 1956); Ronald G. Corwin, *Sociology of Education* (New York: Appleton-Century-Crofts, 1965); Allan C. Ornstein, *Teaching in a New Era* (Champaign, Ill.: Stipes Publishing Co., 1976).

[6] *Economic Status of the Teaching Profession, 1972–73,* Research Report 1973–R3 (Washington, D.C.: National Education Association, 1973), Table 21, p. 26; see Table 6.5.

been low. In 1961 it was estimated that as many as 24 percent of elementary teachers had not completed their bachelor's degrees, although this percent has sharply decreased in the 1970s.[7] Another reason the status of the profession suffers is its large membership—as a rule, the larger a profession the lower its entry requirements and the more its members approximate the ability levels of the general population. The standing of the profession reflects the fact that often students are taught for long periods by substitute teachers, as well as by teachers who lack adequate training in their area of specialization.[8]

TEACHING AS A PROFESSION

A persistent issue among educators has been whether teaching can be considered a profession in the fullest sense. A number of educators have attempted to view professions in terms of ideal characteristics and, by rating teaching on these, to accord it greater recognition as a profession. Table 8.1 lists the characteristics of a profession as defined by three educators in ten-year intervals since the 1950s. Not only is there considerable overlap among these evaluations, but the general conclusions are similar: Teaching is not a profession in the fullest sense; it does not possess many of the characteristics professions are supposed to possess; and at best it can be viewed as a semiprofession or a vocation in the process of achieving these characteristics. If readers were asked whether the teaching profession is marked by the characteristics listed in Table 8.1, it is quite possible that some answers would be yes, some no, and others would be ambiguous. The general conclusion should follow that teaching is partially but not entirely a true profession at the present time.

Of the 13 characteristics of a profession listed in Table 8.1, perhaps the four most important are: (1) A defined body of knowledge beyond the grasp of laymen, (2) control over licensing standards and/or entry requirements, (3) autonomy in making decisions about selected spheres of work, and (4) high prestige and economic standing. The discussion of these characteristics that follows clearly indicates that the teacher profession does not possess them all, but no profession has achieved the ideal state.

A Defined Body of Knowledge

All professions have a monopoly of knowledge, which separates their members from the general public and exercises control over the vocation.

---

[7] *Status of the American Public-School Teacher, 1970–71,* Research Report 1972-RD (Washington, D.C.: National Education Association, 1972), Table 1, p. 12.

[8] Morris L. Cogan, "Current Issues in the Education of Teachers," in K. Ryan (ed.), *Teacher Education,* 74th Yearbook of the National Society for the Study of Education, Part II (Chicago: University of Chicago Press, 1975), pp. 204–29.

Members of a profession are learners; they have mastered a body of knowledge which establishes their expertise and protects themselves and the public from quacks, untrained amateurs, and special-interest groups. However, there is no agreed-upon specialized body of knowledge that is "education" or "teaching." Whereas the behavioral sciences, physical sciences, and health fields can be guided by extensive applicational theory, rules of procedure, and established methodologies, education lacks a well-defined body of knowledge which is applicable to the real world of teaching, or which has been validated and agreed upon by most authorities. The field of knowledge that might be reasonably associated with teacher training largely consists of a list of do's and don'ts, a few tricks or methods which are relative to the individual's personality and the students in the classroom.

Related to the question of knowledge is the fact that professionals should be fully qualified in their areas of specialization. Not only are education courses frequently with little substance, what James Conant labeled "mickey mouse," but content and academic standards frequently are minimal.[9] And not only are many teachers ill prepared to teach their subject matter, they sometimes take an inordinate number of education courses (in the past as many as 40 to 60 credit hours) and elective courses that are outside their field of specialization.[10] Moreover, it is estimated that nearly one third of present teachers working in the secondary schools are teaching out of license; in other words, teachers of English did not major in English in college, nor are they certified to teach English. This problem is especially acute in the areas of science and mathematics teaching,[11] although it has declined with the recent surplus of teachers.

The degree of defined body of knowledge is also determined by training standards. Despite state regulations requiring a certain number of education courses, minimal requirements and content vary among states. As late as 1946, only 15 states required a bachelor's degree for elementary teachers;[12] in 1976 only three states required that its teachers hold a master's degree.[13] In 1958, 13 percent of the 1,200 colleges preparing

---

[9] James B. Conant, *The Education of American Teachers* (New York: McGraw-Hill Book Co., 1963).

[10] James D. Koerner, *The Miseducation of American Teachers* (Boston: Houghton Mifflin Co., 1963); Robert M. Weiss, *The Content Controversy in Teacher Education* (New York: Random House, 1969).

[11] Myron Lieberman, *The Future of Public Education* (Chicago: University of Chicago Press, 1960); Elizabeth H. Woellner, *Requirements for Certification for Elementary Schools, Secondary Schools, and Junior Colleges, 1972–73* (Chicago: University of Chicago Press, 1972).

[12] Ronald G. Corwin, *Sociology of Education* (New York: Appleton-Century-Crofts, 1965).

[13] Allan C. Ornstein, "Characteristics of a Profession," *Illinois School Journal*, Winter 1976–77, pp. 12–21.

teachers were two-year institutions, and 150 of the 1,060 four-year institutions were not credited; only 28 percent of them were accredited by both regional and national associations.[14] In 1961, about 33 percent of the graduates preparing to teach were not approved by the national accrediting agency, and in 1975, as many as 40 percent of the 1,350 colleges involved in training teachers were not credited by the national accrediting agency.[15]

Teachers must gain decision-making influence, to bring about acknowledgment of a specialized body of knowledge, to enhance specialization for teachers, and to upgrade weak teacher training institutions, areas in which state and local departments of education have been lax. Teacher organizations have the potential muscle and leadership to work with interested parties, such as the major teacher training institutions, to develop exemplary models. Teacher training institutions that do not fall in line might not be permitted to send their student teachers to work in nearby school systems, and their graduates would not be considered licensed to teach in the schools.

Control over Licensing Standards and Entry Requirements

Whereas most professions have uniform standards and requirements to ensure minimum competencies, this is not the case in the teaching profession. The problem is twofold, concerning who enters teacher education programs, and what kind of products emerge from these programs and are subsequently certified to teach.

Teacher education programs attract a wide range of student talent and a disproportionate number of less qualified students in academic rank and standardized test scores. For example, in a report published by the Carnegie Foundation some 40 years ago, it was found that the median IQ for 26,000 unselected high school students (including those not going to college) was higher than the median of the candidates for education.[16] The results of Graduate Record Examinations published by the Educational Testing Service in 1965 show that for candidates of 57 major fields of study, education majors had the fourth lowest mean verbal score (higher

---

[14] Anthony La Bue. "Teacher Certification in the United States: A Brief History," *Journal of Teacher Education,* June 1960, pp. 147-72.

[15] Egon G. Guba and David Clark, "Selected Demographic Data about Teacher Education Institutions," paper presented at the First Annual Conference on Teacher Education, Indiana University, Indianapolis, November 1975; Allan C. Ornstein, "Educational Poverty in the Midst of Educational Abundance: Status and Policy Implications of Teacher/Supply Demand," *Educational Researcher,* April 1976, pp. 13-16.

[16] William S. Leonard and Benjamin D. Wood, *The Student and His Knowledge* (New York: Carnegie Foundation for the Advancement of Teaching, 1938).

only than candidates of agriculture, home economics, and physical education), and the fifth lowest mean quantitative score (higher only than candidates of library science, nursing, physical education, and social work). The mean verbal score for all candidates was 534, compared to education majors, who scored 448. The mean quantitative score for all candidates was 540, compared to education majors, who scored 427.[17] Ten years later, the College Entrance Examination Board reported that SAT scores averaged 435, down 21 points from 1965 (and 38 points from 1962). Students checking teaching as an occupational choice consistently averaged 10 to 20 points lower than the mean scores each year during this ten-year period.[18]

In teacher licensing requirements there is tremendous variation among states and even within states, since individual institutions of higher learning vary in terms of academic standards and outcomes. There are no uniform standards or minimum, agreed-upon teacher quality. Every state has its own licensing and certification procedures; the variations among states are beyond imagination. A survey published in 1973, for example, revealed that in Nebraska a prospective teacher of art needed only 12 semester hours to qualify for a certificate to teach art; in Connecticut the requirement was 40 semester hours. In Georgia 6 semester hours were needed to qualify for a certificate to teach English; in New York the requirement was a minimum of 36 semester hours. In some states, such as Hawaii, Minnesota, Nevada, North Dakota, Pennsylvania, and Vermont, the number of semester hours required to teach academic subjects was not indicated; these states required the teacher to have a major in the subject field or an "approved curriculum," and the hours required were left to the training institution. The requirements for professional education courses also varied from 8 semester hours for elementary teachers in Nebraska to 36 semester hours in Mississippi, and from 12 semester hours for secondary teachers in New York to 24 in Tennessee.[19]

Whatever they may think about these differing requirements, teachers do not have a say on such matters. The outcome is that teacher mobility is limited from state to state by the different licensing procedures. Most

---

[17] *Graduate Record Examinations: An Analysis of the Graduate Record Examination Scores by the Undergraduate Major Field of Study, 1963–64* (Princeton, N.J.: Educational Testing Service, 1965).

[18] *College-Bound Seniors, 1974–75* (New York: College Entrance Examination Board, 1975); *College-Bound Seniors, 1975–76* (New York: College Entrance Examination Board, 1976).

[19] T. M. Stinnett, *A Manual on Standards and Developments Affecting School Personnel in the United States, 1973,* National Commission on Teacher Education and Professional Standards (Washington, D.C.: National Education Association, 1974); Martin Haberman and T. M. Stinnett, *Teacher Education and the New Profession of Teaching* (Berkeley, Ca.: McCutchan Publishing Corp., 1973).

people, including teachers themselves, reject teacher regulation of licensing requirements because they are publicly employed. From an educator's point of view, however, the exercise of professional autonomy would be enhanced if teachers could establish licensing laws, or if certification standards were functionally recognized by states. It is in the public interest to place control of professional standards and requirements in the hands of teacher organizations rather than to continue to allow laymen who know very little about teaching to make such decisions.

Autonomy in Making Decisions about Selected Spheres of Work

In a profession every member of the group, but nobody else, is assumed to be qualified to make professional judgments on the nature of the work involved. Professionals usually establish laws of exclusive jurisdiction in a given area of competence, and custom and tradition are relied on to maintain effective control over matters relating to work and dealing with clients. Indeed, lay control is considered the natural enemy of professions; it limits the power of the professional and opens the door to outside, unfriendly interference.

Teachers accept the notion that local and state officials have the right to decide on the subjects, instructional materials, and books to be used. While they sometimes question the wisdom of the community in exercising such rights, the legitimacy of these rights is rarely questioned.[20] At best, teachers are permitted minimal input in curriculum decisions, but they are vulnerable when they seek to introduce textbooks or discussions considered controversial or taboo by pressure groups.

The tragedy is that teachers believe that the democratic process gives the public the right to tell them what books to use and what content to teach. Teachers may be challenged by almost any parent or taxpayer; the community may dictate what they will teach and how, even in opposition to the teachers' professional judgments. Taxpayers are said to "reasonably" claim a share in decision making, since they foot the bill and provide the clients.

The physician and lawyer also provide services that their clients pay for, yet no one in his right mind expects the client or the public to prescribe drugs or write the clauses in a contract. When the client interferes with the decisions of the practicing physician or lawyer, the professional-client relation ends. This protects the client from being victimized by his own lack of knowledge, while it safeguards the professional from the

---

[20] Lieberman, *Future of Public Education.*

unreasonable judgments of the lay public. Professionals recognize the need to service their clients, but not at their own expense. There is a point in the professional-client relation where the professional's self-interest and autonomy suffer — when service to the client is governed by the whims of the client or other laymen. Peter Blau and W. Richard Scott observe that "professional service . . . requires that the [professional] maintain independence of judgment and not permit the clients' *wishes* as distinguished from their *interests* to influence his decisions." The professional has the knowledge and expertise to make judgments, "and the client is not qualified to evaluate the services he needs." Professionals who permit their clients to tell them what to do "fail to provide optimum service."[21]

The same kind of reasoning should hold true with teachers, but they can be told what to do by parents and other citizens, principals, superintendents, and school board members. Although school officials realize they no longer have "the sole right of management," since collective bargaining has resulted in new arrangements between teachers and management, most people still believe that teachers are public servants and therefore accountable to the people and to the school officials who are hired, elected, or appointed by the people. While it is true teachers must not lose sight of the welfare of their clients or those who are in the position to make decisions for the public, they should not surrender the power to determine the nature of the service they render. To err in the first direction is to become rigid and despotic; to err in the second direction is to become subservient and impotent.

In contrast to other professions, a greater portion of the teacher's service is legislated and enforced by lay groups who constitute the membership of local and state regulatory agencies. Decisions within these agencies are usually politically laden, not professionally motivated to either assist teachers or serve students. The expectation that teachers are supposed to act as models to be emulated *in loco parentis* or *in loco communitas* only increases the power of lay groups over teachers. Harry Broudy points out that not more than 25 years ago, as a result of these two doctrines teachers were expected to reflect the mores and social sentiments of local communities by staying out of bars and gambling halls and always being home by midnight. The expected ideals of honesty, hard work, and sexual chasteness were reflected in the popular image of the American teacher: overworked and underpaid, a spinster school ma'am who was a luminous exemplar of praise and blame to correspond to the community's value system.[22]

---

[21] Peter Blau and W. Richard Scott, *Formal Organizations* (San Francisco: Chandler Publishing Co., 1965), pp. 51-52.

[22] Harry S. Broudy, *The Real World of the Public Schools* (New York: Harcourt, 1972).

296

These doctrines persist today in a new language — reform slogans such as "parent participation" and "community control." The appeal to a local group or diffuse citizenry to save our schools is appealing under the guise of democracy, but it is futile, not because our schools do not need to be improved but because worthwhile reform must evolve from and be carried out by teachers. To encourage lay groups to exercise control over teachers is to be anti-teacher; it reduces professional autonomy, and it ignores the fact that the parents or a group of people who claim to "represent" the community do not have the competencies to make professional decisions and pass judgments on teachers.

Professional autonomy does not mean the total absence of any control over professionals. On the contrary, it means that controls requiring technical competencies are exercised by people who possess such competencies; it calls for the development of controls related to work by members of the profession. This can be enhanced by collective negotiations which define areas in which teachers can make use of their experiences and competencies, by increasing teacher representation on school boards at the local level and teaching licensing and governing boards at the state level, and by helping to elect political candidates to office who are pro-teacher and pro-education.

High Prestige and Economic Standing

There are many variables associated with the prestige rankings of occupations, but salary plays an important role in each. The reasons are relatively clear: American society is materialistic, and money is related to visible and behavioral characteristics by which people judge others. If some teachers cannot afford a decent home or a new automobile, their prestige suffers.

The historical change in teacher salaries has been dramatic: in 1930 the average teacher earned $1,420; in 1940, $1,470; in 1950, $3,126; in 1960, $5,449. In the next decade average salary almost doubled, to $9,638.[23] By 1980 the projection is for an average teacher salary of about $17,000.[24] In terms of purchasing power, teachers experienced a net increase of 10 percent between 1930 and 1950, and 22 percent between 1950 and 1970. The greatest gains were made between 1960 and 1970, the period corresponding with the growth of teacher militancy. During this period, salaries for teachers rose 44 percent and prices rose 28 percent, for a net

---

[23] *Economic Status of Teaching Profession, 1972–73,* Table 21, p. 26; *Survey of Teacher Salaries, 1973–74* (Washington, D.C.: American Federation of Teachers, 1974). Table 4, p. 56.
[24] See Table 6.5.

gain of 16 percent.[25] The 1970s has witnessed a leveling off of purchasing power for teachers (as for other workers and professionals), since inflation has outstripped salary increases.

Although salary gains made by teachers between 1930 and 1970 have been greater (about 15 percent more) than for the average worker in industry,[26] salaries have remained lower (by about 25 percent) than for the average college graduate.[27] Of course, there is no realistic salary comparison between teachers with a master's or doctor's degree and physicians, lawyers, dentists, or top business executives. Although levels of formal education are nearly similar, earnings of the latter group approach $100,000 per year, with some earning as much as $1 million; these groups also have traditionally high occupational ratings.

The conclusion is that while the prestige and income standards of teachers have risen relative to their past station, they have risen only slightly more than for the average worker, while declining in comparison to other professions and groups with similar levels of education. The *status-consistency hypothesis* holds that a group tends to compare its achievements (prestige and salary) with other groups and will strive to bring its achievements up to a level with people who have similar jobs, even similar years of education.[28] If this is true, we can expect teachers to make comparisons with other professional groups, to remain dissatisfied, and to express this dissatisfaction through militancy; in fact, this has been one of the major reasons for teacher militancy since the mid-1960s.[29]

PROFESSIONALISM AND TEACHER EDUCATION

All educators agree that preparation of good teachers rests upon (1) a broad liberal education, (2) specialization in the subject or field to be taught, and (3) professional knowledge and skills. However, the relative emphasis each area should receive provokes strong disagreement. The question is: How much time or credit hours should an education student devote to courses in liberal education, to his or her teaching field, and to professional education?

---

[25] *Economic Status of Teaching Profession, 1972–73; Survey of Teacher Salaries, 1973–74.*

[26] *Digest of Educational Statistics, 1973* (Washington, D.C.: U.S. Government Printing Office, 1974), Table 56, p. 48.

[27] *Economic Status of Teaching Profession, 1972–73,* Table 43, p. 52; Table 43–A, p. 54; Table 48, p. 57; Table 62, p. 68, see Table 6.7.

[28] Gerhard E. Lenski, "Social Participation and Status Crystallization," *American Sociological Review,* August 1956, pp. 458–64.

[29] Ronald C. Corwin, *Militant Professionalism: A Study of Militant Conflict in High Schools* (New York: Appleton-Century-Crofts, 1970); Anthony M. Cresswell and Michael J. Murphy, *Education and Collective Bargaining* (Berkeley, Ca.: McCutchan Publishing Corp., 1977).

Progress toward achieving an acceptable balance between liberal and professional studies has been made, in part coinciding with the trend to reduce the number of professional or education courses required for graduation from teacher education programs. In the late 1950s it was found that 22 percent of the academic program for secondary teachers and more than 41 percent of that for elementary teachers was devoted to education courses—required and elective. The percentages were even higher among those attending teachers colleges: 25 percent for secondary school teachers, and 45 percent for elementary school teachers.[30] Today most departments, schools, or colleges of education require 18 semester credits in education courses (or about 12 percent of the total program) for secondary teachers and 24 credits (or about 20 percent) for elementary teachers. Of course, there are some programs that encourage or even require more than this number of credits, and others that require fewer credits in education.

Another long-standing question has concerned who should teach courses in education, especially the foundation courses such as history of education, philosophy of education, psychology of education, or sociology of education. So bitter was the argument between professors of liberal arts and of education in some institutions in the past that it was not uncommon for the two faculties to refuse to lunch together, or for them to vote on policy solely on the basis of faculty membership.[31] While much of the quarreling has subsided and the idea of professional education courses taught by professors of education seems to have been accepted, uneasiness between both faculties still exists in some colleges and universities.

Today questions over teacher education do not involve subject area or who should teach the subjects, so the arguments are not between professors of liberal arts and professors of education. Rather, they concern theory vs. practice and are pursued by educators themselves. Major questions currently are: What is the proper mix of theory and practice? How many credit hours should be taught on campus and how many in the field? Should professors or practitioners teach field courses? Some educators have tried to reach a compromise by calling for a "clinical professor," one who is knowledgeable in both areas, to teach such courses.[32]

The move to provide more field-based and school-based programs, both at the preservice (undergraduate) and inservice (graduate) level, has also been taking on greater impetus in the 1970s. This is reflected in the teacher-center and internship movements, both of which call for greater

---

[30] Koerner, *Miseducation of American Teachers.*

[31] Conant, *Education of American Teachers.*

[32] Ibid.; B. J. Chandler, Daniel Powell, and William R. Hazard, *Education and the New Teacher* (New York: Dodd, Mead & Co., 1971).

involvement of teachers and other school people and more utilization of school facilities, with deemphasis on courses offered on college campuses.

The teacher center originated in England and Wales, where today there are approximately 600.[33] Inservice education, not preservice, is implemented by the teachers themselves. The teachers are responsible for defining and solving their own problems; they develop the programs and activities. Assistance is provided, and they learn from one another. In effect, the centers cater to the teachers' needs and interests, they are staffed by teachers, and they find solutions to problems proposed by teachers.

Teacher centers in the United States will probably involve shifts in power arrangements, from state agencies and institutions of higher education, who have traditionally been in control of teacher education, to teacher organizations, school administrators, local school districts, and community groups—all of which envision an increase of influence and possibly even control of inservice teacher education. The few teacher centers that have been developed thus far are mainly run by colleges and universities within state guidelines and in conjunction with teachers and local school districts, and college credit is given for participation.[34] Eventually there may be greater involvement by various teacher-school-community groups, and if college credit is not involved, local credit may be given for salary increments. A teacher-center bill has been authorized by the federal government to provide up to $67 million annually, from 1978 to 1981, for local school districts to set up such centers. They are to be operated under the supervision of a policy board which must include a majority of classroom teachers.

The internship program is an old idea, popularized by James Conant, which provides beginning teachers with on-the-job training and help in the form of limited teaching responsibility and the advice of experienced teachers, whose own loads are reduced so they can work with the new teachers in their own classrooms.[35] The internship can also serve as a safeguard for preventing unqualified teachers from becoming permanently certified, since all beginning teachers are evaluated during this internship period. The two major teacher organizations—the NEA and AFT—once resisted the internship idea, maintaining that its evaluation aspects would politicize teaching. Now, for different political reasons, they both advocate the internship, seeing it as a means to provide more

---

[33] Arline Julius, "British Teacher Centers: Practical Applications for America," *Phi Delta Kappan* November 1976, pp. 250-53.

[34] Allen A. Schmieder and Sam J. Yarger, "Teacher/Teaching Centering in America," *Journal of Teacher Education,* Spring 1974, pp. 5-12.

[35] Conant, *Education of American Teachers.*

teaching jobs and to increase demand in the midst of an oversupply of teachers, since a reduced teaching load for some would create a need for more teachers. They also believe internship programs would give them greater control over teacher education and certification.

Another area of interest is competency-based teacher education (CBTE). The notion of CBTE is to provide the learner (the candidate teacher) with a particular task involving a simulated or actual teaching situation. Rather than describing what one might do in a particular situation or selecting the best answer from a list of alternatives, the candidate must perform a task at a minimum level of proficiency. The task coincides with some act of teaching or professional subject matter, and a list of competencies, almost like a portfolio of the candidate's abilities, can be created.

While some educators consider CBTE a viable alternative in this overdue reform of teacher education, others raise serious questions about whether valid competencies can be identified with appropriate proficiency levels, whether reliable and valid instruments can be established for measuring such competencies, and whether such competencies can be translated into certification units and then communicated to licensing authorities.[36]

Between 1973 to 1976 there was a shift in the number of states using and planning to use CBTE to certify teachers. In 1973, 8 state education departments indicated they were using it, 22 had plans to go to it, and 20 had no plans to use this form of teacher education. By 1976, 11 state departments indicated they were using it, but only 5 had plans to use it, and 34 said they had no such plans.[37] These surveys suggest that CBTE is unlikely to become a reality in most states, and the move may fizzle out over the years, as has teacher accountability. Both of these movements (CBTE and accountability) are representative of the behavioral trend in education.

Prescriptions and Projections

As part of the move to upgrade the profession of teaching, several recent commissions on teacher education have drafted recommendations. Two of these "bicentennial" sets of recommendations are highlighted below.

---

[36] W. Robert Houston, *Exploring Competency Based Education* (Berkeley, Ca.: McCutchan Publishing Corp., 1974); Benjamin Rosner, *The Power of Competency-Based Teacher Education*, Task Force Committee on National Program Priorities in Teacher Education (Washington, D.C.: U.S. Government Printing Office, 1972).

[37] Melvin G. Villeme, "Competency Based Certification: A New Reality," *Educational Leadership*, January 1974, pp. 348–49; Melvin G. Villeme, "The Decline of Competency-Based Teacher Certification," *Phi Delta Kappan*, January 1977, pp. 428–29.

In the first report, 50 or so members of the Study Commission on Undergraduate Education and the Education of Teachers, most of whom are among education's more controversial leaders and some of whom are public activists, set forth controversial prescriptions for reforming teacher education.[38] Most educators would point to their efforts as a radical document, whose provisions would strip teachers and professional educators of what little control and responsibility they have over licensing standards and entry requirements, and would further weaken teacher academic standards. Some educators of a liberal-minority persuasion, however, see the recommendations as a departure from the usual treatises dealing with the problems and prospects of teacher education. The principal provisions of this report are:

1. The commission anticipates a future restructuring of schools, through such media as alternative schools, vouchers, differential staffing, and accountability.

2. Arguing that teachers need to know the culture and language of those they plan to teach, the commission recommends mastery of the specific culture in the community wherein teachers plan to teach, in lieu of academic competence.

3. The commission recommends that all teacher preparation, selection, and placement be moved to the consumer and the community, and that teachers be made accountable to the community they serve.

4. While criticizing what it sees as overstandardization in teacher education, ironically, it recommends increased intervention by the federal government, both organizational and financial.

5. Existing national accrediting agencies such as the American Association of Colleges for Teacher Education (AACTE), National Association of State Directors of Teacher Education and Certification (NASDTEC), National Council for Accreditation of Teacher Education (NCATE), as well as the six regional accrediting agencies, such as the North Central Association of Colleges and Secondary Schools (NCASS), are criticized as operating to ensure only the interests of the profession at the expense of the consumer and community. It is charged that racial and sexual discrimination is perpetuated by those agencies.

In short, the commission's report has *control* as its principal focus; it seeks to shift control away from teachers and teacher educators to the public and the federal government. The teacher or teacher trainer intent on strengthening the profession or a local program will find few practical prescriptions for program improvement.

---

[38] *Teacher Education in the United States: The Responsibility Gap,* Study Commission on Undergraduate Education and the Education of Teachers (Lincoln, Neb.: University of Nebraska Press, 1976).

The second report, of a commission chaired by Robert Howsam for the American Association of Colleges for Teacher Education, does provide some help.[39] Among its most important recommendations are:

1. Responsibility for teacher education should be delegated to the teaching profession (particularly to teacher organizations) and to the colleges and universities, with the states decreasing their dominance and providing only support services.

2. Minimum competencies or teacher skills should be established which beginning teachers must perform before certified. These include cognitive skills, research and scholarship skills; knowledge of important social, political, and educational issues; humanistic values and attitudes; and personal teaching skills. All these are supposedly conducive to good teacher behavior.

3. Every college of education should identify its objectives, determine the resources necessary to achieve those objectives at a quality level, and then establish priorities that are realistic for the size and diversity of programs those resources can support.

4. Teachers should be required to study a program consisting of liberal education, preparation in an academic specialization (even for elementary teachers), and professional education. This framework for study should be taught by an interdisciplinary team representing various disciplines and teacher educators.

5. Teacher preparation should be conducted in a five-year sequence, combining both bachelor's and master's degrees.

6. An internship in teacher education or a minimum of one year of supervised employment should be made an integral part of all teacher education programs.

7. Teacher centers should be established for preservice and inservice teacher education with the collaboration of the local schools, teacher organizations, colleges and universities, school boards and communities, and state or intermediate state agencies.

8. School systems should become the chief focus for inservice education, in order to maximize school and community needs. Colleges and universities should contribute relevant resources and personnel when they are available.

9. Colleges and universities should expand their teacher education programs to include the preparation of other human-service professionals (such as specialists in adult education, family-centered education, mass media education, consumer education, and self-education), and the

---

[39] Robert B. Howsam et al., *Educating a Profession,* Bicentennial Commission for the Profession of Teaching of the American Association of Colleges for Teacher Education, (Washington, D.C., 1976).

training and retraining of professional and paraprofessional government personnel.

The more practical and pro-professional education slant of the AACTE report does not disguise the fact that it is also concerned with *control* in teacher education. However, this report seeks to increase control for school people. It encourages input from the community and colleges already involved in teacher education, but in more of a supportive than a policy role. It rejects the notion of a community-specific, cultural-specific, or ethnic-specific teacher education program as narrow and dangerous, because it "reinforces differences and perpetuates biases of individual communities and ethnic groups, intensifying rather than reducing the strife within American society." It advocates instead teacher education which promotes the idea of core values "shared among broader circles and within a matrix of cultural pluralism."[40] In addition, it seeks more field experiences at the school level (such as internships and teacher centers). Recognizing that teacher educators at the colleges and universities would be threatened by such a move, it reaffirms the need for professors to instruct in the liberal arts and specialization areas and the theory and research of teaching, to provide the supportive services, and to expand the application of professional education beyond teacher education. Finally, the report rejects the notion of greater governmental influence at the state and federal levels, reaffirming the importance of the school districts and local school boards.

On the heels of these two reports, a two-year study of the schools, colleges, and departments of education conducted between 1974 and 1976 by David Clark and Egon Guba resulted in the following projections for teacher education.[41] Summed up, they suggest the field is heading for at least a short-range (five- to seven-year) recession.

1. Enrollments in teacher education programs will continue to decline, as will funds to support these programs.
2. Support for research and development in teacher education, along with knowledge utilization and dissemination, consulting services, and grants, will decline.
3. Quality in teacher education will decline, as manifested in staff cutbacks and a move to lower-cost, more conventional instruction and fewer individualized, clinically-based or field-based programs.

---

[40] Ibid., p. 96.

[41] David L. Clark, "The Real World of the Teacher Educator: A Look at the Near Future," *Phi Delta Kappan*, May 1977, pp. 680–87; David L. Clark and Egon G. Guba, "An Institutional Self-Report on Knowledge and Production and Utilization Activities in Schools, Colleges, and Departments of Education," Occasional Paper Series, Research on Institutions of Teacher Education, Bloomington, Ind., 1976.

4. Teacher education colleges and universities will experience greater loss of autonomy and responsibility in program development, operation, and evaluation, and increased input from several competing agencies.

5. Changes in the form or structure of teacher education will be evidenced (for example, in certification or accreditation policy and location of programs), but the essential substance of training programs will remain relatively intact.

In general, growing conservatism is expected to characterize teacher education in the near future. In reaction to what Clark and Guba term a "recession," risk behavior will be unlikely, and defensive rather than offensive behavior will become the norm. Negotiations with external agencies will be conducted guardedly; tensions generated by existing problems will increase, and nonsolutions that offer little commitment in money or expectations will be offered. Whatever margin of excellence has been achieved will diminish as fewer innovations and more cutbacks are evidenced, and marginal institutions with low teacher education enrollments and general fiscal problems will most likely drop their programs.

While the projections do not provide much to cheer about, note that the authors did not use the term "depression." A recession should be considered as a temporary cycle; moreover, such a phenomenon can be averted with appropriate measures. The traditional institutional inertia of teacher education programs may be viewed as a depressant to needed reform, but it will probably protect them from precipitous, destructive changes; moreover, it should offset some of the projections impacting on these programs. Survival plans can and should be developed; those institutions with reasonable plans will weather the recession. An individual institution may not be able to reverse a general trend, but it can protect its own health and state of well-being. Recessions can be headed off or quickly turned about (even when already in progress, which seems to be the case with teacher education) if the intervention is wise and is regional or national in scope.

Finally, the problems confronting teacher education are not isolated from those confronting education in general. It is time for the various groups, rather than battling their competitors and vying for power, to work together for the good of teacher education.

PROFESSIONAL AND BUREAUCRATIC TEACHER TYPOLOGIES

The statement that the American school may be viewed as a bureaucracy is a fact. We may deplore this fact or applaud it, but we should not confuse a statement of what is with our views of what ought to be. In fact, most large organizations — schools, hospitals, government departments, military agencies, and business corporations — are organized as bureaucracies. Perhaps it would be more accurate to say that these organizations possess many of the characteristics of a bureaucracy, for the pure bureaucracy may not exist. Nevertheless, we can define a bureaucratic organization as one that exhibits certain characteristics. A widely accepted list of six characteristics has been delineated by the German sociologist Max Weber.[42] These characteristics are:

1. The activities of an organization are distributed in fixed ways as official duties and tasks. *Specialization* of offices and positions is required because the activities of the organization are too complex to be performed by a single individual or group of individuals who possess a single set of skills.

2. The positions and offices are organized into a *hierarchy* with various levels of authority and subordination. To achieve the required coordination of activities, it is necessary to grant each official the requisite authority to control the activities of the subordinates.

3. The management (administration) of the organization is based on written documents and files. *Written records* must be kept to assure compliance with standards and reasonable uniformity in the performance of tasks.

4. Administrators are expected to assume an *impersonal orientation* in contacts with subordinates (workers) and clients; the clients are treated as cases. Only by performing impersonally can officials assume rationality in decision making.

5. Administrators and subordinates require special *training,* and employment by the organization is considered as a *career* for them. Employment is based upon technical competence, and advancement is mainly determined by some form of seniority.

6. Official decisions and actions are based on a defined set of *rules and policies.* The administrator's task is to apply general rules to specific cases.

In Weber's view, these organizing principles maximized rational decision making and administrative efficiency. Bureaucracy was considered the most efficient form of organization, one in which trained experts were qualified to make decisions. Thus he wrote:

Experience tends universally to show that the purely bureaucratic type of administrative organization — that is, the monocratic variety of bureaucracy — is, from a purely technical point of view, capable of attaining the highest degree of

---

[42] Max Weber, *The Theory of Social and Economic Organization* (New York: Free Press, 1947).

efficiency and is in this sense formally the most rational known means of carrying out imperative control over human beings. It is superior to any other form in precision, in stability . . . and in its reliability. . . . It is finally superior both in intensive efficiency and in scope of its operation, and is formally capable of application to all kinds of administrative tasks.[43]

When the schools are analyzed in reference to Weber's six characteristics, the following points emerge.

1. *Specialization.* School tasks are distributed among people holding various positions; there is a clear-cut division of labor based on rules and regulations which makes a high degree of specialization possible. Specialization entails the need to recruit people on the basis of some standard of expertise, to provide inservice training, and to pay personnel according to their qualifications on paper. Hence teachers, supervisors, and administrators are paid different salaries according to their positions, education, and training.

2. *Hierarchy.* The hierarchical structure of the school is usually in the form of a pyramid, wherein each official is responsible for some subordinates but delegates some authority to them. Regardless of the size of the school, a clear-cut chain of command exists—from teacher to principal. Another administrative chain of command exists within the school system, with the school principal at the bottom and the schools' superintendent at the apex.

3. *Written Records.* Teachers and administrators are usually responsible for keeping records. Records must be complete, accurate, and available on time; often school personnel are indirectly rated by how well they fill in and turn them in to their superiors. Each official has a file or a set of records on subordinates which acts as a basis for making decisions regarding tenure, promotions, and so on.

4. *Impersonal Orientation.* Teachers are expected to maintain a social distance from their clients (students), and administrators are expected to do the same with the workers (teachers). The impersonal relationship between teacher and client is designed to maintain objectivity in grading as well as good classroom management. The impersonal relationships within the hierarchical levels of the organization and between the administration and teachers are designed to prevent personal feelings of the administrators and teachers from distorting their judgments in carrying out their duties.

5. *Training and Career Patterns.* The qualifications of teachers and administrators may be proven by the attainment of certificates or results of examinations. Since administrators are appointed and not elected, they

---

[43] Ibid., p. 337.

are dependent on the good opinion of their superiors, which in turn helps maintain the bureaucratic system. Employment by the school or at least by the school system constitutes a lifelong career for many administrators, and even for teachers. Tenure and pensions are provided; advancement is partially based on seniority. At the higher levels of the administrative hierarchy, advancement is often based on "whom you know" or other political considerations, thus creating an in-group at the top echelons of the school system and a certain amount of homogeneity and maintenance of the system.

6. *Rules and Policies.*   Official decisions and actions are regulated by the rules and policies of the school and the school system. The idea is for the principal of the school and the superintendent of the system to apply the general rules and policies to specific cases. These regulations ensure a certain amount of uniformity and also help eliminate some personal favors and preferential treatment based on background or personalities.

A careful reading of Weber's theory and the above analysis of schools according to his six characteristics of bureaucracy will indicate the interrelations of these characteristics. The sum of these interrelations is supposed to maximize efficiency; this model is considered by many authorities to be the criterion of perfection for structuring complex organizations. However, the approach deprofessionalizes the employees of the organization (in this case the teachers), and thus it undermines professionalism.

In joining the bureaucratic organization (the school and, on a larger scale, the school system), the employee (the teacher) accepts an authority relation which provides considerable power and control over his or her own behavior. Limitations are imposed, both explicitly and implicitly, by the terms of employment set down by the contract and by higher echelon administrators; the employee accepts as the premise of his behavior the orders and instructions directed to him by the organization. As the teacher devotes more years to the school and earns higher income, more tenure rights, and greater pension benefits, he is more willing to perform as the school system instructs him. Sanctions and codes of the profession, the independence of professional judgment, and professional knowledge matter less and less; the school or school system establishes more of a controlling influence over the teacher, and this influence is directed toward optimizing organizational activities, not the profession.

The strength of the bureaucratic organization and the subsequent weakness of the teaching profession are reflected in adherence to school policy. Rules and regulations are spelled out and enforced by administrators, in lieu of judgments sanctioned by professionals and enforced by peers. There is little tolerance for creativity or diffuse behavior. For example, the teacher must clock in at 8:30 a.m., even though his first class begins at 9:10 a.m., or he must not clock out before 3:00 p.m., even though his last class ends at 2:20 p.m. and he may want to spend some time in the city library preparing for the next lesson. Thus the "objective" discharge of everyday business primarily means following rules, with little regard for professional initiative. Individual performance is allocated to functionary work and routine practices, which are supported with records and files. Moreover, greater stress is put on record keeping than on research or innovation. Uniform behavior is more important than the individual work of teachers or the individual problems of students.

In effect, the school organization deals not with persons in their humanized capacities but as perceived objects to be programmed and planned for within a department and the larger organization. Differences in job performance are not captured by differences in individual achievement but by rates of absence, lateness, dress standards, and filling

Table 8.2 / Contrasting Characteristics of Bureaucratic and Professional Modes of Organization

Organizational Characteristics	Bureaucratic Employee Expectations	Professional Employee Expectations
Specialization		
Basis of division of labor.	Stress on efficiency of techniques; task orientation	Stress on achievement of goals; client orientation
Basis of skill	Skill based primarily on practice	Skill based primarily on monopoly of knowledge
Standardization		
Routine of work	Stress on uniformity of clients' problems	Stress on uniqueness of clients' problems
Continuity of procedure .	Stress on records and files	Stress on research and change
Specificity of rules.	Rules stated as universals, and specific	Rules stated as alternatives, and diffuse
Authority		
Responsibility for decision-making.	Decisions concerning application of rules to routine problems	Decisions concerning policy in professional matters and unique problems
Basis of authority.	Rules sanctioned by the public	Rules supported by legally sanctioned professions
	Loyalty to the organization and to superiors	Loyalty to professional associations and clients
	Authority comes from office (position)	Authority comes from personal competence

Ronald G. Corwin, *A Sociology of Education: Emerging Patterns of Class, Status, and Power in the Public Schools,* © 1965, p. 232. Reprinted by permission of Prentice-Hall, Inc., Englewood Cliffs, New Jersey.

out forms properly and on time. Promotion is based mainly on years of work and seniority rather than knowledge or expertise. Loyalty to the organization and one's supervisors is more important than loyalty to the profession or client. By bureaucratic design and the standardization of practices, the teacher loses his professional status and moves toward the status of a bureaucratic employee.

Ronald Corwin has distinguished between bureaucratic and professional modes of organization. He outlines three criteria for conceptualizing these organizational procedures: the degree of specialization of work, the degree of standardization of work, and the amount of authority permitted (Table 8.2). Each of these criteria is viewed as a variable on a continuum from highly bureaucratic at one extreme to highly professional at the other.

1. *Specialization.* Bureaucratic employees have specialized skills and tasks; their job is based on practice and repetition. By contrast, professionals function in a broad capacity; they utilize their knowledge in various situations. Although they may refine their knowledge with practice, practice cannot substitute for the competencies that must guide their decisions in specific cases.

2. *Standardization.* Predictability and consistency of behavior among employees characterizes bureaucracy; administrators discourage creative and original thought or behavior. The bureaucratic ideal is based on routine, rules and records, whereas the professional is permitted and even encouraged to use diffuse procedures and alternative behaviors.

3. *Authority.* In bureaucratic organizations authority is based on the person's position within the hierarchy; the right to give orders is based on rank or title. Professional organizations also have the notion of hierarchical authority, but the last word often goes to the person with the greatest knowledge. In bureaucratic organizations, the source of authority is the administrator, within the chain of command of the hierarchy. Among professionals, associations and peers often serve as the source of authority, especially for personal recognition and problems dealing with clients.

Corwin concludes that teachers tend to be organized by actions and policies that correspond with the bureaucratic employee model, although there is movement by teachers toward the professional employee model.

In short, the characteristics which predispose school bureaucracy and teacher professionalism are in conflict; at best, the relation is not a simple one. Not only are we dealing with theoretical generalizations, but the rise of teacher militancy introduces a counteracting phenomenon. As teacher power increases, the problem of defining and enforcing organizational goals and policies becomes a matter of concern and of potential conflict, for teachers on one side and management on the other side. Teachers will negotiate new relations with school administrators and school board members; these negotiations will center on working conditions and decision-making roles as well as salaries. Teacher militancy may well redefine both the nature of school bureaucracy and the nature of the teacher profession.

TOWARD GREATER PROFESSIONALISM

How can teachers improve their professional status? This is, of course, an important question in the light of historical and future trends. From an educator's point of view, it seems that the possibility of increasing professionalism is linked with teacher militancy. Increasing activism on the part of teachers is to be expected. It need not take the form of self-interest by seeking to advance working conditions alone, but it will probably focus on the needs and concerns of teachers first — and students second. As part of this militant movement, teachers will undoubtedly have much more to say to principals, superintendents, and school boards about the ways in which education is conducted. Four forms of teacher militancy are discussed below:

(1) organizational strength, (2) teacher strikes, (3) collective bargaining and negotiations, and (4) political activism.

Table 8.3 / Membership of the NEA and AFT by Decades, Projected to 1980

Year	National Education Association (NEA)	American Federation of Teachers (AFT)
(1857)[a]	(43)	
1870	170	
1880	354	
1890	5,474	
1900	2,332	
1910	6,909	
(1918)[a]		(1,500)
1920	22,850	10,000
1930	216,188	7,000
1940	203,429	30,000
1950	453,797	41,000
1960	713,994	59,000
1970	1,100,000	205,000
1975[b]	1,500,000	450,000
1980[b]	1,800,000	700,000

[a] Year the organization was started.
[b] Estimates by the author; college professors included.
Source: Adapted from T. M. Stinnett and Raymond E. Cleveland, "The Politics and Rise of Teacher Organizations," in A. C. Ornstein and S. I. Miller (eds.), *Policy Issues in Education* (Lexington, Mass.: D. C. Heath Co., 1976), pp. 90, 93.

Organizational Strength

The demands of individuals are often augmented or opposed by public demands and the sophisticated tactics of organized groups. Since the 1960s, the most visible and powerful organizations to challenge administrative authority and school board policy are teacher groups. The National Education Association (NEA) and American Federation of Teachers (AFT) have emerged as the two most important organizational advocates of teacher interests.

The NEA was formed in 1857 as the National Teachers Association, a confederation of ten state teachers' associations, and the name of the organization was changed in 1879. It has grown to the point that in 1975 it had approximately 1.5 million members, including close to 200,000 administrators and 1.3 millions teachers (see Table 8.3); this was 50 percent of the nation's teachers. These members, mostly in suburban and rural areas, are served through a large bureaucracy including 53 state groups and more than 8,800 local affiliated organizations.

During several decades of domination by the administrative membership within the organization, the NEA opposed collective bargaining and negotiations as well as teacher strikes. In 1968 the organization reversed its historic stand against work stoppages and strikes and passed a resolution permitting both tactics. This reversal was due to pressure from the membership for the group to assume greater responsibility for improving teachers' professional status. Relations between administrators and teachers within the organization grew increasingly tense as the majority of members adopted more militant strategies, and, in 1973, the administrators voted to cut the ties of their groups with the NEA.

The American Federation of Teachers (AFT) was founded in 1918 as an affiliate of the American Federation of Labor. The organization grew from less than 60,000 members in 1960 to more than 450,000 members in 1975, organized in some 500 local affiliates. Traditionally, the AFT did not permit administrators into its organization; it has always had a militant philosophy, and most of its membership is derived from large cities, where there is a history of unionism and militant labor.

The AFT remained quite small until 1961, when the union defeated the NEA local group in New York City and the United Federation of Teachers (UFT) was chosen to represent the New York City teachers. Following their election victory, the UFT engaged in a series of successful strikes which brought improved working conditions, salaries, health benefits, and teacher rights in New York City. These UFT victories encouraged AFT leaders in other cities to press for representative bargaining status in their own locales, and the outcome was increasing competition between the NEA and the AFT during the 1960s.

As the 1970s come to a close, the NEA and AFT are rapidly enrolling professors as members while the traditional American Association of University Professors (AAUP) is gradually losing its membership. In 1970 less than 5 percent of the nation's professors were employed under the terms of a negotiated contract; by 1975 professors at more than 400 of the 2,700 colleges and universities (15 percent) had voted to unionize, especially at the community college level. Of this number, less than 10 percent were organized by the AAUP, 25 percent by the AFT, 40 percent by the NEA, and 17 percent by the NEA and AFT in the state of New York, and the remaining 8 percent were affiliated with independent agents.[44] Myron Lieberman predicts that the unionization of college faculties will be one of the most important developments in higher education, and it will vastly increase the organizational strength of teacher organizations.[45] As financial stringencies, declining student enrollments, and revised tenure provisions threaten professors, and there is a general crisis of survival in colleges and universities, the membership of professors in the NEA and AFT can be expected to grow.

Will the NEA and AFT merge? Since the 1970s there has been a great deal of talk and activity concerning this question. Although competition between the two organizations has increased, differences between them have lessened. The NEA's acceptance of collective bargaining and teacher strikes, and restrictions on membership for administrators — which it once opposed and which caused conflict between the organizations — have reduced philosophical gaps. The NEA has also changed the president's term of office to two years rather than one, with the right of reelection. This should give the president more power to promote a merger.

Since the mid-1970s, however, the AFT has encouraged the unionization and membership of school administrators, a complete turn-about from the past for this group. Moreover, beleaguered by the political environment surrounding today's schools and encouraged by teachers' gains, the growth of administrator-supervisory unionism has been rapid. As of 1975, there were 1,276 local administrators' unions, most of which were located in the cities and affiliated with the AFL-CIO.[46] But the AFT's affiliation with labor remains a problem, and some NEA officials fear that a merger of the two organizations with the AFL-CIO would cause many NEA members to break away and form a more conservative group.[47]

---

[44] *Chronicle of Higher Education*, February 18, 1975, pp. 1, 8; June 9, 1975, pp. 4-5; September 2, 1975, p. 9.

[45] Myron Lieberman, "Professors, Unite!" *Harpers Magazine*, October 1971, pp. 61-71.

[46] Edwin M. Bridges and Bruce S. Cooper, "Collective Bargaining for School Administrators," *Theory into Practice*, October 1976, pp. 306-13.

[47] Martha Gottron, "NEA Pushes for Teachers' Rights," *Change*, February 1975, pp. 17-20.

Affiliation with the AFL–CIO is important not to rank-and-file AFT members but to a few AFT leaders who perceive the benefits and support to be derived from a larger union affiliation.

Another obstacle to merger is the NEA's recent position of guaranteeing 20 percent minority representation on all administrative committees. The NEA has taken the position that any merger must include such a guarantee of quotas, and the AFT leadership has rejected this position. Finally, there is the question of who gets what jobs and what kind of decision-making power in a merged organization. The question is not one of employment, for there are plenty of jobs to go around, but of key positions associated with leadership roles and authority.

While NEA–AFT mergers have taken place on the local level in a few places, such as in Flint, Michigan, New Orleans, and Los Angeles, the NEA dropped its Florida local affiliate in 1972 and created a new one when the leadership of the NEA in Florida negotiated a merger with the AFT. Events in New York State are also counterproductive to possible merger. After four years of cooperation between the NEA and AFT in New York, the only statewide teacher organization both national groups had approved, a split evolved in 1976. More than 70 percent of the membership voted in favor of disaffiliation with the NEA.[48]

The question of merger has been a dominant issue at the annual conventions of the NEA and AFT since 1968. The debates have been heated; talks between the leaders of the organizations have been opened, terminated, and renewed on and off. Common concerns such as tenure laws, accountability, school budget crises and cutbacks, and teacher unemployment are driving the organizations together, as it appears the only intelligent way to combat these dangers is to move toward greater unity. Not only would the money and energy presently being wasted on rivalry be saved, but there are immense political and economic advantages teachers could gain by such a merger. As many as 2.5 million teachers, along with another 1.2 million paraprofessionals, college professors, and miscellaneous educators from local, state, and federal agencies would provide immense power not realized in the two separate organizations. The nearly 1 million teachers who presently do not belong to either organization would be more likely to join the single teacher organization.

Teacher Strikes

Since the 1970s it has become apparent that teacher organizations represent a formidable force in local school policy making. The most

---

[48] "Newsnotes," *Phi Delta Kappan,* April 1976, pp. 558–59.

obvious reason has been their ability to threaten to strike or to actually do so in order to achieve their goals. The teacher strike has been most effective in issues dealing with salaries, working conditions, health and welfare benefits, classroom size, selection and use of materials, parent conferences, student discipline, and so on.

Contrary to popular opinion, teacher strikes are not entirely new; rather their rate and impact have been augmented. Between 1918 and 1962 there were some 130 work stoppages, an average of 3 per year. However, these stoppages were mainly short and ineffective, and they often split teachers into opposing camps—for and against a work stoppage.[49] There were five strikes during the 1963–64 school year, 12 the following year, then 18, then 34, and the number soared to 114 in 1967–68. Then came the all-time high of 181 teacher strikes in 1969–70. The annual figures slightly declined between 1970 and 1974, averaging about 130 strikes per year, and for one year the number was less than 100. But a new record was established in 1975–76 with more than 200 strikes, following in 1976–77 with 155 strikes.[50]

There can be little doubt that the spark for these strikes has been the AFT, starting with the 1961 teacher strike in New York City, the only teacher strike of that year, and their continuous success with strikes in other cities. Commenting on the success of the AFT strikes, Peter Janssen wrote: "Strikes . . . have given the AFT's growth a snowballing effect, advancing its image as a militant fighter for teacher's rights, destroying the picture of the teacher as a silent partner in the educational process."[51]

The dramatic shift of the NEA in adopting the strike as a strategy was a crucial factor in encouraging teacher militancy outside the large cities. Representing 50 percent of the nation's teachers, the NEA had not been involved in a single work stoppage between 1952 and 1963. In 1966, it participated in one third of them. The NEA and its affiliates initiated 70 percent of the work stoppages and strikes between 1960 and 1972, but the AFT accounted for 70 percent of the 6 million man-days lost by teachers through work stoppages.[52] In other words, because of its size the NEA has been responsible for most of the recent stoppages and strikes, but the AFT is more militant and will risk more striking days.

Whereas only 50 percent of the teachers surveyed by the NEA in 1965

---

[49] Ronald W. Glass, "Work Stoppages and Teachers: History and Prospect," *Monthly Labor Review*, August 1967, pp. 43–46.

[50] *Chicago Tribune*, July 5, 1977, p. 16; Ornstein, *Teaching in a New Era.*

[51] Peter Janssen, "The Union Response to Academic Mass Production," *Saturday Review*, October 21, 1967, p. 65.

[52] Ronald G. Corwin, "The New Teaching Profession," in K. Ryan (ed.), *Teacher Education*, 74th Yearbook of the National Society for the Study of Education, Part II (Chicago: University of Chicago Press, 1975), pp. 230–64.

supported the right to strike, by 1970 as many as 90 percent supported some type of group action, and 75 percent approved the strike tactic.[53] AFT members are unanimous in their belief in the right to strike, though circumstances may divide members' opinions. For example, black and white teachers were divided over the 1967 strike in New York City, which pitted the teacher union against community control advocates. Yet most black teachers did support the strike.[54]

The strike obviously creates tension between teacher groups and the public. Traditionally the public has opposed the right of teachers to strike, but a gradual change in this attitude is apparent. A 1969 Gallup poll showed that 59 percent of the parents surveyed opposed the teacher's right to strike. In 1975, 48 percent of the parents surveyed were against teacher strikes. (In both surveys parochial school parents were more adamant against the teacher's right to strike: 62 percent and 52 percent respectively.)[55] The change in public attitude is in part due to people becoming accustomed to seeing striking teachers; however, if the economy continues to worsen and teachers' job security is threatened, resentments may build up on both sides.

In general, the effects of the popularization of the teacher strike can be assessed in terms of changes in teacher power. Prior to the 1960s teachers were politically impotent and had little say in the formulation of school policy. Much of this situation has been reversed as a result of teacher militancy, especially the strike technique.

Collective Bargaining and Negotiations

Up to the mid-1960s, one clear distinction that could be made between the NEA and AFT was that the former relied on professional negotiations and sanctions, while the latter used the tactics of labor, such as collective bargaining and strikes. T. M. Stinnett has commented on these differences. Professional negotiation establishes an orderly method for teacher associations and school boards to negotiate on matters of common concern. Both parties do not advocate "or consider legal the use of a strike as a weapon." In case of an impasse, appeal procedures are established. "The rationale is that schools . . . are not profit-making enterprises, and

[53] Corwin, "The New Teaching Profession"; "Teacher Strikes" (opinion poll), *Today's Education,* November 1969, p. 10.

[54] Sandra Feldman, "The UFT and the School Conflict," *United Teacher,* April 23, 1972, pp. 1–8; Eugenia Kemble, New York's Experiments in School Decentralization (New York: United Federation of Teachers, 1968).

[55] *Gallup Polls of Attitudes toward Education, 1967–1973;* George Gallup, "The Seventh Annual Gallup Poll of Public Attitudes toward Education," *Phi Delta Kappan,* December 1975, pp. 227–41.

management and employees are not natural enemies fighting over divisions of profits." Collective bargaining, however, "employs, in case of impasse, the strike, which is recognized under the laws as the weapon of the employee." Such a procedure is subject to federal and state legal interpretation.[56]

The NEA formerly relied on sanctions as the most extreme tactic, that is, curtailment of the services of teachers to a given school district. A first step involved publicizing the dispute, then, the NEA requested its members employed elsewhere not to accept positions in that particular school district and the college placement offices not to list its openings. This procedure was rarely used, and when it was it tended to be ineffective. The AFT has utilized the strike to interrupt services during the school year if there is a dispute that cannot be settled. In most cases, however, teachers serve out their existing contracts and then negotiate another one, although they may strike over terms of the new contract.

The distinctions between professional negotiations and collective negotiations, as well as between sanctions and strikes, are less important today, since the NEA has moved in the direction of adopting such militant tactics as collective negotiations and strikes. Across the country, school boards have been forced to reexamine their roles and prerogatives as they negotiate agreements with teachers. School superintendents have been identified on the side of the school board in negotiations, and their powers have been redefined too.

In essence, it can be said that collective negotiations between school boards and teachers are conducted in two broad areas: (1) salaries, fringe benefits, hours, and conditions of work, and (2) the making of educational policy. By 1977, 25 states had laws providing for some form of collective bargaining,[57] although they varied considerably. However, negotiations go on even in states which have no legislation in effect. Increasingly state departments of education are employing full-time mediators and fact-finding groups who race from one district to another. Many school boards are employing paid negotiators, usually lawyers, whose fees sometimes eat up a dismaying slice of the operating budget in small districts. Both the NEA and AFT spend several millions of dollars each year on legal advice in behalf of negotiating teachers — providing expertise, probing district finances, and stiffening backbones as needed. Both also lobby for passage of additional collective bargaining laws for teachers and college professors.

It makes little sense to have 25 different state laws on collective negotiations — and 25 states with no law at all. No doubt more states will

---

[56] T. M. Stinnett, *Turmoil in Teaching* (New York: Macmillan Co., 1968), p. 90.
[57] *Chronicle of Higher Education*, March 14, 1977, pp. 1, 8.

adopt collective bargaining procedures, but federal collective negotiation legislation, or some uniform law, is needed to rationalize and standardize the process for the more than 16,000 public school districts. A list of suggested topics for negotiations includes: (1) salary policies, (2) career and tenure policies, (3) work conditions, (4) employee benefits and services, (5) teachers' legal rights, (6) grievances and internal agency appeals, and (7) school board-teacher organizational arrangements.[58] Each of these broad areas could include 100 or so specific items. For example, under salary policies could be listed paid absences, personal leave, sabbatical leave, salary schedules, merit pay, seniority pay, afternoon school asssignments, summer school employment, and so on.

A major difficulty lies in precisely defining the scope of negotiations and determining whether the issues are related to employment or to educational policy. Superintendents and school boards will be reluctant to include in negotiations any item related to policy, such as what foreign languages should be taught and when they should be introduced. Myron Lieberman and Michael Moskow contend that teachers are definitely interested in policy issues and should be consulted with respect to them.[59] Whether they are negotiable is another question. It is important to define where working conditions leave off and educational policy begins.

Political Activism

In an era of political activism and protest, it is perhaps natural for teachers to become more politically sensitive — using the tools of protest and persuasion, organizing collectively around specific issues, lobbying and helping to elect proeducation city, state, and federal officials. The axiom "Keep politics out of education and education out of politics" is no longer relevant; political and collective action is now seen as an attractive recourse. Indeed, it is almost necessary, since there are competing interest groups seeking to influence and shape policy for their own benefit and to exercise control over limited resources. Activism is also considered necessary to protect teachers' interests in view of the facts that the supply-demand situation no longer is favorable; the public is beginning to hold the line on school spending and teachers are no longer considered underpaid. Furthermore, teachers are bearing the brunt of much of the criticism directed at poor quality education, particularly in the inner cities.

---

[58] Patrick W. Carlton and Harold I. Goodwin (eds.), *The Collective Dilemma: Negotiations in Education* (Worthington, Ohio: Charles A. Jones Publishing Co., 1969); Cresswell and Murphy, *Education and Collective Bargaining.*

[59] Myron Lieberman and Michael H. Moskow, *Collective Negotiations for Teachers* (Chicago: Rand McNally & Co., 1966).

Political activity among teacher groups is in three broad areas: (1) the use of persuasion techniques and mild coercion, (2) sanctions and strikes, and (3) direct political action. Persuasion techniques and mild coercion are the oldest forms of political activity utilized by teachers; examples are advertising and other influence of the mass media, establishing friendship ties, becoming members of formal and informal groups, and employing lobbyists to influence legislators. This approach has resulted in rather cordial relations between teacher groups and other power groups, although in some cases the gains for educators have been less than satisfying.

Sanctions and strikes are more aggressive and more visible tactics, part political and part economic, which widely surfaced in the 1960s, as has been noted. With this technique, relations with other groups often become strained, and a win-lose situation may be created in the settlement of issues.

Direct political action, whereby teacher organizations devote services and money to help lobby for the passage of certain bills and elect political representatives who favor education, is a more recent and more sophisticated approach. Its implications are long range and relatively invisible to the public. In 1974, the first year support of candidates was attempted on a large scale, the NEA–approved candidates won 229 of 282 seats in the U.S. House of Representatives and 21 of 28 in the Senate. In addition, 165 candidates in state elections received financial support. These allocations amounted to $25 million in local, state, and federal elections.[60] The same year, in New York City, the United Federation of Teachers (UFT) donated several million dollars to secure the election of school board members who were supportive of teachers; about 80 percent of their candidates were elected to the 32 local school boards.[61] The "mother" organization (AFT) contributed more than $10 million to city, state, and national elections through its branch the Committee on Public Education (COPE).[62]

Teacher organizations no longer rely solely on lobbying activity and bargaining rights to clear the paths to policy makers. By 1975 more than 400 educators were serving as legislators, and dozens of others had left teaching to become members of legislative bodies.[63] Both the NEA and the

---

[60] T. M. Stinnett et al., *Introduction to Teaching* (Worthington, Ohio: Charles A. Jones Publishing Co., 1976).

[61] Eugenia Kemble, special assistant to the President, conversations with the person, Chicago, March 27, 1977.

[62] Rachelle Horowitz, AFT/COPE director, letter to the author, April 14, 1976.

[63] James Browne, "Power Pointers for Teachers, Modern Style," *Phi Delta Kappan*, October 1976, pp. 158–64.

AFT endorsed President Jimmy Carter during the 1976 campaign, the first time either one had publicly supported a presidential candidate. Among the President's task force on education are the presidents of both organizations. Albert Shanker, president of the AFT, may be the most influential person in the task group, due to his affiliation with labor.[64]

Although no estimates are available of the number of teachers serving as members of state boards of education and local school boards, the number seems to be growing—a general reflection of political activism among teachers. The NEA affiliates dominate state-level political activities of teacher organizations everywhere except in Florida and New York, and therefore they often are influential with governors and their advisors. The AFT is at home in Washington, where a Congress long controlled by Democrats has been sympathetic to labor. In fact, education bills in Congress start not in committees of educational groups but in the Committee on Education and Labor of the House of Representatives and the Committee on Labor and Public Welfare of the Senate.

The way in which teachers use their source of political power, and the extent to which they are successful, will determine how much influence they can accumulate in shaping educational policy. Many teachers are seeking answers to some interesting questions. What are the alternative bases of political power which teachers can use to influence education? Can teachers anticipate accurately the political consequences of these alternatives? Political power is not something teachers can expect to monopolize in the average community, since there are many competitive forces. Nevertheless, the power of teachers in the decision-making process is growing, and increasingly it will be utilized in interaction with other groups.

CONCLUSIONS

The professional status teachers are demanding is in many ways incompatible with traditional ideas of administration. Principals and superintendents were originally seen as united in a small-town structure, based on the premise of teacher compliance and justified by law. This image was supported by custom and the fiction that administrators are and can be responsible for literally every facet of what is sometimes referred to as "their" system. Bureaucratic authority and tradition are difficult to reconcile with the notion of teacher professionalism. If classroom teachers are to become professional in the fullest sense, they must gain greater autonomy and control over the key matters that affect their status.

---

[64] *Chronicle of Higher of Education*, September 7, 1976, p. 6.

ACTIVITIES

1. Develop and administer to the class a questionnaire regarding the nature of a profession. Compare ratings teachers receive as professionals with nurses, social workers, lawyers, and one or two other groups.
2. Review at least one major book or commission report on improving teacher education. Cite at least three examples where you approve and three where you disapprove of the authors' recommendations — and give your reasons.
3. Invite a guest speaker from the local NEA or AFT affiliate to speak to the class about the nature and future of the organization.
4. From the literature on the topics, research the relationship between teacher militancy and professionalism.
5. Invite a local political figure to speak on the merits of teachers and teacher organizations entering the political arena.

DISCUSSION QUESTIONS

1. Discuss factors which you believe influence the teacher's professional status.
2. Define the concept of professionalism and explain in what ways teachers are professionals.
3. How would you improve teacher education? What types of standards, courses, and field experiences would you require?
4. Distinguish between the bureaucratic and professional roles of an organization.
5. What are the philosophical differences between the NEA and the AFT? What chances do you see of a merger between these organizations?

SUGGESTED FOR FURTHER READING

Andree, Robert G. *The Art of Negotiation: Roles, Games, Logic.* Lexington, Mass.: D.C. Heath & Co., 1971.

Conant, James B. *The Education of American Teachers.* New York: McGraw-Hill Book Co., 1963.

Corwin, Ronald G. *Militant Professionalism.* New York: Appleton-Century-Crofts, 1970.

Cushman, M. L. *The Governance of Teacher Education.* Berkeley, Ca.: McCutchan Publishing Corp., 1977.

Etzioni, Amitai (ed.). *The Semi-Professions and Their Organization: Teachers, Nurses, Social Workers.* New York: Free Press, 1969.

Howsam, Robert B., et al. *Educating a Profession.* Bicentennial Commission for the Profession of Teaching of the American Association of Colleges for Teacher Education. Washington, D.C.: AACTE, 1976.

Koerner, James D. *Who Controls American Education?.* Boston: Beacon Press, 1968.

Lieberman, Myron. *Education as a Profession.* Englewood Cliffs, N.J.: Prentice-Hall, Inc., 1956.

Ornstein, Allan C. *Teaching in a New Era.* Champaign, Ill.: Stipes Publishing Co., 1976.

Stinnett, T. M., et al. *Introduction to Teaching.* Worthington, Ohio: Charles A. Jones Publishing Co., 1976.

PART IV

SCHOOLS

In the closing part of this book we treat directly with topics related to the schools. Chapter 9 is a descriptive analysis of the different kinds of schools. The schools can be described in terms of grade levels, number and size, types (based on geographical and social settings), and social-class composition. These discussions indicate that there are several common characteristics that can be used to describe the schools.

Chapter 10 examines three strategies for improving American schools: compensatory education, desegregation, and administrative decentralization, with options for increasing community involvement through community participation or community control. Various examples and plans are analyzed for the three reform strategies, problems that remain unresolved are discussed, and related research on student performance is studied.

The final chapter (Chapter 11) is concerned with the role of the government in education. The discussion is divided into four parts covering federal, state, and local aspects of public schooling, and government spending. Of particular importance in the first part is the discussion of the increasing role of the federal government in education and the national obligation to educational research and development. State responsibilities encompass the courts, governors, state legislatures, state boards of education, state departments of education, and superintendents. Under local responsibilities, particular attention is given to school problems and related public opinion surveys of the schools. Various aspects of school financing are discussed in the closing part.

CHAPTER 9

AMERICAN
SCHOOLS AND
SCHOOL SYSTEMS

There are several different ways of looking at American schools and school systems. In this chapter we will discuss the pattern of schools by grade levels, their distribution by number and size, special types and descriptions, and social class and racial characteristics of schools. The four parts to this chapter provide a conceptual framework for looking at American schools. Factors related to special need, size, geography, social class, and race are taken into account throughout the discussion.

SCHOOLS BY GRADE LEVELS

In examining schools according to grade levels, it is important to keep in mind that the school unit came into being as a response to widely recognized needs. The organization of the school is the educators' and the public's answer to what they believe is required to meet these needs: not only the children's needs, but also the constraints of enrollment pressures, existing buildings, state laws, and limited resources. As time passes and new needs and ideas for meeting them emerge, existing grade-level units are either modified or new ones are established. The units described below are generally typical; they may not precisely constitute a grade-level pattern in any one school system, for the exact patterns vary from place to place.

Nursery School and Head Start

Nursery school and Head Start are prekindergarten programs that enroll children who are three, four, and five years old. The first nursery school in the United States was for the children of poor working mothers, founded by a philanthropic worker's organization in New York City in 1854. Public support of nursery programs was provided during World War I and II, not because of concern for the children's welfare but mainly to free mothers for national defense work. At their peak in 1945, nursery schools, then called day-care centers, enrolled 1.6 million children.[1] All the states placed day-care centers within their departments of public welfare except for California, which placed it under its department of education. Coincidental with the day-care centers there was a steady growth of private nursery schools. These were mainly for people who could afford to pay for them and were geared more to play and cooperative social behavior than preschool learning.

The nursery school (public and private), then, was not part of the school unit. However, the situation changed radically when the federal government, through the Economic Opportunity Act in 1964 and the Elementary and Secondary Education Act in 1965, made available funds for prekindergarten poor children. Project Head Start, launched in the summer of 1965, proliferated the prekindergarten movement, and eventually more schools integrated the program into their unit organization. Of the 4.6 million children enrolled at the prekindergarten level in 1974 about 33 percent were housed in public schools; the others were being taught in community action agencies and voluntary and independent schools approved by the federal government.[2] The enrollment represented about 40 percent of the population of three- to five-year olds, 95 percent of which was distributed among three- and four-year-olds (Most of the five-year-olds who attended school were enrolled in kindergarten). Enrollment in the prekindergarten program was higher for black three- and four-year-olds (20 percent and 37 percent, respectively) than for white children of the same ages (15 percent and 33 percent, respectively). More than 67 percent of the children attended school for only part of the day.[3]

The main reason for the present Head Start program is to promote the optimal development of each child, especially to counteract the cognitive

---

[1] Ruby Takanishi-Knowles, "Federal Involvement in Early Childhood Education (1933-73): The Need for Historical Perspectives," paper read at the annual meeting of the American Educational Research Association (Chicago, April 1974).

[2] *Preprimary Enrollment: October 1974* (Washington, D.C.: U.S. Government Printing Office, 1975), Table 1, p. 10.

[3] Ibid.; Verna Hildebrand, *Introduction to Early Childhood Education*, 2nd ed. (New York: Macmillan Co., 1976), pp. 8-9.

deprivation of poor children who often come from homes that are environmentally impoverished. The program is largely based on the methods used by Maria Montessori, who worked in the slum areas of Italian cities. Most of the evaluation studies of Head Start indicate that the program has been unsuccessful in raising cognitive achievement levels of target children matched with children who do not attend these programs.[4] More recent data suggest that early intervention programs for disadvantaged children have been moderately successful.[5]

Kindergarten

Kindergarten education originated with Fredrich Froebel, who based the idea on his experimental school in Blankenburg, Germany. Subsequently it spread to many European cities and, in the United States, became a part of the St. Louis public school system in 1873. Within less than 15 years, kindergartens had been established in all of the major cities of the country. However, with the exception of St. Louis, all of them were under private control and available chiefly for middle-class and upper-middle-class children. By the turn of the century, kindergarten was slowly being introduced into the public school systems.

Today, all schools do not provide kindergarten education, and since it is noncompulsory, all parents do not enroll their children. More than two thirds of the public school systems in the country, and all major cities, provide kindergarten education at which attendance is voluntary.[6] As many as 2.9 million students were enrolled in kindergarten in 1975–76, with five-year-olds accounting for about 85 percent of the enrollment.[7]

The kindergarten is more or less a separate unit in the school system, fully integrated with neither the prekindergarten school program (where one exists) nor the first grade. This separation is usually considered desirable on the basis that rapid growth and development take place between the ages of four and six, and different programs must be developed for each of these ages.

The major purpose of kindergarten is to facilitate the child's readiness to learn. This is characterized by sufficient maturity (mental, physical,

---

[4] For example, see Westinghouse Learning Corporation and Ohio University, *The Impact of Head Start: An Evaluation of the Effects of Head Start Experience on Children's Cognitive and Affective Development* (Washington, D.C.: U.S. Government Printing Office, 1969).

[5] See "Early Intervention Has Lasting Effects," *Phi Delta Kappan*, May 1977, p. 719; also see Chapter 11.

[6] *Educational Directory: Public School Systems, 1975–76* (Washington, D.C.: U.S. Government Printing Office, 1974), Table 2, p. xvii.

[7] *Statistics of Public Elementary and Secondary Day Schools, Fall 1975* (Washington, D.C.: U.S. Government Printing Office, 1976), Table 5, pp. 24–25.

social, and emotional), appropriate visual and auditory experiences, and adequate speech and vocabulary. Some children learn to read while in kindergarten, but many others who have had kindergarten experience are still not ready to begin reading when they enter first grade. However, a child who has had a year's kindergarten experience is usually better prepared to learn the basic skills taught in the first grade than one who has not.

One reason why kindergarten programs seem to be more effective than the prekindergarten (nursery school and Head Start) program is that the latter employs many unlicensed teachers. Furthermore, prekindergarten programs mainly enroll children from impoverished environments. Whatever positive effects of the program may exist, they may be offset by the negative effects of the child's environment. Both of these reasons are speculative.

Elementary School

The traditional grade school in early America enrolled children from grades 1 through 8. The student who finished elementary schooling was transferred to a four-year high school. Since the turn of the century, there has been a move to reduce the elementary school unit from eight to six, five, or four grades. Estimated enrollments for public school students (grades K–8) went from 14.9 million in 1900 to 30.5 million in 1975–76. The later figure accounted for 65 percent of the total public school population.[8]

In an elementary school that has eight grades, often the first three are called primary grades; grades 4–6, intermediate grades; and grades 7–8, upper grades. In the six-unit elementary school, grades 1–3 are called primary grades and grades 4–6 upper grades. The elementary school usually follows a single, general curriculum, with the subject matter usually modified to meet the needs of the children, who vary widely in abilities and interests. In this respect, the elementary school is a comprehensive school.

The elementary school unit usually is the self-contained classroom, which is traditional in nature. The furniture is movable in newer schools so that it can be rearranged according to the activity and individual or group projects. Under this arrangement, one teacher, sometimes with the help of an aide, is responsible for the whole range of activities, and the classroom is supposed to be equipped with all the needed materials and media, in-

---

[8] Ibid.; *Digest of Educational Statistics, 1976* (Washington, D.C.: U.S. Government Printing office, 1977), Table 31, p. 34; *Projections of Educational Statistics to 1985–86* (Washington, D.C., U.S. Government Printing Office, 1977), Table 3, p. 14.

cluding art equipment, a piano, and a record player. Ideally, toilet and washroom facilities are also provided in the classroom.

Students usually leave the classroom for specialized instruction, such as physical education, library work, and remedial reading, or a resource teacher takes over the classroom for one or two periods per week for these instructional activities. The efforts of various specialists such as the school nurse, psychologist, and social worker are coordinated with those of the classroom teacher. In some elementary schools, especially where grades 7 and 8 are included in the same building, subject matter is departmentalized and instruction is handled by various teachers. This type of arrangement is customary in some schools as far down as the fifth grade.

Middle, Intermediate, and Junior High Schools

The school units between elementary and senior high school are the middle, intermediate, and junior high schools. These in-between grade units vary according to the state and local school systems. In most systems, grades 5–8 are considered a middle school; grades 6–8, an intermediate school; and grades 7–9, a junior high school.

The move toward these in-between school units can be traced to 1896, when the city of Richmond, Indiana, placed its seventh and eighth grades in a separate building and revised the curriculum. In this and subsequently other cities, the tendency was for grades 7 and 8 to be viewed as part of the secondary rather than the elementary school. This is one reason why many elementary schools which still house the seventh and eighth grades provide for departmentalization at these grade levels.

The reasons for the in-between units vary. Besides the pressure of enrollments, age and condition of buildings, and changing state regulations, there is an educational philosophy which maintains the importance of putting an age group facing similar social, psychological, and physiological changes together in one school unit, so specialists can facilitate their adjustment. Yet these units do not always fulfill this intended function. As James Conant pointed out after surveying the diversity of junior high schools, the placement of the grades and the rearrangement of the grade span are not so important as the quality of the program and personnel provided.[9]

Senior High School

The senior high school embraces grades 9–12 or 10–12, depending on the school system. The most common arrangement today is the three-year

---

[9] James B. Conant, *Education in the Junior High Schools Years* (Princeton, N.J.: Educational Testing Service, 1960).

Figure 9.1 / Percentage of High School Graduates, Persons 17 Years
of Age, 1880–1980

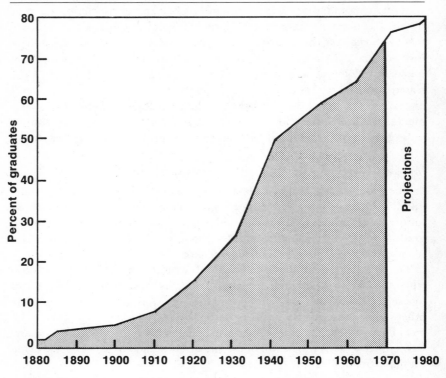

* 1980 estimates made by author and based on Federal projections to 1984–85.
  Note: These figures do not include persons who received high school equivalency certificates; in 1970,
approximately 142,000.
  Source: *Digest of Educational Statistics, 1974* (Washington, D.C.: U.S. Government Printing Office, 1975),
Figure 8, p. 55.

senior high school, that is, grades 10–12. At the beginning of the 20th
century, about 519,000 public and 110,000 private school students, or 11
percent of the population 14–17 years of age, were enrolled in grades 9–12,
with 8 percent of all American youth graduating. By 1975–76, there were
some 14.3 million students in public school grades 9–12 and another 1.4
million in private school grades 9–12, with more than 75 percent
graduating.[10] The percentage graduating exceeds that of any other

[10] *Digest of Educational Statistics, 1976,* Table 34, p. 38; Table 41, p. 43; Table 44, p. 46;
Statistics of Public Elementary and Secondary Day Schools, Fall 1975, Table 5, pp. 24–25;
"Trends in High School Graduates," *American Education,* April 1976, back cover: *U.S.
Catholic Schools, 1975–76* (Washington, D.C.: National Catholic Education Association,
1976), Table 1, p. 3.

nation.[11] Figure 9.1 shows the increasing proportion of high school graduates in each 100 persons of the 17-year-old population over a period of 100 years, from 1880, when it was 2.5 percent, to 1980, when it should reach 80 percent.

The high schools can be divided into three types:

1. *Comprehensive High Schools.* This is the most common type of high school. Its curriculum is aimed to meet the needs of all enrolled in the school, and in theory, special arrangements are made for both slow and talented students. A comprehensive school which largely draws middle-class students will tend to stress college preparatory work and may neglect students who are terminating their educations after graduating from high school. Similarly, a school largely drawing working-class students will tend to stress vocational-type courses and may fail to provide adequate college preparation in foreign language, science, and mathematics.

In his report on the American high schools, Conant pointed out that in 1956 approximately 17,000 of the nation's 21,000 public high schools were too small (graduating less than 100 students per year) to do an adequate job in terms of offering a diversified program to meet the needs of all students. Approximately two thirds of the students attended high schools that were too small by his standards.[12] Subsequently there has been a trend toward consolidating small high schools — which coincides with the general trend to consolidate school systems.

2. *Vocational High Schools.* In most of the large cities in the East and Middle West there are one or more vocational high schools which students may elect. These schools usually enrolled boys or girls separately until very recently and offer one or more of the following programs: trade and industrial, distributive, home economics, agriculture, practical nursing, office, and technical education. The technical schools (also considered vocational schools) usually have selective academic requirements and offer a wide range of skilled and technical programs of study. The two most prominent ones are Brooklyn Technical High School in New York City and Lane Technical High School in Chicago.

For reasons of economy, the education of vocational and commercial students in separate schools is perhaps the most practical arrangement. School boards are either unable or unwilling to allocate sufficient money to purchase the equipment needed for a vocational program in every high

---

[11] Mary J. Bowman, "Mass Elites on the Threshold of the 1970s," in A. Kopan and H. J. Walberg (eds.), *Rethinking Education Equality* (Berkeley, Ca.: McCutchan Publishing Corp., 1974), pp. 104–33.

[12] James B. Conant, *The American High School Today* (New York: McGraw-Hill Book Co., 1959).

school. There is some criticism that the vocational student is stigmatized and placed in a second-class program, and that vocational high schools in large cities predominantly enroll minority students and thus impede integration.

3. *Specialized High Schools.* Some large cities have specialized high schools for students with superior scholastic aptitude or specialized artistic talents. The size of the city is important because the nature of the specialization is often uncommon, and only a large student population will include a sufficient number of talented students to warrant a special school. New York City, the largest school system in the country, has the most specialized schools, including the Bronx High School of Science and Hunter High School, both of which stress academic excellence, the High School of the Performing Arts, and the High School of Music and Art. There is a question whether it would be better to develop more specialized high schools or to work toward making the high schools more com-

Figure 9.2 / Organization of School Systems by Grade Levels

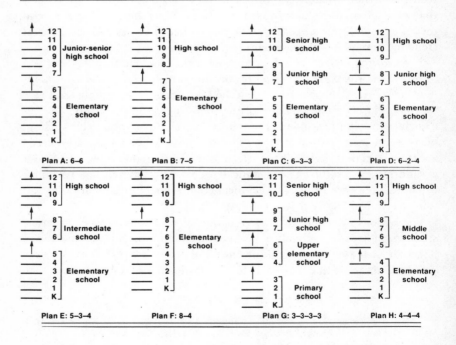

Source: Adapted from James J. Jones, C. Jackson Salisbury, and Ralph L. Spencer, *Secondary School Administration* (New York: McGraw-Hill Book Co., 1969), pp. 96–97.

prehensive as far as the individual characteristics and abilities of the students are concerned.

Grade Patterns of School Systems

The organization of elementary and secondary schools permits several grade patterns and combinations of patterns. James Jones and his associates have identified eight of the more common grade plans,[13] as represented in Figure 9.2.

1. Plan A shows the 6-6 grade pattern often found in sparsely populated or rural areas. The elementary school contains the first six grades, and the last six grades are lumped together as a secondary school, usually called the junior-senior high school.

2. Plan B is the 7-5 grade pattern; the elementary school consists of grades 1-7, and the high school consists of grades 8-12. A few Eastern and Southern states have used this plan.

3. Plan C is the 6-3-3 grade pattern, a common plan for large- and medium-sized school systems. The elementary school consists of grades 1-6, and there is a three-year junior high school and a three-year senior high school.

4. Plan D is the 6-2-4 grade pattern, comprising six grades of elementary school, two grades of junior high school, and four grades of senior high school.

5. Plan E is the 5-3-4 grade pattern, which provides a five-year elementary school, a three-year intermediate school, and a four-year high school. This plan is growing in popularity in some cities.

6. Plan F is the 8-4 grade pattern, the traditional and perhaps still most common arrangement, consisting of an eight-year elementary school and a four-year high school.

7. Plan G is the 3-3-3-3 grade pattern, used only in a few places in the country. The primary grades, 1-3, are organized and housed in a separate building away from the older children in upper elementary grades. There is also a three-year junior high school and a three-year senior high school.

8. Plan H is the 4-4-4 grade pattern, where grades 1-4 consist of the elementary schools, grades 5-8 represent the middle school, and grades 9-12 comprise the high school.

It is difficult to say which plan is better or worse; it varies with the philosophy and the general political and economic situation in the school district.

---

[13] James J. Jones, C. Jackson Salisbury, and Ralph L. Spencer, *Secondary School Administration* (New York: McGraw-Hill Book Co., 1969).

Table 9.1 / Organization of School Systems, by Size and Grade Levels, 1975–76

Size of school system	Total	K-6	1-6	K-8	1-8	K-9	1-9	K-12	1-12	7-12	9-12	Other
Total operating systems												
Number	16,006	393	177	2,949	789	30	7	9,538	1,265	94	537	227
Percent	100.0	2.5	1.1	18.4	4.9	0.2	0.0	59.6	7.9	0.6	3.4	1.4
Systems with 300 pupils												
or more, total	11,542	189	14	1,120	82	22	2	8,671	901	76	328	137
25,000 or more	187	0	0	1	0	0	0	171	8	1	1	5
10,000–24,999	555	3	0	23	0	0	0	466	28	3	16	16
5,000–9,999	1,126	10	0	57	0	0	0	912	92	3	31	21
2,500–4,999	2,050	16	1	120	3	0	1	1,607	227	10	39	26
1,000–2,499	3,467	44	1	312	17	9	1	2,623	282	28	107	43
600–999	1,860	51	2	220	13	4	0	1,372	93	22	69	14
300–599	2,297	65	10	387	49	9	0	1,520	171	9	65	12
Systems with less than												
300 pupils	4,464	204	163	1,829	707	8	5	867	364	18	209	90

Source: *Educational Directory: Public School Systems 1975–76* (Washington, D.C.: U.S. Government Printing Office, 1976), Table 2, p. xvii.

Most of the public school systems operate on a K-12, K-8, and 1-12 grade span; in 1975-76, 9,538 or 60 percent had grades K-12, 2,949 or 18 percent had grades K-8, and 1,265 or 8 percent had grades 1-12. A number of other school systems enroll only elementary school students (K-6, 1-6, 1-8, K-9, 1-9), totaling 1,396 or 9 percent, or only secondary school students (7-12, 9-12), totaling 631 or 4 percent. Table 9.1 shows how school systems are distributed according to grade span and size.

Colleges and Universities

The first colleges were established in the 12th century in Paris, Oxford, and Cambridge. In the United States, the first college was Harvard, founded in 1636, followed by William and Mary in 1693, Yale in 1701, Princeton in 1746, and Columbia in 1754. These were private colleges, church affiliated, were the beginnings of many Ivy League schools. The Morrill Act of 1862, which granted public lands to the states for purposes of agricultural and mechanical training, was the basis for many of the Big Ten universities, such as Indiana, Michigan State and Ohio State. Today some public and state universities have become organized giants, with campuses in several areas of the state and thousands of students. On the East Coast is the largest state system of higher education, the State University of New York (SUNY), which offers two-year, four-year, and advanced degrees on 72 different campuses and enrolls more than 200,000 students. On the West Coast is the University of California, enrolling more than 150,000 students in its several branches.

Institutions of higher learning can be divided into three types, junior colleges, colleges, and universities.

1. *Junior Colleges.* The junior college — public or private — is a two-year post-high school institution which usually serves a community and is often referred to as a community college. In the late 1950s approximately 20 percent of students began their undergraduate studies in a junior college. In the late 1960s 33 percent did so, and by the late 1970s nearly 50 percent began higher education in a junior college.[14]

In the junior college a large proportion of the program is typically devoted to courses which can be transferred to a four-year college or university and which fit into a program leading to a bachelor's degree. However, there is also emphasis on a two-year terminal degree in business, service, and technical fields.

---

[14] *Digest of Educational Statistics, 1973, 1975* (Washington, D.C.: U.S. Government Printing Office, 1974, 1976), Table 91, p. 76; Table 99, p. 83; Table 81, p. 80. *Projections of Educational Statistics to 1985-86,* Table 5, p. 16; Table 8, p. 19.

2. *Colleges.*   A college—public or private—is a four-year institution which offers a bachelor's degree in the arts, sciences, business, or education. Technology and economic growth have led to the rapid expansion of college enrollments, with approximately 35 percent of the 18-21-year-old population attending some form of higher education on a full time basis; this is expected to increase to 40 percent by 1985-86.[15]

A college may be autonomous or part of a university. The university is far more comprehensive than the college, offering a wider range of specializations and degrees beyond the bachelor's degree. Local four-year colleges tend to be characterized by low costs, relatively easy admission standards, and a predominance of students from working-class families; many of the students work part time, and almost all commute to school. (In many respects, this also characterizes the junior colleges.) Small, private, liberal arts colleges, many of them church related, have comparatively high admission standards and high tuition costs, and students mainly come from middle-class families. Women's colleges were first established in the mid-19th century; today the trend is to coeducation, and between 1960 and 1975 approximately half of the 300 women's colleges in America closed down or became coeducational.

Black colleges were founded in the South after the Civil War; traditionally, they have provided opportunities for higher education for disadvantaged black youth, since admission opportunities to white institutions were limited in the past, due to both racial discrimination and academic admission requirements. As of 1975, there were slightly more than 100 black colleges, including two universities—Atlanta and Howard—which offered the Ph.D.[16]

3. *Universities.*   The combination of college and university instruction under a single administration is characteristic of American universities. The university offers a master's degree, which is a one-year degree beyond the bachelor's, as well as the doctor of philosophy (Ph.D.), which is considered the most advanced degree. There are a few universities where individuals can pursue postdoctorate work, mainly by focusing on research in their field. In addition to the master's and doctorate degrees, some universities offer professional degrees in law, medicine, and dentistry.

In 1965-66 the number of master's degrees earned in the United States totaled 140,550; it increased to 316,000 in 1975-76 and is expected to reach 405,000 in 1985-86. Earned doctorate degrees numbered 18,250 in

---

[15] *Projections of Educational Statistics to 1985-86,* Table 15, p. 32; Table 6, p. 17; Table B-3, p. 133.

[16] Robert J. Havighurst and Bernice L. Neugarten, *Society and Education,* 4th ed. (Boston: Allyn & Bacon, 1975); William Van Til, *Education: A Beginning,* 2nd ed. (Boston: Houghton Mifflin Co., 1974).

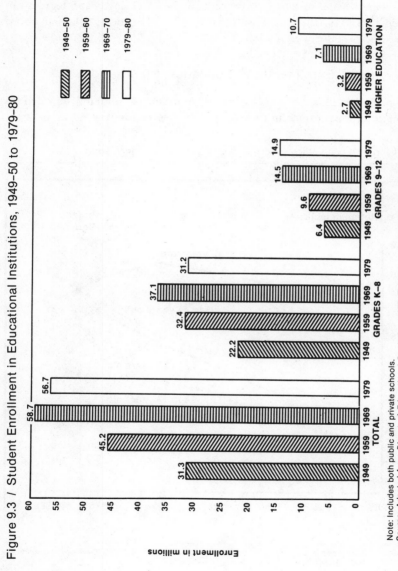

Figure 9.3 / Student Enrollment in Educational Institutions, 1949–50 to 1979–80

Note: Includes both public and private schools.
Source: Adapted from *Digest of Educational Statistics, 1973*, Table 3, p. 7; *Projections of Educational Statistics to 1983–84, 1985–86* (Washington, D.C.: U.S. Government Printing Office, 1975, 1977), Table 2, p. 17; Tables 2–5, pp. 13–16.

1965–66 and 35,000 in 1975–76, with an expected 42,000 in 1985–86. The number of earned master's degrees in education has represented between 50 to 55 percent of the total master's degrees obtained during these 20 years; and the number of doctorate degrees earned in education has represented between 25 to 40 percent of the total doctorate degrees obtained.[17] Today, there is a well-known glut of students with advanced degrees, especially in education.

Summary of Enrollments in Educational Institutions

Figure 9.3 illustrates the growing number of students enrolled in educational institutions in the United States over the past 40 years or so,

Figure 9.4 / Population of School-Age Groups, 1950–1980

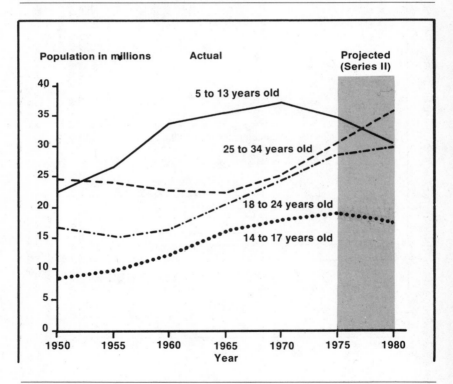

Source: *The Condition of Education, 1977,* vol. 3, Part I (Washington, D.C.: U.S. Government Printing Office, 1977), Figure 1.01, p. 6.

---

[17] *Projections of Educational Statistics to 1985–86,* Tables 16–17, pp. 33–34.

reflecting our respect for schooling and an expanding population. Total enrollment in regular educational programs from kindergarten through graduate education increased for 26 years before reaching an all-time high of 59.7 million in the fall of 1971. Slight decreases first occurred in elementary school enrollments in 1972-73 and the downward trend has continued, reflecting the fact there are now fewer children 5 to 13 years of age than in the recent past.

Enrollments rose at the high school level to about 15.5 million and began to taper off in 1977, reflecting the reductions in elementary school graduates. While colleges and universities rapidly expanded in the 1960s and 1970s, a decrease in numbers of traditional college students (18-21 years old) will become evident in the early 1980s, reflecting the forthcoming decline in numbers of high school graduates. Total enrollments at institutions of higher learning will peak at about 12 million in 1981 or 1982, and to what extent they will decline will be determined by emerging trends such as the labor market demand for college students and whether the recent increase in women, minorities, and adults attending college continues. In short, these school enrollment patterns reflect the changing patterns in the school-age population, which has been decreasing at the elementary schools for several years and is now starting to decrease at the secondary level (Figure 9.4).

NUMBER AND DISTRIBUTION OF SCHOOL SYSTEMS

Before the present school district system of elementary and secondary education began to prevail, the pattern set by the Massachusetts law of 1647 was followed. Each legislature in each state passed its own school laws. As the nation moved westward the one-teacher, one-room, eight-grade elementary school, called "country schools" or "schoolhouses," evolved, in contrast to school districts in cities and towns, which had more students in the area and could establish complete systems, including secondary schools. Often the eighth-grade graduates of the rural schools were permitted to transfer to a nearby town or city school.

As the nation's population increased, the states were kept busy changing district boundaries to meet changing needs. By 1930 there were more than 130,000 school districts; in 1950, 83,718; by 1970, 17,995. Figure 9.5 illustrates the declining number of school systems from 1930 to 1970 in ten-year intervals, with estimates for 1980.

Between 1930 and 1970 the number of school systems decreased 86 percent. The most noticeable decline in school districts occurred from 1950 to 1970, when the number decreased by more than half during each ten-year interval. Nearly 80 percent of the decreases occurred in the Midwest, the region that still has close to one-half of the school districts in the country. The degree of fragmentation is illustrated by the fact that in 1953, one school system, New York City, enrolled more students than the statewide enrollments in 40 states. It enrolled more students than all of the

Figure 9.5 / Number of Public School Systems, 1930–1980

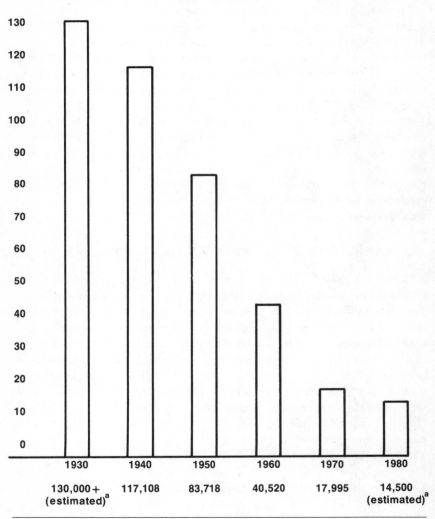

	1930	1940	1950	1960	1970	1980
	130,000+ (estimated)[a]	117,108	83,718	40,520	17,995	14,500 (estimated)[a]

[a] Author's estimates.

Source: *Digest of Educational Statistics, 1972* (Washington, D.C.: U.S. Government Printing Office, 1973), Figure 7, p. 53; Table 63, p. 54; *Fall 1976 Statistics of Public Schools: Advance Report* (Washington, D.C.: U.S. Government Printing Office, 1977), Tables 1–2, pp. 5–6.

2,052 school districts in Iowa, the 2,600 school districts in Minnesota, or the 3,800 school districts in Nebraska during the 1958-59 school year.[18] In the early 1960s, Iowa, Nebraska, North Dakota, and South Dakota, which educated less than 5 percent of the children in the nation, had about 25 percent of the nation's school districts.[19] Despite the continuing trend toward consolidation, as of 1978 there were still four states with over 1,000 systems: California, Illinois, Nebraska, and Texas, accounting for 27 percent of all the districts in the nation.[20]

A great many of the reorganized school districts are still too small to provide a comprehensive educational program and adequate specialized personnel to meet the needs of all students. While the trend toward consolidation continues in the rural and small school systems, there is a recent trend in city school systems to break up the large systems into smaller ones.

What is the ideal size for a school district to be effective, that is, to have enough students to justify offering diversified programs, services, and personnel to meet modern educational requirements? As early as 1934, Howard Dawson's careful study of city and county school systems concluded that a minimum of 10,000 to 12,000 students were needed to justify a specialized and adequate staff as well as a varied program, to ensure reasonable costs of the educational program. At that time, Dawson was severely criticized by many educators who believed that a district of that size was unattainable and impractical.[21]

Paul Mort developed a method for measuring the effectiveness of school system size based on an adaptability index which was correlated with school characteristics such as financial policies, curriculum innovation, community and staff participation, location, and size. His studies considered the maximally effective school district to be comprised of 100,000 students.[22] This estimate was confirmed by others,[23] but recently other

---

[18] American Association of School Administrators, *School District Organization* (Washington, D.C.: National Education Association, 1958).

[19] Willard R. Lane, Ronald G. Corwin, and William G. Monahan, *Foundations of Educational Administration* (New York: Macmillan Co., 1967).

[20] *Educational Directory, Public School Systems, 1977-78* (Washington, D.C.: U.S. Government Printing Office, 1978).

[21] Howard A. Dawson, *Satisfactory Local School Units*, Field Study No. 7 (Nashville, Tenn.: George Peabody College for Teachers, 1934).

[22] Paul R. Mort and Francis G. Cornell, *American Schools in Transition* (New York: Teachers College Press, Columbia University, 1941); Paul R. Mort, William S. Vincent, and Clarence Newell, *The Growing Edge, An Instrument for Measuring the Adaptability of School Systems*, 2 vols. (New York: Teachers College Press, Columbia University, 1955).

[23] Stanton F. Leggett and William S. Vincent, *A Program for Meeting the Needs of New York City Schools* (New York: Public Education Association, 1947); Donald H. Ross, ed., *Administration for Adaptability* (New York: Metropolitan School Study Council, 1958).

Table 9.2 / Distribution of Public School Systems and Number of Students by Size or System, 1975-76

Size of School System	Public School Systems		Public School Pupils	
	Number	Percent	Number	Percent
Total operating systems	16,006	100.0	44,231,874	100.0
Systems with 300 pupils or more .	11,542	72.1	43,719,168	98.8
25,000 or more.	187	1.2	12,533,059	28.3
10,000 to 24,999.	555	3.5	8,070,851	18.2
5,000 to 9,999.	1,126	7.0	7,820,441	17.7
2,500 to 4,999.	2,050	12.8	7,153,477	16.2
1,000 to 2,499.	3,467	21.7	5,682,631	12.8
600 to 999.	1,860	11.6	1,453,505	3.3
300 to 599.	2,297	14.2	1,005,204	2.3
Systems with less than 300 pupils	4,464	27.9	512,706	1.2

Source: *Educational Directory: Public School Systems, 1975-76,* Table 1, p. xvi.

educators have put the ideal figure at around 20,000 to 25,000.[24] Among the 16,006 public school systems that existed in the 1975-76 school year and the 44.2 million public school students enrolled in them, 742 school systems had 10,000 or more students, to account for 20.6 million students, or 46.5 percent of the total. The 187 school systems with enrollments of 25,000 or more accounted for 12.5 million students, or 28 percent of the total. Thus 4.7 percent of the school systems (those with 10,000 or more students) accounted for 46.5 percent of the public school enrollment, and 1.2 percent of the school systems (those with 25,000 or more students) accounted for 28 percent. At the base of this pyramid there were 4,464 school systems with 300 or fewer students; this represented 28 percent of the school systems but only 1.2 percent of the total student enrollment. Table 9.2 shows how school systems are distributed according to enrollment size.

Most of the larger school systems are located in California, Florida, Texas, Ohio, and Maryland and in or near cities, the largest being the New York City system with slightly less than 1.1 million students as of 1978, followed by Los Angeles with slightly less than 600,000 students. (Two other large school systems, in Puerto Rico and Hawaii, span an entire territory and state, respectively.) The smaller school systems are generally located in the midwestern states and in rural areas.

[24] Robert J. Havighurst and Daniel U. Levine, *Education in Metropolitan Areas,* 2nd ed. (Boston: Allyn & Bacon, 1971); A. Harry Passow, *Toward Creating a Model Urban School System, A Study of the Washington, D.C., Public Schools* (New York: Teachers College Press, Columbia University, 1967).

Thinking Small for the Future

One of the great problems facing the schools over the next decade or so is the high probability of declining enrollments. This decline hit the elementary schools in the early 1970s and has recently moved to the high schools and will most likely affect the college enrollments in the early 1980s. Americans are ill equipped for the management of decline; for several generations, we have enjoyed growth in almost all aspects of social and economic life. We have had continuous growth in population and almost continuous growth in per capita real incomes, in productivity, and in gross national product. Almost all our institutions, including our schools, have been geared to accelerating growth.

This age is coming to an end, not only for schools but also for almost all social and economic institutions. The prospects for the next 10 or 20 years, barring a major catastrophe such as nuclear war, suggest that we are entering an age of slowdown and relative smallness. The rate of overall productivity is likely to decrease. As student populations decrease, the school industry will be curtailed.

Of general interest is Kenneth Boulding's analysis of the changes in Colorado school districts between 1960 and 1970.[25] Many superintendents were unaware that their own districts had experienced decline, especially in areas where the turnover of administrators was high. They were absorbed in current problems and not aware of what the system had been like years ago. However, in declining school districts, and especially where superintendents were aware of these declines, there was a higher quality of education than in the expanding ones. This suggests, according to Boulding, that decline in enrollments may result in opportunities for improving education, as measured by such crude indicators as class size, number of dropouts, and performance on tests. Another conclusion was that the larger districts undergoing decline were able to make successful adjustments — probably because there were more things and people to move around. This suggests that many smaller districts are likely to go bankrupt, and there may be a concentration of larger districts in the future. This does not seem too unreasonable; in fact, it coincides with present school consolidation trends, as well as experiences of small businesses which go under or merge during hard times or in a period of decline.

There are also questions of local school spending in relationship to size. A demand for thrift to be exercised by school boards in order to cut expenses, reduce budgets, and lower tax rates can be expected. The general need for conservation of resources as opposed to runaway consumption is

---

[25] Kenneth E. Boulding, "The Management of Decline," *Change*, June 1975, pp. 8–9, 64.

rapidly gaining acceptability. As in the automobile and energy industries, with food and other national resources, the school industry is going to have to think in terms of trimming the fat—if school districts are to survive. In the interests of economy, the following considerations are likely to influence school spending.

1. Classroom size may increase. The data on classroom size and student achievement are contradictory, however, and most studies show no significant differences. When differences are found, they are about as likely to favor large classes as small.

2. Instead of building new schools, it is cheaper in many cases to maintain and modernize older schools. Older schools were usually better constructed, and in an era of declining birth rates those not in distress should be saved. Moreover, older buildings are not necessarily detrimental to student learning.

3. Small schools are cheaper than large schools, especially if they are well insulated and use space effectively. The increasing costs of heat and light are factors to be considered in plans to build big, expensive cafeterias, auditoriums, or gymnasiums. Not only do they add greatly to construction costs, they are unoccupied most of the time and cost a great deal to maintain, to heat, and to light.

4. To hold down energy costs, schools will reduce temperatures during vacations, delay warming the school before classes each morning, switch to the night-heat cycle earlier in the day, and reduce heat in the hallways and other specialized areas. Custodial care will be scheduled during the day, and pipes, walls, and windows will be insulated. There will be more cold lunches, shorter lunch and activity periods, a shorter school day, and, if things get rough, holidays and even the school year may be rescheduled to coincide with warmer seasons.[26]

Thinking small, the U.S. Office of Education's report, *The Education of Adolescents,* strongly recommends a reversal of the recent trend toward larger and larger schools.[27] It cited research showing that when enrollment rises above 1,000 students, school cost per student declines little, while there is abundant evidence that educational effectiveness of such institutions decreases with size. The comprehensive high school, blamed in part on Conant's recommendation for larger schools in the late 1950s, is

---

[26] School energy costs jumped 48 percent in two years, from 1972-73 to 1974-75, according to the Federal Energy Administration; costs jumped another 27 percent in 1975-76, although schools were actually reducing energy consumption by 3 percent. See David Savage, "The Energy Crisis: A Continuing Disaster," *Phi Delta Kappan,* December 1976, p. 353. For additional heat-saving measures, see Kathy E. Davis, *Report on Methods of Conserving Heating Energy* (Memphis, Tenn.: Board of Education of the Memphis City Schools, 1976).

[27] *The Education of Adolescents* (Washington, D.C.: U.S. Government Printing Office, 1976).

cited as a highly negative influence on secondary education. The report does not consider economic or energy factors, but it does discuss social and psychological reasons for advocating smallness: bigness promotes disciplinary problems, student alienation, class and racial segregation, and even fails to achieve its main goal, to provide a breadth of courses. "The solution is obviously not bigger schools," the report concludes. "The negative effects are too overwhelming and obvious." The USOE panel suggested "smallness" in contrast to "bigness."

In England, high schools with more than 500 students are considered too large. This was also the maximum number of students suggested by the President's Science Advisory Committee, chaired by James Coleman.[28] This report found that schools with large enrollments result in bureaucracy, segregated student strata, institutional blandness, youth alienation, and a tendency for students and teachers to withdraw into separate worlds.

DESCRIPTIVE TYPES OF SCHOOLS

The large number of schools and the diversity of types suggests many ways of describing and categorizing American schools. A number of categories of schools, both elementary and secondary, are discussed below.

Geographical Settings

Schools can be classified into geographical settings corresponding to the population of the area. The descriptions below can apply to schools and in many cases to entire school systems.

1. *Rural Schools.* About 35 percent of public school enrollments are located in rural (or nonurban) areas. These schools are often unable to offer a diversified program. Many of the students are from low-income families, especially in the Appalachian and rural New England schools.

2. *Suburban Schools.* About 40 percent of public school enrollments are in suburban areas. While differences between city and suburban schools are usually striking, the differences among suburban schools are sometimes almost as great. One reason suburbs are thought to be homogeneous and middle class is that they tend to be racially homogeneous. Nevertheless, student populations by suburbs can vary greatly in income. Similarly, the schools vary in size; many are large and offer diversified programs; others are small and have limited curricula.

---

[28] James S. Coleman et al., *Youth: Transition to Adulthood,* report of the Panel on Youth of the President's Science Advisory Committee (Chicago: University of Chicago Press, 1974).

3. *City Schools.* About 25 percent of the public school enrollments are in cities; in some cities the number is decreasing with the out-migration of middle-class families to the suburbs. City schools are often large and overcrowded, and double and triple sessions are not uncommon — especially at the high school level. As a group, city students perform below the national norm on reading and mathematical standardized tests. There are two types of city schools, outer city and inner city, and they vary as much as city and suburban schools do.

a. Outer-City Schools. These schools tend to be populated by working-class or lower-middle-class groups. Many are located in white ethnic neighborhoods or those with changing racial characteristics.

b. Inner-City Schools. These schools are usually located in black and Spanish-speaking areas. Most of the students are from lower-class families. For the past 15 years, they have been the focus of attention by the federal government and educational reformers, while outer-city schools have frequently been overlooked.

4. *Metropolitan Schools.* A few schools draw on both city and suburban student populations. The Nashville-Davidson County and Louisville-Jefferson County Metropolitan school systems are examples of large city systems which has recently combined with a suburban system to form a single metropolitan school system.

5. *County Schools.* These schools usually cut across city, suburban, and rural boundaries to draw on a diversified student population. County school systems include Dade County (Miami), Florida; Montgomery County (Baltimore), Maryland, and Clark County (Las Vegas), Nevada.

6. *Regional Schools.* These schools exist only on paper; the idea is for an appropriate state agency or group of states to mandate the establishment of a school offering a specialized educational capability. The school could cut across municipalities within a state or be located in an area where there is suitable interstate transportation to serve students from nearby states.

Social Settings

To a considerable extent the social atmosphere and internal workings of a school depend on the teachers and administrators; the parent-teacher organizations; the teaching materials, books, and instructional media; and, most important, the student-teacher interactions. Therefore attempts have been made to describe types or categories of schools by looking at the entire school, rather than only geographical location or the socioeconomic characteristics of the students.

In his study of 40 elementary schools in the Chicago metropolitan area, Russell Doll interviewed and observed the 40 school principals and 185 teachers and made short observations of the students in the classroom, at recess and lunch, during change of periods, and after school. Four types of elementary schools were identified:[29]

1. *High-Status Schools.* These schools are generally found at the edges of the city in high-income areas and in upper-middle-class suburbs. The students are well prepared to meet the demands of the schools; achievement scores are high, and there are few disciplinary problems. Parents are well educated and take an active part in school life. Teacher morale is high, and turnover is low.

2. *Conventional Schools.* These schools are generally found in lower-middle-class areas and working-class or industrial suburbs, as well as in areas where parents are experiencing upward mobility. The students are academically oriented but a few are considered to be disciplinary problems, and some perform below grade level. Parents mainly support the schools and teachers, but some are unsure about their role in relation to school and withdraw from school activities. Teacher morale is high, and turnover is low.

3. *Common-Man Schools.* These schools are usually found in stable working-class areas in the city and modest suburbs. There is great diversity in student body and home background and ethnicity. The students are less academic than vocational oriented. Many of them do not identify with the school or its personnel. Although there are disciplinary problems, they are not as consistent, overt, or hostile as in inner-city schools. Parental support for the school varies and the family cannot always be counted on to work with the teacher or school or see to it that studies are done at home. For the greater part, teacher morale is positive, and they see themselves in a better situation than if they were in the inner-city schools.

4. *Inner-City Schools.* These schools are usually located in slum areas characterized by low income, high transiency, high delinquency, and predominantly black or Spanish-speaking family background. For the greater part, students perform below grade level, lack inner control, and express covert and overt hostility toward teachers. Many parents are unable to provide support at home or to see that their children study. Teachers find themselves in an unrewarding and difficult school climate; morale is low, and turnover is high.

The high schools may be classified in much the same way as the

---

[29] Russell C. Doll, "Categories of Elementary Schools in a Big City," research paper, University of Chicago, 1969.

Figure 9.6 / Selected Occupations for Defining the SER

Upper-Middle Class (UM)
   Professional, technical, and kindred
   Proprietors, managers, and officials
   Farm owners and managers (10 percent of the total population)

Lower-Middle Class (LM)
   Sales and clerical occupations
   Farm owners and managers (40 percent of the total population)

Upper-Working Class (UW)
   Foremen, craftsmen, and kindred
   Operatives and kindred occupations
   Farm owners and managers (40 percent of the total population)

Lower-Working Class (LW)
   Service workers and household workers
   Laborers and farm workers (10 percent of the total population)

Source: Robert J. Havighurst and Daniel U. Levine, *Education in Metropolitan Areas*, 2nd ed. (Boston: Allyn & Bacon, 1971), pp. 55–56; Robert J. Havighurst and Bernice L. Neugarten, *Society and Education*, 4th ed. (Boston: Allyn & Bacon, 1975), p. 236.

elementary schools. When Daniel Levine and associates classified the high schools of the Kansas City, Missouri, metropolitan area, they were able to identify five types: [30]

1. *Middle-Class Schools.* These schools are generally found at the edge of the city, in high-income areas, and in upper-middle-class "dormitory" suburbs. More than 75 percent of the graduates go on to college.

2. *Comprehensive High Schools.* These schools are the most common and serve a cross-section of the population in socioeconomic terms. About 40 to 75 percent of graduates go on to college.

3. *Working-Class Schools.* These schools serve a predominantly working-class area. There is a high dropout rate in the ninth and tenth grades, and about 40 percent of graduates go on to college.

4. *Small Schools.* These schools draw from outlying parts of a metropolitan area or rural districts. They enroll less than 500 students, and less than 100 graduate each year. They fall between the comprehensive and working-class type schools in terms of socioeconomic status and are similar to the working-class schools in proportion of graduates entering college.

5. *Private Schools.* These are mostly Catholic schools, although there are a few Protestant and high-status nonsectarian high schools. The

[30] Daniel U. Levine, Edna Mitchell, and Robert J. Havighurst, *Opportunities for Higher Education in a Metropolitan Area: A Study of High School Seniors in Kansas City* (Bloomington, Ind.: Phi Delta Kappa, 1970).

church-related schools are similar to the comprehensive schools in socioeconomic composition and number of students going on to college.

SOCIOECONOMIC COMPOSITION OF SCHOOLS

The effects of socioeconomic segregation in the schools can be analyzed by employing a ratio of middle-class to working-class families from the census data in a given school district or geographical area. There are several ways of calculating this ratio, called the socioeconomic ratio (SER), but perhaps the best known procedure is shown in Figure 9.6. Family occupations of the head of the family are placed in four categories. The upper-middle-class occupations (UM) are weighted twice as heavily as the lower-middle (LM), and, in the opposite direction, the lower-working-class occupations (LW) are weighted twice as heavily as the upper-working class (UW). The reason for the weighting is that UM is higher on the social scale than LM, and LW is lower than UW, that is, they represent extremes of the middle class and working class. The ratio is calculated by the formula: $2UM + LM/UW + 2UW$.

There are some obvious generalizations and possible errors in these categories. For example, policemen and firemen are included as service workers (LW), but they tend to have more status than many sales and clerical occupations (LM) and to earn as much or more than many assistant professors (UM). The unemployed are not included in any category, yet they could be added to the LW category, or possibly another category such as lower-lower class should have been added to take into account the long-term unemployed. Nevertheless, the SER can be used to show the socioeconomic stratification in a given metropolitan area or school system. For our purposes, we will show how this ratio can be used to illustrate the social compositions of schools.

Figure 9.7 shows SERs of types of high schools. School A represents a typical high school in a small town or city which has only one high school. The high school is a communitywide, comprehensive school which draws students from the entire town. The SER is 1.0; that is, it is well integrated on a socioeconomic basis. The elementary school population in this community will probably not be distributed as well, since the elementary schools will tend to coincide with the population of local neighborhoods within the town.

School B is predominantly upper middle class, probably located in a suburban area. The SER is .60. School C shows the SER (.13) of a high school which mainly serves students of working-class backgrounds. The school is probably located in an outer city, where there may be a majority of lower-working-class families, but since these children tend to drop out of

349

Figure 9.7 / Socioeconomic Composition and SERs of Three Types of
High Schools

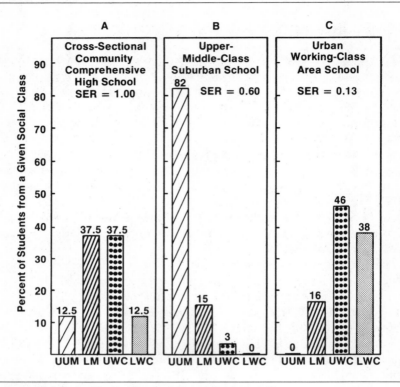

school early the actual composition of the high school shows a majority of
students of upper-working-class students.

There is probably a "critical" or "tipping" point in the SER of city
schools where most middle-class parents are likely to become concerned
and consider moving to an area with a higher socioeconomic level. What
happens is that middle-class parents fear the effects growing proportions of
working-class students will have on their children's education and friendships. They fear a drop in academic standards, changes in the curriculum,
increasing discipline problems, and negative influences upon their
children's motivation in school. When this point is reached, flight by
middle-class families with children to the suburbs is likely. The point at
which a school becomes undesirable in the eyes of middle-class parents is
subjective and will vary with their attitudes and experiences, as well as the
racial composition of the school.

Research tends to show that such attitudes on the part of parents are not altogether unfounded. When student bodies vary in proportion to social class, students develop different educational and occupational aspirations as well as demonstrate different academic performance. Higher-status children have lower educational and occupational aspirations in predominantly lower-status schools than in predominantly higher-status schools; lower-status children tend to have higher aspirations and to drop out less in predominantly higher-status schools than in lower-status schools.[31]

Schools in upper-middle-class and middle-class areas tend to have more students reading on level and going to college. Schools in lower-income areas have more students who exhibit low intelligence, low achievement, and behavior problems and are dropouts. This is confirmed by comparisons of schools in big cities such as Chicago,[32] Detroit,[33] New York

Table 9.3 / Socioeconomic Composition and Characteristics of Public High Schools in the 45 Largest Cities

Socioeconomic Class	Percentage of Schools in Each Category	Average Percentage of Entering Students in College Preparatory Programs	Average Percentage of Entering Students Who Are Economically Disadvantaged	Average Number of Foreign Languages Offered at Fourth Year Level	Average Percentage of Entering Students Who Are Two Years or More Retarded in Reading
Upper middle class predominates (UM)	21%	80%	0%	3.0	5%
Middle class and lower middle class (LM)	30	55	5	2.6	15
Lower middle and upper working class (UW)	28	35	15	2.0	25
Working class predominates (LW)	21	25	35	1.3	55

Source: Adapted from Robert J. Havighurst, Frank Smith, and David Wilder, *A Study of Large City High Schools* (Washington, D.C.: National Association of Secondary School Principals, 1970), Tables 2.3a–2.3e, pp. 23–25.

[31] Herbert H. Hyman, "The Value Systems of Different Classes: A Social Psychological Contribution to the Analysis of Stratification," in R. Bendix and S. M. Lipset (eds.), *Class, Status and Power* (New York: Free Press, 1953), pp. 426–42; Theodore M. Newcomb, "Attitude Development as a Function of Reference Groups: The Bennington Study," In E. E. Maccoby, T. M. Newcomb, and E. L. Hartley (eds.), *Readings in Social Psychology* (New York: Holt, Rinehart & Winston, 1958), pp. 265–75; Alan B. Wilson, "Residential Segregation of Social Classes and Aspirations of High School Boys," *American Sociological Review*, December 1959, pp. 836–45; Alan B. Wilson, "Sociological Perspectives on the Development of Academic Competence in Urban Areas," in A. H. Passow (ed.), *Urban Education in the 1970s* (New York: Teachers College Press, Columbia University, 1971), pp. 120–40.

[32] Robert J. Havighurst, *The Public Schools of Chicago* (Chicago: Board of Education of the City of Chicago, 1964).

[33] Patricia C. Sexton, *Education and Income* (New York: Viking Press, 1961).

351

Table 9.4 / Racial and Socioeconomic Factors of Public High Schools in the 45 Largest Cities

Socioeconomic Characteristics of Students	Racial Characteristics of Students					
	Over 80% White	61–80% White	21–60% White and Black	61–80% Black	Over 80% Black	Other Ethnic Mixtures
Upper-middle class predominates	1 n:110 %: 16.4	4 n: 15 %: 2.2	7 n: 18 %: 2.7	10 n: 16 %: 2.4		14 n: 7 %: 1.0
Middle class and lower middle class	2 n: 116 %: 17.3	5 n: 39 %: 5.8				
Lower-middle and upper working class	3 n: 52 %: 7.8	6 n: 43 %: 6.4	8 n: 17 %: 2.5	11 n: 19 %: 2.8	12 n: 49 %: 7.3	15 n: 20 %: 3.0
Working class predominates			9 n: 16 %: 2.4		13 n: 67 %: 10	16 n: 29 %: 4.3

Note: Asian-American schools not in typology, n = 6 or 1.0%; other schools not used because of some missing data, n = 31 or 4.6%; all schools, n = 670 or 100%.
Source: Havighurst et al., *A Study of Large City High Schools*, Table 2.5, p. 28.

City,[34] Oakland, and San Francisco.[35] Data on a nationwide basis tend to confirm these impressions, too. Results of a recent study of 640 public high schools of the nation's 45 largest cities are shown in Table 9.3: upper-middle-class schools have higher proportions of students in college preparatory programs, offer more foreign languages at the fourth-year level, and have lower proportions of disadvantaged students and entering students who are two or more years behind in reading. Schools that become less middle class and more working class in composition exhibit the reverse characteristics. The table also indicates that most big-city high schools predominantly enroll lower-middle-class and upper-working-class students.

As one might expect, racial factors interact with socioeconomic factors. Looking at the public schools of the 45 largest cities in terms of race and class, shown in Table 9.4, most schools are either predominantly white or black. Only 2 percent of the schools which were 60 percent or more black could be considered middle class, while 42 percent of the schools 60 percent or more white were middle class. If, as the literature tends to

---

[34] Richard Bloom, Martin Whiteman, and Martin Deutsch, "Race and Social Class as Separate Factors Related to Social Environment," paper presented at the annual conference of the American Psychological Association, Philadelphia, September 1963; Miriam L. Goldberg, "Factors Affecting Educational Attainment in Depressed Areas," in A. H. Passow, M. L. Goldberg, and A. J. Tannenbaum (eds.), *Education of the Disadvantaged* (New York: Holt, Rinehart & Winston, 1967), pp. 31–61.
[35] Wilson, "Aspirations of High School Boys."

purport, social class is the most important factor related to school learning, then predominantly black schools (segregated by social class, too) do not provide equal educational opportunity for their students.

There is reason to believe that the racial tipping point, where white parents become anxious and start to think of moving away, is lower than the socioeconomic tipping point. When a school reaches 20 to 25 percent black, the school may no longer be considered integrated; rather it is changing from a predominantly white to a predominantly black school. The interaction effects of social class and race are complex. If there were an equal distribution of low-income white and black families, perhaps whites would not flee from city schools as rapidly as they have in the past.

Besides prejudice, there are other reasons for whites to flee from schools which are becoming increasingly black. Racial disharmony, delinquency, and discipline problems tend to increase; in short, the problems of the ghetto and society spill over into the schools, and this in turn affects academic performance.[36] In addition, school integration tends to correlate with declining achievement scores for white students, about a half a grade level difference by the time the students have reached the ninth grade, all of which cannot be explained away by social-class differences.[37]

CONCLUSIONS

Enrollment in the nation's schools and colleges approximated 58 million in 1975–76. In addition, 3.1 million persons were employed as teachers and professors, and another 300,000 were working as supervisors and administrators. Midway into the 1970s, then, education was the primary occupation of some 61.5 million Americans. In a nation with a population of nearly 215 million, more than 3 out of every 10 persons were direct participants in the educational industry.

Schools can be categorized in many ways, the most popular being by grade levels. They also can be categorized according to size, geography,

---

[36] Nathan Glazer, "When the Melting Pot Doesn't Melt," *New York Times Magazine*, September 10, 1972, pp. 12–13 ff.; Andrew Hacker, "The Violent Black Minority," *New York Times Magazine*, May 10, 1970, p. 25 ff.; Thomas A. Sowell, *Black Education: Myths and Tragedies* (New York: David McKay & Co., 1973); U.S. Riot Commission, *Report of the National Advisory Commission on Civil Disorders* (New York: Bantam Books, 1968).

[37] James S. Coleman et al., *Equality of Educational Opportunity* (Washington, D.C.: U.S. Government Printing Office, 1966); Nathan Glazer, "Ethnic Group and Education: Towards the Tolerance of Difference," *Journal of Negro Education* (Summer 1969), pp. 187–95; George W. Mayeske et al., *A Study of the Achievement of Our Nation's Schools* (Washington, D.C.: U.S. Government Printing Office, 1971); Daniel P. Moynihan, "Sources of Resistance to the Coleman Report," *Harvard Educational Review*, Winter 1968, pp. 23–36; Robert C. Nichols, "Schools and the Disadvantaged: A Summary of the Coleman Report," *Science*, December 1966, pp. 1312–14.

social setting, social class, and race. In general, the schools are viewed as institutions for everyone. The desire of the American people to extend educational opportunities to the higher level is answered in part by the junior college, the newest extension of free, or nearly free, popular education.

ACTIVITIES

1. Visit an elementary school, middle school, and senior high school in the community in which you live or study. How are the programs you observe related to the age group of the students in the three schools?
2. Visit the campus of a junior college, preferably a community college, in your area. Talk with the administrators about the role and future of the junior college.
3. Invite a guest speaker, preferably from a nearby black college, to talk about the future of the black college.
4. Arrange a debate among members of the class about the pros and cons of increasing college enrollments.
5. Explain the computation of the socioeconomic ratio, and illustrate how this ratio applies to a nearby school.

DISCUSSION QUESTIONS

1. What educational level most appeals to you as a teacher? Why?
2. Why is there presently little or no formal education in America for the years from birth to age three? Why is this education desirable? Undesirable?
3. Can you see any reasons to prefer a junior high school or middle school for the middle years of schooling, as opposed to an elementary and senior high school education?
4. Why are the junior colleges booming in student enrollments? What advantages and disadvantages are there in this form of educational organization?
5. Discuss the various geographical and social types of schools in terms of stereotyping. In which type of school (geographical and social) would you prefer to teach? Now, are you stereotyping?

SUGGESTED FOR FURTHER READING

Conant, James B. *The American High School Today.* New York: McGraw-Hill Book Co., 1959.

Cremin, Lawrence A. *The Transformation of the School.* New York: Random House, 1961.

Goodlad, John I. and Shane, Harold G. (eds.). *The Elementary School in the United States,* 72nd Yearbook of the National Society for the Study of Education, Part II. Chicago: University of Chicago Press, 1973.

Gordon, Ira J. (ed.). *Early Childhood Education,* 71st Yearbook of the National Society for the Study of Education, Part II. Chicago: University of Chicago Press, 1972.

Morphet, Edgar L., Jones, Roe L., and Reller, Theodore L. *Educational Organization and Administration.* Englewood Cliffs, N.J.: Prentice-Hall, Inc., 1974.

Riesman, David, and Jencks, Christopher. *The Academic Revolution.* New York: Doubleday, 1968.

Rubin, Louis, (ed.). *The Future of Education: Perspectives on Tomorrow's Schooling.* Boston: Allyn & Bacon, 1975.

Tyack, David B. *One Best System.* Cambridge, Mass.: Harvard University Press, 1974.

Van Til, William, (ed.). *Issues in Secondary Education,* 75th Yearbook of the National Society for the Study of Education, Part II. Chicago: University of Chicago Press, 1976.

Zwerling, Stephen. *Second Best: The Crisis of the Community College.* New York: McGraw-Hill Book Co., 1976.

CHAPTER 10

REFORM
STRATEGIES FOR
AMERICAN
SCHOOLS

The public schools in the metropolitan areas of the United States, especially those in big cities, are in serious trouble. They have failed to teach an increasing number of their students, especially the poor and minorities, at acceptable academic levels. Not only are many of these students performing below national norms in reading and mathematics and unable to write or communicate in formal English, they also are not acquiring acceptable social skills.

Out of this and related problems has grown the need to reorganize the schools and to provide reform alternatives. While the emphasis in considering the different reform and reorganizational strategies is on big-city schools, we must recognize the need to be concerned with *all* schools, and with non-poor and white students as well as the poor and minorities. This chapter focuses on the problems of big-city schools while presenting a broader view which considers American schools in general. The discussion is divided into three parts: (1) compensatory education, (2) desegregation and integration, and (3) administrative decentralization and community involvement.

COMPENSATORY EDUCATION

The move toward compensatory education coincides with expressions of concern for the disadvantaged child. Generally, children from this background exhibit lower achievement levels than middle-class children. It is presumed by most educational and social reformers that an improved school environment offering remedial programs and special activities can largely compensate for their educational disadvantages.

Most compensatory programs have been funded by the federal government, although state and local money is also available. The Elementary and Secondary School Act (ESEA), passed in 1965, immediately provided $1 billion to supplement and improve the education of poor and minority group children. Twelve years later, ESEA money totaled $2 billion per year, or about $250 per disadvantaged child; over this period, $21 billion had been appropriated.

Although federal programs for school-age children usually are ESEA-supported, there are other federal sources of compensatory money: the Manpower Development and Training Act of 1962, the Vocational Education Act of 1963, the Civil Rights Act of 1964, the Economic Opportunity Act of 1964, and the Higher Education Act of 1965.

Types of Programs

A variety of programs, from preschool to higher education has been authorized, with emphasis on reducing classroom size and providing remedial programs, special personnel, and enrichment experiences. An overview of these programs shows they include the following areas.[1]

1. *Infant Education and Intervention in Family Life.* Research indicates that parent-child and family relationships are important factors in the cognitive and social development of children. Programs of infant education and parental involvement range from helping the mother become a teacher of her child to improving family stability.

2. *Early Childhood Education.* Head Start and Follow Through are the most common programs under this category. Whereas Head Start attempts to help disadvantaged children achieve "readiness" for the first grade, Follow Through concentrates on sustaining readiness and supplementing in the early grades whatever gains are made during a year's experience in Head Start.

3. *Reading, Language, and Basic Skills Development.* Poor academic achievement is linked with abilities in basic reading and language areas.

---

[1] A. Harry Passow, "Urban Education in the 1970s," in A. H. Passow (ed.), *Urban Education in the 1970s* (New York: Teachers College Press, Columbia University, 1971), pp. 1–45; A Harry Passow, "Compensatory Instructional Intervention," in F. N. Kerlinger and J. B. Carroll (eds.), *Review of Research in Education* (Itasca, Ill.: F. E. Peacock Publishers, 1974), pp. 145–75; Doxey A. Wilkerson, "Compensatory Education," in S. Marcus and H. N. Rivlin (eds.) *Conflicts in Urban Education* (New York: Basic Books, 1970), pp. 19–39.

More than half of the ESEA projects deal directly with the improvement of reading and language skills through various materials, machines, and personnel.

4. *Bilingual Education.* Emphasis and content of these programs vary, but they commonly focus on children whose mother tongue is not English. Spanish-speaking, American Indian, and Asian children are the major target groups in these programs.

5. *Curriculum Revision.* Curriculum efforts have involved different objectives and content to coincide with subjects pertaining to black, Spanish-speaking, and American Indian identity and pride. These changes have included greater student and community involvement and a proliferation of ethnic studies.

6. *Instructional Materials.* A flood of new materials has focused on disadvantaged and minority children. Major changes in textbooks have appeared, and a variety of multisensory materials have been developed and marketed. These include simple computer printouts to sophisticated language laboratories.

7. *Guidance and Counseling Programs.* Various social, psychological, and vocational services have been provided for the disadvantaged. Social workers and community aides have also been involved to help bridge the gap between school and home.

8. *Tutoring Programs.* Individual and small-group tutoring programs have increased rapidly. This has involved volunteer and paid student tutors, community adults, and aides. The programs at the public school level usually provide a positive model in an older student or adult.

9. *School Organization.* Many schools serving the disadvantaged have been funded for the purpose of offering a variety of organizational changes, ranging from extended school days and extended school years to open classrooms and flexible schedules.

10. *Dropout Prevention Programs.* Along with vocational and career education, a number of programs have been aimed at preventing school dropouts. Numerous work-study programs, on-the-job-training programs, and financial incentives have been offered. Some of these programs have been incorporated into the regular school program; others have been offered in special centers. They are offered during the day, evening, and summer breaks.

11. *Personnel Training.* A great many preservice and inservice training programs have been funded to help beginning interns and experienced educators (teachers and administrators) to gain insight into teaching the disadvantaged. The National Teacher Corps is the best known preservice program, and the National Defense Education Act

(NDEA) Institutes for Advanced Study are the best known inservice programs, although funding in these areas has decreased.

12. *Auxiliary School Personnel.* There has been revised recruitment and training of teacher aides and paraprofessionals, along with nonpaid volunteers. The emphasis is on employing low-income workers from the local community, in order to provide jobs and enhance school-community relations.

13. *School Desegregation.* Money has been provided to aid schools and school personnel to deal with desegregation problems and to provide technical assistance, grants to school boards, and workshops.

14. *Higher Education.* Special programs in this area include the following: (*a*) identifying students of college potential early in the secondary schools and enriching their program; (*b*) special provisions and lower academic requirements for college admissions; (*c*) open enrollment admission criteria whereby every high school graduate has the opportunity to attend a two-year or four-year college, thus favoring low academic achievers who might not otherwise be granted admission; (*d*) transition programs to increase the probability of success for disadvantaged youth once admitted into college; and (*e*) special scholarships, loans, and jobs based solely on financial need and minority status and not on scholarship.

15. *Adult Education.* The most rapidly growing part of education is adult education. A large portion of this trend focuses on illiterate adults and others who need training in basic job skills. Programs are usually offered at public schools, colleges, private industries, and special centers located in impoverished areas.

The Failure of Compensatory Education

The prime criterion of success or failure of these programs is academic achievement. On this basis, the overwhelming majority of compensatory programs have been judged ineffective in raising cognitive levels of target students. This outcome may not be liked but it should be understandable, since the central thrust has been to bring disadvantaged children up to levels of performance comparable to those of children with whom the school feels it succeeds.

Almost all of the programs considered "successful" are based on descriptive comments; reports by participants, personnel, or observers; or hearsay from selected sources. Programs which have been evaluated on the basis of reliable and valid data collection techniques have recorded few successes. For example, when the more than 1,000 programs originally judged successful in 1968 were later reassessed, only 21 had been successful in raising academic levels of the target students on the basis of standardized test scores.[2] Similarly, of the more than 1,200 compensatory programs evaluated between 1970 and 1972 and originally judged to be successful, only 10 were found effective on the basis of statistical reanalysis.[3]

A Rand Corporation study by Harvey Averch et al. points out that, with regard to school spending and compensatory programs, we are already spending too much in terms of what we are getting in return. In the early stages of compensatory education, input increments have a high marginal return, but they gradually diminish until the exchange of input for output is no longer equal, and finally reach the point where input is wasted because there is virtually no increase in output. It is concluded that a "flat area" has been reached where there is less output in relation to input or, even worse, no return.[4]

Kenneth Boulding presented the same thesis about the entire educational industry, noting that extra input in school programs was not yielding more output. The point of maximum return had been passed long ago, and the possibility of increasing school productivity was highly questionable. Private industry operating in the same manner as the schools would have long since been closed down because of the losses.[5]

Trying harder does not seem to make much difference, either. Daniel Moynihan suggested that the ideological commitment and profit motives of those who dispense social and educational services result in some people demanding more. No matter how hard the government tried to produce more output, it could not, so the original prophecy about the indifference of government or the system was endangered.[6]

Another factor to consider is that compensatory (and other social and educational) programs have been affected by a law of bureaucracy: Organizations once formed try to maintain their existence and extend their influence over the external environment. Individuals and interested groups

---

[2] David G. Hawkridge et al., *A Study of Selected Exemplary Programs for the Education of Disadvantaged Children: Final Report* (Palo Alto: American Institute for Research, 1968).

[3] Richard L. Fairley, "Accountability's New Test," *American Education,* June 1972, pp. 33-35.

[4] Harvey A. Averch et al., *How Effective Is Schooling? A Critical Review and Synthesis of Research Findings* (Santa Monica, Ca.: Rand Corporation, 1972).

[5] Kenneth Boulding, "The School Industry as a Possible Pathological Economy," paper presented at the annual conference of the American Educational Research Association, New York, February 1971.

[6] Daniel P. Moynihan, "Equalizing Education in Whose Benefit?" *Public Interest,* Fall 1972, pp. 68-89; Daniel P. Moynihan, *Coping: On the Practice of Government* (New York: Random House, 1975).

that gain from these organizations (and their programs) try to maintain their position and extend their power and profit—in short, to keep their jobs. Organizations are always changing; they either grow or decline. The idea is for the organization to arrest the entropic process which leads to decline or death. The opposite of entrophy is growth, and the most common type of growth is multiplication—a change in quantity rather than quality. In the same way animal or plant species grow by multiplication, the educational-compensatory bureaucracies have attempted to add more programs of essentially the same types. The idea is to maintain some continuous inflow of energy, new money, and new programs, so the various bureaucracies set up to administer these programs can grow and the jobs created by the system can continue.[7]

A judgment of to what extent compensatory education has failed depends on the temperament of the observer and how much evaluation research has been carefully read. The general impression is fairly solid: compensatory education has not resulted in substantial or lasting improvement in students' academic achievement. Several hundred evaluations have been undertaken in different school systems on programs with different emphases and under varying conditions. The data are imperfect, but the uniformity of the results cannot be ignored. Compensatory education has failed to overcome the education deficits of the disadvantaged child.[8]

According to Harry Miller, the disillusionment with compensatory education among educators and the informed public has taken three major forms.[9]

1. Lessened optimism, especially among those who have a considerable stake in financed programs operating under the compensatory umbrella. Those who have chosen this response have lowered their original expectations and claims but have taken heart from selected evidence, at least on a local level, that marginal gain is possible from compensatory efforts.

---

[7] Ibid.; Allan C. Ornstein, "The Cost of Federal Funding? Who Benefits?" *Education and Urban Society*, August 1974, pp. 469–96; Allan C. Ornstein, "Evaluation and Reform of Federal Intervention Programs," *Contemporary Education*, Winter 1977, pp. 92–97.

[8] David K. Cohen, "Policy for the Public Schools: Compensation and Integration," *Harvard Educational Review*, Winter 1968, pp. 114–37; David K. Cohen, "Segregation, Desegregation, and Brown," *Society*, November 1974, pp. 34–40; Gene V. Glass et al., *Data Analysis of the 1968–69 Survey of Compensatory Education, Title I* (Boulder, Colo.: Laboratory of Educational Research, University of Colorado, 1970); Milbrey W. McLaughlin, *Evaluation and Reform: The Elementary and Secondary Act of 1965/Title I* (Cambridge, Mass.: Ballinger Publishing Co., 1975).

[9] Harry L. Miller, "Student Achievement, Teacher Behavior, and Accountability," in A. C. Ornstein and S. M. Miller (eds.), *Policy Issues in Education* (Lexington, Mass.: D. C. Heath & Co., 1976), pp. 69–82.

2. Acceptance of social reality by those who view a decade of compensatory efforts as a disaster and are unwilling to accept the high cost of marginal gains that can be obtained by their continuance.

3. A search for alternatives based on a conviction that the schools, far from being unable to close the performance gap between minority and mainstream children, are unwilling to do what is necessary to achieve that goal.

The conflict arises between the advocates of the second and third choices. Advocates of the second position take on a conservative slant; they seek to curtail wasteful funding, or at least to implement programs on only a modest basis, to test them before expanding them, to define goals and priorities, to effectively coordinate activities, and to postpone making promises until the results are in.[10] Advocates of the third position put the blame on the attitudes of teachers, their laziness or incompetence; the unfairness of civil service examinations by which minority teachers may be disqualified; the nature of schools and society, with reference to racism, poverty, and bureaucracy; and the misleading and culturally biased theories of social scientists.[11] They argue that compensatory education was never really given a fair chance, and more money and programs are still needed.

In general, compensatory education has been criticized for: (1) its hasty planning and piecemeal approach, (2) mismanagement and misappropriation of funds, (3) unethical grantsmen who justify their conduct on the basis that "everyone does it," (4) large consultant fees charged for work not done or for shoddy work, (5) inadequately trained personnel at the state and local levels, (6) high salaries for people at the administrative levels, (7) disregard for and lack of teacher participation, (8) vague objectives, (9) poor evaluation procedures, and (10) increased quantity of services substituted for change in the quality or content of the program.[12] Critics have characterized compensatory funding as using scattergun

---

[10] See Peter F. Drucker, "Can the Businessman Meet Our Social Needs?" *Saturday Review*, March 17, 1973, pp. 41–44; Peter F. Drucker, "Rejoinders," *Saturday Review*, March 17, 1973, pp. 48, 53; Edith Green, "Education's Federal Grab Bag," *Phi Delta Kappan*, October 1972, pp. 83–86; Moynihan, *Coping;* Allan C. Ornstein, *Race and Politics in School/Community Organizations* (Pacific Palisades, Ca.: Goodyear Publishing Co., 1974).

[11] Andrew Billingsley, "Black Families and White Social Science," *Journal of Social Issues,* Summer 1970, pp. 127–42; James E. Blackwell, *The Black Community: Diversity and Unity* (New York: Dodd, Mead & Co., 1975); Kenneth B. Clark, *Dark Ghetto* (New York: Harper & Row, 1965); Edmund W. Gordon, "Education of the Disadvantaged: A Problem of Human Diversity," in N. F. Ashline, T. R. Pezzullo, and C. I. Norris (eds.), *Education, Inequality, and National Policy* (Lexington, Mass.: D. C. Heath & Co., 1976), pp. 101–123; Edmund W. Gordon and Adelaide Jablonsky, "Compensatory Education in the Equalization of Educational Opportunity," *Journal of Negro Education* (Summer 1968), pp. 280–90.

[12] Edith Green, "The Educational Entrepreneur—A Portrait," *Public Interest,* Summer 1972, pp. 12–25; Howard A. Glickstein, "Federal Education Programs and Minority

approaches, and producing slipshod work, poor results, or no results at all. The prevailing idea is that the money is there to be given away, without expecting real benefits.[13] In effect, the ESEA movement seems to have undermined America's blind faith in education and in educators.

Advocates of compensatory spending claim that most of these problems can be remedied over time, and the real problem lies in the anticipation that disadvantaged children will not succeed. Americans are obligated to find solutions that will reach these children and provide the necessary equality of opportunity. Moreover, it is contended that in most instances (1) money was made available in such haste that the quality of planning and development was limited, (2) many programs have been operative for too brief a period to be effectively evaluated, (3) many programs were funded at insufficient levels, and (4) some student successes have been reported in the affective domain.[14] Some effects of compensatory programs have been positive; they have (1) stimulated Congress to pass many other aid to education bills, where previously it had taken a hands-off policy, (2) spotlighted the needs of disadvantaged children, (3) fueled other movements toward equality of educational opportunity, (4) encouraged parental and community involvement in the schools, and (5) indirectly started the accountability movement, with its emphasis on measuring educational outcomes.[15]

Problems of Evaluating Compensatory Programs

One cannot point with confidence to the difference, if any, that most compensatory programs cause in the lives of the target group. It has not been established that one approach has been more effective than another in reducing poverty or providing quality education for all the target children. In short, we do not know what works under what conditions and to what extent. Lack of a solid, well-defined information base of past and present programs pose future limitations on the government's ability to map out effective programs. While research evaluations of compensatory programs are better designed than they were in the mid 1960s, when the

Groups," *Journal of Negro Education,* Summer 1969, pp. 303-14; Allan C. Ornstein and Barney M. Berlin, "Social Policy and Federal Funding," *Journal of Research and Development in Education,* Summer 1975, pp. 82-91; William W. Wayson, "ESEA: Decennial Views of the Revolution: The Negative Side," *Phi Delta Kappan,* November 1975, pp. 151-56.

[13] Ibid.; Boulding, "The School Industry," Harry L. Miller, *Social Foundations of Urban Education,* 3rd ed. (New York: Holt, Rinehart & Winston, 1978).

[14] Gordon and Jablonsky, "Compensatory Education"; Adelaide Jablonsky, "Status Report on Compensatory Education," *IRDC Bulletin,* July 1971, pp. 1-19; Alfred Lightfoot, *Urban Education in Social Perspective* (Chicago: Rand McNally & Co., 1978).

[15] Samuel Halperin, "ESEA: Decennial Views of the Revolution: The Positive Side," *Phi Delta Kappan,* November 1975, pp. 147-51; Wilkerson, "Compensatory Education."

programs were first evaluated, this area of inquiry still suffers from a number of weaknesses. Many of them are simple technical weaknesses; others are more basic, some seemingly inherent in the field. The aspects can be summed up in three broad problems: (1) inadequate sampling, (2) failure to establish comparable experimental and control group, and (3) techniques of data collection that make reliability and validity suspect.

Miriam Goldberg details seven problems that interfere with the sound evaluation of compensatory programs: (1) pressures for "solutions" which call for results and preclude careful, objective evaluation; (2) evaluation which is performed as an afterthought without prior criteria and valid pretest and posttest data; (3) failure to formulate clear objectives and to determine important content; (4) failure to design assessment procedures which discriminate among programs and strategies appropriate for varied populations; (5) unwillingness to develop large-scale research and cross-community evaluations; (6) reluctance to distinguish between short-term and long-term consequences; and (7) failure to develop long-term programs and corresponding longitudinal evaluations.[16]

To this list of problems, A. Harry Passow adds the following: (8) problems of attrition due to high population mobility; (9) problems of obtaining equivalent samples to serve as control and comparison groups; (10) difficulties in using randomization procedures in assigning units to control and comparison groups as well as treatment conditions; (11) disparities in the goals of participants, personnel, and sponsors involved in the programs; (12) changing components of treatments, making comparisons of outcomes difficult; (13) inadequate outcome measures or scales; and (14) political pressure for policy decisions before research results become available.[17]

Doxey Wilkerson mentions four additional problems: (15) programs are ill defined, so that the labels attached to the programs are unreliable guides as to the inputs, treatment conditions, and outputs; (16) intervention variables are multifaceted, and it is seldom clear which variables are related to measured outcomes; (17) cognitive scores tend to be stressed at the expense of measuring growth in the childrens' self-esteem and social interaction; and (18) assessment instruments associated with the latter indices tend to be unreliable and invalid.[18]

[16] Miriam L. Goldberg, "Problems in the Evaluation of Compensatory Programs," in A. H. Passow (ed.), Developing Programs for the Educationally Disadvantaged (New York: Teachers College Press, Columbia University, 1968), pp. 47-57.

[17] Passow, "Compensatory Instructional Intervention."

[18] Doxey A. Wilkerson, "Programs and Practices in Compensatory Education for Disadvantaged Children," Review of Educational Research, December 1965, pp. 426-40; Doxey A. Wilkerson, "How to Make Educational Research Relevant to the Urban Community," Journal of Negro Education, Fall 1972, pp. 299-302.

Added to all these problems is censorship of data. If educators are committed to a specific social policy (say compensatory education) and its related programs because of political and economic reasons, and not because of real educational benefits which can be proven, then, as stated elsewhere, "there is good reason for maintaining ignorance, preventing research, slanting findings, screening the research, or hiring inside or politically [safe] researchers who will guarantee 'positive' findings."[19] The results of evaluation have great potential impact when people are committed by ideology, or when politics and jobs are tied to evaluative results. The people who are committed "never seriously entertain in advance the possibility that results would come out negative or insignificant."[20]

Evaluative research is best conducted in an atmosphere where there is room for failure, and where the focus of interest is honestly to improve the program—to learn why a program is succeeding or failing. To the extent the program has ideological overtones, or where different interest groups are competing for a shrinking amount of federal funds or the evaluation is linked to future allocation of jobs, resources, and money, the information obtained from the evaluation is potentially threatening. Therefore there is greater likelihood that the evaluation will be restricted, slanted, or even censored prior to publication.

The federal government—members of Congress who appropriate the money and members of HEW who make decisions regarding who will be funded—is aware of most of these problems and has expressed concern. Nevertheless, there is no nation-wide system for planning, executing, and using evaluation studies of compensatory programs. As Joseph Wholey puts it, "The whole federal machinery for making policy and budget decisions suffers from a crucial weakness: it lacks a comprehensive system for measuring program effectiveness."[21]

As noted in the list of problems in evaluation, too often programs are designed and funded with no knowledge of how they are to be evaluated. There are no provisions for control or experimental groups to be matched and compared and pre- and posttested, and data related to the objectives are either unavailable or insufficient. Input and output measures and cost-effectiveness criteria are not comparable for similar programs, and methods for yielding quantifiable information on the effects of programs are not specified. Local administrators, staff, or evaluators are not entirely

---

[19] Allan C. Ornstein, *Teaching in a New Era* (Champaign, Ill.: Stipes Publishing Co., 1976), p. 145.

[20] Peter Rossi, "Boobytraps and Pitfalls in the Evaluation of Social Action Programs," in C. H. Weiss (ed.), *Evaluating Action Programs* (Boston: Allyn & Bacon, 1972), p. 227.

[21] Joseph S. Wholey et al., *Federal Evaluation Policy* (Washington, D.C.: Urban Institute, 1973), p. 23.

to blame for inadequate research designs; the federal government lacks a uniform and well-designed method of program development or funding, as well as evaluation. While it now requires a statement of objectives, they are usually written only to fulfill a requirement to obtain funds and are therefore vague and unrealistic. The unplanned and uncoordinated system for evaluating compensatory programs has resulted in a proliferation of noncomparable, poorly designed evaluative studies which provide few substantial data on which sound conclusions and policy could be based. Until HEW and other federal departments establish nationwide minimum evaluative criteria, haphazard studies and noncomparable findings will be the rule.[22]

It is up to the federal government to develop a broad, national policy for coordinating efforts to evaluate compensatory programs at the local level. Evaluation money can best be spent for a unified approach which utilizes "outside" and local evaluators who are considered to have technical expertise and professional integrity. An overall system for objective evaluation of the immediate and long-range effectiveness of programs in meeting their objectives and to assess their impact on other parts of the target institution and various sectors of society is needed. At present, little consideration is given to the fact that many intervention programs affect many more people than the intended recipients.

National Evaluation of Compensatory Programs

Because Title I has continuously received the majority of funds authorized by ESEA (about five-sixths annually), it has been the primary object of attention from lawmakers and school people. ESEA required the U.S. Office of Education (USOE or OE) Title I staff to review the effectiveness of compensatory programs, but "the USOE had had little experience in administering programs of that size, and no experience with evaluation."[23] Although the reporting responsibilities of the USOE were left ambiguous in the 1965 legislation, in time it was forced to justify large-scale funding of compensatory programs to Congress. The growing feeling among many legislators has been that the money was being wasted and the programs had to be justified.[24]

At the outset, explicit decisions were made to avoid evaluation issues that might frighten local or state administrators: not to insist on uniform reporting standards, not to require measurements with standardized tests,

---

[22] Ornstein, *Teaching in a New Era.*
[23] McLaughlin, *Evaluation and Reform,* p. 17.
[24] David K. Cohen, "Politics and Research: Evaluation of Social Action Programs in Education," *Review of Educational Research,* April 1970, pp. 214–38; Moynihan, *Coping.*

not to compare black and white students or school districts, and not to suggest preferred components of effectiveness. Michael Kirst notes that "sophisticated methodological procedures, with control groups and reliable and valid instruments, were rejected as against the grain of state and local officials."[25] The fear was that they might "lead in the direction of a national assessment of schools effectiveness — a development long feared and resisted by school administrators throughout the country."[26] The potential sensitivity of comparative data in judging different student groups or school districts was another basis for this rejection.

As ESEA got underway there was little interest within the USOE in making school people responsible to their constituencies, or "making educational achievement the touchstone of success in judging ESEA."[27] It took the growing concern among legislators, coupled with the threat of federal cutbacks in funding, for the USOE to move in the direction of nationwide assessments of Title I compensatory programs.

The first annual report on Title I submitted to Congress was a glowing account of program successes. The report concluded that it was "bringing about an educational revolution. . . . Hundreds of diverse and innovative projects sponsored in communities across the nation testify to the creative energies released by Title I."[28] However, the substance of the report was based on impressions from local reports, testimonial data, and photojournalism; there was no empirical evidence to support the claims. The second annual report,[29] which examined various programs in 39 cities, was similar in format and substance — what one observer later called an "urban eyewash,"[30] and another observer termed "useless" and done merely to satisfy federal evaluation requirements.[31]

With mounting pressure from lawmakers and educators for comparative school data and cost-effectiveness data to be used in future planning of compensatory programs, the first large-scale nationwide evaluation was

[25] Michael W. Kirst, "Administrative Problems in the Evaluation of Title I of the Elementary and Secondary Act," paper prepared for the Urban Institute, Washington, D.C., December 1969, pp. 17-18.

[26] Stephen K. Bailey and Edith K. Mosher, *ESEA: The Office of Education Administers a Law* (Syracuse, N.Y.: Syracuse University Press, 1968), p. 112.

[27] Samuel Halpern, "ESEA: Five Years Later," *Congressional Record* (September 9, 1970), pp. 8492-94.

[28] U.S. Office of Education, *The Status Report: The First Years of Title I, Elementary and Secondary Education Act of 1965* (Washington, D.C.: U.S. Government Printing Office, 1967), p. 7.

[29] U.S. Office of Education, *Title I/Year II* (Washington, D.C.: U.S. Government Printing Office, 1968).

[30] See Robert A. Dentler, "Urban Eyewash: A Review of Title I/Year II." *Urban Review*, February 1969, pp. 32-33.

[31] See Joseph S. Wholey et al., *Title I: Evaluation and Technical Assistance* (Washington, D.C.: Urban Institute, 1970), Appendix B, p. 1.

awarded to the TEMPO Division of the General Electric Company for a cost/benefit analysis. Known as The TEMPO study it was designed to examine exemplary Title I projects and identify features of successful compensatory programs throughout the nation. Specification of successful programs, it was reasoned, would eliminate future program waste. Data for the study were limited to 11 school districts plus five in-depth case studies, chosen on the belief that successful programs were in operation in at least some of these schools. TEMPO analysts were unable to identify any significant achievement gains of Title I students; in fact, there appeared to be a slight decline in average student achievement in the Title I schools studied. No correlation, plus or minus, could be shown between expenditures and changes in achievement scores; furthermore, no consistent pattern could be shown for Title I populations, treatment variables, or programs in general.[32] The results were disappointing; "the TEMPO study did not show anything at all," according to Alice Rivlin, "only how hard it is to find out anything about input-output relations in education."[33]

The Office of Education proceeded next to survey state and local educators to determine the characteristics of students, teachers, school facilities, and compensatory services in Title I schools, and what services at what cost could lead to how much gain in achievement. It was concluded that while schools selected as participants in compensatory reading programs students with low scores in reading, there was no difference between participating and nonparticipating students in rate of progress in reading. For both, the deficits grew progressively greater in each succeeding grade level.[34] In plain language, wrote one observer, compensatory education "seemed to be having no effect at all. Student achievement continued to be correlated most closely with family background, and to be unaffected by educational intervention."[35]

The USOE survey of compensatory education was no more successful in showing a relationship between educational spending and student achievement; in fact, participants seemed to make slower rates of progress than nonparticipants. This was explained away by the fact that participants had lower pretest scores, and gain scores were more difficult for groups starting with greater deficits. In short, compensatory reading

---

[32] *TEMPO: General Electric Company* (Washington, D.C.: U.S. Government Printing Office, 1968).

[33] Alice N. Rivlin, *Systematic Thinking for Social Action* (Washington, D.C.: Brookings Institution, 1971), pp. 82-83.

[34] U.S. Office of Education, *Education of the Disadvantaged: An Evaluative Report on Title I Elementary and Secondary Education Act of 1965, Fiscal Year 1968* (Washington, D.C.: U.S. Government Printing Office, 1969).

[35] McLaughlin, *Evaluation and Reform: The Elementary and Secondary Act of 1965/Title I*, p. 59.

programs yielded no evidence that the fundings was making any significant impact. The survey also concluded that family background was the strongest predictor of student achievement, and school intervention did not mitigate social-class differences.[36]

While these 1968 and 1969 surveys of compensatory education were being conducted, the Westinghouse–Ohio University report on the impact of Head Start, the best known compensatory strategy and one of the few programs considered a success at the time by reformers, was released. From a sample of 104 Head Start centers, the report concluded that there were no significant differences in learning between participant children and nonparticipant (matched) children, and the program failed to help disadvantaged learners catch up to their middle-class counterparts or to alleviate their cognitive deficiencies.[37]

One year later, in 1970, the Educational Testing Service published the results of a longitudinal study of Head Start and Follow Through programs since 1967. The most compelling finding was "the wide range of individual differences exhibited in a relatively restricted sample. Low-income youngsters are not a homogenous group."[38] Differential growth patterns in cognitive and social development could not be associated with the programs; it was assumed other factors (such as the home or community) influenced their development.

For a period of four years the American Institute for Research (AIR) was contracted to evaluate the impact of Title I by identifying, analyzing, and describing programs which yielded measured benefits in cognitive growth. The first study consisted of site visits to 98 programs in 31 urban centers in 16 states.[39] By presenting sufficient data to document that 18 compensatory programs worked and pointing to specific ways they did so, this research supported legislative investment in education and was considered a resounding success.

Two follow-up studies by AIR, however, found that "successful" programs exhibited the regressive tendencies typical of innovation efforts that have been described since the Hawthorne industrial experiments some 40 years ago. Not only did student gain scores fade over time, but most compensatory programs kept inadequate records, and used poor sampling, design, and testing procedures. Numerous programs originally earmarked

---

[36] Glass, *Data Analysis of 1968–69 Survey.*

[37] Westinghouse Learning Corporation and Ohio University. *The Impact of Head Start: An Evaluation of the Effects of Head Start on Children's Cognitive and Affective Development* (Washington, D.C.: U.S. Government Printing Office, 1969).

[38] *Disadvantaged Children and Their First School Experiences* (Princeton, N.J.: Educational Testing Service, 1970), p. 222.

[39] Hawkridge et al., *Study of Selected Exemplary Programs.*

for evaluation had to be skipped over because their research methodologies were inadequate.[40]

Besides these nationwide studies, a series of smaller, unrelated studies by various investigators across the country in the 1960s, considered together, took on nationwide implications.[41] These studies, noted for their sophistication of measurement, utilized various experimental and control groups, most of whom were followed through grade 3 and beyond, in some cases up to grade 8. Independently, these investigators basically reached the same conclusion: the effects of compensatory education were at best short-lived and small in magnitude, and in many cases no differences between control and experimental groups could be observed.

The lesson of these and the other national evaluation studies suggest that assessment of compensatory programs is a difficult task. USOE does not run Title I or other compensatory programs; the design and content of more than 30,000 Title I projects, not to mention other compensatory projects across the country, are determined by local and state administrators. Consequently, the use of federal money reflects multiple and diverse goals which are not easily transformed into reasonable, common objectives and research designs. Not only do variables differ among programs, but to ensure local and state cooperation, comparisons are not made among specific student groups, schools, districts, or areas. At present most educational reformers are faced with a dilemma: they are unable to show whether cognitive gains can be made by target students, and then to show whether these gains produce lasting and measurable effects.

Recent Positive Findings

In the midst of general pessimism about the effectiveness of compensatory education, a few small, scattered programs offer promise.

---

[40] M. J. Wargo et al., *Further Examination of Exemplary Programs for Education of Disadvantaged Children* (Palo Alto, Ca.: American Institute for Research, 1971); M. J. Wargo et al., *ESEA Title I: A Reanalysis and Synthesis of Evaluation Data from Fiscal Year 1965 through 1970* (Palo Alto, Ca.: American Institute for Research, 1972).

[41] For example, see Martin Deutsch et al., *The Disadvantaged Child* (New York: Basic Books, 1967); David J. Fox, *Expansion of the More Effective School Program* (New York: Center for Urban Education, 1967); Susan W. Gray and Robert A. Klaus, "The Early Training Project: A Seventh Year Report," *Child Development*, December 1970, pp. 909–24; Jerome Hellmuth (ed.), *The Disadvantaged Child: Head Start and Early Intervention*, vol. 2 (New York: Brunner/Mazel, Inc., 1968); Merle B. Karnes, *A Research Program to Determine the Effects of Various Preschool Intervention Programs* (Urbana, Ill.: Institute of Research in Exceptional Children, University of Illinois, 1968); Phyllis Levenstein, "Cognitive Growth in Preschoolers through Verbal Interaction with Mothers," *American Journal of Orthopsychiatry*, April 1970, pp. 426–32; David P. Weikart et al., *Perry Preschool Project*

Although they have been in operation for several years, reports of success have only recently been disseminated. For example, a ten-year study of Head Start and Follow Through in the Hamden–New Haven area of Connecticut, found that target students made greater cognitive gains than students in a matched, controlled group in three of six selected academic areas in the third grade. Further, these gains persisted through the eighth grade for nearly 90 percent of the children, although the gain scores were somewhat below the national norm. In short, there was no fading of the intervention effects five years later.[42]

Francis Palmer's longitudinal study of black children in the Harlem section of New York City showed that test scores of children of age two and a half increased eight points higher than those of a matched control group after intervention, but they lost that advantage when they were tested in the first grade. However, when they were retested in the fifth grade, they scored nine points higher on their IQ tests and three months higher on their reading tests compared to the original control group.[43] This phenomenon has been labeled the sleeper effect — improved performance which does not become apparent until several years later.

A summary of the 5-year distar program (an offshoot of the Bereiter-Englemann drill approach for teaching the disadvantaged; see Chapter 3) adopted by a school district on the south side of Chicago for elementary students, prekindergarten to grade 3, reported repeated successes. Target students test 30 percent higher than the city's inner-city reading mean, but after they are mainstreamed, they score no better than other children unless they continue to receive supplementary training. Those that receive another three years of intervention continue to perform above the inner-city mean and close to the national norm, but they lose about two months per year for each year after the end of the supplementary program. In short, most of the cognitive skills can be retained if the compensatory efforts are long-term and intensive.[44]

Progress Report (Ypsilanti, Mich.: Public Schools of Ypsilanti, 1964); Max Wolf and Annie Stein, Long Range Effects of Preschooling on Reading Achievement (New York: Graduate School of Education, Yeshiva University, 1966).

[42] Victoria Seitz, Nancey H. Apfel, and Carole Efron, "Long Term Effects of Early Intervention," paper presented at the annual meeting of the American Association for the Advancement of Science, Denver, Colo., February 1977.

[43] Francis H. Palmer, "The Effects of Minimal Early Intervention on Subsequent IQ Scores and Reading Achievement," paper presented at the annual meeting of the American Psychological Association, Washington, D.C.; September 1976; Francis H. Palmer, "The Effects of Early Childhood Intervention," paper presented at the annual meeting of the American Association for the Advancement of Science, Denver, Colo., February 1977.

[44] J. S. Fuerst, "Report from Chicago: A Program that Works," Public Interest, Spring 1976, pp. 50–69; J. S. Fuerst, "Child Parent Centers: An Evaluation," Integrated Education, May 1977, pp. 17–20.

Rick Heber's Milwaukee Project has had the most impressive results, not only because reported test score gains have been impressive but also because his intervention program started with children, at the earliest possible stage, who might have been expected to perform at very low cognitive levels. An infant education center was started in the slum area of Milwaukee for children with IQs below 80 whose mothers also had IQs of 80 or less. The children had their own teachers (a 1:1 ratio) until they were two years of age; for the next year they were taught in a group of five to eight children, and in succeeding years, the size of the class was increased to 8 and then 11. When, at the age of 42 months, the children were posttested, they exhibited an average gain of 37 IQ points; moreover, they were learning at a rate in excess of the norm for their age peers.[45]

The Milwaukee Project has provided the most encouraging news for compensatory advocates and has been used to oppose Jensenism, and to lend support to the environmentalists. However, critics have maintained there was biased selection of treatment groups, failure to specify the treatments, and contamination of IQ tests (the children were taught the test). Further, they say the children were below the age when IQ tests are thought to be reliable, and, in general, the gains are too large to be valid.[46] Skepticism was increased because Heber initially refused to publish his findings except for studies in the popular press and in speeches.[47]

On a nationwide basis, HEW's office of Child Development reports that early intervention programs have been moderately successful and that many disadvantaged students do make cognitive gains, and some of these gains persist.[48] The Follow-Through Programs, originated by the Bank Street College of Education and Far West Laboratory in San Francisco, two of the original 22 sponsors of the Follow-Through models, have been successfully adopted by entire school systems in Trenton, New Jersey; Elmira, New York; and Macon County, Alabama.[49] Also, some tutoring programs and some alternative high school programs, such as the Harlem

---

[45] Rick Heber, "Research on Education and Habilitation of Mentally Retarded," paper read at the Conference of Sociocultural Aspects of Mental Retardation, Peabody College for Teachers, Nashville, Tenn., June 1968; Rick Heber and Herbert Garber, "An Experiment in the Prevention of Cultural Familial Retardation," in *Environment, Intelligence and Scholastic Achievement*, U.S. Senate Select Committee on Equal Educational Opportunity, June 1972.

[46] William Havender, "A Comment on Arthur Jensen's Critics," unpublished paper, no date; Arthur Jensen, *Genetics and Education* (New York: Harper & Row, 1972); Harry L. Miller and Roger Woock, *Social and Urban Foundations of Education*, 2nd ed. (New York: Holt, Rinehart & Winston, 1973).

[47] A number of psychometrics and researchers managed to secure a report of Heber's study from the agency which funded it; it no longer makes the report available.

[48] *Council Grams*, National Council of Teachers of English, May 1977, pp. 31-32.

[49] Carol Travis, "Compensatory Education: The Glass Is Half Full," *Psychology Today*, September 1976, pp. 63-70, 73-74.

Prep School in New York City and CAM Academy in Chicago, and some free schools in Boston and Berkeley have provided viable options for inner-city students.[50]

Each year the National Advisory Council on Education of Disadvantaged Children (NACEDC) reports to the President and Congress on changes taking place in compensatory programs, citing progress as well as continuous problems. Recent NACEDC reports indicate that successful programs have (1) clearly stated objectives, (2) materials relevant to objectives, (3) parental involvement, (4) small classes, (5) personalized and individualized instruction, (6) diagnostic prescriptions, and (7) intense remedial treatment.[51]

These recent findings and trends suggest that a cautious optimism is appropriate regarding the impact of early-intervention programs and compensatory programs in general; they raise new hopes and present data that should be considered before the final verdict.

DESEGREGATION AND INTEGRATION

Desegregation refers to racially mixed schools and the elimination of racial imbalance. Integrated schools are racially mixed, have desegregated classrooms, and may also have programs designed to reduce racial tension. Much of the legal support for desegregation stems from the 1954 *Brown* v. *Board of Education* decision. This case, involving students from five different states and including reports by several prominent social scientists, indicated that segregation made black children aware that whites considered them inferior and thus their learning was impaired. Hence racially segregated schools were considered inherently inferior. As argued by the NAACP and social science advocates, the crucial question was: "Does segregation of children in public schools solely on the basis of race, even though the physical facilities and other 'tangible' factors may be equal, deprive children of the minority group of equal educational opportunities? We believe that it does."[52] It has been pointed out that the reports of the social scientists were based on inadequate or questionable

[50] See Mario D. Fantini, *Public Schools of Choice* (New York: Simon & Schuster, 1973); Jonathan Kozol, *Free Schools* (Boston: Houghton Mifflin Co., 1972).

[51] *Annual Report to the President and Congress* (Washington, D.C.: National Advisory Council on Education of Disadvantaged Children, 1973); *Compensatory Education: What Works to Help Disadvantaged Children* (Washington, D.C.: National School Public Relations Association, 1973); also see *Early Children Education in Action—the Second Year* (Sacramento, Ca.: California State Department of Education, 1975).

[52] "*Brown* v. *Board of Education of Topeka, Kansas*, 347 W.S. 483 (1954)," in D. Fellman (ed.), *The Supreme Court of Education* (New York: Teachers College Press, Columbia University, 1960).

data from a methodological point of view,[53] and what accounted for the decision was recognition that separate but equal is against the spirit of the U.S. Constitution. Since it was impossible to have segregation and full equality, de jure segregation, that is, segregation imposed by law was ruled illegal.

Schools and communities in the border states—Delaware, Kentucky, Maryland, Missouri, Oklahoma, and West Virginia—responded positively and with "all deliberate speed," as required. Attempts to desegregate school systems in the heart of the South were not easy or quick, and violence accompanied the early moves to achieve racial balance, especially in Little Rock, Arkansas; Clinton, Tennessee; New Orleans, Louisiana; and Jackson, Mississippi. Stall tactics and bureaucratic mishandling of transfer applications eventually replaced the violence. Virginia even made it legal for the state to pay the tuition of students in private schools where public schools did not exist, and Prince Edward County proceeded to close the public schools for two years. Official opposition to desegregation ended by the mid 1960s in the South, and with the exception of a few private academies that have recently enrolled white students in Tennessee and Mississippi, school desegregation has come to the South.

As the Northern and Western cities experienced a major immigration of blacks in the 1950s and the 1960s, de facto school segregation, that is, based on patterns of residential segregation, became apparent. Concern was mounting to alleviate school segregation in the North, and the New York City Board of Education took the lead in a 1954 statement of objectives to implement the spirit of the *Brown* decision. Attendance boundaries were modified, and free transportation was given to students who wished to transfer to other schools. The total effect was limited, however. The Cleveland and Detroit schools followed with similar statements and procedures, and limited results, in the late 1950s. For the greater part, the official policy of the schools outside the South was "color blind." Several court cases in the North were brought by black plaintiffs to force school boards to take active steps to reduce segregation, or "racial imbalance" as it was called, and many decisions of the lower courts in the early 1960s (regarding Boston, Massachusetts; New Rochelle, New York; and Englewood and Teaneck, New Jersey) ordered school systems to abandon segregated education.

Due to legal maneuvering, the desegregation movement did not gain impetus until ten years after the 1954 *Brown* decision, and it was mainly directed at Southern schools. Thus by 1970, the once all-segregated schools

---

[53] Hadley Arkes, "The Problem of Kenneth Clark," *Commentary*, November 1974, pp. 37–46; Steven I. Miller and Jack Kavanagh, "Empirical Evidence," *Journal of Law and Education*, January 1975, pp. 159–71.

Table 10.1 / Number and Percent of School Districts That Desegregated, by Source of Intervention and by Year of Greatest Desegregation

Time Period	Courts		HEW		State-Local		Total	
	No.	%	No.	%	No.	%	No.	%
1901–53	—	—	—	—	7	3	7	1
1954–65	13	6	18	12	53	21	84	13
1966–71	168	81	122	80	126	49	416	68
1972–75	27	13	12	8	69	27	108	18
Totals	208	34	152	25	255	41	615	100

Source: Adapted from the U.S. Commission on Civil Rights, *Fulfilling the Letter and Spirit of the Law: Desegregation of the Nation's Public Schools* (Washington, D.C.: U.S. Government Printing Office, 1976), Table 2.4, p. 135.

of the 11 Southern states were more integrated than the rest of the country; government statistics showed that 38 percent of black students in the South were attending desegregated schools (50 percent or more white), compared to 27 percent in the North and West. This gap has steadily increased, and decreasing de jure segregation in the South has been offset by increasing de facto segregation in the North and West.

The U.S. Commission on Civil Rights surveyed 1,292 school districts in school year 1975–76, representing 8 percent of the nation's 16,006 public school districts and nearly 70 percent of the nation's minority students enrolled in public schools. Results of this survey, shown in Table 10.1, showed that 608 out of 993 school districts, or approximately two-thirds, had taken substantial steps to desegregate since 1954, with the greatest effort taking place between 1966–71; seven school systems had desegregated prior to the *Brown* decision. Of those that claimed to have desegregated as of 1975–76, the courts were the most important impetus in 34 percent of the cases, HEW in 25 percent of the cases, and state-local pressures in 41 percent. The courts and HEW played the most active roles during the period 1954–71. While local-initiated plans have assumed greater importance recently, this may be due to spin-off effects and potential anxiety about the courts and HEW.

The Role of the Courts

Recent court decisions on the subject of school desegregation are noted below.[54] Since 1973, there has been a focus not only on schools outside the

---

[54] Thomas H. Flygare, "Can Federal Courts Control an Educational Program?" *Phi Delta Kappan,* April 1976, pp. 550–51; Thomas H. Flygare, "Rehnquist's Dayton Decision and System-wide Desegregation Plans," *Phi Delta Kappan* (October 1977), pp. 126–27. Daniel U. Levine, "Recent Court Cases Bearing on Regional School Integration," mimeographed, November 1975; Allan C. Ornstein, *Introduction to the Foundations of Education* (Chicago: Rand McNally & Co., 1977), pp. 553–54.

South but also on the concept of metropolitan (city and suburbs) desegregation.

1. *Brown* v. *Board of Education of Topeka, Kansas* (1954). The Court rejected the "separate but equal" doctrine and decided that racial segregation in public schools was "inherently unequal."
2. *Brown case* (1954). In a follow-up decision, the Court did not order immediate segregation of public schools but required change "with all deliberate speed."
3. *Griffin* v. *Prince Edward County School Board* (1964). The Court claimed there was "too much deliberation and not enough speed" and declared that the closing of the public schools in Prince Edward County, Virginia, to avoid desegregation, was unconstitutional. Tuition grants to private white schools set up after the public schools were closed and were declared unconstitutional, too.
4. *Greene* v. *New Kent County* (1968). The Court maintained that local school boards were required to plan desegregation proposals that promised to be effective.
5. *United States* v. *Montgomery County Board of Education* (1969). The Court ruled that a federal judge had the right to order school boards to integrate the schools' staffs according to specific ratios.
6. *Alexander et al.,* v. *Holmes County Board of Education, Mississippi* (1969). The Court ruled that school districts must end segregation "at once" and integrate the schools "now and hereafter."
7. *United States* v. *Charlotte-Mecklenburg County, North Carolina* (1971). The Court supported busing and other devices, e.g., racial quotas, pairing, and gerrymandering of attendance zones, to remove the South's state-imposed school segregation.
8. *Bradley* v. *School Board of the City of Richmond, Virginia* (1973). With one Justice taking no part in the decision, the Court split on the permissibility of crossing boundaries of city districts with a predominance of black students to include adjacent suburbs for purposes of desegregation.
9. *Bradley* v. *Milliken* (1974). The concept of metropolitan busing in the Detroit area was rejected on the basis that before separate and autonomous school districts may be set aside, "it must be shown that there has been a constitutional violation within one district that produces a significant segregation effect in another district."
10. *Keyes* v. *School District No. 1, Denver, Colorado* (1974). While not dealing directly with integration on a metropolitan basis, the Court ruled that if schools are racially segregated in a proportion of a city as a result of deliberate official acts, then the entire school district must be desegregated.

11. *Morgan* v. *Hennigan, Boston, Massachusetts* (1974). Based on the Supreme Court decision in *Keyes,* the district court found that the entire school system in Boston had to be desegregated.
12. *Newburg Area Council of Jefferson County Board of Education* v. *Board of Education of Louisville, Kentucky* (1975). In accordance with *Milliken* standards (black students in Jefferson County schools were required to attend schools in Louisville in 1954), this judgment ordered implementation of a merger of the Louisville schools and the surrounding Jefferson County suburban schools.
13. *Evans* v. *Buchanan* (1975). In Wilmington, Delaware, as in Louisville, the case hinged on the fact that black students had been required to cross district lines before 1954 to attend schools in the city of Wilmington. Desegregation relief embraced intradistrict and interdistrict action involving the Wilmington schools and the surrounding suburbs.
14. *Pasadena Board of Education* v. *Spangler* (1976). The Court held that a school board, having once reassigned students to achieve racial balance, does not have to continue doing so, even if residential patterns have since resegregated some schools.
15. *Runyon* v. *McCrary* (1976). The Court upheld a lower court's decision that a child cannot be denied admission to a private school on the basis of race, rejecting the argument that it violated certain constitutional principles, including freedom of association, right of privacy, and right of parents to decide on their children's education.
16. *Brinkman* v. *Gilligan, Dayton, Ohio* (1977). The Supreme Court held that the existence of predominantly white and predominantly black schools in a school system does not alone constitute a violation of the Constitution, and that a desegregation remedy must coincide with the Constitutional violations found by the courts.

The immediate effect of the Detroit decision ruled out the possibility of school desegregation in that city, but it still provided interdistrict or metropolitan remedies in individual cases. The Louisville and Wilmington cases illustrate that if plaintiffs can show past discrimination, as prescribed by the U.S. Supreme Court in the Detroit case, the lower courts will rule in favor of desegregation of city schools with surrounding suburbs. This has obvious effects for all Southern and border states, as well as possible implications for some Northern states. Plaintiffs can match neighborhood census tracts with school enrollments to show past segregation which may have been established by assigning black students to schools across the boundaries of white school districts.

The immediate effect of the Denver case, followed by Boston, is also important. Legal suits challenging de facto segregation in the North and

West have been filed which coincide with the *Keyes* decision. To encourage this trend, the Supreme Court in 1976 refused to review and rescind busing orders in Boston, despite continuous turmoil in the city and the fact that following the court decision white enrollments dropped so drastically (from about 70 to 40 percent in two years) that minorities outnumber whites in most schools, and in effect the original desegregation intentions have been nearly washed out.

The Wilmington case is also important because of the Court's analysis and emphasis on housing discrimination as a cause of segregation in city and suburban schools. Following this precedent the Supreme Court ruled in 1976 that federal courts can (this does not mean they will) order the creation of low-cost public housing in the suburbs. The case was based on *Gautreaux* v. *Chicago Housing Authority,* which noted that few neighborhoods were left in Chicago where nonintegrated housing could be achieved by building new housing units or other methods. The Court advocated an integrated society, which should involve a comprehensive metropolitan plan.

The Pasadena case may provide a way out for school boards, once they have implemented a desegregation plan; the Court may have been concerned with white flight from the cities and the possibility that a desegregation move on the heels of another a few years before would only accelerate the trend.

The impact of the *Runyon* decision is directly limited to only a few hundred private schools in the South and border states which are principally meant to provide an alternative to the desegregated public schools. But it does not alter the economic and social reasons behind all-white private schools with no policy of racial exclusion, nor does it prohibit all-black private schools, funded by federal or foundation money, to continue to operate in the ghettos, though they rarely attract white students. In the long run, the significance of the case is likely to be a public awareness that there are no longer any ways, within the law, to exclude minority children from private schools.

As a result of the *Brinkman* decision, the courts must determine whether there was any action by the school board which was intended to, and did in fact, discriminate against minority students, teachers, or staff. If such violations are found, the lower courts must determine how much segregative effect these violations had on the racial distribution of the school population as presently constituted, when that distribution is compared to what it would have been in the absence of such constitutional violations. The remedy must be designed to redress only that difference, and only if there has been a systemwide impact may there be a systemwide remedy. The lower courts must now carefully show the segregative acts committed by the boards of education and ascertain precisely the effects those acts have had on the present assignment of students. Only after such careful analysis will the courts have the authority to order desegregation, and then only to correct the effects of the official segregative acts. The *Brinkman* case not only offsets the *Keyes* decision, but we can now also expect a number of school systems to be faced with delays and reversals.

Table 10.2 / Desegregation Plans Implemented and Considered Most Effective by Superintendents Enrolling 50,000 or More Students

School Desegregation Plan	Percent Implemented	Percent Considered Most Effective
1. Altering attendance areas.	20.5%	19.3%
2. Establishing magnet schools, which incorporate specialized programs and personnel and tend to attract students from various parts of the city's school system.	12.3	10.2
3. Changing elementary school feeder patterns to secondary schools.	11.9	12.1
4. Permitting students to attend schools outside their neighborhood (free-choice transfer).	11.4	12.2
5. Busing students, involving two-way routes.	11.0	14.4
6. Busing students, involving one-way routes.	9.1	9.1
7. Offering open enrollment from predominantly minority schools to predominantly white schools so long as space is available.	8.7	4.8
8. Pairing schools, where two schools in adjacent areas are brought together in one zone. For example, school A may enroll all students from grades 1–4; school B enrolls all students from grades 5–8 (Princeton Plan).	7.8	8.3
9. Bringing together three neighborhood schools to make one attendance zone, thereby increasing the pool of students and achieving better racial balance than if tried with two schools (triad plan).	3.7	4.6
10. Creating four to eight attendance zones, with the narrowest point of each located in the inner city and the broadest at the city's edge (pie-shaped plan).	1.8	3.4
11. Exchanging white and minority students on a one-to-one voluntary basis.	0.9	2.5
12. Establishing educational parks, which provide for a large concentration of schools and facilities in a section of the city on a racially neutral site or at the edge of the city.	0.5	0
13. Merging together the city and surrounding suburbs into a single school system (metropolitan complex).	0.5	1.0

Source: Allan C. Ornstein and Glen Thompson, "A Status Report on the Desegregation of Schools Enrolling 50,000 or More Students," *Illinois School Journal*, 1978, in process.

Desegregation Plans

As desegregation pressures have mounted, first in the South and now gradually outside it, a variety of plans have been tried with varying degrees of success. The ranking of these plans in order of implementation and effectiveness by the superintendents of school systems enrolling 50,000 or more students are shown in Table 10.2. The first five plans listed in the table — altering attendance areas, establishing magnet schools, changing elementary school feeder patterns to secondary schools, free-choice transfers, and two-way busing — comprised 67 percent of the responses regarding implementation, and the last three plans — voluntary transfers, educational parks, and metropolitan complexes — comprised 2 percent. The top five choices for most effective plans were similar to the plans most often implemented, although the ranking was slightly dissimilar. Two-way busing, which often invokes emotional reactions from both educators and citizen groups, was considered the second most effective plan. Metropolitan complexes, which were the lowest choice for implementation and second lowest for effectiveness, should gain in ranking in the future as the courts look for a remedy to desegregate city schools by including surrounding suburbs.

Feasibility of Desegregation

A major stumbling block for school desegregation has always been the attitudes and resistance of the majority of whites who have sought to maintain their neighborhood schools. Traditionally Northern whites were able to resist desegregation by posing the question of Southern de jure as opposed to Northern de facto segregation. Adding to the problem is the growing number of black spokesmen who are opting for local control of their schools rather than desegregation, under the banner of black pride and power. Granted there are subtle differences between whites who advocate neighborhood schools and those who are segregationists, as there are between blacks who advocate power and those who advocate separatism. The effects are the same, nevertheless.

Besides attitudinal resistance to desegregation, there is the obstacle of increasing concentrations of blacks in large cities; typically, the neighborhoods are more segregated racially than in previous generations, and the percent of blacks in many cities has increased to the point where school desegregation is nearly, if not entirely, impossible. Furthermore, attempts to desegregate a decreasing number of white students with an increasing number of black students only increase the out-migration of white families to the suburbs. The result is an increasing number of black students in the cities attending predominantly black schools.

380

Table 10.3 / Percentage of Blacks and Spanish-Speaking Americans in Predominantly Minority Schools, by Geographical Area, 1970 and 1972

Area	Percentage of School Population	Schools under 50% Minority	Schools over 50% Minority	Schools over 80% Minority	Schools over 90% Minority
A. PERCENTAGE OF BLACKS IN PREDOMINANTLY MINORITY SCHOOLS					
National					
1970	14.9%	33.1%	66.9%	49.4%	38.2%
1972	15.2	36.3	63.7	45.2	34.8
Northern and Western					
1970	10.6	27.6	72.4	56.6	43.1
1972	10.9	28.3	71.7	55.9	43.3
Border states and D.C.					
1970	17.2	28.7	71.3	61.9	54.7
1972	17.4	31.8	68.2	59.8	53.0
Southern					
1970	26.1	40.3	59.7	38.6	29.2
1972	26.3	46.3	53.7	29.9	21.1
B. PERCENTAGE OF SPANISH-SPEAKING AMERICANS IN PREDOMINANTLY MINORITY SCHOOLS					
National					
1970	5.1%	44.2%	55.8%	33.1%	22.9%
1972	5.4	43.5	56.5	32.9	23.4
Southwest[a]					
1970	18.3	45.4	54.6	30.3	19.9
1972	19.2	43.8	56.2	29.6	20.5
North[b]					
1970	6.0	24.9	75.1	52.4	41.1
1972	6.6	26.9	73.1	53.5	41.1
Florida					
1970	4.6	47.0	53.0	30.1	14.8
1972	5.4	45.1	54.9	32.5	14.5
Remaining states and D.C.					
1970	0.7	81.5	18.5	9.1	5.3
1972	0.8	80.3	19.7	8.6	5.5

[a] Includes Arizona, California, Colorado, New Mexico, and Texas.
[b] Includes Connecticut, Illinois, New Jersey, and New York.
Source: Adapted from Fall, 1972 *Racial and Ethnic Enrollment in Public Elementary and Secondary Schools* (Washington, D.C.: Office of Civil Rights, 1973), Tables 2A–2B, p. 11.

Table 10.3 shows the extent of segregation by geographical area in 1970 and 1972 for black and Spanish-speaking children. While limited progress has been made concerning blacks, nationwide nearly two-thirds still attend schools enrolling over 50 percent minority students and half still attend schools enrolling over 80 percent. As expected, the greatest progress has been made in the South. As for Spanish-speaking students, ethnic isolation has slightly increased on a nationwide basis, as well as in the Southwest and Florida, which comprise the largest percentages of such students. Nationwide more than half attend schools which are over 50 percent minority students and one-third attend schools which are over 80 percent.

Estimates are that the numbers of black and Spanish-speaking school-age children will continually increase into the mid-1980s, while numbers of white school-age children will decrease.[55] This trend will make it more difficult to desegregate the schools. Furthermore, the increasing concentrations of minority students in the cities[56] are making it still more difficult to improve the racial and ethnic mix of these schools. Thus school desegregation depends not only on the courts, or on political or school leadership, but also on the racial and ethnic composition of school districts.

Another problem is that prior to the 1970s the courts had been remiss in enforcing Northern desegregation, and HEW had used federal aid as a stick to enforce desegregation only in the South. According to one policy report, the priority that emerged in the North was delay, which resulted in the denial of fundamental rights of hundreds of thousands of children, and the granting of millions of dollars of federal tax money to school systems that denied these rights.[57] With the *Keyes* court decision, coupled with HEW's threat to cut off federal aid to Northern school systems (Boston in 1971 was the first city to be so threatened) the trend is now toward compliance in the North; the *Brinkman* decision, however, may lead to new stall tactics.

By 1977 about 25 school systems, most of them in the North and West, were subject to court action which could demand that they conceive some kind of desegregation plan. But opposition to busing children has reached a new high, both in Congress and among the public. According to a 1975 Gallup Poll, only 18 percent of all Americans favor busing, and 72 percent favor a constitutional amendment to prohibit it.[58] And a recent Harris poll found that 81 percent of the American public is opposed to busing for integration purposes: 85:9 among whites and 51:38 among blacks. According to *Ebony* magazine, a growing number of blacks oppose busing outside their neighborhoods to achieve desegregation, 58 percent, to be precise.[58a]

The *Congressional Record* reports that "there is a significant silent black majority view on busing that . . . is opposed to it, though black leaders, who get media exposure on the subject, tend to be in favor of it. The majority of blacks, it is concluded, favor "equality—not integration."[59]

---

[55] *The Condition of Education, 1977,* vol. 3, Part I (Washington, D.C.: U.S. Government Printing Office, 1977), Figure 1.02, p. 7.

[56] See Chapter 4, Table 4.3.

[57] *Justice Delayed and Denied* (Washington, D.C.: National Policy Review, 1974).

[58] "Opposition to Busing Reaches Peak in Congress and Nation," *Phi Delta Kappan,* January 1976, p. 356.

[58a] *Congressional Record,* May 13, 1977, p. E-2292.

[59] Ibid.

There is also increased opposition to forced busing in both houses of Congress, and the belief is that there is not enough support to get a two-thirds vote to approve a Constitutional amendment, at least not in the 1970s. Public statements by the last three Presidents and by key members of the legislative branch, including the directors of HEW and the Justice Department, have been against mandatory busing, suggesting instead limited busing orders and other alternatives.[60]

Even James Coleman has misgivings. Originally one of the prime movers of school desegregation, Coleman now points out that busing has tended to cause the flight of white families to the suburbs and has been counterproductive. Redrawing school attendance lines can and often does reduce segregation sharply in small cities. In large cities with large, racially homogeneous residential areas, and often one or more ghetto areas, however, extensive desegregation requires busing. In the 125 largest cities he analyzed, there was a continuous loss of white students from the schools between 1968 and 1973, and the loss was greater (1) in the larger cities, (2) in school systems that had a higher proportion of black students, and (3) where racial disparity between city and suburbs was great. Although the evidence is not conclusive, according to Coleman, accelerated loss of whites appears to occur one and two years after desegregation, and then there is a continuing but slower loss in subsequent years. In general, substantial desegregation hastens the shift of the city and school system to predominantly black, thus causing more segregation.[61]

Coleman's "white flight" thesis, a familiar one in parlor debates on the subject, was immediately attacked by Thomas Pettigrew and Robert Green, in the *Harvard Educational Review*[62] and *Phi Delta Kappan*[63] and subsequently summarized in several weekly news magazines and public debates. The critics charged that Coleman never interviewed a single white

---

[60] Ibid.; *Chicago Sun Times*, June 15, 1976, pp. 1, 14; *New York Times*, June 6, 1971, Sect. 4, p. 2; "Support for Busing to Achieve Racial Integration Waning?" *Phi Delta Kappan*, January 1975, p. 287.

[61] James S. Coleman, Sara D. Kelley, and John Moore, *Trends in School Desegregation, 1968-1973* (Washington, D.C.: Urban Institute, 1975).

[62] Thomas F. Pettigrew and Robert L. Green, "School Desegregation in Large Cities: A Critique of the Coleman 'White Flight' Thesis," *Harvard Educational Review*, February 1976, pp. 1-53; James S. Coleman, "Response to Professors Pettigrew and Green," *Harvard Educational Review*, May 1976, pp. 217-24; Thomas F. Pettigrew and Robert L. Green, "A Reply to Professor Coleman," *Harvard Educational Review*, May 1976, pp. 225-33.

[63] James S. Coleman, "Racial Segregation in the Schools: New Research With New Policy Implications," *Phi Delta Kappan*, October 1975, pp. 75-78; Robert L. Green and Thomas F. Pettigrew "Urban Desegregation and White Flight: A Response to Coleman," *Phi Delta Kappan*, February 1976, pp. 399-402; James S. Coleman, "A Reply to Green and Pettigrew," *Phi Delta Kappan*, March 1976, pp. 454-55; Robert L. Green and Thomas F. Pettigrew, "The Coleman Debate Continued," *Phi Delta Kappan*, April 1976, p. 555.

parent about why he or she left the city; white flight to the suburbs had been going on at a rapid rate prior to busing; the research design was inadequate; and they could not replicate his study in 19 selected cities. Coleman vigorously defended his data; he reported that the loss rates of whites in cities corresponded with forced desegregation, and explained that his data were not replicated because Pettigrew and Green used a different set of cities and a cut-off date of 1972 rather than 1973, which obscured or missed much of the white flight. Coleman also argued that the white loss rate from the cities in 1974 and 1975 had jumped even more than the 1973 rate, thus strengthening his original data.

Other critics pointed out that what is often considered white flight is, in fact, a class as well as racial phenomenon, and white flight in the 1960s and early 1970s was less a result of school desegregation than an overall trend of whites to emigrate from the cities; that is, desegregation is one of many causes for this population shift.[64] The critics also asserted that Coleman had failed to consider the differences in birth rates between blacks and whites, so that the number of black students in inner cities had increased proportionately more than that of whites. Limiting their data to between 1955 to 1970, Meyer Weinberg et al. found that white flight in Southern cities had slowed down, and they concluded that apprehension in the early stages of desegregation tends to be resolved through time; although problems remain, large-scale white flight is a myth.[65] But Coleman argued that had these critics used a 1973 or more recent cut-off date a link between school desegregation and the white exodus to the suburbs would have been found; furthermore, the drastic increase of white private schools in the South had been ignored.

Memphis, Tennessee, provides a striking example of Southern whites withdrawing from desegregated schools. Shortly after the Memphis busing order, white enrollments fell by 20,000, while the number of private school students rose by 14,000. Memphis lost 46 percent of its white public school students between 1970 and 1973. A similar example can be found in Jackson, Mississippi, where in one and one-half years white enrollment dropped from 55 percent before busing to 36 percent in 1973.[66] Similar examples can be found in other Southern states where private schools have opened, or in the North where there are parochial schools.

Coinciding with the critics' point of view, the U.S. Commission on Civil Rights claimed that 82 percent of the more than 600 school systems which

---

[64] Reynolds Farley, "Racial Integration in the Public Schools, 1967-72," *Sociological Focus,* January 1975, pp. 3-26.

[65] Meyer Weinberg et al., *Three Myths: An Exposure of Popular Misconceptions About School Desegregation* (Atlanta, Ga.: Southern Regional Council, 1976).

[66] Robert G. Wegmann, "White Flight and School Resegregation: Some Hypotheses," *Phi Delta Kappan,* January 1977, pp. 389-93.

reported they had desegregated since 1954 had done so without major disruption, and only 10 percent reported a decline in educational levels. For every Boston and Louisville, "there are a dozen communities," the Commission stated, "which have received no headlines . . . where desegregation is proceeding without incident." Initial resistance was noted in many communities, but the report concluded that school people and parents have generally supported desegregation efforts. It was also reported that loss of white students due to desegregation between 1968 to 1972 was only 6 percent, although it was 15 percent where black enrollments initially exceeded 40 percent.[67] (Coleman, of course, made the point that the loss of white students began to accelerate in 1973.) Also, it has developed that, in its eagerness to demonstrate the effectiveness of school desegregation, the Commission sacrificed a good deal of its objectivity. One of its own researchers and several state advisory members protested that the research was slanted to ensure positive findings, and the Commission had instructed its field members to collect data mainly from those school systems in which desegregation plans seemed to be working and where there were minimal problems.[68]

Regardless of who is right, Coleman or his critics, very little can be done to desegregate many city schools which are 50 percent or more black, unless, of course, the suburbs are included in some kind of transfer busing program. This seems hardly likely unless it is forced down their throats by the courts, and where it has been forced in the suburbs, white flight is just as apparent—which corresponds with Coleman's new position on busing. For example, when a court ordered desegregation of schools in the Los Angeles suburb of Inglewood in 1970, about 38 percent of the population was nonwhite; by 1975 the minority population had grown to 80 percent, and the court order was dropped. In 1972, the court-ordered busing program of Pontiac, Michigan changed the black/white ratio from 1:9 to 1:5 in three years. America's largest suburban school system — Prince George's County, Maryland—began a busing program in 1973; by 1975 the white enrollment had dropped 15 percent.

Desegregation and Student Performance

Legal issues and controversy over busing notwithstanding, the question ultimately arises as to what extent students benefit from integrated schools. Are students academically better off and happier when they are racially

---

[67] U.S. Commission on Civil Rights, *Fulfilling the Letter and Spirit of the Law: Desegregation of the Nation's Public Schools* (Washington, D.C.: U.S. Government Printing Office, 1976), Table 2.7, p. 144.

[68] *Chicago Daily News,* October 5, 1976; *Time,* November 29, 1976.

mixed? Although there is voluminous research in this area, it is inconsistent and contradictory. There are data to suggest a relationship between integration and academic achievement[69] (although most of the differences have been attributed to socioeconomic integration), but data which suggest the opposite—even a negative relationship—can also be cited.[70] Similarly, data can be cited which show a positive correlation between integration and the students' sociopsychological development, as well as no correlation or even a negative one. The kinds of interpersonal contacts among black and white students which evolve as a result of desegregation also vary, from a healthy relationship to intense hostilities in which the police are needed to keep order, or no relations (that is, the groups do not associate with each other).

One of the most influential documents purporting to show the positive effects of desegregation and black achievement has been the 1966 Coleman report. The "Summary," which went through a number of versions before being released, has been used both by HEW and the Office of Civil Rights as a powerful weapon in the desegregation effort. The 1975 Coleman report, besides questioning the merits of busing, takes a much softer stand on the academic gains related to desegregation. In a subsequent publication Coleman notes that: "The achievement benefits of integrated schools appeared substantial when I studied them in the middle 1960s. But subsequent studies . . . have found smaller effects, and in some cases none at all."[71] When *The National Observer* interviewed Coleman, his replies indicated he had sharply modified his attitude toward desegregation:

. . . [D]isorder clearly comes from lower-class schools . . . [M]any observations of ghetto-school classrooms describe an enormous degree of disorder in those classrooms. It is very hard to blame any white parents, or any black parents for that matter, who would like to see their children out of that classroom, given the degree of disorder and the degree to which schools as they're presently constituted have failed to control lower-class black children. . . . The theory is that children who may themselves be undisciplined, coming into classrooms that are highly disciplined, would . . . be governed by the norms of the classrooms. . . . What sometimes happens, however, is that characteristics of the lower-class black classroom—namely, a high degree of disorder—come to take over and constitute the values and characteristics of the classroom in the integrated school.[72]

---

[69] For example, widely cited documents to prove this point are the 1966 Coleman report; U.S. Commission on Civil Rights report entitled *Racial Isolation;* and various studies by Daniel Levine, Thomas Pettigrew, Meyer Weinberg, and Alan Wilson.

[70] For example, widely cited documents to prove the opposite point are the studies by David Armor, Nathan Glazer, Daniel Moynihan, and Herbert Walberg.

[71] James S. Coleman, "Racial Segregation in the Schools: New Research with New Policy Implications," *Phi Delta Kappan,* October 1975, p. 77.

[72] "A Scholar Who Inspired It Says Busing Backfired," *The National Observer,* June 7, 1975, p. 18. Reprinted with permission from *The National Observer,* copyright Dow Jones & Company, Inc., 1975.

Coleman's 1975 data, coupled with his interview with *The National Observer,* have the potential for a profound impact. At best, they will lead to confusion of federal officials and judges. At worst, they will serve both white and black separationists as a weapon against desegregation.

The most comprehensive review of desegregation research is the evaluation of 120 studies by Nancy St. John. The dates of these studies start with 1956, with emphasis on post-1966 Coleman data. Her basic findings were that desegregation has a mixed impact on academic achievement. The evidence is also mixed regarding aspirations, self-esteem, and race relations. While most of the studies lack good statistical controls and suffer from methodological weaknesses, the tighter the design, the more often is no achievement difference found between segregated and desegregated minority children. Where significant gains are reported, they tend to appear in the primary grades—usually in arithmetic. Contradictory findings are the rule, however. Contrary to the expectations of many people, the general direction of the findings is that both the self-concept and the aspirations of black children tend to be stronger in segregated schools. Desegregation may reduce prejudice and promote interracial friendships, but it may also promote stereotyping and interracial cleavage and conflict.[73]

Many of the conditions associated with effective integration and positive educational outcomes are under the control of school people themselves, according to an Educational Testing Service study. Based on a two-year survey of 118 elementary schools and 93 high schools between 1974 and 1975, this study concludes that schools with good race relations among students generally have principals who get high ratings as "supportive" from both black and white teachers. The survey set out to identify school characteristics that distinguish between those who do and do not achieve effective desegregation, with effectiveness measured in terms of student achievement and racial attitudes. The investigators found five variables "most consistently related" to good racial attitudes on the part of students: (1) teaching and school activities designed to promote biracial association and support, (2) positive evaluation of school principals by teachers, (3) positive racial attitudes of teachers, as reported by themselves and as perceived by their students, (4) general support for integration by all concerned—students, staff, parents, and so on, and (5) absence of conflict, not just about race but about other educational and social concerns as well.[74]

---

[73] Nancy St. John, *School Desegregation: Outcomes for Children* (New York: John Wiley & Sons, 1975). Also see Nancy St. John, "Desegregation and Minority Group Performance," *Review of Educational Research,* February 1970, pp. 111-33.

[74] *Conditions and Processes of Effective Desegregation* (Princeton, N.J.: Educational Testing Service, 1976).

In general the research on the effects of desegregation and integration are complicated by statistical and sampling problems; inability to set up control and experimental groups; control of influential variables; varying definitions of social class and income; different percentages of blacks and whites used to define desegregation; and the lack of longitudinal data to show cumulative effects of desegregation at various grade levels. The facts that data are reported on a district or schoolwide basis, which often does not reflect the classroom racial mix, and that desegregation usually involves simultaneous changes in spending and other aspects of schooling must also be considered. There is the strong possibility that blacks who attend desegregated schools come from relatively more stable homes than those who live in the core of the inner city, and the counterpossibility that whites who remain in desegregated and changing schools come from relatively lower income homes with less press for educational achievement. Growth in academic achievement or changes in attitude measured between two points in time can be due to maturation, factors in the community or nation, and other school factors, but such factors are not often considered. Finally, several other factors impact on the child's education, ranging from the number of siblings at home, number of books at home, whether the home has one head or two, and so on; desegregation may be only one factor, and a small one at that, in a composite measure of school performance.

Despite data to refute reform or egalitarian beliefs about desegregation, when everything is said and done the most compelling reason for integration is a moral one with political overtones: the idea that two separate "nations" cannot continue to exist in America without serious repercussions. Though it might be possible to improve the results of disadvantaged students by providing compensatory education, though there are growing demands for black-controlled schools, and though the research results on desegregation have been contradictory, the move toward desegregation (and then integration) is morally and legally right, and it should be a part of our national policy.

ADMINISTRATIVE DECENTRALIZATION AND COMMUNITY INVOLVEMENT

Increasing pressure from the minority community, compounded by increasing reform pressure from educators, has played a part in forcing school authorities in many large school systems to decentralize and increase community involvement in the schools. What has emerged are the following administrative-community alternatives for governing metropolitan schools: (1) administrative decentralization, (2) community participation, and (3) community involvement, with either participation or control usually accompanying decentralization; the categories are not mutually exclusive.

Administrative decentralization is a process whereby the school system is divided into smaller units; the locus of power and authority remains with a single central administration and board of education. Although decentralization need not lead to increased community involvement, this often happens along the decentralized school boundaries. *Community participation* connotes the formation of advisory communities or groups beyond the usual parent-teacher associations. The committees that are formed may operate at various levels within the system — the local school, decentralized unit, or central level. The main function of these groups is to make recommendations (not policy) and to serve as a liaison between the schools and community. *Community control* implies a legal provision for an elected local school board. Decision-making authority and power are to be shared between the local and central school boards, and some of the powers of the professionals and central school board members are usually abridged and transferred to community groups.[75]

The three alternative models can be collapsed into two options: administrative decentralization with community participation v. administrative decentralization with community control. Most educators advocate the first option because their decision-making influence remains relatively intact. However, an increasing number of liberal and minority spokesmen favor the second option as a means for transferring power to the community, at least to people who claim to represent the community.

In reality there is little controversy over decentralization per se, because most people, including the defenders and critics of the system, accept this organizational model. The professional educators see a need for it in terms of reducing school bureaucracy and accept it because it allows them to retain power; the critics accept it because they view it as a first step toward community control. The controversy concerns community control: which group — the professional educators or community groups — will have power and authority to run the schools. The main concern is not limited to education, which is commonly emphasized in the literature on community control, but extends to politics and related issues of self-interest, group ideology, and jobs.

---

[75] Allan C. Ornstein, *Metropolitan Schools: Administrative Decentralization* v. *Community Control* (Metuchen, N.J.: Scarecrow Press, 1974); Allan C. Ornstein, "School Decentralization: Descriptions of Selected Systems," *National Association of Secondary School Principals Bulletin*, March 1975, pp. 24–33.

Decentralization of the School Systems

Table 10.4 reports the results of surveys of the decentralization plans of 69 or 90 percent of U.S. school districts (or systems) with 50,000 or more students. The districts are listed according to student enrollment, with the largest one first. At the time of the study (1973), 42 school districts had decentralized and 8 were considering it. Larger school systems had been

Table 10.4 / Administrative Decentralization Plans of School Districts Enrolling 50,000 or More Students, 1973–74

School District (or System)	Enrollment 1973–74	Status of Decentralization	Date	Units
New York, N.Y.	1,200,000	Decentralized	1969[a]	32 community districts
Los Angeles, Calif.	621,000	Decentralized	1971[a]	12 areas
Chicago, Ill.	558,000	Decentralized	1968[a]	3 areas; 27 districts
Philadelphia, Pa.	290,000	Decentralized	1968[a]	8 districts[b]
Detroit, Mich.	277,500	Decentralized	1971[a]	8 regions
Dade County, Fla.	240,000	Decentralized	1965[a]	6 areas
Houston, Tex.	225,000	Decentralized	1971	6 areas
Baltimore, Md.	190,500	Considering decentralization[c]		
Hawaii, state	181,500	No plans		
Prince George's County, Md.	162,500	Decentralized	n.d.	3 areas
Dallas, Tex.	155,000	Considering decentralization[c]		
District of Columbia	140,000	Considering decentralization[c]		
Memphis, Tenn.	139,000	Decentralized	1971	4 areas[b]
Fairfax County, Va.	136,000	Decentralized	1967	4 areas
Baltimore County, Md.	132,000	Decentralized	1965	5 areas
Milwaukee, Wis.	129,000	Decentralized	1967	14 clusters[b]
Broward County, Fla.	129,000	Decentralized	1968	5 areas and 1 complex
Montgomery County, Md.	126,500	Decentralized	1971	6 areas
San Diego, Calif.	125,000	No plans		
Duval County, Fla.	110,500	No plans		
New Orleans, La.	110,000*	Decentralized	1968	4 districts
Hillsborough County, Fla.	105,000*	No plans		
St. Louis, Mo	104,000	Decentralized	1970[a]	5 districts; 10 units
Indianapolis, Ind.	97,500	Decentralized	1969	3 regions; 10 areas[d]
Boston, Mass.	97,000	Decentralized	1966	6 areas[b]
Jefferson County, Ky.	96,500	No plans		
Atlanta, Ga.	96,000	Decentralized	1956	5 areas
Denver, Colo.	95,000	Decentralized	n.d.	9 areas[b]
Pinnellas County, Fla.	88,000	Considering decentralization[c]		
Fort Worth, Tex.	86,000	No plans		
Orange County, Fla.	86,000	Considering decentralization[c]		
Nashville-Davidson County, Tenn.	85,000	Decentralized	1966	3 districts
Albuquerque, N.M.	85,000	Decentralized	1969	3 areas

Table 10.4 (Continued)

School District (or System)	Enrollment 1973–74	Status of Decentralization	Date	Units
San Francisco, Calif.	80,500	Decentralized	1971	7 zones[d]
Charlotte-Mecklenburg, N.C.	80,000	Considering decentralization[c]		
Cincinnati, Ohio	79,000	Decentralized	1973	4 elementary districts; 2 secondary districts
Anne Arundel City, Md.	77,000	Decentralized	1973	4 areas
Clark County, Nev.	76,000	No plans[e]		
Seattle, Wash.	74,000	Decentralized	1970	2 regions; 12 areas
Jefferson County, Colo.	74,000	Decentralized	1971	9 areas[b]
San Antonio, Tex.	73,500	Decentralized	1969	3 areas
Newark, N.J.	73,000*	No plans		
Pittsburgh, Pa.	70,000	Decentralized	1970	3 areas
Tulsa, Okla.	70,000	No plans		
Portland, Ore.	69,000	Decentralized	1970	3 areas
Buffalo, N.Y.	68,000	Considering decentralization[c]		
Palm Beach County, Fla.	68,000	Decentralized	1969	4 areas
Kansas City, Mo.	68,000	Considering decentralization[c]		
East Baton Rouge, La.	67,500	No plans		
Mobile, Ala.	66,000	No plans		
Brevard County, Fla.	63,000	Decentralized	1969	3 areas
Omaha, Nebr.	62,500	No plans		
El Paso, Tex.	62,500	Decentralized	1972	3 areas
Granite, Utah	62,000	Decentralized	1971	3 complexes
Minneapolis, Minn.	61,500	Decentralized	1967	1 area; 2 pyramids [b, f]
Oklahoma City, Okla.	60,500	No plans		
Oakland, Calif.	60,000	Decentralized	1971	3 regions
Greenville County, S.C.	57,500	Decentralized	1972	4 areas and 1 experimental area
Wichita, Kans.	57,000	No plans		
Jefferson County, Ala.	57,000	No plans		
Austin, Tex.	56,000	Decentralized	n.d.	11 clusters[b]
Fresno, Calif.	56,000	Decentralized	1973	6 areas
Polk County, Fla.	55,000	Decentralized	n.d.	4 areas
San Juan, Calif.	54,000	No plans		
Akron, Ohio	54,000	No plans		
Dayton, Ohio	53,000	Decentralized	1971	3 units
Kanawha County, W.Va.	52,000	No plans		
Garden Grove, Calif.	51,500	Decentralized	1970	3 areas
Norfolk, Va.	51,000	No plans		

[a] The school district has decentralized in stages with the specific year representing the latest major administrative-community changes.

[b] Based on feeder schools to a high school.

[c] Considering decentralization: Baltimore considering 6–9 areas; Dallas, undetermined; District of Columbia, undetermined; Pinnellas County considering 3–4 areas; Orange County, undetermined; Charlotte-Mecklenburg, undetermined; Buffalo considering 5 districts; Kansas City, Mo., undetermined.

[d] Decentralization limited to elementary schools.

[e] Moved from decentralization and returned to centralization.

[f] Decentralization is mainly limited to inner-city schools.

* Denotes student enrollment figures based on 1972–73 student enrollments.

Source: Allan C. Ornstein, "Administrative/Community Organization of Metropolitan Schools," *Phi Delta Kappan,* June 1973, pp. 670–71.

decentralized more than smaller ones; 19 out of 23 (83 percent) of the school districts enrolling 100,000 or more students had decentralized or were considering it, while 31 out of 46 (68 percent) of school districts enrolling between 50,000 and 100,000 students were in this category.

The overwhelming majority of the school systems had started the decentralization process in or after 1967. Even the larger districts (New York, Los Angeles, Chicago, Philadelphia, Detroit, Dade County (Florida), and St. Louis) had implemented a major decentralization plan since 1967. Eight school districts (Philadelphia, Memphis, Milwaukee, Boston, Denver, Jefferson County (Colorado), Minneapolis, and Austin) reported decentralization based on attendance feeder patterns where students go from elementary and/or junior high school or middle school to senior high school.

Two school systems (Indianapolis and San Francisco) had decentralized only the elementary schools, and one school system (Minneapolis) had decentralized only the inner-city schools. In addition, the Cincinnati schools decentralized into separate elementary school districts and secondary school districts. The decentralized units varied, using such terms as districts, areas, zones, regions, complexes, units, and pyramids, with the first two (districts and areas) combined being used in about 80 of the cases. In four cases (Chicago, St. Louis, Seattle, and Minneapolis), the decentralized unit was subdivided into smaller units. (Since the survey, Chicago has eliminated one of its administrative layers — the three areas — to save money.) The number of decentralized units varied from as little as one area and two pyramids in Minneapolis to as many as 32 community districts in New York City, with three decentralized units as the most frequent organization plan (in 14 school systems) and four decentralized units as the second most frequent (in 8 school systems). Most frequently the number of students per decentralized unit was between 15,000 and 25,000, with a range from 2,500 to 8,500 in Milwaukee to 154,000 to 216,000 in Chicago.

In a supplementary survey, the major purposes for administrative decentralization were reported as being to: (1) reduce the administrative span of control, (2) provide greater staff sensitivity to local populations, (3) enhance school-community relations, (4) provide greater articulation and continuity in the K-12 programs, (5) provide more efficient maintenance and support of the school unit, and (6) reduce bureaucratic overlap and waste.[76]

Oddly enough, sufficient evidence was not found to support the generalizations about administrative decentralization or any concurrent

[76] Ornstein, *Metropolitan Schools.*

plans for community involvement. The reasons generally were based on a combination of intuition, logic, and polemics from the literature, and pressure to do something which suggests reform. Very few of the school systems indicated an evaluative procedure for their new organizational models or pointed out the need for pilot testing some of the related assumptions, goals, and recommendations.

Problems related to administrative decentralization are usually ignored by the advocates of this organizational model. Although it is often stated that decentralization will lead to greater innovation and flexibility, it may actually promote traditionally conservative and highly dependent systems. In fact, the tendency is for the most innovative school systems to be those that are consolidating their resources or localities, thereby broadening the scope and range of their activities. Nor does it seem that decentralization eliminates bureaucracy, inefficiency, and unnecessary costs. On the contrary, it establishes another layer of bureaucracy which sometimes performs the same dull administrative chores that are presently centralized — only with greater duplication and cost.[77] It is also said that smaller units can be reformed more easily than larger units; while this may be true in a few cases, the opposite is the general rule. Reform measures are usually achieved when a system is able to influence state or national levels of government, so coordinated and centralized efforts give school reforms greater impact. Whatever progress can be made locally usually depends on the moral and political sustenance of the central school system, as well as centralized state and federal governments and big business.[78]

Community Control v. Participation

New York City and Detroit differ from other large school systems in that administrative decentralization has led to community control plans in which elected school boards function in conjunction with the central school board. Far more frequently, administrative decentralization has brought the appointment of advisory committees at the level of the neighborhood school, decentralized unit, or central board. These committees are usually appointed by school officials; in only a few cases are they elected by the community. When guidelines are established, the school boards usually retain their authority and expectations that the advisory committees will abide by the rules and regulations of the central system. In many instances, it is further specified that they cannot act as

---

[77] Richard Saxe, *School-Community Interaction* (Berkeley, Ca.: McCutchan Publishing Corp., 1975); Albert Shanker, "Cult of Localism," in P. A. Sexton (ed.), *School Policy and Issues in a Changing Society* (Boston: Allyn & Bacon, 1971), pp. 213-24.

[78] Amitai Etzioni, "The Fallacy of Decentralization," *Nation*, August 5, 1969, pp. 145-47.

pressure groups or disturb the operation of the schools and that rules of procedure can be amended at any time by the boards. Thus the power and authority of the school boards are reaffirmed by keeping the community groups participatory or advisory in nature.

In the main, school officials have been willing to encourage community participation, and this trend is increasing across the country.[79] Based on a survey of hundreds of examples of community participation, Mary Stanwick has identified ten general areas in which citizen groups function in concert with school officials, at either the decentralized level (if there is one) or central level.[80] These groups help to: (1) identify goals, priorities, and needs, (2) set budget priorities, (3) select and evaluate principals, (4) select and evaluate teachers, (5) evaluate and develop curricula, (6) evaluate or implement extracurricular programs, (7) improve community support for schools, (8) investigate student or parent problems and complaints, (9) raise money for schools, and (10) recruit volunteers for schools, or serve as volunteers themselves.

However, school officials have been generally reluctant to transfer power to community groups; moreover, many school systems, such as Los Angeles, Philadelphia, and Portland, have clearly stated in policy reports that community control has the potential for more harm than good. Although community control has the appeal of a viable alternative for involving the community in the educational process, it seems to bring out the worst in people as they struggle for power or control. The purpose is to find some way in which schools can be improved, but the evidence seems to indicate that disruptions and radical politics of small local groups have been the order of the day in New York City and Detroit.[81]

Traditionally, school administrators have run the schools. The only pressure groups to successfully challenge the authority and power of administrative groups have been teacher organizations. Now community

---

[79] See Don Davies (ed.), *Schools Where Parents Make A Difference* (Boston: Institute for Responsive Education, 1976). The editor escorts the reader across the country where parental and community participation has recently increased, from rural Wayne County, W.Va., to the Indian reservations in New Mexico and Montana, to the small towns of Cape Cod, Mass., and East Palo Alto, Ca.

[80] Mary E. Stanwick, *Patterns of Participation* (Boston: Institute for Responsive Education, 1975).

[81] See Bernard Bard "The Battle for School Jobs: New York's Newest Agony," *Phi Delta Kappan,* May 1972, pp. 555-58; Sandra Feldman, *The Burden of Blame-Placing* (New York: United Federation of Teachers, 1969); Nathan Glazer, "For White and Black, Community Control Is the Issue," *New York Times Magazine,* April 27, 1969, pp. 36-37 ff.; William R. Grant, "Community Control vs. School Integration—the Case of Detroit," *United Teacher Magazine,* November 7, 1971, pp. 1-4; Robert F. Lyke, "Political Issues in School Decentralization," in M. Kirst (ed.), *The Politics of Education at the Local, State, and Federal Levels* (Berkeley, Ca.: McCutchan Publication Corp., 1970), pp. 111-32; Ornstein, *Metropolitan Schools.*

Table 10.5 / Superintendents' Attitudes toward Community Participation and Control in Four Areas of School Policy

Variable	$\overline{X}$	2-Tail Probability
Curriculum[a]		
Participation	11.651 ⎱	.001
Control............................	14.604 ⎰	
Student Policy		
Participation	13.521 ⎱	.001
Control............................	16.062 ⎰	
Finances		
Participation	10.746 ⎱	.001
Control............................	13.057 ⎰	
Personnel		
Participation	15.540 ⎱	.001
Control............................	17.303 ⎰	
Total		
Advisement	51.325 ⎱	.001
Control............................	60.818 ⎰	

Note: The higher the mean score, the less positive the attitude toward involvement by community members in school issues.

Source: Harriet Talmage and Allan C. Ornstein, "School Superintendents' Attitudes toward Community Participation and Control," Educational Research Quarterly, Summer 1976, p. 42.

groups, or people claiming to represent the community, are making inroads, not only in New York City and Detroit but in selected communities (usually in the inner city) of some big cities such as Boston, Buffalo, Milwaukee, and New Haven, Connecticut.[82] It is to be expected, of course, that those who presently run the schools would hold more negative views toward community control than toward community participation, since control connotes a shift in power from the professionals to the people, whereas participation suggests a status quo in the present power structure.

In a recent survey of superintendents in school systems of 15,000 or more students (399 systems) throughout the United States, significant differences (.001 level) in attitudes were evidenced toward community participation, defined as input related to advising on school policy, and community control, defined as related to determining school policy (Table 10.5). Superintendents were more favorable in their attitudes toward community participation, inasmuch as control entailed the forfeiture of the superintendents' perceived or actual decision-making power. Further, their attitudes about community involvement differed in four areas of school management: curriculum, student affairs, school finances, and personnel; some of these areas are traditionally regarded as shared responsibilities and others as central to the superintendents' power. The

---

[82] See Davies, Schools Where Parents Make a Difference; Marilyn Gittel, "Critique of Citizen Participation in Education," Journal of Education, February 1977, pp. 7–22.

superintendents looked more favorably on community participation in school finances than in the other three management areas, and were least favorably disposed to community advice on personnel matters. In this connection, many communities have traditionally had varying levels of involvement on local tax questions, per-pupil expenditures, new construction, and school repairs. Recently, many state and federal guidelines for proposals to obtain funds have insisted on community participation in the proposal development stage. On the other hand, personnel matters have been zealously guarded by school administrators, who are protective of their rights to recruit new faculty and to determine fitness (evaluation), promotion, and tenure.

Community Control, Pros and Cons

The issues involving community control are more emotional and more threatening to most teachers and school administrators than community participation, as the issues listed in Table 10.6 demonstrate. The first column gives arguments against community control and the second presents the responses of proponents of the concept. The procedure is reversed in the second part; proponents of community control outline their reasons, and critics respond in the opposite column.

The crux of the community control matter lies in political power and economic self-interest: Who will control the schools? Who will get the high-paying jobs? Spin-off problems concerning the hiring and firing of personnel on the basis of race and the question of who actually represents the community have erupted. Because the concept of black power has been an underpinning of community control, many white teachers and ad-

Table 10.6 / A Debate Between the Critics and Proponents of Community Control

PART I	
Arguments against by Critics	*Responses by Proponents*
1. Community control will impede integration.	a. Integration connotes white assimilation. b. The schools in most cities are more segregated now than prior to the Supreme Court's *Brown* decision in 1954. c. Most whites and now many blacks do not want to integrate.
2. Community control will balkanize the cities.	a. Most cities are already balkanized.
3. Community control is a scheme for alleviating pressure from the black community.	a. The parents are motivated to action because their children are failing in school. b. They will be motivated to seek high-quality education for their children.

Table 10.6 (Continued)

4. Parents and community residents (especially from low-income areas) are inexperienced and inept in dealing with complex educational issues.	a. As for inexperience, train the incoming local school board members. b. As for ineptness, this is insulting. How do we know this, if these people have not had the opportunity to run the schools?
5. Community control will destroy the merit system.	a. Competitive examinations are white oriented. b. There is no proof that those who pass the examinations are "fit and qualified" for their jobs. c. Maintain the list of eligibles and permit the local school boards to select personnel from the list.
6. Community control will weaken the teacher's union.	a. It is already splintered by political and racial issues in most cities. b. The union is already weakened, not by community control, but by depleted school budgets, the citizens' revolt against higher taxes, and the surplus of teachers.
7. Community control is a distraction from the greater need for money to educate children, especially ghetto children.	a. This is only one method of reform. b. We can implement community control and still seek increased finances.
8. Community control will enhance black racism.	a. What about 400 years of white racism? b. Black children need an education that will help them cope with white discrimination.
9. Community control will lead to rejection of white participation.	a. Whites who are sensitive to the needs and interests of black children will be encouraged to remain in their schools.

PART II

Arguments for by Proponents	*Responses by Critics*
1. Community control will make teachers and administrators accountable to the people.	a. It will lead to vigilante groups (as in the case of New York City and Detroit). b. It is questionable if anyone can objectively assess the performance and even the output of teachers and administrators, much less parents and community representatives, since the experts in the field of testing and evaluation find it difficult if not impossible to evaluate teachers and administrators with reliability and validity. c. Many community representatives have already reached the conclusion that professional educators are the only ones responsible for student failure; other variables such as the home, community, and the students themselves must be taken into consideration.
2. Community control will lead to educational innovation.	a. The local school boards will concentrate their interests on politics and issues of self-interest and ideology. b. Innovation is based on pilot testing and evaluating programs; community control has not been sufficiently pilot-tested or evaluated.

Table 10.6 (Continued)

3. Community control will lead to greater parental and public participation.	a. The majority of the people, including parents, are indifferent to educational issues—or at least do not participate in school meetings or vote on educational issues. b. Politically oriented groups, ranging from black militants to white segregationists, will gain control of the schools for their own purposes (as in the cases of New York City and Detroit).
4. Community control will enable local boards to hire qualified principals and superintendents (on the basis that they can relate to ghetto children and serve as models to emulate).	a. This will lead to increased ethnic and racial favoritism in appointing and promoting administrators (a pattern already evident in city school systems).
5. Community control will enhance flexible hiring and promotion practices and attract teachers and administrators with more initiative and innovative capacity.	a. "Flexibility" connotes that competitive performance, experience, and objective tests can be replaced by patronage, nepotism, and pork-barrel practices. b. Initiative and innovation are difficult to define; they mean different things to different people. For some they are euphemisms for reverse discrimination.
6. Community control will raise student achievement.	a. There is no proof that this will happen. We should pilot-test this assumption before mass changes are implemented. What happens if achievement is the same or even declines with community control? b. There is no evidence that black teachers and administrators can do a better job in raising achievement among black students. Check the record in school systems where there is a majority of black teachers and administrators.(e.g., southern black schools; Washington, D.C.; Philadelphia; St. Louis; Baltimore; Gary; Newark; etc.).
7. Community control will promote self-government for blacks, as well as for other minorities.	a. It is a return to the myth of "separate but equal." b. It will foster white ethnicity and backlash. c. Inherent in this concept is the surrender of the suburbs to white domination while blacks obtain control of the ghetto—a ghetto depleted in finances and saddled with decay, drug addiction, violence, crime, traffic congestion, pollution, overpopulation, etc.
8. Community control will lead to educational reform.	a. It thwarts future possibilities for school desegregation, which should be the immediate goal of educational reform. b. Despite the present retrenchment in federal government, it is recognized as the only institution with the strength, expertise, and financial resources to reform school and society. (In the past, virtually all major social reform—education, welfare, housing, health services—have been initiated by the federal government.)

Source: Ornstein, "Administrative/Community Organization of Metropolitan Schools," pp. 672–73.

ministrators have been forced out of black-controlled schools.[83] Charles Billings says, the "conflict over community control . . . of schools represents nothing more or less than a struggle for power between black and whites."[84] Stokely Carmichael and Charles Hamilton maintain that blacks must gain "control of the public schools in their community: hiring and firing . . . determination of standards." They argue that "it is crucial that race be taken into account in determining policy," and claim that this is not reverse racism but "a method of emphasizing race in a positive way."[85]

Confrontations between black moderates and militants for community control frequently are based on the improvement of schools only in name.[86] Local administration units have not been made participatory; in New York City, voter turnout for the first two community school board elections was 15 and 11 percent. Often those elected to local boards have not been well enough informed to function effectively, and they have exercised their power to secure personal gains and the employment of friends and relatives.[87] While community control does lessen the heat from the community, it seems to be a strategy for accommodating to the demands of a relatively small number of militant groups in the hope of preventing an "explosion." It serves as a way to satisfy black and more recent Latino demands for change without having to invest enormous resources in schools, jobs, and housing.[88]

Decentralization, Community Control, and Student Achievement

A few years ago, Mario Fantini, one of the major proponents of administrative decentralization and community control, criticized those who urged caution because there was a lack of empirical evidence. He wrote:

The first question [of the skeptic] usually is: What evidence is there that neighborhood control of urban schools improves student achievement? The answer

---

[83] Bard, "The Battle for School Jobs"; Glazer, "For White and Black, Community Control Is the Issue"; Shanker, "Cult of Localism."

[84] Charles E. Billings, "Community Control of the School and the Quest for Power," *Phi Delta Kappan*, January 1972, p. 277.

[85] Stokely Carmichael and Charles V. Hamilton, *Black Power* (New York: Random House, 1967), p. 166.

[86] Sandra Feldman, *Decentralization and the City Schools* (New York: League of Industrial Democracy, 1968); Martin Mayer, *The Teachers Strike: New York* (New York: Harper & Row, 1968); Daniel P. Moynihan, *Maximum Feasible Misunderstanding* (New York: Free Press, 1969); Ornstein, *Urban Education* (Columbus, Ohio: Merrill, 1972).

[87] Bard, "Battle for School Jobs"; Virgil A. Clift, "Organizing Metropolitan Schools," in A. C. Ornstein and S. I. Miller (eds.), *Policy Issues in Education* (Boston: D. C. Heath & Co., 1976), pp. 43–57; Mayer, *The Teachers' Strike;* Saxe, *School-Community Interaction.*

[88] Shanker, "Cult of Localism"; Theodore R. Sizer, "Report Analysis," *Harvard Educational Review*, Winter 1968, pp. 176–84.

is that if there is no evidence it is because there really are no community controlled urban public schools. . . . However, what we do have ample evidence of is the massive failure that the standard, centrally controlled urban school has produced. It is ironic, therefore, that those in control of a failing system should ask others offering alternatives to demand results before there has been any chance for full implementation.[89]

Terry Clark reviewed current books on administrative decentralization, using the term interchangeably with community control, and concluded:

What a considerable portion of the literature on decentralization to date amounts to is special pleading for a particular solution. . . . Very little attempt is made to develop ideas coherent enough to warrant the term "theory," and the casual use of favorable examples seldom justifies the label of empirical research. Where knowledge is incomplete but problems immediate . . . one can still expect generalizing intellectuals and amateur politicans to come forth with solutions.

[D]ecentralization . . . may ameliorate some pressing problems. Such efforts can serve as useful vehicles for social as well as social-scientific experimentation. But unless there is more systematic social-scientific analysis of these efforts than we have generally had to date, we may never understand their many consequences.[90]

These two statements clearly reflect the position differences between the reformer and the social scientist–researcher. The former may seek change for the sake of change, while the latter holds out for evidence before implementation.

The fallacy of many reform educators is that their ideas are often based on "bandwagon wisdom." They urge the adoption of untested programs, using fashionable terms and clichés and expecting others to accept their ideas on faith. Many reformers would rather think up new programs than try to implement them.

Not only has the pace of school reform been slow, but it is becoming increasingly questionable whether present plans for reform of the schools will help them solve any of the major problems of society. While the failure of ghetto schooling has been demonstrated, there is no evidence that administrative decentralization or community control will reform the schools. Without quality research, reform efforts are based at best on bandwagon wisdom and at worst on political ideology. Claims based on unsupported evidence, intuition, and logic, and testimonials from the advocates of change and ideologies can always be found. If there is no adequate research on the effects of decentralization and community control on student achievement, opponents' criticisms will have little effect. Moreover, opponents of untested reform strategies are put on the defensive, criticized for resisting change and branded as caretakers of the Establishment and the status quo.

[89] Mario D. Fantini, *Community Control and the Urban School* (Washington, D.C.: National Education Association, 1970), p. 52.

[90] Terry Clark, "On Decentralization," *Polity*, Summer 1970, pp. 509, 514.

This is what happened in Ocean Hill–Brownsville, New York. The advocates of community control claimed favorable changes: "Ocean Hill had already achieved academic success"; innovative methods had "succeeded in raising the reading levels of many children in the districts in a remarkably short time"; within two years "every youngster in the school system [would] be classified as a reader." The opponents could only note that there were no available statistical data, since "it was the only district in the city which had not participated in the standardized city-wide reading tests."[91] Eventual comparison of reading scores showed the experiment to be a failure; nevertheless, the New York City school system had been pressured into a citywide policy which provided for a strong measure of community control.

If a school system initiates an across-the-board-change such as community control, or almost any other reform measure, without evidence that it will have positive effects on learning, the change may be not only educationally unsound and irresponsible; it may also indicate that education is not the real issue. Many of the issues related to community control are political and ideological.

Kenneth Clark, one of the original advocates of decentralization and community control in New York, now says that the evidence does not add up to any indication that these changes are making "for a better break for our children in schools." Those involved in decentralization and community control "have forgotten what the purpose was. The purpose was not a struggle for power or control." He claims that if we find we are "wasting our time and people are going to squabble and fight and . . . neglect the children, then we [should] try to find other ways in which the children will be given priority."[92] The problem is that it is too late; community control in New York City is a fact, and it is not going to go away, regardless of how the original advocates may feel. They should have realized the potential for conflict; they should not have been so naive. Elsewhere Clark reports that "school decentralization has been a disastrous experience in which the basic issue, teaching children, has been substituted by selfish forces. . . . These forces include the radical politics of small local groups."[93] How could anyone argue for decentralization and community control without taking into account the political implications? Any group that gains power is unwilling to surrender it. Indeed, the process of schooling is largely political—who makes what decisions—and linked to economic considerations—who gets what jobs, now and in the

---

[91] Diane Ravitch, "Community Control Revisited," *Commentary*, February 1972, pp. 71–72.

[92] Kenneth B. Clark, news article in *The New York Times* (May 8, 1973), pp. 1, 26.

[93] Kenneth B. Clark, news article in *The New York Times* (December 3, 1972), p. 7.

future. As John Goodlad says, "Schooling is conducted within a framework of power and struggle for power. It is no more protected from abuse of power than are other political enterprises."[93a]

The stakes are high, of course, especially for the proponents of change and for those who stand to gain (or lose) jobs. Many advocates of community control would like to limit evaluation or at least control it so that the "findings" are known before the report is written. Lack of comparable data and concrete evidence tends to work in favor of those who end up controlling the new policies and making decisions on who is to be held accountable and what criteria are to be used to determine accountability. As Donald Campbell writes, "Given the inherent difficulty of making significant improvements . . . and given the discrepancy between promise and possibility . . . there is safety under the cloak of ignorance. . . . If [a group] has committed itself in advance to the correctness and efficacy of its reforms, it cannot tolerate learning of failure."[94] Similarly, Peter Rossi points out that those who advocate new policies are often against research and evaluation because they "might find that effects are negligible or nonexistent.[95]

In point of fact, it seems likely that community control may have little or no effect on student achievement because there are so many variables associated with school learning over which the schools have little control. Before adopting any plan for change, there must be evidence that it works. From the educator's viewpoint, this is especially important in dealing with school policy and matters that can threaten the job security of teachers and administrators. This may seem a selfish concern to some readers, but we are dealing not only with students but also with those who have devoted their careers to teaching them.

In the past, the racial climate of large city schools made it difficult for social scientists to conduct valid research on decentralization and community control. Very little empirical data are available on the effects of these concepts, and the data that are available tend to be negative in terms of student achievement.[96] There is a wealth of expository literature on these two organizational strategies, but the content is highly intuitive,

---

[93a] John I. Goodlad, "What Educational Decisions by Whom?" *Science Teacher*, (May, 1971), p. 16.

[94] Donald T. Campbell, "Reforms as Experiments," in C. F. Weiss (ed.), *Evaluating Action Programs* (Boston: Allyn & Bacon, 1972), p. 188.

[95] Rossi, "Boobytraps and Pitfalls," p. 227.

[96] See George R. La Noue, "Politics of School Decentralization: Methodological Considerations," paper presented at the annual conference of the American Educational Research Association, New York, February 1971; Allan C. Ornstein, "Research on Decentralization," *Phi Delta Kappan*, May 1973, pp. 610-14; Diane Ravitch, *The Great School Wars* (New York: Basic Books, 1975); Saxe, *School-Community Interaction.*

subjective, and presented in terms of a debate or a specific position for or against. Although data are available to suggest that community participation in the traditional sense of involving parents in learning activities has beneficial effects on student learning,[97] this should not be equated with the effects on community control or even community participation as it is presently evolving.

What kind of research in urban schools is feasible and potentially useful? If pilot programs were implemented with randomized and controlled comparisons and valid pretests and posttests, data would be forthcoming to tentatively validate or invalidate hypotheses. The findings should be replicated in similar settings, because it is misleading to take the results of one or a few experiments as conclusive evidence. There are no totally typical cities, no entirely typical communities, no typical decentralization plans, no typical community control plans. Longitudinal studies for five to ten years would supply a wealth of data, but because of politics and pressure we cannot wait that long; therefore this type of study might be conducted in conjunction with the case study approach, with tentative findings being disseminated every year. Not only ought we to conduct rigorous testing in the initial pilot program, but once it has been decided it is to be adopted as standardized practice throughout a system, we need to evaluate it experimentally in each of its stages.

The issues related to administrative decentralization, community control, and community participation have not been satisfactorily resolved by the various interest groups. Do the students and society really benefit? There is little research evidence that administrative decentralization or community involvement improves education, that the implementation of community participation or community control alone has positive effects, or that decentralization and community involvement combined have any effect at all. If no systematic response to these issues is provided by the proponents of the various administrative and community strategies they are operating on unsupported assertions or questionable assumptions, and many of their conclusions, either stated or implied, are unjustified.

The lack of data on administrative "solutions" (decentralization, community control, even community participation) means there are more slogans than carefully worked-out concepts with consequences understood

---

[97] See Richard A. Cloward and James A. Jones, "Social Class: Educational Attitudes and Participation," in A. H. Passow (ed.), *Education in Depressed Areas* (New York: Teachers College Press, Columbia University, 1963), pp. 190–216; Mario D. Fantini, *The People and Their Schools: Community Participation* (Bloomington, Ind.: Phi Delta Kappa Educational Foundation, 1975); Edmund W. Gordon and Doxey A. Wilkerson, *Compensatory Education for the Disadvantaged* (New York: College Entrance Examinations Board, 1966); Carol Lopate et al., "Decentralization and Community Participation in Public Education," *Review of Educational Research*, February 1970, pp. 135–50.

and accounted for. We assume that the "community" voice is the most vocal and articulated, and we have yet to hear from the majority of silent parents who have their own aspirations for their children and their own ideas about how the school should fulfill them. Once adopted on a systemwide basis, these plans would be very difficult to reverse in large school systems, especially where ideology and racial conflict are apparent. Indeed, we need a partnership between practitioners and researchers, among the various interest groups, and especially between blacks and whites, if a breakthrough is to be made to a higher level of mutual understanding and quality education for children and youth.

CONCLUSIONS

Underlying the various alternatives for school reform — compensatory education, desegregation and integration, administrative decentralization and community involvement — is the assumption that they will lead to improved education and increased levels of student achievement. As of the present, the assumption has not been borne out by the research. While there is available literature about the need and presumed effectiveness of these reform alternatives, student achievement — probably the most important dependent variable — is the most difficult to determine. Given the numerous variables that impact on learning, especially the problems related to poverty and discrimination, we cannot anticipate noticeable improvements due to any particular school model. However, school achievement constitutes only one of several goals behind these alternatives; there are social, moral, political, economic, and racial dimensions to consider; in short, social policy issues that affect schools affect the larger dimensions of society.

ACTIVITIES

1. Arrange a debate among members of the class concerning the advantages and disadvantages of compensatory education, desegregation, and administrative decentralization.
2. Visit a school heavily funded with compensatory money and speak to as many teachers and administrators as possible. Report to the class about the problems and prospects associated with these programs.
3. Visit an integrated school and speak with as many teachers and administrators as possible. Report to the class about the problems and prospects associated with integration at that school.
4. Visit a school which is part of a school system which has decentralized and has increased citizenry involvement and speak to as many teachers and administrators as possible. Report to the class about the problems and prospects associated with these plans.

5. Invite two guest speakers to class who represent different or opposing views concerning compensatory education, desegregation, and administrative decentralization.

DISCUSSION QUESTIONS

1. What are some of the problems involved with evaluating compensatory education, desegregation, and administrative decentralization?
2. What evidence is there that compensatory education has failed? Is succeeding?
3. What evidence is there that desegregation has failed? Is succeeding?
4. Why might decentralization impede desegregation?
5. What are the advantages and disadvantages of community participation and community control?

SUGGESTED FOR FURTHER READING

Coleman, James S., Kelley, Sara D., and Moore, John. *Trends in School Desegregation, 1968–1973*. Washington, D.C.: Urban Institute, 1975.

Davies, Don (ed.). *Schools Where Parents Make a Difference*. Boston: Institute for Responsive Education, 1976.

Fantini, Mario, Gittell, Marilyn, and Magat, Richard. *Community Control and the Urban School*. New York: Frederick A. Praeger, 1970.

Levine, Daniel U., and Havighurst, Robert J. (eds.). *The Future of Big-City Schools*. Berkeley, Ca.: McCutchan Publishing Corp., 1977.

Lightfoot, Alfred. *Urban Education in Social Perspective*. Chicago: Rand McNally & Co., 1978.

McLaughlin, Milbrey W. *Evaluation and Reform: The Elementary and Secondary Act of 1965/Title I*. Rand Educational Policy Study. Cambridge, Mass.: Ballinger Publishing Co., 1975.

Ornstein, Allan C., Levine, Daniel U., and Wilkerson, Doxey A. *Reforming Metropolitan Schools*. Pacific Palisades, Ca.: Goodyear Publishing Co., 1975.

Passow, A. Harry (ed.). *Urban Education in the 1970s*. New York: Teachers College Press, Columbia University, 1971.

St. John, Nancy. *School Desegregation: Outcomes for Children*. New York: John Wiley & Sons, 1975.

Saxe, Richard A. *School-Community Interaction*. Berkeley, Ca.: McCutchan Publishing Corp., 1975.

CHAPTER 11

GOVERNMENT AND
SCHOOLS

A national system of education in this country does not exist in the same sense that there is one in France, England, Germany, Russia, China, or the Latin American countries. Education is considered a state function; we have 50 different state systems and many differences among local school systems in the same state. In this chapter we will examine the various governmental levels — federal, state and local — and how they impact on the schools, both public and nonpublic. We will also discuss our method for financing schools, with primary attention to federal, state, and local roles.

FEDERAL RESPONSIBILITIES

The Constitution makes no mention of public education, but the Tenth Amendment reserved to the states the powers not delegated to the United States or the federal government or prohibited to the states by the Constitution. Under this interpretation of the Constitution, the subsequent acts of the states and the character of public education as a function of the states have been legally recognized. Federal recognition of the states' responsibility for education was clearly embodied in the Northwest Ordinances of 1785 and 1787. The Ordinance of 1785 reserved "lot No. 16 of every township for the maintenance of public schools within the said township." This marked the beginning of federal grants for public education, but grants for nonpublic or sectarian schools were deliberately excluded. Article 3 of the Ordinance of 1787 stated that "schools and the means of education shall be forever encouraged" by the states.

The Northwest Ordinances to Sputnik

The Northwest Ordinances represent the first instance of federal assistance to education. With these acts the federal government recognized its commitment to education and the autonomy of state and local schools, while assuring its responsibility for a public function of national interest. For the next 170 years, up to 1957, the federal government was cautious in lending assistance to the states for education of American students, in line with the majority belief that the federal government should have little to do with education, and that education was a state function. The most noted programs and procedures enacted by the federal government to support educational activities up to this period were:

1. *First Morrill Act, 1862.* Authorized public land grants to the states for the establishment and maintenance of agricultural and mechanical colleges.
2. *Smith-Hughes Act, 1917.* Provided for money grants for support of vocational education, home economics, and agricultural subjects.
3. *School Lunch Programs, 1933.* Provided assistance in school lunch programs, enlarged in 1936 with the use of surplus farm commodities.
4. *Civilian Conservation Corps, 1933.* Provided employment and vocational training for unemployed youth, as well as to conserve and develop natural resources.
5. *Lanham Act, 1941.* Provided aid for construction and maintenance of schools in impacted areas and in communities with greatly increased student populations.
6. *Occupational Rehabilitation Act, 1943.* Provided educational and other assistance to disabled veterans.
7. *Servicemen's Readjustment Act, 1944.* Better known as the GI bill, this act provided funds for the education of veterans.

During this period, the most dramatic increase in laws related to education took place during the Great Depression and then after World War II, to correspond with the return of veterans, the baby boom, and the Cold War.

Sputnik to the Present

The launching of Sputnik in the U.S.S.R. in 1957 resulted in increased pressure for better American schools and federal funding. This was surpassed by the domestic pressure of the civil rights movement and the War on Poverty in the early and middle 1960s, which resulted in massive funding for the education of disadvantaged groups. The era influenced many to demand that the federal government increase its role and responsibility in education in order to find solutions to contemporary problems. Between 1957 and 1965 federal funding doubled; during the next fiscal year, with the funding of several compensatory programs, it reached $6.8 billion. By 1975, federal funds had doubled again and it increased another 25 percent by 1977.[1] The major acts proposed during this period, from 1957 to 1977, were:

1. *National Defense Education Act (NDEA), 1958.* Provided assistance to state and local school systems for strengthening instruction in science, mathematics, foreign languages, and other critical subjects; funded numerous teacher training institutes, including those for teaching the disadvantaged; increased student loans and scholarships for higher education; and provided funds for educational technology and vocational and technical education.

2. *Manpower Development and Training Act, 1962.* Provided training in new and improved skills for unemployed youth and adults, with emphasis on ghetto areas.

3. *Civil Rights Act, 1964.* Provided special training of instructional staff to deal with problems of desegregation, and required non-discrimination in federally assisted programs.

4. *Economic Opportunity Act, 1964.* Provided grants for work-study and job-training programs for low-income youth; authorized support of community action programs, Head Start, Follow Through, Upward Bound, and Volunteers in Service to America (VISTA) programs.

5. *Elementary and Secondary Education Act (ESEA), 1965.* Combined five titles (increased to seven titles in 1968 and 1970), for spending and improving educational programs for the disadvantaged at all levels of education, from prekindergarten to higher education. Title I of ESEA represented the largest commitment, involving in the 1960s more than $1 billion per year and in the 1970s close to $2 billion per year, or nearly 50 percent of the total funds under the act.

6. *Higher Education Act, 1965.* Provided grants for colleges and universities in training and research, educational opportunity grants, student loans and scholarships, and teacher training programs.

---

[1] *Digest of Educational Statistics, 1974, 1975, 1976* (Washington, D.C.: U.S. Government Printing Office, 1975, 1976, 1977), Table 138, pp. 124–25; Table 141, pp. 150–51; Table 139, pp. 143–44.

Amended in 1968 to also assist disadvantaged students in college and again in 1977 to tighten student loans for higher education.

7. *Education Professions Development Act, 1967.* Amended the Higher Education Act of 1965 for the purpose of improving the quality of teaching to help meet critical shortages in selected areas.

8. *Drug Abuse Education Act, 1970.* Amended in 1972; provided for the development, demonstration, and evaluation of educational programs to meet drug abuse problems.

9. *Emergency School Aid Act, 1972.* Provided support to local schools in a variety of ways (e.g., new curriculum, remedial programs, in-service education) as long as funds contributed to decreasing racial isolation and to the alleviation of problems associated with the desegregation of schools.

10. *Family Educational Rights and Privacy Act, 1974.* This act, based on the Buckley Amendment, added new requirements in the keeping of student records, prescribing access of student information to students and parents and restricting the access of others to files without student or parent consent.

11. *Indian Self-Determination and Education Assistance, 1975.* Provided for increased participation of Indians in the establishment and conduct of their education programs and services.

12. *Career Education Incentive Act, 1977.* Provided funds to authorize career education programs in elementary and secondary schools, higher education institutions, and adult education centers.

In addition, several educational amendments from 1972 on were introduced to authorize new bureaus and commissions, including the National Institute of Education, state advisory councils on community colleges, the Bureau of Occupational and Adult Education, and the Office of Indian Education. Additional acts were passed to assist Indian education and education of the handicapped. Appropriations were also made to assist state and local agencies in implementing programs for (1) the use of the metric system; (2) gifted and talented children at preschool through secondary school levels; (3) medical education, vocational education, adult education, consumer education, sex education, bilingual education, and environmental education from elementary to college levels; (4) school desegregation involving students as well as staff; and (5) women's educational equity and affirmative action policies.

Federal assistance during this period and up to the present largely focused on providing assistance for poor and minority groups, thus extending equal educational opportunity. By far, ESEA funds represent the most comprehensive provision by the federal government to assist

Table 11.1 / Percentage of Total Revenues Received Annually for Public Elementary and Secondary Education from Government Sources, 1930–1985

Year	Governmental Level		
	Federal	State	Local
1930....................	0.4%	16.5%	83.2%
1940....................	1.8	30.3	68.0
1950....................	2.9	39.8	57.3
1960....................	4.4	39.1	56.5
1970....................	8.0	39.9	52.1
1980[a]....................	8.5	41.5	50.0
1985[a]....................	9.0	42.0	49.0

[a] Estimates by author.

Note: Figures do not add to 100% because of rounding.

Source: U.S. Bureau of the Census: *Statistical Abstract of the United States* (Washington, D.C.: U.S. Government Printing Office, 1971), p. 115.

Table 11.2 / Estimated Expenditures for Education by Government Sources, 1965–66, 1971–72, 1976–77 (in billions)

	1965–66	1971–72	1976–77
All Levels			
Total, public and nonpublic............	$45.2	$83.2	$131.1
Federal..........................	5.0	9.2	13.8
State............................	13.1	25.8	45.9
Local............................	15.1	26.7	37.4
All other........................	12.0	21.5	34.0
Elementary and secondary schools			
Total, public and nonpublic............	30.0	54.0	81.9
Federal..........................	2.1	4.6	6.4
State............................	9.6	18.0	31.0
Local............................	14.7	25.6	35.4
All other........................	3.6	5.8	9.1
Institutions of Higher Education			
Total, public and nonpublic............	15.2	29.2	49.2
Federal..........................	2.9	4.6	7.4
State............................	3.5	7.8	14.9
Local............................	0.4	1.1	2.0
All other........................	8.4	15.7	24.9

Source: Adapted from *Projections of Educational Statistics to 1985–86* (Washington, D.C.: U.S. Government Printing Office, 1977), Table 30, pp. 61–62.

disadvantaged groups, corresponding with other governmental efforts to meet the challenges of hunger, crime, housing, employment, and Medicaid for the disadvantaged. On a general level, the 20 years between 1957 and 1977 saw the enactment of an estimated 40 major acts geared to increasing federal assistance in education, compared to 30 major acts over a 170-year span between 1787 and 1957.[2] From 1975 to 1977 Congress

---

[2] *Digest of Educational Statistics, 1974; Digest of Educational Statistics, 1976* (Washington, D.C.: U.S. Government Printing Office, 1977).

amended more than 35 laws and bills involving education, making clear its intention to play an active role.[3]

The Increasing Role of the Federal Government

It may seem that power in education remains in the hands of the states and local districts, as it always has, because most revenues for education come from state and local sources (Tables 11.1 and 11.2). Since the early 19th century Congress has worked to strengthen state supervision of education, and the states have delegated many of their responsibilities to the local level. Local school districts, of course, wield enormous influence on personnel, curriculum, and instructional policies as they manage the school on a day-to-day basis, but on matters from teacher certification to the length of the school year and the quality of lunches, they take their orders from the state. More important, the state has always had the power (although it rarely exercises it) to rescind or modify many of the policies of the local district.

While local control and state powers over local districts are considered so established as to be almost folklore, and while the federal government has traditionally come out a distant third to state and local efforts in education, the situation is changing. The most dramatic factor in the increasing influence of the federal government has been the judicial branch, specifically the U.S. Supreme Court. The Court has taken an active role in education since the 1954 *Brown* decision which involved school desegregation, followed by the 1967 *Gault* and 1968 *Tinker* cases, which involved student rights. The Court's influence now includes such areas as student discipline, student dress, and local grading systems. In addition, the Court has given state and local courts wide latitude to change the present system of school financing—and these rulings may be as significant as the *Brown* decision.

A second area of increased federal activity in education is related to the new role played by Congress. While the legislative branch has always been uneasy about no educational responsibilities being included in the Constitution, it has taken on an active, problem-solving orientation which has led to increasing impatience with state and local educators. Writes Samuel Halperin, "In Congress's perception, state authorities and educators alike are defaulting on different problems. Name any major social issue of our time . . . and educators are viewed as tardy at best or as lacking in commitment." Confronted with growing awareness that educators are failing to educate a large segment of students, and influenced by the

---

[3] *Chronicle of Higher Education*, September 7, 1976, pp. 14–15; December 12, 1977, p. 14.

concept of equal educational opportunity, Congress tends to react by passing a law. In the 1960s, money was Congress's antidote; now the new fiscal realities of huge deficits and inflation mean that Congress has fewer dollars to spend on schools. Halperin says today "Congress uses sticks instead of carrots — it legislates and it regulates, what is considered by some critics as ill-conceived and harmful social policy."[4]

Federal money has always meant some regulation to assure it is spent for the purposes it was given, but since the 1960s the concept of program purpose has been enlarged to mean that federal financial assistance to one program purpose subjects any other program or activity to regulation. In other words, by accepting federal money for any aspect of the school or college program, the recipient institution is open to federal regulation on all fronts. This new set of controls and regulations extends the whole range of federal relationships and statutory requirements to schools and colleges, public and private.

A third area of increased federal activity involves the executive branch of government, in particular the information and compliance agencies of the Departments of Health, Education, and Welfare; Labor, and Justice. There has been a manifold increase in the regulatory behaviors, standards, and procedures imposed by various governmental agencies pertaining to the enforcement of the law. States former President Gerald Ford, "We have unwittingly created a heavy burden of varying regulations, differing standards, and overlapping responsibilities. Too often we ask whether federal forms have been properly filled out, not whether children have been properly educated."[5] This is illustrated by the hundreds of forms, reports, and studies state and local schools must respond to, as regards federal regulations about student records and information, school safety and heating systems, vandalism and violence, financial reporting, and the enforcement of school desegregation and affirmative action policies. Examples are the compliance documents related to personnel practices and the Civil Rights Act of 1964, which forbids discrimination on the basis of race, religion, or national origin; Executive Order 11246 and Revised Order No. 4, pertaining to the hiring of minorities and women; and Title IX of the Education Amendments of 1972, which forbids sex discrimination and contains related policies pertaining to vocational education, athletic, and extracurricular programs. These regulations constantly change, which puts school and college administrators on the defensive and tie them up in grievance committees, legal procedures, and

---

[4] Samuel Halperin, "Federal Takeover, State Default or a Family Problem?" *Phi Delta Kappan*, June 1976, p. 696.

[5] Gerald Ford, "If I am Elected," *Change*, May 1976, p. 49.

the courts. In addition, many title programs require a comprehensive advance proposal to secure the money, and most grants require considerable documentation and formal evaluation.

In short, the bureaucratic procedures and paper work generated by local, regional, and Washington agencies for purposes of providing information, inspection, and compliance with various federal laws in turn generate for the school procedures and paper work, committees and meetings, guidelines to be followed, and administrative and clerical jobs to be filled. The requirements have increased out of proportion to the federal dollars received. While federal expenditures account for less than 10 percent of the dollar outlay for public and private schools and less than 15 percent for colleges,[6] there has been a dramatic increase in the amount of time and energy needed to secure federal money and to reduce the likelihood of federal court suits. Further, federal control is growing at a time when federal financial assistance is declining, both in relative importance to institutions and in total real dollars (considering inflation) appropriated. Joseph Cronin notes that "millions of person-hours and dollars [are now] required just to develop procedures, personnel systems, and forms to implement the law. By 1980 the phenomenon of 'federal take over' may appear to be an understatement of the problem."[7]

Along with the growing regulatory scope of the federal government, there has been a striking change in the manner in which it has expended its monetary commitment to education. Federal funds for education are now earmarked for specific categories: vocational education, teacher corps, bilingual education, and so on. Consequently, the funds have a more precise impact; withdrawal can wipe out a program overnight and play havoc with an entire segment of a local school or college. This funding strategy is quite different from the former one, which provided general aid with few or no strings attached to the money. The resulting impact is summed up by Michael Kirst: "this targeting of federal resources has endowed federal funds with more stimulating power and leverage than the small amount of total expenditures would permit had federal officials merely 'put money on the stump and run.' "[8]

Why doesn't anyone stand up against the new federal funding policies? First, the voices of local and state educators are scarcely heard in the nation's capital. The political and professional rivalry of different

---

[6] See Table 11.1 and 11.2 above.

[7] Joseph M. Cronin, "The Federal Takeover: Should the Junior Partner Run the Firm?" *Phi Delta Kappan*, April 1976, p. 500.

[8] Michael W. Kirst, "The Growth of Federal Influence in Education," in G. W. Gordon (ed.), *Uses of Sociology of Education*, 73rd Yearbook of the National Society for the Study of Education, Part II (Chicago: University of Chicago Press, 1974), p. 448.

organizations and groups and poor communication between federal and state or local agencies make education an ineffective pressure group. State and local educators are only now showing awareness of the implications of the federal governments' less than 10 percent contribution to educational expenditures.

Summing up, the data clearly show that the federal government comes out a distant third to state and local funding, but it no longer follows that the most power lies with the state and local authorities. The state and local school districts are increasingly being regulated by the government, that is, being told what to do by federal agencies which formulate, interpret, and enforce the law.

Federal Agencies and Activities

All the executive Departments of the federal government engage in some kind of educational activity. Some operate schools to train government personnel. The Department of State gives instruction to all newly appointed diplomatic and counsular officers. The Department of Defense administers the naval, military, and air force academies, as well as schools on military bases located within the United States and abroad. The Treasury Department maintains a training school for Coast Guard and Internal Revenue Service employees. The Department of Justice trains its own personnel and often acts in behalf of the federal government in school desegregation cases. The Department of Agriculture provides funds for and administers the school lunch program. Indian Education is the responsibility of the Department of Interior. In general, the executive Departments' educational activities are of great magnitude, but the major Department concerned with education, because it oversees and funds educational activities, is the Department of Health, Education, and Welfare (HEW).

HEW was created in 1953 and is headed by a Secretary in the President's Cabinet. The rationale is that a single agency with major status in the federal bureaucracy is essential to provide the needed health, education, and welfare leadership for the nation. HEW's recently enlarged scope and increased funding are highlighted by its share of the nation's budget. Whereas traditional items such as defense spending, space, highways, and farm subsidies accounted for 70 percent of the budget in fiscal year 1955, only 21 years later they amounted to 32 percent of the $374 billion federal outlay. The "human resources" sector of the budget—health, income maintenance, community development, and education—which traditionally represented a small portion of federal spending has dramatically increased, for example, from $10.5 billion, or 21 percent, in 1955 to $199.7 billion, or more than 50 percent, in 1976.[9]

In 1976, from this federal spending pipeline flowed $77 billion for social security, $32 billion for health care, $24 billion for public-assistance programs, $22 billion for education, $20 billion for unemployment benefits, and $19 billion for veteran benefits.[10] At current growth rates, federal social outlays will range between $250 and $300 billion in fiscal year 1980, most of it under HEW. HEW's funding in 1976 represented 37 percent of the $22 billion in federal money for education, and the U.S. Office of Education (within HEW) represented 28 percent of this.[11]

Ten other federal Departments (Agriculture, Commerce, Defense, Housing and Urban Development, Interior, Justice, Labor, State, Transportation, and Treasury), plus a vast network of agencies under them, are also involved in funding education. This scattering of federal education efforts is of concern to many educators who point to the frustration and problems state and local school districts experience in dealing with a variety of agencies. The concentration of educational leadership under one federal agency is often recommended to eliminate conflicting rules and regulations relative to grant programs and affirmative action policies, but other educators express fears that too much power would be concentrated in one Department, and the system of education might become nationalized.

The largest educational agency operating within the auspices of HEW is the Office of Education (USOE or OE). The Office started as an independent Department of Education in 1867 and shifted to Bureau status in 1870 under the Department of Interior. The original mandate was to conduct surveys, provide resource data, and maintain a low profile vis-à-vis state and local partners in education. In 1939 it was incorporated into the Federal Security Agency. When HEW was created in 1953, the Office became a part of this Department, where it has remained. From a small and somewhat shaky beginning, with a staff of 300 and a budget of $40 million in 1950, the Office of Education has gained in strength, status, and significance. In the 1960s and 1970s there were dramatic increases in federal activity in education and expanded delivery of services. In 1977 the operation comprised more than 3,000 staff members and more than 100

---

[9] John F. Due and Ann F. Friedlaender, *Government Finance: Economics of the Public Sector*, 6th ed. (Homewood, Ill.: Dorsey Press, 1977), Table 8.3, p. 157; *U.S. Budget in Brief, Fiscal Year 1976* (Washington, D.C.: U.S. Government Printing Office, 1975).

[10] See Due and Friedlaender, *Government Finance*, pp. 159-68; David A. Stockman, "The Social Pork Barrel," *Public Interest*, Spring 1975, pp. 3-30.

[11] Telephone conversation with Vance Grant, National Center for Educational Statistics, January 24, 1978.

branches and centers, and it had a budget of approximately $6.5 billion. The Carter administration has announced plans to consolidate and streamline the Office and possibly to establish a separate Cabinet-level Department of Education, independent of HEW.[12]

The growth of USOE has made the top officer, the Commissioner of Education, a highly visible and important leader in education. The Commissioners from 1867 to 1963 were known by only a few educators; now they are well known, and their proposals and speeches have widespread influence within and outside professional education circles. The Commissioner can not only use the position to exert moral persuasion and to question basic education assumptions, he or she can also influence federal funding in specific areas. And the power of the pursestring represents real power.

The Federal Role in Educational Research and Development

Prior to the mid-1960s it was fashionable among educators and researchers to bemoan the low level of coordination and development in the educational research community. In the past decade, a great many organizational and supportive changes have been made, spearheaded by HEW and USOE.

The federal role in educational research from 1867 to 1953 largely consisted of the responsibility to collect statistics on the condition and progress of education at local, state, and federal levels. During these years, the federal organization conducted surveys and disseminated reports to help the states and local school districts deal with a variety of educational problems.[13] It might be said that the Department of Education and the federal government were bystanders as the field of educational research moved from its early emphasis on philosophic inquiry prior to the 20th century to concern with psychologically based empiricism and tests and measurements, from the turn of the century to the 1950s.

In 1954 passage of the Cooperative Research Act authorized the Commissioner of Education to enter into contracts or jointly finance cooperative arrangements with colleges and universities and state educational agencies to conduct research and demonstrations in the field of education. Although the legislation was not considered dramatic in

---

[12] *Chronicle of Higher Education,* April 18, 1977, p. 9; April 25, 1977, p. 14; May 9, 1977, p. 9; Halperin, "Federal Takeover, State Default, or a Family Problem?" pp. 696-97.

[13] Stephen K. Bailey, "Significance of the Federal Investment in Educational R & D," *Journal of Research and Development in Education,* Summer 1969, pp. 34-37; Stephen K. Bailey et al., *Schoolmen and Politics* (Syracuse, N.Y.: Syracuse University Press, 1962).

terms of providing actual funds, Congress thereby recognized the feasibility of improving the educational delivery system through research, and the federal government assumed the initiative and cost.[14] Within six years the Cooperative Research Programs had stimulated many researchers from other disciplines outside schools of education to undertake work on education. The number of research proposals from professors outside education increased fourfold between 1955 and 1963, while the number from schools of education remained the same. By 1963, the majority of research proposals in education originated with other disciplines.[15]

Outside the USOE, the National Science Foundation (NSF) provided most of the funds in research, design, and dissemination of new curricula in science and mathematics. In 1958 the National Defense Education Act (NDEA) was passed, with provisions for the support of research on language, media, and science. Through projects in various subject areas, the USOE extended its research program to include the development portion of educational R & D. In 1963 it extended this capacity by establishing nine federal-funded, university-based R & D centers and several other regional laboratories.[16]

The next major breakthrough came in 1965, with the passage of the Elementary and Secondary Act (ESEA), in which Titles III and IV broadened the authorization for federal programs in support of educational R & D. Concern for disadvantaged students, demonstrated by ESEA funding, generated a host of compensatory programs as well as research-related activities on poverty, deprivation, and minority education. These research activities ranged from direct support of experiments in local school districts, colleges, and universities to training programs for educational researchers in institutions of higher learning. Research funds increased from $15.8 million in 1965 to $49.8 million in 1966.[17]

The establishment of Educational Research Information Centers (ERIC) by the Office of Education was another attempt to strengthen educational R & D. Thirteen centers were funded in 1966, and ten years later there were 16. These centers provide a storage and retrieval system for

---

[14] David L. Clark, "Federal Policy in Educational Research and Development," *Educational Researcher*, June 1976, pp. 3–9.

[15] Sam D. Sieber, "Federal Support for Research and Development in Education and Its Effects," in C. W. Gordon (ed.), *Uses of the Sociology of Education,* 73rd Yearbook of the National Society for the Study of Education, Part II (Chicago: University of Chicago Press, 1974), pp. 478–502.

[16] Clark, "Federal Policy in Educational Research and Development."

[17] Hendrick Gidenonse, *Educational Research and Development in the United States* (Washington, D.C.: U.S. Government Printing Office, 1970); Sieber, "Federal Support for Research and Development in Education."

educational information and research; they are helpful to doctoral students and researchers who wish to review the literature or to disseminate their own research findings. It is estimated that the 16 ERICs are used more than 10 million times a year.[18]

In the 1960s a network of new research agencies was formed within the USOE under the Bureau of Research to oversee research in language development, media, international education, foreign currency, professional training, guidance and counseling, education of the handicapped, vocational and adult education, and so on. Increasing funds, amounting to nearly $30 million by the end of the decade, were placed at the disposal of the Bureau. With the exception of handicapped, vocational, and adult educational research, these new agencies were subsequently transferred to the National Institute for Education.

The National Institute for Education (NIE), established in 1972 under the USOE and now an independent agency under HEW, is considered the major educational research agency in the federal government. While the NIE was established with considerable support from the educational research community, it has had numerous problems getting off the ground. Its annual budget has been continuously trimmed by Congress, and behind-the-scenes political activity and bureaucratic struggles to separate the agency from USOE have plagued the agency. There have been serious communication gaps between NIE leaders and Congress; congressional dissatisfaction with NIE funding procedures; lack of support for many of their programs; and strong criticism of the agency by other educators, including state school officers, teacher groups, and college administrators.[19] At one point, the Senate Appropriations Committee recommended zero dollars for NIE in fiscal year 1975, to show its dissatisfaction with it, but written statements of support from several educational associations ensured that NIE was funded.[20] Today, the shape and direction of NIE are still in doubt, and controversy over many of their funding procedures and programs continues.

Nearly all research money in education comes from the federal

---

[18] *Educational Research in America, Annual Report 1975* (Washington, D.C.: National Institute of Education, 1976), p. 27.

[19] John Brademas, "A Congressional View of Education R & D and NIE," *Educational Researcher*, November 1972, pp. 12-15; Patricia E. Stivers, "NIE: Learning about Congress the Hard Way," *Educational Researcher*, November 1973, pp. 8-9; Arthur E. Wise, "The Taming of the National Institute of Education," *Phi Delta Kappan*, September 1976, pp. 62-65.

[20] Patricia E. Stivers, "NIE: Another Appropriations Crisis," *Educational Researcher*, November 1974, pp. 9-15.

government. Local educational agencies (LEAs) have been sluggish in setting up viable R & D activities, and state educational agencies (SEAs) are not doing much to promote educational R & D at the local level.[21] Less than 9 percent of the total support for educational R & D comes from the state and local level, including higher education institutions, academic associations, and teacher organization as well as state departments of education and local school districts.[22]

Many school people at the state and local levels lack the technical skills to understand, much less conduct, research, and much of the research is considered by practitioners to be irrelevant to their daily activities. Moreover, they are reluctant to participate in research if the results can be used to make comparisons at the state or local level, or even to compare student groups.[23] In any case, it is not a simple matter for a state or local educational agency to adopt a new method or machine, regardless of what the research purports about the innovation. Machines cost money, and new methods may mean teachers have to be retrained.[24] There is no profit motive or competition, as in the private sector, to encourage adoption of the best or most effective program. In short, there is no incentive to cooperate in research endeavors or to adopt new programs based on research findings. These attitudes of state and local school people are ample justification for the increasing federal R & D involvement.

The federal role in educational research and development is more comprehensive, vigorous, and supportive than it has been in any previous era. Yet considerable doubt and dissatisfaction with the federal investment exist within the executive and legislative branches. The investment has been dramatically increased, but decision makers have not been convinced that the outcome of educational research has real value or that it will improve schooling. Educational R & D has become, in effect, an obligation without an effective constituency. Continuing difficulties are illustrated by the fact that the NIE — the umbrella agency for educational research — has lost the confidence of Congress and many educators.

But the problem of educational R & D goes beyond NIE and the federal government. It involves groups and individuals in leadership positions, competition for limited funds, and favors and partisan agreements among

---

[21] Bailey, "Significance of the Federal Investment."

[22] Educational Research in America, Table 6, p. 30.

[23] Milbey W. McLaughlin, Evaluation and Reform: The Elementary and Secondary Education Act of 1965/Title I (Cambridge, Mass.: Ballinger Publishing Co., 1975); Allan C. Ornstein, "Bridging the Gap between Researchers and Practitioners," Illinois Schools Journal, Winter 1975-76, pp. 35-48.

[24] Claiborne Pell, "Building Partnerships for Educational Research and Development," Educational Researcher, January 1975, pp. 11-12.

Table 11.3 / Federal R & D Obligation by Function, Fiscal Years 1969–1976 (in millions)

	1969	1970	1971	1972	1973	1974	1975	1976
Total functions	$15,641.1	$15,340.3	$15,564.2	$16,511.9	$16,821.2	$17,438.2	$18,905.1	$21,651.9
National defense	8,353.7	7,976.3	8,106.1	8,897.7	8,997.9	9,011.5	9,498.5	11,358.1
Space	3,731.7	3,509.9	2,893.0	2,715.6	2,608.9	2,501.9	2,554.0	2,897.4
Health	1,113.0	1,112.6	1,323.4	1,567.1	1,596.9	2,064.2	2,158.7	1,904.0
Energy	327.9	317.3	323.6	382.7	441.6	570.6	933.6	1,276.8
Science and technology	513.4	524.6	523.7	601.2	604.4	687.7	772.8	860.4
Natural resources	373.5	418.2	517.1	588.3	583.5	575.6	744.5	825.4
Transportation and communication	458.1	590.2	778.7	612.8	627.1	698.8	676.0	711.9
Remaining functions: social, economic, housing, crime prevention, etc.	615.0	744	910	954	1,146	1,154	1,409	1,498
Education	154.8	146.6	186.1	190.7	214.2	173.5	157.8	318.2
Education R & D as percent of total federal R & D	0.9%	0.9%	1.2%	1.2%	1.3%	1.0%	0.8%	1.5%

Source: National Science Foundation, *Analysis of Federal R & D Funding by Function* (Washington, D.C.: U.S. Government Printing Office, 1976), pp. 66–74.

Table 11.4 / Total Federal Expenditures on Schools (Public and Private, All Levels), 1969–1976 (in millions)

	1969	1970	1971	1972	1973	1974	1975	1976
Total federal expenditures in education...........	$8,054.5	$9,220.4	$10,927.7	$11,771.0	$12,689.7	$13,078.8	$16,545.5	$16,211.9[a]
Federal expenditures for education R & D (from Table 11.3)...........	154.8	146.6	186.1	190.7	214.2	173.5	157.8	318.2
Federal expenditures for educational R & D as percent of total expenditures in education (derived by author)........	1.9%	1.6%	1.7%	1.6%	1.7%	1.3%	1.0%	2.0%

[a] 1976 figure of 16.2 is an estimate provided by the government.
Source: *Digest of Educational Statistics, 1975* (Washington, D.C.: U.S. Government Printing Office, 1976), Table 142, p. 152.

bureaucrats in Washington and state and local school grantsmen and university professors. The triviality of much of the research, the irrelevance of most research to what goes on in schools, and poor communication between researchers and practitioners are other problems.[25]

In summing up the federal role in educational R & D, it should be noted that federal support of this obligation is greater than that of state and local agencies. As of fiscal year 1976, the federal investment in educational R & D (loosely defined to include innovations, diffusion, and evaluation) approached $318 million, twice the amount in 1969 and 26 times the amount in 1963. Of this amount, HEW and USOE received $291 million (of which NIE received $80 million), and NSF received $27 million. But as indicated in Table 11.3, federal R & D obligations for all functions totaled $21.7 billion in 1976, with national defense comprising 53 percent and research for education representing only 1.5 percent. Although this seems low, it represents the highest percentage of total federal R & D, compared to previous years. Put in a different perspective, total federal expenditures for all aspects of public and private education approximated $16.2 billion in fiscal year 1976, as shown in Table 11.4, and the total federal investment in educational R & D ($318 million) represented 2 percent of the federal commitment to education; this also is the highest it has ever been. If another $30 million, the approximate expenditures for educational R & D by state and local school agencies, and another $50 million from foundation sources are added to the federal investment, total expenditures for educational R & D in fiscal year 1976 were about $398 million.[26] With total expenditures for education in school year 1976–77 at $131 billion, .26 or one fourth of one percent of the educational budget was being allocated for R & D.

Considering the size of the field it is supposed to affect, the proportion of research expenditures is severely limited. For some reason, other enterprises that are less intellectual than education treat research more seriously. About 10 percent of the defense budget goes to research; private industry and the agriculture and health fields spend about 5 percent.[27] In short, the current system of producing and consuming educational research does not seem to be well established.

[25] See Francis C. Caro, "Evaluative Researchers and Practitioners: Conflicts and Accomodation," *Journal of Research and Development in Education,* Spring 1975, pp. 55–62; David R. Krathwohl, "An Analysis of the Perceived Ineffectiveness of Educational Research and Some Recommendations," *Educational Psychologist,* no. 2 (1974), pp. 73–86; Carol Weiss (ed.), *Evaluating Action Programs* (Boston: Allyn & Bacon, 1972).

[26] See *Digest of Educational Statistics, 1975,* Table 142, p. 152; *Educational Research in America,* p. 30.

[27] Ornstein, "Bridging the Gap between Researchers and Practitioners"; Edward Wynne, "Educational Research: A Profession in Search of a Constituency," *Phi Delta Kappan,* December 1970, pp. 245–47.

STATE RESPONSIBILITIES

State school codes are a collection of laws which establish ways and means to operate schools and conduct education in the state. Every state, by constitution, statute, and practice, assumes that education is a function of the state, and federal and state court decisions have supported this interpretation. The state, of course, cannot enact legislation which is contrary to, or conflicts with, the federal Constitution. State statutes can be divided into two groups: mandatory laws which establish the minimum program of education, and permissive laws which define the functions that are delegated to the school district under appropriate conditions.

In general, the state accepts responsibility for the support and maintenance of the public schools. Local schools are considered creatures of the state which have been devised for the purpose of running a system of schools. The state may go very far in limiting the control of parents over the education of their own children. Being responsible for the schools, the state enacts legislation; determines school taxes and financial aid to local school districts; sets minimum standards for the training, recruitment, and salaries of personnel; determines student policy; decides on the curriculum (some states establish "approved" textbook lists, too); makes provisions for accrediting schools; and provides special services (e.g., student transportation, free textbooks). Although state constitutions and statutes may simply direct state legislators to provide for the establishment and maintenance of a uniform system of schools, provisions in many states are usually quite detailed concerning methods of operation.

Impact of the State Courts

State courts are subject to constitutional restrictions and may be overruled by federal district courts or the U.S. Supreme Court. Even though state courts may serve to set a precedent, decisions rendered in one state are not binding in another. Moreover, there are instances (e.g., matters dealing with teacher tenure, teacher strikes, and student rights) in which a decision in one state appears to be in conflict in another state. In spite of areas of apparent conflict, on major issues relating to control of schools there has been consistency among the state courts.

State courts have repeatedly held that public education is a function of the state, and the ultimate control of school affairs is vested in the law-making power of the state. The state courts have also made it clear that the state controls the schools for the fulfillment of the public good, not for the benefit of the individual. The state courts have also taken the position that a local school has no inherent powers of government, and its boundaries may be changed or the district may be abolished at the will of the state legislature, unless prohibited by the state constitution. State courts have upheld the power of the legislatures to levy taxes for school purposes, to confer upon other governmental units (municipalities, counties, towns, or school districts) such taxing power, and to allocate the monies to schools.[28] This tax matter was affirmed by the Supreme Court in the *Rodriguez* decision in 1973 and will be discussed later in detail.

The Governor and State Legislature

Although the powers of governors vary widely among states and, with time, in a given state, their authority on educational matters is spelled out in law. Usually a governor is charged with making educational budget recommendations to the legislature. In many states the governor has legal access to any accumulated balances in the state treasury, and these monies can be used for school purposes.

The governor can appoint or remove school personnel at the state level. These appointive or removal powers often have restrictions, such as approval by the legislature. In a majority of states the governor can appoint members of the state board of education and, in a few states, the chief state school officer. A governor can kill educational measures through his veto powers or threaten to use them to discourage the legislature from enacting educational laws he opposes.

In most states, the legislature is primarily responsible for establishing and maintaining the public schools and has broad powers to enact laws pertaining to education. These powers are not unlimited; there are restrictions in the form of federal and state constitutional provisions and court decisions. But within these restrictions, the legislature has the full power to decide basic school policy questions in the state.

The state legislature usually determines how the state boards of education will be selected, what will be their responsibilities, how the chief state officer will be selected, what will be the duties of this office, what the functions of the state department of education will be, what types of local and regional school districts there will be, and what the methods of selection and powers of local boards will be. The legislature usually decides on the nature of state taxes for schools, the level of financial support for education, and the taxing power for schools to be allocated on a local or municipal level. The legislature may determine what may or may not be taught, how many years of compulsory education will be required, the

---

[28] See Commission on Educational Governance, *Public Testimony on Public Schools* (Berkeley, Ca.: McCuthchan Publishing Corp., 1975); E. Edmund Reutter and Robert R. Hamilton, *The Law and Public Education*, 2nd ed. (Mineola, N.Y.: Foundation Press, 1976).

length of the school day and school year, and whether or not there will be community colleges and adult and vocational schools. The legislature may also determine staff and student policies and testing and evaluation procedures, authorize school programs, set standards for building construction, and provide various auxiliary services (e.g., student transportation and school lunches). Where the legislature does not enact these policies, they are usually the responsibility of the state board of education.

The nonpublic or private schools within a state are not exempt from the action of the legislature; there are general laws that apply to nonpublic schools, including parochial schools, pertaining to health standards, building codes, welfare of children, student codes, and so on. Legislative bodies in many states have passed laws to benefit nonpublic schools and, at public expense, to provide aid in such areas as student transportation, health services, dual enrollment or shared-time plans, school lunch services, purchasing of books and supplies, student testing services, teacher salary supplements, student tuition, and student loans. Although the courts have generally held that the legislature has the right to pass laws providing for the supervision of nonpublic schools, rarely has a state legislature enacted comprehensive regulatory requirements—and where they do exist on the books they are not strictly enforced.

Neither the governor nor the legislature is likely (or ought) to endorse proposals merely because they are submitted by a state education agency or any other group. Edgar Morphet and David Jesser recommend that "Insofar as practicable all major proposals should be prepared and submitted by the state education agency within the context of comprehensive planning for effecting improvements with which all agencies of state governments presumably are concerned."[29] In some cases, it may be appropriate to establish a blue-ribbon committee representative of various groups to make recommendations, since many groups and agencies in each state have some interest about education. As Ewald Nyquist notes,

Traditional forces of institutional autonomy are being displaced by emerging patterns which emphasize interdependence in the improvement of education. Local public schools, colleges, and state education departments are finding that they need to cooperate more effectively, not only with each other, but also with other agencies and groups in order to make education more effective.[30]

For either the governor or members of the legislature to formulate educational policy without consulting representative educators or the state

---

[29] Edgar L. Morphet and David L. Jesser, *Emerging State Responsibilities for Education* (Denver, Colo.: Improving State Leadership in Education, 1970), p. 56.

[30] Ewald B. Nyquist, "State Organization and Responsibilities for Education," in E. L. Morphet and D. L. Jesser (eds.), *Emerging Designs for Education* (New York: Citation Press, 1968), p. 36.

education agency, and possibly representatives of private industry and pressure groups, would seem to be an arbitrary and indefensible act. Both the governor and the legislature have available staff members and agencies to help with analysis and interpretation of data and can obtain additional information on matters of educational concern as needed.

State Boards of Education

The state board of education is usually the most influential and important state education agency. Almost all states have some sort of state board of education which is dependent on the state legislature for appropriations and authority and serves an advisory function for the legislature. (The famous Board of Regents of New York State represents a strong and respected state board of education, far more than other state boards.) In addition, many states have a separate governing board for state colleges and universities; thus there are often two separate state boards, one for elementary and secondary education and the second for higher education, from junior college to graduate study. States vary with respect to the arrangement of governing boards for colleges and universities; some have a separate board for each institution of higher learning. In four states, Florida, Idaho, Montana, and New York, the state department of education has control over the entire program of education, from prekindergarten to graduate study.

With the exception of Wisconsin, all the states have boards of education. As of 1976, 33 were appointed by the governor of the state, 12 were elected by popular vote, 2 were elected by the state legislature and 1 by a convention of local school board members, and 2 were ex officio state boards. They varied in size from 3 members in Mississippi to 24 in Texas, with 33 states having from 7 to 11 members, and in the kinds of people serving on them, length of office, and responsibilities.[31] The quality sought in board members is comparable to that of judges with respect to the law. The political aspects of being appointed by the governor or running for election are well known. Most state boards seek to disqualify individuals employed in education or in textbook companies. The problem is to find qualified lay citizens who understand education and are sympathetic to teachers, administrators, students, and parents alike and who have few axes to grind.

---

[31] Roald F. Campbell, Edwin M. Bridges, and Raphael O. Nystand, *Introduction to Educational Administration*, 5th ed. (Boston: Allyn & Bacon, 1977); Luvern L. Cunningham et al., *Educational Administration: The Developing Decades* (Berkeley, Ca.: McCutchan, 1977).

The duties and responsibilities of state boards of education vary by state, but generally the board is charged with certain functions.[32] These are:

1. Adopting and enforcing policies, rules, and regulations necessary to implement legislative acts related to education.
2. Establishing qualifications and appointing personnel to the state department of education.
3. Setting standards for teacher administrative certificates.
4. Establishing standards for accrediting schools.
5. Managing state funds earmarked for education.
6. Keeping records and collecting data needed for reporting and evaluating.
7. Adopting long-range plans for the development and improvement of schools.
8. Creating advisory bodies as required by law.
9. Acting as a judicial body in hearing disputes arising from state policies.
10. Representing the state in determining policies on all matters pertaining to education that involve relationships with other agencies (including the federal government).
11. Advising the governor or legislature on educational matters.
12. In some states, appointing the chief state school officer, setting minimum salary schedules for teachers and administrators, and adopting policies for the operation of institutions of higher learning.

State Departments of Education

Another major state education agency is the state department of education, which usually operates under the direction of the state board of education and is administered by the chief state school officer. State department of education staffs range in size from slightly less than 100 to more than 1,000. In 1972, only nine states had professional staffs of less than 100, and in three the staff exceeded 1,000. The number of staff members in state education departments of most states has increased since the mid-1960s, corresponding with the increased activities of the federal government in education. For example, in 1962 only 10 states had departments of more than 100 professionals, and 21 had fewer than 50

---

[32] *Ibid;* Ralph Kimbrough and Michael Y. Nunnery, *Educational Administration: An Introduction* (New York: Macmillan Co., 1976); Edgar L. Morphet, Roe L. Johns, and Theodore L. Reller, *Educational Organization and Administration,* 3rd ed. (Englewood Cliffs, N.J.: Prentice-Hall, Inc. 1974).

staff members. As a general rule, the more populated the state, the higher the degree of centralization and the larger the staff.[33] Less populated states have smaller and decentralized staffs.

Traditionally, state departments of education functioned primarily as agencies to collect and disseminate statistics about the status of education within the state. Today they provide the following services:

1. Leadership and advisory services, by preparing publications, sponsoring conferences and workshops, and consulting with appropriate school people.
2. Supervisory and regulatory services, by making certain that state regulations are observed, accrediting schools and issuing teaching and administrative certificates, and running programs.
3. Fact-gathering and appraisal services, by compiling data and records, conducting research, evaluating programs, and issuing reports.
4. Public relations services, by explaining the schools to the people and reporting on how taxes are spent on education.

The Chief State School Officer

The chief state school officer serves as the head of the state department of education and is usually called the state superintendent of education, the state superintendent of public instruction, or the state commissioner of education. In 35 states the position is provided for in the state constitution, and in the others it is authorized by legislative act.[34] The position dates back to its creation in New York State in 1812.

The chief state officer is usually a professional educator, not primarily a politician. The office is filled in one of three ways: by the governor, the state board of education, or popular election. In 1972, 5 states filled the position through appointment by the governor, 26 states through the state board of education, and 19 states by popular election. The terms of 21 chief state school officers were indefinite, that is, at the pleasure of the governor or the state board of education. Definite terms ranged from one to five years, and four was the most common term.[35]

The duties of the chief state school officer and the relation of the position with the state board and state department vary from state to state, and usually depend on whether the official was appointed or voted in to office. Where appointed for an indefinite term, greater dependence is likely; where elected, the chief officer tends to have greater independence.

---

[33] Sam P. Harris, *State Departments of Education, State Boards of Education, and Chief State School Officers* (Washington, D.C.: U.S. Government Printing Office, 1973).

[34] Ibid.

[35] Ibid.

Because of differences in method of selection, in the legal relationship with state boards of education, and the degree of state versus local district control of schools, the responsibilities of the chief state officer vary widely. However, the major responsibilities associated with the office are likely to include certain functions.[36] These are:

1. Serving as the chief administrator of the state department of education.
2. Selecting personnel for the state department of education.
3. Recommending improvements in educational legislation and educational budgets.
4. Ensuring compliance with state educational laws and regulations.
5. Explaining and interpreting school laws of the state.
6. Deciding impartially controversies involving the administration of the schools within the state.
7. Arranging for studies, committees, and task forces as deemed necessary to identify problems and recommend solutions.
8. Reporting on the status of education within the state to the governor, legislature, state board of education, and public.

Every chief state school officer has some staff, commonly referred to as the state department of education. Usually, the heads of departments of education change with changes of political party control, but the professional employees, such as the statisticians, secondary administrators, clerks, and secretaries, are civil service employees. This type of arrangement can lead to another problem. While civil service protects professionals in government from partisan politics, it also protects mediocre personnel. By and large, staff members of the state departments of education are recruited from public school personnel and from local schools and colleges.

LOCAL RESPONSIBILITIES

The local district or school district is a creation of the state which encompasses a local area and operates the schools for boys and girls within a community. It is the avenue through which local citizens act in establishing districtwide policies in education. However, because a school district operates to carry out a state function — not a local function — local policies must be consistent with the statewide policies set forth in the state school code. The local district can be compared to a limited corporation whose powers are granted by state laws: those granted in expressed powers and

---

[36] Roald F. Campbell et al., *The Organization and Control of American Schools*, 3rd ed. (Columbus, Ohio: Charles E. Merrill Publishing Co., 1975); Stephen J. Knezevich, *Administration of Public Education*, 3rd ed. (New York: Harper & Row, 1975).

those discretionary powers essential to its operation. Subject to the restrictions of the state constitution, the legislature can modify the local district's jurisdiction, change its boundaries and powers, or even eliminate it.

Originally, school districts were small and the state legislatures permitted them to be almost autonomous. Gradually, through the years, the states assumed more powers of control over local school districts, and local districts were reorganized and consolidated into larger entities. In 1930-31, the first year for which adequate information was available, there were approximately 130,000 local school districts in the United States; in 1975-76, the figure was slightly more than 16,000.[37]

The Board of Education

The local boards of education have been delegated powers and duties by the state to assure that the schools of the community are properly operated. The schools are agencies of limited power and can exercise only those prerogatives specifically delegated to them by the state legislatures. Nevertheless, by law and custom, school boards have assumed significant decision-making responsibility. For the most part, the state sets up a framework of procedures, with minimum requirements for operating local public schools and certain restrictions on financial accounting. Local boards are given the power to raise money through taxes, with a debt limitation. They exercise power over personnel and school property. Some states leave curriculum and student policy pretty much in the hands of the school board, but others, by law, insist on specific requirements. In general the school board conforms to state guidelines to qualify for state aid, as well as with federal guidelines.

Methods of selecting board members are prescribed by state law. The two basic methods are by appointment and election, and popular election is the common practice. In 1976, 28 states elected all their local board members, and in 7 other states 90 percent or more of the boards were elected. The few exceptions were in large and medium-sized school systems, where members were appointed or nominated by another government agency. About 95 percent of the school boards across the country are elected.[38]

Most states specify a standard number of board members; others specify a permissible range, and a few have no requirements. Most fall within a

---

[37] *Fall 1976 Statistics of Public Schools, Advance Report* (Washington, D.C.: U.S. Government Printing Office, 1977), Table 1, p. 5.

[38] National School Boards Association, *Fifty State School Boards Associations* (Washington, D.C.: 1977).

three-to-nine member range, with the largest known having 19 members. A minimum-maximum number for efficient school board operation has not been determined. Some large city school boards have increased their size to avert disruptive forces in the community, to limit the effects of partisan politics, and to acquire a broader representation.[39] There are three general types of board meetings: regular, special, and executive. The first two are usually open meetings to which the public is invited. Open board meetings are obviously beneficial for enhancing school-community relations and allowing parents to understand the problems of education and air their concerns. The use of closed board meetings to reach major policy decisions is generally disdained but is evident in the practices of central school boards in some large cities as conflict and tensions increase.[40]

As noted in Chapter 10, because of a variety of political, economic, and social factors, there has been pressure from diverse sectors of the population to broaden formal participation in educational policy making. School boards have, for the most part, been controlled by a few persons, generally white, upper-middle-class business and political opinion leaders. Only recently have minority groups gained substantial representation on school boards.

The School Superintendent and Central Office Staff

One of the most important responsibilities a school board has is to appoint a competent superintendent of schools. The superintendent is the executive officer of the school board, while the board is the legislative policy-making body. Since the school board consists of lay people who do not profess to be experts in school affairs, it is their responsibility to see that the work of the school is properly performed by professional personnel. The board of education often delegates many of their own legal powers to the superintendent and staff. The superintendent's policies, of course, are subject to board approval.

One of the major functions of the school superintendent is to gather and present data so that school board members can make intelligent policy decisions. Increasing reliance on the superintendent and staff is evident as school systems grow in size. The superintendent advises the school board

---

[39] Diane Ravitch, *The Great School Wars* (New York: Basic Books, 1975); Richard W. Saxe, *School-Community Interaction* (Berkeley, Ca.: McCutchan Publishing Corp., 1975).

[40] Jay Scribner and David O'Shea, "Political Developments in the Urban School Districts," in C. W. Gordon (ed.), *Uses of the Sociology of Education*, 73rd Yearbook of the National Society for the Study of Education, Part II (Chicago: University of Chicago Press, 1974), pp. 380-408.

and keeps members abreast of problems; generally, the school board will refuse to enact legislation or make policy without the recommendation of the school superintendent. However, it is common knowledge that when there is continuous disagreement or a major conflict over policy between the school board and the superintendent, the latter is usually replaced.

Since the superintendents' powers are broad, the duties are many and varied. Besides being an adviser to the board of education, he or she is usually responsible for certain functions.[41] These are:

1. Serves as supervisor and organizer of professional and nonteaching personnel (e.g., janitors and engineers).
2. Makes recommendations regarding the employment, promotion, and dismissal of personnel.
3. Ensures compliance with directives of higher authority.
4. Prepares the school budget for board review and administers the adopted budget.
5. Serves as leader of long-range planning.
6. Takes needed steps in developing and evaluating curriculum and instructional program.
7. Determines internal organization of the school district.
8. Makes recommendations regarding school building needs and maintenance.

In addition, the superintendent is responsible for the day-to-day operation of the schools within the district and serves as the major public spokesperson for the schools.

To fulfill these responsibilities the superintendent is assisted by a central office staff, as well as by support personnel, consultants, and citizen groups. The larger the school district, the greater the number of central administrators and staff needed to assist the superintendent. In large districts, the central office staff may have as many as five or more levels in the hierarchy, and there will be several titles, ranging from deputy superintendent, associate superintendents, assistant superintendents, directors, department heads, and supervisors responsible for various facets of the school operation. Also, many of the larger school systems have decentralized their schools into smaller units, usually called areas or districts, comprising a number of schools and headed by a superintendent who also has a staff to assist in their operation. This field superintendent is usually responsible to a superintendent at the central office—an associate or deputy superintendent or the superintendent of schools.

[41] Kimbrough and Nunnery, *Educational Administration;* Morphet et al., *Educational Organization and Administration.*

432

The School Unit

As a usual practice, each school has a single administrative officer, a principal, who is responsible for the operation of the school. In small schools this person may teach part time as well; in a very large school consisting of more than one building there may be a supervising principal responsible for the total center and a building principal for each separate facility. In a large school, in addition to the principal, there may be one or more assistant or vice principals. The administrative hierarchy may also consist of a number of department chairpersons, a discipline officer (e.g., dean of boys, dean of girls), a director of guidance, and so on.

Although functions vary by locality and size, the principal is primarily responsible for administering all aspects of a school's operations. It is common practice for the principal to work with some type of community lay group for the improvement of the school. Traditionally, this took the form of a parent-teacher association and various advisory school-community committees which had little influence or real power. Since the 1960s, however, lay people have voiced a demand for greater input in the operation of the schools their children attend, particularly in the cities, and as teachers have become more militant, principals are being more careful to follow contract provisions and to also include teacher representatives in policy-making decisions for the school unit. In addition, the student unrest of the 1960s resulted in student representatives, especially at the secondary level, being consulted in many schools in such areas as curriculum and student policy.

School Pressures and Problems

Although the school board–superintendent relationship is the focal point for local policy development, many other groups and individuals attempt to influence decisions made at this level. Several years ago Neal Gross, in a landmark study, asked school board members and superintendents from approximately half of the school districts in Massachusetts to state who exerted pressure on them. The responses of 508 school board members and 105 superintendents, with each group having equal weight, showed they placed at the head of the list: (1) parents or PTA, (2) individual school board members, (3) teachers, (4) taxpayers' association, and (5) the town or city council. At the bottom of the list were welfare and poverty groups.[42] Ten years later, Marilyn Gittell and T. E. Hollander studied six urban school systems and concluded there was little community

---

[42] Neal Gross, *Who Runs Our Schools?* (New York: John Wiley & Sons, 1958).

Table 11.5 / Ranking of Major Problems Confronting Schools, 1969–1976

	1969	1970	1971	1972	1973	1974	1975	1976	Average Ranking
Lack of discipline................	1	1	3	1	1	1	1	1	1.3
Integration/segregation...........	5	2.5	2	2	2	2	2	2	2.4
Lack of proper finances...........	4	2.5	1	3	3	3.5	3	3	2.9
Difficulty in getting good teachers....	3	4	6	4	4	5	4	5	4.5
Size of class....................	—	—	—	5	6	6.5	5	7.5	6.0[a]
Use of drugs....................	—	5.5	5	9	6	3.5	6	6	6.6[a]
Poor curriculum.................	8	7	9	7.5	5	—	7	4	7.2[a]
Lack of proper facilities..........	2	5.5	4	7.5	7	9	9.5	11.5	7.4
Parents' lack of interest..........	6	8	7	6	8	6.5	11	7.5	7.6
Pupils' lack of interest...........	9	11	10	—	11	10	9.5	9.5	8.7[a]
School board policies.............	—	10	8	—	10	8	—	9.5	9.3[a]
Crime/vandalism.................	—	—	11	—	—	—	8	11.5	10.3[a]
Lack of transportation............	7	9	—	—	—	—	—	—	[b]

[a] The cumulative average is based only on the years the problem appears.
[b] There is no cumulative average for lack of transportation, since it only appears twice on the list.

Source: Adapted from *The Gallup Polls of Attitudes toward Education, 1969–1973* (Bloomington, Ind.: Phi Delta Kappa, 1973), pp. 26–27, 66, 101, 136, 177; September 1974 issue of *Phi Delta Kappan,* p. 22, December 1975 issue, p. 236; October 1976 issue, p. 188. Also see *The Condition of Education, 1977,* vol. 3, Part I (Washington, D.C.: U.S. Government Printing Office, 1977), Table 1.15, p. 158.

input in these systems; poverty and minority community interests were served the least.[43] The same year Robert Crain made a similar observation in his study of eight urban school systems. Although school boards represented various racial, ethnic, and religious groups, they did not represent lower-class interests.[44]

The push toward participatory democracy, the rise of black and (more recently) Latino power, the call for responsiveness to ethnic and social class differences, and other political movements to broaden the local schools' decision-making base have threatened established influences on policy making at this level. Teacher groups have also increased their influence over decision making by superintendents and school boards since the mid-1960s.[45] Recent studies of six urban school systems[46] and of 18 large and medium-size school systems in cities and suburbs[47] indicate that welfare, antipoverty and minority groups are now active and influential forces in determining the policies and practices of big-city school-systems across the country.

School problems have changed, too. In the Gross study cited above, the major problems listed by superintendents and school board members were ranked as (1) demands for the school to emphasize the 3Rs, (2) demands that the school teach more courses and subjects, (3) protests about the use of particular textbooks, (4) protests about the views expressed by some teachers, and (5) demands that teachers express certain views.

Since 1969 *Phi Delta Kappan* has published a nationwide survey conducted by the Gallup organization. The primary focus of the poll is public attitude, but beginning in 1973 a sample of professional educators was included among the respondents. The survey has been established as a major source of information on opinion in education matters, representing a probable nationwide sample and a cross section of local school districts. Although comparisons between the Gross study and the *Kappan* surveys are not recommended because they used different respondent groups, the latter survey can be used as a basis for ranking the types of problems confronting public education in order of priority as shown in Table 11.5.

---

[43] Marilyn Gittell and T. E. Hollander, *Six Urban School Districts: A Comparative Study of Institutional Response* (New York: Frederick A. Praeger, Inc., 1968).

[44] Robert L. Crain, *The Politics of School Desegregation* (Chicago: Aldine Publishing Co., 1968).

[45] Myron Brenton, *What's Happened to Teacher* (New York: Coward-McCann, Inc., 1970); James W. Guthrie and Patricia A. Craig, "Who Controls the Schools?" In A. C. Ornstein and S. I. Miller (eds.), *Policy Issues in Education* (Lexington, Mass.: D. C. Heath, 1976), pp. 59–67.

[46] George R. La Noue and Bruce L. Smith, *The Politics of School Decentralization* (Lexington, Masss.: D. C. Heath, 1973).

[47] Allan C. Ornstein, *Metropolitan Schools: Administrative Decentralization vs. Community Control* (Meutchen, N.J.: Scarecrow Press, 1974).

Each year the surveys sample the opinions of approximately 1,600 adults, 18 years and older, mainly parents of school children who can be described as providing a modified probability sample of the adult nation.

The public schools, like other public institutions, reflect the major trends in society. Throughout the 1970s there has been a nationwide shift toward more traditional values, conservatism among the public, and an emphasis on moral values and going back to the basics in education. The table shows discipline continuing to head the list of major school problems, as it has in seven out of eight surveys. In second place are the problems associated with integration and segregation. Next is concern over school finances. Fourth, over the years, has been the difficulty of finding good teachers. A reversal in opinion is noted concerning problems dealing with facilities; classroom size is becoming of greater concern, while facilities in general are less of a concern. The use of drugs and curriculum matters are becoming more of a concern, undoubtedly because of wide publicity related to teen-age drug addiction and national test scores.

It is difficult to discern whether the public's concern over the schools reflects the persistence of problems in the schools, persistence in the public's perceptions of their importance, or the inseparability of the school's problems from society's problems. It is important for the public to have confidence in the people running the schools because educational institutions rely on the public for financial support, and the climate created for education is communicated to both students and teachers. The proportion of the public expressing "a great deal of confidence" in those in

Table 11.6 / Relation of Gross National Product to Total Expenditures for Education (Public and Private, All Levels), 1929–30 to 1984–85

Calendar Year	Gross National Product (in millions)	School Year	Total Expenditures in Education (in millions)	Education Expenditures as Percent of GNP
1929 . . . . $	103,095	1929–30	$ 3,234	3.1%
1939	90,494	1939–40	3,120	3.5
1949	256,484	1949–50	8,796	3.4
1959	483,650	1959–60	24,722	5.1
1969	930,284	1969–70	70,077	7.5
1979[a]	192,400,000	1979–80	155,844	8.1
1984[b]	253,600,000	1984–85	197,808	7.5

Note: GNP reported in calendar years; educational expenditures reported for corresponding school year.
[a] Projections for 1979–80 and 1984–85 are based on extrapolations by author; they do not consider declining enrollments, the possibility of rapid inflation, or other factors.
[b] By 1984 the GNP is expected to increase less rapidly than in the past, due to energy and labor costs, and the lower proportion of people working vis-a-vis an aging population. Although total expenditures in education per student are expected to increase slightly, it is expected to drop off as a percentage of GNP due to decreasing student enrollments.
Source: *Digest of Educational Statistics, 1974*, Table 27, p. 26; *Projections of Educational Statistics to 1983–84*, Table 35, pp. 87–88.

Table 11.7 / Estimated Expenditures for Public Elementary and Secondary Education by Level of Government, 1929–30 to 1984–85

School Year	Amount (in millions)				Percentage of Expenditures[a]		
	Total	Federal	State	Local	Federal	State	Local
1929–30.........	$ 2,089	$ 7	$ 354	$ 1,728	0.4	16.9%	82.7%
1939–40.........	2,261	40	684	1,536	1.8	30.3	68.0
1949–50.........	5,437	156	2,166	3,116	2.9	39.8	57.3
1959–60.........	14,747	652	5,768	8,327	4.4	39.1	56.5
1969–70.........	40,267	3,220	16,063	20,985	8.0	39.9	52.1
1979–80[b].......	92,950	7,901	38,574	46,475	8.5	41.5	50.0
1984–85.........	122,500	11,025	51,450	60,025	9.0	42.0	49.0

[a] Figures do not add to 100% because of rounding; 1929–30 percentages slightly different than Table 11.1., due to different source.
[b] Projections for 1979–80 and 1984–85 expenditures are based on extrapolations by author which include estimated total expenditures in education listed in Table 11.6 and percentages based on Table 11.1.
Source: Digest of Educational Statistics, 1974, op cit, Table 7.1, p. 60; Projections of Educational Statistics to 1983–84, op cit, Table 2, pp. 17–18.

charge of educational institutions has ranged between 30 and 50 percent from 1973 to 1976 — not too good a rating. The public expresses more confidence in people running medical institutions, but less in those in charge of major companies and the press.[48]

EDUCATIONAL FINANCING AND GOVERNMENT SPENDING

Total expenditures in education (for public and private schools and elementary, secondary, and higher education) have steadily increased from $3.2 billion in 1929-30 to an estimated $197.8 billion in 1984-85 (Table 11.6). The largest increases have come since the 1960s, corresponding with the nation's recent emphasis on human resources and its expanding gross national product and increasing percent of GNP devoted to education. However, the rate of increase of the GNP will probably taper off in the 1980s due to economic problems, and so will expenditures for education as percent of GNP, due to declining student enrollments.

State and local money remains the basic source of revenue for public education. Table 11.7, which focuses on elementary and secondary education, shows that federal expenditures now represent between 8 and 8.5 percent; the state proportion of expenditures doubled from 16.9 percent in 1929-30 to almost 40 percent in 1959-60 and has leveled off at about that point, while the local share declined from more than 80 percent in 1929-30 to approximately 50 percent. Not shown in the table is funding for public higher education; the federal share for this now represents about 15 percent.[49]

It must be noted, however, that averages and percentages are deceptive and vary by states. In school year 1975-76 the federal, state, and local contributions, as illustrated in Table 11.8, were 8, 43.7, and 47.8 percent, respectively (with the remaining 0.5 percent derived from intermediate or other sources). In Hawaii, where the state funds education, local revenues in 1975-76 represented less than 1 percent of total receipts. At the other end of the continuum, local school districts in New Hampshire were responsible for contributing 85 percent of the total receipts. In 1975-76 local governments contributed more than 60 percent of revenues in nine states and less than 30 percent in nine other states. Similar differences can be made about the federal contribution, which was over 20 percent in Mississippi and New Mexico and less than 5 percent in Connecticut, Iowa, Massachusetts, Michigan, New Jersey, and New York.

---

[48] *The Condition of Education, 1977*, vol. 3, Part I (Washington, D.C.: U.S. Government Printing Office, 1977), p. 19.

[49] *Projections of Educational Statistics to 1983-84, 1985-86* (Washington, D.C.: U.S. Government Printing Office, 1977), p. 80; pp. 68-70.

Table 11.8 / Percentage of Estimated Expenditures for Public Elementary and Secondary Education from Federal, State, and Local Sources, 1975–76

	Federal	State	Intermediate	Local
United States	8.0%	43.7%	0.5%	47.8%
Alabama	16.1	63.5	—	20.4
Alaska	15.1	64.9	—	20.0
Arizona	10.5	47.8	0.4	41.2
Arkansas	15.5	52.2	—	32.3
California	9.2	40.4	—	50.4
Colorado	6.8	39.8	NA	53.4
Connecticut	4.1	27.7	NA	68.2
Delaware	8.0	67.7	—	24.3
District of Columbia	17.8	—	—	82.2
Florida	6.2	54.6	—	39.2
Georgia	12.1	51.9	—	36.0
Hawaii	7.3	92.7	—	—
Idaho	10.9	49.5	2.9	36.7
Illinois	6.2	46.2	0.1	47.6
Indiana	5.7	40.6	0.4	53.3
Iowa	4.6	38.0	—	57.4
Kansas	11.6	43.8	—	44.6
Kentucky	14.6	54.3	—	31.1
Louisiana	17.5	55.7	—	26.8
Maine	8.1	44.6	—	47.3
Maryland	5.7	39.5	—	54.8
Massachusetts	4.1	23.5	—	72.4
Michigan	3.8	51.7	—	44.4
Minnesota	5.5	54.7	0.4	39.3
Mississippi	21.2	55.0	—	23.8
Missouri	8.2	35.0	5.9	51.0
Montana	6.1	57.6	7.2	29.1
Nebraska	7.4	17.6	3.2	71.8
Nevada	5.5	40.4	—	54.2
New Hampshire	6.0	9.4	—	84.6
New Jersey	4.1	29.4	—	66.5
New Mexico	20.6	63.4	—	16.0
New York	4.6	39.9	—	55.5
North Carolina	13.1	66.3	—	20.6
North Dakota	7.2	48.8	8.6	35.4
Ohio	5.9	36.6	—	57.5
Oklahoma	11.1	50.0	4.9	34.0
Oregon	5.9	29.0	17.2	48.0
Pennsylvania	8.7	48.1	—	43.2
Rhode Island	7.9	35.9	—	56.2
South Carolina	14.7	58.8	—	26.5
South Dakota	14.5	14.2	0.8	70.6
Tennessee	11.1	53.0	—	35.9
Texas	10.4	50.2	0.2	39.2
Utah	7.4	57.9	—	34.8
Vermont	6.0	29.5	—	64.5
Virginia	11.0	30.6	—	58.4
Washington	8.3	51.5	—	40.2
West Virginia	12.3	56.3	—	31.4
Wisconsin	7.5	32.1	0.1	60.3
Wyoming	6.9	32.9	21.6	38.6

Source: *Statistics of Public Elementary and Secondary Day Schools, Fall 1975* (Washington, D.C.: U.S. Government Printing Office, 1976), Table 10, pp. 34–35.

The States' Ability to Finance Education

In most states the distribution of education funds is based on some type of equalization plan which is designed to provide extra money for less wealthy local districts in order to help provide equality of educational opportunity. Basically there are two types of equalization plans — the *foundation* plan and *power-equalizing* plan.[50]

Traditionally the foundation plan has been the common approach; as of 1977–78 about 60 percent of the states utilized this approach for financing education. Its purpose is to guarantee a minimum annual income per student for all school districts, irrespective of local taxable wealth per student. The trouble is, most foundation plans do not provide enough funds to pay for what would be considered even a minimum level of education; the level is so low that there is generally a need to exceed it, and the wealthier the district, the easier the task of raising the expenditure level.

The power-equalizing plan is more recent; about 30 percent of the states have adopted it. Under this scheme, the state pays a percentage of the locally determined school expenditures, in inverse ratio to the wealth of the district. In both programs, the school district has the right to establish its own expenditure level, but in the power-equalizing approach, wealthier districts are given fewer matching state funds. A poor district might receive 65 percent of its school funds from state sources, and a wealthy district, 35 percent. The program is so constrained with upper and lower ratios, however, and in limits permitted that in effect its approaches a foundation plan.

Another problem with these plans is that state resources vary considerably. For elementary and secondary education in school year 1974–75, as an example, California spent $1,373 per student, while Alabama spent $993 and Mississippi spent $921. For California and Alabama, the expenditures represented 4.15 percent of their personal income; for Mississippi they represented 4.49 percent.[51] On the basis of comparative economics, the California and Alabama efforts were equal, and Mississippi made a greater effort than either one, though it was clear that California was spending 30 percent more than Alabama and Mississippi. One of the features of ESEA funding is that it provides a partial solution by granting larger allocations to the poorer states — in other words, it applies the

---

[50] Marvin C. Alkin, "Revenues for Education in Metropolitan Areas," in R. J. Havighurst and D. U. Levine (eds.), *Metropolitanism: Its Challenges to Education,* 67th Yearbook of the National Society for the Study of Education, Part I (Chicago: University of Chicago Press, 1968), pp. 123–47; Charles S. Benson, *Education Finance in the Coming Decade* (Bloomington, Ind.: Phi Delta Kappa Educational Foundation, 1975).

[51] *Digest of Educational Statistics, 1975,* Tables 70–71, pp. 70–71.

Table 11.9 / Financial Statistics for Selected Local Districts in California, 1968–69

County and District	Assessed Value per Pupil	Tax Rate	Expenditure per Student
Alameda			
Emery Unified.................	$100,187	$2.57	$2,223
Newark Unified................	6,048	5.65	616
Fresno			
Coalingo Unified	33,224	2.17	963
Clovis Unified.................	6,480	4.28	565
Kern			
Rio Bravo Elementary	136,271	1.05	1,545
Lamont Elementary	5,971	3.06	533
Los Angeles			
Beverly Hills Unified	50,885	2.38	1,232
Baldwin Park..................	3,706	5.48	577

Source: *Serrano* vs. *Priest* (1971); adapted from court proceedings.

equalizing concept on a national basis. But the amount does not make up for the present disparities among rich and poor states.

Local Ability to Finance Education

On a local level, variations within states are just as wide, again reflecting not so much differences in interest in education as in ability to raise money. In 1977–78 about 95 percent of local revenues collected by school districts came from property tax collections, and disparities among local expenditures mainly reflected assessed property valuation per student. Although the local school districts in any state could be used as an example, California, the one selected for Table 11.9, provides the data used in the historic *Serrano* v. *Priest* decision, to be discussed below.

The table shows that the Baldwin Park school district spent $577 per pupil in 1968–69, while the nearby Beverly Hills school system spent $1,232. The major source for this variation was the difference in local assessed property values per pupil. In Baldwin this figure was $3,706 per pupil, while in Beverly Hills it was $50,885 — a ratio of 1 to 13. Furthermore, the Baldwin citizens paid a higher school tax of $5.48 per $100 of assessed valuation, while the residents in Beverly Hills paid only $2.38 per $100 — a ratio of more than 2 to 1, representing a severe strain on the poorer community of Baldwin. In other states some school districts with low expenditures per pupil have correspondingly low tax rates, but in most cases the opposite is true. Often local districts (as with Baldwin) have low expenditures but high tax rates as a result of their limited tax base, while the tax rate is relatively low (as with Beverly Hills) in wealthier districts.

These kinds of discrepancies exist throughout the country today. Comparing inequities in property valuation between the suburbs and cities indicates that the financial ability to finance education is worsening, due primarily to the out-migration of middle- and upper-middle-class residents from the cities to suburban areas and the influx of low-income citizens to the cities. While these population trends slightly decreased in the 1970s, compared to the population exchanges of the 1950s and 1960s, there has been a recent trend by which private industry and big business are moving to the suburbs (as well as to the sunbelt). In short, the cities, especially those in the North and Midwest, are losing their tax base as the suburbs increase theirs. The problem is further compounded for cities because city property is increasingly being devoted to public housing, transportation, and other public uses and therefore it is no longer taxable. Furthermore, many of the cities are experiencing urban decay, and the assessed valuation of taxable property is declining.

Some city tax bases are alarmingly low compared to the statewide basis. For example, in 1973 in New Jersey, the 17 urban districts all together had an equalized assessed valuation per student almost 30 percent less than the state average, and Newark had 62 percent less.[52] Overall, however, many city property tax bases remain high compared to state property bases.[53] Nevertheless, the property wealth of cities has been declining relative to surrounding suburban areas since the 1950s, especially as more cities experience population changes and once viable communities turn into slums.

Severe financial demands for noneducational public functions, due to population density and the high proportion of disadvantaged and low-income groups in cities, place another burden upon city tax bases. Local taxes for noneducational public functions in cities compared to outlying areas in metropolitan areas were 91 percent higher in 1967.[54] Large-city per capita expenditures for noneducational functions were 13 percent higher than state averages for police protection, 91 percent higher for fire protection, 87 percent higher for waste collection, 66 percent higher for sewers, and 70 percent higher for health and hospital services in 1969–70.[55] These noneducational cost pressures on city tax bases have not diminished over the years. As cities continue to lose industrial and business activity to

[52] Aaron S. Gurwitz, *Urban Schools and Equality of Educational Opportunity in New Jersey* (Newark: New Jersey Education Reform Project, 1974).

[53] John J. Callahan, William H. Willken, and M. Tracy Sillerman, *Urban Schools and School Finance Reform: Promise and Reality* (Washington, D.C.: National Urban Coaltion, 1973), Table a-1, p. 26.

[54] Seymour Sacks, David Ranney, and Ralph Andrew, *City Schools–Suburban Schools: A History of Fiscal Conflict* (Syracuse, N.Y.: Syracuse University Press, 1972).

[55] Callahan et al., *Urban Schools and School Finance Reform*. Table a-4, p. 24.

the suburbs, continue to gain low-income families, and generally decline in their tax bases compared to outlying suburbs, noneducational expenditures will create fiscal competition for educational expenditures.

There are other comparisons to be made. A larger percentage of the enrollment in city schools is in technical, vocational, and trade programs, which cost more per student than a regular academic high school program. The city schools have more senior teachers than their suburban counterparts, since the latter have as a matter of policy traditionally replaced many experienced teachers with new teachers to save money. The differences in teacher salary costs are crucial; nearly 65 percent of the education budget goes for salaries. The cities also tend to have a greater percentage of disadvantaged and handicapped students, who cost more per student to educate. For example, compared to outlying school districts, New York City schools have twice the proportion of students scoring at least two grades below state norms in reading and more than three times as many children from welfare families.[56] In New Jersey the 17 largest city districts have 50 percent more students in special education than does the state as a whole; these districts also have three times the state average in percentage of Spanish-surnamed students.[57] Nonwhite school populations for the 15 largest cities in the United States increased from a district average of 38 percent in 1960 to 56 percent in 1970 to 63 percent in 1975.[58]

Not only is there a false image about suburban wealth, based on images of Scarsdale, New York; Gross Pointe, Michigan; Winnetka, Illinois; or Beverly Hills, California, but the new middle-class suburban communities usually have a great many more public expenses than older, wealthier suburbs. When sewage, utilities, roads, hospitals, and schools have been recently built, property tax rates are high. Thus there are also differences in property taxes and expenditures for education among the suburbs; in fact, many of the working-class suburban and rural school districts experience more strain than some cities do in financing education.[59]

The Courts and School Financial Reform

The courts have become a major issue in meeting the educational needs of students. One of the first statements on the role of the courts dates back

---

[56] Joel S. Berke, *Answers to Inequality: An Analysis of the New School Finance* (Berkeley, Ca.: McCutchan Publishing Corp., 1974), Table 3.10, p. 89.

[57] Gurwitz, *Urban Schools and Equality of Educational Opportunity,* Chart 3.

[58] Berke, *Answers to Inequality,* Table 3.5, p. 79; John J. Callahan et al., *Big City Schools: 1970–75—A Profile of Changing Fiscal Pressures* (Washington, D.C.: National Conference of State Legislatures, 1977), Table 2, pp. 202–205.

[59] Robert O. Bothwell, *State Funding of Urban Education under the Modern School Finance Reform Movement* (Washington, D.C.: National Urban Coalition, 1976).

443

to Arthur Wise, who compared court action to protect an individual's rights to vote and to have legal counsel with the right to receive an equal education.[60] The argument that education represents a fundamental human right was subsequently developed by John Coons and his colleagues. They argued that public education played a vital role in maintaining the American system of democracy, that schools are the major institutions to educate children and they are a planned and continuous service provided by the state, and that it is the responsibility of society to ensure that children have the educational services they need.[61]

In 1971, the California Supreme Court, ruling in *Serrano* v. *Priest*, accepted the arguments of Wise and Coons that public education was a "fundamental right in which children should receive equal protection of the laws." It ruled that the state's system for financing public education violated the equal protection clause of the California Constitution and the 14th Amendment of the U.S. Constitution. Stress was placed on the differences in tax burdens needed to raise school funds (see Table 11.9). The court noted that in the Baldwin Park district taxpayers had to pay almost twice as much in taxes per $100 of assessed property value as did those in the Beverly Hills district, yet the Baldwin schools spent far less per student than the Beverly Hills schools. In summing up its position, the court recognized the fundamental interest of the state in education and stated it should not be conditioned on wealth. The California schools were instructed to equalize school financing.

A number of similar cases followed *Serrano* in the states of Michigan, Minnesota, New Jersey, and Texas—where it was ruled that disparities resulting from taxable wealth among the local school districts did not serve the state's interest and violated the state's constitution. The Board of Education of Texas appealed the decision to the U.S. Supreme Court. By its 1973 decision in the *Rodriguez* v. *San Antonio Independent School District* case, the Court effectively stopped, at least temporarily, school reform through federal action. By one vote, it supported existing school financing system in Texas. The majority opinion asserted that (1) there is no group who because of poverty (based on income or property) is excluded from, or absolutely deprived of, public education; (2) the presence of relative deprivation is not sufficient to identify another suspect group; (3) low-income people live in both rich and poor school districts; and (4) the importance of a service does not establish its status as a fundamental right. Most important, the Court noted the historic relationship of the

---

[60] Arthur E. Wise, *Rich Schools, Poor Schools: The Promise of Equal Education Opportunity* (Chicago: University of Chicago Press, 1968).

[61] John E. Coons, William H. Clune, and Stephen D. Sugarman, *Private Wealth and Public Education* (Cambridge, Mass.: Harvard University Press, 1970).

federal and state roles in education. Nowhere does the Constitution explicitly guarantee the right to education, and education was reaffirmed as a function reserved for state government.

The Court noted that the Texas system was similar to systems in almost every other state. The power of local property taxation for education, the one most commonly used, was also reaffirmed as the perogative of the state. But by leaving the question of education finance up to the state, the Court provided an opportunity of reform through the states.

Redress of the problem is securing positive results in state supreme courts. For example, a few months after the *Rodriguez* decision, the New Jersey court gave the state legislature 18 months to approve a new system of financing schools to replace the local property tax. The legislature failed to meet the Court's deadline, and in the summer of 1976 the court closed the schools. Eventually the legislature passed a state income tax which in essence diverts money from wealthy communities to poorer ones. The Connecticut Superior (lower) Court in 1974, followed by the Connecticut Supreme Court in 1977, declared the state system of financing education unconstitutional (that is, it violated the concepts of free public schooling and equal educational opportunity), and a legislative commission was established to define a more equitable method of school taxation and allocating new funds to poor school districts by no later than 1978.

State Financial Reform

The harsh fact is that attainment of equal tax rates or equal expenditures will not ensure equality of educational opportunity. The needs of school districts differ substantially. A basic premise is that children in different schools must be funded on a different basis, and the need can be devised according to two formulas: the learning requirements of individual students, and prices of educational goods and services (the purchased inputs of the educational process). Recognition of these two factors will cause the states to spend different amounts of money in different school districts.

First, school districts do not have the same proportions of disadvantaged and nondisadvantaged students (or expensive and inexpensive students). Some states have been exploring the possibility of using an index of education need. New York State is a pioneer in these efforts, having devised a density correction factor in the early 1960s which provided an additional 10 percent, subsequently increased to 17.5 percent, to the six largest city districts.[62] In addition, the Fleischmann Commission noted

[62] James V. Vitro, *State Aid to New York School Districts, 1964–65* (Albany, N.Y.: State Education Department, 1966)

445

differences in the needs of students and specified that low achievers should be assigned a value of 1.5, as compared with a value of 1.0 for achievers (50 percent more), to govern the distribution of educational resources. In addition, an extra $500 million per year would be made available to emotionally and physically handicapped children.[63]

While these intentions are certainly positive, there is no rational basis for selecting the 10 percent, 17.5 percent, or 50 percent figures. Research should be conducted to identify the important variables usually attributed to need—reading scores, delinquency rates, poverty or family income levels, average number of siblings in a family, percentage of homes without a father, educational levels of parents, and so on. Using these data as independent variables, a prediction model, or index of educational need, could be developed, with achievement scores as dependent variables.[64]

A related plan is for categorical aid, whereby the state takes into consideration cost differences of programs due to geographical locations. For example, transportation costs are usually higher in rural areas than in urban areas because many children live further from their schools, but facilities cost more in the cities because of higher property costs for new facilities, as well as the costs of vandalism and higher insurance premiums. If the state does not provide additional support to meet particular needs, some students will be penalized because of where they live.[65]

The kinds of categorical problems a school district might have vary widely; they depend on location and the characteristics of the student population. The most widespread need is for compensatory education; here, a funding precedent has been established by the federal government. But states can also provide or at least partially fund construction, transportation, school lunches, classroom size reduction, and other areas related to the costs of educating poorer school districts.

Block Grants and Vouchers

The federal government can assist in financial school reform by providing block grants to the states with no strings attached (to overcome the fear of big government), to be disbursed at their discretion. It is expected that poor states would receive most of the money, and in turn, the states would disburse the money mostly to poor school districts. This plan would have the effect of providing an equalizing schedule for state and

[63] *The Fleischmann Report on the Quality, Cost, and Financing of Elementary and Secondary Education* (New York: Viking Press, 1973).

[64] Alkin, "Revenues for Education in Metropolitan Areas."

[65] Charles S. Benson et al., *Planning for Educational Reform: Financial and Social Alternatives* (New York: Dodd, Mead, 1974).

local governments. In the past, most states were decidedly rural and not expected to help the cities particularly. Recent court rulings that have demanded redistricting of states in order to achieve more balanced representation of metropolitan areas have made these block grants feasible.

Another proposal to reform school financing is the use of educational vouchers. The essential idea, originally put forth by Milton Friedman and Christopher Jencks,[66] is to provide parents with an entitlement or voucher representing financial value when applied to placing a child in a given school of their choice. But the school could select students freely among applicants which might result in racial or social segregation. The USOE has made grants for vouchers to school systems in Gary, Indiana, Seattle, Washington; and San Jose, California. The San Jose project was evaluated by the Rand Corporation in 1974. This experiment did not result in segregation by race or social class; however, differences in academic outcomes of the experimental and control students "were inconclusive or absent."[67]

These reform suggestions represent only a few of the alternatives for financing schools. The basic questions remain as to whether one school district with a more stable or declining school population, where education costs are leveling off or declining, should help pay for another school district where the school-age population is increasing and costs for new facilities and teachers are causing budget strain and property tax increases. Why should districts that purchase minimal facilities assist those that buy lavish ones? Can we expect wealthier districts to redistribute revenues to poorer districts? Should the federal government become more involved in the funding of schools? Will new federal demands and regulations and paper work make the initial reform plan not worth the effort? These are tough questions; they are not easy to answer.

CONCLUSIONS

In the overall picture of education in America, three levels of government—federal, state, and local—influence policy. The relationship does not remain constant for any great length of time; changes at the federal level produce changes at the state and local levels, or a new state law may

---

[66] Milton Friedman, "The Role of the Government in Education," in R. A. Solo (ed.), *Economics and the Public Interest* (New Brunswick, N.J.: Rutgers University Press, 1955), pp. 139–56; Christopher Jencks, "Education: Cultivating Greater Diversity," *New Republic*, November 7, 1964, pp. 33–40.

[67] D. Weiler et al., *A Public School Voucher Demonstration: The First Year at Alum Rock, Summary and Conclusions* (Santa Monica, Ca.: Rand Corporation, 1974), pp. vii–viii.

modify the local-state relationship. Although federal funding approximates 8 percent, a percentage that has remained fairly constant since the mid–1960s, there has been steady growth in the concern, influence, and participation of the federal government in many aspects of education. Very large extensions of federal influence have emanated from judicial rulings and regulatory activities involved in acceptance of federal money.

Because a classroom teacher's welfare and professional role are inevitably affected by changes in government activities, especially if the shifts are sharp, no teacher should remain a mere spectator in changes outside his or her classroom. As a member of one or more teacher organizations, the teacher should evaluate educational changes brought about by governmental provisions, support those that seem desirable, and challenge those that are judged unworthy through collective bargaining, lobbying, and support of political candidates who will provide leadership.

ACTIVITIES

1. As a possible research paper, identify and explain the conditions which have caused greater federal participation in the local operation of the schools.
2. Interview a local HEW or USOE official to obtain his or her viewpoint on government participation in education.
3. Interview a local state board of education official to obtain his or her view on government participation in education.
4. Develop an instrument listing a number of problems in education. Take a neighborhood pool of at least 50 adults. Compare the results with the annual Gallup poll listed in Table 11.5.
5. Invite a guest speaker to discuss the principles and prospects of school finance.

DISCUSSION QUESTIONS

1. Identify and explain three ways in which the federal government is involved in public education.
2. How would you describe the status and future of research in education?
3. What are the major responsibilities of the chief state school officer? How does this compare with the responsibilities of the chief local school officer?
4. What are the advantages and disadvantages of the property tax as a source of revenue for the operation of schools?
5. Explain the concept of equalization from a school finance viewpoint.

SUGGESTED FOR FURTHER READING

Benson, Charles S. *Education Finance in the Coming Decade.* Bloomington, Ind.: Phi Delta Kappa Foundation, 1975.
Berke, Joel S. *The New Era of State Education Politics.* Cambridge, Mass.: Ballinger Publishing Co., 1977.

448

Campbell, Roald F., et al., *The Organization and Control of American Schools.* 3rd ed. Columbus, Ohio: Charles Merrill Publishing Co., 1975.

Gross, Neal. *Who Runs Our Schools?* New York: John Wiley & Sons, 1958.

Johns, Roe L., and Morphet, Edgar L. *The Economics and Financing of Education.* 3rd ed. Englewood Cliffs, N.J.: Prentice-Hall, Inc., 1975.

Koerner, James D. *Who Controls American Education?* Boston: Beacon Press, 1968.

Morphet, Edgar L., and Jesser, David L. *Emerging State Responsibilities for Education.* Denver, Colo.: Improving State Leadership in Education, 1970.

Reutter, E. Edmund, and Hamilton, Robert R. *The Law and Public Education.* 2nd ed. Mineola, N.Y.: Foundation Press, 1976.

Sacks, Seymour, Ranney, David, and Andrew, Ralph. *City Schools–Suburban Schools: A History of Fiscal Conflict.* Syracuse, N.Y.: Syracuse University Press, 1972.

Wirt, Frederick M., and Kirst, Michael W. *Political and Social Foundations of Education.* Berkeley, Ca.: McCutchan Publishing Corps., 1975.

Alexander, C. Norman, 99, 100, 102n
Alkin, Marvin C., 440, 446n
Allen, Dwight, 285
Alloway, David N., 124n
Allport, Gordon, 121
Anderson, Archibald, 3
Anderson, E. L., 166n
Anderson, James, 101
Anderson, James G., 146n
Anderson, Ralph, 263, 265
Andree, Robert G., 321
Andrew, Ralph, 442n
Angell, Robert C., 7n
Apfel, Nancey H., 371n
Armer, J. Michael, 98n
Armor, David, 386n
Ashline, N. F., 362n
Ashton-Warner, Sylvia, 250
Astin, Helen S., 200n, 208n
Ausubel, David P., 73, 85
Averch, Harvey, 108n, 360
Ayres, Leonard, 152n

Bachman, Jerald G., 185n
Bacon, Margaret, 34n
Bagley, William, 3
Bailey, Stephen K., 367n, 416n, 418n
Bain, Robert, 101
Bakke, Allan, 198
Banfield, Edward C., 56n, 133n, 205n
Banks, James A., 20n
Bard, Bernard, 244n, 394n, 399n
Barker, R. G., 263n
Baroni, G., 175n
Barr, A. S., 278n, 280
Barry, Herbert, 34

Bauer, Raymond A., 21n
Bayer, Alan F., 199n, 200n
Beardslee, David C., 221n
Bearison, David J., 82n, 145n
Bell, Bernard, 195n, 200n
Bell, Daniel, 9, 158, 180n
Bell, Robert R., 6n
Bellack, Arno, 273, 274
Ben-David, Joseph, 13n
Bendix, Richard, 161n, 351n
Benedict, Ruth, 32, 35, 153
Bennett, George K., 230n
Benson, Charles S., 446n, 448
Bereiter, Carl, 84, 137
Berelson, Bernard, 52n
Berg, Ivar, 180, 210
Berger, Brigitte, 58n, 192n
Berke, Joel S., 443n
Berlin, Barney M., 363n
Berlyne, Daniel E., 79n
Bernstein, Basil, 80, 81
Biddle, Bruce, 267, 270, 277n, 285
Billings, Charles, 399
Billingsley, Andrew, 133n, 134n, 135, 362n
Bird, Caroline, 187, 188
Black, James A., 28
Blackwell, James E., 134n, 362n
Blau, Peter M., 160n, 164n, 181, 182n, 296
Blauner, Robert, 134n
Bloom, Benjamin, 73, 74, 114
Bloom, Richard, 352n
Bloomgarden, Carol R., 259n
Bobbitt, Franklin, 7
Bode, Boyd, 3
Boocock, Sarane S., 56n, 114, 151n
Borich, Gary D., 285, 277n

451

THE BOOK MANUFACTURE

Composition:	Fox Valley Typesetting
	Menasha, Wisconsin
Printing and Binding:	Kingsport Press
	Kingsport, Tennessee
Internal design:	F. E. Peacock Publishers
	art department
Cover design:	Sandy Mead
Type:	Times Roman with Helvetica
	display